Splendours of Royal Mysore

Praise for the Book

'The book is the due result of the earnest desire of the author to know about those who ruled the erstwhile State of Mysore [...] After reading this book, a reader would feel that Mysore is not just a city but it is indeed a city of palaces and culture. The contributions of the city are so remarkable that it is rightly called the cultural capital of Karnataka.'

—**Maharajkumari Meenakshi Devi Avaru,**
Princess of Mysore

'Vikram Sampath has done some fresh churning, taken pains, collected unknown or not so known facts on various aspects of Mysore's history [...] His straying off from his regular professional path is welcome, and I congratulate him for this mammoth effort!'

—**Suryanath U. Kamath,** former Chief Editor, Karnataka State Gazetteer and former Director, Karnataka State Archives

Splendours of Royal Mysore

The Untold Story of the Wodeyars

Vikram Sampath

RUPA

Published by
Rupa Publications India Pvt. Ltd 2008
7/16, Ansari Road, Daryaganj
New Delhi 110002

Sales centres:
Prayagraj Bengaluru Chennai
Hyderabad Jaipur Kathmandu
Kolkata Mumbai

Copyright © Vikram Sampath 2008, 2009, 2023

The views and opinions expressed in this book are the author's own and the facts are as reported by him which have been verified to the extent possible, and the publishers are not in any way liable for the same.

All rights reserved.
No part of this publication may be reproduced, transmitted, or stored in a retrieval system, in any form or by any means, electronic, mechanical, photocopying, recording or otherwise, without the prior permission of the publisher.

ISBN: 978-93-5702-858-5

Third impression 2025

10 9 8 7 6 5 4 3

The moral right of the author has been asserted.

Typeset by Mindways Design, New Delhi

Printed in India

This book is sold subject to the condition that it shall not, by way of trade or otherwise, be lent, resold, hired out, or otherwise circulated, without the publisher's prior consent, in any form of binding or cover other than that in which it is published.

Dedicated to
the ever-lasting memory of
Ajji, my grandmother,
who, though not around in flesh and blood
to see this day, will continue to remain
a constant source of inspiration
in all my creative endeavours.

CONTENTS

Acknowledgements — ix
Foreword — xi
Preface — xv
Introduction — xix

Section – 1

Preface — 3
1. The Genesis AD 1399–1578 — 7
2. The Age of Glory AD 1578–1617 — 21
3. Peril At the Gates AD 1617–38 — 45
   Looking Back: Section 1 — 57

Section – 2

4. The Golden Period—I (AD 1638–73) — 63
5. India in the Seventeenth Century — 88
6. The Golden Period—II (AD 1673–1704) — 102
7. The Dalavoy Regime AD 1704–34 — 129
   Looking Back: Section 2 — 138

Section – 3

8. The Early Years of Haidar Ali AD 1734–61 — 143
9. Haidar Ali: The Supreme Dictator AD 1761–82 — 167
10. Haidar Ali: The Man and His Legacy — 212
11. Sultanat-e-Khudadad Mysore AD 1782–91 — 223

12. The Sword of Tipu Sultan AD 1791–99 . . . 265
    Appendix to Chapter 12 . . . 293
13. The Legacy of Tipu Sultan . . . 308
    Looking Back: Section 3 . . . 346

Section – 4

14. The Restoration and Thereafter 1799 . . . 371
    Appendix to Chapter 14 . . . 386
15. The Survivor Statesman Dewan Purnaiya's Life and Times . . . 396
16. The Beckoning of Doom AD 1812–30 . . . 420
17. A Country on the Boil . . . 440
18. Commissioners' Rule and the Issue of Rendition AD 1831–68 . . . 467
19. Towards Rendition . . . 492

Section – 5

20. The Reformer King Chamarajendra Wodeyar X . . . 505
21. The Rajarishi . . . 521
22. Political, Social and Economic Development of Mysore . . . 549
23. The Struggle for Swaraj . . . 577
24. The Beginning of the End . . . 594

Section – 6

25. Defining Culture . . . 623
26. The Lives and Times of Mysoreans: Classical Music . . . 627
    Appendix to Chapter 26 . . . 663
27. The Lives and Times of Mysoreans: Classical Dance . . . 668
28. The Lives and Times of Mysoreans: Folk Arts and Popular Traditions . . . 677
    Appendix to Chapter 28 . . . 686
29. The Lives and Times of Mysoreans: Painting, Coinage and Architecture . . . 690
30. The Lives and Times of Mysoreans: Literature, Theatre and Journalism . . . 703

Conclusion . . . 718
References and Bibliography . . . 720
Index . . . 727

Acknowledgements

Mine is certainly not the only hand in the mammoth task of writing this book. I owe my heartfelt gratitude to Yaduveer Krishnadatta Chamaraja Wadiyar, Scion of the Royal House of Mysore, for agreeing to write the Foreword. I am also grateful to eminent historian, Dr Suryanath Kamath, for having agreed to go through the manuscript in detail and for verifying its historical accuracy and for the preface. I offer a humble thanks to Maharajkumari Meenakshi Devi Avaru, Princess of Mysore and daughter of Shri Jayachamaraja Wodeyar, for her praise for this book. I also thank her sister-in-law, Smt Bharati Raj Urs, for all her help and suggestions. Mere words will not suffice to thank Dr Mamatha Gowda, secretary to the Chief Minister of Karnataka, for all her help, support and encouragement.

I am also grateful to the authorities at the Bangalore palace for all their help. The book was transformed for the better by the painstaking and tireless efforts of the editor, Dr Lata Ramaswamy, who did not live to see this day. My sincere thanks are also due to eminent author, Dr Shashi Deshpande, who mentored me through the entire course of publication. A special note of thanks goes to eminent scholar and author Prof P.V. Nanjaraja Urs, noted Kannada litterateur Dr Srinivasa Havanur and the late Mr S.R. Prabhu, former chairman of Canara Bank, for their valuable inputs and guidance.

Dr J.V. Gayathri, deputy director of Archaeology, Museum and Heritage Department, Mysore, and Shri Gavisiddhayya, archivist-in-charge, Divisional Archives, Mysore, provided me with rare and unpublished photographs of the royal family from the archives. Dr Meera Rajaram Pranesh, eminent musician, musicologist and scholar, and the Vanamala Art Foundation offered little-seen photographs of the Mysore musicians, as did Dr Raghavendra and the Ananya Sangraha, Bangalore. Shri

M.A. Narasimhan helped me with valuable information on the Mysore Pradhans.

I am grateful to Vidushi Jayanthi Kumaresh, one of India's leading veena artists, for sharing information regarding the Mysore Bani of veena playing. I also thank Smt Lalitha Srinivasan and Kumari Bhanumathi—noted Bharatanatyam dancers and students of Dr Venkatalakshamma—for inputs regarding the Mysore *shaili* of dance.

It is with a sense of humility that I acknowledge my ever-loving and encouraging parents and my late grandmother who have stood by me in all that I have done. Despite being totally allergic to history, my mother managed to read one draft and give me valuable insights from a layman's perspective. She also helped me type this voluminous document.

Words are insufficient to acknowledge the role of Dr Uma Narain, my professor, friend, philosopher and guide, with whom every conversation is an inspiration and provides food for more thought. I could not have broadened my outlook in matters of publication but for my friend Aruna Chandaraju, an accomplished journalist. I have to place on record my immense gratitude to a host of people who helped me procure valuable material: Mr Thejaswi Shivanand, my hitherto 'virtual friend' who was more than willing to help me in the endeavour; Mr S.N. Jois and his daughter, Smt S.N. Geetha of Mysore for lending me old and valuable manuscripts; Mr Subbanna of National College, Basavanagudi, Bangalore; Smt Geetha Murthy and Smt Uma Shashi, both from the Bangalore University; Shri Muralidhar of Suhaas Graphics, for giving me beautiful and hard-to-find photographs of Mysore and the royal family, and for their meticulous work on the maps.

My special gratitude to my uncle Mr Krishnamurthy, a die-hard Marxist who has always widened my outlook on life and who, in this case, joined me tirelessly in the pursuit of books. My thanks are also due to Smt Aditi Vashisht, my principal at Sri Aurobindo Memorial School; my school teachers, Smt Jayashri Ravindra and Smt Sheela Raghu, Mrs Hilda Peacock and Mr Vincent Jeyakaran and to my friends Smt Gayathri Indavara and Mrs Malini for their encouragement and help. I must of course thank my publishers Rupa & Co. and Sanjana Roy Choudhury for reposing trust in me. I also thank the editor Anamika Mukharji, whose meticulous and tireless efforts helped chisel the book for the better.

Yet, my real obeisance and gratitude is due unto the Divine, without whose guidance not a word could have been written.

The Palace
Mysore

9th May 2023

FOREWORD

My family's history is intertwined with that of the formation of the modern state of Karnataka. We claim to have descended from the tribe of Yadu, and the two brothers, who founded the state, came down from Dwarka to have darshana of the famous Sri Cheluvanarayana Swamy at Yadugiri, now known as Melukote. After establishing their rule, their successors were able to slowly increase their influence and power and nearly two centuries later, under the illustrious Raja Wadiyar, came to occupy the ancient seat of the 'Mahamandaleshwara' or Viceroy of the Karnata Samrajya, in Srirangapatna during the sunset years of that great empire.

My family's history is part of an ancient aspiration of many dynasties and rulers of the Deccan towards the Karnata Samrajya and becoming the Karnata Chakravarti. Indeed, the rulers of Vijayanagara Empire, often referred to themselves as Karnata Chakravarti and their state as the Karnata Samrajya.

After Raja Wadiyar, a number of famous rulers like Kanteerava Narasaraja Wadiyar and Chikka Devaraja Wadiyar strengthened the state, continued the tradition of Dasara, like their overlords at Vijayanagara, and built a strong military state that maintained relative autonomy during a time of great turmoil all over the country. During the middle to latter half of the 1700s, the Dalvoys of the Mysore army gained tremendous influence over the affairs of the state as weak or young rulers were often at the helm. This dark period saw several wars and turmoil throughout the state resulting in finally ousting the usurpers in 1799, with a return to power for the Wadiyars.

During the subsequent century-and-a-half, the kingdom of Mysore blossomed into a model state for India. A number of the legacy institutions that formed the strong base, from which our modern state of Karnataka grew into a powerhouse, was indeed founded during the time of the Kingdom of Mysore. Culture, education, the Kannada language, the arts, healthcare and upliftment of backward classes, amongst other causes, were given the utmost importance. Indeed, the state was so renowned for its administration that it was often used as an example to show how well Indians could govern themselves during the Independence struggle.

Sri Vikram Sampath has, in his book *Splendours of Royal Mysore*, narrated the history of our Mysore family, documenting our victories, our struggles, our tumultuous half century when we nearly lost our kingdom, to the glorious days of what we now refer to as the Golden Age of Karnataka, under the rule of H.H (Nalwadi) Krishnaraja Wadiyar IV and finally, our welcoming of Independence and the subsequent changes. Throughout his narration, he has placed heavy emphasis on historical sources and relevant references thereby making this book one of the best contemporary sources to gain knowledge on my family's history.

I am privileged to write this foreword for the 15th year anniversary of the release of *Splendours of Royal Mysore*. To say that the book, in its 15 years of existence, has contributed to a greater appreciation of the contributions of some of the illustrious rulers of Mysore, would not be inaccurate. This book is an important chapter of Karnataka's history and a contemporary account was much in need during the time this book was released.

Sri Vikram Sampath has always been a staunch defender of writing a true account of history, no matter whether it suits an agenda or not, and more such authors are required to ensure that the vast sea of India's glorious history is given its due importance. I wish him more success in his every endeavour and I hope this book reaches more such milestones in the future.

Yaduveer Wadiyar

Dr. SURYANATH U. KAMATH
M.A., Ph.D.
Historian

President : **Karnataka Itihasa Academy**

No. 798, 'KEERTI', 11th Main,
6th Cross, Hanumanthanagar,
BANGALORE - 560 019
Phone : 26624806
Mobile : 9341903242

(Formerly : ♦ Reader in History, B'lore University; ♦ Chief Editor, Karnataka Gazetteer
♦ Director, Karnataka State Archives; ♦ President, Mythic Society)

PREFACE

On this unique princely state of India—Mysore—there had been no modern book of the type that we have now in our hands. The author is an electronics engineer and MBA and an employee of a leading bank. His duties require him to keep dabbling with figures and banking rules. I have said this to point out that he is not a trained historian and to write on a dynasty like Mysore Wadiyars, some specialisation in the subject is necessary. Despite that, the author has undertaken the writing of the work by sheer love and devotion and made it an extremely readable and interesting account.

The history of the Mysore Dynasty is filled with myths and legends and many times the extra-ordinary achievements of princes of the dynasty appear to be suspect when the role of legends tries to glorify them. I had advised the author to water down such legendary accounts to make the narrative look factual. But a common reader is more attached to these myths and legends as he is accustomed to read Puranas. History has to be a factual account so that it looks to be an account of humans like us and guide us and teach lessons.

Mysore's history helps us to trace the past of a small principality of some villages (definite information is secured after it had 30 villages and earlier it could have been just three or four or five villages) and its growing into a territory of over 80,000 square miles, with various stages of its enlargement clearly marked. Some of the princes were renowned for their prowess and they enlarged their territories, as in the case of Kanthirava Narasaraja Wadiyar I or Chikkadevaraya. They were great administrators by contemporary standards, meticulous as revenue administrators, religious by temperament, helped and expanded agriculture and extended irrigation. Concessions were given to peasants bringing new lands under the plough. If a peasant deserted the village, the village accountant was punished. They founded *agraharas* to encourage learning and had increased industrial activities. Chikkadevaraya had invited weavers from the Baramahals in Tamil Nadu to Bangalore. He was a man of letters and also encouraged literary men. His allowing his dumb son to succeed him helped the emergence of new centres of power, the Dalavayis, and this paved the way for Haidar's ascendancy.

Chikkadevaraya accepted Mughal suzerainty for the sake of acquiring Bangalore and its surroundings. This resulted in his being a feudatory of the Mughals for this limited area. The Nizam and the Marathas later repeatedly came to collect the feudal dues (by way of Chauth and Sardeshmukhi) from Mysore. These powers were authorised to collect the dues from the southern Mughal Subahs by the Mughals. This point is ignored by Mysore records and they simply state that Chikkadevaraya 'purchased' Bangalore from the Mughals. Newly discovered Mughal records in Persian have belied this statement, as pointed out by Sethumadhava Rao Pagadi.

The story of usurpation by Haidar, achievements of Tipu and subsequent developments under British rule are interesting chapters. The accounts of post-rendition period, including the growth of Mysore as a modern and model state are well presented. Mysore, the third largest princely state under the British, achieved all-round progress in agriculture, industry, education, culture and other finer aspects of human activity. Power production at Shivasamudra (1902) helped the founding of the prestigious Indian Institute of Science in Bangalore (1909), emergence of modern industries (even under the public sector) and Bangalore growing in our times as a unique hub of IT, BT and nano-technology. Men like Sir M.V. and Sir Mirza Ismail had paved the way for such developments.

Krishnaraja Wadiyar IV was an enlightened prince. But he did not yield to the demand for responsible government despite the fact that there was a Representative Assembly in Mysore and the British had provided the facility of responsible rule in their own Presidencies. The rigid policy of Mysore led to the Vidurashwatha tragedy. Later in 1947, Jayachamaraja Wadiyar, by his adamant stand over the matter provoked the massive 'Mysore Chalo' movement and caused the death of over 20 persons by police firing. These are some black spots amidst a glaringly bright reign of the Wadiyars.

Vikram Sampath has done some fresh churning, taken pains, collected unknown or not so known facts on various aspects of Mysore's history. His presentation is lucid and smooth. His love for the dynasty has not prevented him from telling us about the not-so bright aspects, wherever necessary. His straying off from his regular professional path is welcome, and I congratulate him for this mammoth effort!

Suryanath U. Kamath
Former Chief Editor,
Karnataka State Gazetteer and Director,
Karnataka State Archives

INTRODUCTION

The artistic representation of history is a more scientific and serious pursuit than the exact writing of history. For the art of letters goes to the heart of things, whereas the factual report merely collocates details.

—Aristotle

I

I must have been a boy of twelve when the 'Mysore bug' bit me for the first time. The provocation was a controversial teleserial—*The Sword of Tipu Sultan*—aired on national television in those days and based on an eponymous novel by Bhagwan S. Gidwani. The serial did not go down too well with lots of Kannadigas, and Bangalore, my hometown, witnessed quite a few protests because of a certain raw nerve that the serial had attempted to touch, which, incidentally, was something the novel never did.

Bangalore and a large part of modern-day South Karnataka had been part of the erstwhile princely state of Mysore. The state was ruled for over 600 years by the Yadava dynasty who called themselves the Wodeyars of Mysore. It was after India's Independence that the princely state merged with the northern parts of modern Karnataka to become, first the state of Mysore and later, Karnataka after unification. Though it has been just about half a century since the royal family ceased to wield power, the twin torments of indifference and debate dog its long history. Also, the general populace holds the royal family and its icons in reverence. This applecart was upset by the way this serial portrayed members of the royal family. The eighteenth ruler of the family, Immadi Krishnaraja Wodeyar and his wife, the celebrated Rani of Mysore, Lakshmammanni, were not shown in a good light—the former portrayed as a buffoon and the latter as a scheming woman. That is what led to the voices of dissent. To learn the truth behind this falsehood was what prompted my little voyage of discovery at that time. Being a mere middle-school student back then, and one for whom history had always meant memorising dates and boring details of battles and wars, the study of Mysore's sovereigns came as a whiff of fresh air; more so as it was entirely self-motivated and not done under duress.

Thus began a series of unending trips to Mysore, its palace, numerous libraries in Bangalore and Mysore, rustling up old contacts—basically doing everything possible under the sun to get the information that I was looking for. Being a complete novice and totally ignorant of the ways and means of historical research, I had to fall back on my grandmother and parents for help and support and that I got it in far greater measure than expected needs to be placed on record. While my parents would dutifully take me to Mysore during almost every vacation and wait patiently for hours on end as I sifted through dusty books in the libraries there, Ajji, my loving grandmother, would leave no stone unturned in contacting her old acquaintances and friends or making trips to libraries and older parts of Bangalore, where the probability of finding material on the topic would be higher. What began as a study of just the two sovereigns I mentioned above slowly broadened into a study of the whole dynasty across the 600-odd years of its reign. It was, however, disconcerting to note that there were hardly any books readily available that covered the entire story of the Wodeyar dynasty from 1399 to 1950. People really didn't seem to care much, like they never do all over India, about telling the story of their past in a manner that interests, excites and inspires.

It would not be an exaggeration to say that in the course of my study, which developed from a novice's child-like curiosity to a more serious pursuit of the subject, I found one disturbing trend. The veil of time and the kind of historical documents that existed have slowly blurred the facts. The issue gets more complicated in the case of Mysore's history as it includes a forty-year-long interregnum when the Hindu dynasty of the Wodeyars was temporarily dislodged by a Muslim adherent Haidar Ali—a man the monarch had rescued as a boy by buying him from his tormentor for a paltry sum. Haidar and later his son Tipu Sultan ruled

Mysore over a span of forty years, in which wars with the neighbouring states of Pune, Hyderabad, Carnatic and Travancore and especially the English East India Company became the order of the day. It was with the fall of Tipu in 1799 that power was restored to the Wodeyar dynasty at the behest of the British.

I called the above fact a complicated one for two reasons. One, you have two competing parties each with their claims and grouses against the other. History, in my view, is the handmaiden of the ruler. Naturally the historical records of the times tend to be invariably biased towards the ruling party. The pro-Wodeyar records berate the House of Haidar as a barbaric and dogmatic clan, while the contemporary Muslim records heap encomiums on the father and son. To complicate matters further, you have English historians who, seized with rabid hatred for Haidar and particularly Tipu, portray them as the worst villains mankind could have ever seen. In the midst of such totally contrasting records, where does a modern, unbiased commentator on history, such as myself, go? Who am I supposed to believe and what am I to take as the truth? In such a context the belief that history is after all an interpretation of the person who wrote it becomes more germane and hence I began with the quote of Aristotle that alludes to history being an art by virtue of the inherent judgmental nature in its representation. A commentator on history can at best see all these differing records and come to a lowest common denominator of acceptance. This, he must do, without tilting the scales favourably on either side, since none of us can be certain of the truth without a time machine!

The other reason for the complex nature is the fact that the communal angle gets into the whole story. India has long been vivisected by the Hindu-Muslim debate. These two communities have always been at odds with each other, perhaps since they are different in so many ways. In this case, since a Hindu monarch's kingdom was usurped by a Muslim, it is natural for each side to paint the other in a poor light on communal grounds. There are Hindu records that speak of mass conversions to Islam under Tipu's short and stormy rule, uprisings and revolts in different parts of Mysore, such as Malabar, Coorg, South Kanara and so on, offering people a choice between the Koran and the gallows. At the same time there is evidence of Tipu's patronage of Hindu pontiffs and temples across the state, including the world-famous Sringeri Mutt of Adi Shankaracharya—the harbinger of Hinduism's Advaita philosophy. Is that yet again a dead end for the historian?

Further, in the political climate of India today, people want definitive answers. Was he communal or was he secular? The demand for instant classification of characters of the past into categories set by us in the present, to pander to our present-day exigencies, encourages a tendency to oversimplify history by painting characters black or white with no place for shades of gray. The breed of Marxist historians do no great service in this department, causing more harm in fact, as they have specific agendas to pursue in their depiction. As Arun Shourie notes in his *Eminent Historians*, the game plan adopted is very repetitive and predictable:

> Tarnish every person, institution, period from which people may derive pride, confidence; ascribe tolerance and magnanimity to the intolerant; portray the inclusive, open tradition as the one out to swallow the others and the exclusivist, totalitarian ideology as the ideology of peace, tolerance...

In short, a deep malaise that strikes at the very heart of history writing and documentation. If we are not to believe colonial, Marxist, court or community-specific historians, on which sources do we rely? Any surprise then that history gets so easily 'saffronised' and subsequently 'detoxified' to suit the political climate of the day?

Perhaps one way out is the manner suggested by celebrated historian Arnold J. Toynbee in his *Study of History* (Volume I):

> Its (history's) true concern is with lives of societies in both their internal and their external aspects. The internal aspect is the articulation of the life of any given society into a series of chapters succeeding one another in time and into a number of communities living side by side. The external aspect is the relation of particular societies with one another, which has likewise to be studied in the two media of time and space.

Lord Acton, one of the greatest minds among modern Western historians has similar thoughts when he says:

> By Universal History, I understand that which is distinct from the combined history of all countries, which is not a rope of sand, but a continuous development, and is not a burden on the memory, but an illumination of the soul. It moves in a succession to which the nations are subsidiary. Their story will be told, not for their

own sake, but in reference and subordination to a higher series, according to the time and degree in which they contribute to the common fortunes of mankind.

Luckily, in this aspect of the humane study of history, there aren't as many controversies as in the political history I was speaking about. The narration therefore ends with a chapter dedicated to the unique legacy of the socio-cultural aspects of Mysore's history, one that, though subservient and dependent on the political scenario of the times, is still independent and based more on the aspirations and voices of the common people.

The decision to include a discussion on the economic growth of the state in the murky nature of its political story was also driven by a motive. Present-day Karnataka, and Bangalore in particular, has reached the pinnacle of material success with the growth of the information technology and biotechnology industries for which it is hailed as the veritable capital in India and the Silicon Valley of the East. In such times, it is but natural to lose touch with one's roots. Traditionally, Kannadigas have been the most welcoming, hospitable and amiable set of people, to the extent of being oblivious to their own glorious past and traditions and worse still, apologetic and even bearing a sense of inferiority at times among more vociferous neighbours. In these modern and changed times, however, it is essential that, while you soar in the skies, you have your feet firmly on the ground. Like many Bangaloreans, I too have been asked why and how Bangalore got into this IT/BT revolution. The most simplistic answer that people give is that it has such a salubrious climate and that is what drives the whole engine. But can weather be the only driver? If that were so, why would companies not set up shop in hill-stations like Shimla or Kodaikanal? Why choose Bangalore?

That's when a Bangalorean's complete ignorance about his own past comes to the fore. Under the erstwhile rulers of Mysore and its illustrious dewans, like Sir M. Vishweswaraiya and Sir Mirza Ismail, the state in general and the city in particular had attained a high degree of industrial growth by the time of Independence. Mysore state became one of India's first states to have a democratic system of local governance and was hailed as the 'Model State' of India by the founding fathers of the country in view of the large-scale material, cultural and spiritual progress of the state and its people. While Mysore city was the cultural capital of the state, Bangalore emerged as the intellectual capital of India with research centres, such as IISc and later on IIM, as well as the largest number of engineering colleges in India. Bangalore was also prominent on the strategic map of India's defence with HAL, BHEL and similar companies housing their operations here. With such a large pool of talent and advantages, the nascent Indian IT industry, which is a knowledge-based one, naturally chose Bangalore as its starting point. So the sound fundamentals of the economy were laid courtesy the progressive maharajas of Mysore, something for which we could perhaps gloss over the fact that they were completely under the tutelage of the British Crown after their Restoration in 1799. This book intends to instil among residents of Karnataka that sense of pride about their own culture and past, about the achievements that have come about through years of vision and planning, the ability to see patterns in the scheme of things, identify the symbols of the past around them that connect them to bygone days and not foolishly assume that it all happened one fine morning because of some magic wand waved by hordes of outsiders who poured into the state.

Perhaps this sense of pride and achievement would be all the more necessary in the year that Karnataka celebrates its 'Suvarana Rajyotsava' or the golden jubilee of its formation after Independence. This book is my humble tribute to this everlasting spirit of my state.

At the same time, while history's intention is to instil pride and comfort about the achievements of the past, it also needs to infuse a sense of responsibility about the present. While people of the past might have undoubtedly won laurels, are we, as present day citizens, doing enough to preserve this glory? With regular reports of the crumbling infrastructure in Bangalore and the flight of industry, can't history inspire us to act, and act fast? Perhaps the words of C. Rajagopalachari, the first governor general of Independent India are apt to quote here. In the address he gave to the newly formed government of independent Mysore during his visit to the state he said:

> I may say without hesitation, not as an old citizen of Mysore State, but as the Governor General, and an objective judge, that Mysore is really the most beautiful city in India. I have been feeling it all the time since I came here. In fact I did not get good sleep last night, because I was feeling as if I had just come back after paying a visit to 'Fairy Land'! The State has now been handed over to democratic machinery. Successive and able administrators

under His Highness' predecessors have built this province to an enviable degree of progress and glory. The new Government has taken over the responsibility. If I were here, I would not sleep happily. You have taken over a glorious thing. My colleagues in national agitation and struggle have taken over, I feel, a very high responsibility. It is not easy to maintain the State and keep it up to the level it had reached through the talent, industry, devotion and patriotism of previous administrators.

This is the sense of ownership and responsibility that history needs to instil in its readers, even while puffing them up with pride about past achievements.

II

The travails of an Indian student who finishes his schooling and is forced to branch into one of the two divine disciplines of engineering or medicine brought me to Sri Jayachamarajendra College of Engineering (SJCE), Mysore, acclaimed as one of the premier institutes of Karnataka. I was all the more thrilled to be in Mysore, a city that had always been little short of utopia for me, with the *tongas* that hurry past you as they would have past your grandfather or his father, the ever-benign countenances of the maharaja's statues that one encounters at every road intersection, and where all roads lead to the sprawling palace. Mysore was always a pleasant addiction and the special interest that I nurtured for the history of the place only made this addiction all the more chronic. Even as our train checked into the narrow Mysore railway station, the freshness of the air beckoned us—a totally alien experience these days in my hometown Bangalore, which has got itself entangled in the cesspool of modernism.

That evening, as we hired an autorickshaw to look for the paying guest accommodation that I wanted, the pleasantness and polite manners of the auto driver struck us—the same class in Bangalore is a most despised lot responding only with grunts and angry rebuffs. Caught in the maze of strikingly similar houses, we lost our way and had to ask at one such house for directions. We were touched by their earnestness to set us back on the correct route. The lady of the house took it upon herself to phone the person concerned from her house and even ventured to come with us to show us the house we were looking for, and all this at about 9 pm. While the whole exercise took more than fifteen minutes, the driver did not even demand extra money.

It is this social ethos that Mysore has been able to maintain, even as the rat race rushes on unabated elsewhere. It is a city that has not yet opened its eyes to avarice, urbane sophistication and the materialistic way of life. You cannot help but get transported into the past when you are in Mysore, because history for the average Mysorean is not dead, found in the cold storage of text books giving sleepless nights to many a student, but a more vibrant and enlivening aspect of their daily lives that makes them shoot at least cursory glances at all those forts, palaces, statues of their erstwhile rulers and remind themselves of the legacy they inherit. The kingdom may be long gone, but it still lives among the people, their attitudes, their daily discussions, musings and reminiscences.

The next morning we visited the breathtaking palace of the maharaja; it seemed to embrace the solitude and serenity of the surroundings with its high walls, merging with the colour of the sand of the adjoining courtyard. As I strolled past the sprawling fort surrounding the majestic Mysore palace, built in the Indo-Saracenic style, with large gateways and central archways, and a beautifully maintained garden of roses, apart from the *spathodia campanulate*, gulmohars and rain trees, I was awestruck imagining the grandeur and pomp of the inhabitants. Mysore and its majestic palace had always been my addiction and a feast for my eyes. As I left through the Varaha gate at the southern end of the complex, those large portraits of the legendary painter Raja Ravi Varma, those chandeliers, mirror cases and richly carved doorways flashed across my mind.

As I walked along, I could not but help catch sight of a small temple on the outer ramparts of the fort surrounding the palace. Inside was a small image of Lord Bhairava with four hands. He holds a trident, a drum, a skull and a sword. To his left is Bhadra Kali, holding a sickle. Both these gods of the Hindu pantheon symbolise death and destruction. But in the case of Mysore, like the phoenix, they ushered in a new era in its resplendent history.

Located around 770 metres above sea level and 135 kilometres from Bangalore at 12.18° N and 76.42° E, Mysore represents a cultural melting pot of the present-day Indian state of Karnataka. According to ancient legends, the area around Mysore was once the domain of the demon king Mahishasura who had grown increasingly invincible and wrought havoc on the world at large. It was then that the gods propitiated the feminine power in the form of Durga or Chamundeshwari who vanquished the demon in a massive battle waged over a period of ten days. Chamundeshwari is also known as Mahishasura Mardini or the slayer of the demon Mahisha. This epic battle between the forces of divinity and evil has captured the imagination of Indians who celebrate it across the length and breadth of the country as Dasara or Dussehra, the consummation of the nine nights of strife against evil, the Navaratri. Mysore retains the name of the slain demon as the anglicised version of 'Mahisuru', the *ooru* (Kannada for town) of Mahisha. Goddess Chamunda is supposed to have slain Mahisha atop a hill and to this day her image resides on the same hill which benignly overlooks the town of Mysore.*

---

* It is noteworthy that this story behind the name is most likely a mythical one. The first reference to the name 'Mysore' is actually found in an inscription of more than 1,000 years ago which refers to the place as 'Mayysoor'.

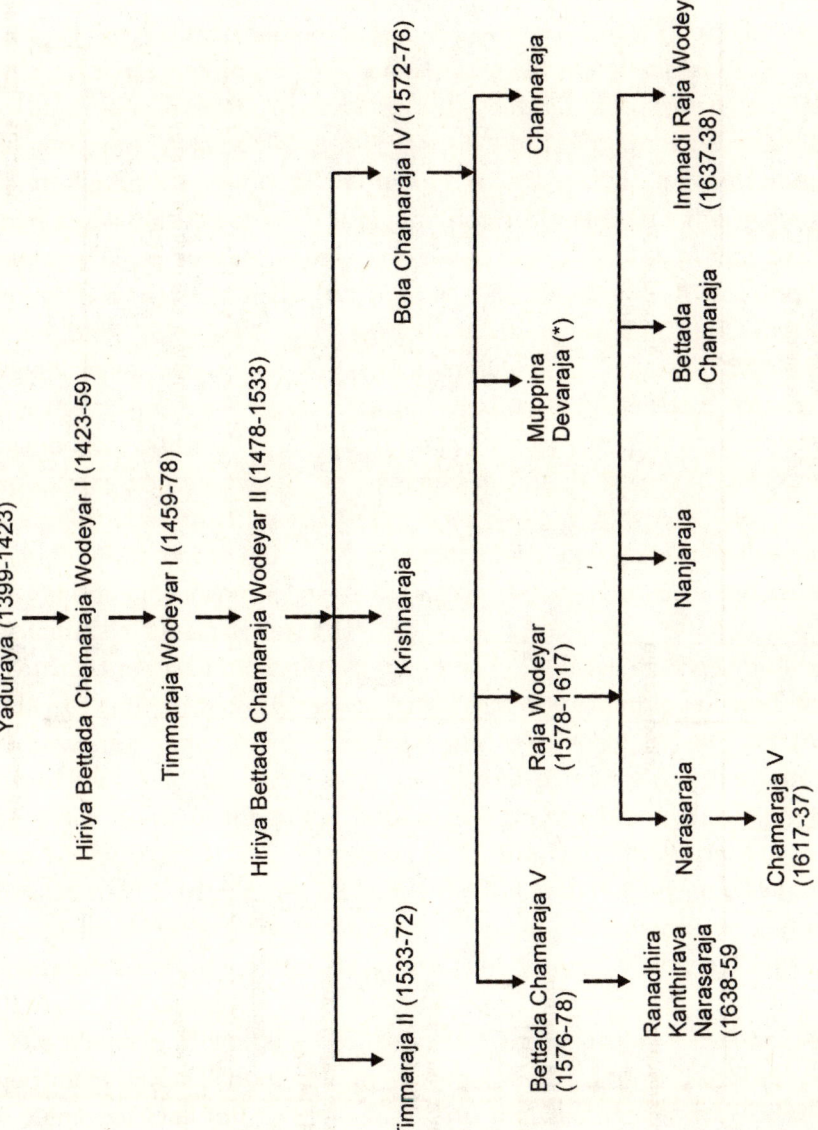

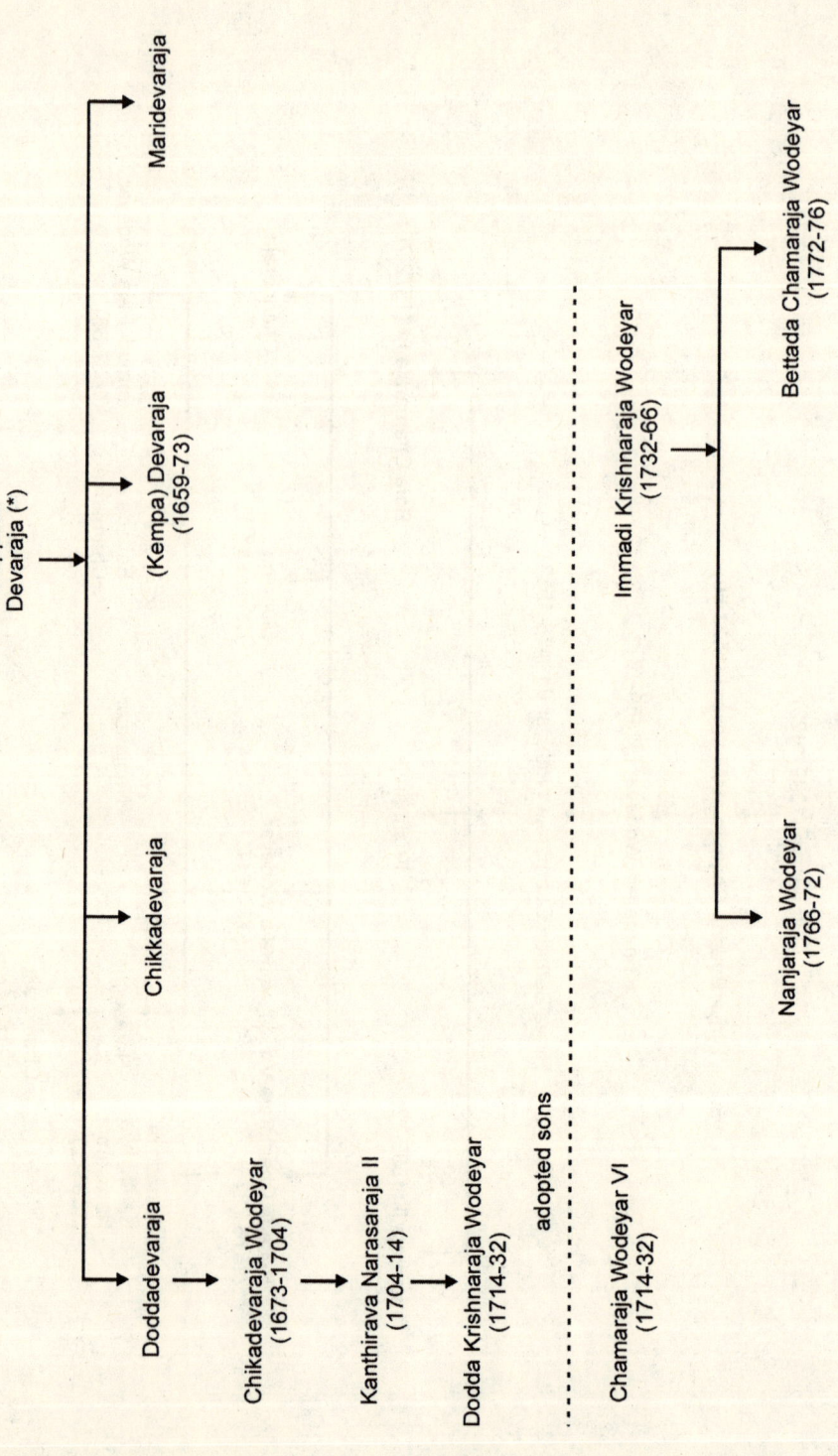

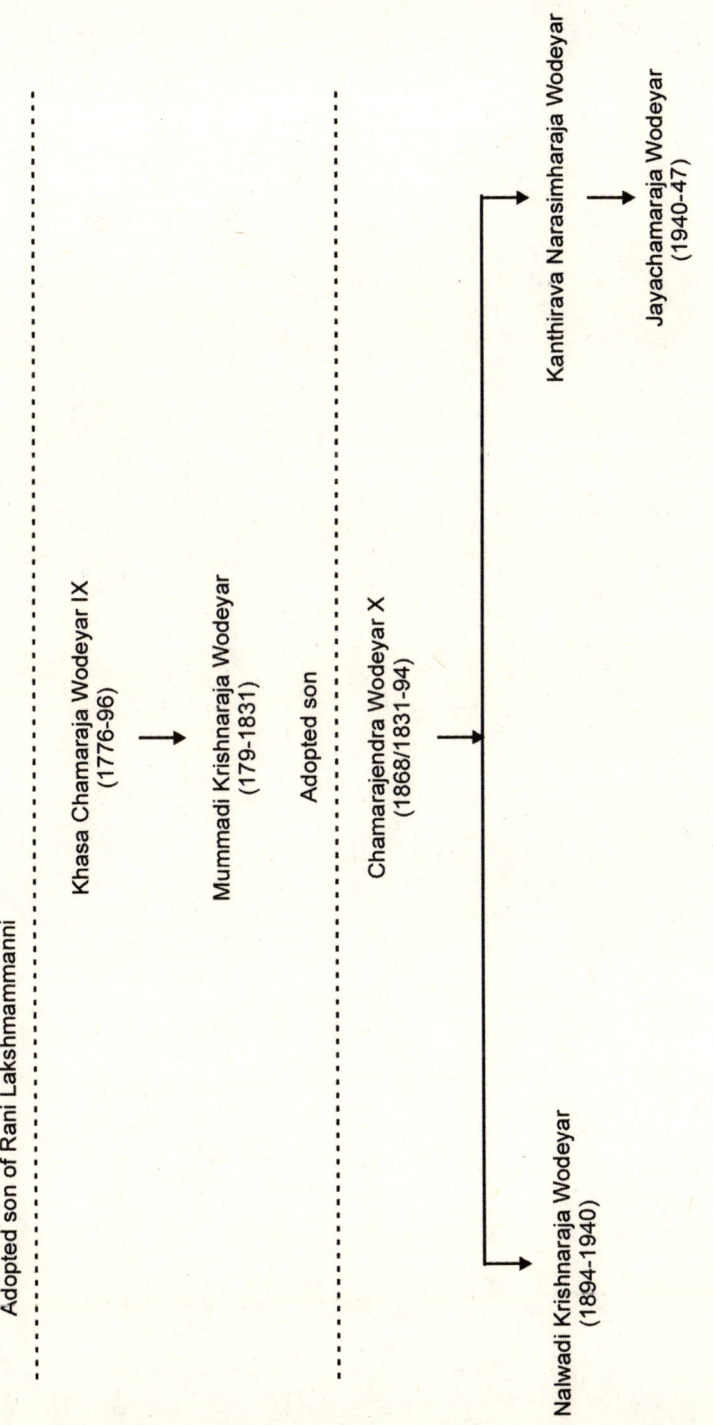

Section 1
The Period of Legend and Fable
(AD 1399–1638)

Raja Wodeyar: AD 1578-1617

PREFACE

This section, dating back to the very origins of the dynasty, has taken shape through much reliance on folklore. There are various sources available to a historian to reconstruct the past: manuscripts, documentation, travelogues, biographies and autobiographies of monarchs, archaeological excavations, monuments and folklore. In this long list, rationalists and historians have no quarrel with any of the sources except the last named, and the frown of disapproval becomes almost instantaneous when they hear the word 'folklore'. The term is usually associated with something traditional, old fashioned, quaint, rustic, backward and primitive. Some might even use it derisively as bordering on the limits of nonsense and falsehood, and rubbish it away as 'Oh, that's mere folklore, it's gibberish'.

But folklore is much more than that. It is a part of the experiences and practices of our everyday life, which only goes to suggest that in some way, all of us as individuals are involved in transmitting folklore, though not consciously. Dan Ben Amos in his essay, 'Toward a Definition of Folklore in Context', in the *Journal of American Folklore*, defines it as 'artistic communication in groups'. He classifies this artistic communication into the three categories of what people say (folk literature or verbal lore/ oral literature), what people do (folk custom) and what people make (material culture). Thus it wouldn't be an exaggeration to link folklore directly with something as lofty and abstract as the 'culture' of a group of individuals or of a community at large.

All over the world, the study of folklore and legend is being accepted as one of the means through which history reveals herself to those who seek her. In Britain, for example, for over a thousand years, storytellers have spun tales of King Arthur, his Queen Guinevere and the circle of his noble knights. Why do these stories endure? How have fables, songs and ballads twisted and turned over the centuries and have they in any way defined and reflected our expectations of heroism, governance, achievement and well being? These are questions that invariably emenge when we scratch the surface and go a little deeper.

Folklorists in Scotland, Ireland, France, Germany, the USA, Scandinavia and Eastern Europe went professional when, in the manner of sociologists and anthropologists in the first half of the twentieth century, they began to describe themselves as 'ethnographers'. Unfortunately, in India the amount of seriousness and thought that has gone into the study of folklore is conspicuous by its absence in the course of exploring Indian history. The first chair in folklore was founded in Helsinki as early as 1886, and an important international conference was held in Paris in 1937, but nothing as significant has happened in India to date. This is rather disconcerting considering the fact that India and Indians are, and have been, congenital storytellers. It comes so naturally to us. Most of the visible forms of our cultural expression are linked to the process of spinning a yarn. The epics *Ramayana* and *Mahabharata* constitute, without doubt, the bedrock of Indian storytelling. You have different versions and variations that are local adaptations of the same epics. We have even heard of versions where Rama and Sita are siblings. But apart from stories with a religious orientation, others, with a view of imparting moral education—be it the *Panchatantra* or the *Jataka* tales—have also been handed down over centuries to us. Could the study of history benefit from these stories? Could they give us an insight into the ways or lives of those times? Have we done enough to dissect these stories as a tool of reconstruction?

The early history of the Wodeyars of Mysore features many fascinating stories and ballads. Some of these fables were originally spun by court historians to heap encomiums on the incumbent king and to bolster the divine right theory of kingship. So it may be easy to rubbish away concepts of divine dispensation that guided the founders of the dynasty or a fable like that of the blind man regaining sight upon the king's touch, but one certainly needs to evaluate the impact they have had on popular imagination, right down to the present day.

Nowhere else did I get to see legends being so much a part of daily life than at Talakad. I was there at the recently held conclave of the *Pancha linga darshana* and was overawed by the sea of humanity that had congregated in a rare pursuit of faith. While I stood there marvelling at the beauty of the harsh and rugged landscape around me, my thoughts were interrupted by the wails of a woman that seemed to reverberate in the sandy environs. They were emanating from the CDs and cassettes that a hawker was selling to curious onlookers. Could something as eerie as this be a saleable commodity, I wondered. On listening more closely I realised that the wails and the remorseful dialogues were intended to be that of Rani Alamelamma. She laments the indifference of the Lord of Doctors, Vaidyeshwara, in whose town her family has taken refuge to ensure that her husband is cured of his ailment. But the God has failed her. To add to her misery, the King of Mysore is hounding them. So in utter frustration arising out of helplessness, we hear this woman showering the famous three-line curse before plunging into the Cauvery. And to my surprise I found people all around me, literate or semi-literate or completely unlettered, talking confidently and knowingly about this 'historical' event of the seventeenth century. Would it matter to them that some rationalists and historians actually are debating the very existence of this medieval queen and the event? This is because none of the early records—Wilks' mammoth account and Francis Buchanan's elaborate travelogue—mention the queen who jumped into the river and cursed the royal family of Mysore. Would they, who recorded every detail, have missed something as important as this? And if it were so much a part of public debate and consciousness, would they not have, in the course of their interviews with the local populace, got some insight into this event? Would it thus not suggest that this whole story is a concoction prepared at some later date with vested interests in mind? This is the line taken by rationalists and historians.

But then, we should also consider whether such rationalisation changes the beliefs that are so deeply entrenched by virtue of frequent repetition. If it does, what would happen then to the many hawkers for whom the curse is a means of livelihood during this jamboree? It is always so easy to sell a book or a CD that supposedly harps on a medieval curse as it instantly attracts customer attention and curiosity. While these thoughts cross my mind, I also wonder if history is what lies below what is recounted by the masses at large or it is that which academics debate and decide as the truth in closed door meetings.

A tale, like that of Rani Alamelamma, for whatever it is worth, talks of a deep socio-political and cultural truth of the times. It speaks of the delicate balance that existed those days between the victor and vanquished.

It gives us a glimpse into the mind of a woman of that century and how honour was more precious to her than her own life. It also acts as a connecting factor between the past and the present, where greed and avarice seem to be traits that never get satiated.

So which group owns the truth—popular belief or academic debate? What actually gets distilled and accepted as 'true history'? One should neither debunk nor bank completely on these myths of the past but rather use them to draw valuable inferences. At the end of the day it reinforces the balance between art and science on which history does its tightrope walking on. To tilt it to either side would mean destroying this fine equilibrium.

Medieval ideas, such as curses and omens, that have a visible impact till date add a dash of romance and thrill to any account. But it all comes as a package—facts that can be substantiated and rational arguments along with a lot of mumbo-jumbo and rumour-mongering. If nothing else, it gives the historian a chance to turn novelist—a temptation that I have succumbed to as well!

1
THE GENESIS AD 1399–1578

AD 1399

In the early hours of the morning, Mahisuru looked more gorgeous than ever against the artistic backdrop of the hills that overlooked the place. A few washerwomen were engrossed in their gossip as they sat thumping clothes on a stone beside the Devarajasagara tank. One of them remarked: 'Oh God! What decadence are we facing! Times have really worsened!'

The ignorant companion asked, 'Why? What's wrong? Is all well with the palace and our chieftain? You obviously know more as your husband guards the chieftain's private apartments.'

'Oh you ignorant fool! Do you have no sense of what is happening to our kingdom? Late last night, Chamaraja Bhupati died.'

'What?'

'Yes! No sooner does the king die than our poor queen is put to so much mental agony. As they say, it's always good to have a son; after all a son is the progenitor of the family. Alas! Chamaraja Bhupati died sonless and left behind his wife and pretty daughter Princess Chikkadevarasi. Don't tell anyone, but Dalavoy Maaranayaka has cast his evil eyes on the kingdom. In the middle of the night, even when our chieftain's family was facing such a tragedy, Maaranayaka—that imp of Satan—barged into the wailing queen's apartments. Fie upon him, has he forgotten all the decorum of the royals? And can you believe what he asked the queen Mother Devajammanni? He threatened her with an attack on the palace if she did not hand over her daughter Chikkadevarasi in marriage to him and said that he had already lined up his soldiers along the fort walls. O poor Queen Mother! Hardly had the vermillion of her forehead been wiped, than she had to face the treachery of an ordinary minister who hitherto was at the beck and call of her husband. God alone save our Kingdom, my friend!'

This conversation of the washerwomen caught the attention of a young and handsome man, Yaduraya. Life had taken strange turns for Yaduraya and his brother Krishnaraya. They were the sons of Raja Deva of Dwaraka in present-day Gujarat and claimed their descent from the lunar dynasty of Lord Krishna of the Hindu pantheon. Yaduraya had a series of inexplicable dreams—dreams which he could barely comprehend—but he was certain that they intended to convey a message, a directive. Just a week ago, he had felt that he had seen a vision of some divine force that coaxed him to leave Dwaraka for the Mahabala Mountains cradled between the Cauvery and Kapila Rivers and worship the presiding deity, Goddess Chamundeshwari.

A troubled Raja Deva called for the royal physician.

'Is there something wrong with my son? He seems to have this sudden urge to leave for the area below the Vindhyas. He remains disturbed by the after-effects of these dreams that he has had.'

The physician was clueless, since the prince had no discernible physical or psychological problems.

'Your Highness! My knowledge of the human body and mind is limited by the education I have received. There are matters that transcend the mundane education, which our intellect cannot perceive. There seems to be a profound reason that is driving the young Prince out of Dwaraka to the Mahabala. Let us not act as obstacles in the way of cosmic dispensation. Let him go where his destiny beckons him.'

Accompanied by his brother and confidant, Krishnaraya, Yaduraya set out on this unknown mission. He had no idea what he was supposed to do once he got there, but was sure that he had to go to the land of Mahisha. They reached the Mahabala Mountains on horseback. The scenic beauty of the mountainous region and the guiding mantra of Goddess Chamundeshwari inspired them to explore the land further. They travelled southwards and reached the beautiful township of Mahisuru, where they were completely enamoured by the loveliness of the place. As they aimlessly wandered around the town, the sun was beginning to set and they were in desperate need for shelter. Their eyes caught sight of a small temple on the banks of the Devarajasagara tank. It was that of Lord Bhairava who, with his consort Bhadra Kali, signified death and destruction in a mundane sense, but liberation and ultimate release from a spiritual perspective. The brothers were too tired to look any further and decided to spend the night in the temple with the gory images of the gods overlooking them. Little did they realise that while they slept comfortably in the temple, catastrophe had befallen the family of the man who ruled this little township.

It was like any another lovely morning in Mahisuru. The hill that overlooked the town was believed to be the one atop which Goddess Durga as Chamundeshwari had beheaded the ferocious demon king Mahishasura. The benign protection that the hills provided to the town and its inhabitants seemed reassuring. Yaduraya was stirred from his sleep by the early rays of the sun and the chirping of the birds. He sauntered along the Devarajasagara tank. All the while, he was confused and perplexed and kept questioning his decision.

'Driven by my strange dreams, I have made the long and tiresome journey to this distant and unknown land, much against my father's wishes. But what now? What am I supposed to do in this beautiful land? What brought me here? Maybe the force that guided me to reach this place will show me the path ahead. But what if it was all a mere hallucination of my mind? What will I tell my father? That I made a wild and thriftless journey to nowhere and returned empty handed?'

His stream of defeatist thoughts was interrupted by the sounds of the thumping of clothes by a couple of washerwomen. Yaduraya happened to hear the whole conversation. As he sat pondering over the conversation, a mendicant or Jangama approached him.

'You seem to be a stranger in this country, who are you?' he asked, trying to conceal a bag within his saffron robes.

'Sire! My obeisance to Your Holiness. I am Yaduraya, the prince of Dwaraka and the man sleeping over there is my brother, Krishna.'

'What brings you here?'

'Your Holiness, I have had strange dreams for quite some time now. Something seemed to be telling me to give up my reverie and leave for Mahisuru. I had never heard of this place before. So I thought there was surely more to it than meets the eye. We decided to act accordingly.'

The Jangama was ecstatic. 'Hail the Mother! Hail the Mother! She knows how to get Her will done! She knows whom to send and where and when.'

Yaduraya was baffled. 'Sire! I do not understand anything that you say. Which mother are you talking about and whom has she sent?'

Pointing towards the hills, the Jangama said, 'The Divine Mother, young lad. There She is, sitting atop that hill, having slain the demon Mahishasura. She protects this place. How could She let it fall into evil hands? You are Her chosen man. Look son, you have a tremendous task to accomplish. Let me explain. The soil on which we sit here today was ruled over by Chamaraja, the successor of Shuradevaraya of the Bhoja Dynasty who had reached this land of Mahisuru from Mathura.

'But, alas! Just last night Chamaraja died after a prolonged illness. The only wish he had was that of a son to succeed him. Sadly, this wish was never fulfilled and he was blessed with a beautiful daughter instead. What sighs does the queen exhale ever since he died. Maaranayaka, the cruel Minister, is planning to usurp the kingdom and abduct Princess Chikkadevarasi. Tormented by his threats, Maharani Devajammanni locked herself in a room and prayed fervently to Sri Hari. There was an immediate message from the Lord directing her to take into confidence two young visitors who would be setting their foot on this land from a foreign country. You are supposed to be the only ones who can redeem her and her family from this peril. She spoke her heart out to me and pleaded with me in such a pitiable manner that even I was moved to tears. After all, she is the queen and if she had to plead with an ordinary man of God like me thus, you can imagine the intensity of her agony. So I started looking for newcomers to Mahisuru and without much trouble I found you and knew that you were the one I was seeking. Son, do not delay, vanquish the evil forces who have cast their eyes on this beautiful land.'

Saying this, the Janagama held out the saffron bag he had been trying to conceal, which contained many weapons, and said, 'Here, these weapons were smuggled out of the armoury at the queen's behest. Make haste son, before it is too late. From the days of yore the forces of evil have always stood vanquished in this land. May the force of the Goddess, which inspired you to come to Mahisuru, guide you on your mission.'

Having said this, the Jangama departed.

It all seemed like a fairy tale to Yaduraya. He rubbed his eyes hard to check if he had perchance slipped into another reverie. Was this another dream? But the array of weapons lying in front of him dispelled these doubts. He quickly rushed to the Kodibhairava Temple and woke his brother to narrate the entire sequence of events. Immediately, both

Yaduraya and Krishnaraya armed themselves and made their way to the palace.

As they reached the main gates, they were stopped by the guards, who were on Maaranayaka's payroll. After a fierce battle, the guards were overcome but danger signals were sent across to Maaranayaka, the self-proclaimed caretaker of the palace. He rode his horse to the spot with his battalion behind him. Meanwhile, the prayers inside the palace chambers had intensified as the queen sat silent with her rosary. Yaduraya and Krishnaraya fought Maaranayaka for several hours, at the end of which they emerged victorious. Yaduraya held Maaranayaka's severed head and entered the palace.

As an attendant informed the Queen of Yaduraya's success, her face beamed with joy and she came hurrying down to the entrance to welcome the victor. 'Son! You don't realise what solace you have bestowed upon our troubled mind by killing this evil man. Could we have ever dreamt that someone who was hitherto a loyalist would betray us this way? But then it is divine providence by virtue of which you and your brother arrived at Mahisuru and came to our rescue at the right time. You have built for yourself a new edifice in our heart. None but you can be a befitting successor to the dynasty and a perfect match for my daughter!' The Princess was only too pleased to think of marrying the man who had protected her father's kingdom from the dark clouds of misery.

Thus, in the Hindu month of Vaishakha in the year AD 1399, Yaduraya ascended the throne of Mahisuru after marrying Chikkadevarasi. The people cheered with joy to see their saviour being led to the throne by a galaxy of priests amidst the chanting of Vedic hymns. Out of gratitude to the deity of Melukote—whose blessings he thought had earned him the kingdom—Yaduraya built a massive fortress on the hill with four gateways and named it 'Melukote', or 'The Fort atop the Hill'. Goddess Chamundeshwari became the family deity as it was Her intervention which supposedly brought Yaduraya to Mahisuru and ensured its subsequent fame. Thus was laid the foundation of the dynasty of the Yadu rulers of Mysore, called the Wodeyar or Wadiyar dynasty ('odeya' in Kannada meant master).

Wilks, the famous historian who has documented the history of Mysore in his book, *Historical Sketches of the South of India in an Attempt to Trace the History of Mysoor*, narrates a similar incident—with minor variants to the episode that led to the founding of the Wodeyar Dynasty.

During the period that the dominions of the rajahs of Vijeyanuggur extended really, or nominally over the greater portion of the South of India, two young men of the tribe of Yedava, named Vijeya and Kristna, departed from that Court in search of a better establishment to the South. Their travels carried them to the little fort of Hadena, a few miles from the present situation of the town of Mysoor; and having alighted, as is usual, near the border of a tank, they overheard some women of the Jungum sect, who had come for water, bewailing the fate of a young maiden of their tribe who was about to be married to a person of inferior quality. The brothers enquired into the circumstances of the case; desired the women to be comforted; and offered their services in defence of the damsel. She was the daughter of the Wadeyar (or Lord of 33 villages) who was afflicted with mental derangement; and in this desolate and unprotected state, the Chief of Caroogully, a person of mean caste, had proposed to the family the alternative of immediate war, or the peaceable possession of Hadena by his marriage with the damsel; and to the latter proposition they had given a forced and reluctant consent. The offer of the strangers was made known, and they were admitted to examine the means which the family possessed of averting the impending disgrace. In conformity to their advice no change was made in the preparations for the marriage feast; and while the Chiefs of Caroogully were seated at the banquet in one apartment, and their followers in another, the men of Hadena, who had been previously secreted for the purpose, headed by the two brothers sprung forth upon their guests and slew them, marched instantly to Caroogully which they surprised, and returned in triumph to Hadena. The damsel, full of gratitude, became the willing bride of Vijeya, who changed his religion (from a disciple of Vishnou he became a Jungum or Lingwunt) and became the Lord of Hadena and Caroogully. He assumed on this occasion, the title of Wadeyar which is uniformly annexed in the manuscripts to the name of every rajah, and still retained by the family after another change of religion which took place about the year 1687. Wadeyar or Lord (in the Kalla Canara) seems at this period, to have indicated the office of governor of a small district, generally of 33 villages.

Here, the reference Wilks makes to Hadena is Hadinadu, Caroogully being Karugahalli. Yaduraya has been named as Vijaya, just as he has been in other contemporary literary works like the *Mysuru Nagarada Purvottara*, an account of the early history of the Wodeyars.

This episode in Mysore's history is an interesting legend, which tries to veil the fact that the dynasty was founded by a humble and adventurous local soldier with a small group of villagers under his control.

The Wodeyar dynasty was the latest entrant in the long and chequered political history of the state. The early history of Karnataka—or Mysore state as it used to be called before India's independence—is replete with sagas of brave dynasties and warriors. Early references to the region are found in Mauryan literature and Ashokan inscriptions. Chandragupta Maurya is claimed to have come all the way to Shravanabelagola with his teacher Bhadrabahu. Although many historians refute this claim, the story points to the hoary past of the region of Mysore. In different time spans of its political history, the region has been ruled by the various dynasties of southern India—the Pallavas (AD 200–430), the Gangas of Talakad (AD 350–1050), the Hoysalas of Dwarasamudra (AD 1022–1342) and the Vijayanagara emperors.

Around the middle of the fourteenth century, the Sultanate of Delhi—founded under the aegis of the Slave Dynasty of Iltutmish and later on his daughter Razia—included almost the whole of India with a few minor exceptions. But the century also marked a kind of assertion of the southern kingdoms against northern hegemony. The Muslim chiefs from the south revolted against the control of Delhi while for the Hindu chiefs it was a matter of national pride and safeguarding their culture and religion against Muslim domination from north of the Vindhyas. This catapulted to prominence the two main kingdoms of the south—the magnificent Vijayanagara dynasty and the Bahamani empire. The people of the Deccan never reconciled to the fact of being governed by invaders who had occupied the throne of power at Delhi. As early as AD 1329, when Muhammad-bin-Tughlaq decided to shift his capital from Delhi to Daulatabad or Devagiri, there were serious reservations about the proposed move.

In 1336, a new era began in the history of the Deccan with the founding of the Vijayanagara dynasty by Harihara Raya and Bukka Raya with the aid of an erudite scholar and religious teacher named Vidyaranya. Under the Vijayanagara kings, many petty chieftains or Palayagaras flourished.

A Palayagara levied taxes on the people, maintained the law and order of his dominion and was almost like a king in his small satrapy. It was in one such small satrapy, Hadinadu, ruled by the chieftain Chamaraja, that the foundations of the royal family of Mysore were laid.

Yaduraya ruled the principality till AD 1423 and in the month of Shravana of the same year died after naming his elder son Hiriya Bettada Chamaraja Wodeyar (1423–59) as his successor. His younger son, Chamaraja Wodeyar, founded the Kenchalgud branch of the royal family of Mysore. The successive rulers were feudatories of the glorious Vijayanagara empire which had touched its zenith under rulers, like Krishnadeva Raya. In 1459, Hiriya Bettada Chamaraja Wodeyar's son, Timmaraja Wodeyar I, succeeded him and ruled till 1478.

On his demise, his son—Hiriya Bettada Chamaraja Wodeyar II—the Aarberal (or six-fingered king, as mentioned in manuscripts) ascended the throne. He had three sons by his wife Goparasammanavaru—Timmaraja Wodeyar II, Krishnaraja Wodeyar and Bola Chamaraja Wodeyar. Krishnaraja Wodeyar is known to have captured many villages and towns by defeating their Palayagaras or Poligars, the chieftains of the Vijayanagara empire, and got the title of 'Shringaarahara'. Timmaraja II, being the eldest son, succeeded his father in 1533. Timmaraja is also designated as Hiriya Bettada Chamaraja Wodeyar III. While history does not have sufficient documentation of the rulers who succeeded Yaduraya, the reign of Timmaraja and those of his successors have been chronicled in various manuscripts and inscriptions. He has had various names—Dodda Chamaraja, Bettendra, Bettarajendra, Betta Chamarat, Betta Chamendra, Sama, Bettada Chama and so on. It seems more likely that his true name was Timmaraja, after his grandfather, and that he was later appellated by these other names. Inscriptions speak of him as a 'mill for grinding the corn, his enemies, victorious in war and delighting in the spoils of victory', 'destroyer of enemies, famous among kings as the moon from the milky ocean'.

He acquired the title of 'Birudentembara Ganda' in strange circumstances. It was said that many chieftains had congregated at the annual car festival of the Lord of Nanjangud. Here, Nanja Shetti of Kalale, who was a loyalist of Timmaraja, was enraged by the fact that his master had no title worth his stature while the assembled chieftains were pompously reeling out their own. He challenged them to the lawful ownership of the much coveted title of Birudentembara Ganda. A scuffle

Deccan in 1525
(Maps are artistic recreations made at Suhaas Graphics, Bangalore)

followed and it was said that the Shetti managed to hold his own against his opponents and proclaim the title for his master. The title has since then been the unique appellation for the kings of Mysore. If nothing else, this incident shows the hollowness of the medieval and feudal society where it was common to witness brawls on such matters as titles and their rightful owners.

Timmaraja is also credited to have laid the foundations of a fort in Mysore by putting up an inner enclosure wall (*valasuttina kote*) in 1524 and naming it Mysuru Nagara. As narrated in a literary work titled *Mysuru Doregala Purvabhyudaya Vivara*, Mysore had till then only an irregular fort (*hoodevoo*) with an outskirt called Purageri, or the main street of the town, along with a Tammatagiri or Drummers' Lane. To the north-eastern end was the temple of God Someshwara built by the Cholas and a lake by its side called the Cholakere. The Chola temples of Bhairava and Lakshmiramanaswamy also stood beside it. Timmaraja also got a tank constructed behind the Chamundeshwari temple atop the hills called Hirikere. In November 1548, he purchased Tippur village for the construction of the temple of Cheluvarayaswamy of Melukote.

It is, however, hard to comprehend the Mysore of this age as a kingdom and these early rulers as kings. It is noteworthy that for over two centuries after the dynasty was established, the jurisdiction of the family was at best limited to the control of thirty-three villages. It was only by the end of the first decade of the seventeenth century that the Wodeyars of Mysore truly arrived on the Indian political scene. Till then, they can at best be considered as subsidiaries of the empire of Vijayanagara which was slowly but steadily heading towards its doom.

Meanwhile, the Indian political scenario was changing. India had stepped fully into the later medieval era. At the apex of the country's political system was a new dynasty that had come in from outside its borders and captured the seat of power in Delhi—the Mughals. The situation in southern India was unexpectedly volatile. After the death of Krishnadevaraya, the Vijayanagara empire slowly began to disintegrate under rulers, like Achyutaraya and Sadashivaraya. Trouble cropped up at this time with a certain Ramaraya playing the pivotal role in the destruction. He had seized power on the pretext of being regent to the infant Sadashivaraya, Krishnadevaraya's nephew, who was now the ruler of the kingdom. After removing many of the old Brahmin nobility, he placed his own relatives and adherents in power. There were five Muslim rulers in the Deccan after the disintegration of the Bahamani kingdom. They sought Ramaraya's help in their mutual squabbles.

On 26 December 1564, the Muslim Sultans joined hands against Vijayanagara, camping at Talikota. The war commenced on 23 January 1565, at a place between the Rakkasa and Tangadagi villages. Initially, Vijayanagara was at an advantage. But the opposing camp won over two pivotal Muslim commanders of Vijayanagara after brainwashing them to fight for Islam rather than side with the Hindus. These two commanded all the Muslim soldiers of Vijayanagara against the empire itself. Caesar Frederick writes:

> ...and when the armies were joined, the battle lasted but a while, not the space of four hours, because the two traitorous captains, in the chiefest of the fight, with their companies turned their faces against their king and made such disorder in his army, that being astounded, they set themselves to fight.*

Ramaraya was captured and killed by Nizam Shah—a member of the Muslim leaders' confederacy formed to fight Vijayanagara. The victorious forces pursued the princes and the army in the course of which 100,000 and more men were slain. Robert Sewell's account, *A Forgotten Empire*, explains the ruin which followed when Tirumala, Ramaraya's brother, fled the city with as much treasure as he could load on 1,550 elephants:

> ... then a panic seized the city ... no retreat, no fight was possible except to a few, for the pack oxen and carts had almost all followed the forces to the war and they had not returned. Nothing could be done but to bury all the treasures, to arm the younger men, and to wait. Next day, the place became a prey to the robber tribes and jungle people of the neighborhood. Hordes of Brinjaris, Lambadis, Kurubas and the like poured down on the hapless city and looted the stores and shops, carrying off great quantities of riches. Couto states that there were six concerted attacks by these people during the day.

It is perhaps due to these plunders that Kannadigas to this day refer to Hampi, the once splendorous capital of the empire where diamonds

---

* Frederick's account has been quoted in Nilakanta Sastri and Srinivasachari's *Advanced History of India*.

were supposedly sold on the streets, as 'Haalu Hampi' or the 'Destroyed Hampi'. Vijayanagara never recovered from this severe blow.

The fall of Vijayanagara meant the end of a glorious era of India's Hindu dynasties. But it also led to the rise of new power centres in the peninsula which were hitherto subsidiaries of the Empire—the Wodeyars of Mysore, the Nayakas of Madurai, Tanjore, Ikkeri or Keladi, Jinji, Chitradurga, Sonda and so on. These families inherited the traditions and heritage of Vijayanagara.

Meanwhile in 1572, in the month of Pushya, Timmaraja Wodeyar II died. He was succeeded by his brother Chamaraja Wodeyar IV. We find at this juncture the practice of polygamy creeping into the family with Chamaraja marrying Veerarajammanni of Sindhuvalli and Depajammanni. He had four sons: Devaraja, Chennaraja, Bettada Chamaraja and Raja Wodeyar. An interesting incident occurred during this time. Once, while returning from the *darshan* of Goddess Chamundeshwari, lightning struck the King's head as he descended the hill, but miraculously just a few strands of hair were charred making him bald. He thus came to be known as Bola Chamaraja Wodeyar or the bald Chamaraja Wodeyar.

Inscriptions speak of him as an expert in archery and in the handling of weapons of war, and as someone possessing great courage and prowess.

Scuffles between Bola Chamaraja and the Viceroy of Vijayanagara were common. In 1574, the Vijayanagara troops laid siege to Mysore for three months. But Chamaraja cleverly intercepted the supplies and reduced the besieging forces to a state of misery. The commandant, Remati Venkataraya, was forced to lift the siege and flee in disgrace. It was a complete victory for Mysore and a fall from grace for Vijayanagara, which had to cede Kalve Kottagala to Mysore. *Mysuru Doregala Vamshavali* states that by 1576 Chamaraja had become an overlord of 33 villages, commanding a force of 300 men and surrounded by hostile neighbours.

The rulers of Mysore acquired many titles, like Timmaraja II who was called Birudentembara Ganda, Bola Chamaraja who was referred to as Suguna Gambhira, and so on. After Bola Chamaraja died in 1576, his eldest son, Bettada Chamaraja Wodeyar V ascended the throne in the Phalguna of 1576. He had two sons, Timmaraja Wodeyar III and Ranadhira Kantheerava Narasaraja Wodeyar. Bettada Chamaraja V was a reckless ruler. Wilks sums up thus:

> ...mild and brave but thoughtless and improvident and in two years had thrown the finances into disorder. Elders of the land

found themselves obliged to propose to his younger brother Raj Wadeyar to supplant him in government. The scale of its affairs at the period may be conjectured from the chief objection of Raj Wadeyar to undertake so weighty a charge; viz., that with an empty treasury, an arrear of tribute of 5000 pagodas that was due to the Viceroy. This difficulty was removed by a contribution of 3000 from the privy purses of the females of the family and 2000 from the elders of the land; and Raj Wadeyar was installed.

Who exactly were these 'elders of the land' who seemed to have so much referent power on the matters of succession? They are often referred as 'Hale Paikis' which literally meant old peons and soldiers. But in reality it meant the old and loyalist adherents who wielded sufficient veto power in deciding who would succeed a ruler or for that matter even depose a sitting king. This quasi-democratic process seems to be a very unique feature of Mysore.

Interestingly, while at the same time, kingdoms elsewhere witnessed many bloodbaths among siblings on matters of kingship and succession, in the case of the Wodeyar family, the decisions were meekly accepted. It would not have been difficult for the deposed Chamaraja V to have assembled a motley crowd of armed men and tried to stage a coup of sorts or to get his brother assassinated. On the contrary, even after his deposition, he is known to have taken up cudgels on behalf of his younger brother and fought the troops of Karugahalli that were menacingly advancing towards their domain. This absence of rancour and ill-will among members of the family seems to be a unique trait of the early rulers of Mysore.

Quoting Wilks again on this rather interesting feature of the Mysore dynasty:

> This deposition of the elder and election of the younger brother, by the elders of the country, is a curious feature of ancient Indian manners, and illustrates the uncertainty of succession which characterizes the Hindoo Law. We find the power exercised, on several subsequent occasions, of deviating from the direct course of lineal descent, for the dangerous and generally delusive purpose, of obtaining a more worthy, or a more compliant successor; and terminating, as in other countries, in faction, usurpation and murder. Various incidents seem to prove that the characters of

the brothers rather the manners of the time, are marked in the disposal and subsequent history of the deposed raja. He was neither murdered nor imprisoned: and on his approaching the hall of audience, where his brother had been just installed, he was informed by the attendants, that the measure had become necessary from the state of the finances; but that he might still be usefully and honorably employed, in representing the family at the court of the Viceroy at Seringapatam; or if he should prefer independent retirement, that also had been provided for him at Mysoor. 'I will reside at neither,' said he, and departed in anger; but shortly afterwards, we find him living peacefully at Mysoor… find this generous and gallant soldier leading the forces of his younger brother, and achieving a variety of petty conquests….

The deposed raja retired to the pleasant village of Gundlu Terakanambi along with his wives and children.

2

THE AGE OF GLORY AD 1578–1617

AD 1610

Talakadu Maralaagali
Malingi Maduvaagali
Mysuru Dhoregalige Makkalagade hogali !

I curse Talakad to be submerged under creeping sands;
May a cruel whirlpool be the scourge of Malingi;
And the kings of Mysore suffer the pangs of childlessness!

With these terrible words on her lips, Rani Alamelamma ended her life in the Cauvery adorned with all the jewels that Raja Wodeyar was seeking that she never wanted to relinquish. Folklore and legends state that it rained sand for ten days after her death and the entire township of Talakad was submerged under sand dunes. A whirlpool in the Cauvery ensured that the town of Malingi came under its sway. The effect on the Mysore family was long lasting: generations of Wodeyars after this remained childless, in the sense that the royal family was never again of lineal descent with a son succeeding his father and so on.

The guards who had gone along with the troops to besiege the palace of the Rani for her jewels rushed to the makeshift tent where Raja Wodeyar had camped. Gasping for breath they conveyed the message: 'Your Highness, the rani jumped off a cliff into the gushing waters of the

Cauvery. She was fully decked in her choicest ornaments. She is dead... she is gone.'

Raja Wodeyar was consumed by immense pathos when the messengers brought him the news of the sad suicide of Rani Alamelamma. He was also shocked. Losing his composure, he sobbed uncontrollably like an infant. 'What have I done? Will I ever be forgiven? An act of haste on my part has caused the death of an innocent woman. Fie upon me!'

The ensuing night was perhaps the most difficult one in Raja Wodeyar's life. He barely managed to sleep. And if at all he did, the image of the bejewelled Rani with dishevelled hair and bloodshot eyes woke him with a shock. This carried on for a few more nights and when he heard the terrible curse that the Rani had spelt out before ending her life, his heart sank.

He called for the royal priest and confessed to his sins. 'Oh Holy One! I have committed a grave sin. Driven by my meaningless and malefic obsession, I have led an innocent woman into such a state of desperation that she was forced to end her life in the waters of the Cauvery. The curse that she pronounced on our family sends a chill down my spine. I have lost the luxury of sleep ever since. Is there some way out, some remedy? You are my only hope.'

The priest thought for a while, pulled out his almanac, did a couple of quick astrological calculations and said: 'My Lord! It is indeed the most unfortunate thing to have happened to your esteemed dynasty. Alamelamma was a woman of great determination. A statement rendered with that kind of conviction, call it a curse or whatever you might please, is bound to have a long lasting impact. In our religious traditions, the killing of snakes is also considered a terrible thing to do. The snake is supposed to avenge this act for seven generations. But conducting the *shraddha* ceremonies or the *sarpa samskara* to propitiate the soul of the deceased reptile is said to impart great benefits. I suggest that you conduct similar ceremonies to mollify the departed rani's soul and install a bronze idol of the Rani in the Palace and pray fervently. It is only prayers and repentance that can wash away the catastrophic effects of the terrible curse. Trust in the Almighty, my Lord. He will show us a way out.'

Accordingly, Raja Wodeyar got a bronze idol of Rani Alamelamma installed. The guilt and shame ensured that he never managed to make eye contact even with the idol. Yet he prayed fervently and conducted all the ceremonies as per the prescribed rituals. In the midst of all these rituals his thoughts invariably went back to the past—a past that had seen a long and stressful relationship between him and Alamelamma's deceased husband.

✥

Raja Wodeyar was born in 1552, to Bola Chamaraja Wodeyar and his wife Sindhuvalli Veerarajammanni. He assumed the leadership of the then principality in the Vaishaka month of 1578 and his reign is replete with contradictions. The Battle of Talikota ushered in the emergence of new centres of power under rulers who were hitherto feudatories of the Empire. One such kingdom which grew from a state of non-existence to one of eminence was Mysore and the man who heralded this transition was Raja Wodeyar. The early years of his reign marked tremendous efforts at consolidation and expansion of the frontiers of the Mysore principality which was now slowly, but steadily, becoming a force to reckon with in the Deccan.

The Vijayanagara empire was in the last phase of its existence. Historians categorise the history of Vijayanagara into four phases, each ruled by different dynasties which were different branches of the collateral line—brothers, uncles, nephews, etc. Harihara and Bukka who founded the empire belonged to the first dynasty, the Sangama dynasty. In 1486 the second offshoot emerged under Saaluva Narasimha, which was the Saaluva dynasty. In 1503, the Tuluva Dynasty came into prominence and Krishnadevaraya was a part of the same. The Battle of Talikota in 1565 and the death of Ramaraya led to the total disintegration of the empire and the last offshoot of the family—the Aravidu dynasty. As stated before, Tirumala, Ramaraya's brother, fled the city on the fateful day of the battle with as much treasure as he could load on 1,550 elephants and later established his supremacy. Six years after Talikota, there was confusion and anarchy, following which Tirumala became king. The Nayaks of Madurai, Tanjore and Gingee became virtually independent monarchs.

The mutual feuds of the sultans of Bijapur and Golconda, however, gave these early rulers of the Aravidu dynasty some breathing space and freedom to govern an extensive realm. Tirumala divided his empire among his sons whom he appointed as Viceroys. His eldest son Srirangaraya represented Penukonda (in Andhra), Sri Rama was placed in Srirangapatna and Venkatapatidevaraya in Chandragiri. Tirumala's reign was short and troubled. After merely eleven months on the throne, he retired and in 1572, his eldest son Sri Rangaraya succeeded him and took over Srirangapatna. The Wodeyars of Mysore and the Nayaks of Vellore and Keladi owed allegiance to the throne of Srirangapatna, which now had its new monarch, Srirangaraya.

Relations between Raja Wodeyar and Srirangaraya were strained from the beginning. The Nayaks of Madurai under Venkatapati Nayak attacked Srirangapatna and being a feudatory, Srirangaraya expected the ruler of neighbouring Mysore to stand by him in his hour of need. But Raja Wodeyar refused to be drawn into this battle of supremacy. He had other ideas in mind. He was looking for a more sovereign and powerful position for the Mysore kingdom in Deccan politics.

By then, Srirangapatna had a new viceroy—Tirumala II, who despised Raja Wodeyar with all his heart. Around 1585, Raja Wodeyar refused to pay taxes to Tirumala II on the excuse of the large-scale destruction of crops in Mysore by wild cattle. To keep away the cattle and thieves, he requested permission for the construction of a fort wall around Mysore. Soon after the wall was constructed, he expelled the Vijayanagara tax collectors from Mysore and openly challenged the authority of the throne. Simultaneously, he also decided to expand and consolidate his domain by defeating the neighbouring chieftains and Palegars. The same year Raja Wodeyar also made a customary visit to the court of Tirumala. But the bitterness was there for all to see.

In 1586 he conquered Rangasamudram, defeated Mallarajayya who surrendered Naranalli and similarly acquired Arakere from Adhataraya, Sosale and Banur from Talkad Nanjarajayaa, Kannambadi from Dodda Hebbar, Narasipura from Lakshmappa Nayak and so on. 1586 also saw Srirangaraya's demise and the succession to the throne by his brother Venkatapatidevaraya or Venkata II, who was to be by far the most significant ruler of the Aravidu dynasty. He ruled from Chandragiri.

In 1590, Raja Wodeyar visited the court of Tirumala at Srirangapatna for a second time accompanied by what Wilks calls his 'usual retinue and rude music'. An interesting incident from this time gives us insight into the social customs of those days. On the way to Srirangapatna, Raja Wodeyar met one Deparaja Wodeyar of Kembal and was enraged to note that he was accompanied by similar music. Music was subordinate to the powerful and the kind of music that 'accompanied' one seemed to suggest the position and power of an individual. An incensed Raja

Wodeyar reached Tirumala's court but asked his music band to stay mum. When questioned about this strange retinue of 'silent musicians' by Tirumala, Raja Wodeyar haughtily replied: 'What is the use of being accompanied by music, if someone like Deparaja, who is inferior to me is also accorded the same status? If music is not the differentiator, then why even have it along?' He then challenged Deparaja to a combat as open contest would be the only way of determining the superiority of either claimant. The latter accepted the challenge. But the very next day Deparaja was defeated and Kembal was annexed to Mysore. If nothing, this incident shows the kind of man Raja Wodeyar was and also the whimsical grounds on which conquests and annexations were made in those times.

Meanwhile, Tirumala II was growing wary of the powerful feudatory in his neighbourhood: Raja Wodeyar, who was slowly but steadily rising right under his nose and there was precious little he could do to prevent the rise. He was also encouraged by all the chieftains of the area who were growing increasingly insecure due to the aggressive designs of the man from Mysore. A political summit of sorts happened in Srirangapatna in 1596 when Tirumala returned from his Madurai campaign. The chiefs made their representations to him there. Raja Wodeyar had sent his Niyogis or political agents to keep a close watch on the developments at Srirangapatna. In a sly plot hatched in the dark corners of the Srirangapatna palace, Tirumala decided to send invitations on palm leaves to all the chieftains under his suzerainty, including Raja Wodeyar, for the Mahanavami festival during Dussehra. Raja Wodeyar accepted the invitation and reached Srirangapatna along with his brother Devaraja Wodeyar. Tirumala met the brothers at a camp on the outskirts of the city where they had taken temporary shelter. A great show of bonhomie was made and promises of everlasting friendship solemnised. But all that seemed to vanish the minute the royal scribe of Mysore read out the titles of Raja Wodeyar. The title of 'Birudentembara Ganda' bestowed on him through his lineage from his grandfather aroused Tirumala's anger. He felt that it was the lawful possession of his own family. When contradicted, he left in a huff but made up his mind to seal the fate of the brothers and break all the vows of camaraderie they had just made.

The next day Raja Wodeyar was to visit the Lord Ranganatha Temple at Srirangapatna. Tirumala had ordered his soldiers to capture the brothers and imprison them while they were offering worship. Luckily for Raja

Wodeyar, the machinations of Tirumala were loud enough to catch the ears of his loyalist Niyogi, Somayaji, who promptly alerted him about the impending disaster. In the dead of night, the brothers fled from Srirangapatna through the Brahmapuri Gate. His trust in Tirumala was now completely shattered.

Their relations then reached a flashpoint when Raja Wodeyar engaged Tirumala and his supporters in a bloody war at Kesare. Initially, Tirumala wanted to besiege the fort of Mysore but was warned by his loyalists about the futility of such an exercise, keeping in mind the fate that had befallen Remati Venkataraya in the past. So they thought it prudent to besiege the fort of Kesare, the gateway to Mysore that was poorly defended by about 30 soldiers only. On 18 August 1596, the Vijayanagara troops, including one lakh foot soldiers, about 12,000 horses and 200 elephants encircled the fort of Kesare headed by the chiefs of Ummattur and Mugur.

But Raja Wodeyar's brothers, Bettada Chamaraja and Chennaraja, proved daunting enemies. The former left his younger brother to lead at Mysore, marched southwards and attacked the hostile chief of Heggadadevanakote. He then crossed the Kabini River near Nanjangud and in the dead of night made an unnerving surprise attack on the enemy camp at Kerehatti, Satajagala and Kirangur. This shook the enemy troops, who were caught completely off-guard. Yet again, this shows the manner in which the deposed king stood up to back his successor and younger brother.

Meanwhile, Raja Wodeyar fell on the enemy troops like a hawk sweeping on its prey and killed Jakka, the chief commandant who was menacingly proceeding towards Hanchega, a premier post. This set the whole enemy camp in complete disarray. Raja Wodeyar took advantage of the prevailing confusion and weaned away many hostile chieftains from being partners-in-sin in Tirumala's grand alliance. Tirumala was thus dealt a crushing blow by the Mysore forces and he was shamed into returning to Srirangapatna to lick his wounds.

Venkata, the emperor, admonished Tirumala for wrecking such disgrace on the Aravidu household and decided to repose less and lesser faith in him. In fact, he began to look more favourably upon Raja Wodeyar, who he thought was more daring and accomplished and a befitting representative of the Vijayanagara kingdom. With this assurance of sorts from the monarch himself and his recent victory at Kesare, Raja Wodeyar felt more empowered and at almost every stage defied the authority of Tirumala II, encroaching upon his domain whenever possible. His aggressive designs continued with the acquisition of Hariharapura in 1597 and a receipt in grant from Tirumala himself in 1598 of vast lands in Belagula.

On his part, Tirumala thought hatching conspiracies was the best way to deal with the situation. In 1607, a fresh attempt was made on Raja Wodeyar's life. Singappa Wodeyar of Belagula was sent to kill him. When he drew out his dagger and was just about to thrust it into Raja Wodeyar, Deparaja of Yeleyur, a nephew, who was hiding behind a pillar, flung himself on the assassin from behind, pushing him away and thereby averting the mishap. Tirumala was yet again frustrated at the failure of his designs.

Tirumala did not share a very cordial relationship with the monarch Venkata either. However, he decided to bury his differences and align with Venkata to vanquish Raja Wodeyar, but the King flatly refused to accommodate his Viceroy. Tirumala was forced to eat humble pie when Emperor Venkata asked him to seek the help of the very man he despised, Raja Wodeyar, to free his officers led by Tirumalarajayya who had been captured by the Palegar of Narasipura, Lakshmappa Nayak. Raja Wodeyar's success in this endeavour endeared him further to the monarch, who was tilting in his favour with each passing day, at the cost of his own viceroy. As luck would have it, Tirumala was also afflicted by an incurable disease. Some records call it *Bennu phani*, which perhaps is the herpes of the spine. Realising that he had lost both political and physical power, Tirumala decided to retire after calling a truce with his long time *bete noire* Raja Wodeyar.

Emperor Venkata II called Raja Wodeyar over to Srirangapatna for discussions. Raja Wodeyar's stars were at their beneficial best. On the one hand, his competitor, the viceroy of Srirangapatna, Tirumala, was too unwell to put up any show of strength. On the other hand, Venkata, unlike his predecessor, was completely in awe of his man Friday. Raja Wodeyar marched victoriously to Srirangapatna in the hope that he would be richly rewarded in the wake of the changed circumstances. His hopes weren't misplaced. Fortune awaited him in the court of Srirangapatna with open arms.

Of course there is a variant to this story which says Raja Wodeyar supposedly dealt the final blow to his foe in January 1610, when he dispatched troops under his son Narasaraja Wodeyar, who drove away all the chiefs loyal to Tirumala and forced him to surrender and retire.

The Annals narrate a rather lengthy dialogue between Raja Wodeyar and Emperor Venkata with reference to the golden throne of the viceroy which he handed over to Raja Wodeyar and which remained the official throne of the Mysore kings ever after.*

Emperor Venkata said:

Do you see that bedecked throne? It has such a long and vibrant history behind it. In the days of yore, it was the property of Dharmaraja Yudhistira who passed it on to his grandson Parikshita. The throne was with the Pandava family for 1,115 years. With the fall of the Pandavas, the king of Magadha, Sumali held possession of it after which 30 kings up to Kadambaraya of Mysore ruled over it for 494 years. It stayed with Lokalokaditya Kadambaraya for another 80 years after which Jayanthi Kadambaraya and 31 successors after him ascended it over 24 years. The throne has seen a rule of 456 years of Durmitaraya and 30 other kings. Then Vikramaditya, the son of the Kshatriya daughter of Veerasena and Govindabhagawan held possession of it for 63 years. For another 41 years, Vikramaraya, the ruler of Malwa, had the opportunity of sitting on the throne. For 64 years thereafter it was the prized possession of Bhoja, the king of Avanti. It then passed on to the Nava Ballalas of Halebid. But then the Badshahs of Delhi captured it and held it for 54 years.

It kept changing hands thus in times of anarchy and falling into the laps of the brave. Then the Tundu rulers of Bidare and Surtal captured the throne. Prataparudra Kakatiya of Oregallu then held it for 421 years when he and his successors sat on the bejeweled throne.

Alas! It had to then fall into the hands of one of the successors, Kampilaraya, who after ruling from it for 13 years secretly buried it one night. But then in AD 1334 Swami Vidyaranya was keen on establishing a powerful force in the South to reckon with the Muslim power that was at its peak in the Northern regions. He decided to invoke the blessings of Goddess Lakshmi. Pleased with

---

* Incidentally, *The Annals* confusingly indicate that it was Srirangaraya who handed over the throne to Raja Wodeyar. But it must be noted that Srirangaraya passed away in 1586 and this incident occurred in 1609-10.

his penance the Goddess supposedly showered gold on the place, famous as the *Suvarna Vrishti* or Golden Rain of Vijayanagara. This indicated that the place was auspicious for the task.

Vidyaranya was on the look out for a befitting ruler for the empire he wanted to build. One day, two young men Hakka and Bukka, who were retrenched from their offices at the court of Oregallu, were resting below a tree when a snake danced on Hakka's head and left. Vidyaranya happened to see this rare spectacle and immediately realised that the golden throne must be buried there, as it was believed that snakes guard secret treasures. On unearthing the place, they found the dazzling throne there! Vidyaranya christened the men as Harihara Raya and Bukka Raya and crowned Harihara as King in 1336, thus marking the foundation of the Vijayanagara Empire.

When the dynasty fell at the battle of Talikota in 1564, the throne went to Tirumala I, Ramaraya's brother. My father, Tirumala I, called us all to his deathbed and divided the kingdom among us. My elder brother, Srirangaraya, held possession of the throne till his death, after which it was the official throne of the Viceroy of Srirangapatna. This has been the glorious history of this throne, which I now hand over to your custody.

Historical records date the throne to a project commissioned by the Maharaja of Mysore in AD 1716. The present shape of the throne was designed in the year 1917.

Historians are divided over whether the throne was handed over by Venkata II to Raja Wodeyar or by Tirumala II who, after being defeated in battle after battle with the Wodeyar, was admonished by the monarch to hand over the throne to the victor or whether he willingly decided to relinquish the throne after being afflicted with the disease. Wilks sums up this dichotomy aptly:

> ...the acquisition of Seringapatnam, in 1610...is related in different manuscripts, with a diversity of statement, which seems only to prove a mysterious intricacy of intrigue beyond the reach of contemporaries to unravel....

Whatever be the sequence of events, what is noteworthy is that the year 1610 marked a triumphant one in the history of the Wodeyars with their supremacy being established in greater measure and the shifting of the capital city to Srirangapatna from Mysore. An inscription of 1612 refers to Raja Wodeyar as 'Sriman Mahaadhiraja', indicating that he was thenceforth a prominent feudatory of the Vijayanagara Empire.

The sick and vanquished viceroy, Tirumala II, gave up his efforts to defeat the Wodeyar, submitting himself to the will of Lord Vaidyeshwara in Talakad on the banks of the Cauvery River and retired to a life of peace and tranquillity at Malingi (a village by the side of Talakad) along with his two wives Alamelamma and Rangamma. Historians differ on whether Tirumala II died in Talakad after succumbing to his illness or, as epigraphical evidences suggested, survived till 1625. Whatever be the case, he and his family were now powerless and at the mercy of Raja Wodeyar.

On his part, Raja Wodeyar was not content to let his *bete noire* beat such a hasty and simple retreat. He was the same man who had tried to trick him and get him murdered. He had more than one axe to grind with his hitherto bitter enemy. Confiscating all that belonged to Tirumala was his top priority. Rani Alamelamma had brought with her all the jewellery that belonged to her. She would supposedly lend the same to adorn the Goddess Ranganayaki Ammal at the Sriranganathaswamy temple at Srirangapatna every Tuesday and Thursday. Raja Wodeyar believed that with the loss of power, the family had also relinquished its authority over these costly jewels and that they rightfully belonged to the Temple. He sent his soldiers to the Rani at Malingi to get the jewels back.

But history blanks out at this stage, which, according to popular legend, was undoubtedly crucial in the story of the Wodeyars. It was to determine the very nature of their genealogy. Historians, geologists, archaeologists, thinkers and rationalists have differed hugely on the veracity of the legend and its long-lasting impact on history and geography. Here, I present the more widely accepted or popularly believed version of the sequence of events, which can by no means be construed as accurate. The accuracy of the story has anyway been wiped out by the sands of time (or the sands of Talakad) and there is absolutely no way of ascertaining the true version—one of the many dilemmas and predicaments that confront people involved in historical research. Facts get drowned in the tide of time and popular legend, by sheer virtue of constant repetition, gets reinforced as truth. History also does not tell us clearly whether Tirumala was alive at this point or whether the disease had already claimed his life. Either way, his Rani was left to fend for herself in the unfortunate circumstances that now befell her.

Totally unaware of the machinations on the part of the new occupant of the throne of the Viceroy, Rani Alamelamma was in a blissful state of spiritual and emotional renunciation on the banks of Talakad. She was baffled to see soldiers from Srirangapatna knock at her apartment.

'The Viceroy of Srirangapatna has sent us to you to collect all the jewels that you send across to Goddess Ranganayaki every week. He says it belongs to the Royal Treasury of the emperor and hence should be kept in safe custody in Srirangapatna.'

'What impertinence! These are family jewels that have come down to us from ages. How can I hand it over to an upstart and a usurper? Please tell your viceroy that I have no such intention.' This was the terse reaction of the Rani.

'Madam, we have been ordered by His Highness that unless we get the said jewels from you, we are not allowed to leave Malingi. So let us not create a scene here. We request you to hand over the jewels to us.'

The Rani finally relented and unwillingly sent across her huge pearl nose ring.

But this didn't satisfy Raja Wodeyar who wanted the entire set. He sent his soldiers again to Malingi with orders to besiege the palace of the Rani and use force if necessary to get the jewellery back.

From the ramparts of her palace the Rani was shocked to see a huge retinue of soldiers marching towards Malingi. She was distressed and irked by the indecent behaviour of the soldiers of Srirangapatna and their new master. 'What more does he want? I relinquished my costliest ornament to him. These jewels are not the property of Vijayanagara, but that of my family. Anyway I send them twice every week to Srirangapatna to adorn the Goddess. Why should they be used by Raja Wodeyar and his harem just because they have vanquished us politically?'

By then the troops had reached the gates of the palace. The personal attendants of the rani rushed to her apartments. 'Your Highness, there is a large army of soldiers knocking at the doors of our palace. I can sense some trouble here. Why don't you escape via the secret route?'

The rani was too shocked to react. She was left numb and speechless due to this indecent behaviour of her husband's foe. 'Ask them to wait, I will give them what they want,' she said and left with a stony silence adorning her pretty face. She put on all the ornaments that she could find in the royal chest and with an air of quiet determination, made her way towards the secret exit from the palace.

By then, the troops were getting restive. Sensing some foul play they broke open the doors and barged into the palace, which bore a deserted look. They rushed towards the Rani's apartments. Through the windows of her room, one of the soldiers saw a dazzling apparition making its way towards the riverside. Sensing that it might be the rani trying to escape, they hastened to follow her. By then she had climbed a cliff that overlooked the gushing torrents of the Cauvery, overflowing in the wake of the monsoons. She cried to the troops from her position there, 'Go tell your viceroy that in life he vanquished us, but not in death. Honour is more important to us than our life and he has tried to play with it. I, my jewels, this territory of Talakad and Malingi will forever remain invincible for that vile man. He can only hope to acquire us all, but his hopes would remain just that—unfulfilled and unconsummated.' Then she blurted out the inevitable. With folded hands and closed eyes, she prayed to Lord Vaidyeshwara and said, 'O Lord! If I have been ever sincere to you as a devotee and a faithful wife of my husband, grant me this dying wish that would be a curse for the arrogant viceroy of Srirangapatna:

Talakadu Maralaagali
Malingi Maduvaagali
Mysuru Dhoregalige Makkalagade hogali !

I curse Talakad to be submerged under creeping sands;
May a cruel whirlpool be the scourge of Malingi;
And the kings of Mysore suffer the pangs of childlessness!

And then, Alamelamma leaped to her death in the waters of the Cauvery, to the utter dismay of the soldiers of Raja Wodeyar.

Penitent and troubled, Raja Wodeyar performed the prescribed rituals in front of the bronze image of Rani Alamelamma, but he could not stop his mind from slipping away into the past, remembering his stressful relationship with her husband. His thoughts were interrupted by the priest who nudged him to perform the final *pinda daan* or rice ball offerings to the soul of the deceased. With a heavy heart, he arose to bid the final adieu to a lady whose death was his handiwork.

✣

Even today on the ninth day of the Dussehra festival the idol of Alamelamma is taken to the main palace from an old outhouse along the outer walls of the palace fort. In a ceremony that is not much publicised and kept strictly private, this idol is worshipped along with that of the family goddess Chamundeshwari. The priests cover their mouths with a cloth, to signal their shame and embarrassment. The Wodeyar is supposed to never make eye contact with her—again out of shame, indignity, trepidation and respect. Over the Internet, the present scion of the Wodeyar dynasty Srikantha Datta Narasimharaja Wodeyar can be seen performing the rituals to venerate Rani Alamelamma.[*] Her pearl nose ring is still preserved in the Ranganathaswamy temple at Srirangapatna. Incidentally, Raja Wodeyar was the one who continued the glorious Vijayanagara tradition of celebrating the Dussehra festival with pomp and grandeur over ten days—a phenomenon that continues in Mysore till today.

Since the days of Rani Alamelamma, every alternate generation of the Wodeyar family has been heirless in the sense that the king did not have a son or even if he did, he wasn't fit enough to ascend the throne as he was born of an illegitimate union or from a woman of low birth. The Wodeyars have had to resort to the practice of adopting sons from the collateral line (children of brothers, uncles, etc.), though after a while even the collateral line ceased and they had to adopt from outside the family. An interesting phenomenon was that every adopted son would have a biological son. But the biological son would be childless and would have to resort to another adoption. Such is the case that even to this day, with all the progress in science and technology at their command, the present scion of the Mysore royal family, who is the son of an adopted heir, is childless.

Strangely the priests who worship the Rani's idol seem to have been affected by the same curse and are childless too. Once, when a priest did beget a son, he died tragically—electrocuted just before the ninth-day ritual during Dussehra. Such is the gory mystery surrounding the legend of Alamelamma, the unfortunate Rani who ended her life after being pushed into a corner by a victorious King. The tale of Alamelamma remains a disturbing chapter in the history of Mysore—one that has no straight answers, no historical and scientific justification, but one that continues to be a living legend.

---

[*] Visit http://www.royalsplendourofmysore.com/videodasara2004.htm, video file 25.

Not only Rani Alamelamma, but also Raja Wodeyar captured the interest of the masses through folklore and vernacular literature abounds with tales about him, for both the right and wrong reasons. *The Annals of the Mysore Royal Family*—one of the more popular records of the royal family—describes a number of miracles centred on his life. The point here is not to test the veracity of the claims, which as the very name suggests is 'folklore' and has been transmitted by word of mouth from one generation to the next. What it definitely suggests is that this King was certainly someone who was popular, respected, and of course, by virtue of the age-old divine right theory of kingship, was bestowed with other worldly powers and capabilities. But at the same time he was also hated by a few for his actions and inactions.

Somewhere around 1595, Veerarajayya, the chieftain of the principality of Karugahalli and a cousin of Raja Wodeyar, failed in his attempts to prevent him from passing through his dominion to the temple of Srikantheshwara at Nanjangud. To avenge this shameful defeat, he thought of a hideous plan to eliminate his rival. He knew that the Wodeyar, being a devout and God-fearing man, regularly visited all the temples in the palace complex each morning before he started off the day's work. One such temple was that of Sri Lakshmiramanaswamy whose head priest Srinivasayya was summoned by Veerarajayya's men. Taking him aside they handed him a bag full of gold coins. The old priest was flummoxed. 'Sir, what is this for? Is it an offering for the Lord?'

'No my man of God, this is for you. This is just the beginning. You can see your future lined with gold if you act according to our plans. We bring you a message from the chieftain of Karugahalli.' They whispered their hideous plan in the priest's ears. His face turned pale with fright.

'No, no, no, this is something I simply cannot do. That will be the biggest sin of my life. The Lord Almighty would never forgive me. I am sorry....'

The hitherto saccharine messengers held a dagger at Srinivasayya's throat. 'But your Lord Almighty would not come down to help you if we decided to slit your throat right now. Don't be imprudent. You have nothing to lose but your life by refusing. But if you comply then you would roll in wealth. Think about it.'

Srinivasayya had no option but to agree.

The next morning, as always, Raja Wodeyar made a visit to the temple to pay his respects. Srinivasayya felt a lump in his throat the minute he saw the King nearing the sanctum. Completely disoriented, he tried to carry on with the rituals. The King could sense that his usually exuberant priest was not his normal self. He used to greet him each morning in a pleasant manner with blessings and words of wisdom on his lips.

'Sir! Is something bothering you? You look weak and tired,' the King enquired.

'Errrr...no Your Highness, I am alright...couldn't sleep last night... so...otherwise...usually....'

His incoherent mumbling astonished the King further. But he let it be.

After the pujas were completed, the priest came out of the sanctum to offer the *tirtha* or holy water to the King. His hands trembled violently while he tried to offer the *tirtha*.

'Sir! Something seems to be bothering you. Your hands are trembling. Shall I send for the royal physician?'

'Oh no, Your Highness, insomnia, old age...they have no cure...I am all right...nothing is wrong...there is nothing wrong with the *tirtha* also.'

'What? What could be wrong with the *tirtha*? It comes with the blessings of the Lord...I don't understand what you are trying to say,' the King was suspicious now.

'Oh foolish, old me! I think I am getting senile. How can anything be wrong with the holy water? It is supposed to cure, not kill. Errrr... what am I saying? Please accept the...'

Raja Wodeyar now knew there was something seriously wrong. He sternly ordered the old man to come out with the truth or face the consequences. Finally, Srinivasayya gave in. Setting the bowl aside, he fell at the king's feet and with tears in his eyes pleaded for mercy. 'Forgive me my Lord! I have sinned. My soul would be condemned to hell fire. Being lured by gold and giving in to the threats of the Karugahalli chieftain, I poisoned the *tirtha*....'

The King was unfazed. 'The *tirtha* is divine water. If anything it should heal and cure, so what if it has poison mixed with it?'

Saying this, he supposedly snatched the bowl of *tirtha* and drank it in one gulp, which according to the *Annals*, 'turned from poison to nectar in his throat'. The priest was punished by being transferred to a temple at remote Kannambadi while the ears and nose of the Karugahalli chief were cut off with a sledge-hammer after a hand-to-hand fight with him on horseback at Kadu Basavanathittu, his fort was destroyed, the booty from his treasury was confiscated and offered to the presiding deity of the Mysore royal family, Goddess Chamundeshwari.

Another such 'miracle' is recorded in the *Annals* which takes us to Tirumala Tirupati, the Seven Hills of Lord Venkateswara—the veritable Vatican of Hindu faith. In this holy place, a devout Brahmin would visit the temple regularly. This man was blind since his birth. Sitting at the doorstep of the Lord, he would lament everyday: 'O! Lord! Grant me the power of vision so that I can see the wonderful world you have created, see myself, my friends, relatives, see you! Till now I have just heard that your world is gloriously colourful. Give me the ability to perceive these colours!'

It was the time of the annual Brahmotsavam celebrations at Tirumala where the deity is taken on a grand procession along the hills. There was grandeur everywhere as the temple authorities and the locals got ready to take out a gloriously bejewelled deity, decked in all His wonderful and choicest ornaments, in a resplendent chariot on the streets of Tirupati. The Brahmin devotee was frustrated at his unfulfilled desire. He vented his frustration and anger on the God whom he had worshipped so far and who he felt had betrayed his trust. 'O! Lord! Till now not a day has passed without my regular visit to your holy presence. I have served you with my body, mind and soul. Yet you have not granted my wish. If I do not get at least one of my eyes to see the festivities, I will end my life at your doorstep.'

Next morning when he woke up, the Brahmin was shaken out of his wits to realise that he had got sight back in one eye. He rushed to the temple and fell at the Lord's feet, thanking him profusely even as tears rolled down from his eyes. But he was like just any other human being whose desires and greed knew no bounds. Each time a wish of ours gets fulfilled, we harbour desires for the consummation of the next one and another. This man began nurturing the desire of getting back his other eye too. So one night, in his dream Lord Venkateswara seems to have appeared and directed him to go to Raja Wodeyar of Mysore if he wanted his other eye as well. At that very instant the man got up, packed his belongings and left for Mysore.

On reaching Mysore he narrated the tale to the Wodeyar who was wonderstruck on hearing the tale. He instructed the man to come over to the Lakshmiramana temple the next day and expressed the hope that the divine will would prevail. The next morning the miracle happened. On

Raja Wodeyar's touch, the man gained sight in his other eye as well. He prostrated himself before the King and ran joyously to Tirupati, narrating the incident to all passers-by.

With these fascinating fables behind us, we move ahead in the political history of the Wodeyars after AD 1610 and the accession of Srirangapatna. With the acquisition of Srirangapatna and the newfound importance bestowed upon the Wodeyar dynasty, Raja Wodeyar decided to consolidate his position in the Deccan through a series of conquests. The expansion of the kingdom continued with the annexing of Siyur and Malavattur from Peripatna Nanjunde Urs in 1610 and 1617 respectively, Srikantharajayya's Suragur in 1612, Terakanambi and Ummattur from Hadinadu Nanjarajayya in 1614, Talakad, Hullahalli, Kalale, Heggadadevanakote, Mugur, Hosakoralu and Ramasamudra in 1615.

Ever since the days of perfidy by the then dalavoy or army general, Maaranayaka, Yaduraya and successive kings had abolished the practice of appointing of Dalavoys.* But Raja Wodeyar deemed it necessary to appoint one and nominated his nephew Mallarajayya as the Dalavoy by giving him the traditional ring of the Dalavoy. After serving for a few days, this man went to his native place, Kalale, and mysteriously sent back the ring through his grandson with no explanation for the same. This became a sore point for Raja Wodeyar in his last days. It was Raja Wodeyar who had saved this Mallarajayya from the clutches of his cruel stepmother Tagadoor Chennammaji and her three sons, Nandinatha, Kantha and Chandrashekara. Young Mallaraja had to escape from Kalale and from the house arrest that these people had placed him under to Mysore to his maternal uncle, Raja Wodeyar who had taken full responsibility for his education and livelihood and now elevated him to the post of army general, which he threw away with such ingratitude. He now appointed Bettada Urs as the new Dalavoy for the kingdom.

---

* Dalavoys occupied a very important role in Mysore's history. They were army generals and determined the military strategies of the kingdom in consultation with the king. At the beginning they were generally subservient to the ruler. As time went by, however, these Dalavoys slowly began to assume extra-constitutional powers beyond their normal jurisdiction and started assuming the title of 'Sarvadhikari'—supreme dictators. Their growth spelt doom for the royal family in the centuries to come.

As if validating the curse of Alamelamma, all the three sons of Raja Wodeyar died in quick succession after he ascended the throne of Srirangapatna. This made him very anxious about the future of the kingdom as his age was steadily advancing. His last days were spent in utter sorrow and despair. His wife Edanahalli Timmajammanni was pregnant at that time. So the King nominated his eleven-year old grandson, Chamaraja, offspring of his son Narasaraja and Chamarajammanni, as his successor. In the Jyeshta month of 1617, Raja Wodeyar, who had led such an eventful life and to whom goes the credit for bringing Mysore to the forefront of kingdoms that existed in the early seventeenth century, breathed his last. He can truly be credited as the man who established the Wodeyar dynasty and Mysore as a powerful and noteworthy force in southern India.

He was also a hero of folklore and fable, and, as indicated earlier, there is no rational, scientific or historical evidence to prove the veracity of the tales about him. They are fables and legends which have been passed down the generations with such conviction that they have almost become a belief. The exact intention of spinning such yarns seems to be to glorify the king of the times and place him on a pedestal above ordinary mortals. However, in the case of Raja Wodeyar there are contradictions galore. A man who was given to such supposedly pious and noble acts was also involved in the most heinous episode that pulls him down to the nadir of human nature from the pedestal on which the glorifying fables placed him. Ultimately, one is at a loss to understand what one needs to believe and what to discount. But finally, the theme of history in fact needs to be like that. The people of the past were not clearly demarcated into heroes and villains. They had streaks of both, like any of us. These stories and fables only highlight the two sides of the same coin, the dichotomy that exists in human nature and character.

THE SANDS OF TALAKAD—MYTH vs SCIENCE

The submerged temples of Talakad, the disappearance of Malingi and the strange phenomenon of the Wodeyar lineage raise questions that perplex any reasoning intellect.

To any rational mind, while the last line of the Rani's curse might seem logical—that of destroying the very family of the Wodeyars for what they had done to her and her family—why the poor towns of Talakad and Malingi had to become scapegoats in this entire drama baffles everyone.

Wouldn't it have been better if she had cursed the capital city of the Wodeyars, Srirangapatna, to death and disaster? In what way did the submergence of Talakad and the whirlpool formations at Malingi affect the Wodeyars? These are questions that do not have a direct answer and remain shrouded in mystery forever.

An unbiased and scientific approach to the story of Alamelamma would naturally cause anyone to question whether she had the power to curse an entire lineage and town to doom. Sadly, there is no known evidence or reference in our historical texts to suggest that she was blessed with supernatural powers, bestowed on her after perhaps years of penance or meditation. Such power is usually found in those who are above all earthly attachments. But in this case, her lust for her gold ornaments was all-encompassing. How often in Hindu traditions do people submit offerings to a deity and then take them back for personal use? Did the social customs of the times permit widows to wear such fancy jewellery? Raja Wodeyar was supposedly demanding these ornaments for the goddess of the Srirangapatna temple and not for the inmates of his harem. A woman who would rather end her life and throw the jewels in the river than submit them to the presiding deity could certainly not have been a saint capable of such powerful curses.

It is noteworthy that historical documentations of the seventeenth and eighteenth centuries make no reference to Rani Alamelamma. In fact even the accounts of British travellers like Francis Buchanan, who has recorded the minutest of details related to the kingdom of Mysore, its people and their traditions, speaks casually of a legend of the 'natives' during his visit to Malingi. He records their belief that the curious sand formation that had submerged many temples in neighbouring Talakad was due to the curse of a local woman drowned while crossing the river to visit the temple. So enraged was she with the God of the place for having denied her *darshan*, that she cursed the temples to be submerged by sand! Nowhere is the reference made to a queen who lost her life under such tragic circumstances. Could someone like Buchanan have missed out on something as important as this—had it been true—even after interviewing several locals for his account? Would the locals themselves have overlooked telling him such an interesting and significant tale? It seems extremely unlikely.

Other contemporary records have similar tales to tell. Lieutenant Colonel Wilks, Political Resident at the Mysore Court who compiled an exhaustive history of the region, misses out on the rani too! These documentations date back to the early nineteenth century. If the Rani episode had indeed occurred in 1610, a full 200 years before, could vernacular and British literature have omitted mention of the episode altogether for so long?

The first time that Rani Alamelamma does make an appearance in the documentation of the history of Mysore is in Rice's *Gazetteer* of 1876. Here, her three-line curse makes its presence felt. The story is further dwelt upon in the *Annals* with a full dramatisation of the events preceding her death. Interestingly the *Annals* were published by the then maharaja himself, and he took an active interest in its contents and publication. If this story was such an embarrassment to the royal family, why did the maharaja not censor it completely? It thus grows increasingly clear that the story of Alamelamma was fabricated in the nineteenth century—maybe towards the 1830s or 1840s—and was most probably created at the behest of the royal family itself. Rationalists argue that Dalhousie's announcement of the Doctrine of Lapse spurred the royal court to concoct this story. The nobility must have witnessed with alarm the annexation of numerous Indian princely kingdoms by the British on the pretext of illegitimate succession or the absence of a legal male heir. That the then king of Mysore had no legitimate male heir was reason enough for them to believe that their kingdom would be next. To avert this, a possible escape route might have been to attribute the childlessness to a curse of yore and try to substantiate it by placing it in a historical and geographical era and circumstance of 1610, Talakad and the Vijayanagara viceroy's family.

Scientists, geologists and archaeologists dismiss these legends as mere mumbo-jumbo. They attribute more plausible reasons for the occurrence of these phenomena. The course of the Cauvery seems to hold the key, they say, as it takes a sharp meander on its route along the Mudukutore Betta or Hill. High school geography textbooks tell us that when a river meanders and turns back on its course, the outer banks of the river obviously get eroded by the waters of the river, but it also exposes the inner banks, which get deposits of sand and sediments. In the mid-fourteenth century, a minister of the Vijayanagara Empire, Madhava Raya, supposedly built the Madhava Mantri dam. This created lower water stages downstream and exposed the deposits of the river that forced the Cauvery to shift its course. This, coupled with large-scale deforestation in the region, created fine sand and silt that was trapped in the topographical area of Talakad bounded closely by the tall temple structures and gradually started accumulating over the entire region. Archaeologists supplement the theory by virtue of their excavations, which reveal that it was no catastrophe that killed people in large numbers or buried their remains in the sands, but a natural and gradual process. The shifting course of the Cauvery in a westward direction exposed the inner banks as stated earlier. But it also eroded the outer banks on which stood Malingi, which was perhaps what was meant by Malingi becoming a terrible whirlpool.

The curse of Rani Alamelamma remains shrouded in mystery. The third part of her curse on the Wodeyar dynasty is also irrational, especially because the very object of her curse, Raja Wodeyar, fathered sons! Since the impact of the curse was not felt in the very first generation itself, its effect on future generations is certainly questionable. The Wodeyar lineage (till the last ruler of the dynasty of fifteen kings who succeeded Raja Wodeyar) shows that the kings may have died sonless only thrice in the family tree. Even in these cases, the king did not have *legitimate* sons from the queen—his countless concubines or other queens did have sons, but they were not acceptable as heirs to the throne. It is but natural for a king with so many wives and concubines to spend the bulk of his time and divert his affection to them rather than the principal queen. Could it be that this was the reason—rather than a curse—for the absence of a male heir? Also, during the eighteenth century, when the kingdom was usurped, it was alleged that the young kings who had been placed as puppets on the throne were surreptitiously murdered by the usurper by the time they reached their puberty. Such young boys could not have had sons at such an early age, necessitating an adoption from the collateral line. Thus, while every rational argument goes against the myth of Alamelamma and her existence, she continues to capture popular imagination. The imagery of an innocent woman being wronged by a man intoxicated with power, and the subsequent suicide of the lady in question, can really affect the psyche of the people, giving rise to myths and legends. No wonder then, that despite the question on the historical validity and rationale of the Alamelamma legend, it still continues to be narrated as folklore with such conviction as merits a documented fact.

Meanwhile, for reasons of geological phenomena or the curse, Talakad stands as a mute spectator to this sudden metamorphosis, wailing amidst a million dunes with the fables of the past swishing with the wind across its arid expanses. The township of Talakad to this day lies submerged in sand dunes, a town on the banks of the river Cauvery that bears the brunt of its hoary past.

But since time immemorial Talakad has been home to innumerable legends; in fact, its name is derived from one such legend.

The temple of Lord Vaidyeshwara at Talakad is among the oldest in the place. It is worshipped as the main deity along with the *pancha lingas*, or five manifested forms of Lord Shiva. The deity has a vertical dent on it. Legend has it that aeons ago a saint, Somadatta, worshipped Lord Shiva at Benaras and prayed that he might realise the truth of the scriptures. In a dream, the Lord of Kashi instructed him to proceed to the quiet abode of sage Richika in Dalavanapura, the Talakad of today. Somadatta and his retinue of disciples set forth upon this hazardous journey to the saint's hermitage past dense forests and uncharted terrain. Before they reached holy Talakad, the entourage was set upon by wild elephants and trampled to death.

Since the saint and his dying disciples thought of wild elephants in their dying moments, they were reborn in the forests of Dalavanapura as elephants, worshipping the secret *linga* of Lord Vaidyeshwara under a tree with the daintiest lotuses from the pond. Two hunters, Tala and Kada, (and hence the name Talakad), intrigued by this sight, struck their axe upon the tree to unravel the mystery of this secret worship. And behold, blood gushed forth from this slit, in a relentless stream, frightening them out of their wits. The hunters then heard a strange voice from the heavens bidding them to pluck a few leaves from the very tree and anoint the wound with the juice of its leaves. Legend goes that the hunters carried out this divine bidding and the blood turned into heavenly milk, upon drinking which the hunters and the elephants, including Somadatta, attained salvation. The dent upon the *linga* is said to be the very spot where the hunters, out of curiosity, slashed the tree with their axe.

The old temple of Vaidyeshwara is probably the most imposing structure in Talakad. The figurines of Durga, Ganesha, Surya, Srinivasa and Saraswati loom in silent watchfulness near the sanctum. Huge gatekeepers, *dwarapalakas*, stand sentinel over centuries of sandy silence. Beside it is the shrine of Goddess Manonmani in Vijayanagara style with a five-foot statue of Goddess Parvati worshipped as Manonmani Amman. The sands bury every temple in their relentless wake. Over fifty temples and thousands of *lingas*, an entire city and palaces lie buried within the treacherous sands, but they never venture to embrace the shrine of the Lord of Doctors, Vaidyeshwara. The base of the Vaidyeshwara shrine is over twenty feet below sand level. An adjoining shrine and a few *lingas* that were excavated recently stand testimony to an ancient civilisation under the sands.

Lost amidst the vast stretch of sands is the temple of Lord Kirtinarayana, Lord of Victory, which is an intricate structure built by the Hoysalas in AD 1117 to commemorate their victory over the Cholas of Talakad. Lost in the silence of the times, the stellate temple houses ancient idols of Ramanujacharya, Hanuman and Garuda surrounded by the lathe-turned pillars that support the structure. In the sanctum, upon a fine lotus pedestal, towers a two-metre statue of Lord Kirtinarayana holding a conch, discus, mace and lotus in his four hands. The ten incarnations of Vishnu are intricately carved upon the archway above the idol.

Near it also stands the small Ganga shrine of the underground Lord Pataleswara, worshipped as one of the *pancha lingas* of Talakad. A flight of steps to a narrow compound wall erected to keep the nuisance of the sands away bring one to the much-renovated shrine surrounded by scattered *lingas* forgotten by time. It is believed that the *linga* mysteriously changes colour during the day in the festive month of Magha. It looks red in the morning, black in the afternoon and whitish in the evening. The shrine of Maruleswara, Lord of the Sands, is about 300 feet away. Quaint figures surround the shrine, which has seen much renovation during recent times. The other lingas of the *pancha linga* fame include Gokarneswara, Anandeswara and Arkeshwara atop the Mudukutore Betta and the hilltop shrine of Lord Mallikarjuna. *Mudala kodu tore* meant 'the hill to the east of the river' and this was corrupted to its shortened form later.

The *pancha linga darshana* or the ritual worship of the five *lingas* is a unique occurrence much awaited by devout Hindus. To this day, on the celestial date of Kartika Bahula Amavasya as per the Hindu almanac, when the sun and moon enter the Vrischika Raashi or Scorpio, which occurs once in twelve years, lakhs of pilgrims visit the shrines of Vaidyeshwara and in ritual sequence each of the little shrines nearby and the four other *lingas* that loom in the Talakad sandscape. This tradition has come down over the years in this hallowed Benaras of the south. In fact, it is believed that the five *lingas* actually represent the five faces of Lord Shiva.

Talakad and the fables surrounding it will continue to occupy and engage people's imaginations. The intriguing and eerie feeling that the arid landscapes of Talakad evoke definitely shakes one up to think about the events—both scientific and fictional—that led it to its present state.

3

PERIL AT THE GATES AD 1617–38

The 14-year-old Chamaraja Wodeyar VI succeeded his grandfather in the year 1617. Born on 21 April 1603, Chamaraja excelled in the fine arts of music and literature. The time of his ascendancy to the throne was strategically significant for the kingdom of Mysore. The death of Vijayanagara's Venkata II had led to a civil war of sorts and a struggle for succession that made the crown one of thorns for the incumbent monarch Ramadevaraya (1617–32). The menacing attitude of the Sultans of Bijapur added to the already weak Vijayanagara polity. The time seemed ripe for a new power to assume its suzerainty and Mysore was not to be found lacking.

Chamaraja being a minor, Dalavoy Bettada Urs served as his regent till 1620. An able and shrewd military man, Bettada Urs seized the opportunity that destiny seemed to be offering Mysore on a platter. The neighbours of Mysore at that time were the powerful chieftain Jagadevaraya of Chennapatna to its north, Muttu Virappa Nayak I of Madurai to its south and local satraps and chiefs to its east and west. Of these, Jagadevaraya was the hardest nut to crack and Urs initiated a series of expeditions aimed at nullifying his influence in the region. Mindful of the political changes in Mysore, the wily Jagadevaraya sent an olive branch of friendship to the new Wodeyar in the form of an embassy to Srirangapatna with costly gifts, an elephant named Ramalinga and 3,000 Varahas.* This was in return for Mysore's support in his conquest of Chikkanayakanahalli.

---

* The Varaha was a currency unit, approximately equivalent to the modern Rs 3.50.

However, it was strategically suicidal for Mysore to play second fiddle to a powerful and inherently hostile neighbour. The Dalavoy therefore rejected the offer and instead launched an offensive on Jagadevaraya's domain of Nagamangala that was under his loyalist Chennayya. Nagamangala was besieged and Chennayya's brother Doddayya slain in battle. A harried Jagadevaraya enlisted the support of his brother and Prime Minister Ankusharaya and Gopalarajayya of Kannambadi. The combined forces spelt disaster for the besieging Mysorean armies. They were driven back to Srirangapatna. But not one to take defeat lying down, Urs realigned quickly and met the same combine in the battlefield. This time, lady luck seemed to favour Mysore. The allied troops were defeated and the township of Hosakote was annexed to Mysore.

Buoyed by the victory, Urs now turned his attention to the southern end of the kingdom and wanted to consolidate his position there vis-à-vis the Nayak of Madurai. Danayakanakote was a frontier post at the southern border and coterminous with the Nayak's realms. Mallarajayya was dispatched to besiege the fort there. An agitated Palegar of Danayakanakote sought the help of the Nayak to ward off the enemy. The latter was too petrified by the rising power that Mysore had become and instead sought a truce with the besieging army. An agent, Chikkappa Shetty, was therefore sent to negotiate the terms of the deal, one that resulted in an annual tribute of 12,000 Varahas liable to be paid by the Palegar to the treasury of Mysore.

Urs carried out a series of annexations following these successes. He ensured that the authority of Jagadevaraya was curtailed in each of his conquests. Maddur and Keregodu were wrested from their chieftain in 1619 and 1620 respectively. The deft military expeditions of Bettada Urs resulted in the extension of Mysore towards Chennapatna, the very seat of power of Jagadevaraya.

While the dalavoy carried on his relentless campaigns, back home at the capital, the King on his part was the king in name only. He fell into bad company, with no one to advise and reprimand him, and his sycophantic servants and friends saw to it that he drifted away from the realm of education and became a reckless drunkard and womaniser. The people in charge of his education, Rama Somayyaji and Ranganatha Dixit, along with the royal physician Bommarasa Pandita were the cause of this drastic change in the young boy's behaviour. Dalavoy Bettada Urs was quick to realise the game plan of these people and threw them out of their positions. He appointed a new set of qualified personnel for the same. But Chamaraja had got so addicted to their company that he had lost his capability to think rationally. He deposed the new appointees and reinstated his old friends. To further punish him, he imprisoned Bettada Urs and publicly blinded him. He did not perhaps realise the importance of a dalavoy who was loyal to both the kingdom and the king. Bannur Linganna was made the new dalavoy.

Conspirators were, however, on the move. In the shady chambers of the palace, Bettada Urs's brother Dodda Chamappa and his son Chikka Chamappa were hatching a plot to depose Chamaraja, partly to avenge Chamaraja's treatment of Bettada Urs. Chikka Chamappa told his father:

> This King has lost all his sense of discretion and fails to see the difference between good and evil. For all his services, my uncle had to undergo such agony. We must avenge this insult to our family. We will either poison him or call the Tantrik to use black magic to eliminate this worthless King, out to undo his ancestors' achievements.

But their whispers were heard by Chennavva, the maidservant of the Queen Mother Honnajammanni. Chennavva ran to the queen mother's apartments, panting for breath. 'Mahamathrushree, trouble is out to befall our King. Dodda Chamappa and his son are planning to poison our King. Make haste, mother, before they succeed in their nefarious designs.'

The terrified Honnajammanni told the king about the motives of the two conspirators, who immediately imprisoned and executed the mischief-makers. Chennavva was rewarded with the appointment of her son Basavayya as the *gurikara*, or sentinel for the inner apartments of the palace. Chennavva also pleaded with the queen mother to bring back her old friend Bommarasa Pandita, the royal physician, not realising what havoc this tiny man would wreak on the future of Mysore.

Meanwhile, the new dalavoy carried on with the strategy of his predecessor. In October 1620 Talakad was annexed from Somarajayya, followed by Malavalli from Jagadevaraya in May 1623 and in December of the same year, Arikuthara from Baloji Nayaka. Bookinakere and Sindhugatta from Jagadevaraya again in 1624, and Satyagala from Hadinadu Nanjarajayya in May 1625 were annexed to Mysore.

All this time, we find the position of the king diminishing to that of a mute spectator; someone who sat by the sidelines and watched his avaricious dalavoys and officers exhausting the treasury of his kingdom and contravening the authority of the throne in every possible manner, but would not raise a finger in protest.

The following year, Linganna besieged Chennapatna—Jagadevaraya's seat of authority—but was unfortunately killed in the assault. So Basava Linganna was made the dalavoy. He conquered Hoganur and Amachawadi from Hadinadu Nanjarajayya in March 1626, Tagadur and Kottagala from Prabhudeva and Lingarajayya in July 1626 and in December of the same year, Jadale from Chamaraja of Heggad. The domains of one Ghatta Mudaliar in the southwest of Mysore were also made subservient in 1627.

A long-standing hostility between Mysore and the dynasty of the Ikkeri (Keladi) kings began in 1626 with a siege of Periyapatna by the dalavoy. The Ikkeri loyalist Singalaraya was chastised and humiliated by having his nose cut off. This proved to be the starting point for long-lasting bad blood between the two royal houses. The King of Keladi, Virabhadra Nayak (1629–45) and his father Hiriya Venkatappa Nayak I were already facing a lot of opposition from chieftains across Southern India. A reference to the unpopularity of these leaders can be found in a passage from a Jesuit letter from Canara, dated 1630, cited in Rev Hera's article, 'The Expansion Wars of Venkatappa Nayaka of Ikkeri'.[*] It points to the unrest and strife that characterised the Deccan of those times:

> The king of Bamguel has rebelled against the said king Virabhadar Naique and the king of Palpare and the king of Mayzur are lending him aid. The following have also rebelled against the said king: the queen of Olala and the queen of Carnate...so that from the Canhorto to Batecalla everything is in revolt and the King Virabhadar Naique is no longer master of anything below the ghats and is in such straits that he will no more be able to recover his losses....

In March of 1630, Basava Linganna was succeeded by the infamous Vikramaraya. True to the post he held, Vikramaraya revelled in military exploits. He had a rich heritage of predecessors who had won laurels for the kingdom on the battlefront. Though his avarice and ambitions far surpassed his military acumen, Vikrama was a brave warrior. In October

---

[*] The article appears in John Lockman's *Travels of the Jesuits* (1701).

1630, Chennapatna, the bastion of Jagadevaraya—the long-standing foe of Mysore—was taken after a siege. In the same year, Nagamangala, long sought-after, was also wrested. By March 1631, some of the last bastions of the beleaguered Jagadeva like Bellur were annexed as well. Between 1631 and 1634, Vikramaraya unleashed a reign of terror on the neighbouring satraps and chiefs. Lakshmappa Nayak, the chief of Holenarasipura, Venkatappa Nayak, the chief of Belur, and many others fell before the magic sword of the dalavoy. Chennarayapatna was the prized possession won from the Belur chief that year and this marked the culmination of his advance towards the northwestern frontiers of the kingdom. Mysore had now emerged as a major feudatory of Vijayanagara. By 1634, it extended towards Chennapatna and Nagamangala to the north, till Periyapatna and Chennarayapatna in the west and northwest and till Malavalli and Danayakanakote to the east and southeast.

On his part, Chamaraja sat well-cushioned in his palace and acquired a plethora of titles. He was eulogised as the *Chatusshashti Kala Praveena* or the expert of all art forms. His court dazzled with some brilliant luminaries from different streams of the fine arts. It was also a legendary meeting-ground for religious and theological discussions between people from various schools of philosophy like Vaishnavism, Shaivism and Jainism.

Despite being a staunch Vaishnavite himself, Chamaraja was known for his religious tolerance. On a visit to the world-famous Jain Shrine of Sravanabelagola in 1631, he is supposed to have heard the story of an eminent Jain monk, Guru Charukriti Pandita Yogindra who had fled the place to Gersoppe, peeved by the constant military combats of the Mysore forces with Jagadevaraya that hindered his peaceful pursuits. Deeply disturbed by this, Chamaraja invited the Guru to his court at Srirangapatna with due respect and made arrangements for his comfortable stay at Sravanabelagola. He also freed the Jain *muth* of all its debts in 1634. His grants and gifts to temples and individuals, creation of the *Chamaraja Samudra Agraharams* or residential layouts in Aladur and Navilur villages, speak of his benevolent nature.

Chamaraja patronised many leading lights of Kannada literature. In 1625, an 18-chapter volume on horses and their upkeep was written in Kannada by Ramachandra. On the same topic, another scholar of the times, Padmanna Pandita, who was also an Ayurvedic expert, wrote *Hayasara Samucchaya* in the literary metre of Kanda. Chamaraja himself is credited with two works. One was the *Brahmottara Khanda* (1630) in a colloquial Kannada prose format on the philosophy of Shaivism. He also composed the *Chamarajokta Vilasa*, a translation of the *Saptakandas* of the Ramayana into Kannada. It is, however, claimed that the latter work was plagiarised from Virupaksha or rather, that the scholar was forced to write it in the King's name. Whatever be the validity of that assertion, while Chamaraja seemed a complete misfit when it came to affairs of administration and military exploits, he was an expert when it came to the arts and religion.

He had five wives: Muddajammanni, Devirammanni, Siddajammanni, Channajammanni and Doddajammanni. In 1637, Chamaraja died and all his wives burnt themselves on his funeral pyre in the ritual of Sati, a custom that had become common among the ruling classes of Hindu society.

In 1617, the very year that Raja Wodeyar died, his wife Edanahalli Timmajammanni gave birth to Immadi Raja Wodeyar or Raja Wodeyar II, who was now crowned in the Vaishaka month of 1637 as the successor of Chamaraja and the 11th ruler of the kingdom of Mysore. Immadi Raja Wodeyar was worse than his predecessor when it came to asserting himself. The powers of the kingdom slowly and steadily made their way into the hands of Dalavoy Vikramaraya who made full use of the powerlessness of the king.

But there was hope for the troubled throne of Mysore which had seemed to helplessly accept weak monarchs as its destiny. In faraway Gundlu Terakanambi, the place to which his father had retired, Ranadhira, the son of Bettada Chamaraja Wodeyar and nephew of Raja Wodeyar I had grown into a young, handsome and brave man. He was truly what Mysore needed in those dark days of treachery and bureaucratic avarice. The explorer in Ranadhira loved to visit new lands and on one such expedition into the countryside, he happened to reach Tiruchirapalli.

The chieftain of Tiruchirapalli had a famous wrestler called Mahamalla. While the chieftain was extremely proud of this invincible wrestler, he was also scared to offend him in any way lest he decided to overthrow him. Hence, he remained a mute spectator each time Mahamalla defeated and killed his competitors by deceit. Mahamalla declared that he would hang his loincloth on the fort door and anyone who dared to cut the cloth would have to face him in the arena. It was more of a symbolic gesture to demonstrate and assert his power in the principality. Any sensible and self-respecting chieftain would have taken this as an affront to his suzerainty. But the chieftain let this, too, go by. Upon entering the fort at Tiruchirapalli, Ranadhira was amazed to see a loincloth hanging over the ramparts. It seemed the most distasteful way of welcoming a visitor. He heard the people of the town lamenting the disgraceful sight they would witness each morning. So he cut the cloth away. The royal guards immediately caught him and dragged him to the wrestling arena where Mahamalla stood waiting for his prey.

Ranadhira was an athletic man and well-versed in the art of wrestling. He very easily defeated Mahamalla in no time. Not one to give up easily, Mahamalla then challenged Ranadhira to meet him in the Vajramushti or adamantine fist contest, where he usually grabbed his opponent and suffocated him to death. He tried to use the same tactics against Ranadhira as well, but the latter was too smart for him. In a split second, Ranadhira snatched a spear from a guard's hands and killed Mahamalla. Ironically, this was precisely the sort of foul play that Mahamalla would resort to which now ended his life. In the ensuing confusion at Mahamalla's death, Ranadhira conveniently slipped away.

While leaving, he left a message for the chieftain on the fort wall which read: 'The man who killed that arrogant villain is a common wrestler of Mysore.' The chieftain's anger knew no bounds. The same man who had had no qualms about the wrestler challenging his authority on almost a daily basis felt terribly outraged and decided to hunt down the impudent visitor.

Ranadhira returned to Terakanambi where Dalavoy Vikramaraya's envoys brought him an ominous and terse message: 'As the deceased king had no direct heir, we have decided to crown you the new king of Mysore.' Ranadhira was shocked to read about his cousin Immadi Raja Wodeyar's apparent death. He had had no inkling of any serious illness that the king might have been suffering from, nor had the king been brave enough to have died in battle. Then what could possibly have caused his sudden demise?

Even as he sat lost in thought, a Brahmin messenger of Queen Mother Edanahalli Timmajammanni came over. He said, 'Prince! I bring to you the message from Her Honourable Highness Queen Mother Timmajammanni. She begs you to proceed to the capital immediately to help your cousin, the young King of Mysore Immadi Raja Wodeyar whose life is in grave danger.'

Ranadhira was flummoxed and unable to understand the implications of this strange message. On the one hand the Dalavoy had already sent out news about the King's demise and made plans for a successor and on the other hand the Queen Mother had sent him a message to save her son's life. There seemed to be more to it than met the eye. He decided to quiz the Brahmin about what necessitated his presence at the palace and what dangers he was referring to.

The messenger replied:

The king has begun to assert himself and is no longer the pleasure-loving weakling that he used to be. As you know, wine and women were his only pastimes, but that was only till recently and this miracle was brought about by none other than the Queen Mother herself. Vikramaraya had taken over the reigns of the kingdom and the King was a mere puppet in his hands. She could bear it no longer and one day she stormed into the King's apartments while he was lost amidst damsels in a state of complete intoxication. She thundered at him and derided him for forgetting his duties towards the state and its people and for betraying the trust placed in him by his father, the late Maharaja Raja Wodeyar the Great. Her disparaging comments were so harsh that they brought the King out of his reverie. He was ashamed of himself and decided to assume his duties in a more responsible manner.

The very next day he paid a surprise visit to the Treasury and found a huge deficit there. Money was being siphoned off on an almost regular basis by Vikramaraya and his goons. The King immediately ordered the arrest of the goons who were carrying out the Dalavoy's orders. But Prince, the day is not far when our King would be forced to take stricter action against the evil Dalavoy as most of the wrongdoings of the state are his brainchild. Smart man that he is, Vikramaraya has surely sensed trouble ahead of him and will make an all-out effort to eliminate the King. This is what worries the Queen Mother and since she has no one to fall back on in the capital, you are her sole hope.

There surely seemed to be a huge gap between what was narrated to him and what might actually be happening in Srirangapatna. So without further delay Ranadhira hurried to the capital. He was welcomed at the gate by Vikramaraya, who hugged him and with feigned sorrow narrated the tale of the sad demise of the king and led him aside to a palace to rest before he could proceed to meet the royal family. He placed his guards outside, instructing them to keep a strict watch on Ranadhira and not allow him anywhere near the main palace. He had plans of getting Ranadhira killed later that night. Ranadhira was getting restive; he realised that he was under virtual house arrest. The guards prevented him from meeting the Queen Mother or getting out of the building. But he defeated them in a small scuffle and rode to the Queen Mother's apartments.

The queen lost her composure on seeing her favourite nephew. She recounted the sad story:

> When my son returned after inspecting the treasury, he complained of headache which was getting unbearable. All the while, he also kept moaning about vague fears he had about Vikramaraya harming him as he was enraged by his efforts to check his misdemeanours. It was I who told him not to worry too much and called for the royal physician Bommarasa Pandita, the friend of that old servant Chennavva. The evil crook came with his bag of herbs and prepared a concoction. The King refused to drink it, but I compelled him to and literally pushed it down his throat, telling him that he needed to get well soon to resume his duties. To please me, he drank the mixture. Soon after taking the medicine, he complained of excruciating pain and felt that his throat was on fire. He kept clasping my hand and yelling out in pain. Even as I looked at Bommarasa to look into the matter, he turned the other way with an air of indifference. I yelled at Bommarasa to examine the King. By then my son gave a loud cry: 'Chamundamba'. The physician examined him and proclaimed him dead. The entire universe with its multitude of stars, planets and galaxies seemed to stand still for a moment. I had lost the only hope of my life, my only son! But even in that moment of sorrow, I suspected Bommarasa and demanded an explanation. On much questioning, he confessed that he had given the King poison as per Vikramaraya's orders.

She then beat her hand on the wall and gave a loud cry of grief:

> Oh! How can I ever imagine that with these hands that once fed him milk, with these very wretched hands I gave my own son poison! Ranadhira, I have killed my own son. Fie on me!

Composing herself after a while she said:

Ranadhira, the palace is without a leader. I am an old woman, desperate and helpless at the moment. It is now up to you to save the Mysore of Yaduraya and Raja Wodeyar from falling into the hands of that villain. Meet me only after you have vanquished that devil. Victory be yours. Hurry! Make haste!

As he walked out of the Queen Mother's apartments, Ranadhira encountered Vikramaraya, who had been baffled to hear that his captive had managed to escape and had learnt the truth about the king's death. With a sneer, he told Ranadhira: 'Prince! I heard from my guards that you were feeling highly restless in the Palace, with no work at hand. Hence I decided to arrange for your entertainment. These two wrestlers, Channa and Ranga, the best of their tribe in Mysore, will keep you occupied.'

Ranadhira's anger knew no bounds but he consented. Vikramaraya had given strict orders to the two wrestlers that come what may, they had to defeat and kill their opponent that night, either by fair play or by deceit. In return he promised them lucrative goodies. At the arena, Channa and Ranga were easily defeated by Ranadhira, who had secretly befriended them. That dark night was a decisive one for Vikramaraya. Decades of his life had been spent plotting and conspiring for the consummation of that night's plans. He could almost see himself ascending the throne of Mysore. He sat drinking wine and enjoying the dance of the courtesans. Channa and Ranga hurried into the room with blood-soaked daggers to inform him that the job was done—Ranadhira was dead. Vikramaraya's joys knew no bounds. He took the two men inside to reward them with lavish gifts. The fulfilment of his long-cherished dream made him feel heady. He embraced the two men in a tight clasp thanking them for their efforts. But at that moment he was stabbed in the back, *literally*. That stroke of the dagger killed him and his dreams of ascending the throne of Mysore. His horrific cry shook the entire palace out of its slumber.

Vikramaraya was dead.[*]

It was actually Ranadhira's plan to kill the iniquitous dalavoy in a manner as cunning and surreptitious as the latter's mechanisations against

---

[*] A later inscription at the Nanjangud temple speaks of him as a layman, which seems to suggest that he did not die and was perhaps merely removed from power.

his opponents had always been. Wilks offers his characteristic variant to this episode as well. He refers to the fateful dark night when Vikramaraya had stepped out of his apartment to answer the call of nature, which was when Channa and Ranga pounced on him and devoured him.

> The detail of this transaction has been preserved in several manuscripts. The two attendants scaled the walls of the minister's courtyard after dark, and laid in wait for an opportunity to effect their purpose. Shortly afterwards the minister appeared, preceded by a torch-bearer; passing towards a detached apartment. The associates first killed the torch-bearer and the light happened to be entirely extinguished. 'Who are you?' said the minister. 'Your enemy!' replied one of the Peons; and made a blow. The minister, however, closed with him, and being the more powerful man, threw him to the ground, and held him by the throat, in which situation he called out for aid. The night was so very dark that the companion was afraid to strike at random. 'Are you uppermost or undermost?' 'Undermost,' cried the half-strangled Peon, and this information enabled his associate to strike the fatal blow. Canteerava Narsa Raj was installed on the following day, and in two days afterwards proceeded to the seat of government at Seringapatam.

Ranadhira approached the Queen Mother's apartments to report the joyous news. Her laughter rose in a crescendo, stunning the people around her. She kept looking towards the skies and saying 'Son! Today is the day of your salvation!' Turning to Ranadhira, she said, 'You have really done a commendable job my son! My blessings are always with you. But I would like to retire to the holy town of Kashi after witnessing your coronation.'

Thus, after vanquishing the evil Vikramaraya, Ranadhira was crowned as the new king of Mysore at Srirangapatna in the Karthika month of 1638. He went to seek the blessings of his aunt and tried to persuade her to stay back and guide him in the affairs of the state. But Timmajammanni was resolute. She said:

> Ranadhira! After my son's death there is nothing in life that is left for me here. I lost my husband at an early age, at a time when I was still pregnant. I had to bring up my fatherless son all by myself. My son, for a large part of his life, remained oblivious

to his duties and when he got his senses back, fate had other designs in mind. I would have killed myself the day his pyre was lit, but stayed on only to ensure that all evil clouds are dispelled from the skies of Mysore and our kingdom is put back on the rails of stability. Now that you are here at the helm of affairs, I have nothing to worry about. I can dedicate the rest of my life now to spiritual pursuits, which would be the only solace for my troubled mind. So I request you not to embroil my mind in these worldly matters of kingship and politics and let me retire. May Goddess Chamundeshwari shower Her blessings on you and guide your way!

With these words the Queen Mother departed.

LOOKING BACK: SECTION 1

The reign of Ranadhira divides the history of Mysore, so to say, between the period of legends and the period of actual documented history. The period of his reign has a mixture of the two. With all the excitement behind his installation on the throne and the events preceding it, history now changes its course to a more sober and scientific path, one that abounds with written material rather than mere oral history. The tone and tenor of this narrative will, therefore, change in the course of the following pages.

But before we leave behind the fascinating legends we have recounted thus far, let us cast a cold, rational eye on them. For instance, a rational mind would always argue about the story of Yaduraya, a prince hailing from Gujarat, stirred into action by overhearing a story told by the washerwomen. How could a man from Gujarat understand the dialect of local washerwomen? Does it then not imply that Yaduraya was after all a local himself or a second-generation migrant to Mahisuru?

If we take a rational look at the turn of events that led to the foundation of the dynasty and discount all the myths of dreams and divine dispensation, isn't it intriguing that the leading lady of the principality—the deceased chieftain's wife—decided to confide in a stranger her family secrets? Would she do that with every passer-by in the principality? Would she dream of marrying her daughter to a complete stranger of unknown antecedents and lineage? It becomes quite clear then that her confidence in Yaduraya must have been so strong that she was convinced of his ability to redeem her family and this confidence is what spurred her to despatch her Jangama as a messenger. By logical deduction, this implies that Yaduraya must have committed acts of heroism, which would have been popular enough in those days, that must have caught the queen's attention?

It is also pertinent to analyse what language the Jangama and this young traveller had in common. If he was indeed from Gujarat, could the Jangama have spoken Gujarati with him or was Kannada known to the people of Gujarat, enabling Yaduraya to indulge in such a complex conversation with the mendicant? All these point definitely to the fact that Yaduraya must have been a local hero whose bravery and exploits instilled such confidence in the queen's mind that he alone could help her in this precarious situation. Some historians do claim that the early Wodeyars belonged to the tribe of local shepherds and potters. This could have possibly enabled Yaduraya to be well informed about local political happenings. But with no substantive evidence on either side, it is difficult to take a confident stand.

What is really true though, not only of the early Wodeyars but of almost all ruling dynasties of India, is that the founders generally came from extremely humble backgrounds. It was either that luck favoured them and they were at the right place at the right time or that they were industrious and ambitious enough to convert a situation to their advantage. The stories woven around them come later and are largely an attempt to invent divine or at least higher-than-human sanction for their success. But, like the tale of the *Suvarna Male* or Golden Rain that ushered in Vijayanagara, these stories get repeated so many times that they become accepted. A historian needs to be circumspect while considering them and separating the chaff from the grain is an onerous task.

But there are times when written records help. For example, a number of inscriptions—lithic and copper plate—from Mysore, Hassan, Tumkur, Bangalore, Salem and Coimbatore have been compiled in the *Epigraphica Carnatica, Mysore Archaeological Report, Inscriptions of the Madras Presidency, The Mackenzie Collection* and *The Madras Epigraphists' Report*. These are in Kannada and Sanskrit and date from the sixteenth to the mid-eighteenth century. They simply document which king gave what gifts and grants to which temple or individuals. This helps to construct some of the events associated with a particular king. So, the epigraphical evidence that a grant of a car was made to the temple of Talakad by a member of the royal family in 1670–80 may seem at first glance of small importance, but it has led rationalists to question the Talakad myth. Why would someone give a grant to a place that is submerged in sand, they quiz. Does not that mean that the occurrence of the sand dunes was not courtesy Alamelamma and her curse, but a later happening?

Perhaps the earliest attempt that was ever made to chronicle the history of Mysore and its kings was by Lt Col Mark Wilks (1760–1831), the British Resident at the court of Mysore, 1803–08. His work, *Historical Sketches of the South of India in an Attempt to Trace the History of Mysoor*, was published in 1810 and has been quoted as an authority on the subject. But Wilks was operating in an India that was completely unaware of techniques of historical documentation. It was either court eulogisers or biased writers who had the onerous job of preserving the past. A lot of Wilks' efforts are based on local sources, memoirs and translations. Like the predicament that faces historians today, the paucity of information till about the time of Haidar Ali (c. 1750s), plagued Wilks too. So to what does a historian, in any century, turn for information in such a situation?

Literary works have always mirrored society and the political situation of the times, and therefore are one option. In the case of the history of Mysore, the seventeenth and eighteenth century works in Kannada and Sanskrit mirror some of the events, but to a limited extent. Many of these are not published works and are still maintained as palm-leaf manuscripts in libraries in Mysore and Madras. But the thrust here seems to be more on religion, philosophy, poetry and literary value of the work rather than a serious and well thought-out process of documenting events and people. Some of them do deal with specific kings of the royal family like the *Kanthirava Narasaraja Vijayam* (c.1648) of Govinda Vaidya, *Chikkadevaraja Vamshavali* (c.1678–80), *Chikkadevaraja Vijayam* (c.1682–86), and *Apratimavira Charitram* (c.1695-1700) of Tirumalaraya, *Soundaryakavya* (c.1740) of Nuronda and so on.

Coins of the time, especially those of Ranadhira Kanthirava Narasaraja Wodeyar and Chikkadevaraja Wodeyar (1673–1704), throw some light on the general state of the economy, political evolution, religion of the king's family and so on. But they also have their limitations. While a number of travelogues, chronicles and letters have been found—*La Mission Du Madure* (1659–86), *Travels of the Jesuits* (1743) of John Lockman, Dr John Fryer's *Travels in India* (1676–1680), Niccolo Manucci's *Storio Do Mogor* (1683–1708) to name a few—these are to be taken with a pinch of salt as they are the jottings of the Jesuit missionaries. They had their specific agendas and biases, were usually misinformed and tended to exaggerate. Some contemporary writings give a glimpse of Mysore and its history in hindsight, like the *Muhammad Namah*—the official history of Muhammad Adil Shah of Bijapur which has chapters dedicated to the war between

Ranadulla Khan of Bijapur and Ranadhira Kanthirava of Mysore. The *Records of Fort St. George*, Madras, the *Diary of Ananda Ranga Pillai* and the *Selections from the Peshwa Daftar* are other pieces of the puzzle we can use to put together the past.

Much later in time, secondary sources were added. These are: *Mysuru Doregala Poorvabhyudaya Vivara* (1710–14), *Mysuru Nagarada Poorvottara* (c.1734–40), *Mysuru Doregala Vamshavali* (c.1800), *Mysuru Rajara Charitre* (c.1800) by Venkataramanayya, *Kaifiyats* (c.1800–04), *Keladi Nripa Vijayam* (c.1800), Linganna Kavi's *Halegannada Chhampu* (c.1830), Devachandra's *Rajavali Kathe* (1838) and of course, the Palace-commissioned work, *The Annals of the Mysore Royal Family*, or *Srimanmaharajaravara Vamshavali* (1864–65). It is in the light of this paucity and confusion that Wilks' maiden effort becomes so appreciable an attempt. Also, in the wake of the uncertainty of the available sources, one tends to turn to the fables and legends for succour. The flavour of freshness they have and the fact of transfer by word of mouth from the time of the happening of the event (of course, discounting the distilling over the generations) makes them a tempting foundation to build our story on. But one must be incisive enough to know where to draw the line and what to take at pure face value.

Section 2
The Golden Period
(AD 1638–1734)

Ranadhira Kanthirava Narasaraja Wodeyar: AD 1638-59

4

THE GOLDEN PERIOD – I (AD 1638–73)

THE REIGN OF RANADHIRA

His ascent to the throne of Mysore brought Ranadhira into the arena of Indian politics. From small scuffles and fights with chieftains and their wrestlers, he was now faced with an Indian political landscape that had vastly changed. The Aravidu dynasty of Vijayanagara was on its last legs. After the death of Venkata II, powerless kings such as Sriranga II (1614–19) and Ramadeva Raya (1619–29) caused the remnants of the kingdom great misery due to their political insignificance. The nobles and satraps indulged in constant bickering and one-upmanship. Mysore was among the few kingdoms that still owed a degree of allegiance to its erstwhile monarch. The Nayakas of Madurai and Gingee were on a constant warpath with the monarch, who was more a monarch in name alone, having been stripped completely of his erstwhile power. After much infighting among the contenders, Venkatapatideva Raya III emerged as the new ruler of the dwindling dynasty in 1630.

The Bahamani kingdom had split into a number of dynasties—notable among them being the Adil Shahi dynasty of Bijapur and the Qutub Shahi dynasty of Golconda. The Adil Shahi dynasty was founded by its illustrious king Yusuf Adil Shah in 1489 while the famed Quli Qutub Shah founded the Golconda line of authority. These kingdoms were constantly at war with each other and generally made common cause only when the enemy in question was the Hindu ruler of Vijayanagara. Up north, the Mughal empire was the new reigning power that had brought almost the whole of India, sans the South, under its control. Under such able rulers as Akbar, Jahangir and Shah Jahan, it was itching to extend its sway below the Vindhyas. The Deccan was made a viceroyalty of the Mughal Empire by Akbar. In 1636 Emperor Shah Jahan signed a treaty with Adil Shah and Qutub Shah of Bijapur and Golconda respectively to define their boundaries, thereby halting the advance of the Deccan's two Shahi Kingdoms up north.

Among the contemporaries of the new King of Mysore were Venkatapatidevaraya and later Sriranga VI (1642–64) of Vijayanagara, Muhammad Adil Shah (1627–56), the celebrated ruler of Bijapur, Virabhadra Nayak (1629–45) and Shivappa Nayak I (1645–60) of Ikkeri, Immadi Kempegowda of Magadi (1585–1633) and Tirumala Nayak of Madurai (1623–55). The new king had enemies all over the place. If a dying Vijayanagara was the safest opponent, the others—the Mughals, the Sultans of Bijapur and Golconda, the Nayakas of Madurai, Tanjore and Ikkeri and smaller barons like Chennayya of Nagamangala, Nanjunda Mudaliar of Periapatna—were all forces to be dealt with in a large or small way. And Mysore's new ruler simply loved battle and revelled in victory.

The Deccan, like other parts of India, was marked by constant infighting among the different feudal overlords and barons, each wanting to prove his supremacy over large tracts of land. The Wodeyars had risen up the ranks in the same manner. The feudalism of medieval times brought with it this characteristic nature of turmoil and power struggles among the many petty local chieftains, each aspiring for a larger slice of the pie. The tottering Vijayanagara empire brought the feudal satraps into open mutual conflicts. Madurai's chieftain Tirumala Nayak declared his independence from the empire and the kings of Ikkeri were in constant conflict with neighbouring chieftains and Palegars.

There was everlasting hostility between Hanumappa Nayak of Basavapatna and Virabhadra Nayak of Ikkeri. Hanumappa sent his envoy to the court of the Sultan of Bijapur, Muhammad Adil Shah, knowing fully well that he could not vanquish Virabhadra without the latter's help. The Sultan sent in a huge retinue of the Bijapur army under its valiant General Rustum-i-Zaman Ranadulla Khan to Hanumappa's aid.

4

THE GOLDEN PERIOD – I (AD 1638–73)

THE REIGN OF RANADHIRA

His ascent to the throne of Mysore brought Ranadhira into the arena of Indian politics. From small scuffles and fights with chieftains and their wrestlers, he was now faced with an Indian political landscape that had vastly changed. The Aravidu dynasty of Vijayanagara was on its last legs. After the death of Venkata II, powerless kings such as Sriranga II (1614–19) and Ramadeva Raya (1619–29) caused the remnants of the kingdom great misery due to their political insignificance. The nobles and satraps indulged in constant bickering and one-upmanship. Mysore was among the few kingdoms that still owed a degree of allegiance to its erstwhile monarch. The Nayakas of Madurai and Gingee were on a constant warpath with the monarch, who was more a monarch in name alone, having been stripped completely of his erstwhile power. After much infighting among the contenders, Venkatapatideva Raya III emerged as the new ruler of the dwindling dynasty in 1630.

The Bahamani kingdom had split into a number of dynasties—notable among them being the Adil Shahi dynasty of Bijapur and the Qutub Shahi dynasty of Golconda. The Adil Shahi dynasty was founded by its illustrious king Yusuf Adil Shah in 1489 while the famed Quli Qutub Shah founded the Golconda line of authority. These kingdoms were constantly at war with each other and generally made common cause only when the enemy in question was the Hindu ruler of Vijayanagara. Up north, the Mughal empire was the new reigning power that had brought almost the whole of India, sans the South, under its control. Under such able rulers as Akbar, Jahangir and Shah Jahan, it was itching to extend its sway below the Vindhyas. The Deccan was made a viceroyalty of the Mughal Empire by Akbar. In 1636 Emperor Shah Jahan signed a treaty with Adil Shah and Qutub Shah of Bijapur and Golconda respectively to define their boundaries, thereby halting the advance of the Deccan's two Shahi Kingdoms up north.

Among the contemporaries of the new King of Mysore were Venkatapatidevaraya and later Sriranga VI (1642–64) of Vijayanagara, Muhammad Adil Shah (1627–56), the celebrated ruler of Bijapur, Virabhadra Nayak (1629–45) and Shivappa Nayak I (1645–60) of Ikkeri, Immadi Kempegowda of Magadi (1585–1633) and Tirumala Nayak of Madurai (1623–55). The new king had enemies all over the place. If a dying Vijayanagara was the safest opponent, the others—the Mughals, the Sultans of Bijapur and Golconda, the Nayakas of Madurai, Tanjore and Ikkeri and smaller barons like Chennayya of Nagamangala, Nanjunda Mudaliar of Periapatna—were all forces to be dealt with in a large or small way. And Mysore's new ruler simply loved battle and revelled in victory.

The Deccan, like other parts of India, was marked by constant infighting among the different feudal overlords and barons, each wanting to prove his supremacy over large tracts of land. The Wodeyars had risen up the ranks in the same manner. The feudalism of medieval times brought with it this characteristic nature of turmoil and power struggles among the many petty local chieftains, each aspiring for a larger slice of the pie. The tottering Vijayanagara empire brought the feudal satraps into open mutual conflicts. Madurai's chieftain Tirumala Nayak declared his independence from the empire and the kings of Ikkeri were in constant conflict with neighbouring chieftains and Palegars.

There was everlasting hostility between Hanumappa Nayak of Basavapatna and Virabhadra Nayak of Ikkeri. Hanumappa sent his envoy to the court of the Sultan of Bijapur, Muhammad Adil Shah, knowing fully well that he could not vanquish Virabhadra without the latter's help. The Sultan sent in a huge retinue of the Bijapur army under its valiant General Rustum-i-Zaman Ranadulla Khan to Hanumappa's aid.

Statue of Demon king Mahishasura atop the Chamundi Hills, Mysore

Yaduraya, the founder of the dynasty (1399-1423)

Idol of Lord Cheluvanarayana, Melukote

Timmaraja Wodeyar I (1459-78)

Hiriya Bettada Chamaraja Wodeyar (1423-59)

Bola Chamaraja Wodeyar IV (1572-76)

Hiriya Bettada Chamaraja Wodeyar II (1478-1533) or (1478-1513)

Hiriya Bettada Chamaraja Wodeyar III (1513-53)

Timmaraja Wodeyar II (1533-72) or (1553-72)

Stone Chariot, Hampi

Bettada Chamaraja Wodeyar V (1576-78)

Ugranarasimha Statue, Hampi

The resplendent Golden Throne

Meandering course of the Cauvery River as seen from atop the Mudukutore Hill, Talakad.

Present scion of the Wodeyar family, Shri Srikanta Dutta Narasimharaja Wodeyar at the annual Dasara festivities in the Mysore Palace

The temple of Lord Vaidyeshwara, Talakad

Chamaraja Wodeyar VI (1617-37)

Immadi Raja Wodeyar (1637-38)

Kirtinarayana Temple, lost amidst the sand dunes

The Golden Period – I (AD 1638–73)   65

Meanwhile, the Sultan was also constantly being instigated by Chennayya of Nagamangala to proceed towards Mysore. He exaggerated the political uncertainties and the power politics that occurred in Mysore under Immadi Raja Wodeyar. Now that a new king had taken over along with a new dalavoy to replace Vikramaraya—one Timmarajayya—he made this an even bigger issue, citing the supposed inexperience of the incumbent and the ripeness of the time for Bijapur to annex Mysore. The Sultan was lured and directed Ranadulla to set his eyes on Mysore after he cleared the mess at Ikkeri.

Accordingly, Ranadulla made his first stop at Basavapatna and defeated Hanumappa Nayak's arch rival Virabhadra in a bloody battle. It resulted in a tremendous victory for the forces of Bijapur. Ikkeri and Bhuvanagiri fell, the entire Malnad region was overrun, places like Sira, Turuvekere and Tumkur ravaged, Bangalore was snatched from its chieftain Immadi Kempegowda and Shahji was appointed governor. The kingdom of Mysore was the only low-hanging fruit for Ranadulla Khan.

He sent word to the king of Mysore demanding the payment of tribute to Bijapur, something Ranadhira flatly rejected. With supreme confidence following the Ikkeri victory and Chennayya as guide, the troops of Bijapur, which consisted of about 50,000 horses, 4 lakh foot soldiers, and 100 elephants, pounced on Mysore. One division was headed by Ranadulla Khan himself and the other by their ally Hanumappa Nayak. On 18 January 1639, the combined forces decided to besiege the Fort of Srirangapatna. Ranadhira personally led the campaign against the menacing enemy. Surprise night attacks were made by the Mysorean armies on the enemy troops, who were ignorant of the topography of the area. The attacks on their camps at Arakere, Hosholalu and Melukote shook the besieging forces. The reverses they suffered prompted Hanumappa Nayak to prevail upon Ranadulla Khan to sign a truce with Mysore. This required payment of tribute for the cessation of hostilities. In return, the King of Mysore was to be made the undisputed leader of the region south of the Cauvery. But Ranadulla was not one to relent. He wanted to script a royal victory for himself and stage a repeat of the success of Ikkeri in Mysore.

The Bijapur forces secretly ascended the ramparts of the Srirangapatna fort and with a blow the wall was breached. But even before the enemies could make their way into the fort, Ranadhira appeared on the scene. Records speak of him being a terrible 'lion' on the battlefield, totally ruthless with the enemies. Commanding the huge Mysorean army, Ranadhira managed to drive away the enemy who had stormed the very doorstep of the kingdom. Badly beaten and bruised, Ranadulla Khan beat a hasty and shameful retreat.

This was the first defeat that Ranadulla had tasted after a string of successes. Chennayya's claims had led him to believe that Mysore would be the easiest victim. But even he was baffled by the valour with which Ranadhira had resisted the forces of Bijapur. The troops were fatigued after such a long series of battles. Ranadulla too had half a mind to sign a truce with Ranadhira and turn back. But Chennayya was not the sort to give up so easily. He had an axe to grind with Ranadhira and coaxed Ranadulla to stay on. Blessed with an agile intellect, Chennayya could win people over with his rhetoric. As he walked along the walls of the fort, he befriended the *gurikaras* or watchmen there and in a subtle manner extracted details of all the secret entries to the fort. He then communicated by way of signs to Ranadulla Khan to attack the most vulnerable part of the fort. As Ranadulla started firing arms, Ranadhira made another heroic appearance and inflicted the most crushing and humiliating defeat on the Bijapur army. When news of this defeat reached the Sultan of Bijapur, he was irked and ordered his commander to make immediate peace with the 'Lion King' of Mysore. Left with no other alternative, Ranadulla dispatched his two Hindu envoys, Kaveri Hebbaruva and Minchu Hebbaruva, to make peace with Ranadhira. The siege of Srirangapatna lasted for just three days and on 21 January 1639 the representatives negotiated the terms of peace with the Wodeyar, according to which the area south of the Cauvery River was to remain the undisturbed possession of the King of Mysore while the area north of the same river was the property of the Sultan of Bijapur. Buoyed by his son's maiden victory, an overjoyed Bettada Chamaraja Wodeyar is said to have sent his son the famed broad sword 'Vijaya Narasimha' from his retreat at Gundlu Terakanambi.

But even as the warring factions were signing the terms of peace in Srirangapatna, Ranadulla had sent a secret contingent to Mysore to attack the fort there. Without further delay, Ranadhira rushed from the capital city of Srirangapatna to neighbouring Mysore to save it from this sudden onslaught.

By the time he reached Mysore, he was pleasantly surprised to find the place completely peaceful. The *Annals* record a miracle of sorts at this point.* The *gurikaras* there had an astounding tale to narrate to Ranadhira. The *gurikara* Verathayya told Ranadhira the sequence of events, with his lips quivering with excitement:

> Doddabuddhi, the evil forces of Ranadulla Khan played foul with you. Engaging you in a peace mission at Srirangapatna, they attacked our fort in Mysore after proceeding from Kadabasavanatittu and capturing Lakkihalla and Veerabhadranakotthala. They killed all the other *gurikaras*, but I was saved as I hid in a safe place. Our officers Thanedar Basavarajayya and Hobalidar Siddha Nayak fought bravely but in vain, Sire. The armies rushed into the fort like a hawk sweeps over its prey. It so happened that Ranadulla Khan's soldiers saw a battalion of women on the topmost ramparts of the fort. As it does not befit the brave to kill women, they decided to get over the ramparts and drive them away. But lo! As they went there to do so, these women with dishevelled hair, bloodshot eyes, armed with weapons assaulted the enemy troops. The enemy ran like a goat out of the butcher shop, as if they had encountered the very devil. After that, it was all calm and to our surprise the women had disappeared when we went up to thank them!

Ranadhira at once realised that it must be the presiding deity Goddess Chamundeshwari's grace that had saved his kingdom from peril. Having thanked her profusely, he returned to Srirangapatna. The exploits of Ranadhira set the entire political scene of the Deccan on fire. The powerful and mighty of southern India sat up and took notice of a man from the hitherto unknown territory of Mysore who had defeated the most successful army of the Deccan. These exploits of Ranadhira reached the ears of the Tiruchirapalli chieftain who wanted to avenge Mahamalla's death but was also petrified that in the process of expanding his kingdom, Ranadhira might attack Tiruchirapalli. He sent twenty-five skilled wrestlers under the leadership of Chandremalla (the brother of Mahamalla) to Srirangapatna.

---

* The veracity of these stories found in the *Annals* is dubious. They were perhaps narrated to enhance the reputation of Ranadhira as a man blessed by the Goddess Herself, and as a chivalrous and romantic warrior, which, in any case, he was.

Chandremalla happened to meet one Nanjarajayya, who was in fact the dalavoy of the kingdom and a friend of the late Vikramaraya. United by a common enemy and goal, they hatched a plot to kill Ranadhira. All twenty-five wrestlers entered the king's chamber one night. The king was in deep slumber. But, sensing shadows on his body, he woke up in a start to see twenty-five enormous men armed with daggers waiting to pounce on him. Being an athletic and agile man, he leapt from the bed and took his sword, Vijaya Narasimha, and fought the intruders alone. On hearing the commotion in the king's apartments, his security guards barged in to their king's aid. Most of the intruders were killed and the rest sent back with their hands and legs chopped off, as gifts to the Tiruchirapalli chieftain. Nanjarajayya was ousted and Lingaraja was made the dalavoy. When the subjects heard of this feat, they were astonished that one man could vanquish twenty-five at a time and praised him as the very incarnation of Lord Narasimha. He was thus christened Ranadhira Kanthirava Narasaraja Wodeyar.

The peace of 1639 with Bijapur was, however, short-lived. The phantom returned the very next year when the tributes that were stipulated to be paid by Mysore (as per the truce treaty signed by Ranadulla) fell into arrears. Like before, Ranadhira haughtily refused to comply when the representatives of Bijapur visited his court to remind him of the terms on the grounds that he owed his allegiance to the throne of Vijayanagara and that no one else had the right to ask him to pay tribute. An angered Adil Shah sent Ranadulla Khan for a second combat. On his way to Srirangapatna, Ranadulla also had the task of quashing the banner of revolt raised by Hanumappa Nayak who had refused to pay his tributes to the Bijapur treasury and the task of slaying Chennayya of Nagamangala who was sent as a negotiator. Ranadulla Khan now decided to align with Hanumappa's rival Virabhadra Nayak whom the combined forces had defeated the last time. They now laid siege to Basavapatna — Hanumappa's seat of power — and as some records state, slew him later. Having tasted sweet victory again, a buoyed Ranadulla decided to rewrite his infamous history at Srirangapatna.

Alarmed by the menacing advance of the Bijapur forces, Ranadhira on his part decided to strengthen all the border areas of Mysore. Ramagiridurga from Immadi Kempegowda and Bagur, Huliyurdurga, Turuvekere — all frontier posts were snatched from the chieftains owing allegiance to Bijapur.

But Ranadulla's dream of seeing his flag flutter on the ramparts of Srirangapatna remained a dream. And it was not Ranadhira this time, but the Lord of Death who stood in his way. Ranadulla's untimely death in 1640 quashed all his hopes of vanquishing Mysore. His successor, Mustafa Khan, decided to pursue the unfinished agenda and marched towards Srirangapatna. Dalavoy Timmarajayya was sent to halt his advance to the capital. Mustafa Khan had camped at Chandanahalli near Bellur on the outskirts of the kingdom and sent word to the dalavoy that either Mysore pay up the stipulated tribute or face the onslaught of a bloody siege. Instead of replying to this embarrassing diktat with an act of his sword, the meek dalavoy just conveyed the ultimatum to his master in Srirangapatna. A peeved Ranadhira immediately stripped him of his post and made Nanjarajayya of Hura—an acclaimed and gallant warrior—the new dalavoy. Accompanying the new and inexperienced dalavoy, Ranadhira made a frontal attack on the Bijapur troops and inflicted another crushing defeat on them. For the second consecutive time, the authority of one of Bijapur's most illustrious sultans, Muhammad Adil Shah, was fairly and squarely rejected by the valiant ruler of Mysore.

Trouble, meanwhile, brewed for Ranadhira on the southern frontier of his kingdom. The neighbourhood of Danayakanokote, the southern tip of his kingdom, was of strategic importance as it was the southern gateway. Any disturbances here meant a direct blow to Mysore. The neighbouring province of Danayakanakote, Samballi, was under the suzerainty of Ghatta Mudaliar's son Pattadayya. The nayak of Madurai instigated him to create trouble in the vicinity, thereby causing a ripple effect on the surrounding domains of the kingdom of Mysore. In March 1641, the dalavoy was sent to be-siege Maratahalli, a dependency of Samballi. Ghatta Mudaliar was thoroughly vanquished and both Samballi and Maratahalli taken over. The reverses stunned the Madurai nayak. His insecurities grew when, in the span of a year, the Mysorean forces occupied other important fronts around his kingdom—Kaveripuram, Toleya and Changappadi. He knew that the ultimate designs of Mysore were in taking over the coveted and fertile land of Tiruchirapalli and that would deal the death blow to his authority.

In 1644–45 the dalavoy was dispatched for a series of annexations and subjugations of hostile satraps that had defaulted on payment of the stipulated tributes. Hole Narasipura and Periyapatna were thus taken from Narasimha Nayak and Nanjunda Arasu respectively. In the latter case, sustaining a fierce nine-month siege of Periyapatna and fighting against the combined forces of the Ikkeri and Bijapur chieftains, Dalavoy Nanjarajayya emerged victorious. Nanjunda Arasu fled and took refuge in the domains of the King of Coorg, Nanjarayapatna, but was hotly pursued by Ranadhira himself. Not only was Nanjunda slain, but Nanjarayapatna was annexed to Mysore. This marked an important advance of Mysore westwards towards Coorg.

Meanwhile, relations between Mysore and Ikkeri, which had always been strained, became worse. It was a long-drawn conflict between two equal powers, each vying to prove itself the sole authority in south Indian politics. Among the many reasons for which the rulers of Ikkeri despised their Mysore counterparts was this rather strange and bizarre custom adopted by the latter of disgracing their enemies in battlefields by chopping off their noses with a sledge-hammer. The Ikkeri rulers called the Wodeyars 'Mayavis' or sorcerers in view of this peculiar habit of theirs.

Rapid changes occurred within Ikkeri at this time. Virabhadra's uncle Shivappa Nayak treacherously deposed his nephew and took over the capital city of Bidanaur. As a gesture of friendship, Shivappa sent emissaries to Srirangapatna eliciting the cessation of past enmities with Mysore. But Ranadhira despised the Ikkeri chief for what he had done with his own nephew and promptly returned the olive branch of peace that he had sent. This greatly enraged Shivappa Nayak who decided to bide his time to avenge this insult.

He did not have to wait too long. The Bijapur commander, Mustafa Khan, was back on his southern expedition. Proceeding by way of Gadag and Lakshmeshwar to Honnalli and then to Sakkarepatna he enlisted the active support of the new chief of Ikkeri. His intention was to recapture Turuvekere, the northern limit of Mysore that he had lost to the Wodeyar in 1642. But the combine was no match for the deft military skills of Dalavoy Nanjarajayya who completely repulsed the invaders. Unfortunately, the able dalavoy was slain in the bloody combat of January 1647. His younger brother Lingarajayya was made the next Dalavoy.

All through, we see Ranadhira remaining a steadfast loyalist of the monarch of Vijayanagara. The copper plates of the times refer to the Wodeyar as 'Mahamandaleshwara' or viceroy of the empire and 'Sriman Maha Maisuraadhipa' or the Great Ruler of Mysore. In 1642, with the death of Venkata II, his son Sriranga VI ascended the Aravidu throne.

Ranadhira continued to remain his loyal subsidiary. Sriranga on his part was happy with the defence that Randhira had put up for the empire's southern provinces against the repeated onslaughts of the Bijapur Sultans. But his worries were far from over. He was a man who revelled in the glories of the past when Vijayanagara was one of the Deccan's undisputed empires. Sriranga did not care that times had changed, with almost all his powerful feudatories, like the chiefs of Tanjore, Madurai and Gingee having asserted their independence, nor that the Ikkeri chief had allied himself with the Sultan of Bijapur. He still loved to live in his world of make-believe—with him as the emperor of south India, though the empire was steadily shrinking.

Realising the vulnerability of this emperor—who did control some tracts of land—Bijapur's commander, Mustafa Khan, now made a frontal attack on Sriranga's territories. The forces of Bijapur and Golconda united, like they had for Talikota a century back, and attacked Sriranga. Already a dispirited monarch with a recalcitrant army, he easily lost ground. The chieftains of Madurai and Tanjore meekly submitted without defending their emperor. Sriranga became a fugitive and kept taking shelter with many of his hitherto feudatories, turn by turn. Once settled in a place he would revel 'in the midst of festivities, feasts and pleasures' (as described in Hayavadana Rao's 1945 *History of Mysore*) only to be thrown out to seek refuge under another chieftain. He was the political football of the south in those times and only a sad reminder of the glorious past of his dynasty.

Ranadhira on his part remained neutral in this shifting coalition of South Indian politics. He preferred however, to continue to owe allegiance to the emperor, though coins that he began to issue from April 1645 onwards indicate a subtle assertion of his independence. His priorities lay strictly in consolidating the kingdom of Mysore and maintaining its territorial integrity. In the mid 1650s Sriranga was shown the door at Tanjore where he had taken shelter and he literally begged the King of Mysore for help. According to a contemporary commentator, Proenza, Ranadhira received Sriranga with all due respect and extended an 'invitation to choose for his stay a province more agreeable to him and assurance of a brilliant treatment worthy of his rank; he eagerly accepted the offer so obliging and found a hospitality which even surpassed the promises made to his ambassadors.' Sriranga took up residence either at Srirangapatna or its neighbourhood.

Instead of spending his time peacefully in the domain of his gracious host, Sriranga kept manoeuvring to stage a comeback and recover lost ground—of course with the help of the Mysorean forces. But Khan Muhammad of Bijapur laid siege to his territory of Penukonda, capturing it in 1653. The very next year he captured Vellore where Sriranga was hoping to raise an army of his own. Frustrated in all his attempts, the monarch sat patiently, waiting for destiny to help him recover his empire.

The King of Mysore on his part provided no active support to any of these machinations. He was just being a cordial host. His priorities were different—expansion and consolidation of Mysore. In this, his valiant dalavoys—Lingarajayya (1647–48), Kemparajayya (1648–49), Lingegowda (1649–50) and Hamparajayya (1650–51) acquired many places for the kingdom that included Hebbur from Immadi Kempegowda, Sulekeredurga, Nayakavadi, Yelahankanadu, Channagiri, Tunnagani, Madapura, Kattarighatta and Basavapatna. The trend was carried on by his father-in-law Kalale Dasarajayya (1651–53), the succeeding dalavoy who annexed the bigger territories of Pennagara, Ratnagiri, Virabhadranadurga, Kenegere Kote, Dharmapuri, Denkanakote and so on.

The string of successes and annexations were enough to send Adil Shah into a tizzy. Feeling the heat of an ambitious southern neighbour, he once again sent Khan Muhammad to cap his rival's power in March 1653. Tirumala Nayak of Madurai aided and assisted the invaders. After a series of victories, Ranadhira's stars seemed to be on the wane and he lost. He was perhaps growing battle weary. Lingegowda, who was reappointed the dalavoy, didn't seem to be a match for the buoyed forces of Bijapur. Speaking about the devastation the *Muhammad Namah* says:

> The Khan marched out of Vellore, pillaged and burnt the Mysore territory down to a 'heap of ashes'…Balaji Haibat Rao who had left Adil Shah's service for that of Mysore was now sent by Kanti Rai against Khan Muhammad. The Khan dispatched Siddi Masaud with his vanguard to meet this army. In the battle that followed, Balaji was beheaded and his army routed. At this time the Rajah of Mysore in mortal terror sent his envoy to the victorious Khan Muhammad, with an offer of submission asking pardon for his offences and praying for safety. He promised to pay 'treasure beyond calculation' as an offering to Adil Shah and regularly deliver tributes every year. By the orders of Adil Shahi, Khan

Muhammad left the Mysore Rajah's devastated Kingdom to him... the Peshkash was realised by Khan Muhammad.

The flourish apart, what comes through is the thorough rout of Mysore at the hands of Bijapur after successfully keeping it at bay for so long. Bijapur seemed to be having it good all the way through. In 1654, both Bijapur and Golconda ended their campaign in the Carnatic region and by 1656 accomplished a clear division of their territories. The belt of territory to the north of Mysore—including Bangalore, Hoskote, Kolar, Doddaballapura and Sira—was called Carnatic-Bijapur-Balaghat while the territory below the Ghats that shared its borders with Mysore's south-eastern frontier was called the Carnatic-Bijapur-Payeenghat region. Shahji was put in charge of this vast tract. Golconda's possessions lay east of this area with the rich eastern plains of today's Tamil Nadu, Chittoor, Gutti, Gurramkonda, Chandragiri, Gandikote, Kanchipuram and so on with Hazrat Anar Sahib as governor of the Qutub Shah.

But this peace and success too was short-lived. Both the Shahi kingdoms got embroiled in a bitter fight with the Mughal viceroy of the Deccan, Aurangzeb. As a consequence they had little time and energy to maintain their acquisitions in the south and left them completely at the disposal of their viceroys and governors. The chieftains of the Carnatic region took advantage of the absence of the two powers. The wily Shivappa Nayak of Ikkeri acquired Vasudhara and Sakkarepatna from Bijapur and other forts of Soraba, Udugani, Mahadevapura and so on. He played a masterstroke by sending feelers to Sriranga, who was aimlessly biding his time in Mysore. He was convinced that it would be suicidal on his part to remain in a kingdom that had been so badly beaten by the Bijapur Sultans. Ikkeri, on the other hand, was the right place for him, having just recorded successes against those very dreaded Shahs to whom the Wodeyar had capitulated so meekly. The avaricious Sriranga heeded his advice and took shelter in the court of Bidanaur from 1656 to 1659.

In 1655, under the new Dalavoy Hamparajayya, Ranadhira's first priority was to wreak revenge on the Nayak of Madurai for his support of the Bijapur forces in that devastating and humiliating decisive battle. The Mysore troops laid a direct siege to Madurai. Normally a powerless nayak would have fled the ground, but he enlisted timely help from the Marava chief Raghunath Setupati. The dalavoy meanwhile, in Proenza's words, was

...too weak to hazard a general action and informed of the approaching arrival of reinforcements which his king had sent him...with his presents won the Brahman commander of the Madura forces. The traitor sought to repress the ardour of his soldiers and put off, from day to day, the time of attack. But the Maravas, impatient at the delay, conceived suspicions, cited treason, threw the Brahman into a dungeon, pounced on the enemies and cut them to pieces. The remains of the defeated enemy took refuge in a neighbouring fortress, where, after some days, the expected reinforcements of 20,000 men joined them. The combat again began with such fury that each army left nearly 12,000 dead on the battlefield...the advantage remained with the Nayak who utilised his superiority to return to the Mysoreans the evils which they had inflicted on his kingdom, and transport the theatre of this bloody war to their possessions...

The king of Mysore had ordered to cut off the nose of all the prisoners; his soldiers to distinguish themselves, executed this barbarous order on all those who fell into their hands, men, women and children, and sent to Mysore sacks full of noses, as many glorious trophies. The Nayak, resenting this procedure, which in the opinion of the Indians, added the most humiliating outrage to cruelty, ordered reprisals; and his troops burst into the provinces of Mysore, seeking not enemies to fight, but noses to cut. It is this which has given to this inhuman war the name of 'hunt for noses'...the King of Mysore, the first contriver of this barbarity, himself lost his own nose, and thus suffered the penalty which he deserved.

Of course the validity of Ranadhira losing his nose in battle is not certain. But the Mackenzie manuscripts too talk of a complete rout for the Mysorean army that was pushed into its own territories as far as Nanjanagud by Madurai (Mahalingam 1972).

When Mysore faced this embarrassing defeat at the hands of Madurai, Ikkeri's Shivappa Nayak—who had been waiting for long to avenge the insult caused to him by the rejection of his offer of friendship—saw this as the right opportunity to hit back. Since he was the host of Sriranga, whose cause he sought to espouse, every act of his was considered fair and in the larger scheme of things beneficial for the restoration of the Emperor. In 1657, he marched southwards and besieged Hassan and Belur, which belonged to the Sultan of Bijapur. The chieftain of Belur, Krishnappa Nayak, sought Ranadhira's help and the latter sent a huge army. But the Mysorean forces were routed by Ikkeri, Krishnappa was defeated and his son Venkatadri taken prisoner. Sriranga was put in charge of Hassan and Belur by Shivappa Nayak and honoured with many titles like Ramabana, Paravaaranavaarana and so on and given costly gifts that included a richly ornamented earring of sapphire, a costly pearl, the royal emblems of the conch and discus and an umbrella called the Jagajhampa, along with the head of a slain enemy. A thoroughly satisfied Sriranga sat gloating on the throne with dreams of a return to his glorious past. But little did he realise that it was he who depended on his feudatories for his existence, and not the other way round. What this virtually led to was a long-awaited event—the logical conclusion—the death of a really old and sick man, and the ultimate demise of the once glorious Vijayanagara empire.

At the same time, the Ranadhira magic that had swept across south India was definitely on the wane. Three successive defeats were a blow to the prestige of Mysore and its heroic king. His personal life was also in shambles at this time. His only son, Chamaraja, from Ayammanni, one among his ten wives, died at the age of five sometime in 1653–54. This, coupled with the political reverses and losses, left him a completely dejected and frustrated man. In 1659, this great hero who shook almost all the regimes of the south with his valour and presence of mind breathed his last at the young age of forty-five. His wives Ayammanni, Lakshmammanni, Channajammanni, Doddananjammanni, Muddajammanni, Nanjammanni, Gowrammanni, Veerajammanni, Somajammanni and Veerarajammanni committed Sati.

MYSORE UNDER RANADHIRA

Ranadhira contributed much to the progress of the kingdom of Mysore. Stories about him abound in Kannada literature, which speaks volumes of his bravery and romance, especially the troubled circumstances under which he assumed power. The famous poet Charana Kavi Govinda Vaidya's *Kantheerava Narasaraja Vijayam* sings paeans to his legendary bravery. By the end of his reign, he was able to present a competent administration, a well-organised army and a considerably extended territory. The kingdom's northern boundary extended to Chennapatna and Turuvekere. In the east it ran alongside the Bijapur kingdom. In the south it extended up to Danayakanakote and Satyamangalam in present day Tamil Nadu, till Kaveripatna in the south-east and till Coorg in the west. Under Ranadhira, Srirangapatna emerged as a major centre of Vedic and Brahminical learning. Poetry, music, dance, the epics and literature were an important part of the lives of the people. The twin cities of Srirangapatna and Mysore were always abuzz with activity.

He was undoubtedly one of the greatest kings the throne of Mysore had seen after Raja Wodeyar I.

Administration

Ranadhira realised that Mysore had now caught the attention of kings across India and attacks on it would henceforth be commonplace. Perceiving this threat to the kingdom of Mysore, Ranadhira got the palaces, forts and armoury at Srirangapatna and Mysore rebuilt and strengthened. The weapons he installed in the Mysore armoury were named Ramachandra, Muddukrishna, Lakshmiramana, Chamundeshwari, Nagaramari, Ranganatha, Bhairavi, Ramabana, Ugranarasimha and Chikkapirangi. The Mysore palace was adorned with departments called Thottis, like the Jantada Thotti, Samukhada Thotti, Soundarya Vilasa Thotti, Namatirtha Thotti and so on. A total of 43,739 cannons were stationed on the fort walls—1,927 old cannons, 6,000 small, 3,000 fairly large, 23,000 of iron and so on. In 1639, the Srirangapatna fort was extended and huge stockpiles of provisions stationed perpetually in cellars and strategic locations for anticipated use during a siege. The armoury was re-fashioned with weapons, like *katthi* (sword), *kathari* (dagger), *gurani* (shield), *tupaki* (gun), *ambu* (arrow), etc. Stables were built for horses, elephants and bullocks.

Another noteworthy feature of his reign was the establishment of a mint or *tenkashala* for the first time ever in Srirangapatna. As stated earlier, this was also a symbol of the autonomy that Mysore had now begun to enjoy vis-à-vis Vijayanagara. Moreover, Ranadhira was also motivated by the fact that a standardisation of currency across the kingdom would enhance administrative efficiency and allow the currency to clearly articulate the religious orientation of the ruler and the royal family. The first coins were struck in his name on 26 April 1645 and have been called Kanthiraya Hana or Kanthirava Raya or Kanthirava Raya Ravi. The other kind of currency he issued was the Kanthiraya Varaha, which later became corrupted to 'Canteroi Pagoda' due to the Anglicised pronunciation. It was made of ten sub-units of a measure called hanam. The weight of one varaha was equal to that of nine hanams. In modern currency terms the varahas were worth Rs 3.50. Copper coins called anekasu were also issued as token currency. The use of the 'Boar seal' by the kings of Mysore, signifying their faith in Varaha—the mythical incarnation of Lord Vishnu as a wild boar—also began around this time.

Ranadhira also settled the land revenue system of tracts that were annexed—something long due. The powers of Palegars were curbed a great deal. Officials like *subedar, thanedar, karanikas* and *gumastas* were appointed for the collection and delivery of revenue to the central treasury.

Among the many confidantes and ministers of Ranadhira's court were Timmarasa, his minister-in-chief or Mantrisha; Lappavarasa, the finance minister; Basavayya, the treasury officer; the royal scribe Narasimha Upadhyaya; Lingegowda, the mayor of Srirangapatna and Kotturaya, his agent at Saligrama.

Ranadhira also got the Narasambudhi dam built across River Kaundini at the Nanjangud temple of Lord Shiva. The Cauvery was bridged along the Srirangapatna fort at convenient locations and a dam constructed near Chandravana. The water thus stored was led to the capital by canals from the bridge. The crops raised under this scheme were to be used for the services of Lord Ranganatha at Srirangapatna. Many more checkdams (among them the Bangaradoddi canal) were raised across the Cauvery and her tributaries. Irrigation thus received a major impetus.

Religion

Sri Vaishnavism, one of the earliest Hindu religious traditions that originated from the Azhvars and Saint Ramanujacharya's Vishishtadwaita philosophy, fascinated Ranadhira and he presented a crown bejewelled with the nine precious gems and several semi-precious gems called the *Kantheerva mudi* to Lord Narasimha, who like Ranadhira symbolised raw energy and valour. The personal faith of the king in the philosophy led to the rapid growth of Sri Vaishnavism all over the kingdom. In fact, the sect was flourishing all over south India. In Mysore in particular, Melukote and Srirangapatna emerged as centres of Vaishnava tradition and culture. The Tirunakshatram festival commemorating the birth anniversary of the seer of Vishishtadwaita or Vaishnava philosophy of Hindusim, Sri Ramanujacharya, would be celebrated as a major festival—*Gajendra Tirunal*—in Melukote. Also prominent on the festival calendar of the kingdom was the car festival or *Rathotsava* of the presiding deity of Srirangapatna, Lord Ranganatha. This was an elaborate ritual and a joyous occasion when the whole city would be tastefully decked up.

The Mahanavami festival that Raja Wodeyar had continued as part of the Vijayanagara traditions was carried forward by Ranadhira too with added gaiety. The first eight days would be marked by the conduct of public durbars or *Oddolaga*. The activities included the presentation of gifts by subjugated chiefs, boxing and athletic feats, acrobatic performances and fights of gallant men with tigers and bears that were let loose on them. Each night the palace and the city would be illuminated and recitals of vocal and veena music reverberated all over, along with poetry sessions and recitations of the epics. A colourful display of crackers and fireworks would end the activities of each day. The ninth day marked the worship of weapons in the armoury and of the horses and elephants in the stables. On the concluding day, the king would proceed in a delightful procession to the outskirts of the city for worship of the Sami tree. The main street from the palace to the mandap where the Sami tree stood would be beautified for the king's reception. Crowded streets with eager onlookers were a common sight. On the striking of a drum, the procession would begin with the army, beautifully caparisoned elephants, horses, chariots, foot soldiers, musicians and Ranadhira dressed resplendently and riding on a horse, followed by his Dalavoy, ministers, courtiers and servants. On reaching the mandap, he would display his archery skills, witness ram fights and athletic displays, perform the ritualistic puja and return riding on the state elephant. A lavish display of light and colours, illumination, crackers and fireworks would conclude the ten-day long jamboree.

Culture and Architecture

The *Kanthirava Narasaraja Vijayam* by Charana Kavi Govinda Vaidya gives graphic details of the state of the kingdom and its capital city. It eulogises Ranadhira as the very incarnation of Lord Narasimha—the half-man, half-lion form of Lord Vishnu, known for His raw energy and valour. He has been described as being born to eliminate the *mlecchas*—those born of a lower caste—indicating the Muslim rulers of Bijapur.

It is a refreshing first-hand account of the lives and times of people of that age. Srirangapatna was an important centre of social and cultural life; it was prosperous, with a well-guarded fort. The entrance to the fort had deep trenches and the rooms of the guards were located at the entrance. The fort had lofty ramparts, bastions and flag staffs. The entrance led to the broad main streets of the city that were named after the sun and the moon. It was lined with multi-storeyed mansions of the elite of the city—princes and nobles. Minor streets and side lanes housed apartments of poets, scholars, musicians, merchants, ministers, courtiers and militia. The principal gates of the fort were the Eastern Gate, the Mysore Gate and the Bijapur Gate. They were lined with stables for horses and elephants.

In the middle of the city was the lavish abode of the king. The palace was a marvellously sculptured building with intricately carved storeys, aesthetically decorated pavilions and apartments like the Lakshmi Vilasa, Soundarya Vilasa, Madana Vilasa, Durga Mandapa, Sharada Mandapa, Bhuvaneshwari, Indira Mandira, Bangara Chauki, Chitrashala (picture gallery), Ayudhashala (armoury), Natakashala (theatre), Majjanashala (bath complex), Bhojanashala (dining-hall), Dolls' Pavilion, Bokkasa Bhandara (treasury) and so on.

The city also had the temples of Lord Ranganatha, Lakshmi Narayana, Tiruvenkateshwara and so on. The striking feature was the similarity of everything with and the indelible traditional influence of the Vijayanagara empire.

The city of Mysore emerged as another important hub of the kingdom, with a well-provided fort and a palace that housed a Durbar Hall, Council Chamber, picture gallery, theatre and temples of Trineshwara, Lakshmikantha, and Bagila Hanuman. The Bhogi Bhushana and Kalabhairava temples stood on the Doddakere tank bund.

The poetry of Govinda Vaidya also portrays at length the culture and living conditions of the kingdom at that time. It speaks of the many-storied mansions of the affluent class, the middle-class houses with flat roofs and plastered pavements and the humbler abodes of the common populace. The cities also had a teeming market-place that had become an index of the economic prosperity of the kingdom. The purchasing power of the citizens could be gauged by their rich tastes in silk and lace fabrics and ornaments of various descriptions in gold and precious and semi-precious gems. Vaidya paints a beautiful picture of the capital with scenes of princes and sons of nobles in public streets parading their horses or witnessing fights of rams, bulls and cocks, sons of chiefs returning from their daily exercises at the gymnasium, princesses passing along in palanquins and people playing chess and dice as common pastimes.

Elaborate descriptions of court scenes marked with characteristic pomp and splendour also makes refreshing reading. The richly ornamented halls of the palace with huge pillars, paintings and canopies hosted the public and private meetings of the king. Ranadhira himself is described as dressing himself up in the choicest of clothes, overlaid with rich pearls, an ornamented overcoat, filigreed turban set with a crest of diamonds and a symbol on his forehead with musk, earrings of pearls and sapphires, necklaces, medallions, rings of precious stones, wristlets, bracelets, waistbands, badges for the feet set with precious stones from the crowns of defeated chieftains and ornamented sandals.

The Nityotsavada Olaga or Daily Durbar was also marked with some ceremonial grandeur and would usually be held at night at the Lakshmi Vilasa chamber to the accompaniment of music and dance. Ranadhira would be seated on a bejewelled throne and 'served by twice-eight fair ones holding chowries in their hands' and honoured with symbols of kingship. Vedic scholars, musicians, disputants, close ministers, the dalavay, accountants, feudatories and others would attend the durbar. Other than music, scholarly debates, drama, politics, grammar, submission of reports by ministers, etc., were some of the activities of the Durbar. On these occasions Ranadhira would be variously addressed as 'Karnataka Chakreshwara' or Emperor of Karnataka and 'Andhra Bala Sangha Karikula' or the leader of the elephant herd that vanquished the Andhra kings.

Ranadhira also constructed many temples, gardens and parks in Mysore. Near the Trineshwara Temple he got the Shringarathota garden constructed. A Kalyana Mandapa or marriage hall was constructed near the Sriranganatha temple at Srirangapatna and many idols of the Vaishnavite pantheon like the Alwars, Garuda, Vishwaksena, etc., were installed. He submitted the *Vaikuntha mudi* crown to Lord Ranganatha at Srirangapatna, installed Panchalingas in the Gangadhara Swami temple and made liberal grants to numerous temples. A Brahmin residential area or *agrahara* called 'Kantheerapura' was established. The older parts of present-day Mysore still have some of these *agraharas*, which have been the citadels of religion, philosophy and culture for aeons.

Art and Literature

Ranadhira was also a patron of arts and literature. Notable among the works written during his rule were the *Behara Ganita* by Bhaskara, a mathematical treatise dealing with compound interest, square measure, chain measure and mint mathematics, *Markandeya Ramayana* by Timmarasa and *Kanthirava Narasaraja Vijayam* by Charana Kavi Govinda Vaidya. Alasingaraya was a noted Vaishnava scholar who was well-versed in the philosophy of Srivaishnavism.

Speaking about the athletes of Mysore who were called *Jettis* Wilks writes:

> Mysoor, I believe, is the only country in the South of India in which the institution of the athlete has been preserved on its ancient footing. These persons constitute a distinct caste, trained from their infancy in daily exercises for the express purposes of these exhibitions; and perhaps the whole world does not produce more perfect forms than those which are exhibited at these interesting but cruel sports. The combatants clad in a single garment of light orange coloured drawers, extending half way down their thigh, have their right hand furnished with a weapon... composed of a buffalo horn fitted to the hand and pointed with four knobs resembling very sharp knuckles...with a fifth of greater prominence, at the end nearest the little finger, and at right angles with the other four. This instrument, properly placed, would enable a man of ordinary strength to cleave open the head of his adversary at a blow; but the fingers being introduced through the weapon, it is fastened across them at an equal distance between the first and second lower joints in a situation, it will be observed, which does not admit of attempting a severe blow, without the risk of dislocating the first joints of all the fingers...the combat is a mixture of wrestling and boxing...the blows are mere cuts inflicted...and before the end of the contest both of the combatants may frequently be observed streaming with blood from the crown of the head down to the sand of the arena....

Regarding the other members of the royal family at this time, Ranadhira's father Bettada Chamaraja Wodeyar passed away at the age of eighty-five in March 1639. The only surviving brother of Raja Wodeyar was Muppina Devaraja Wodeyar who lived at Gundlu with his family and passed away at the ripe old age of 103 in 1656. He had four sons by his second wife Kempammanni. Of them, the eldest Doddadevaraja was born in 1622 and perhaps held charge of Mysore, ruling jointly with Ranadhira by the time of the end of his reign.

Thus ends the story of one of the most heroic kings of Mysore.

Ranadhira was a clever tactician and a ruler of vision, besides being an able warrior. He realised that the dalavoys with a large army under their control and also a hand in the administration could practically become *de facto* rulers and challenge the very authority of the throne. Hence, none of them were kept for too long. In his entire reign there were ten dalavoys. To him goes the singular credit of stemming the advance of Bijapur on Mysore and maintaining the pre-eminence and integrity of the kingdom in south Indian polity. He thus presented to his successor a compact and progressive kingdom, which had emerged as a force to reckon with.

An inscription of the times sums up, though in highly exaggerated terms, this stormy and valiant reign of Ranadhira:

> While he ruled, the Gods sent good rains; the earth brought forth full fruit; all points of the compass were unclouded; the respective orders were diligent in their several rites; all the people were free from disease; the country was free from trouble; the women were devoted to their husbands and all the world was prosperous.

THE REIGN OF DEVARAJA WODEYAR

Raja Wodeyar's brother, Muppina Devaraja had four sons. Of them, the eldest was Doddadevaraja Wodeyar. His third son, born on 25 May 1627, was Kempadevaraja or Devaraja Wodeyar and it was 'this man who was selected to the exclusion of the elder brothers as the male issue' by Ranadhira Kanthirava (Wilks' *History of Mysore, Vol. I*). He succeeded the deceased king in his thirty-seventh year in the Bhadrapada month of 1659.

A series of aggressions greeted the new king's ascent. The Ikkeri ruler Shivappa Nayak was waiting for an opportunity to strike another fatal blow upon Mysore. Espousing the cause of Emperor Sriranga, he enlisted the support of many local chieftains and encamped on the outskirts of Srirangapatna. Dalavoy Hamparajayya was sent to repel this menacing advance. But the Ikkeri forces won a brilliant victory and marched into Srirangapatna. The fall of the city seemed imminent. It was then that dubious methods were used to counter the offensive. The incumbent king, unlike his chivalrous predecessor, decided to resort to means outside of warfare to ward off this frontal attack on the capital city. He bribed the officers and agents of Ikkeri who beat a retreat. Stung by this reversal within his own ranks, Shivappa was forced to retract.

Wilks states: 'Dud Deo Raj is accused by the historians of Bednore of having employed bribery...for the purpose of inducing this army to raise the siege, and retract in confusion and dismay to Bednore.'

The retreating armies were, however, hotly pursued by the defeated Dalavoy Hamparajayya who had found sufficient time to realign himself. They were defeated and, as was practice, lost their noses.

The very next year, Shivappa Nayak passed away and his younger brother Venkatappa Nayak held sway for a short while. This was followed by the ascent of Bhadrappa Nayak in Ikkeri. During this time, there was a quick succession of dalavoys at Mysore as well. In 1660, Hamparajayya was implicated in cases of fraud and dismissed. Mallarajayya was made dalavoy. But he was inefficient and inexperienced. Hence, Muddayya replaced him as dalavoy, but his untimely death made way for Nanjanathayya as the dalavoy. He was a man of rare talent and had two terms as dalavoy with a short intervening period of Kumarayya. Dalavoy Nanjanathayya made full use of the political vacuum that the disappearance of the Shahi kingdoms had left behind in the Balaghat region. In January 1663 he acquired Chelur, Bidare, Sampige and Chikkanayakanahalli and by the end of the year, the Ikkeri dominions of Vastare and Honnavalli.

Meanwhile, a regime change at Ikkeri saw Hiriya Somashekara Nayak taking charge, though he continued the dynasty's avowed hostility for Mysore. He launched an aggressive assault on Mysore but was completely routed in battle by the sagacious dalavoy. He was forced to sue for peace.

If all these reverses upset the ambitions of one man, it ought to have been Sriranga VI. He had made the suicidal move of aligning with Ikkeri against Mysore, his one-time host and friend. The death of Shivappa Nayak and the defeat Ikkeri faced in one battle after another made Sriranga's position in Belur untenable. In a huff, he left Belur for the southern reaches of India in 1663. He reached Madurai and took refuge in the court of the new chief there, Chokkanatha Nayak. History seemed to repeat itself here. What Shivappa Nayak planned against Mysore, using Sriranga as the pawn, Chokkanatha attempted by aligning with forces like Ghatta

Mudaliar. The tragedy was that Sriranga was naive enough to believe that each of these chieftains were furthering his cause and without reading between the lines, sought blind refuge in each of their courts. In January 1667, Devaraja Wodeyar, on hearing about this growing confederacy in the south, attacked and defeated Mudaliar. Dalavoy Kumarayya raided the territories of the Madurai Nayak and in 1667–68, Erode, Dharmapuram, Vamalur, Samballi, etc., were taken. He reached as far as Tiruchirapalli forcing Chokkanatha to submit. The Madurai forces were routed. Lithic records dated 1663 call Devaraja Wodeyar the 'destroyer of the Pandya King'. The brutalities that followed were quite shocking. The heads of the vanquished were cut off and hung on the fort walls and from the booty collected, golden slippers were made for the king. This was done to send cold shivers down the spines of rebellious Palegars who were attempting a similar act. The remaining part of the booty was distributed among the army in recognition of their good work and used for welfare work, like the extension of temples, construction of tanks and temples, and other grants.

Sriranga's last hopes of a possible revival of fortunes were thus quashed and in utter frustration he left for Penukonda where he apparently ruled till 1681 or 1692. Historical records do not give the exact date. During his absence from the south, two scions of the Aravidu Dynasty, Devadeva Maharaya and Venkatapatiraya—Sriranga's son and nephew—held nominal sway. But this is the last that history recounts of the worthless scions of the once mighty Vijayanagara empire. For Mysore, it meant breaking free from the nominal shackles of self-imposed subordination. The name of the emperor of Vijayanagara is conspicuous by its absence in the records of Devaraja from 1665–73. From a mere feudatory existence, Mysore had certainly risen to the status of an independent kingdom. The shifting of the celebrated Tatacharya family of Sri Vaishnava royal preceptors from the court of Vijayanagara to Srirangapatna also signified the shift in the axis of power and the dwindling fortunes of the once mighty empire. The use of the boar seal by the Mysore kings indicated the kingdom's suzerainty. Of course the symbol of the boar, one of the incarnations of Lord Vishnu, also signified the religious orientation of the dynasty. By January 1665, Devaraja assumed the titles of 'Samrat' and 'Chakravarthi', which further symbolised this new power.

This new-found freedom bolstered the ambitions of the Mysorean troops. In 1666, Santavalli and Holenarasipura were annexed,

Huliyurdurga in 1667 and Kunigal in 1668 from Mummadi Kempegowda of Magadi. By 1673, Mysore extended as far as Hassan and Sakrepatna in the west, Salem in the east, Chikkanayakanahalli in the north and Erode and Dharmapuram in the south.

Devaraja was famous for the *Mahadanas* or grants he made in his tenure, which were called the *Shodasha Mahadanas* or sixteen *Daanas* (great grants/gifts/offerings)—*Tulapurusha dana, Hiranyagarbha dana, Brahmanda dana, Kalpavruksha dana, Gosahasra dana, Hiranya kamadhenu dana, Hiranyakshwa dana, Hiranyakshwa ratha dana, Hemahasthiratha dana, Parichalanga dana, Dhara dana, Vishwa chakra dana, Sapta sagara dana, Kalpa lata dana, Ratna dhenu dana* and *Mahabhoota ghata dana*. These were grants of gold, grains, cows, horses, chariots, land, etc., to Brahmins and men of God. Realising the hardships faced by pilgrims in traversing rocky terrain on the way up to the hill-top temple of Goddess Chamundeshwari in Mysore, he got a thousand steps built leading up to the temple. Halfway up the hill, a beautiful granite statue of Nandi or Basava, the Holy Bull that is the vehicle of Lord Shiva, was installed. It is worshipped to this day atop the hill and is a tourist attraction.

The king donated sixty-two houses for the Brahmins of the kingdom and a *muth* for the Jangama Shaivite saints called the Gacchi Muth. The Devarajapura Agrahara was constructed and he also made pious grants to Lord Venkateshwara of Tirupati. He was greatly admired by his subjects for his benevolence and solicitude.

Many scholars resided in Devaraja's court. Most significant among them was the scion of the Tatacharya family, Venkatavaradacharya, who was legendary for his knowledge of the sacred texts, logic and philosophy. Alasingaraya was another eminent scholar, whose son Tirumalaraya or Tirumala Iyengar had a profound influence on his childhood classmate—Devaraja's son Prince Chikkadevaraja. The royal scribe, Lakshmipati, and Lakhappa Sharman, an astrological scholar, were other luminaries at the royal court of Mysore.

Devaraja's reign also saw the beginnings of intercourse with the European nations. In June 1671, the French agent Flacour proceeded from Tellicherry to settle a trade deal at Srirangapatna. Dellon, the physician, who had sailed from France in 1668, intended to accompany him. While he went as far as the mountains of the region, the excessive torrents forced him to retreat. Flacour persisted and managed to reach Srirangapatna and strike his deal.

Devaraja had two wives, Muddajammanni and Devajammanni. His elder brother, Doddadevaraja Wodeyar, who had administered Mysore during the reign of Ranadhira, had retired to Gundlu. His wife Amritammanni gave birth to two sons, Chikkadevaraja Wodeyar and Kanthiravayya. Doddadevaraja died at the age of forty-seven in 1669. His brother and king, Devaraja took over the responsibilities of his young nephews. Chikkadevaraja lived at the fort of Hangal where he led a life of great discipline and learning. Devaraja also got his nephew married to Devajammanni of Yelandur and Devammanni.

Devaraja passed away in the Phalguna month (11 February) of 1673 at the age of forty-six. Though not credited with military talents like those of his illustrious predecessor, Devaraja was known for his diplomacy and shrewdness, which could twist even adverse situations to his own advantage.

THE REIGN OF CHIKKADEVARAJA WODEYAR

Devaraja's nephew Chikkadevaraja Wodeyar was crowned the fourteenth ruler of the Wodeyar dynasty on 28 February 1673. If Raja Wodeyar was gifted with a rare sense of diplomacy and shrewdness and the celebrated Ranadhira with raw energy and power, Chikkadevaraja had a combination of all these qualities, coupled with an amazing sense of administrative acumen and political far-sightedness. He was undoubtedly the man of the moment for Mysore. Born on 22 September 1645, Chikkadevaraja had shown great promise right from his childhood. However, the distractions of youth, in the buzzing capital city of Srirangapatna, made him falter in his twenties. This compelled his uncle and guardian, Devaraja Wodeyar, to ensure that the young man was confined in an environment congenial to his academic and military education. He was packed off to Hangala, a village south of Mysore. This confinement proved to be a boon for young Chikkadevaraja. He came into close contact with meritorious men of his age, who were to have a lasting impact on him. Of these were Shadaksharayya, a Veerashaiva preceptor of the Yelandur family and Vishalaksha Pandit, a Jain scholar from Yelandur. He also became close friends with Tirumalaraya or Tirumala Iyengar, the son of the scholar, Alasingaraya.

After his coronation, one of his first acts was the constitution of a Council of Ministers called the Mantralochana Sabhe. It was a form of

Cabinet headed by Vishalaksha Pandit as its prime minister. Other members included Tirumalaraya, Shadaksharayya, Chikkupadhyaya and Karanika Lingannayya. Kumarayya was retained as the dalavoy of the kingdom.

Vishalaksha Pandit was a Jain scholar who began to wield great influence on the king and the polity. His tenure as prime minister helped in the spread of Jainism in Mysore and he is even credited with the construction of a *chaitya* in Srirangapatna dedicated to the last Tirthankara and endowments to the shrine at Sravana Belagola. Tirumalaraya or Tirumala Iyengar, as he was called, was a Vaishnavite who succeeded Pandit to the post of prime minister. He was a classmate of the king's and a close associate from childhood. Chikkupadhyaya was also a staunch believer of the Vaishnava tenets. He was a poet, philosopher and eminent mathematician, whose real name was Lakshmisha or Lakshmipati. The suffix of Chhikkupadhyaya signified that he had served as junior teacher to Chikkadevaraja in his student days. These two individuals had a great influence on the king's religious orientations in the latter part of his rule. Shadaksharayya was a Veerashaiva who did his bit to ensure that the king remained within the fold he hitherto belonged to, but did not succeed. Lingannaya, a Smartha Brahmin,[*] was in charge of the public accounts and their maintenance.

The challenges and the road ahead for the young ruler of Mysore were daunting. But he had the wherewithal to overcome each of these and transport his own fame and that of Mysore to greater heights.

---

[*] Smartha is a Shaivite Brahmin sect among Kannada, Marathi and Telugu Brahmins.

5

INDIA IN THE SEVENTEENTH CENTURY

At this point, it is worthwhile to pause and examine the geopolitical context of Mysore in the seventeenth century. It obviously did not operate in isolation; being influenced by and in turn influencing the unprecedented changes taking place in the country and outside.

THE RISE OF THE MARATHAS

The birth of military nationalism came naturally in the mountainous regions of Maharashtra, with its arid, uncultivable soil and the large number of easily defended hill forts. The Marathas rose to power in the Deccan after the weakening of the Vijayanagara empire. The promotion of Hinduism became the cause of their political existence and they dreamt of building a vast Hindu empire in India. To this day, the right-wing Hindu nationalistic politicians of India uphold the Marathas and their leader, Shivaji, as one of their role models and leading lights. Maratha nationalism of this time was inspired by the Bhakti literature of the region.

A number of families emerged in the seventeenth century—the Bhosles of Viral, Yadavas of Deogiri, Nimbalkars of Phalten and so on. The Mughal emperor Akbar defeated Malik Ambar of Ahmednagar and a host of Maratha allies. Maloji Bhosle became prominent during this strife. His sons were Shahji Bhosle and Sarafji Bhosle, and the former became the *sipahsalar* or commander of Ahmednagar after his father's death and fought the Mughals in the Battle of Bhatvadi. After Malik Ambar died, Shahji fled to Bijapur and took shelter under Badshah Muhammad Adil Shah (1625–56). In 1638, Ranadhira Kanthirava had his historic war with Bijapur. Ranadulla Khan and Shahji captured Sira, Tumkur and Bangalore.

THE STATE OF THE MUGHAL EMPIRE

Shah Jahan, the Mughal emperor, fell seriously ill in 1658, and his four sons laid claim to his throne. The political situation in India was tense with this turmoil in Delhi. Each of Shah Jahan's sons had considerable administrative experience and military skills, commanded a large military force and had a loyal following. The eldest, Dara Shikoh (1615–59), was resident at Shah Jahan's court as the designated heir; Shuja was governor of Bengal, Bihar and Orissa; Aurangzeb governed the Deccan; and Murad was governor of Gujarat and Malwa. Dara's forces were defeated by Aurangzeb, who occupied the imperial capital of Agra; and Aurangzeb took his own father prisoner. Shah Jahan was imprisoned in the Agra Fort under the special care of a tyrannical eunuch who took great delight in inflicting petty indignities upon the captive and once-powerful emperor.

Shuja's army was routed in battle; and Murad was lured into a false agreement and taken prisoner. Dara eventually collected together another force, suffered defeat as before, and once again fled. But soon he was betrayed by one of his allies and handed over to his brother. Accused of idolatry and apostasy from Islam, Dara was condemned to death, and the sentence was carried out on the night of 30 August 1659, one year after Aurangzeb took over the Agra Fort and assumed the throne. Aurangzeb delivered the head of his brother to their father as a gift.

Aurangzeb was among the last of the great Mughal emperors who took the empire to glory, extending it from Ghazni in the west to Bengal in the east, Kashmir in the north and southward to the Deccan. It can be said that with Aurangzeb, the medieval age of Indian history ends. With blood on his hands—that too of his own siblings—Aurangzeb celebrated his coronation on 15 June 1659.

Aurangzeb was a tyrannical and communal ruler, who destroyed a number of temples, imposed the Jaziya tax on the non-Muslims of his kingdom and led massive conversion drives. The Rajputs in his kingdom revolted against this discrimination. The Sikhs were another rebellious group. The killing of their ninth guru, Tegh Bahadur, caused the Sikhs to align in a rabid anti-Mughal campaign under their tenth guru, Gobind

Singh. In the south, a new power was raising its head against the atrocities of Delhi. The Marathas were becoming a powerful force to reckon with under their new leader Shivaji, whose father, Shahji Bhosle, served under the Sultan of Bijapur.

THE REIGN OF SHIVAJI

Shivaji was born in 1627 to Shahji Bhosle and his wife Jija Bai. His love of adventure, his knowledge of popular ballads and his exciting raids using guerilla warfare tactics, his horsemanship and statesmanship coupled with his vision of a unified Hindu confederacy made him a popular hero among the Marathas. In an irony of sorts, while his father was on the payroll of the Sultan of Bijapur, Shivaji revolted against the same sultan. He recaptured many forts that belonged to the sultan including Pune, which he made his base. The enraged sultan imprisoned Shahji and decided to release him only if Shivaji mended his ways. Shivaji then used the services of Shah Jahan through Prince Murad—who was the Deccan viceroy—to get his father released. The sultan had no option but to release Shahji. Shivaji's exploits continued.

By 1656 he had more than doubled the extent of his geographical sway. The Western Ghat area from Kalyan to Mahad fell into his hands. Heroic stories and legends abound of how he would hoodwink most opponents who came to assault him by deceit. Afzal Khan, the envoy of the Sultan of Bijapur, and the Mughal envoy Shaista Khan were shown the door in a clever and cunning way. Aurangzeb invited Shivaji to Agra for talks and when the latter reached, 'instead of giving him the promised position, which was to be the highest in his audience hall, he caused him to be assigned the lowest place in the first circle of nobles within the golden railing,' (as describd by Niccolo Manucci, cited in Edwards' *A History of India*). Before he could storm out of the court in a huff, Shivaji was arrested by Aurangzeb's guards. The manner in which he cleverly escaped—hiding in a basket of fruit—is a popular anecdote of history. If there was anyone who gave Aurangzeb sleepless nights, it was Shivaji.

In 1664, Shahji died at Hodigere near Chennagiri and his son Ekoji took over the administration of Bangalore. Ekoji kept waging wars against neighbouring Mysore and Devaraja Wodeyar.

Meanwhile in 1677, Shivaji (who had crowned himself 'Chhatrapati' or emperor of the Marathas in 1674) prepared for the most important expedition of his life. With 30,000 cavalry and 40,000 infantry, he embarked on the southern expansion. He captured a number of territories of the Bijapur Sultanate in the Carnatic region including Tiruvannamalai and Vellore. He then turned his attention to Bangalore. Claiming it as his father's *jagir*, he overran Bangalore and adjacent areas of Kolar, Hoskote, Sira and Chikkaballapur and presented Bangalore as a gift to Dipa Bai, wife of Ekoji. Ginjee fort was strengthened and a strong Maratha army was stationed there. He then shifted focus towards Mysore and attacked it in 1677.

But just a few years later, in 1680, the valiant hero died. Shivaji's son Shambhaji succeeded him.

THE ADVENT OF COLONIALISM

None of the these changes had the kind of impact that a new ideology and its representative power, in distant England, were to have on India.

By the sixteenth century vast changes had taken place in Europe. The modern age had set in following the Renaissance and Reformation that heralded the rise of nation-states. In the East, however, the medieval age continued long after Europe had entered the modern era. For thousands of years Europe had imported spices and luxury items from Asian countries via the Middle East. The capture of Constantinople in 1453 by the Ottoman Turks and the obstruction of this hitherto free route constrained Europe to look for alternative and more feasible routes to Asia.

With the Renaissance and the spirit of enquiry and reform it brought, the Europeans set out on their famous voyages to explore distant lands; more so with the idea of exploring, for trade, new lands that till then had been blocked by the Turks. Asia was the front-runner among the lands waiting to be explored by these adventurous sailors, who had the royal sanction of their respective countries and a kind of charter to reach new lands and explore trading possibilities there. It is interesting to note that cuisine constraints were what initially forced Europe to search the world for items, like pepper—an indispensable ingredient in ensuring that preserved meat was edible. The Europeans were thrown into a tizzy when they realised that their route to the pepper lands was blocked.

Columbus of Spain in 1492, Magellan of Spain in 1519 and the Portuguese Bartholomew Diaz tried unsuccessfully to find a route to India, but Vasco da Gama of Portugal met with success. As his ship drew closer to India, the chains of slavery automatically seemed to grip India. In 1498 he set up settlements at Cochin and Cannanore with the supposed intention of spreading the Christian faith. When asked by an Arab trader his intentions behind visiting India, Vasco da Gama reportedly answered, 'We seek Christians and spices,' (Hall 1996). That they got both, in larger measures than they had expected, is history. The initial Portuguese aspirants had to face the hostility of the Arabs who had monopolised Indian trade until that time. But the trouble in Egypt, where the Mamelukes were threatened by the Turks, a divided North India and a disintegrating Deccan helped Portuguese designs. The Portuguese king sent Dom Francisco Almeida as governor (1505–09) and Alfonso de Albuquerque as viceroy (1509–15). Almeida was involved in a bloody battle with the Egyptian and Gujarati fleets off Diu, eventually emerging victorious. As Vincent Smith observed, the moral of his victory set the thumb-rule for all those seeking a share in Indian trade: 'As long as you may be powerful at sea you will hold India as yours; and if you do not possess this power, little will avail you a fortress on shore.'

Albuquerque, his successor as governor, hoped to build a Portuguese empire in the East. By the time of his death, the Portuguese had acquired strategic control of the Indian Ocean by securing bases covering all the entrances to the sea—in East Africa, off the Red Sea, at Ormuz, in Malabar, and at Malacca. Goa, which was acquired by him in 1510, was the principal port of the Sultan of Bijapur and became the first bit of Indian land to be directly governed by Europeans since the time of Alexander.

With all these different groups setting their eyes eastward, India would face a challenge that she had perhaps never before faced in her long and chequered history. She had seen a number of expeditions and foreign invasions in the past; but economic subjugation leading to political domination was unknown to the general Indian psyche.

'In the middle of the seventeenth century, Asia still had a far more important place in the world than Europe.' Thus wrote Pirenne in his *History of the Universe.* He added:

> The riches of Asia were incomparably greater than those of the European states. Her industrial techniques showed a subtlety and a tradition that the European handicrafts did not possess. And there was nothing in the more modern methods used by the traders of the Western countries that Asian trade had to envy. In matters

of credit, transfer of funds, insurance, and cartels, neither India, Persia, nor China had anything to learn from Europe.

THE ENGLISH EAST INDIA COMPANY: ORIGIN AND STRUCTURE

The British were not to be left behind in this quest for new lands. A merchant, Ralph Fitch, inspired the founding of the basis of British power in India—the English East India Company was established on 31 December 1600. After the English defeated the Spanish Armada, opening the passage to the East, Queen Elizabeth I gave a charter with exclusive rights to 'The Governor and the Company of Merchants of London', to trade in the 'East Indies'.

Interestingly, India never featured on the Company's initial strategy. They were looking at the spice islands of modern day Indonesia—pepper from Java, cloves from the Malaccas, mace and nutmeg from the Banda islands. But a series of defeats on the Spice Islands at the hands of the Dutch forced the Company to look for opportunities elsewhere in Asia. India was their first choice now.

In his classic book *The Corporation that Changed the World*, which traces present day multinationals to the East India Company's philosophy and management style, Nick Robbins candidly states:

> The Company had pioneered the shareholder model of corporate ownership and built the foundations for modern business administration. With a single-minded pursuit of personal and corporate gain, the Company and its executives eventually achieved market dominance in Asia, ruling over large swathes of India for a profit. But the Company also shocked its age with the scale of its executive malpractice, stock market excess and human oppression.

Such was the situation when the East India Company began its trading activities in the early seventeenth century. Interestingly, the East India Company was one of a number of companies that were granted a royal charter to seize opportunities in other lands. Some of these were Muscovy (1555), Levant Companies (1581), Company of Royal Adventures (1672), companies targeting Virginia (1606) and Hudson Bay (1670). But the East India Company combined acumen with shrewdness, bribery and corruption to emerge as the ultimate winner. Its very genetic make-up was different from its contemporaries and it is interesting to note its striking similarities with modern-day corporate working mechanisms. Due to the huge capital costs entailed by long-distance voyages to the East, the infrastructure for the same, political and other risks involved in the process, the Company came up with the joint stock mechanism. It had a set of investors who pumped in money to facilitate these operations and a set of managers who manned the day-to-day activities and drove strategies for the company sitting at Leadenhall Street.*

Initially, 218 investors put in a capital investment of £68,373 and financed a small fleet of four ships that sailed out of England in February 1601. Around 1612, the East India Company's docks were constructed on an acre-and-a-half of land at Blackwall. This was envisaged as the commercial hub which would see an inflow and outflow of goods for the people of Britain. By 1620, the Company managed a fleet of 10,000 tonnes, operated by over 2,500 sailors and maintained by 500 ships' carpenters. Successful ships returned after a voyage of two or three years, the goods were unloaded and carted to different warehouses the Company owned. It all thus began with a romanticised idea of adventure that ended up aiming for maximum profit.

The way the Company functioned was very similar to what happens in corporate situations today. If there was a profit, the investors received their dividends based on the ratio of their investments and in case of losses, they were liable only for their paid-up capital. Also, the Company conducted trading as a joint stock company rather than on a member basis, giving it a very unique institutional character when compared to Asian or European trading bodies. The exploits of victory and the infamy of loss not only boosted or destroyed individual reputations, they also had a direct impact on the share price of the Company, which was listed at Exchange Alley. Thus, along with profit and personal aggrandisement, responsibilities to the shareholders and investors and control over the share price were serious concerns for those managing the Company's affairs.

---

* Incidentally, this was not the first headquarters of the Company. That was at the City Mansion of its first chairman, Sir Thomas Smythe, located at Philpot Lane, London.

Despite all this seeming independence, its 'chartered' operations meant that the Company existed and operated at the pleasure of the British Crown. Since it had exclusive rights of trade between England and the Cape of Good Hope, the Company enjoyed the confidence of investors, who trusted in it since it enjoyed such privileges and the confidence of the king of England. Maintaining this amiable relationship with the throne was the constant endeavour of all Company managers. On foreign shores, the Company tried to outstrip its French, Dutch and Portuguese rivals by initially appearing servile towards the local monarchs. This usually paid off; for instance, the Mughal emperor of India favoured them over others, giving them the additional right (in the form of *firmans*) to carry on their activities. At the same time, using military might to resolve a conflict of interest was never ruled out in those days of stiff competition.

The corporate governance in the East India Company functioned very systematically. Depending on the stock amount they owned, shareholders could elect a Board of Directors for four-year tenures and even stand for election themselves. The chairman and deputy chairman were elected by the group of directors from among themselves. Shareholders could even veto the directors' decisions after debating them in an open forum. They often tried to exert their influence to secure good jobs for their kith and kin. Each director was assigned to one of ten committees, of which correspondence, treasury and accounts were the most important. Other committees dealt with buying commodities, warehousing, shipping, managing the East India House headquarters, the legal department, and the Secret Committee that dealt with political and military strategies in times of war.

Entering as 'writers', or clerks, most employees progressed up the ladder in about five years to become 'factors'. After three years, they would at this post be promoted to junior and senior merchant and thereafter the president's council itself if they performed well and were high achievers. The Company had high expectations of its employees and also had the right to dismiss them in case of malpractice. The overseas staff received minimal salaries but had the right to conduct private trade in Asia. This was a great 'employee retention incentive'. The executives loved overseas assignments. Like many contemporary Indian software employees who await windfalls in the form of much-awaited 'offsites', the executives of the Company knew that a post in India would ensure enough wealth for the next two or three generations to live like aristocrats in England.

This digression into the origins of the East Indian Company, the manner in which it was structured, and the motivations of its employees, becomes pertinent and relevant in our study of Indian history. In contrast, Indian monarchs were used to stratify Indian society, which clearly demarcated the ruling class from the trading community. Faced by the structured, planned and financially-driven Company, it is no wonder our Indian kings were completely bulldozed in the Company's ambitions to control Indian trade and then India itself. Mysore's response to the challenge was no better. Devaraja's regime first saw European powers seeking a trade deal with Srirangapatna, and the Wodeyar willingly acquiesced.

THE EARLY YEARS OF THE COMPANY IN INDIA

Driven out of the Spice Islands, the East India Company turned towards India. They had visited Gujarat and the Coromandel Coast looking for cotton textiles. British traders had initially come to India hoping to sell Britain's most popular export item to Continental Europe—British broadcloth, but were disappointed to find little demand for it. Instead, like their Portuguese counterparts, they found several Indian-made items they could sell quite profitably in their homeland. Competing with other European traders, and competing with several other trade routes to Europe, the early British traders were in no position to dictate terms. They had to seek concessions with a measure of humility and offer trade terms that allowed at least some benefits to the local rulers and merchants. While Aurangzeb, (who had, perhaps, seen the connection between growing European trade concessions and falling revenues from overland trade) attempted to limit and control the activities of the East India Company, not all Indian rulers had as many compunctions about making trade concessions. Besides, the East India Company was willing to persevere; fighting and cajoling for concessions; it built trading bases wherever it could along either side of the lengthy Indian coastline. In 1601, their first factory was established at Surat.

In this period, relations between Indians and the British were not lacking in cordiality and the East India Company included employees from both worlds. Friendships between the two nationalities developed not only within the context of business relations, but even beyond, to the point of inter-marriage. Disproving the stereotype of the pompous, stuffy British gentry, the British employees of the East India Company made the most of life in India, dressing in cool and comfortable Indian garments, enjoying Indian pastimes and absorbing local words into their dialect. With as yet unprejudiced eyes, these British traders delighted in the delicate craftsmanship and attractiveness of Indian manufactures and took advantage of their growing popularity in Britain and France. So lucrative was the trade that even though India would accept nothing but silver or gold in return, the East India Company prospered.

Considering the long route (around the African Cape) that the British had to take to reach England, it was surprising that they made as much money as they did. But other factors outweighed this disadvantage. First, owing to their legally sanctioned monopoly status in England, they had substantial control over the British market. Second, by buying directly from the source, they were able to eliminate the considerable mark-up that Indian goods enjoyed enroute to Europe. Third, the East India Company probably enjoyed better economies of scale since their ships were amongst the largest in the Indian Ocean. In addition, they were able to develop new markets for Indian goods in Africa and the Americas.

Finally, and perhaps most significantly, as Veronica Murphy reports, 'although the East India Company was not itself engaged in the transatlantic slave trade, the link was very close and highly profitable'. In fact, in the eighteenth century, the British dominated the Atlantic slave trade, transporting more slaves than all the other European powers combined. In 1853, Henry Carey wrote: 'It (the British System) is the most gigantic system of slavery the world has yet seen, and therefore it is that freedom gradually disappears from every country over which England is enabled to gain control.' The Atlantic slave trade was hence a vital contributor to the financial strength of the East Indian trading companies.

So much so that by the middle of the seventeenth century, the East India Company was exporting Indian goods to Europe and North Africa and even Turkey. Unsurprisingly, this was to have a severely deleterious effect on the Ottomans, the Persians and the Afghans, since the revenues of these states came from Indian trade. It also seriously impacted the revenues of the Mughals, and while the activities of the Arab and Gujarati traders were not entirely eliminated, their trade was much curtailed, and largely reduced to the inter-Asian trade, which continued unabated. In any case, the Mughal state was unable to resist centrifugal forces and rapidly disintegrated. This left the East India Company with considerably more leverage and emboldened it to expand its activities and demand even greater concessions from Indian rulers.

But even as the Indian rulers were granting more concessions, there was a rising chorus of voices bemoaning the loss of European silver to Asia. At the end of the seventeenth century, the silk and wool merchants of France and England were unwilling to put up with competition from Indian textiles, which had become the rage in the new bourgeois societies of Europe. Not only did they seek bans on such trading activities of the East India Company, they also sought and won restrictions on the purchase of these items in their respective nations. These prohibitions, while not entirely eliminating the smuggling of such items, nevertheless squeezed out most of the trade, impacting the revenues of the regional Indian states that had only recently broken off from the centralised Mughal state. Bengal was the first to face the consequences.

Having lost the opportunity to profit from the Indian textile trade, the East India Company did not hesitate to change its character. In 1616, Sir Thomas Roe, an envoy of the East India Company's declared to the Mughals under Emperor Jahangir that war and trade were incompatible. By 1623, factories sprang up at Surat, Broach, Ahmedabad, Agra, Machlipatnam and later at Orissa, Patna, Balasore, Dhaka, Bengal and Bihar. British settlements evolved from these factories or trading posts into major commercial towns under British jurisdiction, as Indian merchants and artisans moved in to do business with the Company and with the British inhabitants living there. Maintaining their presence in Mughal India was a herculean task for the Company. But they emulated the Portuguese and decided to make colonies and settlements for themselves. They signed a truce with the Portuguese at Goa in 1635 and by 1639 Fort St. George was established at Madras. Bombay was acquired by 1668 and gifted to King Charles II when he married the Portuguese Princess Catherine of Braganza.

The East India Company began to spread its tentacles all over India. But a strong rival, not as meek and timid as the Dutch and Portuguese, existed in the form of the French Company, which set up its factories at Surat, Machlipatnam, Pondicherry and Mahe. Both these companies had high commercial and political ambitions. The decline of the Mughal empire and the constant bickering of the southern satraps of Mysore, the Marathas, Hyderabad and Carnatic was a blessing in disguise.

The East India Company's trade was built on a sophisticated Indian economy. India offered foreign traders the skills of its artisans in weaving cloth and winding raw silk, agricultural products for export, such as sugar, the indigo dye and opium, and the services of substantial merchants and rich bankers. The Company's Indian trade in the first half of the eighteenth century seemed to be established on a stable and profitable basis. Those who directed its affairs in London could see no case for military or political intervention to change the status quo. In 1664 it imported a quarter of a million cloth pieces from the Coromandel coast, Gujarat and Bengal. By the 1670s, cotton and silk textiles made up about fifty-six per cent of the Company's imports, relegating to the background the goods they had initially set out to import—spices. pepper, raw silk, indigo, saltpetre, coffee and tea, in that order, formed the other imports. By 1685, textile trade touched eighty-three per cent of the import share and Bengal started emerging as the source where cheap cloth could be bought and exported. Between 1681 and 1685 alone, the Company exported 240 tonnes of silver and 7 tonnes of gold to India. This steady inflow of bullion helped the Indian economy in the initial years, stimulating employment and incomes.

The British did, however, intervene in Indian politics from the 1750s, and revolutionary changes were to come in their role in India. This change can best be explained partly in terms of changed conditions in India and partly as a consequence of the aggressive ambitions of the local British themselves. The seeds of this policy shift were sown by Sir Josiah Child who became the governor/chairman of the Company in the 1680s. His policy of engaging an aggressive Mughal empire under Aurangzeb boomeranged. After much diplomatic humiliation and a payment of Rs 150,000 and damages to the emperor, the Company somehow managed to retain the trade rights. Factories were also bought at Kolkata, Sutanuti and Govindapore villages in Bengal. The death of Aurangzeb in 1707 brightened the prospects of the Company. The Mughal empire gradually declined after his death. The later Mughals were weak and inefficient. The real power lay in the hands of powerful *wazirs* and nobles, like Zulfikar Khan, the Sayyid brothers and Nizam-ul-Mulk Asaf Jah Bahadur. Many new independent and semi-independent states like Bengal, Hyderabad, Awadh, and Carnatic were formed. The Sikhs were divided into their twelve *misls* and the southern kingdoms of Hyderabad, Carnatic, Mysore and the Marathas were constantly at war with each other. By 1716, the Mughal emperor Farrukhsiyar issued three *firmans* that gave the Company duty-free trading rights in Bengal, Hyderabad and Ahmedabad provinces. This gave the Company an opportunity to get directly involved in the petty local disputes of the provinces and act as an unwelcome arbiter in many cases.

R. Mukerji in his *Rise and Fall of the East India Company* describes the motives behind the Company's political ambitions: 'Although monopoly rights assured the India Companies of the exclusive privileges of buying and selling, it did not guarantee that they could buy cheap. For that, political control was essential.' The opium trade of the eighteenth century, which eventually led to the Opium Wars, when the Royal British Navy worked more or less hand in hand with the commercial interests of the East India Company, exemplified precisely such a link between war and trade.

Most Indian kings and satraps of the time lacked the ability and foresight to see through machinations of this magnitude and the profit-driven strategies of a band of traders. The traditional Indian social hierarchy from the times of Manu had been one where the priestly class and the royal clans occupied the higher echelons of the social ladder. The Vaishya or trader class were always considered to be subservient to the warrior tribe of Kshatriyas. They acted on behalf of and at the pleasure of the latter and seldom or never at their own behest, nor were they driven by their personal interests overriding those of the king. That it was the king's duty to create economic conditions feasible for trade was a concept drilled into the Indian psyche. But the rules of the game had changed now and sadly caught the Indians totally unawares. Here was a community of traders that superficially looked like those merchants the king was traditionally accustomed to. They wanted a share in the pie, to export spices and textiles and bring in gold and silver in return. But the equation was more complex. These traders had profit as their guiding motive, to the extent that they wouldn't hesitate to overthrow the very monarch who first facilitated their entrance to the trading arena. But was it just this unfamiliarity with a foreign community or was it the natural Indian mindset of succumbing to fair skin? One cannot ever be sure.

But to give some credit to the Indian kings in the early phase of the East India Company's Indian sojourn, till the early decades of the eighteenth century, the motives of the foreign companies were hardly discernible. It seemed like a perfect win-win situation for both sides. India had been carrying on foreign trade for thousands of years. This seemed like just another harmless addition to the series. It was around the middle of the eighteenth century, when the British and French companies started direct intervention in political matters and battles, that the kings of the time should have sat up and realised the threat they were facing. As we shall see in later chapters, the manner in which the companies infiltrated the political set-up was surreptitious in some cases, but entirely blatant in a few others. It wouldn't have been impossible for a monarch with foresight and a sixth sense to see through this gameplan. But sadly for India, no such ruler existed. Slowly and steadily, her sovereignty and freedom passed into foreign hands.

6

THE GOLDEN PERIOD – II (AD 1673–1704)

TURBULENT TIMES

The rest of India was going through a period of flux and churning. As seen earlier, new entrants into the political arena, from within and outside, complicated matters further. Mysore had just seen a regime change and the new king Chikkadevaraja Wodeyar had to spend the early years of his reign in arduous battles with nearby kingdoms.

With Sriranga VI having disappeared into oblivion and the Shahi Kingdoms of Bijapur and Golconda locked in a fight for survival with the Mughal Emperor Aurangzeb, the Deccan was an open playing-field for the powers of the time—Mysore, Ikkeri, Madurai, Tanjore and Ginjee—with the Marathas making appearances on and off. Ikkeri's Hiriya Somashekara Nayak I was murdered by the scriptwriters of a court intrigue and was succeeded by his daunting and brave dowager Queen Channammaji in 1672. Chokkanatha Nayak continued to hold his sway over Madurai. Shahji's death brought his son Ekoji to the fore.

On 5 March 1673, barely five days after his coronation, Chikkadevaraja was drawn into battle. He undertook an expedition eastwards and captured the forts of Dhuligote, Malali, Paramatti and Salem and encountered Madurai Nayak Chokkanatha and his Dalavoy Venkatakrishnama Nayak. Chokkanatha faced a crushing defeat in the battle with the Mysorean forces. Chikkadevaraja returned to the capital with the spoils of his first victory as king by the end of 1673, capturing Sadamangalam and Anantapur on the way. But the revelry was short-lived. A combined confederacy of Rani

Channammaji and the forces of Golconda and Bijapur under Hussain Khan and Balbal Khan planned an attack on Mysore with the help of Kodandarama I, Sriranga's nephew. The motive was the same hackneyed one of attempting to reinforce Sriranga's supremacy. Dalavoy Kumarayya was sent to counter this menace at Banavar and he succeeded in capturing places like Arakalgud, Sakaleshpur, Angadi, Nuggehalli and Belur, but was defeated by the combine at Hassan.

The political climate in the Deccan of those times was so volatile that each passing day brought new equations to the fore. Tanjore's Nayak, Vijayaraghava Nayagan, died in a skirmish between Madurai and Tanjore. Chokkanatha installed his foster brother Alagiri Nayak as Viceroy of Tanjore but the latter had hopes of overthrowing his brother and benefactor. The deposed Tanjore family's adherents planned a palace coup to restore the kingdom to the original family. Bijapur's help was sought to help install on the throne a young boy from the original dynasty, Chanagamala Das. The Sultan of Bijapur dispatched Ekoji to drive out Alagiri Nayak and install the young boy. This he achieved with no major difficulty, as Alagiri was not a chivalrous military man. The death of Muhammad Adil Shah in 1675 led Ekoji to assert his own authority over the province he had captured. Maratha rule was thus established in Tanjore and Ginjee from 1675 onwards. Ekoji cut off his allegiance to Bijapur and made Tanjore his headquarters, even as he maintained a foothold in his father's *jagir* of Bangalore.

On his part, Chikkadevaraja was consolidating and also expanding the frontiers of Mysore. By 1675, he managed to check Madurai's aggression, advanced till Belur in the west against Ikkeri and conquered vast tracts of land in the Carnatic-Bijapur Balaghat region, which had become more susceptible since the exit of Ekoji. In his *Travels in India*, Dr Fryer mentions 'the Raja of Saranpatam' enjoying 'a vast territory at the back of the Zamerbin', the reference of Saranpatam being to Srirangapatna and the Zamerbin to the Zamorin in the Malabar and Calicut region.

As stated before, the coronation of Shivaji encouraged him to indulge in military exploits. He swept the Carnatic in 1677. His descent to the Carnatic plains was at the behest of Raghunath Panth who complained bitterly to Shivaji about the maladministration of Tanjore by Ekoji. On his way to the south, Shivaji camped at Bhagnagar—present day Hyderabad—and through the Madras plains, entered the Carnatic. Shantaji, another brother and a member of Ekoji's Council in Tanjore, crossed over to the daring

Shivaji's side and was given Ginjee. It seems that Shivaji met his brother Ekoji and the two warring siblings arrived at some sort of conciliation. Ekoji was issued a stern warning to improve his administrative style. Shivaji then turned eastwards into Mysore territory. The country was plundered and overrun. Orme in his *Historical Fragments* mentions that the 'Marathas retired to their country after having some bloody battles with the Naik of Mysore.' That Shivaji reached the gates of Srirangapatna and plundered the territories of Bangalore, Doddaballapur and Hosakote is known. But whether Chikkadevaraja put up a tough resistance or paid Shivaji off is not clear. Kannada accounts of the time, however, state the chivalrous conduct of the young king of Mysore in repulsing the attack and checking Shivaji's advance in South Mysore.

Troubles between Ekoji and his sibling (and hitherto friend) Shantaji got worse after the return of Shivaji. The two met in a bloody battle at Valikondapuram where Ekoji was defeated. Shivaji sent his emissaries to sue for peace between the two brothers. This greatly frustrated the attempts of Chokkanatha Nayak, who had allied with Shantaji to wrest Tanjore back from Ekoji. But calamity befell Chokkanatha soon. Court intrigues accused him of being mentally unstable and he was unceremoniously removed from power. His brother Mutthulinga Nayak was made the lame-duck chieftain, only to be overrun by Rustum Khan, a Muslim adventurer who captured the province of Madurai.

The shock of Shivaji's blitzkrieg in Mysore stirred Chikkadevaraja into action. A series of conquests and acquisitions followed. It was clearly a direct contest between Mysore and the Marathas for supremacy over the South. All the other powers were in such a state of confusion and disarray that they did not matter much. To assert himself, Chikkadevaraja set out on an expedition: in 1678, he captured Andur from Ghatta Mudaliar, Erode, Chikkatotlagere, Korategere, Magadi, Maddagiri, Kudur and Hosur. At Hosur, he met the forces of Ekoji under his prime minister, Yeshwant Rao. Yeshwant was dealt a crushing blow and, in characteristic Mysorean style, lost his nose as well. The annexations of Channarayadurga, Mannekolala, Midageshi, Bijjavara, Gundumaledurga and Bhutipura followed, making Mysorean territories coterminous with those of Shivaji's ancestral property of Sira in the Carnatic Balaghat. Records of the time bolster these successes of Chikkadevaraja who is addressed thereafter as 'Emperor of the South and the Karnataka Country' and as a 'Sultan of Hindu Kings'.

Around the same time, the valiant warrior Shivaji breathed his last and was succeeded by his son Shambhaji. Soon after coming to power in 1680, Shambhaji was locked in a contest with the Sidi of Janjira, Aurangzeb and the English at Surat.

Meanwhile, the deposed chief of Madurai, Chokkanatha sent an emissary to Mysore enlisting support for restoration. The Maravas' help was also solicited.* Dalavoy Kumarayya led a large army against the usurper Rustum Khan and after a bloody contest, Khan was defeated. Chokkanatha's joy knew no bounds. In his ecstasy, he wrote, in a letter dated 8 March 1682 to Fort St. George: 'We and the Naique of Mysore are now good friends.'

But his joy was short-lived. Dalavoy Kumarayya had pledged to his king that he would not appear before him till he had wrested the fertile lands of Tiruchirapalli for the kingdom and collected the tributes payable to Mysore by Madurai. Chokkanatha was shocked by this betrayal. He now sought Maratha assistance and an army came to his aid under Haraji. Kumarayya decided to bribe Haraji and make him retire to Ginjee. He was trying to while away time as he waited for reinforcements to arrive.

Taking advantage of the absence of a large army from Srirangapatna, Maratha generals Dadaji, Jathaji and Nimbhaji attacked Srirangapatna in April 1682. Chikkadevaraja sent an emissary to the Dalavoy to send over a portion of the army to rescue the capital, under his nephew Doddayya. The Maratha generals were stationed in the Kalasagere and Kotthathi regions. Along with the advancing army of Mysore, two to three thousand cattle were let loose from the shed with torch lamps tied to their horns in the dead of the night. The generals, who were woken up from their slumber, were startled by this sea of lights proceeding towards them. The sudden attack by the Mysorean forces also caught them completely off-guard.

The Marathas had always revelled in their expertise in the techniques, of guerrilla warfare but were fed a dose of their own medicine. The generals were slain, the Maratha forces completely routed and a huge

---

* The chieftains of Ramnad (called Setupatis) and the Rajas of Sivaganga—both in Tamil Nadu, were called the Maravas. As warriors, they were temperamentally disinclined to accepting authority. They had hideouts in forests and slowly rose to political eminence in the south by aligning with various powers in their mutual skirmishes.

booty confiscated from them. The noses, ears and limbs of people in the Maratha army were cut off and the head of Dadaji paraded as a trophy in the army while those of Jathaji and Nimbaji were tied to the gate of the Srirangapatna Fort.

But the celebrations were, in fact, premature. The position of Dalavoy Kumarayya, who was trapped at Tiruchirapalli, was getting increasingly untenable by the day. He had hoped to secure an honourable exit for himself. But the Marathas wanted to avenge the fate that befell their generals at Kalasagere. They pounced on his army, took many prisoners, including Kumarayya, and also captured all the forts that Mysore had conquered from Madurai's Nayak. Chikkadevaraja managed to secure the release of his father-in-law and old Dalavoy Kumarayya. The latter was ashamed of the ignominy he had faced at Tiruchirapalli and offered to resign. Doddayya was thereafter made the new dalavoy.

War became imminent for Mysore again. This time the armies of Shambhaji, Basappa Nayak of Ikkeri and the Qutub Shah of Golconda attacked Mysore. It was one of the worst reverses Mysore had faced. Fresh from the debacle at Tiruchirapalli, the war-weary army's morale was at an all-time low. Most of Mysore's fortresses in the east and south were lost.

Aurangzeb had been keeping track of developments in the South. When news of the defeat of Maratha Generals Jayaji, Dadaji and Nimbhaji reached the ears of Aurangzeb, he was delighted. It was music to his ears that the Marathas, his long lasting enemies, were finally routed by a power down south. All he had to do was to befriend his bitter foe's enemy to strengthen his own position in the Deccan. He sent feelers of friendship to Chikkadevaraja Wodeyar. In fact, a Jesuit letter speaks of Aurangzeb being willing to send a 'formidable army against Sambogi at the request of Mysore'. It was a different matter that the supposed help never came as the Mughal ruler was involved in his do-or-die battle with the Shahi Kingdoms of the Deccan. That Mysore was ravaged once again by the lineage of the brave Shivaji becomes amply clear in another Jesuit letter of the times:

> The power of the King of Mysore in Madura begins to grow weak, because, violently attacked in his own dominion by the troops of Samboji, he cannot sustain and reinforce the armies he had sent to these countries. The provinces he had conquered there shake

off his yoke gradually to claim their independence, or become attached to some one of the princes, who have partitioned the shreds of the Kingdom, once so flourished, among themselves.

Peace was finally restored in Madurai with a pact. The kingdom of the erstwhile chieftain was divided into five portions as referred to in the Jesuit letter and divided between the Nayak of Madurai, the Wodeyar of Mysore, the Maravas, Shambhaji and Ekoji. Chokkanatha died in a state of utter frustration after all his thwarted attempts at restoration. His fifteen-year-old son, Mutthu Virappa nayak III was made the titular nayak of the portion allotted to their family.

The ravages of war and an internal rebellion brewing in the kingdom had made life miserable for Chikkadevaraja. But destiny came to his aid in the form of the end of two of his enemies—the two Shahi Kingdoms of Bijapur and Golconda—at the hands of Aurangzeb (in 1684 and 1687 respectively). The Marathas were also engaged in a battle of nerves with the Mughals and their attention was diverted. With vast tracts of the Deccan now under his control Aurangzeb got a little greedy. His commander Kassim Khan marched by way of Penukonda towards Tumkur in March 1687. He also took Chikkanayakanahalli, Kandikere and Tyamagondlu from Ekoji. Ekoji found it difficult to manage the *jagir* of Bangalore from Tanjore. So he decided to sell the place to Chikkadevaraja for Rs 3 lakh.

But just as Chikkadevaraja was to occupy Bangalore, Kassim Khan swept over the place like a hawk and captured it by force. An agreement was thereafter signed between the two whereby Bangalore, Tumkur and Hoskote were taken by Chikkadevaraja on lease (*izara*) from the Mughals. He also agreed to keep an army contingent ready for them. Mysorean records claim that they purchased Bangalore at a cost of Rs 3 lakh. But this seems a travesty of the truth because recently discovered Mughal records, at the Jaipur Palaces clearly mention the Wodeyar's acceptance of Mughal suzerainty. In a way, Mysore had become a feudatory of the Mughal empire by agreeing to the terms of this treaty. Mysore paid a heavy price for this in the long run: in subsequent decades, the Nizam of Hyderabad, the Nawab of Arcot and the Marathas—tax collectors for the Mughals—attacked Mysore regularly. Bangalore remained an integral part of the Mysore kingdom. Chikkadevaraja also got the Venkataramana Swamy temple constructed within the Bangalore Fort, famous to this day as Kote Venkataramana.

Kassim Khan retired to Sira where he was appointed as the Mughal governor. With the Shahi kingdoms destroyed and Mysore almost made a feudatory, Aurangzeb turned on his biggest and toughest foe, the Marathas. But the Marathas were going through tumultuous times. Ekoji died in 1688 and his son Shahji II succeeded him at Tanjore. Shambhaji was captured and executed by the Mughals. The same year, Shambhaji's gallant general, Haraji also died.

It was now time for Chikkadevaraja to make up for all the reverses he had faced in the last few years. The Nayak of Madurai died an untimely death and Queen Mangammal took over. Taking advantage of the entire political spectrum of the Deccan, Chikkadevaraja swept through the territories. In 1688, he acquired Avaniperur, Arasaravani, Hoskote, Manugondedurga, Mannargudi and Vamalur; and in 1689, Dharmapuri, Paramatti, Kaveripatnam and Kunturdurga. By 1690, he was able to acquire all that he had lost in his shameful defeat at the hands of Shambhaji and also reasserted his claim to the title of 'Karnataka Chakravarthi'—the Emperor of Karnataka.

With the execution of Shambhaji in 1689, Rajaram, his younger brother (later known as Shivaji II), became regent to Shahu—the infant son of his deceased brother. The fort of Raigarh and many other principal posts fell to the Mughal assault led by Zulfikar Khan. Rajaram cleverly escaped from Satara to the Carnatic by way of Ikkeri, and received a hospitable welcome from Dowager Queen Channammaji. He managed to reach Ginjee fort by the end of that year. An incensed Aurangzeb sent Zulfikar Khan to reduce Ginjee and capture the fugitive. Rajaram found the assistance of a valiant Maratha sardar, Shantaji Ghorpade. By April 1691, Zulfikar Khan reached the Carnatic and marched as far as Tiruchirapalli and Tanjore. Ginjee was besieged by Asad Khan, Kassim Khan and the Mughal Prince Kam Baksh. The Jesuit letters of the times (1690–97) speak of the vast disturbances in the Carnatic caused by these contesting parties of Mughals and Marathas. But Ghorpade sprang on the invaders like a predator on its prey. In an ironic negation of his name, which means peace, Shantaji's name became synonymous with terror in the Carnatic region. He mercilessly ransacked the Deccan *subahs* of the Mughals. Kassim Khan was cornered, attacked near Dodderi and defeated. It is said that to avoid disgrace, Khan consumed poison and ended his life in 1695.

Realising that the situation was getting out of hand, Aurangzeb sent fresh reinforcements under Bidar Bakht to Ginjee and ordered Zulfikar Khan to chase Shantaji out of the Carnatic till the boundaries of Mysore. Unfortunately for the Marathas, Shantaji was murdered in 1697 and Ginjee captured by Zulfikar Khan, Daud Khan and Dalapat Rao in no time at all. Rajaram again managed to flee to Satara. This triumph consolidated Mughal supremacy over all of India, particularly the Deccan.

On his part, Chikkadevaraja remained a mute and neutral spectator, watching from the sidelines. He maintained cordial relations with the Mughals, especially Kassim Khan, after the initial skirmish at Bangalore, and instead directed his energies against Channammaji of Ikkeri. In 1694, the rani sent a huge army under her Dalavoy Channabasava Setti along with Sabnis Bommarasayya of Koliwad, Yakub Khan, Krishnappa Nayak of Aigur and the Beda chiefs of Chitradurga. Mysore's Dalavoy Timmappayyas put up a tough resistance at Hebbale. Mutual infighting and treachery in the Ikkeri army resulted in huge chaos, with commanders giving contradictory orders to their soldiers. Yakub Khan and Krishnappa Nayak were killed in the aftermath of the confusion, while the Ikkeri dalavoy managed to flee. The victorious Mysore armies took Arakalagud, Aigur, Sakaleshpur and Kodlipet.

In the very next year, however, Channammaji launched yet another offensive in which the dalavoy of Mysore was killed and his son taken prisoner. Kalale Mallarajayya was made the new dalavoy and was later succeeded by Virarajayya and Dasarajayya. But the death of Channammaji in 1697 brought respite to war-weary Mysore and Chikkadevaraja completed his annexations of Salem, Sadamangalam, Paramatti, Namakkal and Tammambaati in the east. His only cause for concern was a possible attack on Mysorean territories by the Mughal army, buoyed by its significant victories in the Deccan. The *Records of Fort St. George* dated 16 June 1698 speak of Aurangzeb ordering 'Dulpatrow and Daud Cawn to remove to Bollegol and Adonee and the Nabob to assist Didar Bux coming against Misore.'

With a long-term strategy of ensuring the territorial integrity of Mysore, Chikkadevaraja decided to send a goodwill delegation to Agra with a message of friendship. An embassy left for Ahmednagar—where Aurangzeb was holding his court—with Chikkadevaraja's good wishes to the emperor under the leadership of Karnaik Lingappayya in 1699. The idea was to align with the Mughals to prevent any possible onslaught on Mysore by the Maratha forces. The delegation is supposed to have returned in 1700 with a signet ring of the emperor bearing the inscription 'Jagadevaraya' or 'King of the World'. It was a subtle sign of permission from the centre of power in India, granting autonomy to the kingdom of Mysore. A seal engraved in Persian characters, the words 'Raja Chikkadevaraj Muhammad Shahi', along with costly gifts and presents and a letter recognising the right to hold durbar seated on the 'celebrated throne of the Pandavas' were also dispatched by Aurangzeb.

This enhanced the prestige of the King of Mysore and his kingdom immensely in the eyes of his rivals who saw him as power friendly to the empire. The victorious delegation was given a rousing reception and paraded in the streets of the capital city.

Wilks, however, takes a different view in his analysis of this momentous event. He opines it to have been more stage-managed and a variant from the truth—a ploy that Chikkadevaraja resorted to in order to ensure that his supremacy among his subjects as well as neighbouring kingdoms and Palegars was kept intact.

> The splendour of the Embassy does not, however, appear to have made much impression at the imperial court; and if we may judge from the trifling sum recorded to have been expended in the entertainment of the ambassadors, the Zemindar of Mysoor (as he was called) was not held to be a person of very high consideration. Whether Aurungzebe actually conferred the high honours which were pretended to be received, would perhaps be a balanced question if it were of sufficient importance to merit a separate discussion. It is sufficient to our present purpose to state that they were publicly assumed, and as far as is known, were never questioned....

As Wilks states, perhaps the Mughal emperor never accorded Chikkadevaraja status higher than that of a 'zamindar' of Mysore. Whatever might be the historical veracity of the diplomatic mission's success, it certainly did enhance Chikkadevaraja's position vis-à-vis the other powers of the south. He managed to advance as far as Coorg and Malabar and took rich gifts and tributes from their chiefs as well as from those of Tigula and Malnad. The period from 1700–04 was marked by peace and tranquillity for Mysore and it also gave Chikkadevaraja ample time to consolidate his rule and introduce a plethora of reforms for which he later became famous.

By 1700 Chikkadevaraja Wodeyar was at the height of his power and Mysore was basking in unprecedented glory. In the north the kingdom extended till Bangalore and parts of Tumkur, coterminous with the Mughal headquarters of Sira; in the west and northwest up to Hassan and Kadur as far as Chikkamagalur and Sakrepatna, coterminous with Ikkeri; and in the east and south, up to and including parts of Salem, Baramahal and Coimbatore districts. Thus, Chikkadevaraja established himself as a major force in the south after the disappearance of the Shahi Kingdoms and those of the Nayaks of Madurai, Tanjore and Ginjee.

Interestingly, all the powers-that-be in the Deccan seemed to want a piece of Bangalore—a coveted township that began to represent political supremacy. The accession of Bangalore to the Bijapur dynasty was a major feather in their cap. Shahji got Bangalore along with Hoskote, Kolar, Chikkaballapur, Doddaballapur, Sira, Kanakagiri, etc., and lived virtually as the king of Bangalore. He built the Gowri Mahal Palace there.

It would be worthwhile to temporarily turn to Bangalore, a city that slowly and steadily emerged as the fulcrum of political activity for Mysore in the medieval ages and went on to occupy a primary position in the affairs of the kingdom in later times. The city of Bangalore, the present day capital of Karnataka, was always a coveted one for warring forces. It played a pivotal role in the history of the Mysore kingdom. 'Flowers, flowering shrubs and creepers blossoming in glorious profusion, snipe (and snakes) abound in the marshes, brilliant butterflies dance in the sunshine...' was how Winston Churchill, the former prime minister of Great Britain had once described the beauty of Bangalore. Blessed with a salubrious climate, this once sleepy city—comprising a residential locality to its northern end, a fort in the south which belonged to its illustrious founder and a deep ditch in the middle—has now been transformed into the power centre of modern Karnataka and the pivot of India's information technology revolution.

There has been much speculation about the origins of the name 'Bangalore'. According to the *Gazetteer of India* Bangalore is an anglicised name for 'Bengalooru', a word in the local Kannada language. The story goes that this word was derived from the phrase *'benda kaalu ooru'*, or 'the town of boiled beans'. It is said that King Ballala of the Hoysala dynasty lost his way in the jungle while on a hunting expedition. Tired and hungry, he encountered a poor, old woman who offered him the only food she had—some boiled beans. Grateful to her, the king named the place Bendakaalu Ooru. However, historical evidence shows that Bengalooru was recorded much before King Ballala's time in a ninth-century temple inscription in the village of Begur.

Another historical figure instrumental in shaping the city of Bangalore is a feudal lord who called himself Kempe Gowda of the Yelahanka Prabhu dynasty, and who served under the Vijayanagara kings. Hunting seemed to be a favourite pastime in those days. During one of his hunting expeditions, Kempe Gowda was surprised to see a hare chase his dog. Either his dog was chicken-hearted or the hare was lion-hearted, but the episode surely made an impression on the feudal lord. He told himself this was surely a place for heroes and heroics, and he referred to Bangalore from then onwards as *'gandu bhoomi'* (heroic place).

Kempe Gowda, who was in charge of Yelahanka, acquired twelve *hoblis** around Bangalore with the help of King Achutaraya. He built the little towns of Balepet, Cottonpet, and Chickpet, all inside a mud fort in 1537. Today, these small areas serve as the major wholesale and commercial market places in the city. Kempe Gowda's son erected the four watch towers at Ulsoor, Hebbal, Lalbagh and Kempambudhi to mark the boundaries of Bangalore and indicate the future expansion of the city. Today, these towers stand almost in the heart of the present city, indicating the extent to which the city has grown—much beyond the dreams of its founder.

The climate of the place, the high ground nippiness of its air and the sheer beauty of its landscape have never failed to fascinate outsiders. 'The most beautiful habitation that nature has to offer to mankind upon earth—chill weather, dammit! And that too, in Southern India,' Churchill had exclaimed.

Thus, right from the seventeenth century, Bangalore had occupied a place of primacy in the politics of the region.

---

* A group of villages.

THE REIGN OF CHIKKADEVARAJA WODEYAR

Socio-Economic Conditions

The most important component of revenue for a feudal society is through land revenues. This was as true in Mysore as anywhere else in medieval India. It was the backbone of the feudal system and defined the entire cultural, social and political class hierarchy even, while it sustained the state's economy. Right from the Vijayanagara empire onwards, the Palegars acted as the intermediaries for the King to levy these land revenues and taxes. They controlled vast tracts of land and lived like virtual kings. Some territories yielded annual revenues of almost 3,50,000–4,00,000 Pagodas of which the Palegar paid a fraction as yearly tribute to the Vijayanagara monarch. This also helped him maintain infantry to protect his domain in cases of aggression by neighbouring kingdoms. As seen during the reigns of weak sovereigns, the Palegars exceeded their brief and acted as independent satraps. For the local people, the Palegar was their king and he was called raja, intrinsically linked to the culture and festivities of his domain. He constructed temples for the people, provided irrigation facilities, and so on. As we have seen earlier, the Mysore rajas also started off as Palegars. Once Vijayanagara's Aravidu dynasty had been completely wiped out, Chikkadevaraja proclaimed complete independence and sovereignty for the Wodeyars. What was till then the responsibility of the Vijayanagara king was now that of the monarch at Srirangapatna.

But this was also a time of intense class struggle and societal churning that arose due to a change in the centre of power.

Resentment, Rebellion and Repression

There were frequent peasant struggles against the oppressive extortionist techniques of the Palegars. In 1684, the famous peasant uprising at Nanjangud, also known as the Hadinadu rebellion, shook the foundations of the traditional feudal set-up. It was symbolic that the uprising sparked off in Hadinadu—the original seat of the Wodeyar dynasty. In the Hadinadu rebellion, peasants hung their ploughs upside down on *peepul* trees at village squares to protest the oppressive taxes exacted by the collection officers. Inscriptions of the time speak of warnings issued to the officers against squeezing the peasants beyond their limits. The concerned officer merited severe punishment if any tiller left his land on account of financial pressures exerted by the taxation system. Despite this, these officers were heartless in their collection of taxes. When the peasants revolted, Chikkadevaraja, who had been sympathetic to the peasants and ignorant of his officers' deeds, refused to compromise with the revolting ryots. It is estimated that as many as 400 peasants were brutally massacred in a blatant measure of suppression.

There are numerous references to this period of unrest that Mysore faced in the 1680s. A Jesuit letter by Louis de Mello to Noyelle, dated 1686, states:

> The King of Mysore incensed at their (subjects) insolence sent an army against them to carry fire and sword everywhere, and toss the rebels on the point of the sword, without distinction of age or sex. These cruel orders were executed. The Pagodas of Vishnu and Siva were destroyed, and their large revenues confiscated to the royal treasury. Those idolaters who escaped the carnage fled to the mountains and forests, where they led a miserable life.

This certainly seems like a gross exaggeration, especially considering the fact that Chikkadevaraja was an ardent Vaishnavite himself. Destruction of temples of Vishnu to fill his coffers seems rather far-fetched and is typical of missionary-driven zealous propaganda.

What is significant though is the fact that the orange-robed Jangama priests, who belonged to the Veerashaiva faith of Shiva worshippers and were pivotal in the establishment of the Wodeyar dynasty, were seen as sympathetic to the cause of the peasants reeling under the effects of excessive taxation. These Jangamas had also lost their local importance, more so after the king turned towards the Sri Vaishnava philosophy. Historical records speak of a plot Chikkadevaraja hatched to eliminate these trouble-mongering Jangamas. Wilks details the same in his inimitable style:

> A large pit had been previously prepared in a walled enclosure, connected by a series of squares composed of tent walls ... audience which were successively received one at a time, and after making their obeisance were desired to retire to a place, where according to custom, they expected to find refreshments prepared at the expense of the Raja. Expert executioners were in waiting in the square, and every individual in succession was so

skilfully beheaded and tumbled into the pit, as to give no alarm to those who followed, and the business of the public audience went on without interruption or suspicion. Circular orders had been sent for the destruction on the same day of all the Jungum muts in his dominion; and the number reported to have been in consequence destroyed was upwards of 700. The disappearance of the 400 Jungum priests was the only intimation of their fate received by their mournful disciples; but the traditional account which I have above delivered has been traced through several channels to sources of the most respectable information, and I profess my entire belief in the reality of the fact...wherever a mob had assembled, a detachment of troops, chief, cavalry was collected in the neighbourhood...the orders were distinct and simple; to charge without parley into the midst of the mob; to cut down to the first selection every man wearing an orange-coloured robe; and not to cease acting until the crowds had everywhere dispersed...system of terror...to the final establishment of the new system of revenue...the Raja exacted from every village a written renunciation, ostensibly voluntary, of private property in the land, and an acknowledgement that it was the right of the State...if such documents ever existed, they were probably destroyed in 1786.

It is unclear how far one can test the veracity of the claims Wilks makes based on these 'traditionary accounts' on which he professes his 'entire belief'. But it was certain that unpopular measures were adopted to crush a brewing revolt to ensure that it didn't develop into a large-scale mass movement. The revolt had been widespread and had far-reaching echoes in the political echelons of Mysore. A large section of the populace also held the Jain Pandit Vishalaksha responsible for these reprehensive measures and were envious of the great power that he wielded over Chikkadevaraja in his earlier years. The Jangamas had their own grouses against him for neglecting what had hitherto been the state religion and the religion of the royal house. The widespread resentment and the manner in which the revolt was put down led to the ultimate assassination of the Pandit. Wilks sums up this entire build-up:

> The first fourteen years of his reign were occupied in these financial measures, interior reforms, and minor conquests, but these reforms

had rendered so unpopular the administration of the Jain Pundit, to whom they were chiefly attributed, that a plan was secretly concerted for his assassination. Chick Deo Raj had, without doubt, in the early part of his life, been educated in the doctrines of the Jungum, which was the religion of his ancestors: he had hitherto, since his accession to the throne, shewn no very marked attachment to any form of worship, but was supposed from particular habits, which he had adopted, and from the great influence of the Jain Pundit, to have conceived the intention of reviving the doctrines of that ancient sect. The Pundit was attacked and mortally wounded, while returning at night, in the usual manner from court to his own dwelling (1686), and as, in addition to religious motives, the Jungum had a deep account of revenge to retaliate, for the murder of their priests...the suspicion of this assassination fell chiefly upon that people, and tended to confirm the alienation of the Raja's mind from the doctrines of their sect...

Confirming this sentiment of resentment is the *Rajavali Kathe* of Devachandra, which also speaks of the Jangamas prevailing upon one Naganna—a skilled archer—to help them accomplish their mission. According to Rao's *History of Mysore*, where he quotes the poet Devachandra, Naganna befriended the Pandit and on that fateful night, when the latter was returning to his abode seated in a palanquin, 'the hireling flung himself at him and pierced him through, having him unconscious, in which state he was conveyed home.' Chikkadevaraja was baffled and rushed to his minister and childhood friend's house. In his dying moments, the Pandit is supposed to have recommended the name of Tirumala Iyengar as the next prime minister. His wish was duly fulfilled by the king. Tirumala Iyengar then succeeded the Pandit and held the post of prime minister till 1704.

Administrative Reforms

Incessant battles, coercive levies and dacoity of goods in transit were horrors that most merchants faced in Chikkadevaraja's Mysore. To add to this was the perennial struggle among the Palegars for petty supremacy. Leo Huberman sums it up in *Man's Worldly Goods*:

The strife between warring overlords frequently meant disaster to the local population, no matter which side won. It was the presence of different overlords in different places along the highways of business that made trade so difficult. What was needed was a central authority, a national state, a supreme power that would be able to bring order out of feudal chaos. The old overlords could no longer fulfil their social function. Their day was gone. The time was ripe for a strong central power.

Chikkadevaraja was aware of the socio-economic rumblings felt across the kingdom. After the successful mission to the Mughal court, he chose to completely reorganise the way administration ran in Mysore. He made it his singular duty to completely eliminate the Palegar class. He made new conquests, disarmed the Palegars and disbanded their armies. He did not always need the sword to vanquish the influence of the oppressive Palegars. To quote Huberman again '…the Rajah brought these powerful chieftains to Seringapatam and gave them various dignified appointments in his household and converted them from powerful chieftains to humble courtiers.' In removing this intermediate social structure, Chikkadevaraja ensured a centralised state apparatus, which was not only directly subservient to him but also retained some of the best elements of the disbanded structure.

One of the hallmarks as well as necessities of any such centralised nation-state is of course an effective defence mechanism, which translates into powerful and effective armies. Under Chikkadevaraja, Karnataka for the first time had a regular and well-organised army of 12,000 horse and 1,00,000 foot. As Huberman states:

> He could hire and pay for a trained army always at his service, not dependant on the loyalty of a lord. It would be a better army too, because its only business was to fight. Feudal troops had no training, no regular organisation, which enabled them to work together smoothly. An army paid for fighting, well trained and well disciplined, and always on hand when needed was a great improvement. Moreover technical improvements in military weapons also called for a new kind of army. Gunpowder and cannon were coming in and effective use of these arms required trained cooperation. And while a feudal warrior could bring his own armour, he couldn't easily bring cannon and powder.

Thus, we see under the reign of Chikkadevaraja, a clear transition of Mysore from the feudal age to the modern age—along lines similar to the developments that occurred in Europe in medieval times. B. Puttaiyya writes:

> His numerous conquests and the subjugation of a large number of local polegars created the necessity of enlarging his army and the strengthening of the forts with cannons and guns. He therefore increased the strength of his army…fully equipped with all weapons of offence and defence and mounts, such as horses, camels, elephants and remounts, such as oxen, carts, tents, etc.

All of this was achieved within a year of his successful mission to the Mughal court. The best of the forces from among the disbanded Palegars were merged with the existing Mysorean forces to set up the *kandachara* or local militia. Each *hobli* had a *kandachara* of 100–400 armed men or *olekars* under the *hoblidar's* command. As Hayavadana Rao details:

> Their duty was to keep in readiness weapons of offence and defence including gunpowder and shot and to be prepared to fight when necessary. Ordinarily it was the duty of the staff of the militia to patrol the unit and safeguard the local treasury… in times of war they were required to be ready with arms and ammunition. The militia seems thus to have occupied an important place in the civil and military governance of the country, useful alike in times of war and peace….

Chikkadevaraja had some amazing administrative skills. He had a vision and knew how to achieve it. The dalavoys continued to hold their post as army generals. The dalavoys who served during his reign were Kumarayya, his son Doddayya, Thimappa (1690–96), Mallarajayya (1696–1702) and Dasarajayya of Devarayadurga (1702–04). To ensure a streamlining of the activities of the government, he divided the administrative work into eighteen *kacheris* or departments, famously called *athara kacheri*. This was largely inspired by the Mughal administrative set-up, but Chikkadevaraja meticulously tweaked that model to suit Mysore's indigenous needs. This was his brainchild after the flirtations he had with the Mughal court, after the return of the embassy from Ahmednagar. These eighteen departments were as follows:

1. *Nirupa Chavadi*: Dealt with the recording of petitions from officials to the king and the same would be disposed off in the form of orders

or *nirupas*. The Secretariat had one *daroga* (superintendent) and three *daftars* (registrars and accountants).

2. *Ayakattuchavadi*: Maintained the civil and military accounts of all the eighty-four administrative units, the central exchequer, the king's household, etc.
3. *Mysuru Hobali Vicharada Chavadi*: A dual department for the administration of Mysore. The kingdom was divided into two administrative zones: Patna Hobli (area north of the Cauvery) and Mysore Hobli (area south of the Cauvery). The Mysore Chavadi looked after the administration in the Mysore Hobli. It had one *dewan* and thirteen *daftars*.
4. *Patnada Hobali Vicharada Chavadi*: A similar set-up as above for the Patna Hobli.
5. *Simeya Kandachar*: Maintained the accounts of civil and military establishments in the units, recording the figures for arms, ammunitions and stores for each unit. It had an accountant for provisions, military troops and all expenses of the provincial troops with one *bakshi* and three *daftars*.
6. *Bagila Kandachar*: Accounts of troops stationed at the headquarters.
7. *Sunkada Chavadi*: Or *kacheri* of duties, road tolls, import-export duties and customs levied within Mysore.
8. *Pom Chavadi*: Pom was a form of tax. In the *taluks* where *sunka* (toll) was levied, an additional tax of half the original amount was also levied on commodities purchased or disposed of by certain classes of people, such as Brahmins and officers.
9. *Tundeya/Thodaya Chavadi*: Was also a tax-collecting department where a quarter of the first duty was collected at the capital city of Srirangapatna.
10. *Ubhaika Vichara Chavadi*: This had two responsibilities under it, for Mysore and one for Srirangapatna. The *Mysuru Hobli Ashtagramada Chavadi* had jurisdiction over eight *hoblis* formed newly under the Devanala canals.
11. *Ubhaika Vichara Chavadi:* This was the Srirangapatna chapter of the above: the *Patna Hobli Ashtagramada Chavadi*. It had jurisdiction over eight *hoblis* formed under the Chikkadevaraja Sagara Canal. These last two departments were also in charge of repairs to dams and canals across the Cauvery and Hemavathy Rivers and maintained accounts of the government's share in the produce of lands irrigated thereunder.

12. *Benne Chavadi*: This was the animal husbandry department (later christened Amrit Mahal by Tipu Sultan—who changed all Kannada names to Persian or Islamic ones) and looked after the breeding of cows for milk, butter, etc., for the royal palace and for domestication.
13. *Patnada Chavadi*: In charge of repairs of forts, the palace and public places, etc.
14. *Behina Chavadi*: This was the department of post and espionage, responsible for the speedy delivery of couriers (*anche harikar*) to and from Srirangapatna and the communication of *nirupas* from the king to the litigants.
15. *Sammukhada Chavadi*: The palace officers, domestic and personal servants, etc., were part of this *kacheri*. It was handled by Gurikar Somarajayya and Appajayya under the direct supervision of the king.
16. *Devasthanada Chavadi*: In charge of recording the daily grants to temples, Brahmins, priests, establishing and repairing temples, and other charitable activities.
17. *Kabbinada Chavadi*: Handled purchase of raw iron ore, its manufacture and sale thereafter. The iron trade was a state monopoly.
18. *Hogesoppina Chavadi*: Tobacco department.

Each department had in common a supervisor (*gotthugara*), three record-keepers (*daftars*), accountants (*gumastas*), writers (*raayasadavaru*), head peon (*daffedar*), menials (*ooligadavaru*), attendants (*gollas*), watchman (*kavalugar*) and torch-bearer (*divatigeyavaru*). As mentioned above, some departments also had a few extra personnel. These eighteen offices formed the fulcrum of the administrative set-up and all the administrative work was clearly demarcated. In fact, the present-day Karnataka High Court in Bangalore, opposite the State Legislative Assembly/Vidhana Soudha, is an impressive two-storied building called Attara Kacheri, built in 1867. It reminds the people of the benevolent ruler and able administrator who first coined this term in administrative parlance.

Revenue collection (done entirely in cash) and land assessment were also structured by Chikkadevaraja. Smaller slices within the kingdom were combined and eighty-four divisions or *gadis* created out of them. These units had the following administrative personnel: peons (*daffedars*), menials (*kalooligadavaru*), treasury attendants (*hastaantari golla*), two watchmen (*chavadi kavalugararu*) and a torchbearer (*deevatigeya jana*). A local militia or *kandachar* was placed in each unit along with a *thanedar*, a *gurikar*, three *shirastedars*, a *hoblidar*, a *daffedar*, an *olekar*, a bugler and a drummer.

Each such division or unit had *hoblis* of eight, ten, twelve or nineteen villages—a model retained from Raja Wodeyar's times. The villages were grouped according to size, population, etc., and formed the *hobli*, which was a larger administrative unit. The *hobli* was headed by the *hoblidar*, who had a retinue of one assistant, three scroll-writers and six accountants. Land classification, land assessment, regularisation of tenures, fixing and collection of revenues, codification of the twenty-four taxes and ensuring their prompt collection became the hallmarks of this new and efficient set-up. Each village had a *subedar*, a messenger or *chikkaparupathyagara*, three *athavanedars* or scroll-writers, six clerks, one postman or *anche harikar*, one *daffedar*, one *hastantri*, one cowherd, two watchmen and one *kaidivitige* or torch-bearer. They formed the core administrative body of the village and reported to their respective *hoblidars*.

The village also had a body of twelve functional heads called the Barabalooti system with one gowda, one to three Shanbogues, one Brahmin, one blacksmith, one goldsmith, one potter, one washerman, one kalasi, one gardener, one talvar, one water supplier and one barber. Between them they represented all the major caste combinations and functional roles of the village. They also got a share of the grains of harvest. The heads of these units—the *subedar* at the village level, the *hoblidar* at the *hobli* level and the *killedar* for the forts performed their duties with the King's sanction, given to them in the form of a signet ring with the words 'De' (for Chikkadevaraja) inscribed between figurines of the sun and moon.

Chikkadevaraja also constructed dams across the Cauvery and built canals for irrigation called Chikkadevarajanala and Devarajanala which helped bring large tracts of the Cauvery basin under irrigation. Towards the end of his rule, Mysore became progressive in its outlook and had undergone a series of administrative and tax reforms that few other kingdoms of India had at that time.

Taxation

Under Chikkadevaraja we see the principles of state landlordism taking root in the revenue model of the kingdom. Land and other taxes were codified and no one was allowed to amass a disproportionate amount of wealth. Official remuneration was paid half in currency and half in food grains. It was decreed that no official should spend more than his income. To maximise revenues the king decided to expand the cultivable land area. As an incentive to the ryots, he granted revenue concessions for a fixed number of years. In the case of superior land the remission granted was two-thirds of the full assessment for a period of five years and for land of medium quality it was one-fourth. Incentives given to the ryots not only encouraged them to increase the agricultural area but also fixed a peasant to a particular piece of land. Distinguished and meritorious soldiers and *kandacharas* were granted lands over which they could claim hereditary rights and obtain exemption from payment of taxes. These holdings were the final blow to the feudal system. This also created an elevation in the economic status of the so-called lower castes of traditional Hindu society. Chief among them were the Vokkaligas, Lingayats, Kurubas, Bedas, Raja Parivaras and Idigas, who were now mini landlords in their own right.

Land tax under Chikkadevaraja's regulation varied, being a quarter, one-third or half of gross produce, which was collected in cash as well as kind. This was a distinct improvement compared to the other South Indian kingdoms, like the Cholas, Vijayanagara Rayas and the Nayaks of Madurai and Tanjore, where the maximum share of land revenue varied in actual practice from half to four-fifths or 50–80 per cent of gross produce against the one-sixth or quarter permitted by Hindu law-givers.

The kingdom had an annual income of 7,20,000 Pagodas or Varahas (estimated at Rs 21,60,000, with a conversion factor of Rs 3 per Varaha). It is said that the maharaja would not have his breakfast each day till the finance minister deposited 2,000 Pagodas in the state treasury. The daily deadline was noon. It is by such financial prudence that the kingdom's coffers were overflowing in no time. In fact, Chikkadevaraja got the title of 'Navakoti Narayana' or the Lord of Nine Crores. The economy of surpluses and the great wealth accumulated under his direct control further enhanced the power and authority of the king. Wilks records that:

> It is certain that the revenues were realised with great regularity and precision, and this Rajah is stated to have established a separate treasury to provide for extraordinary and unexpected disbursements, of which he himself assumed the direct custody. It was his fixed practice, after the performance of his morning ablutions, and marking his forehead with the upright insignia of the Vishnoo, to deposit two bags (thousands) of Pagodas in

his treasury from the cash dispatched from the districts, before he proceeded to break his fast...By course of rigid economy and order, and by a widely extended and well organised system of securing for himself the great mass of plunder obtained by his conquests he had accumulated a treasure, for which he obtained the designation of Nou Kotte Narain, or the Lord of Nine Crores (of Pagodas) and a territory producing a revenue calculated on the estimate of the schedules...of 13,23,371 Canterai Pagodas; a sum which is no further remarkable than in its near coincidence with the value of the territory assigned to the revised state of Mysore after the lapse of another century in 1799...

Of course, this financial prudence had its evil effects as well. The king's obsession with depositing the requisite pagodas in the treasury by noon really pressurised officials all the way down the hierarchy. The compulsion to deliver often made them resort to the extreme step of extortion with the Hadinadu rebellion, a direct fallout of such measures.

Trade and Commerce

Like administration, Chikkadevaraja also regulated trade and commercial activities by fixing weights and measures and defining standards. The prevailing units of weight were *mana* (28 pounds), *dadeya* (1/4 *mana*), *pancheru* (1/8 *mana*), *balla*, *seru* or *seer*, *ardha-seru* (half *seru*), *pavu*, *ardha-pavu*, *kolaga* (8 *seru*) and *chataaka*. Canteroi Pagodas or Kanthirava Varahas were the lowest denomination of currency and given that each Pagoda was identical in weight, three of them weighed one Duddu-Tola. Twenty-four of the latter made a Seru, ten Serus made a Dadeya, four Dadeyas made a Chikka Mana. Fourty-four to fourty-six seers made a Dodda Mana or big mana used to measure grains, jaggery, arecanut, turmeric, tamarind, pepper, chillies and miscellaneous spices. A new kind of currency called the Tandava Krishnamurti Devaraya—a gold Varaha—was introduced. It was symbolic of the triumph of Mysore over Madurai's Chokkanatha Nayak and also the growing influence of Vaishnavism on the royal house. The annual revenues from the different coconut and banyan groves across the kingdom were also standardised. The taxing of fruit trees in gardens and of coconut trees, etc., varied from 15, 18, 25, 28 to 30 Varahas per 1,000 trees. This would be collected annually and transferred to the Srirangapatna treasury. As Puttaiyya summarises:

Finding that weights and measures were not uniform but were much abused, he fixed the standard of each and caused the monogram of his name 'De' to be impressed on each and ordered that all weightments and measurements should be made in these approved weights and measures as a safeguard against fraud. Similarly he caused seals bearing the monogram 'De' to be kept in the custody of local officials to be used whenever necessary for sealing purposes.

This standardisation greatly benefited the merchant class and facilitated free trade, which had suffered hugely after the fall of Vijayanagara and the Adil Shahis and of course under the oppression by the erstwhile Palegars.

Bangalore, Gubbi, Turuvekere, etc., became hubs of commercial activity and centres for the growth of cash crops. In fact, 12,000 weavers were stationed in Bangalore and their products were exported widely. This led to the rise of the textile merchants or Banajigas. Weekly *santhes* or rural markets ensured that all the stakeholders got their proper dues and also a platform to sell and purchase. The acquisition of Bangalore and its development as an urban centre speaks of Chikkadevaraja's vision. Dodda Petes or market-places were established in Bangalore, Gubbi and Turvekere where merchants brought their commercial products like cotton, arecanut and so on, weighed them on the giant scales called *chinataalu*, and later took them to local markets for sale. As Puttaiyya states:

> The rajah thereupon improved the place (Bangalore), built a fort and a shop street, imported a large industrial population, such as the weavers, arranged for the safety of the town and made it a big cloth centre for the export of cotton goods to all parts of the territories. It was in Chikkadevaraja's time that the building of towns with divisions and shop centres was taken up on an extensive scale to deal with merchandise and to provide with settlements for the industrial population. He strengthened the fortresses he had won from the poligars, built towns round them and constructed high streets and shop centres therein and arranged for the weighing and selling of goods in these centres before they were transported to the interior for being sold in retail. It is interesting to note that Bangalore, Gubbi and Turuvekere

were among the first towns so organised by him. As a result of the establishment of these centres, trade developed and the raja found an opportunity to tap fresh sources of revenue and forthwith introduced the octroi system of collecting revenue on all marketable articles such as cloths, drugs, tobacco and similar articles and entertained an establishment for collection work.

One of Chikkadevaraja's pioneering efforts was the wonderful postal system, started by him in 1672. The department was called *anche* meaning swan—a reference to the mythical swan that played Cupid and messenger between the celestial lovers Nala and Damayanti. A romantic name indeed for a state department.

Art and Culture

The king was also a man of letters and a patron of the arts. He is in fact credited with writing two dance dramas: *Geeta Gopala* and *Saptopadaki*. Bharatanatyam and Carnatic music flourished under the Wodeyars. In fact, Mysore was accredited as a seat of music and dance and developed its own inimitable Mysore *shaili* or style. Chikkadevaraja's court was adorned with scholars and poets, like Yelandur Pandita, Tirumalayya, Singarayya, his childhood tutor Chikkupadhyaya, Sanchi Honnamma and Sringaramma. The famous poet Kavi Lakshmisha was a contemporary. Chikkadevaraja, in fact, wrote a masterpiece in praise of the Lord Cheluvanarayana Swami of Melukote. The poem was titled 'Chikkadevaraja Binnapam'.

Religion

An interesting aspect of Chikkadevaraja's reign is his religious transformation and subsequent espousal of his new-found love for Vaishnavism. It also throws light on the kinds of pulls and pressures prevalent in the Hindu society of his times. The domineering nature of the Vaishnava community of the time became apparent in its attempts to ensure its triumph as the preferred faith of the hitherto Veerashaiva royal house. As stated before, in the early phase of his reign, Chikkadevaraja was deeply influenced by Vishalaksha Pandit, a Jain. Between 1673 and 1680, he had a more egalitarian and secular approach to all faiths. His fascination for the tenets of Sri Vaishnavism, maybe under the growing influence of people like, Tirumala Iyengar, his father Alasingaraya, and Chikkupadhyaya, can be seen around 1680. After the death of Pandit in 1686, the transformation became complete. The faith became the chief criteria for classification of the Arasu families in Mysore and emerged as a powerful influencing factor in the court of Mysore. That Tirumala had succeeded as prime minister only made matters better for the faith. By 1693, Chikkadevaraja had become a die-hard follower of the faith and proselytising tendencies took root. In 1693, scholars and priests of different Hindu subsects voluntarily decided to sport Vaishnava marks in a direct acceptance of the superiority of this faith. Chikkadevaraja also performed the *panchasamskaras* or the five rituals—the *Chakrankana, Urdhvapundra, Dasa Namam, Moolamantropasana* and *Narayana Puja*—any Vaishnava had to go through to become a pure-bred, authentic follower.

From 1696 to 1704, Chikkadevaraja had become elevated in his faith. It was now that he began to realise the true depth of the philosophies of Vaishnavism. This was also a period of tranquility in Mysore that gave the ruler ample time to ruminate. His thoughts condensed into spiritual upliftment and a quest for salvation. Gone was the political need for proselytisation; it was now a more intense dialogue of the soul with the Supreme. From a war-enthusiastic ruler who crushed all revolts with an iron fist, he seems to have metamorphosed into a mystic by this time, guided by the doctrines of Sri Vaishnavism. This idea couldn't have been expressed more beautifully by anyone other than Chikkadevaraja himself in his famous eulogy in the 'Chikkadevaraja Binnapam'. A paraphrased, summarised version follows:

> Oh Lord of Yadugiri! Having settled on the famous peak adorning the Karnataka country, Thou hast attained celebrity as the Protector of all people, and as the tutelary deity of the Yadu race. Thou art Parabrahman, the primeval cause of the world, Thou art Infinite, Thou art manifest in the Vedas, Puranas and the 18 Vidyas...Thou art an embodiment of the entire world, being 'One' in diversity...fear of falling into hell vanishes by mere recitation of Thy name; sinners become purified by contemplating Thee. Salvation is an end most cherished by those who are free from mundane cares. All the other ends are evanescent; salvation alone is eternal and it is to be attained by right action, right knowledge and right faith....Oh Lord of Yadugiri! To those who have renounced the world and placed their trust in Thee, Thou art easily accessible...Renunciation of worldly desire...is easiest

to achieve and is powered by the conception of relationship between Master and servant...Let Thy grace dawn upon me... Let Thy accessibility to Thy devotees manifest itself, and may Thou settle in the abode of my heart...I surrender myself at Thy feet and seek salvation.

The Maratha prince of Tanjore taunted Chikkadevaraja that while his kingdom had innumerable temples, Mysore had very few to showcase other than the Chamundeshwari temple at Mysore and the Melukote one. So Chikkadevaraja constructed a series of fine temples which exist to this day. They are the Shweta Varaha Swamy temple at Srirangapatna, the Gopala Krishna temple at Hardanahalli, the Paravasudeva Temple at Gundlupet, the Varadaraja temple at Varkod, the Venkataramana Swamy temple at Bangalore fort, also called Kote Venkataramana, etc. He made lavish grants for their upkeep and maintenance. An ardent Vaishnavaite, he gave prominence to the Vajramukuta festival or Diamond Crown festival in Melkote. He followed the Veerashaiva tenets of Basaveshwara in the early years of his reign. He built a pond at Sravana Belagola for the use of Jain pilgrims.

Srirangapatna

During Chikkadevaraja's reign, Srirangapatna became a flourishing city and a political centre of gravity. A lithic record of 1685 describes the Srirangapatna township as abundant 'with plum, jacks, coconut, plantain, lime, orange, fig and other fruit trees, with houses as high as hills...and with cows and Brahmanas, with trees of plenty, with temples, with fine elephants....with horses neighing like the thunder of clouds, with splendid chariots and fort soldiers...a beautiful city having splendid gateways, an ornament to the lady Earth, surrounded by the Cauvery.'

Among the pantheon of illustrious rulers, Chikkadevaraja Wodeyar occupies primacy alongside Raja Wodeyar and Ranadhira Kanthirava Narasaraja Wodeyar. Believed to have possessed exceptional personal strength, courage and prowess, he was, according to contemporary sources, quoted by Hayavadana Rao, 'a handsome personage with features characteristic of a great man destined to rule as a sovereign, features suggesting a budding manhood, charming round face, large lotus-like eyes, well-proportioned nose, soft arms, round chest, well-built body, pleasing countenance and excellent voice. He was a trained warrior, a good scholar, a notable author, a large-hearted and large-minded devotee and exceptionally capable administrator. He would personally test the weapons, diamonds, horses and elephants required for his use.'

After a long and illustrious reign of nearly thirty-two years, Chikkadevaraja Wodeyar—one of the most illustrious sovereigns Mysore had ever seen—passed away in the Karthika month of 1704.

7

THE DALAVOY REGIME AD 1704–34

Every kingdom and dynasty goes through phases of highs and lows. History has several stories of even the most powerful kingdoms reduced to weak reflections of their earlier supremacy, courtesy the inefficiency of the king in question. The golden era of the Wodeyar Dynasty saw it being established as a major power to reckon with in the politics of the Deccan under such able rulers as Raja Wodeyar, Ranadhira and Chikkadevaraja Wodeyar. After these rulers, however, the kingdom passed through the hands of successive titular puppets who wilfully surrendered to the wishes of their powerful dalavoys. A weak ruler, power without accountability and access to the riches and secrets of the kingdom make a perfect combination for corruption and pilferage to thrive and that is exactly what happened in Mysore. This period of Mysore's history is aptly called the 'Dalavoy regime' and lasted till it spelt ultimate doom for the royal family. It was left to the prudence and shrewdness of a neutral upstart to milk this situation and turn the tide in his favour.

THE POLITICAL SCENE

Born in 1672, Kanthirava Narasaraja Wodeyar II was crowned on 30 November 1704. He had two wives, Chamammanni and Cheluvarajammanni. The latter was the mother of his son, Dodda Krishnaraja Wodeyar. Mute from birth, he was a titular monarch who carried out the affairs of the kingdom in sign language. To facilitate the administration of the kingdom, the kith and kin of the king were appointed as the dalavoys on the presumption that they would be trustworthy. The period thus marked the rise to prominence of the Kalale family as dalavoys of Mysore. Matrimonial alliances between the family of the Kalale nobility and the royal house of Mysore furthered the referent power that the former began to exercise in affairs of state.

Meanwhile, just how tenuous the Mysore–Mughal relationship was became evident after the death of Chikkadevaraja Wodeyar. The hype that surrounded the successful embassy to the Mughal court seems to have vanished. If Signor Niccolo Manucci, a Venetian traveller in India and contemporary chronicler, is to be believed—Aurangzeb mistook the new king of Mysore to be an illegitimate successor and ordered the seizure of his treasure, saying that the 'bear has entered the jaws of death'. Elaborating in his *Storia da Mogor*, Manucci writes:

> Without troubling himself about the increasing ruin to his Empire due to the Mahrattahs, this King (Aurangazib) now plans the renewal of war against Maisur or Saranpattan. His ambition is to capture the great treasure possessed by this Prince. This territory lies near the region of Malabar and the Prince possesses one hundred thousand matchlock men and 10,000 cavalry...he is lord over a large territory defended by over 100 fortresses and many forests.... For this reason King Aurangazib protests that this Prince is not a legitimate succession, and claims the right to take possession. Thus he is making ready for a campaign, and has sent out orders to the Princes of Tanjoor, the Princes of Trichinopoly, and other neighbouring rulers who are his feudatories. They must be prepared to invade Mahisur, and should they refuse compliance, they will, he says, be chastised.

Accordingly Daud Khan was despatched to seize this treasure from the new ruler of Mysore. But as luck would have it for the Wodeyar, Daud Khan was intercepted by the Marathas. Anxious to ward off the Mughal advance on his territory, Kanthirava—a sad and ironical reminder of the other valiant ruler of the dynasty who bore the same name—found it expedient to appear subservient to Aurangzeb and offered him fifteen million rupees and five elephants, so as to escape interference by the Mughals. But conveniently, these remained mere promises on paper and Mysore never wished to act on the same. An enraged Aurangzeb kept sending violent reminders to Srirangapatna on the delay in the tribute due to the imperial treasury at Delhi. The uprisings in north India, however, distracted Aurangzeb and he seemed to forget Mysore for a while.

The death of Aurangzeb in 1707 led to a crisis of succession in Delhi. The lot fell in favour of Shah Alam I (1708–12) and his successor Farrukhsiyar (1713–19). The confusion in Delhi encouraged the Marathas to regroup as a considerable force under Shahu (1708–48), son and successor of Shambhaji. In early 1713, Asaf Jah (Chin Killich Khan, 1671–1748), who was subedar of Oudh under Shah Alam I, became the foujdar of Hyderabad as the new Mughal viceroy of the Deccan under the title of 'Nizam-ul-Mulk', which he received from Emperor Farrukhsiyar. The government of the Mughal areas of the Carnatic, which included Payanghat and Balaghat along with Sira, with its headquarters at Arcot was under Aurangzeb's trusted commanders, Zulfikar Khan and Daud Khan. With the latter being recalled to Delhi during the 1707 civil war there, the Mughal Carnatic passed on to Daud's Dewan Sadatullah Khan. He was recognised as the Nawab of Carnatic by the Peacock Throne of Delhi. Thus, political equations had changed in the Deccan with the entry of new players. The older ones, like the Madurai Nayaks under Rani Mangammal and Vijayaranga Chokkanatha and Tanjore under Shahji II and Serfoji, were in the throes of dissolution.

The death of Aurangzeb and the political turmoil in Delhi encouraged Mysore to advance northwards. In 1710, Dalavoy Nanjarajayya was sent to capture Chikkaballapur from its chieftain Baiche Gowda. In early 1711, he marched further and captured Doddaballapur and, later on, Midageshi. This extended the kingdom of Mysore to the very gates of the Mughal Empire's southern heartland of Sira. The advance of Mysore was being watched with amusement by Sadatullah Khan, the Mughal protégé in the Carnatic. In August 1711, he joined hands with the subedar of Sira, Amin Khan, and attacked Mysore. The intention was also to remind the kingdom of its promise to the late Aurangzeb, that of paying tribute to Delhi. The Wodeyar was obliged to make a payment of Rs 5 lakh, after collecting which Sadatullah retired to Arcot. Thus, Mysore became a lame-duck province for the Mughal empire's representatives in South India. On 18 February 1714, Kanthirava Narasaraja II died at the age of forty-two and his twelve-year old son Dodda Krishnaraja succeeded him on 3 March 1714. Devarajayya was made the new dalavoy after his predecessor Veerarajayya of the Kalale family stepped down. Devarajayya and his brother Karachuri Nanjarajayya were to play a pivotal role in the future of Mysore. Another Nanjarajayya of the Kalale lineage and cousin of Devarajayya was made the Sarvadhikari. With a titular and spineless ruler unable to control them, this trio made hay while the sun shone, thus ensuring that power was concentrated in their hands.

Up north, catastrophe awaited the tottering Mughal empire. Under monarchs, like Farrukhsiyar and his successor Muhammad Shah (1719–48), the last proverbial nail in the Mughal coffin seemed to have been fixed. The hitherto protégé of the Mughal throne, Nizam-ul-Mulk declared his independence and the entire country below the Ghats, known as the Carnatic-Bijapur-Balaghat and Carnatic-Bijapur-Payanghat, south of Hyderabad, came under his suzerainty. He divided the Carnatic Hyderabad region among three feudatory Pathan chiefs, designated as nawabs, from Savanoor, Cudappah and Kurnool. He became the de facto absolute ruler of the Deccan, with Sadatullah being relegated to Arcot.

The Nizam had a contender to the position of absolute authority over the Deccan in the form of a new Maratha power centre—the Peshwas. Chhatrapati Shivaji had appointed Moropant Trimbak Pingle as his first peshwa or prime minister. But with time, the descendants of Shivaji became titular rulers called 'Swami' and the peshwa emerged as the virtual king of the Maratha dominion. The appointment of Baji Rao I as peshwa by Chhatrapati Shahu in 1719 made this post hereditary. They were given considerable powers to command the Maratha armies and also to collect the taxes of Chauth and Sardeshmukhi from the Mughal provinces and feudatories in the Deccan. Mysore inevitably was on this list of feudatories of the Mughals from the days of Chikkadevaraja and this brought the Marathas on repeated conquests to Mysore.

Meanwhile, Amin Khan, the nawab of Siras was feeling increasingly threatened by his colleagues in the region. The growing friendship between Sadatullah Khan of Arcot and the Pathan Nawabs of Savanoor, Cudappah and Kurnool, as also the threatening moves of the contender to the chieftainship of Sira, Tahir Khan, prompted Amin to send feelers of friendship to Mysore. In a suicidal move, Mysore decided to extend its support to the beleaguered Amin Khan, thus earning the wrath of the other Mughal officers of the South. Keeping an eye on these moves, the Nizam ordered a grand confederacy (that included the Pathan nawabs, the nawab of Arcot, Siddhoji Ghorpade of Gutti and Ikkeri) to rout Amin Khan. The combined forces under Ikkeri's Dalavoy Rohile Lingappa routed Amin Khan in 1724 and Tahir Khan was made the new nawab of Sira. The anger of the combined forces was now directed against Mysore, which had unwittingly, and for no benefit, become embroiled in this crossfire. The Fort St. George dispatch dated 11 February 1725 speaks of the Nizam ordering both Sadatullah and Tahir to 'attack the King of Misore'. The huge army led a violent attack on Srirangapatna. A baffled king was forced to buy them off with a huge bounty of a crore of rupees, which also included the arrears of tributes due to the Mughals. Sadatullah divided Rs 60 lakh of this tribute among his five confederates and apportioned the rest to himself, marching back to Arcot, victorious.

Meanwhile, seized by zeal and a new-found authority, the peshwas attacked neighbouring kingdoms regularly. Mysore was always on their radar. The recent reverses of Mysore encouraged them to strike whenever the iron was hot. Led by Peshwa Baji Rao, the Marathas attacked the kingdom of Mysore, reaching up to Chitradurga and, in 1727, marched victoriously through Hukkeri, Samanagada, Belgaum, Sonda, Lakshmeshwar, and Bidnaur and laid siege to Srirangapatna. The weak ruler of Mysore paid twenty-one lakhs to send Baji Rao back. This inspired the Marathas to attack Mysore repeatedly to collect the dues payable to the Mughals, as they were assured that the titular ruler on the Masnad of Mysore would offer the least resistance and generously fill their coffers. Thus, under Dodda Krishnaraja Wodeyar, Mysore was increasingly weakened and susceptible to enemy forces.

The only noteworthy success for the Mysorean forces in this tragic phase of their history was the subjugation of Mummadi Kempa Virappa Gowda of Magadi in 1728. Dalavoy Devarajayya blockaded the fort of Magadi and took the chieftain prisoner; he later died in prison at Srirangapatna. The hill fort of Savandurg was reduced and the accumulated treasure of ages was taken. The Mysore army advanced till Salem, but the already drained treasury of Srirangapatna could no longer sustain these military campaigns.

THE DECLINE OF THE WODEYARS

On 5 March 1732, in the month of Phalguna, Dodda Krishnaraja passed away at the age of thirty. His short rule destroyed the eminent position that Mysore had begun to occupy under the reign of Chikkadevaraja. He was content with delegating his authority to his vicious officers and Dalavoys. He was, however, a devout Vaishnava like his predecessors. He invited the Parakala Guru Srinivasa Yatindra, a famous Sri Vaishnava luminary, to the capital. He also made lavish grants to the Vaishnava shrines of Melukote, Belur and Tirupati, expanded the Kalale Lakshmikantha temple, founded *agraharas* and excavated a tank there. His principal queen was Devajammanni, daughter of Chikke Urs of the Kalale family. He also had eight junior queens, of which four were from the Kalale household. Cheluvamba was his favourite queen and a great litterateur, poet and scholar herself.

Since he died childless, his wife, the powerful dowager Rani Devajammanni adopted Ankanahalli Devaraja Urs' sons Chamaraja and Krishnaraja. Chamaraja Wodeyar VII was crowned the seventeenth king of the Wodeyar dynasty in 1732. During this time, power had virtually passed over to the Dalavoy Devarajayya and his cousin Nanjarajayya, who was appointed the Sarvadhikari or administrative head in his thirtieth year. To quote Wilks' *The History of Mysore*:

> The profligacy of Nanjaraj made a shameless job of the revenue by the appointment of his own menial servants nominally to the office of the Amildar, but retaining them about his own person leaving to them to provide deputies and exacting a certain proportion of their income as a joint fund for himself and his brother.

Taking advantage of the political crisis threatening to destroy Mysore, the two vicious brothers looted most of the revenue coming from the *taluks*. Of the revenue from each *taluk*, which was lawfully the property of the royal treasury, 2000–3000 Varahas went into the brothers' pockets. Even some of the provisions coming to the palace every week conveniently found their way to the storehouses and kitchens of the brothers. An additional 100–200 Varahas from each *gadi* or administrative unit were deceitfully drawn for them and their faithful accomplice Pradhan Venkatapatayya. On receiving intelligence of the treachery of the brothers, Chamaraja made up his mind to punish them. But Dalavoy Devarajayya secretly overheard the king's plans and rushed to the Queen Mother's chambers.

In a dramatic way, he began to brainwash the Rani:

> Mahamatrushree! This son that you have adopted is out to bring disrepute to Your Highness. He wants to totally eliminate the influence of the late king and your husband on the state. He has killed many people who were considered close to the deceased

monarch and is plotting to remove loyalists like me from power. We in fact overheard him expressing the evil desire of throwing Your Highness out of the Palace and sending the provisions and other essentials in half their usual amounts to your future residence. Please do something Your Highness before that servant of yours overpowers you.

The ignorant rani's anger knew no bounds. 'Oh! So this boy has got the audacity and temerity to annul our influence on the state, does he? Devarajayya, try all means, by hook or crook, to dethrone this arrogant fool. Your efforts would have my sanction. From today you would be our instrument in ousting the evil powers and would be amply rewarded.'

Having received encouragement, Devarajayya embarked on his evil designs. The troops were let out of the fort on Fridays for exercises. On one such day when all the troops had left the fort, Devarajayya installed those forces which were under his pay on all the ramparts of the fort. They were supposed to prevent the return of the forces that had gone out for exercises. The inmates locked up the doors for protection when they realised this but, with his elephant Ramabana, Devarajayya broke open the palace doors. Chamaraja came rushing out and pleaded with his dalavoy. 'For the first eight months of my rule, you were my Regent. Now that I have started assuming independent charges, you are vexed with me. So henceforth, I appoint you as my Regent and will virtually hand over the reigns of the state to you. Please don't kill me.' The king of the resplendent throne of Mysore had been reduced to such a pathetic state.

But Devarajayya was too ambitious to listen to him. He snatched the Shikhamohar ring— worn as a symbol of kingship—from the king's hands. He ordered his soldiers to arrest the king and his family. They were packed off as prisoners to the jail at Kabbaludurga. On 10 June 1734, Chamaraja Wodeyar VII was unceremoniously deposed and condemned to die in prison.

Devarajayya then approached Rani Devajammanni, who had unknowingly been a party to these misdemeanours, and advised her to coronate Chamaraja's younger brother Krishnaraja as king. Accordingly, in the Jyestha month of 1734, the six-year old was crowned the eighteenth ruler of Mysore as Immadi Krishnaraja Wodeyar or Krishnaraja Wodeyar II. He had three wives—Puttammanni, Devirammanni and the daughter of

Katti Gopalaraje Urs, Lakshmammanni, who was to play a pivotal role in the history of Mysore. His two sons were Nanjaraja Wodeyar and Bettada Chamaraja Wodeyar VIII.

THE FOREIGN HAND

Meanwhile, the rivalries between the British and the French peaked during this period and they invariably supported rival sides among the warring Indian satraps. The fallout of this rivalry was first experienced in the Deccan in the form of the Carnatic wars. The term 'Carnatic' is a generic one for the region of southern India that includes parts of present-day Karnataka, Tamil Nadu and Andhra Pradesh. It is in this region that the Indian classical music style of south India—Carnatic music—was nurtured. As seen earlier, the collapse of the Mughal empire led to the formation of the dynasty of the Nawabs of Carnatic at Arcot with Sadatullah (1710–32). His death was followed by a war of succession, which put Anwar-ud-din on the throne. Both the British and the French powers had cast their evil eyes on the fertile and prosperous lands of the Carnatic, watered by the River Cauvery. There followed a long period of a series of wars for seven years, called the Carnatic wars.

The immediate cause for the First Carnatic War (1744–48) was the Austrian war of succession that broke out in Europe in 1742. England and France joined the war on opposite sides. Their interests clashed in India and America. In 1745, the English threatened Pondicherry but failed to capture it. With the help of a fleet from Mauritius, the French General La Bourdonnais captured Madras in 1746, and reached an agreement with the Company to hand it back for a sum of money. But Dupleix, the French governor of Pondicherry and arch-rival of La Bourdonnais, refused to honour this agreement. He had promised Madras to the Nawab of Carnatic, Anwar-ud-din. Anglo-French rivalry erupted in the form of the First Carnatic War. While the two French leaders were engrossed in this unseemly battle, a gale of unusual severity in the monsoon season damaged the French fleet. La Bourdonnais was recalled to Mauritius and then to France. Dupleix succeeded in holding Madras, one of the key positions of the British in the Deccan where they had built Fort St. George. The nawab demanded that Madras be granted to him as per the agreement, but Dupleix was in no mood to acquiesce. This enraged the nawab, who attacked Dupleix's forces with a large battalion. But the cavalry of the nawab was no match for the musketry and field artillery of the French and the latter won an easy victory. It exposed the weakness of the Indian army. The British possessions in the South were reduced to the fort of St. David. The French were very proud of their victory and the English were feeling the pinch of humiliating defeat and waited to strike back. The Austrian war ended in 1748 with the signing of the Treaty of Aix-la-Chapelle and Madras was restored to the English.

In 1739, Sarvadhikari Nanjarajayya died on the banks of the Cauvery in Srirangapatna. In a short tenure of five or six years, he had amassed so much ill-gotten wealth that future generations of his family need not have bothered to earn a living. But strange are the ways of fate—he died childless.

Before his death, he issued a proclamation, recorded by Wilks in *History of Mysore*:

> The Marathas are untrustworthy. We better befriend the Mughals. It is futile to invest powers in the hands of Mahmud Shahabaz Sahib's brother, Haidar Ali Khan, who has been granted 50 horses, 100 adherents on Your Highness' wishes and to appoint him to assist Katti Gopalaraje Urs at Bangalore. May not be today, but in a few more years, this Mussalman may prove to be a threat to the throne of Mysore and its Maharaja.

Ex-post facto, his words seem prophetic.

LOOKING BACK: SECTION 2

As the era of the dalavoys leads to another significant span of Mysore's history, the Interregnum, it is worthwhile to stop and introspect over certain disturbing lessons and insights that this phase has to offer. What comes out clearly is that the canker of corruption and abuse of political power for personal use is an age-old tradition in India, if we may use that term. Quoting Manu, the ancient law-giver, may be politically incorrect in today's India, but his words in the *Manusmriti*, (Chapter VII, v.143) are timeless:

> That monarch whose subjects are carried from his kingdom by ruffians, while they call aloud for protection and he barely looks on them with his ministers, is a dead and not a living king.

Corruption is indeed an abstract term to define precisely. According to the 1997 Report of the World Bank, abuse of public power for private gains is described as corruption. But this appears too simplistic an explanation of the term. It is, in fact, a multi-headed dragon, which gradually kills a system. A basic conflict between the ethos and the system has weakened Indian polity.

The problem with India and Indians is that we revel in and glorify our past to the extent that we would prefer to live in the past rather than the present. How often we hear laments like, 'Oh! Those were the days,' or, 'India in the past had achieved almost everything the West now hopes or dreams to discover!' This is a suicidal version of history. Of course, India has a glorious past and resorting to Marxist interpretation by belittling successes and symbols of the past is not an encouraging practice. We did indeed make great strides in the arts, spirituality, our own systems of medicine and health and developed a uniquely Indian way of looking at life—one that continues to attract and inspire people from different parts of the world. But there can be no worse tragedy for a nation than to think that all that was the best, all that was the most magnificent has already happened. That tendency leaves little inspiration for the present and the future becomes more of an attempt at weak imitation of the superlative past. We need to understand that while we excelled in various fields, we had terrible shortcomings in others and corruption certainly is one such malaise. History offers us a package of good and bad and to pick only the former is selective cherry-picking at its worst. The tendency to milk the state, use public funds for personal pilferage and abuse power vested in one's hands is something deeply ingrained in the Indian psyche from times immemorial. Recently, this has earned us the dubious distinction of being listed among the top nations in the World's Corruption Index.

When we are convinced that this is a phenomenon, not merely of the wretched present but of the glorious past as well, it gives us the self-confidence to work in the present for a better future, rather than suffer from a mighty inferiority complex vis-à-vis the bygone era. In the case of Mysore, the same tendency of the ministers in power to assume a larger-than-life image and the corresponding inadequacy with which the monarch responded to these challenges aggravated the situation completely in favour of a third party.

Section 3
The Interregnum Period
(AD 1734–99)

(A portrait of Haidar Ali: AD 1761-82)

8

THE EARLY YEARS OF HAIDAR ALI AD 1734–61

AD 1796

In the grimy and dingy inner apartments of the Natakashala the glimmer of a candle was all there was to dispel the darkness. Straining under its flicker to see and write coherently, but at the same time aware of the perils of illuminating the room and thereby waking the soldiers who guarded her closely, Rani Lakshmammanni, the old widow of Immadi Krishnaraja Wodeyar, signed off the letter with her characteristic *nom de plume* 'Sriranga'. She heaved a long sigh and re-read the contents of her letter to see if she had covered all she wished to convey to her confidante Tirumala Iyengar.

> We have been writing to you of our affairs from time to time. It is twenty-two years since you left this kingdom. We are daily being persecuted by Tippu. We cannot say at what moment he may send assassins and get us murdered. And for the restoration of our kingdom, you have been exerting your best, winning the sympathies of English Sirdars in our favour and entering into treaties with them. And all this with what amount of sacrifice and suffering? For our sake 700 families of your kith and kin have been ruthlessly murdered, all your immense wealth has been spent, and you are a ruined person.

And all along it has also been our greatest anxiety to see our Kingdom justly administered with you as our right hand in Srirangapatna and our pious gifts to Brahmins and temples rightly upheld, and thus, leading a holy life under the sacred influence of God Sriranga, end our days in quietness and peace.

But while we note the projects of the Mahomedan tyrant, we despair of our life. For now we learn that the French Vakeel at the Court of Tippu has been strongly advising him to put us all to death, as we may possibly one day be the cause of his ruin.

We send along with this a copy of the treaty which Tippu has lately made with the French. If you show this to the Governor of Madras and get him to invade the country with a large army before the arrival of French assistance to Tippu, it will save not only us, but the English also. But if, on the contrary, there be any vacillation as on the two or three previous occasions, Tippu and the French will unite like fire and air, and the whole country will be ruined. Please tell the Governor and the English there that if they may not care for us, at least in pure self defence, in order to preserve their own safety, they must put down Tippu at once before he gets French aid.

Under these circumstances, you will see, our life is quite uncertain, and when we are no more, as you are the best wellwisher of the state, you should keep exerting your best, see Tippu destroyed, and get a member of our Royal Family placed on the throne and administer the country with an eye on justice and truth and maintain our pious and charitable institutions, in such a way that our soul may rest with satisfaction in the other world. If, however, by God's grace we should also be alive, and the English conquer Tippu and restore to us our kingdom, we shall pay the English army to the extent of one crore of pagodas. And for this they must abide by the terms of our old treaty with Sullivan and Macartney. You should communicate all this to the English and get the army to march at once. And it cannot arrive here at a more opportune moment, for Tippu is acting here in the most foolish manner. He does not know who his best friends are and who his worst enemies. And hence he has lost control even over his army. He has no good military officers. And everybody here is wishing for his discomfiture and he is very unpopular. By whatever route the allied armies may come now, they can have ample supplies and good water.

If you will therefore exert your best now without delay and with your usual zeal, ability and intelligence, I have no doubt that God will second your efforts and victory will be ours this time. As for further particulars, the Brahmin bearers of this will explain.

Sriranga*

She sealed the letter and closed her eyes in a small prayer. Her troubled mind took her thirty years back in time, when Immadi Krishnaraja Wodeyar lay on his death-bed. He clasped her hand tightly and said: 'Lakshmi! What sins have I committed to die this way, a refugee in my own palace? What did I not do to help this ungrateful man? Don't you remember me telling you about Devarajayya narrating to my deceased father the distressing condition of those fatherless fiends and how he had taken pity on him and recruited him and his elder brother in the Mysorean services? My heart is heavy; my soul would find no salvation.'

Battling her tears the young rani had promised her husband, 'My Lord! There is nothing else left for me in life. The easiest option before me now is to jump into the fire that lights your pyre. But I make a solemn promise to you this day. The mission of the rest of my life would be the liberation and restoration of the kingdom. Your soul will rest in peace, my Lord, in the gardens of Paradise. If I fail in my endeavour, then hellfire be upon me. Give your worries to me and leave.' Her soothing words had assuaged the worries of the dying man and with a smile on his face, he had breathed his last.

Rani Lakshmammanni's ruminations were rudely interrupted by a violent banging on the door of her apartments. It was daybreak and the palanquin had come to take her to the only outing she was entitled to in the day—a visit to the temple of Lord Venkataramana, whose idol she had brought from Balamuri and consecrated in the palace compound. She hid the letter beneath the flowers and incense sticks she carried to the temple for the daily *pujas*. Upon reaching the temple she signalled to the priest to lay the letter at the feet of the Lord and by sleight of hand ensured that the letter was passed to the Brahmin who stood secretly within the sanctum sanctorum impersonating the priest's attendant. All

---

* This letter is a rough translation of the original letter in the *Annals*.

the while aware that the five armed men accompanying her watched her every move, she communicated with the Brahmin with her eyes. The Brahmin nodded reassuringly, conveying that the work would be done. With a satisfied smile, she got back into the palanquin to endure another day of house arrest.

Rani Lakshmammanni lived in the past and the future. The present sent shivers down her normally resolute spine and she would rather not think of living through it in her musings as well. The future held a ray of hope for her, but the past brought a bitterness and frustration she wanted to eschew. Still, who could prevent the flow of thoughts? They involuntarily led her to the genesis of this whole sordid affair. Seventy years was a long time—she was not even born then. She was told that that was when Devarajayya had approached her father-in-law with the sad story of a young boy whose father had been treacherously murdered.

⁂

IN THE DECCAN, 1728

Dalavoy Devarajayya was not the kind of man to be moved by the piteous condition of fellow human beings. He and his siblings were motivated purely by greed, and he would twist any rule to achieve his heart's desire. But something turned inside him when he heard the story narrated by Maddagiri Mallarajayya and his commander of 200 foot-soldiers and 50 cavalry, Ghulam Haidar Ali Saib. Standing with them was a veiled woman, Majida Begum. The veil might have concealed her tears, but her body language gave away her immense misery. Without further ado, Devarajayya took the delegation to the king's court. Dodda Krishnaraja Wodeyar was in the midst of a discussion when the messengers informed him about the arrival of the dalavoy and his guests. The king let the rapacious dalavoy in.

The delegation suggested that the grievous story be narrated in the first person by Majida Begum herself. In a faltering voice choked with emotion, the veiled woman sought the king's mercy even as she recounted the sad turn of events. The ancestors of her husband Fateh Mohammad hailed from Arabia. One Ashraf Ali had left Arabia for India with his family and personal adherents and settled down at Bijapur in the service of the sultan of that state. A descendent of Ashraf Ali, followed by his wife and three sons, came to Kolar from Bijapur. After his death, his three sons found their own way. The first son was Majida's husband Fateh Mohammad, who served the Nawab of Sira, Dargah Quli Khan, as commander of 400 infantry and 100 cavalry. He proved daunting at the Ganjikota attack and also gained the village of Gummanahalli. Fateh Mohammad had two sons by his younger wife Majida Begum, Shahabaz and Haidar. Haidar had been born seven years ago at Budikota, near Kolar, in 1721. Fateh Mohammad's younger brothers were Ghulam Haidar Ali Saib and Ghulam Ali Saib. Ghulam Haidar was serving Mallarajayya of Srirangapatna. He was childless. Ghulam Ali Saib served the Doddaballapur Palegar and was childless too.

Things were going well for Fateh Mohammad and his family. His courage at the Ganjikota attack attracted the attention of the nawab of Sira, who rewarded him generously. At the same time it stoked the fires of jealousy among his contemporaries and rivals. In the meantime, the death of the nawab of Sira led to disturbances among various contenders and in one such battle between Abdul Rasool Khan, the son of the deceased nawab, and Tahir Khan, the subedar of Sira, Fateh Mohammad was made the scapegoat.

Majida Begum's voice seemed to be drowning in emotion as she told the royal audience how one Ramazan night, she and her two sons sat waiting in their Doddaballapur residence for Fateh Mohammad to get back from the battle and break the fast with them. The boys were delighted to hear the sound of an approaching army, anticipating it to be that of their victorious father. But they were shocked to see the corpse of their father flung down and Abbas Quli Khan, the son of Abdul Rasool Khan, planting his feet on its chest. Abdul Rasool and his son Abbas Quli Khan despised Fateh Mohammad for the favours he had managed to procure from the late nawab. This was their payback time. Fateh Mohammad owed Abbas Quli Khan money and the latter demanded that his loans be settled at once.

As if the sudden, ugly turn of events was not bad enough, the financial burden brought Majida and her sons to their knees. They pleaded for some time to repay the debts. But the tormentor was in no mood to relent. Shahabaz and Haidar were locked in a *nagara* or drum, which was beaten upon by the adherents of Abbas Quli Khan. Even Majida Begum was imprisoned but she managed to escape and reached her brother-in-law, Ghulam Ali Saib, for help. But he said he himself was hopelessly indebted and could do little to help her. She then approached Ghulam

Haidar Ali Saib, who took her to Maddagiri Mallarajayya, making her promise that if the benevolent maharaja of Mysore helped them, they would remain ever loyal to him.

Majida fell on her knees and requested the king of Mysore to take pity on her condition. Krishnaraja was moved beyond words. He made up his mind that the two boys need to be saved from the clutches of the tyrant. He accordingly decided to buy Shahabaz and Haidar for 10,000 Varahas. Abbas Quli Khan was paid off and the boys were recruited into the Mysore service. Ghulam Haidar Ali Saib was made commander of the army and on his death Shahabaz became commander under the leadership of Karachuri Nanjarajayya, the new dalavoy and brother of Devarajayya. Young Haidar was sent to Bangalore to aid Katti Gopalaraje Urs. His tumultuous childhood deprived him of the advantages of education and he remained illiterate to the end of his days.

Of course, in the years that followed history took a dreadful turn for the benefactor king. The caprice and ambitions of Devarajayya ensured that Chamaraja Wodeyar was unceremoniously deposed and the baton passed on to Immadi Krishnaraja. The young man felt stifled under the guidance of the same villain who had caused untold misery to his elder brother and family. But there was little he could do; Devarajayya had the covert support of Queen Mother Devajammanni. So he sat biding his time till he could find an individual who would be his saviour and outmanoeuvre the cunning schemes of Devarajayya and Sarvadhikari Nanjarajayya. The latter died with his famous prediction about the threats the king of Mysore could face from an ordinary adherent, like Haidar Ali. Spoken by a known traitor, these words seemed unimportant and Krishnaraja Wodeyar did not think them worth a second thought.

The exit of Sarvadhikari Nanjarajayya brightened the fortunes of Karachuri Nanjarajayya, the brother of Devarajayya who was appointed the new dalavoy. Since Haidar was working under the command of Nanjarajayya, his destiny seemed to be inextricably linked with that of his mentor.

DISORDER IN THE DECCAN

The 1740s saw tumultuous times in the Deccan. Rivalries between the nawab of Arcot, the kingdom of Mysore, the nizam of Hyderabad—the subedar of the Mughals who had assumed independence, the peshwas of the Maratha kingdom and the rajas of the Malabar coast, as well as rivalries within kingdoms, ensured constant ferment in the region. The two foreign powers present there—the French and the English—did not hesitate to exploit this unrest to their own advantage.

In the Carnatic, Dost Ali Khan succeeded his uncle Sadatullah Khan as nawab of Arcot. The period was marked by strife and petty attacks on neighbouring territories. Mysore bore the brunt of a lot of these misguided attacks. Relations between Mysore and Sira were troubled, especially after the king of Mysore helped Fateh Mohammad's family. Zahir Khan, nawab of Sira, dispatched Qasim Khan and Murad Khan to capture Srirangapatna. But they were stopped at Chennapatna and slain by Devarajayya. In 1746, Nasir Jung, son of Nizam-ul-Mulk of Hyderabad attacked Mysore. During that time Karachuri Nanjarajayya was away at Coimbatore. Unable to face Nasir Jung, Devarajayya bribed him and sent him away after signing a contract at Thonanur.

In 1749 the Mysore army laid siege to Devanahalli, an outpost on the frontiers of Mysore. Haidar made his first appearance here as a volunteer horseman along with his brother Shahabaz who commanded 200 cavalry and 100 foot-soldiers. It was at this siege that his skill as a soldier was first revealed. After eight months of war, Devanahalli was annexed. The daring feats of young Haidar in the Devanahalli campaign attracted the attention of Dalavoy Nanjarajayya, who made him commander of 50 horse and 250 foot. Thus began Haidar's meteoric career, which eventually saw him becoming the de facto ruler of a large part of southern India.

Meanwhile, the aged Nizam-ul-Mulk died in 1748 and his son Nasir Jung succeeded him. But Muzaffar Jung, the dead nizam's grandson and Nasir Jung's nephew, fought his uncle, claiming that his grandfather had nominated him as successor. This dispute led to the Second Carnatic War in which, yet again, the English and the French took opposite sides. Nasir Jung mustered the support of the Pathan nawabs of Cudappah, Kurnool and Savanoor, Morari Rao Ghorpade and the maharaja of Mysore. Around the same time, one Chanda Sahib who was released from prison by the Marathas laid claim to the throne of the nawab of Arcot. Thus, the Deccan seemed a potpourri of disaster in which the two European forces decided to test their strength.

Dupleix decided to support the claimants for the positions of the nizam and the nawab of Arcot, in this case Muzaffar Jung and Chanda Sahib respectively. The Frenchman had his own brand of thought and strategy—best summed up by Ananda Ranga Pillai, his secretary of many years, as follows:

> ... (his) method of doing things is not known to anyone, because none else is possessed of the quick mind with which he is gifted. In patience he has no equal. He has peculiar skill in carrying out his plans and designs in the management of affairs and in governing; in fitting his advice to times and persons; in maintaining at all times an even countenance; in doing things through proper agents; in addressing them in appropriate terms; and in assuming a bearing at once dignified towards all.

With the French position known, the British had no choice but to fall in on the other side of the divide. The British general Major Lawrence was sent to the aid of Nasir Jung in his fight against his nephew. Krishnaraja Wodeyar sent a troop under the command of Berki Venkata Rao, which joined Nasir Jung at Madhugiri. Haidar and Shahabaz were also present in this troop. On the battlefield, Nasir Jung sent an elephant to an ally of his, the Cudappah Nawab and saluted him. But the ambitious nawab had other plans. He received the salute with a volley of bullets that pierced Nasir's chest. Soon, Nasir's head impaled on a spear announced his fate to his army. This sudden turnaround on the nawab's part comes as no surprise. The Frenchman Dupleix is said to have encouraged sedition among Nasir's army and allies through a Brahmin intermediary, Ramadas of Srikakulam. Discontented at the way he treated them, the Pathan nawabs of Cudappah, Kurnool and Savanur were the chef architects in the conspiracy to kill Nasir. In fact, as John Malcolm writes:

> Dupleix had evinced throughout these extra-ordinary scenes a mixture of European and Asiatic character, which marked him as the fittest of all instruments for a government which cherished a wish, as it appeared the French did at this period, to obtain through the influence of alliances with native states, the superiority over all their European rivals in India; and gained, as he merited, a rich reward from Muzuffer Jung, both by a share in the treasures of the late subadar, and a Commission which constituted him governor over all the countries south of the Kitsna (Krishna river); making Chunda Saheb his deputy of Arcot.

The Early Years of Haidar Ali AD 1734–61

In the huge chaos that ensued, Haidar, along with the aid of the tribal Bedar peons, looted the army of his own ally, Nasir Jung, gaining many camels laden with Akbari *mohurs* (gold coins), 500 muskets and 350 horses. These he brought triumphantly to Srirangapatna and offered a part of the exploits as *nazar* or tribute to the maharaja. This was when the king took notice of this bright young lad whom he had once saved from the clutches of penury and misery. He gifted Haidar three camels laden with *mohurs* as a reward for his services.

Now began Haidar's ascent on the ladder of fortune. There was no looking back. The strife in the Carnatic and shifting loyalties proved that each political player looked out for his own gains alone. But these warring rulers failed to recognise that all this while the advantage lay with the foreign powers supposedly standing by them, but actually nurturing far-sighted dreams and long-term goals.

With Nasir Jung out of the way, the French were satisfied. They had vanquished their rival and his allies. Dupleix was at the height of his fame and was free to complete his designs in the Carnatic. He had a burning desire to vanquish the British and establish French supremacy in South India. He made Muzaffar Jung the nizam and sent a huge force under De Bussy to be stationed at Hyderabad for the nizam's protection. In return, they received large grants and vague titles such as 'Ruler of India south of the Krishna'. Muzaffar's glory was, however, short-lived. He was assassinated and the French ensured the accession of Salabat Jung to the throne. But the bright days of Dupleix's political career were by now on the wane. While Hyderabad had proved to be the lucky charm for French designs, Arcot had other things in store for them.

From Ginjee, where the battle against Nasir Jung had occurred, Muhammad Ali—the son of Anwar-ud-din, the deceased nawab of Arcot—fled to Tiruchirapalli. He was pursued by his rival for the Arcot throne, Chanda Sahib, who besieged the fort of Tiruchirapalli. A desperate Muhammad Ali sent Sheshagiri Pandit to Mysore to beseech the maharaja for help in return for the prosperous and fertile lands of Tiruchirapalli and all the territory extending till the Cape of Comorin. Against the wishes of the maharaja and his brother Devarajayya, Nanjarajayya, tempted by the offer, took his army along with Haidar to aid Muhammad Ali. With 5,000 cavalry and 10,000 infantry they marched towards Tiruchirapalli.

Meanwhile, Chanda Sahib's health declined rapidly. Food was scarce and he saw no advantage in continuing with the siege. Resigned to his fate, he mildly left all authority in the hands of his officers. He requested the Tanjorean General Monajee to help him. The latter invited him to his palace, where Chanda Sahib was 'seized and put in irons and the next day was secretly murdered at the instigation, it is said, of Muhammad Ali'.

Muhammad Ali had emerged triumphant in this war of nerves. Fair play demanded that he keep his promise to his allies, who had stood by him in this crisis. But he was not one to count gratitude among his virtues. He procrastinated about handing over Tiruchirapalli each time Nanjarajayya reminded him. After two months, he half-heartedly decided to accede to Mysore, Srirangam and adjacent areas. When the Mysore troops under Katti Gopalaraje Urs reached his palace to sign the terms of the handover, he seized their weapons, turned some of them out of the fort and even fired a few bullets at the Mysore army.

Nanjarajayya was enraged. His entire professional honour was at stake. It had been his brainchild to enter this conflict, despite opposition from all sides. He had named Tiruchirapalli as the prize for the involvement. So he wanted Tiruchirapalli at any cost. Sensing that the French were licking their wounds in the aftermath of their ally, Chanda Sahib's assassination, he decided to take their help from Pondicherry to annex the land.

The British troops under Dalton and Lawrence naturally aligned themselves with Muhammad Ali and attacked the Mysorean troops on 10 May 1753. Veeranna, the chief commander of the Mysore forces, yielded to temptations offered by the British and turned traitor. Dupleix sent 3,000 of Morari Rao Ghorpade's corps, 300 Europeans and 100 regular sepoys for Nanjarajayya's help, attacked Lawrence and blocked supplies from reaching the enemy. Lawrence withdrew. With the British dithering, Muhammad Ali had only one strategy for survival—to break the strength of the allied opposition and weaken them. He and the raja of Tanjore prevailed upon Morari Rao to leave the Mysorean forces and join them. A shrewd man, Rao knew that taking sides would not bring him material benefits. It was a war of equals and which way the pendulum would swing was anybody's guess. He knew that the worthless campaign at Tiruchirapalli had emptied the Mysore treasury and that Devarajayya would be unable to settle his dues. Seizing the chance, he declared his intention to quit the Mysore forces and demanded the settlement of his arrears. On 11 May 1754, he left the Mysore troops, but not before taking another three lakhs from Muhammad Ali for promising that he would never step into the Payeenghat region of the Carnatic again. He had also taken about half a lakh from Nanjarajayya before withdrawing. Thus, in two men's war, the third party profited the most.

By 14 April 1755, Nanjarajayya and the troops were recalled to Mysore. The four-year-old thriftless campaign, which was largely Nanjarajayya's personal ego-aggrandisement agenda, had impoverished the state treasury. It was a political debacle from which Nanjarajayya never did recover. In the process, Mysore's position became more and more susceptible. Always alert to weakness, the Marathas under the peshwas contemplated an attack on the impoverished and war-fatigued kingdom. Meanwhile, Salabat Jung attacked Mysore along with the French armies, who had ironically supported Mysorean troops in the four-year-long confusion at Tiruchirapalli. With the army away at the Tiruchirapalli siege, Devarajayya had to pay Rs 56 lakh to Salabat Jung. But the treasury was exhausted. Thus plates and jewels from temples, as well as jewellery and precious items belonging to the royal family were pawned to send Salabat away. Despite all these efforts, only one-third of the said amount could be realised. Loans from *sowcars* (the moneylenders and unofficial bankers of the times) became necessary to buy Mysore's freedom. The once magnificent kingdom of Mysore had been reduced to total bankruptcy and helplessness.

The expensive campaign in the Carnatic took most of the sheen off all the major players. The French retained their territorial possessions and their special position in Hyderabad, but their desire to gain a chunk of the Carnatic and vanquish the British was throttled. The French reputation for superiority was destroyed. The relative positions of the two European players were reversed. They had played a major role in Indian politics and one of them emerged successful. This totally discredited the Indian rulers, whose existence was now obviously irrelevant to the success or defeat of the Europeans. This was a huge morale-booster for the foreign powers. They grabbed this opportunity for further expansion. The fact that the Indians used their public offices to settle personal scores and rivalries made it all the more lucrative to intervene in all existing disputes or to create them if they didn't exist, thus usurping all powers of the hitherto ally. This seemed to be the constant mantra for success.

Indian soil was not virgin and invasions had been common ever since the time of Alexander the Great right down to Muslim invasions. But this was perhaps the first time India and Indians had to contend with European diplomacy. Muslim rulers who decided to make India their home took an interest in her existing culture and, by a process of exchange and integration, fostered fresh developments, like the Hindustani classical style, which was born out of Indian *dhrupad* and Persian/Arabic music, and the emergence of a new literary language, Urdu.

But with the European powers this was not the case. They meant business and did not care for local traditions or culture. For them, India was the goose that laid golden eggs and they wanted to exploit her fully before having her for dinner. It was beyond the political acumen of the petty rulers of India to sense this, primarily because they couldn't see beyond their personal ego clashes with warring neighbours or ambitious relatives. They lent themselves to European exploitation time and again and this fact was borne out in the Deccan as well. The Indians were the losers in this game—the Nizam became a puppet, Mysore's maharaja was totally discredited and so was the architect of the debacle, Nanjarajayya, who had undoubtedly committed political suicide.

If there were two parties which emerged triumphant, they were the British forces and, of course, the undaunted Haidar Ali. Their success in southern India encouraged the British to engage their rivals in other parts of India as well. They turned their attention eastwards, to Bengal. In the Battle of Plassey (1757), the British under Robert Clive won a convincing victory over Nawab Siraj-ud-daulah—the successor of the Mughal viceroy, who had declared his independence. This laid the foundations of the British empire in India. Bengal then consisted of modern-day West Bengal, Bangladesh, Assam, Bihar and Orissa. It was a large geographical expanse, extremely profitable from an agrarian and industrial viewpoint. Thus, from trader to intervener in political disputes to a full-fledged political entity—the metamorphosis of the English East India Company was complete. And luckily for them, there was no looking back.

For Haidar, it was a golden period. He had caught the maharaja's attention from the time he displayed his valour and craftiness in the battle against Nasir Jung. His was a classic case of running with the hare and hunting with the hound. Both the maharaja and Nanjarajayya, who hated each other from the depths of their hearts, seemed to repose the greatest trust in Haidar and his acumen. Not one to fall short when presented with opportunity, Haidar used it to the fullest. He had come a long way since the time he was beaten upon, locked in the *nagara* by Abbas Quli Khan. He was fiercely ambitious and luck was seemingly on his side. Such was the goodwill he had earned in the eyes of the maharaja that, sensing trouble in and around Dindigul due to British presence, Haidar was dispatched by the king to the region as the foujdar or commander. The raja bestowed on him the title of 'Bahaddar'—the Brave. Erode, Satyamangalam, and Dharapuram, which was worth three lakh Gopalivarahas, came under his jurisdiction. The raja perhaps saw Haidar as a possible bulwark against the impulsive and corrupt brothers he was so averse to dealing with.

In 1755, Haidar left for Dindigul with 25,000 horse, 3,000 infantry, 2,000 peons, and 4 guns, defeating the rebellious Palegars on the way. Haidar maintained a regular force of Pindaris and Bedar peons who, Wilks observes, were not generally augmented with regular pay, surviving on looted money instead. Tribal class that they were, they remained loyal to the master who gave them the chance to loot and earn their livelihood. Haidar had a good team to assist him as well, which included his childhood friend Ghazi Khan. He left his old friend and Brahmin *mustaddi* (accountant) Khande Rao at Srirangapatna. Khande Rao, Haidar's close confidante, was an expert manager of accounts, strategy and other aspects of statecraft. The accountant was bold, sagacious and individualistic. He knew how to convert unprofitable wars into a regular stream of cash flows. Haidar, himself illiterate and ill at ease with numbers, marvelled at Rao's mathematical and computation skills. The Pindaris on their part maintained a good rapport with both Rao and Haidar. They got their regular pay and half the looted booty—a profitable arrangement for all parties.

On the personal front as well, Haidar couldn't have asked for more. He had been childless for long and that was a source of worry for him. His pretty wife Fakhrunnissa had tried all kinds of prayers at temples and *dargahs* to beget a son. Finally, she reached the tomb of the Sufi saint Tipu Mastan Oulia at Kolar, known to be rather strange. There was an unwritten law that women could never enter the tomb, as the Sufi saint had been a strange man who had lived on twigs and herbs, renounced worldly pleasures, lived on a hilltop and abhorred women. But the daring Fakhrunnissa made the arduous journey to Kolar to seek the blessings of Oulia. She vowed at the tomb that if she were blessed with a son, she would hand him over to the path of Sufism and Godhead. Finally, her many prayer bells and rosary beads were answered and the couple was blessed with a son on 20 November 1750. They named him Tipu, after

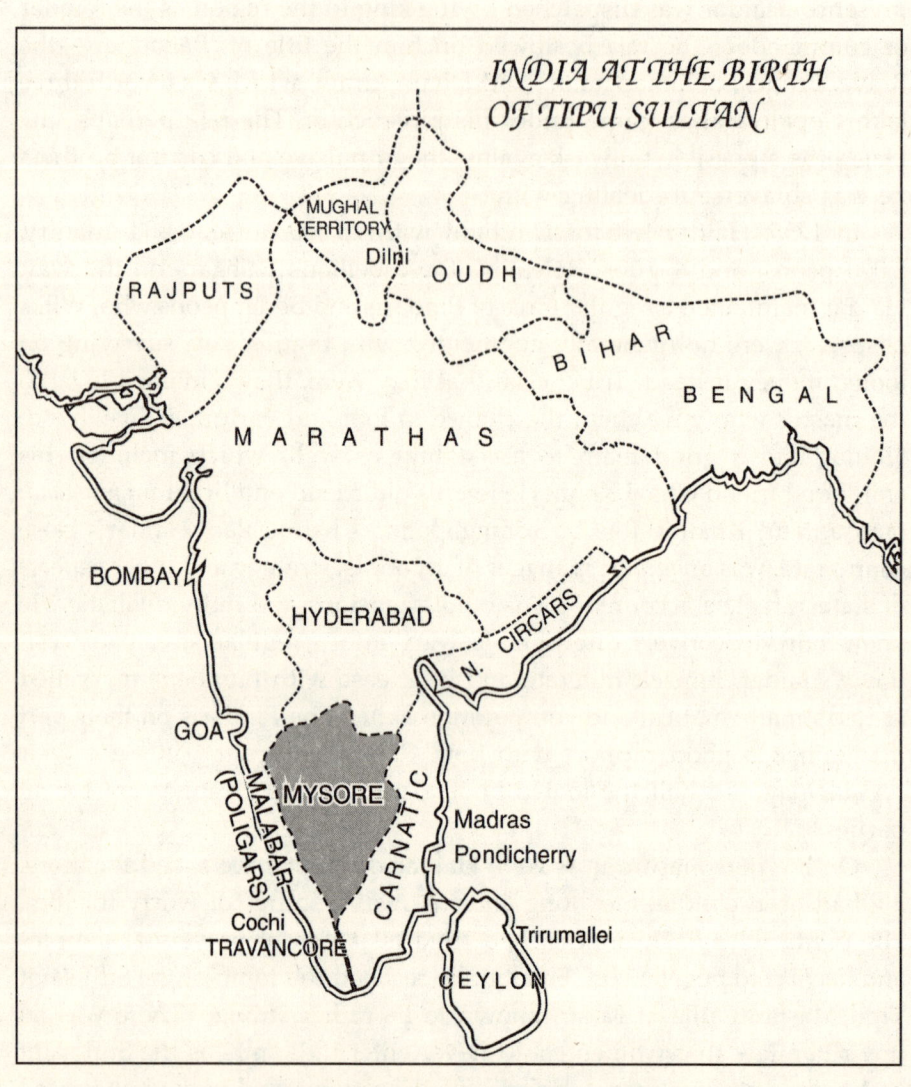

India at the birth of Tippu Sultan, 1750
(Maps are artistic recreations made at Suhaas Graphics, Bangalore)

their patron saint. The infant seemed to usher in good luck for Haidar, because his career graph soared ever upwards after his birth.

At Dindigul, Haidar obtained skilled French artificers to reorganise arsenal and artillery from Tiruchirapalli, Pondicherry and Srirangam, realising that military might was quintessential for success. On the other hand, at Srirangapatna, Khande Rao wasn't content playing second fiddle to Haidar. He had ambitions for himself. He exaggerated the political crisis and Haidar's exploits at Dindigul. He spun fictitious tales to poison Nanjarajayya against Haidar, urging him to augment the forces and use revenues from other *taluks* for the purpose.

Meanwhile, the maharaja was feeling suffocated—finding it intolerable to leave the affairs of the kingdom to people, like the vicious brothers who held him as a virtual captive. Nanjarajayya had fallen from grace after leading the worthless campaign at Tiruchirapalli against the king's wishes, which ended up draining the exchequer. So he decided to strip them of their powers. But receiving intelligence of this plan well in advance, Nanjarajayya pleaded with his brother, Devarajayya to quash the idea. The latter was already most unpopular for his shameful acts against the earlier Maharaja Chamaraja. So in a holier than thou approach, he refused to support Nanjarajayya.

Nanjarajayya decided to carry on with his clandestine plans all by himself. He lined up his forces near the palace and shot at its door, which had been locked from within by the bewildered inmates when they heard about the forces gathering outside. Entering the palace, he found the so-called defenders of the palace hiding in the *zenana*, the women's quarters. He cut off the ears and noses of these cowardly soldiers, right in the presence of the maharaja, who, though seated on a bejewelled throne, was in a most unenviable and helpless position, suffering the torment of treachery. This was the last straw for the maharaja as far as Nanjarajayya—whom he never trusted again—and Devarajayya were concerned. The latter left Srirangapatna for Satyamangalam in 1757 with his family, 1,000 cavalry and 2,000 infantry. The fortunes of Haidar and those of his political mentor, friend, philosopher and guide, Nanjarajayya, seemed to be inversely proportional to each other. What Nanjarajayya achieved with this action and why he indulged in repeated political suicide is unknown. Perhaps the only explanation is that he was impulsive, and not given to careful and deft strategising.

The royal treasury bore the brunt of repeated wars and political instability. The coffers were empty and the king couldn't even pay their regular salaries to the soldiers. In 1757, the troops at Srirangapatna revolted. They demanded that their wages be paid. The maharaja turned to Haidar, his blue-eyed boy, to come to the capital to pacify the troops and work out a settlement. Haidar did as required, thus elevating his status in the king's eyes. But it is said that misfortune seldom comes alone. No sooner had the problem of the soldiers' salary been resolved than the Marathas under Peshwa Balaji Rao attacked Mysore in March 1757. Nanjarajayya agreed to pay thirty-two lakhs to send them back, but could realise only five lakhs. To pay the rest he surrendered Nagamangala, Belur, Kadur, Chikkanayakanahalli, Huliyurudurga and nine other *taluks*. The Marathas departed but left behind their agents to exact the revenue from these districts. Mysore's position thus grew weaker with every passing day. Each invasion and the knee-jerk reaction to it exposed the hollowness of state polity.

But Haidar's fame had spread across the borders. The Nair raja of Palghat requested Haidar's help to defeat his enemies, the raja of Cochin and the Zamorin of Calicut. So he dispatched a unit of 2,000 horse, 5,000 infantry and 5 guns under his brother-in-law Mokdum Saib's command. The two rajas were vanquished and decided to end the war in favour of peace, agreeing to restore all the territory they had taken from the Palaghat Nair Raja and make a payment of 12 lakhs. But they despised the idea of having terms dictated to them by a Muslim and wrote to Devarajayya, who still seemed to call the shots from Satyamangalam. Devarajayya sent his trusted Rajput accomplice Hari Singh to replace Mokdum Saib.

This of course did not go down well with Haidar. He disliked Hari Singh anyway and it angered him that even though he himself had won the war and appointed Mokdum Saib as the negotiator, his wishes were ignored. Haidar made an attempt to reconcile Devarajayya and Nanjarajayya, who had fallen out with each other over what he saw as a non-issue. Devarajayya haughtily rejected the proposal. But Haidar besieged the fort at Satyamangalam and fired a few shots which scared him out of his hideout. In establishing peace between the two brothers, Haidar actually managed to intimidate Devarajayya, and so got back at him for his interference in Haidar's matters.

In March 1758, Haidar and his men ascended the Ghats through the Gejjelhutty Pass, reached Hardanahalli, where they halted for fifteen days, and reached Mysore. Leaving Devarajayya there, Haidar and Khande Rao proceeded to Srirangapatna. It was the same old issue of troops protesting over pay. Each time this happened, Haidar would use his good office with the soldiers and the raja would sail through the crisis. But this time it had assumed larger proportions. The men had seated themselves in a *dharna* outside Nanjarajayya's house, cutting off supplies of food, water and provisions to the residents. Nanjarajayya sent frantic messages to Haidar, who with his rhetoric and glib talk, pacified them and promised to pay them their arrears soon.

From Mysore, Devarajayya sent his conditions for reunion with his brother—demanding a public atonement for the latter's indecent behaviour with the royal family. He of course conveniently forgot his own similar actions with another member of the royal family. At a special durbar in Srirangapatna, the maharaja issued two political documents in favour of Nanjarajayya, which clearly prove the evils of excessive devolution of power on the dalavoy, the *bhashapatra* or deed of promise and the *nambige niroopa* or order of assurance. A salute was fired from all the guns of the garrison to announce that the maharaja had forgiven Nanjarajayya and recruited him back into service.

It is impossible to believe that the king, who had been humiliated in the worst possible manner, could have pardoned the perpetrator of such an act. It was clearly a stage-managed show organised at Haidar's behest. This was his way of getting back at his erstwhile mentor and also proved the extent of Haidar's influence on the king's decisions—something the Queen Mother Devajammanni and Queen Lakshmammanni abhorred. On 13 June 1758, the king forgave the two brothers. A mere six days later, on 19 June, Devarajayya died of dropsy. Haidar was made the dalavoy. Nanjarajayya was a totally crestfallen man. His own misadventures, the pandemonium and confusion in the army, the bankruptcy of the kingdom, and the death of his brother broke him completely. He considered Haidar his only source of support in this mess.

Meanwhile, Hari Singh failed to get the stipulated twelve lakhs from the Rajas in Kerala due to the untimely death of his mentor Devarajayya. He left Malabar for Avanasi in Coimbatore on the pretext of resting the troops but had secret plans of quitting the Mysorean service for good and joining the raja of Tanjore. Haidar sent Mokdum Saib with a large army and the latter gleefully killed his long-time rival Hari Singh at Avanasi, looted his camp and obtained 300 horses, 1,000 muskets and 3 guns.

Haidar urged Nanjarajayya to secure to him the due payment of three lakhs, which Devarajayya had borrowed from the *sowcars*. Nanjarajayya put up the matter before the king, who readily agreed and allotted the revenues of Coimbatore to Haidar to clear the debt.

In early 1759, peril once again struck Mysore in the form of the Maratha invasion under Gopal Hari and Ananda Rao Raste. They attacked Mysore, besieged Bangalore and occupied Chennapatna. With the treasury virtually bled dry and the troops on their perennial protests, Nanjarajayya couldn't resort to his usual defence—paying off the enemy. So Haidar was called for help. He stationed his troops at the forts of Maddur and Malavally under Latif Ali Beg and his uncle Mir Ibrahim respectively. Latif's spies were on the move and informed Haidar of the arrangement of the Maratha troops. Haidar had perfected the art of guerrilla warfare and surprise attacks in the dead of night. He used these tactics against the Marathas repeatedly and the war carried on for over three months. The Marathas began losing their patience; they were also running out of food supplies. Gopal Hari finally agreed to retreat after claiming thirty-two lakhs, which Haidar coughed up through loans from *sowcars*.

Haidar's sagacity, as compared to the hastiness of the capricious and quirky Nanjarajayya, did not go unnoticed by the maharaja. He invited Haidar to a specially ordered durbar in 1759 and gave him the title of 'Nawab Haidar Ali Khan Bahaddar', presenting him with horses, elephants, Mahtab Khillats and Naubats, which were awards and titles accompanied by cash rewards for the victorious soldiers. Haidar continued his journey up the political ladder. He got Bangalore as *jagir*. He annexed the districts of Baramahal Javajipalaya, Tiruputtoor, Krishnagiri and 13 other places to Mysore.

Mostly away on political campaigns, Haidar remained blissfully ignorant of the games his accountant was playing. Stationed in Srirangapatna, Khande Rao had ample opportunity to meet the raja and his Queen Mother Devajammanni, an astute lady who wanted to free Mysore from Haidar's clutches. She could not bear the fact that a Muslim, whom they had bought for a few varahas just a couple of years ago, had the audacity to exercise such influence over matters of state, marginalising the king himself. Her anger against Nanjarajayya was more pronounced, for, apart from her grievances against him for his many misadventures and political follies, she also considered him the reason for Haidar's ascent. The two thought that Nanjarajayya was the oxygen that kept Haidar

The giant Nandi statue atop the Chamundi Hills

Devaraja Wodeyar
(1659-73)

Chikkadevaraja Wodeyar
(1673-1704)

The European ships of exploration

The emblem of the English East India Company

Kempegowda, the founder of the city of Bangalore

Kempegowda's watchtower at Lal Bagh, Bangalore

The Attara Kacheri—the High Court Building in Bangalore that keeps alive the memory of Chikkadevaraja

Dodda Krishnaraja Wodeyar (1714-32)

Kanthirava Narasaraja Wodeyar II (1704-14)

Immadi Krishnaraja Wodeyar (1734-66)

Chamaraja Wodeyar VII (1732-34)

Dupleix: the master strategist

Nanjaraja Wodeyar (1766-70)

Muhammad Ali Khan Walahjah: the wily Nawab

A painting of Tipu in his younger days

Bettada Chamaraja Wodeyar VIII (1770-76)

'Khasa' Chamaraja Wodeyar IX (1776-96): the chosen man

The first governor general of India, Warren Hastings

Sir Eyre Coote

A mural of the Battle of Polilur on the walls of the Daria Daulat Bagh in Srirangapatna

Haidar's tomb in the Lal Bagh garden: an artist's impression

Dungeons of death: Srirangapatna

Tipu Sultan: Supreme dictator of the Sultanat-e-Khudadad Mysore

Lord Cornwallis

An artist's impression of the northern entrance to the Bangalore fort

Tearful farewell: sons of Tipu being surrendered as hostages to Lord Cornwallis

Kille Venkataramana Swamy temple: the God that brought about change

The breach in the fort wall that welcomed the British in 1799

A view of the once invincible fort wall of Srirangapatna

Distant view of Seringapatam from Meadow's redoubt

West View of Seringapatam from the middle of the river

War scene: the final storming of the Sriran gapatna fort, 1799

The last fight of a chivalrous hero: Tipu defends his kingdom and honour

Identification of the body of Tipu

Keeping Tipu's memory alive

Grieving family members of Tipu

The Obelisk: British victory monument at Srirangapatna

Resting in peace: Tipu with his parents, Gumbaz, Srirangapatna

Fateh Haidar *Abdul Khaliq*

Mahizuddin *Moizuddin*

The Tiger of Mysore

Inner view of the Daria Daulat Bagh in Srirangapatna

Tipu's toy

The Sword of Tipu Sultan

Masjid-e-Ala, Srirangapatna

Gumbaz, Srirangapatna

alive and that cutting off the former would automatically bring the latter to his knees. They conspired against Nanjarajayya by encouraging troop anger against him for his lax dealings in salary matters.

But little did Rani Devajammanni know that Haidar had other plans in mind. Having reached a degree of self-sufficiency and prominence, he no longer considered Nanjarajayya his mentor. He was in fact embarrassed to be associated with a man who had brought disrepute upon himself and the royal family and earned public abhorrence. So, even before the Queen Mother and Khande Rao could get their act together, Haidar had embarked on his agenda to see his former political mentor out of the way. With a show of pressure and false protests followed by an interview with the maharaja, he put forth the demand that Nanjarajayya must surrender his office, retaining only the title of Sarvadhikari, that he should have a 3 lakh pagoda yielding *jagir* to maintain 1,000 horse and 300 infantry, and that he should leave the capital immediately.

Caught totally unawares by this volte-face Nanjarajayya was forced to surrender. He left Srirangapatna in June 1759 for Nanjanagud to worship the God there, but stopped at Mysore due to illness. Knowing that this could be a ruse to linger on, Haidar took great exception to his stay at Mysore and ordered him to proceed without further delay. Nanjarajayya was furious. He sent back a message saying that he took orders only from the maharaja and none other. Haidar besieged the fort at Mysore and demanded that Nanjarajayya surrender the Sannad* of his office, which the latter was unwilling to relinquish as it had come down the generations to him. Haidar then opened fire with all arms, guns and muskets on the fort. Once friends, the two now fought for more than three months.

Lack of provisions and ammunition finally compelled Nanjarajayya to give up. He, along with his family, reached Haidar's camp as hostages. Haidar decided to let them live at Konanur and give them a *jagir* on the western frontier of Mysore. Nanjarajayya left for Konanur in utter disbelief and disgust at the way the tide had turned against him, cursing himself for having supported such an ungrateful wretch as Haidar. The maharaja granted Haidar further allotments of revenue to settle arrears and for regular pay for the troops. He appointed Khande Rao as Haidar's pradhan—his second-in-command. Nearly half of Mysore's territories

---

* The official seal.

came under Haidar's jurisdiction. Politically, Nanjarajayya was finished and he knew that better than anyone else.

It is said that in politics there aren't any permanent friends or enemies, only permanent interests. Haidar seemed to personify this more than anyone else. No one could switch sides at convenience as well as Haidar. He used Nanjarajayya as the ladder to his political success, used him to impress the ruler, and once the king's favour was won, he conveniently dumped Nanjarajayya. Little did Haidar realise, however, that many of his own colleagues could have been playing the same game with him as well.

THE FINAL BLOW: KHANDE RAO'S TREACHERY

Rani Devajammanni was dumbstruck by the chameleon traits of political opportunism that Haidar had displayed. Her efforts had been futile but she was not the kind to be cowed down so easily. She knew about the bitterness between Khande Rao and Haidar. Like the *chitu* bird that sits waiting for the rain, she was on the lookout for an opportunity to trap Haidar. And luckily for her, the opportunity came sooner rather than later. Haidar was camping with fewer troops than usual since a major section of his troops had been dispatched to help the French against the British. Seizing the opportunity, Devajammanni called on the maharaja and Khande Rao. She managed to convince the maharaja about the motives of the man he had been favouring all through. If he could betray his political mentor and friend, he could do the same any day with his benefactor, the man who had bought him a couple of decades ago. The maharaja was now certain that scruples were not Haidar's priority. He began to see some merit in this argument against Haidar and agreed to partner his adoptive mother in her plans.

The three of them secretly congregated at the Sri Ranganatha Swamy Temple at Srirangapatna. In the inner recesses of the ancient temple, an elaborate plot was hatched and the three vowed to overthrow Haidar. The *Annals* record that many chiefs, such as Kollegal Veeranna Shetty, Pradhan Venkatapathayya and others were also a part of this plot. It was thought that the presence of the Maratha forces under Visajee Pandit Binniwale at Doddaballapur was a good omen, as it would distract Haidar's attention. A secret army was also appointed to assist the maharaja to overthrow Haidar. In the dead of night, plans and plots were outlined, Devajammanni being the coordinator of this meeting. With their plans made, the group dispersed, waiting anxiously for daybreak when they would execute their plans.

On the fateful morning of 12 August 1760 Haidar, as usual, reached the fort after his pre-dawn exercises, but found that the gates would not be opened for him and also that intimidating gunshots were being fired from the top of the fort, striking close to where he stood, but luckily not hitting him. Completely shaken, he summoned Khande Rao and learnt that it was Khande Rao himself directing the fire from the ramparts! Realising Rao's treachery, he rushed with a small band of the troops who had accompanied him on his exercises and found cover in a hut out of reach of the ongoing firing. He used the boats kept in the hut to get away. Khande Rao's plan was to invite the Marathas at this very moment and capture him while Haidar was mentally and militarily weak. But as luck would have it for Rao, there was a delay in the arrival of the Maratha troops, giving Haidar ample time to flee.

Before leaving, he tried to negotiate with Rao, telling the latter that he owed his present success to him (Haidar) and that he had admired him more than anyone else in his life for his shrewd brain. But Rao was nonchalant. He told Haidar matter-of-factly that it was all being done as per the maharaja's wishes and was by no means a personal grudge; that the maharaja and his mother considered Haidar a nuisance now and wished him to quit the service of Mysore and seek employment elsewhere. Haidar knew that no amount of coaxing and flattering could budge Khande Rao. So he secretly made his way out and managed to reach the opposite side of the river before nightfall. Some say he swam the entire distance. He also managed to ship across a good deal of jewellery, money on 100 horses with six officers, two camel *harkars* and twenty spare horses. Khande Rao had clearly not been as vigilant as required. The slip between the cup and the lip was evident— plotting conspiracies in dark corners is easy, executing them is daunting. Before the Marathas could arrive, Haidar was out of reach. Khande Rao was astonished to find Haidar's apartments deserted; he looted his treasures and imprisoned the family Haidar had left behind, which included, among others, Haidar's nine-year-old son Tipu and Karim, his second son, prematurely born just the previous day.

Haidar went to Anekal and, with his commander Ismail Ali, reached Bangalore, where the killedar, Kabir Beg, was a loyalist. He took a loan of 4 lakhs from the *sowcars* of Bangalore and tried to reorganise his army.

It was a decisive phase for him. His entire life and its achievements were at stake and losing them to a traitor was the last thing he could swallow. He was determined to win this battle of nerves. His faithful accomplice Mokdum Saib, on his way to Bangalore, was stopped at Baramahal by the Maratha forces under Visajee Pandit and Gopal Hari. Mokdum rushed for shelter to the Anchetidurga Fort from where he sent an urgent message seeking reinforcements for Haidar that should be commanded by Fazalullah Khan. At this juncture, Haidar was helpless and could have been easily defeated.

But mysterious are the ways of fate. It was the year 1761, the time of the Third Battle of Panipat, where the Marathas suffered great reverses against the invader Ahmed Shah Abdali. The peshwa at Pune recalled all detachments of Marathas on expedition to assemble at Pune. The Marathas hence negotiated with Haidar that they would leave Mysore if he gave them Baramahal and three lakhs. On receiving the news of Visajee Pandit being summoned back to Pune by the peshwa and of the debacle of the Marathas at Panipat, Haidar decided to conveniently 'forget' paying the said dues to Visajee Pandit. The defeat of the Marathas at Panipat created a huge political vacuum and Haidar took full advantage of their absence in the south by defeating all their allies and regaining his lost reputation.

Haidar then requested the French to help him and a French force of 200 cavalry and 100 infantry joined him at Nanjangud. Buoyed by his resurgent good luck, he decided to make his way back and reclaim what he had lost. He crossed the Cauvery at Sosale, where Khande Rao mounted a surprise attack on him. Haidar was defeated in the very first encounter. Terrified by this defeat he rushed to his hitherto friend-turned-foe, Nanjarajayya's house and fell at his feet begging pardon for his treachery and ingratitude. Nanjarajayya was as opportunistic as Haidar. He knew that he had nothing left to lose, that Haidar would somehow triumph over these troubles and that riding piggyback on him in the future would be the best saving grace for Nanjarajayya. So he conveniently forgot Haidar's past actions, forgave him, and gave him 2,000 cavalry and infantry. He also dispatched letters under the forged seal of the king conveying the idea that he would be reinstated as sarvadhikari with Haidar as his dalavoy.

Khande Rao was camping at Katte Malalavadi, twenty-six miles southwest of Srirangapatna, with a view to looting Nanjarajayya's possessions, when he came to know that Haidar was being supported by him. Haidar prepared false letters with the seal of Nanjarajayya to capture Khande Rao. These letters were sent to Khande Rao's army in the name of Sarvadhikari Nanjarajayya. The army was dismayed. They had earlier received letters in the name of the maharaja that Nanjarajayya had been reinstalled as sarvadhikari and it would therefore be their duty to act according to the sarvadhikari's orders and capture their own commander, Khande Rao. Hearing about the confusion in his own army, Khande Rao fled to Srirangapatna in February 1761 with his army in hot pursuit. Haidar's forces, meanwhile, made surprise attacks on the leaderless and disorganised army of Khande Rao. Haidar descended from the Ghats through Gejjelhutty Pass to reclaim all the territory he had lost to Khande Rao, receiving large amounts of *danda* or fine from Rao's allies.

Haidar reached Khande Rao's camp and made a false appeal of negotiation at Chandgal in late 1761. He camped on the opposite side of the river and every evening, for eight days, pretended to be exercising his troops. On the eighth day, on the pretext of parade, he crossed the river and made a sudden attack on Khande Rao's army, seizing his equipment and troops. Khande Rao was imprisoned. Haidar, with his prize hostage, reached Ganjam in Srirangapatna and wrote to the maharaja:

> Khande Rao was my servant initially. But since he is now under your Highness's service, I request you to surrender him to me and pay my dues and I will gladly leave Mysore to find employment elsewhere if that is what your Highness wishes.

But the financially bankrupt and impoverished maharaja had no funds to pay him the balance and agreed to surrender Khande Rao instead.

On the opportune date, Haidar presented himself before the maharaja in a private sitting of his court. Perhaps never before had the king of Mysore felt so helpless and embarrassed. The man he and his family had tried to eliminate through their supposedly astute plan was there right before them, triumphant and defiant. Standing beside him in chains was the confidante who had been the royal family's partner in sin, Khande Rao. Rani Devajammanni couldn't conceal her anguish when she saw her loyalist in such misery. The maharaja had little option but to surrender the administrative powers of his kingdom to his favourite. He was in no position to pay Haidar off and dispense with his services and Haidar ensured that he demanded his pound of flesh in true earnest. Krishnaraja

Wodeyar's heart sank as he placed the royal *firman* that authorised the transition of power into Haidar's hands. At the same time wails were heard from the ladies' quarters upstairs. Queen Mother Devajammanni and the young Rani Lakshmammanni couldn't believe their eyes and had burst into tears.

The maharaja couldn't afford that luxury, however, and kept a straight face even as he passed on secret documents of the kingdom and those related to the treasury into the usurper's custody. 'Is this the helpless boy we bought a couple of decades back?' was the constant question that the maharaja's grim and stoic face seemed to ask. But then, he had only himself to blame for the sad state of affairs. Fortune has an uncanny tendency to favour the brave and if there was one virtue that the Wodeyar successors of Chikkadevaraja singularly lacked, it was courage and chivalry. After all, had Krishnaraja not capitulated to the machinations of his capricious dalavoys and used different office bearers as pawns and buffers in the political game of chess, this day of ignominy would never have dawned upon him.

This decisive event of 1761 marked the transfer of the kingdom's administration to Haidar's control. He deposed the maharaja and assumed the powers of a supreme dictator. The maharaja reserved a *jagir* yielding three lakh Pagodas for the nominal maintenance of the royal family and a *jagir* worth one lakh for Nanjarajayya. There was much drama before handing Khande Rao over to Haidar. Here was the man who had helped the royals in all their endeavours, but could not be saved by his own benefactors. The least they could do was request Haidar to treat him well. The maharaja and Queen Mother Devajammanni made Haidar promise not to take harsh action against Khande Rao. Haidar replied: 'Khande Rao is my man. I will look after him as mercifully and endearingly as I would look after my parrot.'

He kept his promise. Khande Rao was imprisoned in a huge iron cage and fed only milk and rice for the rest of his life.

9

HAIDAR ALI: THE SUPREME DICTATOR
AD 1761-82

The Muslim Interregnum in Mysore's history, as it is called, had begun with Haidar assuming supreme charge of the kingdom. The centuries-old reign of the Wodeyars had ended and they had only themselves to blame for this situation. After Chikkadevaraja Wodeyar the kings— none of whom deserved their posts—let power slip into the hands of the powerful dalavoys. Finally, it was Haidar who emerged successful. However, he stopped short of assuming the title of king. He continued to act on behalf of the maharaja, who was retained as the nominal or titular head of state. There could be two reasons for this. For all his lack of gratitude to others in the past, Haidar had immense respect for the maharaja. After all, it was this man who had saved his family from disaster in his childhood. To depose him completely and occupy his place was perhaps something his conscience didn't allow. The other reason was that the people still held the royal family in great esteem. It would have been unthinkable for them to be ruled by a Muslim upstart whom their benevolent ruler had bought a decade or two back. Fearing public outcry against such a brazen act, Haidar decided that he had nothing to lose in allowing the titular head to carry on. Orders would be issued in the maharaja's name though it was he who was instrumental in drafting those orders. Within twelve years of his debut in Mysorean politics, Haidar reached the pinnacle of success that had eluded the Nanjarajayyas and Devarajayyas of the world, despite their best efforts. His fate seemed to shine throughout his political career, as he ascended rung by rung the ladder of fortune. History has seen few like Haidar, who turned every adversity to his own advantage.

HAIDAR ALI IN CHARGE

Haidar's first act after taking over the reins of the kingdom was to consolidate and expand its frontiers. He wanted to establish Mysore as a force in the Carnatic. He helped Basalat Jung, a successor of the nizam, to conquer Hosakote from the Marathas. The latter were still reeling under the tremendous blow to their power and prestige after the Third Battle of Panipat, where Ahmad Shah Abdali vanquished them totally. Haidar's next target was Doddaballapur, which was under Killedar Abbas Quli Khan. Quli Khan fled to Madras upon hearing of this attack, though he left his ailing mother and family behind. Haidar conquered Doddaballapur without firing a single gunshot, but magnanimously promised his enemy's old mother that he would treat them with all the respect they deserved. He then conquered Sira from Maratha Killedar Triumbak Krishna, defeated the combined forces of Morari Rao of Gutti and the Palegar of Chikkaballapur and annexed the township to Mysore. Haidar then made his way towards Chitradurga. Advisors to Madakari Nayak V, the Palegar of Chitradurga, advised him not to antagonise Haidar and so the former paid off two lakhs Varahas to send him away. Haidar emerged victorious in a series of battles with the kings of Bidnaur, Hardanahalli and Rayadurga.

In the war camp, Madakari Nayak introduced Haidar to one Chennabasavayya, described as the adopted son of Raja Basavappa Nayak of Ikkeri (also called Keladi). The kingdom of Ikkeri shared a long and stressful relationship with Mysore under the Wodeyars. It was among the many Hindu principalities that sprang to prominence under the leadership of Chowda and Bhadra after the fall of Vijayanagara. The ruler Basavappa Nayak (1739–55) was dead and his adopted son Chennabasavayya had been put on the throne. But intrigues had reached a climax under the dead king's widow, Rani Veerammaji. She was unpopular not only among the subjects but also among the leading officers and influential persons of the kingdom due to her affairs with the state's Dewan Nimbayya. The last straw was when she allegedly got the adopted son Chennabasavayya murdered, hoping to usurp the reigns of the kingdom.

If Chennabasavayya was murdered, who was the man introduced to Haidar in his war camp?

He was an impostor propped up by the Chitradurga chieftain who had an axe to grind with Rani Chennammaji. Haidar did not care about the true heir to the throne of Ikkeri. He wanted to make as much hay while the sun shone. He promised the fake Chennabasavayya freedom from the adoptive mother who had thrown him out of power. He attacked Ikkeri in 1763, dividing his troops into four columns. The rani had imprisoned one Linganna, a faithful minister of the deceased raja, whom Haidar freed. In his gratitude, Linganna shared all the information on secret routes to the fort with Haidar.

The rani tried to negotiate with Haidar but the latter replied that he would return to Srirangapatna and lift the siege only if she handed over Keladi, as compensation for which she would receive a residence at Srirangapatna. The rani proudly rejected the offer and resolved to defend her kingdom. The Nawab of Savanur Abdul Hakim Khan supported her. Haidar besieged the fort but the clever rani held it for a year. Fearing the onset of the monsoon, Haidar ordered the troops to attack the fort as fiercely as possible and stream in. The troops did so and this time the rani could not resist the attack. She set the palace on fire, burnt many of her jewellery boxes and pounded her ornaments in an iron mortar lest they fall into the enemy's hands. With Nimbayya and a few other confidantes she fled to the fort of Kavaledurga but was pursued by Haidar. Even here, she held the fort bravely for a month but finally gave up the futile exercise.

As in the past, Haidar conveniently forgot his promises! He sent Rani Veerammaji and Nimbayya as prisoners to the fort of Madhugiri but bundled along Chennabasavayya too, whose cause he had been claiming he represented. Ikkeri was merged with Mysore. Haidar got a large booty from whatever was left after the place was burnt down by Veerammaji—two–three boxes of pearls and diamonds, two boxes of jewelled chains for the foot of an elephant, two sets of gold and silver bells for the necks of royal elephants and two gold saddles were among the things he carried back home after appointing Raja Ramachandra the caretaker of the capital, which he named Bednore or Haidar Nagar.

On his way back, Haidar and Fazalullah Khan attacked the nawab of Savanur to avenge the latter's support to Veerammaji and defeated him, acquiring 'elephants, camels, tents of velvet, bechobas embroidered with gold, Burhampur cloths of great value, arms and ammunition.'

Haidar's attention then turned to the Malabar. But the brave raja of Malabar put up a strong resistance as Haidar arrived at Kodathanad. The Zamorin of Calicut, Raja Mana Vikrama decided to surrender on 11 April 1766 after being vanquished by Haidar. The victorious Haidar demanded twelve lakhs. Meanwhile the Zamorin's troops, believing that their king was already a prisoner, thought it prudent to disappear. The helpless Zamorin could neither make the stipulated payment nor defend his kingdom without an army. Hopeless and defeated, he locked himself in his room and set himself on fire.

The following day, Haidar took over Calicut and appointed Putta Madanna as caretaker. His troops then marched to Coimbatore, subduing the rajas of Cochin, Palaghat, Kottayam and Travancore. Another revolt by the brave Nairs of the Malabar pulled him back to Malabar where the Nairs were defeated in a deadly war and imprisoned. As early as 1765, Haidar entered into an agreement with Raghunath Rao, uncle of Peshwa Madhava Rao, hoping to ensure everlasting peace between Mysore and the Marathas.

While Haidar was engaged in quashing the Nair revolt in Malabar, the Maharaja of Mysore, Immadi Krishnaraja Wodeyar, died in the year 1766 at Srirangapatna. His sudden death dealt a great blow to Queen Mother Devajammanni, who had still hoped to redeem Mysore from Haidar's clutches. She decided to crown Nanjaraja Wodeyar (Kalale Devajammanni and the deceased king's son) as king in 1766, when the boy was merely four years old. Hayavadana Rao, however, makes a different point in *History of Mysore*, Volume III, where Nanjaraja is described as the elder son, aged eighteen at the time of his father's death, and Bettada Chamaraja as the younger son. Rao (1945) believes that Haidar preferred Nanjaraja Wodeyar, even though popular opinion dismissed him as a weakling, favouring instead the younger prince. Of course, Haidar was the one whose opinion mattered—a true king-maker, he always had his way.

Haidar believed that the king of Travancore had instigated the Nair revolt in the Malabar and decided to punish him for his mischief and also extend the domain of Mysore to the coast. By the end of the Nair campaign, in 1765, Haidar returned to Coimbatore and started preparations for the Travancore invasion. The kingdom was ruled by Balarama Varman, the successor of Martanda Varman. Martanda Varman was the maker of the modern state of Travancore who had had his troops disciplined in the European fashion by a Flemish officer called De Lannoy. The state of

Travancore, though small, had an excellent defence mechanism and also the historic fort of Travancore lines or *Netum Kotta*—a forty-mile-long fort. Haidar was determined to make a concerted attack on Travancore and decided to win the British over to his side in this campaign by permitting them to open a factory at Honnavar. He decided to befriend the Marathas and pre-empt a possible Maratha attack on Mysore while he was away. He also wanted to make Nizam Ali into an ally through their common friend Mahfuz Khan. But no sooner did Haidar leave for Travancore than a combination of forces attacked Mysore.

The political situation was changing rapidly at this time, especially in southern India. In 1763, the English and the French signed the Treaty of Paris after the Seven Years' War. This transformed both these parties into political players rather than mere merchants or 'allies to the Circar' as they had so far pretended to be. It also altered the power equations among the different players in the South, especially the Carnatic. Article XI of the Treaty captures these changes:

> In the East Indies, Great Britain shall restore to France, in the condition they are now in different factories, which that crown possessed, as well as the coast of Coromandel and Orixa (Orissa), as on that of Malabar, as also in Bengal, at the beginning of the year 1749. And his most Christian Majesty (France) renounces all acquisitions which he made on the Coast of the Coromandel and Orixa since the said beginning of the year 1749. His Most Christian Majesty shall restore, on his side, all that may have been conquered from Great Britain, in the East Indies, during the present War; and will expressly cause Nattal and Tapanoly, in the island of Sumatra, to be restored; he engages further, not to erect fortifications, or to keep troops in any part of the dominion of the Subah (the Mughal Subedari) of Bengal. And in order to preserve future peace on the coast of Coromandel and Orixa, the English and French shall acknowledge Muhammad Ali Khan for lawful Nawab of the Carnatic, and Salabat Jung (who was deposed by his brother Nizam Ali on 27th June 1762) for lawful Subah of the Deccan; and both parties shall renounce all demands and pretensions of satisfaction with which they might charge each other, or their Indian allies, for the depredations or pillage committed on the side or the other during the war.

The treaty was political suicide for the French who unwittingly surrendered their territories on the eastern coast. It was also the first time two foreign powers were deciding the claimants of the throne and *subedari* and also the dominion of the Mughals, while all along they had claimed to be mere auxiliaries and allies of the Indian political establishment. It also awoke in Muhammad Ali ambitions of expansion by deposing the nizam of Hyderabad, the raja of Travancore and Haidar Ali of Mysore. The treaty empowered him to stand against his masters hitherto, the Mughal emperor and his deputy in the South, the nizam.

On his part, Nizam Ali felt betrayed at being replaced by Salabat Jung and within seven months of the treaty and the appointment of Salabat as nawab, he attacked and killed his brother to take over the Carnatic. In 1765, in a successful campaign south of the Krishna, Nizam Ali subjugated his brother Basalat Jung as well. This double victory emboldened him to attack Haidar and Muhammad Ali.

The English failed to secure a lease of the prized Northern Circars from Nizam Ali, something he had offered to Muhammad Ali, the nawab of Arcot, earlier despite the higher negotiating price they offered. The British, led by Lord Clive, were determined to obtain this crucial deal, which the French were eyeing as well. In 1765 Clive received the diwani of Bengal from the Mughal emperor and during this time he managed to convince the emperor to hand over the Northern Circars[*] as well. The victorious British sent an embassy to Nizam Ali thereafter, asking him to gift the area as a tributary dependency. Accordingly, on 12 November 1766, a treaty was concluded at Hyderabad by General Calliaud that stipulated an auxiliary force at Nizam Ali's disposal. It was also stipulated that this force should help Nizam Ali in his plans of conquest against the Marathas

---

[*] The Northern Circars was a former division of British India's Madras Presidency, which consisted of a narrow strip of territory lying along the western side of the Bay of Bengal in the present-day Indian states of Andhra Pradesh and Orissa (comprising the districts of Krishna, East Godavari, West Godavari, Vishakhapatnam, Vijayanagaram, Srikakulam, Prakasam and Guntur, as well as the Gajapati and Ganjam districts of Orissa). The territory derived its name from Circar or Sarkar, an Indian term applied to the component parts of a *subah* or province, each of which is administered by a deputy governor. There were five Northern Circars: Chicacole (Srikakulam), Rajahmundry, Ellore, Kondapalli and Guntur, covering a total area of about 30,000 square miles.

and Mysore. It suited the British policy of setting one principality against the other and enjoying the advantages of the ensuing unrest.

Meanwhile, back home in Mysore, the death of Immadi Krishnaraja encouraged the old acquaintance of the throne, Nanjarajayya, who had been granted a *jagir* earlier, to try and regain his lost power. After seeking his support in the troubled days following Khande Rao's treachery, Haidar had forgotten his benefactor. Nanjarajayya could not take this anymore. He sent emissaries to Nizam Ali Khan and Peshwa Madhava Rao to have Haidar killed. But Haidar's spy system was far too efficient to bypass the intrigues of Nanjarajayya. Haidar paid a visit to Nanjarajayya's house, in all humility executing an agreement or *kararnama* with him and agreeing to arrange a lavish wedding for his son Virarajayya. In a show of false camaraderie, Haidar even invited Nanjarajayya to 'come and encamp with his little army in the island of Seringapatam'. Nanjarajayya knew this would be suicide. Seeing no other option, he consented, after making Haidar swear on the Koran that no harm would come to him. The book on which Haidar took his oath was apparently an ordinary one with just the splendid cover of the Koran placed over it! On reaching Srirangapatna, his little army was encircled by Haidar's troops on the pretext of arranging a grand reception for the old man. Hayavadana Rao records the description given by a contemporary historian:

> On the day appointed, Nand Raj without any mistrust, made a pompous entrance into Syringpatam, at the head of his little army, the cannon firing, and the troops beating to arms and saluting him. Being arrived at his palace, his attention was taken up by the compliments of the great men of the city, who were admitted by few at a time, on the pretended account of not making too great a crowd. Moctum (Saiyyad Mokhdum) then entered the city, followed by a number of officers and made a sign to the troops, not to pay him any honors: he went directly to the palace of Nand Raj, where every one supposed he was going to pay his respects; and dismounting, he caused the first company of the battalions of sepoys who guarded the gate, to follow him. As soon as he came into the presence of Nand Raj, who came to meet him, he acquainted him, that Ayder, being informed that he was surrounded by people who gave him bad advice, had sent him to remove them from about him: at the same time he commanded

all present to leave the palace, which was done without uttering a word; the grenadiers followed them; and Moctum remaining with Nand Raj, his two sons and some officers, the conversation was carried on with the greatest politeness. Moctum acquainted the two princes that they were to make the campaign; and that instead of one father they would find two in Ayder and himself. During this short conversation, the women and all the family of Moctum were announced. Moctum took his leave, carrying the two princes with him, to whom he represented, that it became their dignity to wait upon the Nabob and give him an account of all that had passed. These young noblemen departed, accompanied by many of Moctum's officers; neither they nor Nand Raj expressing the least astonishment or chagrin. After their departure, Moctum spoke a word to Nand Raj's general, who ordered his troop to ground their arms, which was done with great silence. All the gates and windows of Nand Raj's palace that looked towards the street were afterwards walled up, except the principal entrance...

Thus, Haidar imprisoned Nanjarajayya and his family and sent them to Srirangapatna. Nanjarajayya found himself a prisoner in his own palace, his guards captured and Haidar's sentinels in command. His accomplices, including one Mallu Anna were heavily fined while those who had helped Haidar (such as Obalayya and Kalappa) got important positions in the treasury office. Haidar also paid the arrears due to Nanjarajayya's troops and confiscated his *jagir* worth Rs 4 lakh. Half of this was assigned to Nanjarajayya along with the principality of Kalale for his maintenance. The remaining half was set aside for his sons, who followed Haidar in his campaign against Muhammad Ali.

The Mysore records speak no more of Nanjarajayya, who finally died in captivity in 1773, thus ending the dalavoy legacy in Mysore and all the treachery that went with it. After his death his principality of Kalale was taken back by Haidar. When he decided to show some compassion to his former benefactor's son, Virarajayya remained indifferent, thus angering Haidar, who threw him back into the prison.

TIPU

A constant source of worry for the estranged royal family and the dowager Rani Devajammanni was Haidar's budding Samaritan son Tipu.

As promised at the tomb of the Sufi saint, Tipu was handed over to the path of Sufism. But Tipu's brother Karim, whom Haidar had planned to make a great warrior and befitting successor, turned out to be the most timid weakling. He shuddered at the very sight of the sword and even had terrible convulsions once after Haidar forced him into combat. Haidar changed his mind about letting Tipu live as a Sufi. Describing these early years of Tipu's education, Hayavadana Rao writes:

> Haidar, who lamented more deeply than we will ever be able to discern or measure, the lack of education in himself, not only encouraged Mullahs for teaching the elements of Persian and Hindustani, but also, what is more interesting, entrusted the care of Tippu, his son and successor, to a duly qualified Muslim teacher. His attempt at educating Tippu in the traditional mode is a chapter of history by itself. It is said that Tippu's teacher was never questioned by Haidar as to the progress made by the boy for many years, at the end of which period, he one day conducted a public examination of Tippu. This showed that the boy had not obtained the training required for a soldier's son; instead he had had everything that would be requisite to turn him into a good Moulvie. Haidar's displeasure knew no bounds and he exclaimed, much in the strain of Aurangzib, that his boy had not been taught the things that would make him a great and good ruler. He had not been taught; he thundered forth, the modes of warfare he should know, the manner of conquering countries or conducting diplomacy with the surrounding nations, or even the duties of kingship. Instead, Haidar protested, everything requisite for converting him into a religious zealot had been done and his mind filled with notions and fancies which had made him hate everything not connected with Islam. Everything indeed had been done, concluded Haidar in his anger, to ruin his family and his kingdom and nothing to advance either.

Convinced that Tipu's education was not to his liking, and realising Karim's soft nature, Haidar Ali redirected young Tipu from the path of Islamic studies towards a thorough training in various modes of warfare. Haidar was conscious of the impact the extreme, rabid training had had on Karim and therefore ensured that Tipu expanded his mind with a wider range of religious and secular literature.

Tipu, who was to have held the olive branch in his hand, instead had the sword thrust on him and was pushed into the battlefield by a father who did not want to lose his grip on the kingdom at any cost. With a heavy heart, Tipu shed his Sufi robes and entered the camps of Ghazi Khan—another trusted associate of Haidar's. Here he was subjected to tremendous physical exercise and martial training and we find a sudden, yet beautiful metamorphosis in this young man of fourteen when he made his debut in the battlefield by plundering the plains of the Carnatic. He invoked the wrath of the British, ushering in the battle commonly referred to by historians as the First Anglo-Mysore War.

THE FIRST ANGLO-MYSORE WAR

After charting a series of successes in the Carnatic and Bengal, the British forces were full of exuberance. After Plassey, the East India Company was able to enforce the cultivation of opium in sufficient quantities in India, and procure enough tea for the British market, reaping significant profits. Yet, military attacks were now also to be directed against Indian, and other Asian, ships engaged in the inter-Asian trade. These attacks were to lay the groundwork for the battles against the southern rulers and the Marathas whose revenues from this trade had dwindled. While Plassey may have been a matter of survival for the East India Company, the subsequent battles can certainly not be classified as such. Some historians tried to argue that competition with the French precipitated the battles in South India, but such a view is contradicted, ironically, by a Frenchman. Abbe de Pradt, author of *Les Trois Ages des Colonies, Paris, 1902* wrote that with the victory at Plassey and the establishment of sovereign rights, England had demonstrated to all of Europe that it was no longer necessary for Europe to send precious metals obtained from the New World to India. It could trade on the basis of revenue acquired from taxing subjects and commodities, whereas other European countries had to trade at a loss with metal currency. The extension of English sovereignty in India would prevent Europe from sending capital into India. De Pradt said:

> The people who have enough control over India to reduce substantially the exportation of European metallic currency into Asia rule there as much for Europe's benefit as for their own;

their empire is more common than particular, more European than British; as it expands, Europe benefits, and each of their conquests is also a real conquest for the latter.

Chastising European opponents of the British conquest, he wrote:

All the sound and fury now echoing across Europe about England's hegemony in India are the shrieks of a blind delirium, as an anti-European uproar; it might be thought that England was taking away from every European state what it was conquering from those of Asia, whereas, on the contrary, every part of Asia that she takes for herself, she, by that very fact, takes for Europe.

Meanwhile, the young maharaja of Mysore was feeling increasingly stifled by the growing popularity of Haidar and his son Tipu. He was also constantly heckled and provoked by the two queens, his grandmother Devajammanni and her daughter-in-law Lakshmammanni. He sent emissaries to the Peshwa Madhava Rao for help in getting rid of Haidar and Tipu. The Marathas had recovered from the disastrous defeat at Panipat under the stewardship of the young and energetic Madhava Rao. Their resurrection offered a gleam of hope to the beleaguered Wodeyars.

But as ill fate would have it, Haidar learnt of Nanjaraja's mischief and sent Mohabat Ali to the peshwa for negotiations. The peshwa refused to concede—burning with the fire of revenge, he fell on Mysore in January 1767 like a hawk swoops in on its prey. He crossed the Krishna River and advanced rapidly towards Sira, halting at Savanur. He was joined there by the forces of Murari Rao of Gutti and the Palegar of Chitradurga. Sira was guarded by Haidar's brother-in-law, Mir Ali Raza Khan, with 4,000 cavalry and 6,000 infantry. After defending the fort for over fifteen days, he finally gave up. Madhava Rao then moved towards Maddagiri and released his former ally Rani Veerammaji and her son Chennabasavayya, proceeding thereafter to Channarayadurga. Sardar Khan of Mysore, with 2,000 foot soldiers and 1,000 irregulars, put up a tough defence before falling before peshwa might. The Maratha flags fluttered proudly across Mysore as places fell like pawns before Madhava Rao's onslaught—Hoskote, Chikkaballapur, Doddaballapur, Kolar, Mulbagal and Gurramkonda.

Haidar marched from Coimbatore to Srirangapatna to halt the Maratha advance. He tried several tactics, from frontal attacks to guerrilla warfare to strange techniques of tiring the enemy by 'breaking down the embankments of tanks, poisoning the wells with milk-hedge, burning all foliage and presenting a scorched earth to the enemy.' Finally in April 1767, the negotiations began. Haidar was forced to conclude the war. He sent a clever diplomat, Appaji Rao, along with Karim Khan, and a large sum of 35 lakhs. The peshwa restored all districts of Mysore to the southeast of Sira and returned to Pune on 11 May 1767, only to attack it again later, in January 1770.

Meanwhile, Nizam Ali had been on the move. Trying to fish in troubled waters, he, his brother Basalat Jung and a detachment of English troops under Colonel Joseph Smith had joined Madhava Rao and marched towards Srirangapatna by April 1767. Sadly for Nizam Ali, the Mysore–Maratha war ended at this time. Still, this sudden move of Nizam Ali's petrified Haidar, who began negotiating with him through Mahfuz Khan, the eldest son of Anwar-ud-din and the lawful nawab of Arcot. The Dewan of Nizam Ali, Rukn-ud-daula, mediated in the matter and Haidar bought peace with Hyderabad at a cost of 30 lakhs. It was also decided that Tipu would marry Mahfuz Khan's daughter and that Mahfuz Khan would surrender his claims to the Arcot throne in favour of Tipu. The two forces decided to make common cause against Muhammad Ali. Raza Ali Khan, son of Chanda Sahib, was to give up, in return for the principality of Tanjore, any claims he may have had to being the nawab of Arcot. The entire deal was clinched so surreptitiously with an aim to enable a Mysore–Hyderabad joint occupation over the entire Carnatic region that it even missed prying English ears. Nizam Ali was a master politician, playing with great finesse his game on both sides. Colonel Smith was alarmed by Nizam Ali's betrayal. Not only had he joined the Maratha campaign towards the end in a token, mock participation, he had also entered into family ties with the house of Haidar Ali through his allies Mahfuz Khan and Rukn-ud-daula to consolidate his positions.

To ward off English fears, the wily Nizam Ali and his minister fooled Colonel Smith, swearing by the unswerving nature of their friendship and instigating him to attack Bangalore, promising that he would never want for support. Smith marched towards Bangalore only to see Nizam Ali's troops heading off in the opposite direction without any explanation. Smith's fears and bewilderment were further accentuated when the joint forces of Haidar and Nizam Ali decided to descend on the English and Muhammad Ali. In a letter to Lord Clive he exclaimed: 'Although it was as plain as noon day to every person (except the Council) that they (Nizam Ali and Haidar) were preparing to enter the Carnatic jointly, no measures were taken to establish magazines of provisions in proper places nor any steps to supply our army in time of need.' Haidar, thus, pulled off a royal coup on the British by breaking the usual tripartite confederacy of the British, the nizam and the Marathas against him.

Tiruchirapalli had been a sore memory for Mysore since the days of the colossal misadventures of Nanjarajayya. To see it occupied by the same deceitful Muhammad Ali hurt Mysore's ego all the more. Haidar sent letters to Muhammad Ali to surrender Tiruchirapalli and honour the earlier treaty, but the latter chose to ignore it. Haidar also sent letters of warning to the British asking them not to help Muhammad Ali, whom he planned to subjugate. The British however, stuck with their ally Muhammad Ali. This caused hostilities across southern India. Also, Mysore was among the prized possessions in the peninsula that eluded the British. The neighbouring kingdoms felt threatened by Haidar's expansionist policies—he had annexed one principality after the other since assuming office. It was precisely these insecurities the British played on to engage Mysore in a long-drawn series of wars that lasted for eighteen years and became famous as the Anglo-Mysorean Wars.

Haidar initially joined hands with Nizam Ali of Hyderabad to curb the British forces in the south. The combined forces of 50,000 men and 100 guns made a quick round-up and in 1767 took over Vaniyambadi, Changama, Tirupattoor and Kaveripatnam and laid siege to the Krishnagiri fort. The English tried in vain to stop the growing alliance. A section of the Mysore force led by Tipu and Berki Srinivasa Rao raided the areas surrounding Arcot. Muhammad Ali and Colonel Smith decided to repel the Mysore–Hyderabad joint attack. As head of the cavalry, Haidar entered the Carnatic on 25 August 1767 by one of the passes near Krishnagiri and besieged Kaveripatnam fort. A battle ensued between Haidar and Smith in late August and early September near Tiruvannamalai. Despite suffering some initial losses, Haidar pushed through, his guns still active, surrounding, plundering and killing the English forces. Haidar hounded Smith, driving him all over the place as he ran from one region to the other in quest of food. The northeast monsoon added to Smith's misery and the British decided to evacuate their troops from Tiruvannamalai and move the wounded and exhausted forces to Settupattu. A sudden reinforcement of troops and provisions bolstered Smith's position.

The confederate forces were stopped by Colonel Smith on 26 September 1767. Nizam Ali turned out to be a traitor and showed the trait he was best known for—duplicity. Abandoning the confederate forces, he retreated through the Changama Pass to Singarapettai in the middle of the night. Smith saw the confusion in the enemy camp as an opportunity to regain lost ground and mounted midnight attacks under Major Fitzgerald. He decided to proceed to Madras after garrisoning Tiruvannamalai, Vaniyambadi and other outposts, leaving his army behind at vulnerable places, like Arcot, Vellore, Gingee, Kanchipuram, Wandiwash and Tiruchirapalli.

Hostilities resumed in November 1767 after a brief lull. Nizam Ali rejoined the side, apologising profusely for his sudden flight and swore again to stand by the alliance. He was by far the most untrustworthy and wily partner in any military alliance. His troops, however, marched to Hosakote and Haidar recaptured Vaniyambadi and Tirupattoor forts on 5 and 7 November 1767. Haidar then laid a fierce siege of the fort of Ambur, which was held by the dwindling forces of Captain Culvert for over twenty-six days. Just when Culvert seemed to be giving in, he received a huge reinforcement from Vellore and that forced Haidar to move up the valley again.

However, Captain Culvert attacked Vaniyambadi and forced Haidar to get away from the Carnatic and retreat to Kaveripatnam. On 14 December 1767, Haidar received intelligence of the Nair revolt brewing in the Malabar. He sent off his heavy guns and baggage westwards under Tipu and Ghazi Khan's command to assist the provincial commander Lutif Ali Beg. Mangalore, Kumta and Honnavar had been captured by the British. At the same time, English troops from Bengal landed at the Northern Circars under Colonel Peach and, in a bid to divert Nizam Ali, attacked his province of Warangal. The latter opened a secret dialogue with Smith to buy peace with the British. He was, in any case, a master in this game of double-speak. He finally made his intentions clear by concluding a peace treaty with Muhammad Ali and the English on 23 February 1768.

Haidar subdued the Nairs while Tipu annexed Mangalore in May 1768. But the wily British, under Colonels Smith and Wood, invaded Mysore from the south, conquering Salem, Erode and Coimbatore, overrunning Krishnagiri and Baramahal and besieging Bangalore. The very heart of Mysore was threatened. Almost half its territories and pivotal areas were under enemy control. Haidar was the last man to be dismayed by such a turn of events. Realising that the age-old dispute with Muhammad Ali had given rise to all these conflicts, he sent peace emissaries. But the demands made by the English and their ally Muhammad Ali were too unreasonable to accept. The war carried on for a couple of years. Haidar resorted to his usual guerrilla tactics, false alarms and surprise attacks. The British army, which was more used to systematic warfare, was taken by surprise. Places began to fall before Haidar's advance. He managed to recapture Mangalore, laid siege to Hosur, forced Smith to raise the siege at Bangalore and inflicted a crushing defeat on the British by reaching the very gates of their headquarters, Madras. Seeing the forces of Haidar barely five miles away from Madras, the British were panic-stricken and sued for peace. Initial peace overtures made by Captain Brooke in January 1769 did not meet with much success. By 29 March 1769 Haidar's troops had reached Tindivanam and St. Thomas Mount on the very outskirts of Madras city. Charles Bourchier, the governor of Madras, decided that calling for peace was the only way to save the English forces an embarrassing defeat.

On 3 April 1769 the peace treaty was signed at Madras between the two parties after the negotiators from both sides—Vissaji Pant from Mysore and Du Pre and George Bouchier of the British side—reached mutual consent. The treaty decided that there should be perpetual friendship between Mysore and the British and also provided for the mutual restitution of all conquests; for mutual aid and alliance in defensive war and absolute liberty of commerce between Mysore and the East India Company's settlements. The English ended up promising to help Haidar in case he was attacked by any other power. It was a big jolt to British pride, which had earlier enjoyed a string of successes. The First Anglo-Mysore war thus crushed the myth of British infallibility. Another treaty was signed between Haidar and Muhammad Ali, according to which the latter was to evacuate Hosakote and pay Mysore an annual tribute of six lakhs. Both were to respect the borders that existed before the commencement of hostilities.

It is interesting to note that though the British signed the treaty, they did so under duress and were already thinking of avenging this defeat rather than abiding by the terms and conditions of this treaty. The very negotiators and signatories defended their decision in the Court of Directors:

Much invective hath been circulated in this colony and nearly in the terms in which you express your sentiments of the peace 'dictated at the gates of Madras' and we find it hath been used as industriously at home to establish the same ideas. If an indifferent person were to read of an enemy dictating peace at the gates of a fortified town, the idea that would immediately occur would be that the enemy came with a superior force; that the garrison, seeing no hope of dislodging the enemy, and fearing for their own town, their lives and property, accepted the terms prescribed. This is the idea that men have endeavoured at home and abroad to propagate; how justly will appear. Our army had been in pursuit of the enemy in the southern part of the Carnatic for nearly four months without being once able to come up with him; at the last march before the peace he gave our army the slip, and arrived at the Mount about 48 hours before our army halted at Vandaloor 12 miles short of the Mount. One of the first points he insisted on was, that an order should be sent to Colonel Smith to halt at 10 coss (about 25 to 30 miles) from him, and declared that although he came to negotiate peace, he would not remain there, unless an order was sent, but march immediately to the northward of Madras, or Tripasoor, where he could be more conveniently supplied with provisions and provender. As a peace was necessary to us, and every day increased our distress, it appeared better to us to negotiate with him near at hand than at a distance, and it was very material to save as much of the Jaghir as possible from plunder. It missed Colonel Smith, but the messenger returning overtook him at Vandaloor, twelve miles from the Mount. What then, it might be asked, could induce us to make peace, if the enemy was so much afraid of our army? The motives are clearly and fully assigned in our reasons entered in Consultation on the 10th April 1769. This being the case, we cannot see why it was more disgraceful to negotiate at the Mount than at 100 miles distant.

In a letter dated 29 June 1769, the Governor of Madras, Charles Bourchier writes about this humiliating defeat of the Company.

We have at length happily put an end to the enormous expenses occasioned by the war by concluding a peace with Hyder, who, having led Colonel Smith a dance of near a month, had the address, after drawing him as far as Villaporam, to slip by him and making a march of no less than 45 miles the first day, got so much ahead of our army that he reached the Mount three days before they got the length of Vendaloor. On his arrival there, he wrote to me that he was come, so near to make peace with us himself. In the extremities we were reduced to we gladly embraced the opportunity of opening the Conference again; for the country being entirely at his mercy, our army being incapable of protecting it or bringing him to a decisive action, and daily diminishing by sickness and fatigue; the promised succors of horse by Nabob Mohamid Aly and Mora Row not arrived nor likely to be for some months, and our distress for money great; our whole dependence being on the Nabob, who though he promised largely, we had doubts of his performing; and it being also the Company's positive orders to make peace, we were under the necessity of doing it almost at all events.

A PERIOD OF UNREST

Mysore: Internal Politics

Haidar had no respite. No sooner did he wind up a successful campaign at Madras than the Marathas struck again. Mahimaji Sindhia, commanding 400 horses and a powerful confederacy of Palegars, attacked Mysore. The Mysore army of 5,000 cavalry, 4,000 infantry and 4,000 irregulars under Mir Ali Raza Khan and Berki Srinivasa Rao drove him away. Incensed by this and by Haidar's attempts to levy taxes on the Palegars of Cudappah, Kurnool, Gadaval and of territories thought of as Maratha, Peshwa Madhava Rao decided to strike himself. He seized Kadur and Hassan, overran Doddaballapur, Chikkaballapur, Nandidurga, Kolar and Mulbagal.

A decisive battle then took place between the Mysore forces and the Marathas at Chinkurli, about 11 miles from Srirangapatna, on 6 March 1771. At daybreak a severe artillery action followed during which Trimbaka Rao was slightly wounded by a bullet passing through his ear. He and Balwant Rao beat a hasty retreat and it seemed like the Marathas were going to lose. But then a shot from one of the Maratha cannons struck a few rockets on the Mysorean side. These rockets had been laden on camels and when they exploded they caused great disarray among the animals, which started running helter-skelter. The fire soon spread to the ammunition boxes and blew them all up. Seeing the confusion in the enemy camp, with the soldiers running around in distress, the Marathas made a frontal attack. What followed was a scene of absolute slaughter at the hands of the enemy Pindaris who looted Haidar's army. Among those who fell in this disaster were Mysoreans – Narayana Rao, Srinivasa Jivaji and Lala Mian, Haidar's elder brother's son-in-law, Mir Ali Raza Khan, Ali Zaman Khan, Abdul Muhammad Mirdhe and Yasin Khan Wunti Koodri—all of Haidar's chief officers were taken prisoners. Yasin Khan was mistaken for Haidar and captured by the enemy, though treated with respect as a state prisoner. The 'Chinkurli disaster', as it is known, was the most shocking and embarrassing defeat the Mysore army had faced in recent times.

Along with his associates, including Ghazi Khan, Haidar fled in fright to Srirangapatna, hotly pursued by the enemy till the very suburbs of the capital. By midnight Haidar arrived near the tomb of Khadar Wali in Srirangapatna. He was joined here by Tipu, who had escaped the field with his followers in the guise of a travelling mendicant.

Overjoyed at the loot they had got, the Marathas unwittingly allowed Haidar time to recover even as they enjoyed the spoils of war. They were complacent because they thought they had already captured Haidar Ali. By the time they realised their mistake, the real Haidar Ali had escaped to his hide-out. The 10-day gap was enough for him to realign. He strengthened the fort on all sides by erecting new works and mounting guns on all sides. Realising his folly, Trimbaka marched forthwith to attack the fort of Srirangapatna and laid siege to it for nearly two months. Haidar easily lured away the battle-weary Maratha soldiers, enticing them with money. His Commandant Mohammad Ali made a surprise attack on the Maratha army resulting in a terrible carnage. The siege was lifted and the Marathas descended through the Gejjelhutty Pass and planned to attack the Mysorean districts of Coimbatore, Palaghat and Dindigul. But they were chased away by two divisions of the Mysore army under Tipu and Mohammad Ali. Tipu inflicted a crushing defeat on Trimbaka Rao near Dharmapuri, while Mohammad Ali achieved success at Kaveripatnam and also secured the release of many prisoners of Chinkurli.

Undeterred, the Marathas continued their repeated attacks on Srirangapatna throughout late 1771 and early 1772. Haidar despatched

Appaji Rao to negotiate peace with them. But Appaji was detained by a haughty Trimbaka who prepared to raid and pillage the wealthy province of Bidnaur. To halt them, the Mysorean army rushed to Bidnaur but was badly defeated. Haidar made piteous representations to the Marathas to revive the peace talks under Appaji. Sixty five lakhs was the final negotiated war indemnity that Haidar had to pay. Loans were sought from *sowcars* to pay about 40 lakhs and the territories of Gurramkonda, Sira, Kolar, Hosakote and Doddaballapur were ceded to the Marathas to make up for the rest of the dues.

Even with all the military campaigns and the constant unrest, Haidar never forgot to pay his symbolic obeisance to the throne of Mysore and its titular occupant. He loved to call himself a humble servant of His Highness. Peixoto, a Portuguese officer in Haidar's army, records in his memoirs a meeting on 27 February 1770 between Haidar, the young maharaja, and his mother Kalale Devajammanni, eleven days after Haidar's arrival at the capital after the Maratha campaign.

> The Nabob quitted his Palace and went to that great king, and was received by the King with attention in the customary form, which is, the King remains sitting, and the Nabob to throw himself at his feet. The King wanted to exempt the Nabob from this humble ceremony, but the Nabob did it instantly. The King then ordered him to sit down, which he did, after saying he could not sit in his presence. There was with the King his mother, who, it is said is a lady of good judgment, and daughter of the Rajah Nande Rajah...and after the compliments were over, during which the Queen mother looked very grave, the Nabob told the King that the Maratta was come with great power to contribute that kingdom, and that he asked a very great sum which seemed to him too much, wherefore he would rather fight and show him that his kingdom dreaded not his power, that he hath been in the field on that account and hath already shown his intentions...that he, the Maratta, did not stand to give battle, but only took satisfaction to ruin the country as much as possible, breaking, burning and totally ruining the inhabitants, which he could not hinder him from, as the Maratta force did consist in cavalry, and his own in foot. Wherefore he acquainted him, that he might order him what he thought proper in this particular. The King answered

him, 'I and this whole Kingdom do not dread any invasion of the Maratta, nor any other enemy as long as God preserves your life. All what you do for the utility, conservation and ease of the people, are precious enamels with which you augment your name. The security and defence of the Kingdom is in your hand, and in me the confidence that you will prosper in everything.' The Nabob remained mute without answering the King, and without any farther longer stay, took his leave and came to his Palace.

It was a rather strange relationship that Haidar and the throne shared—replete with symbolism and duplicity. Both parties knew where the real power rested. Yet they made a sham of false respect and misplaced graciousness. Whether it was for mere public consumption or for the consummation of some exalted objective is completely unknown. But the drama continued, though not for long. The young maharaja passed away all of a sudden on 2 August 1770. It is interesting to note that this very commentator, Peixoto—who paints the master-slave relationship that existed between the raja and his so-called sarvadhikari—nails Haidar as the villain of the piece; as someone who got the young maharaja murdered in cold blood! However, it is impossible to think what Haidar could have possibly gained from murdering a man who was anyway subservient to his wishes. This is yet another instance of the difficulty that contemporary historians face with depictions of the Interregnum where characters are painted in black or white, seldom or never in shades of gray. To quote Peixoto, however:

> He was not sick, but was found dead on the morning of the said day. This did cause great inward sorrow to all, not only his vassals, but even to the most part of the grandees of the camp, for...he showed such a Royal presence of spirit by which it was judged that he would not suffer much time the subjection he was kept by the Nabob, but Death made an end of these hopes. The author of this success is known, of whom fear does not permit to make mention of. In the night in which he died, which was at 2 o' clock in the morning; he hath drank, after supper, a cup of milk which the Nabob hath sent him. As soon as it was day, and it was divulged that the King was dead, the Nabob seemed to be sorry, and sent instantly to examine into the cause of this success; sent for the surgeon who attends annually in the Royal Palace

and asked him the motive of that success; he knew to answer no more than that after it was already night, he hath retired from the Palace to his House and that he hath left the King in health and that this was all he could say to the Nabob. The surgeon was put prisoner and condemned to pay a great sum into the Royal Treasury, accusing him greatly of the King's death and in this manner the Nabob shews his sorrow by the surgeon's prison, and by the condemnation, utility to his Treasury, where all the Nabob's interests do centre...

While bolstering a lot of these conspiracy claims, eminent historian Hayavadana Rao points out:

In the midst of his savage purpose, Haidar was, we have to concede, a man. He was not a mere monster, who mechanically perpetrated cold-blooded deeds. Despite the tendencies of the times and his own baser instincts, to which he fell a prey sometimes, there is enough in him to show that he was a humanised being. It is this humanising touch in him that helped to individualise him and make him convincing as man among men. That explains to some small extent the great hold he had upon the imagination of the men of his time...we have seen in him thus far the play of at least three conflicting motives and passions—his love of money as means to an end, the end being political mastery; his hatred for everyone who comes in the way of his attaining that mastery; and worse than either of these, his personal animosity against Nanjaraja, whom he dreaded far more for his cunning than even for the power that he might, perchance, wield against him to his discomfiture at a moment when he least expected it.

Without playing devil's advocate, I must stress that this dichotomy makes amply clear to the reader the complexities facing the historian. What source are we to rely upon? What inferences are we to draw about the perceived motives of people, which none but they themselves would be privy to and which have evanesced with their descent to their respective graves? Haidar had faced the worst backlash from the royal family during Immadi Krishnaraja Wodeyar's reign with the master plot being hatched by the maharaja, the queen mother and Khande Rao. Did that make him dread the royal family when any intelligence of their silent moves to reclaim power reached him? Did he not want any king of the family to attain majority and did he therefore systematically poison them all? Was Haidar—whom the mighty English and the neighbouring kingdoms feared—himself afraid of a powerless, titular teenager whom he could squash like an insect under his feet at free will? To ward off these supposed dangers, would he have resorted to those most inhuman acts stated above? If yes, why do other historians paint such a wonderful and humane picture of a man guilty of the worst form of murder? Or are their depictions, too, as biased and favourable to the powerful as most historical accounts usually are? These are questions lost in the tomb of time and our interpretation is our own truth—perhaps one of the biggest banes to afflict modern and unbiased narration of ancient history.

On 16 August 1770, fifteen days after the death of Nanjaraja Wodeyar, Rani Lakshmammanni placed on the Mysore throne Bettada Chamaraja Wodeyar VIII, the 11-year-old son of Immadi Krishnaraja.

Administrative Changes

Haidar made changes in the administration set-up during this time. In 1775, he bifurcated the Revenue Department or the Mahalati Kacheri under the designation of Balaghat Kacheri and Payanghat Kacheri. The former was placed under Nazim-ud-din Khan of Arcot as dewan with Jadir Rama Rao as chief accountant (munshi) and records (daftar) under Puttayya, Singayya, Appaji Rao, Keshava Rao, Koneri Rao and Lala Lingo Pant. The Payanghat Kacheri came under Mir Ali Nakim and his younger brother Mohammad Ghouse, with Kadim Shamaiya as the chief accountant and Kacheri Krishnayya, Subba Rao and Kushal Chand in charge of the daftar or records. Grave irregularities prevailed in the collections of land revenue. Embezzlement of government money became the order of the day.

On receiving intelligence news of these malpractices that had crept in, Haidar abolished these new offices, re-amalgamated the kacheris and placed them under Anche Shamaiya in August 1779. A devout Sri Vaishnava Brahmin, Shamaiya belonged to Sulakunte in Kolar and had known Haidar since his youth. He began to wield supreme power over affairs of state. Venkatapatayya was made in-charge of the daftar and the dewanship of the kacheri was given to Mir Muhammad Sadak, son of Mir Ali Nakim. On Shamaiya's advice, the police, finance and espionage departments were merged and given supreme powers. A special commission was formed for the investigation of embezzlement, which enabled the detection of actual frauds, but in establishing apparent proof of alleged malpractices that had never occurred. Shamaiya misused the authority vested in him to the hilt and unleashed a reign of terror against everyone he hated. *Sullu-pattis* or false statements were a perennial Damocles' sword over officials' heads regardless of their integrity. Once caught by the financial irregularities committee, punishment was certain. Many old rivals of Shamaiya paid the price for this rivalry. Harikara Nayaka Shamaiya was heavily taxed, flogged and imprisoned, and his brothers Singaiya and Sheshaiya severely tortured. Salayat Khan and Muhammad Ghouse of the erstwhile Mahalati Kacheri weren't spared either, and the former died from the wounds inflicted on him. In fact even Purnaiya, a collections officer of the Kacheri, wasn't spared—111,000 Varahas were exacted from him, he was tortured and forced to prepare false returns or *sullu-pattis*. He would have surely met his death but for the timely intervention of Bacche Rao and other benefactors, like Annadana Setti and Narasa Setti. Berki Srinivasa Rao used to plead to Haidar the case of Purnaiya and to reduce his punishment to merely keeping him under guard. Many amildars and officials were similarly punished—tied to elephants' feet, flogged to death or pierced with needles.

Haidar, however, had great regard for Shamaiya and the latter was honoured by him with an umbrella, medal, pearl necklace, palanquin, a cash reward of 5,000 Varahas, an allowance of 1,000 Varahas and a pair of rich shawls. His elder brother Rangaiya was granted an additional allowance of thirty Varahas and the younger one, Aprameya, placed in charge of the records of the toshikhane or treasury, cavalry, infantry and other establishments.

In 1779 Haidar despatched a grand embassy to Delhi to secure for himself the imperial grants of the *subadari* of the two Carnatics of Bijapur and Hyderabad. The motive, as Wilks states, seems to be 'in order that an exterior dignity which still commanded some respect, might accompany the possession of an authority, which he had now an early prospect of conferring on himself.' His dreams, however, remained just dreams.

External Troubles

Meanwhile, the Marathas weren't likely to give up. Madhava Rao was sick, but he sent his commander Trimbaka Rao to attack Mysore. Trimbaka 'Mama', as he was called (being the peshwa's maternal uncle), besieged Gurramkonda commanded by Sayyid Saab and nephew Mir Saab and captured it after two months. Accompanied by the perennial trouble-maker Murari Rao and the Palegars of Chitradurga, Ratnagiri, Midageshi, etc., he then proceeded westwards. He then annexed Tumkur, Devarayadurga and other places. The main Mysorean army was stationed at Srirangapatna and Bangalore and Haidar sent them to repel the Maratha invasion. He left no stone unturned in defending Mysore's sovereignty. The Mysore commander Mohammad Ali crossed the Cauvery at night, attacked the Maratha camp, captured their battery and plundered their possessions. One day, when the Marathas had gone to bathe at the Sangam at Srirangapatna, near the foot of the Karighat hills, Ghazi Khan and Mohammad Ali accompanied by 4,000 Pindaris fell on them like wolves, killing many Maratha warriors. Trimbaka continued to plunder Mysore from Periapatnam in the west to Dindigul in the south. But catastrophic news from Pune awaited him.

The young and dynamic Peshwa Madhava Rao was seriously ill and lay on his deathbed. All army contingents were recalled to Pune. On 17 June 1772, Trimbaka was forced to leave Mysore. In November 1772, Madhava Rao passed away. His untimely demise shook the Maratha kingdom. It would be no exaggeration to say that had Madhava Rao lived on, India's history would have unfolded differently, and the East India Company would have had a tougher time subjugating the country.

The new peshwa was Madhava Rao's young and tactless brother Narayana Rao, and his uncle Raghunath Rao was regent. Raghunath Rao (or Raghoba, as he was called) had been nurturing dreams of peshwaship. It didn't augur well for him that he was sidelined and his inefficient nephew made the peshwa. He had lost the opportunity twice—once after the death of his brother Balaji Baji Rao and again now. His wife Anandi Bai's scornful taunts and jibes deepened his ambition. Anandi kept attacking his passivity, taunting him to wear bangles and sit at home rather than play perpetual regent for all minor peshwas. Narayana Rao, sensing that trouble would brew, began to negotiate with Haidar and the nizam to imprison Raghoba. He was arrested, and in prison, along with Sakaram Bapu and others, he conspired with the Gardis—a Pindari-like tribe—in charge of the prison. Raghoba gave them a letter which proved decisive. For an exchange of five lakhs and three forts, he issued a forged document to the Gardis with the message 'Capture the Peshwa'. The message found its way to the apartments of Anandi Bai for her perusal.

So angered was she with the shabby treatment meted to her husband that she appended the message with the phrase 'put him to death'.

On 30 August 1773, Narayana Rao was resting in the courtyard after lunch when the Gardis rushed in and demanded their arrears. The spirit of the Maratha kingdom, which had been founded on the high ideals of Shivaji, would have certainly suffered at the sight of its peshwa running around the palace with the Gardis in hot pursuit. He was finally caught and butchered by one Sumer Singh Gardi. Raghoba became the peshwa the following day.

Raghunath Rao tried in vain to attack Mysore but the domestic turmoil at Pune forced him to conclude a peace treaty with Haidar and agree to cede Sira in return for his acknowledgement of Rao's claim to the Peshwaship. Raghoba was building up support for his treacherous act among the southern powers, lest he be treated as a political pariah. It was agreed that the entire area north of Srirangapatna up to the banks of the Krishna River extending to Badami, Jalahalli, Sira, Maddagiri and, Chennarayadurga would be restored to Haidar.

Meanwhile, Nana Phadnavis, Phadke, Pethe, Patwardhan and other trusted nobles of the kingdom formed the *Barabhai* (twelve brothers), a union to oust Raghoba from the peshwaship. Around this time, Narayana Rao's widow Ganga Bai gave birth to a boy who was named Sawai Madhava Rao. The *Barabhai* tied the mohur of peshwaship to the child in his cradle and titled him 'Srimantha Peshwa Sawai Madhava Rao Saib' with Nana Phadnavis—the wise statesman—as regent and guardian. Anticipating trouble, Raghoba fled to Bombay and in 1775 signed the Treaty of Surat with the British to help him regain the peshwaship.

The Zamorin, taking advantage of Mysore's troubles with the English and the Marathas and the political flux, instigated the Nairs and Moplahs to revolt in 1773. Haidar sent his agents, *harikars* Rangappa Naik and Ramagiri Chennarajaiya for negotiations, but they were treacherously murdered by the Nairs. An enraged Haidar decided to descend on the Malabar himself. In 1773–74, he led an expedition to the Malabar region. Taking immediate possession of all the land belonging to the Zamorin and the kings of Kadatanadu, Cotiote and others, he despatched a force of 40,000 men under Berki Srinivasa Rao, his pillar in all troubles, along with Sayyid Saab. The force reached Calicut, hearing which the Zamorin hurriedly concluded a treaty with the French—seeking their protection—on 12 January 1774. An undeterred Srinivasa Rao marched on to Calicut and took the fort by storm. The wily French left the scene for Mahe and the Zamorin himself fled to Travancore with his family. The Nair chieftains were punished and subjugated. Srinivasa Rao was appointed fouzdar of the Malabar.

Fighting the British

By 1780 the Indian rulers formed a confederacy against the British. Who inspired and created this confederacy is a matter of debate and speculation; it is widely opined that the wise Maratha statesman Nana Phadnavis was the chief architect of the alliance, though others opine that it was formed on Haidar's advice. All the players—Haidar, Nana Phadnavis, the Sindhia, the Nizam, the Bhosles under Madhoji Bhosle—had an axe to grind against the British, their common foe. They drew up a plan for simultaneous attacks against British positions everywhere to expel them from India. This was perhaps the first time Indian rulers united for a common cause beyond their narrow personal interests and prejudices. It was decided that the Marathas would attack the British locations in Bombay and its dependencies; Sindhia and Bhosle were to invade Bengal, the Nizam was to subjugate the Northern Circars and Haidar was in charge of the invasion of Madras and the Carnatic. Haidar swept down the Carnatic like a torrent with 80,000 men and 100 guns. In October 1780 he captured Arcot, defeating an English army under Colonel Braille. But the British managed to break the alliance between the raja of Berar, Mahadji Sindhia, the nizam and Haider. Sadly, the other members of the confederacy didn't take up the plan with enthusiasm; otherwise they may have ensured the complete subjugation of the British, who were already precariously placed. The confederacy failed to take off because of duplicity and mutual suspicions among the allied forces even though Maratha forces—under Mahadji Sindhia, the nizam of Hyderabad and Haidar—defeated the British and Raghoba between 1775–82 and, through the Treaty of Salbai, demanded that the British hand Raghoba to the Marathas, thus ending his ambitious flight.

Mysore vs Coorg

During the Maratha onslaught on Mysore, Haidar had requested the rulers of Aigoor and Coorg to assist him. The former did but the raja of Coorg refused. This started the bickering between Mysore and Coorg. Haidar sent Farzullah Khan with a large army to annex Coorg. Coorg, or

Kodagu as it is called, is hailed as the 'Scotland of India'. Coorgis have historically been a warrior class—brave, handsome men and beautiful women being their hallmarks. They have their own indigenous culture, customs and traditions, and a language distinct from Kannada. They revel in the fact that they could never be conquered due to the remote, mountainous location of Coorg and the inaccessibility of the region, especially in the monsoons. Since the early medieval period the little kingdom of Coorg began to prosper, because of the silver, gold and salt trade that came through its mountains from the Kerala coast to the great cities of the Deccan plateau. Coorg's relative wealth attracted several invaders, including the kings of Vijayanagara and the medieval Deccan sultanates, but the fierce Coorgi men repulsed all of them. The Coorgis had always been great lovers of freedom and guard their sovereignty very dearly. The region was ruled by the Virashaiva Haleri Palegara family. About a third of the population consisted of Kodavas—a group that had begun its transformation to caste much later than in the plains of Karnataka and had therefore retained a lot of its tribal past. This was displayed in the form of holding land and accompanying labour operations with cooperativist tendencies.

During Haidar's time, the throne of Coorg was shared by Mudduraja of Haleri and Muddhiaharaja of Hormale. Their combined forces under Lingaraja defeated Farzullah Khan. Haidar had to sign a treaty under which he surrendered Bellare territories. But with the death of the two kings and the installation of the weak monarch Devrajappa, coupled with the usual palace intrigues and skirmishes, Haidar found the time ripe to invade Coorg again. He attacked the kingdom in 1773 and annexed it. Appaji Raja was made the titular ruler on the promise of a tribute of Rs 24,000. In 1776 Appaji Raja was killed in a campaign to capture Wynad and Lingaraja became king. He submitted Elusavirasime, Amara, Sulya, Panje and Bellare to Mysore.

The region had the Jamma ryots composed of a combination of castes, like Kodava, Amma Kodava, Heggade, Eimbokala, Airi, Koyava, Mapilla and Arey Gowdas. These Jamma ryots were enraged by the new revenue system. Lingaraja and his son Viraraja capitalised fully on the discontent among the ryots, leading to guerrilla warfare and peasant uprisings in Coorg on a regular basis—a thorn in the flesh for Mysore. It was not until 1782 that Haidar finally captured Viraraja and Lingaraja, though the discontent was far too deeply entrenched to be so easily quashed. He erected the fort of Mercara in the most central location and confirmed the landholders in their possessions for moderately higher revenue. As Hayavadana Rao mentions:

> Compared with the revenue raised in the Mysorean territories that which had been arranged for Coorg was extremely low; but their standard of comparison was not what had been levied from others, but what they themselves had formerly paid. The very highest rate of assessment in Coorg had been a tenth of the produce. In general, it was much lower and a considerable portion of the landholders, exclusively of the military service, paid an acknowledgement to the Raja which was merely nominal. Hyder deemed his moderation to be excessive in requiring not much more than the old Hindu assessment of one sixth.

Battling On

Meanwhile, in 1775 a combined force of Basalat Jung of Adoni and Morari Rao of Gutti, along with Nizam Ali's commander-in-chief Ibrahim Khan Dhoonsa, attacked Bellary. Caught unawares, Haidar steadily marched from Srirangapatna with his light horse and regular and irregular foot soldiers. He struck the besieging troops with surprise attacks from the rear. Basalat's camps were routed and many of his warriors killed. Haidar then set out to Adoni and exacted ten lakhs from Basalat Jung and reimbursed himself with one lakh Pagodas. On 23 November 1775, he arrived at Kenchanguda and captured it along with Adoni, Penagonda, Ratnagiri and Kurnool. Morari Rao—with his dillydallying and betrayal tactics—had spelt trouble for Haidar since the days of the Tiruchirapalli campaign. Morari on his part always allied with Haidar's enemies in all the major wars, adding to the latter's dislike of the Gutti ruler. Haidar's overtures for reconciliation were scoffed at by Morari Rao. Towards the end of January 1776, after besieging the fort for five weeks, Haidar took the fort by storm and looted the place. Morari's messages to Pune and Hyderabad for help met with little success. His peace envoys were rejected by Haidar saying that the tribute money offered grossly undervalued the real worth of Gutti. He attacked the fort again and by the end of it, Morari Rao capitulated. He was captured and sent away to Srirangapatna as prisoner. Morari's territories were annexed to Mysore. On his return, Haidar annexed many territories like Anegondi and made his victorious way to Srirangapatna in August 1776.

In 1773, Warren Hastings had been appointed the first governor general of India. While Clive had been content with creating the impression that the nawab of Bengal remained sovereign, subject to the diktat of the Mughal emperor only in some matters, Hastings moved swiftly to remove this fiction. The nawab was stripped of his remaining powers and the annual tribute paid to the Mughal emperor was withdrawn. Hastings supported the kingdom of Awadh (Oudh) against the depredations of the Rohillas, chieftains of Afghani descent, and he took measures to contain the Marathas, though they could not be prevented from attacking Agra, Mathura, and even Delhi, the seat of the Mughal empire. He had heard ballads about Haidar and his legendary bravery and was determined to crush him.

A New Ruler

On 16 September 1776, the 17-year-old Maharaja Bettada Chamaraja Wodeyar died, throwing the royal family into utter despair. The childless raja left no heirs. Haidar rushed to Srirangapatna to offer his condolences to the bereaved family. Maharani Lakshmammanni desired to crown her brother-in-law's son Narasarajayya or her co-wife's son Siddharajayya. But Haidar intervened, asserting that these boys had physical deformities which prevented their adoption under the Hindu law of succession. He told her that since the Yadu family of the Wodeyars must shine with a reputed leader, she could not just crown anyone without proper scrutiny of his worth. It was public knowledge that Haidar just wanted to defy the maharani and to ensure that a powerless infant sat on the throne. Although terribly angry, the maharani, fearful of Haidar's wrath, agreed.

All the children of the royal family, the nobility, and the Urs families were called in for the special kind of examination Haidar set up in a manner where the final decision rested with him. The children were left in a huge room strewn with a variety of objects—fruits, sweetmeats, flowers, toys, books, money bags, male and female ornaments, weapons and so on. The boys were asked to pick whatever they wanted. Haidar was most satisfied by the actions of Chamaraja, a two-and-a-half-year old who picked up a mirror and a sword, symbolising his equanimity between pleasure and duty and also the transparency with which he intended to run the affairs of the state. Haidar loudly proclaimed: 'He is our new king!' He then directed all the people assembled there to stand up in reverence and placed the child on a couch. He sent his word to the horrified maharani that this was his decision and seemed to seek her acceptance. The powerless maharani accepted his choice. But deep in her heart she nurtured tremendous hatred for the boy, who had been handpicked by the usurper of her husband's throne. On 27 September 1776 (Bhadrapada month), the young lad was crowned as the twenty-first ruler of Mysore—Khasa Chamaraja Wodeyar IX, 'Khasa' meaning legitimate. Born on 28 February 1774, he was the son of Devaraja Urs of Arikuthara and Honnajamma.

Lakshmammanni made life miserable for the young boy and on many occasions tried to eliminate him. Haidar came to know of her designs and, foreseeing the possible harm that could befall the young monarch, shifted Lakshmammanni away from the capital, to the Natakashala Bokkasada Thotti—the fine-arts section of the palace of Nazarabad—where she was held under house arrest. Although she left in anger, being away from Haidar's gaze proved to be a boon—giving her ample opportunities to attempt secret negotiations with the British.

Maharani Lakshmammanni

Born in 1742, this daughter of Katti Gopalaraje Urs was one of the most heroic and sagacious queens Mysore had ever seen. She found that Haidar's hold on the kingdom's royal family as well as its subjects never slackened and burned with the desire to rid the family from this eclipse. As Joyser describes her, she was a widow at twenty-four, 'while yet looking forward to a long career of womanly and queenly happiness, Lakshmammanni was left a dowerless widow, without offspring, without husband, without kingdom, with princely orphans to maintain and a powerful usurper to fight against!' Had she been a weak woman, she may have fallen into despair, but fortunately she was made of sterner stuff.

If there was one community Maharani Lakshmammanni could trust wholeheartedly, it was that of the Sri Vaishnavas, popularly known as the Mysore Pradhans. The families of Sri Vaishnavas or Iyengars had settled in Karnataka many years before the arrival of the Vaishnavite pontiff Ramanujacharya in the state. They had enjoyed a position of respect under the benevolent monarchs of the Hoysala, Vijayanagara and Wodeyar dynasties. Apart from royal patronage they also occupied prominent positions in the administration either as the gurus of the kings or as senior bureaucrats. In fact, it was a member of the family of the Mysore Pradhans, Govindarajayya, who solemnised the marriage of

Maharani Lakshmammanni with Immadi Krishnaraja Wodeyar. It is said that in 1765, Haidar sent his men to plunder the Pradhan's family of his wealth but found nothing as the latter had secretly buried the treasures and refused to disclose their location. In frustration, the soldiers strangled him to death. Govindarajayya's sons, Tirumala Rao and Narayana Rao, decided to avenge the death of their father by teaming up with the maharani.

The trusted duo of Tirumala Rao and Narayana Rao, nephews of Anche Shamaiya, were employed as the maharani's pradhans who acted as her agents to the 'Company Bahaddars'. Through them she sent emissaries to Haidar's foes to enlist their support against him. She even sent a messenger to Pune to request military aid from the Marathas and though the Maratha contingent came, Haidar cleverly made peace with them and sent them away. Tirumala Rao was banished to Cudappah by Haidar. The maharani suffered her biggest setback with the appointment of Muddu Malamma—her late husband's illegitimate wife and mother of the current ruler Bettada Chamaraja—as the regent of the young king. She found it an affront to her womanly honour to be seen genuflecting to the diktat of her husband's mistress and hated Haidar for inflicting this insult on her.

She began her negotiations as early as 1760, through one Rayadurga Srinivasa Rao, with the first emissaries being sent to Lord Pigot, governor of Madras, for recovering the lost grandeur of the family in the wake of the interregnum. Pigot responded, saying that vanquishing a powerful man, like Haidar, would require a permanent and trusted envoy of hers to station himself at Madras and inform the British regularly about Haidar's movements. But the changes the Carnatic during this time prevented the English from taking any firm action.

After a brief lull, the rani heard that Pigot had helped the native ruler of Tanjore to occupy his lawful throne. Emboldened by this, she prevailed upon the Rao brothers to carry her message to Pigot. This was an assignment fraught with risk as incurring Haidar's wrath could prove fatal for the envoy. She managed to bribe Tirumala at Cudappah with the promise—conditional on his help in her time of need—of the hereditary dewanship of the kingdom after it passed back to the Wodeyar family and also an annual salary of ten per cent of the state revenue. Haidar got wind of this plan and sent his soldiers to Cudappah to arrest or kill Tirumala Rao. But the latter managed to escape to Madras and met Lord Pigot who advised them to take shelter at the court of the raja of Tanjore. No sooner had they reached Tanjore that they received news of Pigot's death. They were now caught in no-man's land and didn't know where to proceed.

But Sullivan, the British Resident of Tanjore, introduced them to the new Governor Lord Macartney, who readily agreed to help the rani of Mysore. On 18 October 1782, the governor of Madras and Maharani Lakshmammanni signed a treaty, as Wilks records, for the 'conquest of Hyder Ally and the restoration of Hindoo supremacy'. For the English services she undertook to pay up to Rs 1 crore to the English army and 30 lakhs as a reward. The treaty had about fifteen articles in all, attested and authenticated by Rev. Schwartz and shared with Tirumala Rao and John Sullivan, the Company Representative. Hayavadana Rao describes the terms and conditions: in the very first article, the Company stated that 'they are willing to assist with their troops in reducing Hyder Ali and in re-establishing the Rajah in his hereditary dominions upon the conditions proposed in the first, second, third and fourth Articles.' A successive scale of payment of money on the rani's part is suggested in the treaty for the 'favours'. On taking over and delivery of the Coimbatore country, 3 lakh Canteroi Pagodas, on the English Army ascending the Balaghat (Mysore) and taking Hardanahalli and other forts, a sum of one lakh Pagodas. 'On the surrender of the fort of Mysore and the government of the country being given over to our Rana[*] or whoever she may adopt,' another one lakh was to be paid and finally upon the 'fall of Seringapatam', another 5 lakhs to be paid, 'in all the sum of ten lakhs of Pagodas'. The English were also to maintain an army in Mysore whose expenses were to be paid by the rana. The Company agreed not to interfere in the internal management of the country nor in the 'business of the Polygars, in the collection of the Revenue, or in the nomination of Killedars etc. but will support and assist all officers who may be appointed by the Government of Mysore.' If the Company failed to 'reduce Hyder Naig' and were 'obliged to make peace with him,' it would take over the protection of the royal family and reimburse it of the money advanced 'on account of our Rana for the purposes being mentioned'. But if they achieved success in their endeavour, the rana would be put in possession 'of all conquests made by Hyder Ali' and they would 'protect her and her successors in the same.'

---

[*] Though a rani, she was referred to as Rana in recognition of her bravery in a man's world.

Haidar Ali: The Supreme Dictator AD 1761–82

Some of the details of the above stated terms of the Treaty of 1782 make interesting reading:

We will pay to the Company 3 lakhs of Kandirayeen pagodas as soon as their troops shall have driven the enemy out of the Coimbatore, etc., countries on this side of the mountains. As soon as the English troops shall have ascended the Balaghat and possessed themselves of the forts of Ardmelli or Viseyburam we will pay the further sum of one lakh of pagodas. Upon the surrender of the fort of Mysore and the Government of the country being given to our Rana or whoever she may adopt, we will pay another lakh of pagodas. Upon the fall of Seringapatam we will pay 5 Lakhs of pagodas, that is to say, in all, a sum of ten lakhs of pagodas, that the Company shall not interfere in the management of the country nor for the managements for the peshcush and chout; that the killadars, amildars and other officers who may be appointed by the Rana for the management of the country shall be employed and none others in the collections, and that they shall be supported by the Company's troops in the execution of their office, and further that the Company shall not interfere in the business of the Paleyagars. That the Company will order to be delivered over to us whatever jewels, treasures, elephants, horses, military stores, and effects of every kind belonging to Hyder Naig and his officers that may be taken. That Hyder Naig and all prisoners of rank who may be taken shall be delivered over to the Rana's Officers. That Seringapatam being a place of religious worship no troops shall be stationed within the walls of that place except in times of actual war. That the Governor and Council of Madras must procure a Sunnud from the Company in England to confirm to our Rana and her successors the full possession and Government of all the countries that may be taken as before mentioned from Hyder Naig for ever and ever, upon the conditions herein definitely expressed.

It is another story altogether that at the end of the day, the British didn't honour a single article of the above treaty and yet, driven by complete desperation, Maharani Lakshmammanni agreed to the new terms and conditions laid out by the Company 'Bahaddars'.

Lord Macartney wrote to her in a letter the same year:

God bless you! I received the letter you sent with Narayana Rao, and have noted the contents with pleasure. I have always been anxious to serve your interests. The ingratitude and injustice of Hyder to your Royal Family are well known to everybody. It has become a matter of necessity not only for us, but for others also, to punish him for his misdeeds. I write this in accordance with the treaty with you. If God blesses the efforts of the company it will be seen how your rights will be respected. We also count much upon the services of Tirumal Rao and other such intelligent noblemen on your behalf. And hence you may be rest assured that your Kingdom will be restored to you. Hyder has declared war against us and our allies through enmity. We shall therefore necessarily invade his territories from all quarters. And by the grace of God we will restore to the rightful owners those territories, which Hyder had occupied by fraud and force. The English and the Company will see to this with special care. And we shall always do what is just and upright. The Ranee and her partisans should join in this noble work. And there is no doubt that good will result in every way.

After the conclusion of the Treaty of 1782, to help the British pass through the Gejjelhutty Pass in their march towards Srirangapatna at the height of the Second Mysore War, the Pradhans collected 300 horses and accompanied Colonel Lang and his army towards Karur. On 2 April 1783, Karur was captured, followed by Vijayamangalam on 6 April and Dindigul on 4 May. Lang was succeeded by Fullarton who annexed Palghat, Dharapuram and Coimbatore.

Though she remained in seclusion in the *zenana*, Maharani Lakshmammanni showed herself as undaunted as some of her letters to the well-wishers of her family show her quiet faith in the Mercy of Providence to relieve the misfortune that befell her family; that the night would pass away and the sun would rise. 'May Lord Ranga help us,' was how she rounded off most of her letters. The locals and the subjects still had great respect for her and fondly called her Mahamathrushree. Thus, while Haidar remained busy with innumerable campaigns, he remained blissfully unaware of the manipulative enemy within, who was showing the secret doorway to his most hated enemy, the British, and striking at the very roots of his establishment. Whether he underestimated her prowess or was afraid to take action against a female member of the respected royal family or if it was a gross intelligence failure on the part of his otherwise astute spy system is unknown. But one thing was certain: the foundations of Haidar's kingdom were being weakened, brick by brick.

HAIDAR'S CONQUESTS

In early 1777, the confederate armies of the Marathas and the Nizam launched a combined assault on Mysore. While the Maratha army, estimated at around 30,000 men, assembled near Miraj on the left of the Krishna with a view of taking over Savanoor, the Nizam's army of 40,000 under Ibrahim Khan Dhoonsa was to attack the southern frontiers. Receiving intelligence of this plan, Haidar fixed his base at Gutti and reinforced the Mysorean army commanded by Mohammad Ali. He managed to buy the Nizam with the lure of gold. Two people failed to fall in line on this occasion—Abdul Hakim Khan, the Cudappah Nawab and Madakari Nayaka, the Palegar of Chitradurga. The latter had joined Trimbaka Mama in 1770, sided with the Marathas in the siege of Nijagal and allowed Sivarama Bhao, nephew of Morari Rao, to escape after the fall of Gutti.

The Palegar of Chitradurga, Madakari Nayaka, seemed to pose a big threat to Haidar by befriending the peshwas. The Mysore army hurried to besiege the fort of Chitradurga in 1777 and Tipu was despatched to conquer the fort after befriending the minister of the chieftain of Rayadurga, Krishnappa. But the fort and its dependencies were so well guarded and fortified that even Tipu found it impossible to annex it. The Maratha army sent for the help of the Nayaka under Phadke and Parasurama Bhao were generously bribed by Haidar, who tried to annex the fort by hook or crook. He came to know through insiders that the fort had only one small entrance, which one had to crawl through to enter. It was this *kindi* or narrow opening that offered a ray of hope for Haidar. He hatched a clever plan to send his soldiers one by one into the fort through this opening. When a sizeable number of soldiers had entered, they could open arms on the inmates all of a sudden.

The Mysore troops kept a close watch on the movements of the watchman who guarded the ramparts. They decided to sneak into the fort one hot afternoon when the guard went home for lunch. In the middle of the lunch, the guard wanted some water to drink. But they had run out of water at home and so his wife Obavva decided to fetch water from a small stream that flowed near the *kindi*. She was shocked to see the soldiers of Mysore lined up to enter the fort. She rushed home to alert her husband. But finding him totally engrossed in his lunch, she decided to save the day for Chitradurga all by herself. She took the *onake* or the long club meant for pounding paddy grains and rushed towards the *kindi*. As the soldiers tried to crawl in, Obavva smashed their skulls with her *onake*. After killing each soldier she would put aside the corpse and wait for the next victim to enter. Soon several soldiers had entered and met this fate. Obavva was unfazed that she was a lone woman combating the skilled soldiers of a kingdom that had shaken even the English East India Company. She saw herself merely fulfilling her duty to her chieftain by protecting the fort. Eyes flashing, and covered in perspiration, she stood like a bloodthirsty vampire, her upraised *onake* waiting for the next prey. The guard, on his return, was shocked to see the grotesque and eerie scene of Obavva standing with a blood-soaked *onake* and several dead bodies around her, like the Goddess Kali. He blew the bugle and aroused the slumbering troops. Obavva's work was done, and she encouraged the troops to attack the invaders. But the excitement proved too much to bear and she died of exhaustion, though not before ensuring that the enemy troops were being dealt with. The story of this heroic woman of Chitradurga, popularly known as 'Onake Obavva', has assumed iconic proportions and is known to every child in Karnataka. She is remembered to this day for her valiant attempt to put off the Mysorean troops.

Unfortunately, Obavva's sacrifices went in vain. The army of Chitradurga wasn't as brave or efficient as the lady who guarded its ramparts. Also, Haidar managed to bribe all the Muslim soldiers of the Nayaka's army in the name of Islam and they literally escorted him into the fort. The traitors soaked the guns in oil to destroy them and thus the Palegar didn't even have the opportunity to defend himself. Madakari Nayaka surrendered the township in 1779; his brother Parashurama Nayaka, wife and children were imprisoned and despatched to Srirangapatna, where Madakari Nayaka died later that year. From all over Chitradurga thousands of young teenagers were forcibly brought to Srirangapatna, circumcised and converted to Islam. A special contingent of these, called the 'Chela Batallion', was created at Haidar's behest.

Haidar's commander Fazalullah Khan defeated the Palegar of Hardanahalli, besieged the forts of Ujjini and Kittur, captured Gudikota,

Jarimale, Kanakuppe, Molakalmuru and Dodderi. The same year, Haidar besieged Cudappah. The Nawab of Cudappah, Abdul Hakim Khan, sent 60 Pathans to behead Haidar by nightfall. These people slowly crept towards the tent where Haidar slept. But his loyal watchman warned him and Haidar leapt in self-defence. He made a dummy figurine of himself with pillows and shawls and escaped to rouse the other soldiers. As the trespassers tried to stab 'Haidar', he and his soldiers attacked them from behind and cut off their hands and legs. He then besieged Cudappah, took the fort by storm, looted the place, captured and deposed the Nawab and his family, sending them to Srirangapatna. The hands and feet of the assassins were cut off and some others dragged round the camp tied to the feet of elephants!

SECOND ANGLO-MYSORE WAR

Meanwhile, internationally the situation was getting tough for the British. The American War of Independence broke out in 1775. It began more as a colonial revolt against the economic policies of the British empire but eventually widened beyond British colonies in North America with France, Spain and the Netherlands entering the war against Great Britain. The British forces in India had just recovered from the shameful debacle in the Maratha war where they had to give up their loyalist Raghunath Rao to the combined forces. It was the worst timing for Hastings. The strain of the American war reduced the possibility of reinforcements in India; British sea power was severely constrained and gave the French a chance of recovery. The French declared their war against the British in 1778 and Haidar, who had remained a trusted ally of the French, threw his lot in, to fight what came to be known as the Second Anglo-Mysore War.

Tiruchirapalli and the Carnatic were a blot on Mysore's history and a personal failure for Haidar. Right from the conquest of Tiruchirapalli by Nanjarajayya to the time of the First Anglo-Mysore War, Mysore tried in vain to annex Tiruchirapalli. In 1774–75, Haidar set his eyes again on the Carnatic-Payenghat region. By 1776, detailed strategies were created to attack Tiruchirapalli again under the command of Sayyid Mokhdum and Tipu. In 1779, a detachment of 10,000 cavalry under Murarji Mama and Berki Srinivasa Rao was despatched to cross Kaveripatnam towards the Changama pass and then divide into four branches. One was to remain there, the other to invade Tiruchirapalli, the third to move towards Ambur and the fourth to approach the Carnatic region. Haidar wrote to Muhammad Ali yet again, demanding that he respect the earlier treaty and hand over Tiruchirapalli to Mysore. When the latter remained indifferent, Haidar prepared for the final assault on Tiruchirapalli in June 1780 with a force of about a lakh—perhaps the largest army confederacy ever assembled in southern India. It further proved the importance of the accession of Tiruchirapalli in the larger scheme of things for Mysore.

Proceeding by way of Maddur, Chennapatna and Bangalore, Haidar crossed the frontier at Hosur and traversed Madanahalli, Palukode, Kaveripatnam and Singarapettai to reach Kilpauk by end-June 1780. Here, the army was split into two parts. The larger division stayed with him. The other one, consisting of 20,000 cavalry, was despatched to conduct simultaneous raids on the entire southern peninsular and Carnatic regions from Machlipatnam in the north to Arcot, Chengelpet, Vellore, Pondicherry, Kumbakonam, Tiruchirapalli, Madurai and Rameswaram in the south. Balavant Rao was despatched with 500 horses to Karur to intercept the English forces before they reached Tiruchirapalli, and Sardar Khan at Calicut was to guard Telichery. With such an extensive strategic movement of the army, Haidar finally attacked the heart of the Carnatic on 20 July 1780.

Individual regiments were also sent to important locations to guard or take by storm. Haidar captured a sequence of forts and places—Tiruvannamalai, Chetput, Tiruvattoor, Gulwa, Kaveripak, etc., before laying siege to Arcot on 21 August 1780. Achanna Pandita, the chieftain of the Arcot fort, held his territory in a gallant battle.

No movement was made till smoke was seen from St. Thomas' Mount, where Sir Hector Munro commanded some 5,200 troops. Taken by surprise, the British sent their commanders in defence of their ally Muhammad Ali. Corps were despatched under Colonel Harper in Guntur; Colonel Baillie commanded the army towards the southern parts of Kalahasti and Tirupati, and Colonel Braithwaite moved to Chengelpet. Reinforcements were sent to salvage Arcot and to important locations like Udaiyarpalayam, Gingee, Karnatakgar and Wandiwash. However, the Commander-in-Chief, Sir Hector Munro decided otherwise midway and directed the troops to assemble at Kanchipuram. Accordingly, before end-August, the regiments regrouped there—General Munro with a force of 5,209, Colonel Braithwaite and Colonel Baillie with 2,813 men. The move was intended to distract Haidar from Arcot and the motive was accomplished. Haidar turned defensive, lifting the siege of Arcot on 29 August 1780 and marching towards Kanchipuram.

By the time they reached Kanchipuram, Munro's provisions seemed to be running out. They were amazed at Muhammad Ali's reported inability, when approached for help, to bail them out at this critical juncture. Colonel Baillie, however was camped on the wrong side of the River Kortalaiyar and with the seasonal floods, they were stranded on that bank. Tipu attacked Baillie's already exhausted and dissipated forces, completely encircling the troops. To add to Baillie's discomfort, Haidar sent his infantry, guns and forces to Permabakum and Polilur where Baillie was being trapped. The fierce battle that followed resulted in the total destruction of Baillie's force of 2,800 on 10 September 1780. Of the 86 European officers, including the staff and surgeons, 36 were killed or fatally wounded and 50, of whom 34 were wounded, were taken prisoner along with 3,820 soldiers (including 508 Europeans) and Baillie himself.

This was a major blow to the British, who had already suffered an ignoble defeat in the First Anglo-Mysore War. It was in fact the first and most serious setback the English had suffered in India. The whole detachment was either killed or taken prisoner. This defeat caused much consternation in Madras. Sir Hector Munro, the hero of Buxar, who had defeated three rulers of India (Mughal emperor Shah Alam, Nawab of Oudh Shuja-ud-daula and Nawab of Bengal Mir Qasim) in a single battle, was petrified at the prospect of facing Tipu. He ran for his life to Madras, throwing all his cannons into the tank of Kanchipuram.

Tipu had taken great interest in the Mysore-Maratha war of 1769–72. After the death of Peshwa Madhava Rao in 1772, he was sent to the northern part of Mysore to recover the territories previously occupied by the Marathas. By the time of the Second Anglo-Mysore War, he had gained great experience both in warfare and diplomacy. In September 1780 he inflicted a crushing defeat on Colonel Baillie near Polilur.

The terrified British were severely critical of Munro, who had been the chief planner of the Kanchipuram strategy which had boomeranged badly on the British. Innes Munro said:

> In a review of this melancholy and fatal event, that no imputation may fall on any individual, it is necessary to recur to the origin of the ill-concerted expedition. It was first suggested, as has always

been observed, by the Nabob of Arcot (who was very naturally solicitous to save his capital), and eagerly embraced by the Council. The only plausible reason which they could adduce in support of a measure of such singular hazard was the impossibility of supporting the army, when reinforced in the vicinity of Madras. No provisions had been laid in by them, nor the smallest preparation made for the support even of a force so inconsiderable. They, therefore, without any consideration of probable contingencies, resolved upon sending out the army to forage for themselves, who were to be joined by another still worse provided than they were. Had Lieutenant Colonel Baillie's detachment been ordered to repair to St. Thomas' Mount, as proposed by Sir Hector Munro and Lord Macleod, it is probable it would have accomplished the junction without molestation, as Hyder's whole army was then before Arcot. When united they might then have had the ability to execute any judiciously concerted plan which might have tended to the relief of the settlement.

After pursuing Munro on his flight to Madras, Haidar camped at Arcot yet again. With the guidance of French officers, he commanded the simultaneous firing from two columns of his army under Maha Mirza Khan and Tipu. Finally, on 28 November 1780, Arcot fell to Haidar, and Achanna Pandita, Arshed Beg Khan, Chistiyar Khan and Sayyid Hamid of the fort were taken prisoner. It seemed like the death knell for Muhammad Ali. Haidar advanced down south as far as Tanjore and took Chambargarh, Dhobigarh, Kailasgarh, Karnatakgarh, Satgarh, Sholingur, Tripasore, Tindivanam and many other places of the Carnatic and Payenghat. Tipu was proclaimed 'Nabob of the Carnatic'.

Warren Hastings had to act fast. Matters were out of control. He sent from Bengal Sir Eyre Coote, one of the chief architects of the Battle of Plassey. Sir Charles Smith, a Senior Member of Council replaced Whitehill as Governor of Madras. The British had to change strategy if they didn't want to upset the southern applecart. The Carnatic was already out of their hands. On 17 January 1781, Eyre Coote marched to salvage Chengelpet, Wandiwash and Carnagooly. All the three were annexed and Haidar forced to decamp from Wandiwash. Haidar moved to Porto Novo and from there attempted a siege of Tiruchirapalli in June 1781 along with Tipu, assisted by French forces under Monsieur Lally.

But Coote diverted him by attacking Chidambaram, which was Haidar's strategic entry-point to the Carnatic.

The two met head on in the famous Battle of Porto Novo on 1 July 1781. Coote dealt Haidar's forces a crushing defeat at Porto Novo and won the battle despite odds of five to one. This victory is regarded as one of the great feats of the British in India. As Innes Munro recounts:

> Upon the conclusion of this hard-contested business, how mortifying was it to find that no other advantage had been gained by us after such extreme fatigue than the simple possession of the field? — A compensation very inadequate to the loss of so many gallant soldiers. This might have been one of the most glorious and decisive victories ever obtained, had the General permitted the line to advance at an earlier period of the day. There cannot be a doubt but it would have finally terminated the war, as most of the enemy's guns must have inevitably fallen into our hands; for it was with the utmost difficulty they got them reconveyed across the nullah during the pursuit, a labour in which, by Meer Sahib's gallantry, and our own tardiness, they were singularly favoured. It was also a matter of surprise to many in the army that the British cavalry were not ordered to pursue the fugitives, there being, with Mahrattas and others, a thousand in the camp, a number that might have done considerable execution against a flying enemy if properly conducted, particularly as they had eight light three-pounders dragged by horses constantly attached to them.

This was closely followed by another bloody war in Polilur, where Haidar had crushed the British during the First Anglo-Mysore war. But luck did not favour him this time. He suffered a second defeat before Coote's forces on 27 August 1781. Munro quotes Coote's description of this war:

> Had not Hyder Ally from a principle of superstition, which we know regulates in a great measure the actions of the natives, chose to have met me at the ground on which he had been formerly successful, I could not have moved one mile further to the westward in quest of him, but must have been, for want of provisions, reduced to the necessity of returning without action...

Hyder Ally's army was strongly posted. His troops, covered in hollow ways and ranged just behind the summit of the rising ground in our front, would not stand when pushed. Their loss consequently (was) not so considerable as it would have been had they waited the decision of the day from our musketry, but this they in general avoided, always drawing off their guns, and retiring before we can bring them to close action.

A month later, on 27 September, the Mysore forces lost yet again to Coote at Sholingarh. Haidar's forces were pushed towards Kaveripauk and the army of Mysore suffered more than 2,000 casualties. Lord Macartney had taken over as the new governor of Madras and his first priority was to relieve Vellore. Additional provisions were sent to Vellore and Haidar's supplies blocked en route to Chittoor. Despite the reverses, Haidar's army carried on with their surprise attacks, forcing the British to retreat and join the main army at Madowady. However Tipu, who had besieged Wandiwash, was forced to raise the siege even as Coote marched menacingly towards the place.

Tipu, however, avenged the three successive defeats of the Mysorean forces at British hands. He inflicted a serious and humiliating defeat on Colonel Braithwaite at Annagudi near Tanjore on 18 February 1782. This army consisted of 100 Europeans, 300 cavalry, 1,400 sepoys and 13 guns. Tipu seized all the guns and took the entire detachment prisoner. The total force, of a few hundred Europeans, was the standard size of the colonial armies that had caused havoc in India before Haidar and Tipu. In December 1781 Tipu had successfully seized Chittoor from British hands. Thus, Tipu had gained sufficient military experience towards the end of the Second Anglo-Mysore War.

On 17 May 1782, the Treaty of Salbai, signed between the British and the Marathas, decided Raghoba's fate. It meant some reprieve from war for Mysore, though the terms were inimical to Mysore. Haidar had to relinquish all territories taken from the Marathas after his earlier treaty with the late Madhava Rao in 1767 and had to evacuate the Carnatic. To add to it, there was an insurrection in the Malabar and rebellion in Balam and Coorg. The French contingent arrived, though much later than promised, with about 300 men and an African regiment. Haidar conferred with Monsieur Cossigny and Admiral Suffrein, hoping that Monsieur Bussy would come to his aid in the South with a large contingent, as promised. The English kept track of the clandestine deals between Haidar and the French and sought to stop Bussy's arrival through naval actions off Trincomalee in April 1782. Haidar, however, made four divisions in the Mysore army, the biggest being led by him and the other three by the faithful Palegars, Monsieur Lally and Commandant Mohammad Ali and Tipu. They secured Cuddalore and Permacoil and moved towards Arni. The Battle of Arni with the British forces took place on 2 June 1782. The English incurred considerable losses and were forced to beat a hasty retreat to Vellore, with nearly 2,000 of their soldiers taken prisoner. Attempts at peace bore no fruit as Haidar was determined that Muhammad Ali cede Tiruchirapalli to Mysore—an idea the latter decisively dismissed.

DEATH OF HAIDAR

In the midst of the war at Narasingarayapet near Chittoor, Haidar fell seriously ill. Tipu was at that time away in the Malabar to crush the Nair revolt and also to enlist French support for rebuilding the artillery. Haidar had a trusted commander Sheikh Ayaz, to whom he had granted the governorship of Bidnaur. Unknown to Haidar, the man had been bought by the British, to whom he regularly leaked important state secrets. Wilks speaks of Ayaz's early life and career, which began with Haidar's first Malabar invasion of 1766:

> Among the many prisoners carried off in the first inhuman emigration from Malabar was a young Nair, from Chercul, who had been received as a slave of the palace, and to whom on his forced conversion to Islam, they had given the name of Sheikh Ayaz. The noble port, the ingenuous manners and singular beauty of the boy, attracted general attention; and when at a more mature age he was led into the field, his ardent valour and uncommon intelligence recommended him to the particular favour of Hyder, who was an enthusiast in his praise, and would frequently speak of him, under the designation of 'his right hand in the hour of danger'. Ayaz soon conveyed the impression of an affectionate and trustworthy humble friend in the estimation of Hyder. To the endowments which have been stated, incessant and confidential military service has superadded experience beyond his years; and Hyder selected him for the important trust of civil and military

governor of the fort and territory of Chitteldoorg. But modest as he was faithful and brave, Ayaz wished to decline the distinction, as one to which he felt himself incompetent...

Despite being rewarded lavishly by Haidar, Sheikh Ayaz seemed to foster bitter memories and was perhaps biding his time for revenge. On his part, Tipu never really liked Sheikh Ayaz, because he was his father's favourite. Haidar would publicly shower praise on Ayaz and contrast him with his own son—something Tipu despised with all his heart.

Meanwhile, Haidar's health was deteriorating by the day. The *hakims* and *vaids* had given up hope of an immediate recovery. Purnaiya, his trusted associate, was at the helm of affairs in the war camp. News of Haidar's ill-health was concealed from the general public and the army, lest it create confusion. So the only people, other than Purnaiya, who were privy to the news were Commandant Mohammad Ali, Krishna Rao, Badar-u-Zumaun Khan, Maha Mirza Khan, Ghazi Khan and Abu Muhammad Mirdha. Purnaiya decided to send the message to Tipu and did so through three emissaries—Ghulam Mohammad, Amir Khan and Sadhuram. Mohammad was in Ayaz's pay and carried the confidential letter straight to his master's chambers. The British got the news in this manner but, since the coded message meant for Tipu could not be entirely deciphered, were not sure of Haidar's exact condition. Even the watchmen outside Haidar's tent did not know if their master was dead or alive. Amir Khan was killed on the way and it was Sadhuram alone who managed to reach Malabar and convey the message of his father's critical condition to Tipu.

But by then a different kind of situation prevailed in the war camps at Narasingarayanapet. A frustrated Sheikh Ayaz spread rumours through Shamsuddin and Mohammad Araman that Purnaiya had murdered Haidar. All this was done to create confusion and anarchy in the already thwarted army. But the enraged Purnaiya dealt with the situation with all firmness. He immediately ordered the arrest and execution of the mischief-makers. To instil confidence in the troops, bugles and drums were played outside the tent as usual, as if on Haidar's orders. The troops prayed for their master's recovery. Had the situation gone out of control it would have ensured disaster for Mysore. The British were waiting in the wings to deal their final blow and there was no dearth of traitors either.

Finally, on 7 December 1782, Haidar, who from his humble origin had risen to the corridors of power and royalty, usurping the very kingdom whose king had once bought his welfare, who had been relentless in his hatred and battle against the British who were out to plunder the country, prayed for the last time to his Maker and dropped down dead.

These were testing times for Purnaiya. The news of Haidar's death was to be kept a secret lest it create anarchy in the army. As part of an elaborate plan, huge chests were brought in and announced as gifts sent by the Ottoman Caliph of Constantinople wishing Haidar a quick recovery. The caliph was considered the ultimate symbol of Islamic power and therefore his name was brought into this entire deception. This practice continued for a few days, as if Haidar had seen the gifts, accepted them and ordered that they be sent to the treasury of Srirangapatna. When the people got used to this practice, Purnaiya decided to use the chests to send Haidar's body to Srirangapatna, before the stench of the rotting body could raise the troops' suspicions. The chest was despatched with an abnormally heavy escort and the body was taken to Kolar where Haidar's father Fateh Muhammad lay buried.

Tipu finally arrived. Shaken by his father's untimely demise, he wanted to renounce everything. He was, however, inspired and advised by Purnaiya and the others to realise his duties and work for the cause for which his father had laid down his life. After the burial ceremonies at Srirangapatna, Tipu resolved to carry on the war against the British. Thus ended the story of one of Mysore and India's greatest warriors—a man blessed with an insurmountable spirit coupled with a cunning and sharp intellect; someone who had the courage to face the challenges of life and turn the tables against destiny.

10

HAIDAR ALI: THE MAN AND HIS LEGACY

Haidar Ali, who captured popular imagination with his meteoric rise, and who stayed at the top through a unique mix of leadership, cunning and manipulative skills, has been much studied by historians. Macaulay wrote:

> About thirty years before this time a Mohammadan soldier had begun to distinguish himself in the wars of Southern India. His education had been neglected; his extraction was humble. His father had been a petty officer of revenue; his grand father a wandering darvise. But though thus meanly descended, though ignorant even of the alphabet, the adventurer had no sooner been placed at the head of a body of troops than he proved himself a man born for conquest and command. Among the crowd of chiefs who were struggling for a share of India, none could compare with him in the qualities of the captain and the statesman. He became a general; he became a sovereign. Out of the fragments of old principalities which had gone to pieces in the general wreck, he formed for himself a great, compact and vigorous Empire. That Empire he ruled with the ability, severity and vigilance of Louis the Eleventh. Licentious in his pleasures, implacable in his revenge, he had yet enlargement of mind enough to perceive how much the prosperity of subjects adds to the strengths of Governments. He was an oppressor; but he had at least the merit of protecting his people against all oppression except his own. He was now in extreme old age; but his intellect was as clear and his spirits as

high as in the prime of his manhood. Such was the great Hyder Ali, the founder of the Mahammadan Kingdom of Mysore and the most formidable enemy with whom the English conquerors of India have ever had to contend.

Nothing could have summed up Haidar's life and times more aptly. He had strenuously and painstakingly worked his way up the ladder of fame, leaving behind a legacy of his own in the pages of history. But, as mentioned in an earlier context, we find contradictions galore when it comes to an authenticated account of his nature and psyche. Unlike the Mughals who were either great poets or writers themselves, Haidar was illiterate, and so he took his thoughts, strategies and dreams to the grave with him. The accounts we have are merely those of subservient courtiers or of antagonistic documenters who supported the royal family. Some of the latter, as we saw earlier, have depicted him as the murderer of the teenage kings of Mysore to ensure the elimination of the dynasty itself. Author Mirza Iqbal strongly criticises Haidar's regime, and rather surprisingly for a fellow Muslim of the times:

> By his power mankind were held in fear and trembling; and from his severity God's creatures, day and night, were thrown into apprehension and terror. Cutting off the nose and ears of any person within his territories were the commonest things imaginable and the killing a man there was thought no more of than the treading on an ant. No person of respectability ever left his house with the expectation to return safe to it.

Thus, records of this period tend to be viewed with a lot of apprehension. While the Hindu records sing paeans of glory to the royal family of Mysore and heap scorn on the 'upstart usurper', and British records do only the latter, Muslim records exalt him as a personification of all that was good and noble in the world. However, one could not dispute his sense of tolerance, amply brought out in this anecdote:

A Muslim saint, Peer Ladha, complained to Haidar that the Hindus of Srirangapatna had beaten up his followers, the true soldiers of the army of Allah. On investigation, Haidar learnt that the fault lay with the Muslim followers, who had attacked a religious procession of the Hindus and triggered off this violent reaction. When Peer Ladha tried to justify the Muslim action, saying that the very fact that such a procession could take place was an insult to Islam and must not be tolerated by Haidar as the 'head of a Mussalman Government', Haidar replied, 'Who told you that it was a Mussalman Government? I am sure I never did.' The priest then threatened to leave Srirangapatna and Haidar dismissed him, saying he could go wherever he pleased.

FATEH HAIDAR

Among the many aspects of Haidar's life, we have a glimpse of him as a warrior and soldier with a never-say-die attitude that kept him going till his last breath. The other facets of his life are those of an administrator while he assumed the supreme dictatorship of the kingdom and importantly, the man himself. As stated before, the paucity of authentic information limits our deeper exploration of these facets of Haidar's long and inspiring life.

Credit for the consolidation of the kingdom, which had endured severe bouts of political instability and turmoil under the vicious dalavoy regime, goes to Haidar. Apart from making Mysore a force to reckon with in the geopolitical environment of the Deccan and India, Haidar streamlined the administration of the kingdom, which expanded under him to roughly 80,000 square miles, yielding an annual return of Rs 2 crore. The kingdom was divided into 20 main *tukdis* or sub-divisions. The *daftar*, *khajana* and *fouz* were the three main administrative units. The administrative machinery was run by a dewan, three bakshis in the Capital city, 20 Fouzdars for the 20 divisions of the state, 100 mamaledars, 100 shirastedars, killedars and 1,700 harikars, apart from the large militia guarding the borders.

One particular aspect of Haidar's personality—reflected both in his administrative model as well as in his personal dealings—was a deep-rooted suspicion of everyone around him. Since he had risen up the ranks the hard way and faced the most treacherous onslaught from the royal family and his own one-time ally Khande Rao, Haidar simply refused to trust people around him for too long. Most of his dewans enjoyed the post only for short periods of time. Haidar did not believe in concentrating power in a few hands and was convinced that absolute power corrupts absolutely. So he sacked his dewans at regular intervals. There were five dewans during his tenure—Venkatappa, Chinnayya, Asad Ali Khan, Silahat Khan and Mir Sadak. Mir Sadak was the only one who enjoyed Haidar's confidence and lasted at his post longer than the others could have ever dreamt of doing. In fact, Sadak continued even after Haidar's death, though eventually Tippu made a grave mistake in continuing to have faith in his father's trusted lieutenant. Purnaiya, who headed the Daftar Department as its bakshi, was another close associate of Haidar's and almost a part of his family. Krishna Rao headed the *khajana* or treasury as Purnaiya's senior. Haidar's brother-in-law Mokhdum Saib was the bakshi of the *fouz* or army.

Probably mindful of the high-intensity negotiations Rani Lakshmammanni and other members of the royal family were indulging in, Haidar had a vast network of spies spread all over Mysore. There were occasions when people would comment that even walls and doors could have been planted with ears by the 'Nawab'. His spies had an uncanny flair for mingling freely with the local populace and, in the course of common talk, extracting valuable news of goings-on in the kingdom. Haidar gave regular audience to these spies.

Curbs were also imposed on the freedom of the subjects of the kingdom fearing the sort of mobilisation that would be detrimental to his interests. People could not assemble in large groups or talk in public gatherings. They had to obtain prior permission from Haidar's office even for events, such as a marriage in the family. In fact, Haidar's men could loiter into a marriage party, get some goodies from the bride or bridegroom's side and also collect secret information from the casual conversation at such get-togethers.

His *mohar* or signet ring had the name 'Fateh Haidar' inscribed on it in Persian while his *durbar mohar* or royal insignia had the proud declaration: 'Fateh Haidar has taken birth to conquer this world. There is none who can match his bravery and the power of his sword.'

The employees of the kingdom received their salaries through a system called *patta*. This had two broad categories—Shamsi and Khamri—which corresponded to the months of the Muslim calendar. The wages were seldom paid for a whole month; months of the Muslim calendar with fewer days earned them lower wages. On an annual basis, employees got their salary for just 9–10 months of a traditional 12-month year. But they got plenty of 'gifts' in kind—either loot money after successful expeditions or some gracious bonus awarded by the 'Nawab'. They had to wait patiently for these to be sanctioned. His natural suspicion also ensured that Haidar Ali resorted to various means, including torture, for extraction of information and punishment. Errant and corrupt government officials were subjected to the severest torture the kingdom had ever seen. Thus Mysore, under the Interregnum Period of Haidar Ali and Tippu, saw a curious combination of medieval practices and progressiveness. A more comprehensive assessment of the administrative set-up and reforms that emerged in the 40-year rule of the house of Haidar has been presented towards the end of this section.

THE MAN HIMSELF

Moving on to other interesting aspects of Haidar's life—his personality, what his typical day was like, what anecdotes or glimpses we have of the way he thought, interacted with people around him and so on—this picture of the heroes of history is essential to de-mystify them and to help us relate to their human side. However, as stated earlier, the lack of comprehensive and credible information impairs our voyage into these aspects of Haidar's life. Historian Hayavadana Rao quotes Wilks on Haidar:

> It is impossible to withhold homage from the great natural talents, which raised an unlettered adventurer to the supreme control of a powerful kingdom, or the indomitable energy and fertility of resource, which found the most desperate reverses but fresh opportunities of rising...he could neither read nor write any language, though he spoke fluently Hindustani, Kannada, Marathi, Telugu and Tamil. The sum of his literary attainments consisted in learning to write the initial of his own name, H, to serve as his signature on public occasions; but either from inaptitude to learn, or for the purpose of originality, he invented its form, and signed thus, hh. In person he is described as robust and of medium height, of dark complexion, with an aquiline nose and small eyes. Contrary to the usual custom of Mussalmans, his face was clean shaven, even the eyebrows and eyelashes being removed.
>
> The most striking article of his dress was a scarlet turban, flat at the top and of immense diameter. His uniform was flowered white satin, with yellow facings and yellow boots, and a white silk scarf round his waist. He was fond of show and parade on great occasions and at such times was attended by a thousand

spear-men, and preceded by bards who sang of his exploits in the Kannada language. He was an accomplished horseman, a skilful swordsman and a dead shot. He had a large harem of six hundred women, but his strong sensual instincts were never allowed to interfere with public business. From sunrise to past noon he was occupied in public durbar; he then made his first meal and retired to rest for an hour or two. In the evening, he either rode out or returned to business. But frequently, the night was enlivened with the performances of dancing girls or of actors of comedies. He took a second meal about midnight and retired to rest, sometimes having drunk freely.

A couple of anecdotes from contemporary writers, like Kirmani and Mirza Iqbal, give us a glimpse into Haidar's personal life and nature. To quote Kirmani:

On most occasions, Hydur used patiently to bear with the petulance and coarseness of the brave men in his service. As, for instance, one day, in the Nawaub's court, or assembly, some recollections of the battle of Churkoli (Chinkurli) were introduced. The Nawaub said, that on one day his whole army had followed the path of cowardice; that they had run away before his face; that no one with his sword in his hand had exerted himself faithfully; and that they (the officers), to save their own lives, had sacrificed those of their men. Among those who were present there, was Yaseen Khan Wunti Koodri, who had followed the path of faith and honour in that battle and who had there devoted, as a charitable donation to the sword and fear, the whole of his body, and one eye; and he said in answer, 'Yes, Huzrut, what you say is true; for such occurrences arise from fate, and depend on the will and power of no man. Yet, this eye of mine, for what was it put out? And for what man did I lose the blessings of sight, the pleasures of beholding the lights and shades of the many coloured world, the object and delight of life?' The Nawaub smiled at this and said—'I did not mean you.'

Kirmani writes on another occasion:

Sometimes he was fond of sporting his wit, or of joking, with his associates or companions, particularly with Ali Zuman Khan.

At the time the Souba of Sira was conquered, the Nawaub one day mounted his horse to look at the city, that there are many tombs in front of the doors of the houses, and also in the streets or roads. The Nawaub, therefore asked those who were with him, how these tombs became placed in the middle of the town. Those persons replied that apparently, the whole space had been formerly waste land; but now, men seeing that God's people were protected, and the peasantry, encouraged by His Highness, they had assembled from all parts and had built the city. The Nawaub said, 'A truce to your compliments! Do you not know that these men and women died fighting for their houses?'

Mirza Iqbal states:

In his Durbars or levees, no one dared converse, or even whisper. If any one had a wedding in his house, he could not invite any friends; except through the Nawaub, and the agency of his servants; and even then he gave his Wordi Hurkaras orders to go and see and hear what was said and done. These men, therefore were in general bribed not to tell the truth; but he believed all they told him. If he had advanced anyone of his servants money, the third part of his pay was stopped until the amount was refunded; and if anyone paid the debt on demand, he was accustomed to demand interest, under the pretence that he had borrowed the money from a banker for him. But when he obtained the interest, he said, 'This man is rich, why did he borrow money from me? Seize his goods'; and accordingly, his property was sometimes confiscated or stolen by thieves set on by Hydur's authority.

Haidar never had elaborate or fancy dietary habits. He never insisted on the cooking of his favourite dishes—perhaps he did not have any favourites. The food and the way it was eaten were not commensurate with the high post he held and he retained the ruggedness of an average Mysorean solider all his life. He preferred sour and spicy dishes to sweet ones. Dried grams or rotis made of rice flour, wheat and ragi were his staple during war times and travel.

Despite being illiterate, Haidar had a sharp intellect and common sense. He was a veritable face-reader, a skill he had picked up out of insecurities born of suspicion. He had an infallible memory as well and recollected people and incidents even several years later. He seldom met visitors from unknown lands and that too after they were subjected to stringent cross-examination to verify their objectives. He had a cheerful disposition, made interesting and witty conversation interspersed with jokes. But it was just as easy to incur his wrath—he was infamous for his nasty temper, losing control over his speech and shooting the worst of invectives on the hapless victim.

Tuesdays and Fridays were the stipulated days for his elaborate shaves. No one dared to disturb him while he was busy with this, usually till about noon. For some strange reason, after assuming kingship, he preferred his head to be completely hairless. The shave would begin from a tonsure to shaving of his facial hair—beard, moustache, eyelashes and eyebrows. This caused his sharp features to seem all the more prominent!

The towns and villages of Mysore would abound with nomadic women playing the *dolu* (drum) and singing melodiously to entertain people. A regular feature of Mysorean weddings and get-togethers, these nomads were soon placed under Haidar's pay and they secretly gathered information about the happenings of the kingdom as well as of pretty women in the countryside. Haidar's men would then go to the suggested house and, either through coercion or wilful surrender, bring those beauties to his harem in Srirangapatna. Soon, commoners were petrified at the voice of the *dolu* woman—the woman who was believed to usher in good fortune now became a harbinger of doom for the young women in any household. The captive women were classified into four groups in the harem and distinguished by the colour of their dress—red, green, blue and white. Each group was assigned different chores under the supervision of a female head, who finally reported to Haidar's principal wife Fatima Begum. Not all were subjected to Haidar's licentiousness and lust—some he seldom spoke to. They ended up being domestic slaves who also added a touch of glamour to the royal household. He also started a Natakashala (to guard the treasury of which he exiled Rani Lakshmammanni)—a centre for performing arts where these captive women were sent if they had a talent for music, theatre or dance. They were trained there and later utilised for the Nawab's entertainment.

Each time Haidar entered Fatima's apartments, he would bring along the costliest of jewels and other valuables as gifts. The entire harem of captive females would wait on him and fan or caress him. But he seldom looked at them; he had eyes only for his darling wife. Despite all his love for Fatima, he was also extremely scared of her! She was 'blessed' with the most caustic tongue and Haidar used to dread its wagging! This prevented him from engaging in any verbal duel or argument with her. If the decibel levels soared far beyond his comfort, he would make a hurried exit and join his friends for a drink, lamenting Fatima's acid-tongue and exclaiming that encountering the British was a better proposition for him than facing the domestic harangue!

Tipu seemed to be under the sway of his mother as well. After the conquest with the British in 1771, Haidar had on his return from Madras via Arcot selected a bride for Tipu. But his wife and son had other plans, preferring instead the daughter of Lala Amin, one of the heroes of the Chinkurli episode. They went ahead and selected this pretty nymphet. Although this greatly angered Haidar, he later consented to Tipu's marriage to both these young women as per Islamic laws. Thus, Tipu wedded on the same day the woman of his choice and another of his father's choice. In 1778, Tipu's brother Karim was married but this did little to change him. He remained a recluse and had transformed into an ascetic Sufi. Lost in his own thoughts, Karim was a constant source of worry for Haidar in his last days.

In his memoirs, De La Tour, a Frenchman in charge of Haidar's artillery, talks extensively about the routine followed by Haidar. Hayavadana Rao sums these up in the following way:

> Haidar rose daily with the sun, about six o'clock. Immediately thereafter, the military officers, corresponding to adjutants-generals in attendance on duty overnight and those who relieved them, entered and made their reports and received orders for transmission to the ministers and generals. The couriers then entered next, the couriers who had come in the night or at daybreak, and presented their despatches. Meanwhile he finished his toilet, which took him two or three hours! The toilet, however, was given up, when any military operations required his attention. Between 8 and 9 a.m. he arrived at his assembly room, where the officers waited for him. He passed the letters received by him, with instructions as to the replies to be sent. Then, he met here his sons and other near relations, besides friends.
>
> At 9 a.m., they also had refreshments served to them with himself. Next, he appeared at a balcony and received the salute

of his elephants and horses. Next, tigers passed by led by the hand and were fed by him with sweetmeats. At half past 10 a.m., the repast ended; he entered the audience-hall, or the grand tent, if at the army. He seated himself on a sofa beneath a canopy, not infrequently in some balcony, fronting an open space. Some relations sometimes sat by him here. Many came to seek audience, those who had business to transact being introduced by Chobdars or macebearers and accompanied by the officers concerned, so that immediate relief may be granted to the party…couriers arrive almost every instant, and are conducted with great noise and bustle. A secretary kneeling takes the packet, and sitting on his hams, opens it and reads the letter. Ayder immediately dictates the particulars of the answer, and the letter is carried to the office of a minister…the letters signed by Ayder are closed by the seal of the sovereign, of which the principal secretary is guardian. There were special letters written by him, to which were affixed a particular or private seal which he always wears on his finger or in that case he himself carries the packet.

The audience closed at 3 p.m., when Haidar returned to his apartment to a siesta and returned to the audience hall at 5:30 p.m., from whose balcony he saw the troops exercise or the cavalry exercise or the cavalry defile before him…at 6:30 p.m. when the day closed in, a great number of mussalchys, or bearers of flambeaux, appeared in the courtyard and saluted Haidar as they passed on the side of the apartment where he was. Haidar's apartments were all illuminated in a moment with tapers in chandeliers of exquisite workmanship, ornamented with festoons of flowers of the utmost lightness and delicacy…. about nightfall, at 8 p.m., there was for the most part lasting till 11 p.m. entertainment intermixed with dances and songs.

During its progress the Arabsbequi (chamberlains) continued near the strangers…careful to ask, if any chose to drink or eat, in which case they caused sherbet, fruits or confectionary to be presented to them…Haidar, to whom entertainments on stage were very indifferent, discoursed with his ministers or ambassadors or sometimes passing into a cabinet to speak with more secrecy, without seeming to be busy…almost always before the end of the performance, flowers were brought to him in a basket of filigram, out of which he himself gave a few to those who were about him... if a battle had been won or any glorious event had occurred in favour of Haidar, the court-poet announced it on his first entering the apartments with due pomp and in courtly language....the entertainers were all women, who were all specially trained to their work by the directress, who was likewise manager. At 11 p.m. or about midnight, the entertainment broke up and everyone retired, except those who stayed over to sup with Haidar...

This mode of life pursued by Haidar is, as may be easily imagined, interrupted in the army. It is likewise occasionally interrupted by hunting parties, by excursions on foot or horseback, or by his attending to assist at the exercises and evolutions made by considerable bodies of troops.

Such was a day in the life and times of a valiant hero of Mysore, a man who epitomised the proverbial rags to riches story; someone who had a whole lot of shortcomings, but never fell short of courage and valour and his singular hatred for the enemies of Mysore.

11

SULTANAT-E-KHUDADAD MYSORE AD 1782–91

Haidar's death brought yet another hero of Mysore to the fore—Tipu Sultan, a child given to the path of God who metamorphosed into a valiant warrior in the long course of battles he fought alongside his brave father. Tipu had promises to keep and the image of Haidar to live up to. He had an urgent and unfinished task at hand. The Second Anglo-Mysore War was still brewing. With Haidar gone, the entire burden of this decisive war was on his shoulders. Lord Macartney was keen on preventing Tipu's re-entry into the Carnatic. He urged Major General Stuart, who had succeeded Sir Eyre Coote as the commander-in-chief, to take the field before Tipu could return from the west coast. Tipu's overtures of peace were haughtily rejected by Macartney and this compelled the former to storm the Carnatic.

Tipu marched with the army towards Kaveripauk. The rains having abated, he camped at Arni, where a French contingent of over 1,000 troops joined him from Cuddalore towards the end of January 1783. This was followed by the Battle of Wandiwash where General James Stuart was defeated and arrested by Tipu. All the prisoners of war were packed off to Srirangapatna and condemned to the dungeons there, where they lived, and most died, in the most inhuman conditions.

THE SECOND ANGLO-MYSORE WAR CONTINUES

To divert Tipu from the Carnatic, the British sent their Provincial Commander-in-Chief Brigadier General Matthews to create trouble on the western coast of Mysore. In January 1783, Rajahmandurg and Honavar fell to his assault as Matthews marched victoriously towards Kundapura, closest to Bidnaur, which the British were eyeing. The traitor Sheikh Ayaz had a way of ensuring that Tipu's orders and letters found their way to his camp. Himself illiterate, Ayaz had the letters read to him and thoroughly scrutinised every detail in strict confidence. Around 24 January 1783, one such intercepted letter from Tipu sent shivers down Ayaz's spine. It contained orders to his commander Latif Ali Beg to march to Coorg and thereafter to Bidnaur and put Ayaz to death if the latter resisted. The unfortunate letter-reader was instantly put to death by Ayaz so as to prevent discovery. The news of Matthews' presence in the vicinity of Bidnaur was very welcome to Ayaz, who decided that aligning with Matthews was the safest bulwark against Tipu's designs.

On 29 January 1783, as Matthews marched towards Bidnaur, he was pleasantly surprised to see the fort gates open in welcome. Sheikh Ayaz decided to surrender to the forces of Matthews and in return negotiated that his own private property be secured and that he continue to remain in the same state of dignity and position under British tutelage. He hated Tipu and could not imagine being subservient to him. Thus, the British occupied Bidnaur without firing a single shot.

The new allies' eyes fell on Anantapur (not the modern-day Anantpur of Andhra Pradesh, but Anandapura of Shimoga district), which they were determined to annex. The commander there, Narayana Rao, refused to surrender. Rao's army had 500 men and Rao was surprised to find his fort besieged by the British. After putting up a brave resistance, Anantapur was captured on 14 February 1783. Of the 500 men, 440 were killed. The patriotic Narayana Rao refused to surrender even as he lay grievously injured and even spat at Matthews! He was immediately slaughtered. Matthews ordered the killing of every man in Anantapur. This was followed by mindless plunder of the town and large-scale rape of its women.

Following the tragedy at Anantapur, Tipu left his command in the Carnatic under Sayyid Saab and marched through the Changama Pass, Devanahalli, Maddagiri, Sira and Chitradurga, reaching Bidnaur in March 1783. Sheikh Ayaz fled to Bombay on hearing of Tipu's arrival. Tipu divided his army into two columns—one took the southern route of Kavaledurga and Haidargarh, which were easily captured. The other took a northeastern route to reconquer Anantapur and Bidnaur. After five days of incessant heavy firing, the British were completely outnumbered. Captain Fetherson, who had been sent to aid Matthews, was killed. Matthews was also plagued by fellow officers' allegations of unfair distribution of plunder and money taken at Bidnaur. Completely routed and short of provisions, Matthews finally surrendered in April 1783.

A treaty was concluded with Matthews, in which the English relinquished the forts of Bidnaur, Kavaledurga and Anantapur. In return they were to be given free exit to Bombay via Goa. Tipu was determined to teach Matthews a lesson. Concluding the treaty, as Matthews and his army left Bidnaur after laying down arms, they were surrounded by the Mysorean forces and captured. They were then sent off to different jails across Mysore—Srirangapatna, Bangalore, Gutti, Chitradurga and Kabbaladurga. Tipu took full possession of Bidnaur and then marched towards Mangalore.

On 19 May 1783, Tipu attacked Mangalore with an army of 60,000 cavalry, 30,000 disciplined sepoys, 600 French infantry under Colonel Cossigny and Monsieur Lally's corps, 100 pieces of artillery and 1,40,000 fighting men. The army was commanded by Tipu in person, accompanied by his brother Karim Sahib and Mohammad Ali, one of Haidar's most trusted commanders. He laid siege to the fort of Mangalore and inflicted a crushing defeat on the English army led by Campbell. After fifty-six days of conflict at Mangalore, around 19 July, the French refused to cooperate with the Mysore forces any longer. After a brief interlude of flirting with the British hostages, the French forces under Cossigny retreated, despite Tipu's threats and remonstrance. Undaunted by this volte-face of the French, Tipu carried on the siege from August to December.

Earlier an armistice had been signed with the British, according to which the latter could buy provisions for up to ten days at a time. Determined to break the British stronghold, Tipu began a systematic violation of this armistice. While the bazaar to provide the provisions was made available, every commodity was so exorbitantly priced that it was beyond the capacity of the British to purchase. Hayavadana Rao records that prices were raised on a daily basis 'till a fowl sold from nine to twelve rupees, a seer of rice for four, a seer of salt for three and a frog for six pence'. Seven boats laden with provisions were sent in from Bombay, but Tipu seized them all, revelling in the British discomfiture.

The British, however, had some temporary success with the capture of Palghat and Coimbatore by Colonel Fullarton between October and

December 1783. The fall of Coimbatore seemed to provide direct access to Srirangapatna for the British. Fullarton opened negotiations with the adherents of the royal family, who continued to provide grain and repair of carriages to support Fullarton—who seemed to be riding a crest of success—hoping that he would further the cause of the displaced Wodeyars.

Trouble awaited Tipu on the home front as well—a revolution of sorts was brewing at the capital. The chief architect this time was Anche Shamaiya, the terror-kingpin during Haidar's times, who was with Tipu at Mangalore and secretly commanded his allies in the capital. His brother Rangaiya and Narasinga Rao, the paymaster and town mayor were co-actors in the plot. Subbaraja Urs of the royal family was also part of the game. The idea was to take advantage of Tipu's absence from the capital and the proximity of the British troops in the Carnatic. They would invite the British to Srirangapatna and prevent the return of Tipu to the capital. The support of the Marathas, the Palegars and the Coorgis was also solicited. Narasinga Rao was in charge of the execution of the plot and he chose 9 am, 24 July 1783 as the time they would strike. This was when Asad Khan, the killedar of the Fort, distributed payslips to the troops, who normally assembled unarmed in the court to collect their salaries. *Jetties* or professional athletes were paid to kill the commandants and the soldiers and prepare ground for the English arrival.

Unfortunately for the conspirators, the killedar got wind of the whole plot. Letters written by Narasinga Rao to the British army were intercepted, Rao taken prisoner and tortured to confess. The conspirators were captured, stripped and dragged on the streets of the capital, tied to the legs of elephants and with their ears and noses cut off. Some of them were flogged in public view and hanged from the Fort ramparts. Narasinga Rao, Subbaraja Urs and others were later executed, while Shamaiya and Rangaiya were imprisoned in huge iron cages and rubbed with chilli powder. Till their last breath the brothers seem to have denied their involvement in the rebellion. Strict curfew orders were imposed in Srirangapatna and citizens told not to assemble in groups or in the dark of the night on the threat of similar punishment. Tipu ordered mass persecution of the kith and kin of Subbaraja Urs and Tirumala Rao. About 700 families of the Mysore Iyengars, men, women and children alike were chained and thrust into the dungeons of Srirangapatna. Narayana Rao was captured but he managed to escape. The *jagirs* and properties of the pradhans and their relatives were confiscated. On Tipu's return to the capital city, all the captured conspirators were ruthlessly executed on the festival day, Naraka Chaturdashi, just before Deepawali. To this day, the descendants of the Iyengars of Mysore observe the day not as a festival but as a day of *shraddha*, the Hindu ritual to propitiate the souls of the dead.

Interestingly, historians are unaware of whether this entire operation was carried on with the consent of or at the instance of Maharani Lakshmammanni. As Wilks states:

> Neither evidence, nor the unlimited use of the torture, had directed the slightest suspicion towards the imprisoned Ranee; it is just possible that she might afterwards have been induced…to assume a disguise in her confidential conversations with the late Sir Barry Close, and with the author; but the absence of even suspicion, when so strongly excited by circumstances, added to her uniform and consistent assurances, convinced them both of her entire ignorance of every part of the correspondence conducted in her name…but that conviction must not be understood to impugn the reality of Tremalarow's (Tirumala Rao) projects for the subversion of the actual government.

Back in the camp at Mangalore, things were not at all easy for Tipu. He suspected Rustum Ali Beg, the killedar of Mangalore, of treachery for not having dealt effectively with the siege. But Rustum's case was strongly defended by Mohammad Ali, one of Haidar's most trusted confidants and friends. Still, so convinced was Tipu about Beg's misconduct that he ordered the latter's public execution. Keen to save his close friend, Moammad Ali rescued the prisoner and openly declared that he would not suffer him to be executed and cried out, 'justice, in the name of God'. The following day Mohammad Ali was packed off in irons to Srirangapatna. Saddened by the behaviour meted out to him, he strangled himself to death, using the common groom's cord for leading a horse. Strangely, on hearing the news of Ali's death, Tipu was so overcome with grief that he ordered the imprisonment of Shaikh Hamid, the man he had appointed to take Mohammad Ali to Srirangapatna!

Shaken by the sudden and planned revolt back home, the death of Mohammad Ali and the weariness setting in among the troops with the long-drawn battle at Mangalore, Tipu desired a truce. Campbell's troops were exhausted and, having run out of provisions in the long siege, were reduced to eating frogs and rodents for survival. So exhausted was Campbell at the end of this ordeal that he quit the service on 15 February and in less than a month, died on 23 March 1784.

PEACE

By 25 December 1783, peace negotiators arrived from Madras. The Madras government had appointed commissioners to carry on the negotiations with Tipu. But Sadleir and Staunton, who made up the two-man commission, had deep differences regarding their approach to the negotiations. Macartney had to finally appoint a third commissioner, John Huddleston, to balance things. The sole purpose of this commission was to ensure the release of all prisoners—this took precedence over the restitution of Mangalore. It was also decided that both parties should relinquish their possessions and restore the status quo. The British were so desperate that Colonel Fullarton seemed to have been coaxed to relinquish all that he had captured in the Carnatic to encourage reciprocation.

Tipu treated the commissioners with the utmost disregard. He refused to meet them on various pretexts each time they sought an appointment. He continued his acts of hostility, as Hayavadana Rao reports, by 'erecting gibbets opposite to the tent doors of each of the Commissioners, carrying by surprise a post dependent on Honawar, cutting up a subaltern detachment from Col. Fullarton's army, and putting to death Gen Matthews and several other English officers in prison'. With every passing day the English woes increased and Tipu enjoyed their discomfiture. But this did not last long. The British government at Calcutta was getting increasingly restive at the suicidal actions of Macartney's southern campaign. Governor General Warren Hastings had almost reached a treaty with the Peshwa and the Sindhia to effect a combined attack on Tipu. Alarmed by the developments, Tipu thought it prudent to end the war from a position of strength rather than vacillate.

Since Tipu's resumption of war with the English, the negotiations for peace actively engaged the latter's attention. The preliminaries began in February 1783, when Lord Macartney sent a Brahmin diplomat, Sambhaji, to solicit better and more humane treatment of British prisoners of war languishing in Mysore's jails. Tipu gladly welcomed him and directed his own *vakil*, Srinivasa Rao, to accompany Sambhaji on his return to

Madras, with an equivocal letter addressed to himself under Tipu's seal, authorising him to confer on the subject of peace. As recorded in a contemporary document:

> Then the Agent proceeded to mention the grounds of the war on the part of Hyder, which were, the break of the express and solemn engagements that had been made by Mahommed Ally Cawn (Nabob of Arcot) to deliver to the Mysorean, Madura and Trichinopoly, besides a large sum of money lent to Mahommed Ally for which he had given his bond still due and bearing interest, with other grievances against him for encroachments and violences on the limits dividing the Carnatic and Hyder's territories, and suggested the justice of a redress of such grievances and a compliance with engagements which Mahommed Ally neither fulfilled nor adjusted by any subsequent agreement. The President Lord Macartney in answer informed the Agent that the treaty between the Governor and Council of Fort St. George and the Nabob Hyder Ally Cawn Bahadure made in the year 1769 was in behalf of the Honorable East India Company expressly for the Carnatic Payanghaut, and that such treaty was therefore a final adjustment of all claims relative to the country whether upon the Company or Mahommed Ally Cawn who had the Government of it under their protection, and that therefore all demands founded on transactions prior to the year 1769, were absolutely inadmissible.

The siege of Mangalore was lifted on 29 January 1784. The Second Anglo-Mysore War ended with the Treaty of Mangalore on 11 March 1784. It is an important document in the history of India—perhaps the last occasion when an Indian power dictated terms to the English, who were the humble supplicants for peace. Warren Hastings called it a humiliating pacification, and appealed to the English king and Parliament to punish the Madras government, saying that the British nation's faith and honour had both been violated. The English could not accept this humiliation, and worked hard from that day to subvert Tipu's power.

This treaty is to the credit of Tipu's diplomatic skills. He had honourably concluded a long-drawn war. He frustrated the Maratha designs to seize his northern possessions. The great advantage was the psychological impact of his victory over the British, with a highly satisfactory conclusion. The march of the commissioner all the way from Madras to Mangalore, seeking peace, made Munro remark that such indignities were throughout poured upon the British, that 'limited efforts seemed necessary to repudiate the Treaty at the earliest time'. Such public opinion in the country highly gratified Tipu, who felt it was his great triumph over the English. That was the only bright spot in his contest with the English, the only proud event which had humbled a mighty power. It was also for Tipu a glowing tribute to his father, who had fought the British till his last breath.

Concluded over 10 articles and executed by the Commissioners Sadleir, Staunton and Huddleston, the treaty had the following provisions:

1. Peace and friendship to be immediately established between the Company and the Nawab Tippu Sultan Bahadur and their respective friends and allies, including the Rajahs of Tanjore and Travancore and the Carnatic-Payanghat on the English side and the Beebi of Cannanore and the Rajas and Zamindars of the Malabar coast on the Nawab's side. The British were not to attack Tipu directly or indirectly, nor assist his enemies or wage wars against his allies.
2. Tipu had to completely evacuate his troops from the Carnatic, and release all prisoners of war—a measure to be reciprocated by the British.
3. The British had to give up Honavar, Karwar, Sadashivagarh and adjoining forts to their original masters as also Karur, Aravakurichi, Dindigul and Dharapuram districts to Mysore.
4. Cannanore was to be restored to its queen Ali Raja Beebi. Tipu was to relinquish claims over Amburgarh and Satgarh forts in the Carnatic.
5. Tipu had to give up all earlier claims on the Carnatic region.
6. Prisoners were to be reunited with their families.
7. Tipu was to maintain peace with the Rajas and Zamindars of the Coromandel Coast.
8. Mysore had to renew and confirm the commercial privileges and immunities extended to the British Company by the late Haidar and honour the treaty signed between the two on 8 August 1770.

Speaking extensively about the Treaty of Mangalore, Innes Munro, participant in the long war, opined:

Peace is generally considered by those who have toiled through the hardships of war as such a blessing, that the acquirement of it is generally applauded, however humiliating or repugnant to the real interests of the state the terms may be upon which it is obtained...it is to be hoped that the treaty of peace, which the Company have lately concluded with Tippoo Sahib, is only meant to be temporary. Such, I am certain, must be the wish of every Briton actuated by the sentiments of patriotism and capable of feeling the indignities which may have been uniformly heaped upon the British name. Can any Englishman read of the sufferings of his unfortunate countrymen, in the different prisons of Misore, without dropping a tear of sympathy? Or can he peruse the account of the repeated indignity and contempt with which his nation has been treated by the present usurper of Misore, without being filled with indignation and burning with sentiments of retaliation and revenge?

It must be allowed that the distresses, in which we were involved during the war, in this quarter of India, were in a great measure occasioned by our own imprudence and misconduct. Want of unanimity amongst our rulers laid the foundations for miscarriage and defeat; and the ardour of our armies was invariably checked by the want of supplies, withheld through the anarchy and dissensions that generally prevailed in the councils of Madras. The rocks, upon which we have split, are now perceptible to every eye; and it is to be hoped that future rulers may be directed by them to shun the fatal disasters into which the affairs of the settlement have lately been plunged. To retrieve our sinking reputation in India must be the united effort of labour and wisdom; and I should humbly conceive that no measure would be more likely to effect this desirable purpose than to crush the object of our just revenge, the present usurper of the Misore Throne; and, by observance of rigid integrity in our future engagements with the country powers, to wipe off the odium and distrust now universally attached by them to the British name.

Prudence and policy will clearly dictate that the deposing of Tippoo Sahib, in attempting which little is to be dreaded, and establishing the lawful sovereign upon the throne of Misore, are objects of the most essential consequence to the interests of the

India Company in the Carnatic. By such means the Mahrattas would be kept as much in awe as at present; and the Company, in the King of Misore, would most likely secure a peaceable neighbour and a powerful ally.

THE NEW SCENARIO

The British

This disastrous war was the last nail in Lord Macartney's coffin. He was constantly plagued with scarcity of provisions and money during the campaign of 1781–82. The arrears due to the army were not cleared until 1789. His difficulties were compounded by non-cooperating commanders-in-chief and serious ego clashes with Sir Eyre Coote. Macartney however made a great deal of his position as member of the Supreme Council at Calcutta and insisted on having his way at Madras. But Coote's successor, Stuart, was no better. From the time of his succession, Stuart took up a position completely opposed to the government upon almost every subject. His defiance and assertion of independence ensured that he was arrested on charges of subversion. Macartney also had to live with the complexities of a strained relationship with the government in Calcutta, something even his critics (like Dr Vincent Smith) acknowledge by stating that 'the interference of Calcutta sometimes was practised in an irritating way'.

Mysore

The treaty and the amicable way in which the war ended dashed the hopes of the maharani of Mysore and her pradhans. To assuage their fears, Lord Macartney and Sullivan assured the pradhans they would further their cause in the days to come and that the temporary reprieve was needed for purposes of realignment. The pradhans retired to Tanjore and decided that the best policy was to watch with fingers crossed as events unfolded. They were conferred a pension of twenty pagodas per month in accordance with the 12th article of the Treaty of 1782. However, Huddlestone, Sullivan's successor as resident in the Tanjore court, bargained with the company authorities to increase the measly sum. Tipu's persecution ensured that Tirumala Rao's stay at Tanjore was short-lived and he had to flee to Travancore to take refuge there for two years.

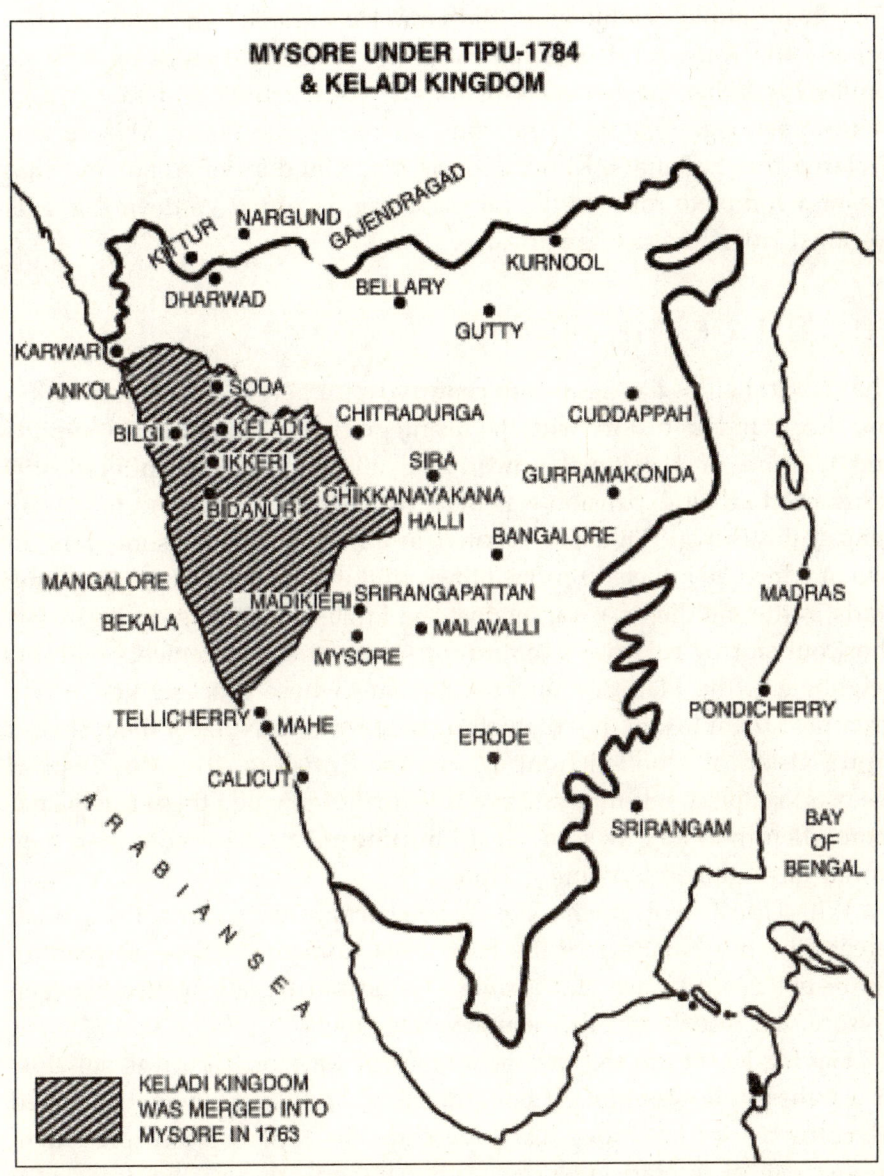

Mysore under Tipu (1784) and the Keladi Kingdom
(Maps are artistic recreations made at Suhaas Graphics, Bangalore)

Meanwhile, Tipu was made the sarvadhikari of Mysore on 4 May 1784 in a simple ceremony at Bidnaur. He assumed the title of Tipu Sultan—the King—and declared himself the de facto ruler of Mysore. Unlike his father, he felt no love for the royal family and saw it as a mere appendage of little or no consequence to the polity. Mysore was declared the 'Sultanat-e-Khudadad' or the 'Kingdom of Allah' and that meant a complete rout for the lingering family of the Wodeyars and its so-called ruler Khasa Chamaraja.

THE RISE OF THE BRITISH

The second half of the eighteenth century was a period of great confusion and flux in Indian history with the disintegration of many Indian empires and the rise of a colonial power. The only state which offered stiff resistance to their expansion was Mysore, fighting not one but four wars against the British. Tipu participated in all those four Mysore wars, in two of which he inflicted serious blows on the English. In fact, Tipu's rule starts in the middle of a war against the English and ends similarly. His short but stormy rule was eventful for his several engagements with his neighbours—the Marathas and the Nizam—whose short-sighted policy prompted them to join the colonials against Mysore. None of them shared Tipu's vision of a united front against the British to drive them out of the country; petty self-interests and insecurities plagued these rulers and, more often than not, they ended up hurting themselves more than they would have gained by joining Tipu.

With Tipu's involvement, Mysore had become 'the terror of Leadenhall Street', the headquarters of the East India Company. These 40 years of Tipu—both as a prince and a ruler—witnessed bloody battles between Mysore, the British and the neighbouring rulers.

Having learnt the western techniques of warfare, Tipu was not slow to use these. He was himself bold, dashing, and a person of undaunted adventurous spirit. Under his leadership the Mysore army proved to be a school of military science to other Indian princes. The dread of a European army no longer deterred Tipu, whose attack on British might in the First and Second Mysore Wars damaged their reputation as an invincible power. Alexander Dow wrote, 'We were alarmed, as if his horses had wings to fly over our walls.' Such was the valour of the man who began to be hailed as the 'Sher-e-Mysore'or 'Tiger of Mysore'.

Tipu's initiation into battle began, as mentioned before, when he was barely thirteen years old and his parents withdrew him from the path of religion. He had his first experience on the field in the Malabar, where Haidar was always busy crushing the Nair revolts. He displayed great courage and there was no looking back. He was present during Haidar's negotiations with the Nizam in the First Mysore War when his tact and resourcefulness impressed the Nizam, helping to win him over to Haidar's side. It was Tipu who obtained the ratification of the Treaty of Alliance between the Nizam and Haidar in 1767. Tipu had gone to the Nizam's camp at the head of 6,000 troops and successfully concluded the treaty. This was Tipu's first diplomatic assignment and he was well received by the Nizam, who conferred on him the title of 'Nasib-ud-daula' (fortune of the state) and also 'Fateh Ali Khan'. The Maratha war of 1769–72 and the Second Mysore War—where he displayed great courage and presence of mind—enhanced his status as a military leader.

Shortly after the conclusion of the Second Mysore War, Tipu began his march through Balam and quelled a brewing revolt among the mountain-dwellers of that region. He got a new fortress built there, named Munzirabad.

The Treaty of Mangalore, which concluded the Second Anglo-Mysore War, carried the seeds of strife with the Marathas, disappointing their expectations of playing mediators and recovering their losses in the north of Mysore. Tipu had emerged with enhanced prestige at the end of the war, invincible against even the mightiest empire of the world. This made the Nizam and the Marathas terribly insecure and they were on the look-out for protection against any possible strike by Tipu in his expansionist zeal. The Nizam, who regarded himself as the overlord of the entire South, loathed Mysore and expected that Haidar and Tipu would be subservient to his wishes. Militarily very weak, he allied himself either with the Marathas or the English to distress the Mysore rulers. There was always a pro-British party at Hyderabad that dissuaded the Nizam from being cordial to Tipu.

MYSORE–MARATHA WAR

In early 1785, trouble brewed with the Marathas. Haidar had promised the Marathas territories south of the Krishna, which were now being demanded by Nana Phadnavis. Tipu refused to meet the demand, sparking off the long-drawn Mysore-Maratha war. He claimed instead that the chief of Nargund, Kala Pandit, who was related to the Maratha strongman Parashuram Bhau, owed Mysore dues that he had been refusing to pay. Burhan-ud-din, the Mysorean commander-in-chief and Tipu's cousin and brother-in-law was dispatched to Nargund at the head of 5,000 cavalry and three *kushoons* or regiments of foot. The army laid siege to the fort of Nargund. Kala Pandit and his clever guerrilla tactics gave Burhan-ud-din and his men a tough time. But the Mysorean batteries and forces were quite a daunting prospect for Kala Pandit. He sent emissaries to Parashuram Bhau who sent aid in the form of a contingent from Poona. Reinforcements for the Mysore troops came in from Srirangapatna under Tipu's cousin Kumr-ud-din. The combined forces of Mysore successfully routed the Poona armies and also took Ramdurg fort on 5 May 1785. By August 1785, Nargund was captured and Kala Pandit packed off as a prisoner to Srirangapatna. Kittur, another neighbouring principality of a Deshayi or Chieftain, was also annexed.

Kumr-ud-din was however recalled to Srirangapatna owing to mutual jealousies and ego clashes between the two cousins. On being recalled to Srirangapatna, Kumr-ud-din spread a wild rumour that the Sultan was dead and the funeral procession of an eminent person of the kingdom organised at the Sultan's behest was in fact the funeral of the Sultan himself. This created momentary confusion and disarray among Mysorean troops while the British gloated. This, coupled with alleged secret negotiations he was carrying on with the Nizam, earned him Tipu's wrath and Kumr-ud-din was condemned to a life of imprisonment and disgrace. The incident underscores the tenuous nature of the polity and circumstances under which Tipu had to operate, one that was rife with rumours and where almost everyone, even members of his own family, seemed to wish his downfall.

Meanwhile, Nana Phadnavis was determined to avenge the shameful retreat at Nargund. He decided to align with the Nizam for a combined attack on Mysore. They began their blitzkrieg with a siege of Badami and followed it up with a string of successes in Dharwad, Julihul, Gajendragarh, Navalgunda, and Nargund and in fact the entire northern side of the Tungabhadra. The Palegars of Sirahatti, Damul, Kanakagiri and Anegondi quickly shifted allegiance to the Marathas and the Northern Carnatic region seemed to be quickly slipping from Tipu's hands.

Tipu personally took to the field in June 1786 and marched on to Bangalore with six branches of regular infantry, three regiments of regular cavalry, 10,000 irregular foot, 30,000 horses and 22 heavy guns. From here he marched and laid siege to Adoni, a strong frontier post of the Nizam's which was under Mohabat Jung, son of Basalat Jung and nephew of Nizam Ali. Burhan-ud-din was advised to take on the Marathas. The siege of Adoni was intended to divert the confederate armies from their position. Mohabat Jung and his widowed mother sent feelers of goodwill to Tipu; but the latter's condition for saving Jung's life—disassociation from his uncle, the Nizam—seemed unacceptable to Mohabat and he decided to defend the fort of Adoni. The confederate armies rushed to Adoni to save the place and the relatives of the Nizam were trapped in the fort. Tipu quickly gave them the slip and raised the siege, allowing them to flee with all the women who were held hostage. While they were escaping, he followed. Mir Sadik was left behind to take Adoni, which he did on 11 July 1786.

The Mysorean forces with Tipu in command and with several daring leaders of the army, like commander-in-chief Burhan-ud-din, Ghazi Khan, Maha Mirza Khan and Badr-u-Zaman Khan made many surprise attacks by night at Sirahatti, some miles away from the fort of Savanur. The Maratha and Nizam armies faced considerable losses. By October, Tipu managed to dislodge the confederates from the vicinity and left their ally—the Savanur Nawab, Abdul Hakim—high and dry. He fled by night and left his son Abdul Khira Khan behind, who was imprisoned by the Mysore troops. Savanur was looted of all its innumerable treasures, right down to the last brick. The Mysorean forces captured Padaspur, Hosakote, Soda, Jamboti, Khanapur and other Maratha territories.

The war abruptly ended with a peace treaty towards the end of 1786. An interesting message of peace was sent to Tukoji Rao Holkar, the leader of the Maratha forces, by Tipu:

> You have obtained experience in feat of arms, and are distinguished among the chiefs for superior valour. Now that war has commenced its destructive career, and thousands are doomed to fall, why should we longer witness the causeless effusion of human blood? It is better that you and I should singly descend into the field of combat; let the Almighty determine who is the conqueror and who the vanquished, and let that result terminate the contest.

Or if you have not sufficient confidence in your own single arm, take to your aid from one to ten men of your own selection, and I will meet you with equal numbers. Such was the practice in the days of our Prophet, and though long discontinued, I desire to renew that species of warfare. But if prudence should dictate your declining the second proposition also, let the two armies be drawn out, select your weapons, and let us, chief opposed to chief, horseman opposed to horseman, and foot soldier to foot soldier, engage in a pitched battle, and let the vanquished become the subject of the victors.

But this peace was short-lived, quickly followed by the war against the combined forces of the Nizam and Marathas on the banks of the Gandaki River. The armies fought a pitched battle at Gajendragarh and some of the Hindu soldiers in Tipu's army who had been bought over by the Marathas were severely punished by Tipu—their noses and ears were cut off and the leader, Hanumant Naik, had his legs amputated. The war ended on 14 February 1787 with the Treaty of Gajendragadh by which Tipu ceded Badami to the Marathas, hoping to win their support against the English or at least to prevent them from joining the English. It was agreed that Mysore, Hyderabad and Poona would act as a combined confederacy in the Deccan and if any fourth party attacked any of the allies, the others would join to repel the hostile attempt. But as events unfolded in the years to come, it was evident that this was not to be. Tipu also had to pay the Marathas four years of accumulated arrears that Haidar had agreed to pay them for being acknowledged as 'the undisputed master of everything south of the Krishna from sea to sea'. This amounted to about Rs 30 lakh. Kittur and Nargund were surrendered to the Peshwa along with Badami and Gajendragarh; Adoni to Mohabat Jung and the Nawab of Savanur, Abdul Hakim was reinstated. Thus, the troubled relationship between Mysore and Poona ended temporarily in a brief reprieve.

Tipu also had to concentrate his energies on Coorg and Malabar where trouble kept brewing.

TROUBLE IN COORG

The valiant Coorgi tribe could not digest the thought of external rule after their territories were annexed by Haidar. They made repeated attempts to establish their independence. In fact, even in the middle of the Second Mysore War, Tipu overran Coorg and crushed a rebellion in 1782. Zain-ul-Abidin Mehdavi was made the fouzdar and given all powers to permanently quell the menace. But no sooner had Tipu left for Srirangapatna than trouble started brewing again. In late 1784, Tipu despatched Raja Kankeri to lead the Mysorean army against Coorg but he was defeated on his way to Madikeri. This was followed by a year-long skirmish where Tipu made repeated attacks on Coorg to contain the situation. But the guerrillas of Coorg put up a formidable defence. Tipu's attempts at Islamising the region (Madikeri was renamed Zaferabad) further enraged the already discontented rebels in Coorg. The alleged attempts of Tipu's handpicked fouzdar, Mehdavi, to molest the sister of Momuti Nair—a minister of the local chief—further enraged the Coorgis. The rebels attacked the fort of Zaferabad and reduced the hostages and the fouzdar, to a state of utter despair. Mehdavi was forced to send urgent requests for help to Srirangapatna.

In September 1785, Zain-ul-Abidin Shustari, the sipahadar of a *kushoon* was sent with an abundance of stores and 2,000 irregular foot soldiers. To quote Hayavadana Rao:

> The Sipahadar, marching quickly, arrived at the ghat leading to Coorg, only to find himself attacked on all sides by the rebels with their arrows and muskets...he soon retired in despair on the plea of ague and fever to the pass of Sidapur, despite the remonstrances of his followers. Also he wrote to the headquarters that nothing but Tipu's own presence with the main army would terminate the war.

Accordingly, in October 1785, Tipu marched personally towards Coorg as head of 20,000 regular infantry, 12,000 irregular foot soldiers, 10,000 cavalry and 21 field pieces. Entering the region in two columns, he left his horse at the pass of Sidapur, Periapatna and Munzirabad and along with his irregular foot soldiers, *kushoons* and artillery crossed the pass and overran the territory by burning and destroying the patches of vegetation in the countryside. He had a face-to-face encounter with the rebels at Kushalnagar. After vanquishing them, he rode to Madikeri and took the fort with ease. Many of the rebels surrendered and some of them fled for refuge to the woods and mountains of the region. A huge repression drive began. Large bodies of troops were sent to punish and torture the captives. Lally proceeded to the Cardamom Ghats, Shustari and Hussain Ali Khan Bakshi towards Kurumbanad and the rest of the sipahadars towards Talakaveri and Kushalpur. The territory was completely overrun and several men captured and tortured. It was also alleged that a huge drive of conversions to Islam was carried out during this time—perhaps as a means to display the military subjugation of Coorg and the superiority of Mysore.

Little did they know that it wasn't all that easy to suppress the ferocious tribes of Coorg. They quickly reorganised themselves, bolstered by the escape of their captured leader Viraraja in 1788. Ghulam Ali led the Mysorean attack against the newly organised troop of Viraraja in 1789. After suffering initial losses, Viraraja regained his strength and completely vanquished Ghulam Ali at the Kodanthur Pass. Though Tipu sent reinforcements led by four captains, the force was no match for Viraraja who defeated the lot at Heggala. An alarmed Tipu sent his brother-in-law Burhan-ud-din. The nature of the insurgence in Coorg was such that skirmishes and constant give and take of territories among various players was very common and occurred frequently.

The remarkable nature of the Coorg revolts was that they were entirely driven by peasant discontent. There was thus an almost endless supply of fighters from among the brave Coorgis. In terms of strength the guerrillas were just about 5,000 organised men but they managed to take on the might of the Sultanat-e-Khudadad of Mysore—an army six times its size. This peasant-guerrilla warfare was also sustained by the fact that the rebels knew the terrain infinitely better than the Mysorean army. They utilised this knowledge to make sudden and mobile wars characterised by surprise attacks, utilising the countryside to surround towns, avoid decisive conflicts and fight only when victory was certain, completely routing their enemy's supplies and communications, leaving him helpless and dispirited in a largely unknown, rocky forest terrain. There was tremendous damage caused by the Coorgis and Nairs of Malabar to Mysore and its army. Haidar and Tipu grossly underestimated the might of both these coastal satraps.

Finally, realising the futility of the aggression in Coorg, Tipu decided to extend a hand of peace in 1791. A *parwana* or order was issued to the Patels of Coorg seeking a compromise: 'It is well known to me that you have for a long time experienced much trouble in your country and under this consideration I forgive everything of what has happened. You may now fulfil your several duties as subjects and observe all the customs of your religion agreeably to ancient practices and whatever you formerly paid to your own Rajas, the same, I repeat, you will now pay to this Circar.' It was perhaps among the most disgraceful retreats Mysore had faced after the reckless and expensive campaign at Tiruchirapalli in the past. In the twenty-five years of this bloody campaign, Mysore's army faced more damage and casualties than in all their conflicts with the British. Such was the valour and courage of the people of Coorg. The *parwana* ended the political conflict with the Coorgis but their hatred for Mysore remained. The difference of language also ensured that the Coorgis preferred to maintain their distinct identity. The latent anger and simmering discontent resulted in the Haleri king of Coorg finally joining hands with the British against Tipu by 1799, proving very helpful to the British troops against their common Mysorean foe.

ARRIVAL OF LORD CORNWALLIS

The year 1786 saw Tipu facing a new challenge—possibly the toughest of his life. Lord Charles Cornwallis took over from Sir John Macpherson as the English Governor General at Madras. Cornwallis was fiercely patriotic. A pompous man out to gain glory for the Crown, he had neither Macpherson's cunning nor Hastings' avarice. He was upright, fair and just in all his dealings except war with his enemy, when he forgot all tenets of mercy and humanity.

Born on 31 December 1738, Cornwallis attended the military academy at Turin, and rose to Lieutenant Colonel while serving in Germany during the Seven Years' War. On succeeding to his father, Earl Cornwallis's title as the second Earl in 1762, Cornwallis became politically active with the Whigs and took his seat in the House of Lords where his abilities and connections led to several high-profile appointments. Although opposed to the measures that provoked the American Revolution, he accepted a position in North America as Major General. Cornwallis served with distinction during the American Revolution.

However, for all his success against the American rebels, he could do little against the military talents of American commander-in-chief, George Washington. Choked with tears and shame, he had to surrender at Yorktown on 19 October 1781. It is torture for any brave solider to be vanquished in war and surrender his country's flag to the enemy.

Cornwallis was therefore set upon redeeming himself and saw India as the opportunity he needed. As Cornwallis made his way to India, he was cognisant of the fact that he had a reputation to repair. He decided it would be his bounden duty to vanquish the obstacle to British progress in India—Mysore and its ruler Tipu Sultan. He saw Washington in every rival and each defeat he inflicted on his opponent would help him forget the trauma of Yorktown. As his ship sailed majestically to the shores of Madras and he set foot on Indian soil, his vision of success and the consummation of his desires urgently beckoned Cornwallis.

Without any further delay he reached Hyderabad, where he received a warm welcome from that faithful ally of the British, Nizam Asif Jah Bahaddur, and his worthless minister Mushir-ul-Mulk. A pact of understanding was signed between the two. The British were to align with the Nizam in a joint attack on their common foe Tipu. From Hyderabad, Cornwallis headed straight to Poona to win over the Marathas. There was a huge debate in the Maratha camp on whether they should go ahead with this alliance with the British. Nana Phadnavis was apparently against the idea, but eventually the Marathas agreed to become a part of the Grand Alliance. Rumblings were being heard from within the Mysore camp as well; Mir Sadik, the commander, was secretly negotiating with Cornwallis. This Grand Tripartite Alliance decided to finish off Tipu once and for all and the strife that followed led to the Third Anglo-Mysore War.

THE INVASION OF TRAVANCORE

The immediate provocation for the Alliance's attack on Tipu was his invasion of Travancore, a British protectorate. Travancore was more of an en route invasion in Tipu's larger plan of purchasing the fort of Cochin from the Dutch. Tipu also argued that the Travancore Lines were actually built on his property and intersected the country of his tributary of Cochin. He tried to sell his point of view to the government of Madras, which he knew would now see him as an aggressor and a violator of the 1784 treaty. At the same time he also sent emissaries to the Maharaja of Travancore asking him to surrender the culprits of the Malabar revolt, whom he had hospitably hosted, and also to give up his claim to the Lines. A defiant reply from Travancore incensed him and he attacked the Lines on 29 December 1789.

The first attack ended in a surprising disaster for Mysore. Hayavadana Rao describes how Tipu had personally led the attack 'seated in his palankeen and proceeding with two Risalas and two thousand regular horse...' but by daybreak 'his palankeen remained in the ditch, the bearers having been trodden to death, his seals, rings, personal ornaments and dagger fell as trophies into the hands of the enemy, and the fortunes of a day, which was turned by twenty men, cost his army upwards of two thousand.' Humiliated and enraged, Tipu swore to again attack the small province of Travancore that had defied his authority. After a few months of preparation, Mysore attacked Travancore in April 1790. This time fortune favoured Tipu. About 4,000 Travancoreans were killed and wounded and the Lines were surrendered to a triumphant Tipu by 15 April 1790. That eyesore—the Travancore Lines—was demolished. Tipu set the example by dealing the first blow with a pick-axe. All his officers and courtiers gladly followed suit. Within six days, the Lines was razed to the ground.

Interestingly enough, Tipu had all along kept the government at Madras apprised of his dealings with the Travancore Raja and the British had maintained a diplomatic silence despite the latter being their ally. But with the destruction of the Lines, danger signals flashed in Madras. Tipu's subjugation of Travancore would assure him of easy access to the southern provinces of the British domains. Conveniently, the British decided to attack Tipu on the pretext of helping their ally, the Maharaja of Travancore. Embroiled in the French Revolution, the French, who were on Tipu's side, could not help him much.

Tipu had to single-handedly tackle the combined forces of the British, the Marathas, the Nizam, the rajas of Travancore and Cochin along with the Palegars of Kangundipalya, Chikaballapur, Punganur, Madanapalli, Anekal, etc. Cornwallis's army consisted of about 22,300 combatants along with nearly 80,000 modes of transport, including camels, elephants and ponies. This marked the beginning of another long skirmish between Mysore and the Company—more commonly known as the Third Anglo-Mysore War.

THE THIRD ANGLO-MYSORE WAR

Major General William Meadows commanded the grand army that attacked Mysore in May 1790. Tipu sent overtures of peace to the English army, suggesting that the usually upright mind of the general was somewhat dust-coated, to which he received a reply that the English, who would not accept an insult just as they could not inflict one, had always considered the war having begun the moment he attacked their ally, the king of Travancore.

In June–July 1790, Meadows occupied the frontier posts of Karur—abandoned by the Mysoreans—and advanced towards the weak forts of Aravakurichi and Dharapuram, which were guarded by just thirty men. The attainment of a chain of posts closely connected with each other, extending from the Coromandel coast to the foot of the Gejjelhatty Pass, was evidently an essential strategy to any initial invasion of Mysore. The acquisition of Tanjore, Trichinopoly, Karur, Erode and Satyamangalam served this very purpose. By the time Meadows reached Coimbatore he was stunned to see the city virtually empty. The chieftain, his family and the subjects had all fled. Meadows made Coimbatore his headquarters from where he sent Colonel James Stuart to Dindigul, Colonel Oldham to Erode and Colonel Floyd towards Mysore.

Hyder Abbas, the brave killedar of Dindigul refused to surrender and fought bravely. Major Skelly then brought to Stuart an old, villainous man Shah Abbas, Hyder Abbas's uncle, who was now under British pay. He was bribed to convince his nephew to surrender. Hyder Abbas fell for the offer of a gold-lined future and surrendered, getting a huge treasure in return from the British. On reaching home, he faced an angry family, disappointed in his treachery. His brother, Sheikh Abbas killed him, but was himself stabbed by a dying Hyder. Their aged mother died of shock upon seeing both her young sons lying dead. Was this the golden future for which Hyder had sold himself?

The sad truth of our glorious land is that our countrymen do not lack in wisdom, courage and intellect; but they do not lack in treachery, cunningness and avarice either. The smell and sight of gold is enough to send all our patriotism down the drain. We were certainly conquered by the external enemy, but more significantly by the enemy within. The misfortune, however, remains that we have not learnt any lessons from history, which they say repeats itself because nobody was listening the first time, and continue to divide ourselves along narrow, petty lines.

Meanwhile, Colonel Stuart occupied Palaghat and Colonel Oldham Erode. Colonel Floyd was in Gejjelhatty, thirteen miles from the route to Mysore where Tipu was camping. Tipu's sudden descent into the

Coimbatore district was so sudden, silent and skilful that it took the British by surprise. A fierce action followed at Satyamangalam on 13 September 1790. The massive British troops were routed by the Sultan. With heavy casualties on his side, Colonel Floyd was forced to retreat to Coimbatore, abandoning the post of Satyamangalam.

A centre division of the English army from Bengal left Burhanpur and reached Kanchipuram by August 1790. The force had been augmented to 9,500 men, including three regiments of European infantry, one regiment of Indian cavalry and formidable artillery. They assembled at Arni under Colonel Kelly's command. He intended to besiege Bangalore and reduce the districts adjacent to it. But his untimely death foiled the division's plans. His successor Colonel Maxwell joined the troops of General Meadows in their invasion of Baramahal. After a few months of skirmishes, Tipu extended the olive branch to Meadows through his vakils Mir Sadik, Ali Raza and Appaji Ram. Meadows replied (as recorded by H. Rao) that he would not mind entering into a treaty with the Sultan 'but that before he does so, he must have some person or place of consequence put into his hands as security for the Sultaun's being in earnest, when the first Article will be the unequivocal release of every English officer, known to be still in existence and in confinement in the Mysore country'.

With the peace mission making no headway, the battle raged on even as Tipu swept across the Carnatic. His requests for French help did not meet with much success as King Louis XVI—a figurehead after the French Revolution was concluded—was sceptical of offering any assistance. H. Rao reports his remark that 'this resembles the affair of America, which I never think of without regret. My youth was taken advantage of at that time, and we suffer for it now; the lesson is too severe to be forgotten.' He is said to also have been amused with the 'shabby finery of Tippu's miserable presents to himself and the queen, trumpery to dress up dolls!' Tipu was therefore left alone to defend his kingdom.

Later, on the banks of the river Bhavani, the English forces were defeated and pushed back. Coimbatore, Karur, Aravakurichi, Dindigul, Palaghat and the Carnatic passed back to the Sultan's hands. Two years of war had yielded nothing. Cornwallis was getting increasingly restive and irritated. He had nightmares of the Yorktown debacle happening in India. He also feared losing his allies—the Nizam and the Marathas—following these ignoble defeats. 'I conceive it to be possible that my presence in the scene of action would be considered by our Allies as a pledge of our sincerity, and of the confident hopes of success against the common enemy, and by that means operate as an encouragement to them to continue their exertions, and abide by their stipulations,' he declared, and decided to enter the fray himself (H. Rao 1945).

A series of reaffirmations with the allies at Hyderabad and Poona followed. Sir Charles Warre Malet at Poona and Captain John Kennaway at Hyderabad negotiated the strengthening of ties with the Peshwa and the Nizam respectively on principles of mutual aid and reciprocal partition. Accordingly, a formidable Triple Alliance was formed in June–July 1790. According to H. Rao, Cornwallis held that the rationale for such alliances 'was founded solely upon the expectation of their being guided by the common influence of passions and by considerations of evident interest, which ought to dispose them to seize a favourable opportunity with eagerness to reduce the power of a Prince whose ambition knows no bounds and from whom both of them have suffered numberless insults and injuries.'

Accordingly, to achieve his heart's desire, Lord Cornwallis took the field in person in November 1790, 'to bring the war to a happy conclusion; to cement an everlasting connection between the Mahratta State, the Company and Nizam; to punish a wanton insult; and circumscribe the dangerous power of Tippoo.' The British army marched straight to Bangalore and besieged the fort in March 1791.

The Fall of Bangalore

The fort of Bangalore had been completely rebuilt and strengthened by Haidar and Tipu. It was almost of an oval form and had round towers at intervals, five powerful cavaliers, contained a faussebray and a good ditch. There were two gateways—the Mysore Gate and the Delhi Gate, the latter stood opposite the Pettah or town of Bangalore. The Pettah was surrounded by an indifferent rampart and excellent ditch, with an intermediate berm planted with well-grown thorns.

Speaking about the siege, Wilks says:

> Few sieges have ever been conducted under parallel circumstances; a place not only not invested, but regularly relieved by fresh troops; a besieging army not only not undisturbed by field operations, but incessantly threatened by the whole of the enemy's force. No

day or night elapsed without some new project for frustrating the operations of the siege; and during its continuance, the whole of the besieging army was accoutred, and the cavalry saddled, every night from sun-set to sun-rise.

Incessant firing by the British troops led to a breach in the strong fort. Kumr-ud-din had stationed himself in the neighbourhood of Basavanagudi, which was within a mile and a half of the Mysore Gate, to assist the besieged killedar. But the news of the battering down of the fort walls by British guns alarmed Tipu and he dispatched Toshikhana Krishna Rao for assistance.*

The day came to an end and Tipu decided to resume the defence by dawn. But the British had different plans—through the night they climbed the ramparts of the fort, which was guarded by the French. Unfortunately, the French betrayed Tipu. They did not defend the fort to the hilt. The British breached the fort walls, entered and killed the Killedar Bahaddar Khan. The whole of Bangalore was ransacked by Abercromby on the General's orders. Writing about the siege and fall of Bangalore, Wilks says:

> It was a bright moonlight; eleven was the hour appointed, and a whisper along the ranks was the signal appointed for advancing in profound silence: the ladders were nearly planted, not only to ascend the faussebray, but the projecting work on the right, before the garrison took the alarm, and just as the serious struggle commenced on the breach, a narrow and circuitous way along a thin shattered wall, had led a few men to the rampart, on the left flank of its defenders, where they coolly halted to accumulate their numbers, till sufficient to charge with the bayonet. The gallantry of the Killedar, who was in an instant at his post, protracted the obstinacy of resistance until he fell; but the energy of the assailants in front and flank at length prevailed. Once established on the ramparts, the flank companies proceeded as told off by alternate companies to the right and left, where the resistance was everywhere respectable, until they met over the Mysore Gate:

---

* Kirmani talks of Krishna Rao's treachery at this juncture and of his passing on hints to the English about Tipu's moves. However these charges have not been substantiated by any other contemporary accounts.

separate columns then descended into the body of the place; and at the expiration of an hour, all opposition had ceased.

On ascending the breach, a heavy column was observed on the left, advancing from the embankment described, to attack the assailants in flank and rear; but this also had been foreseen and provided for, and they were repulsed with great slaughter by the troops reserved for that special purpose; a similar column, lodged in the covered way on the right, had been dispersed at the commencement of the assault, by a body appointed to scour it, and draw off the enemy's attention from the breach; and at the moment the flank companies had met over the Mysore Gate, another column was perceived advancing along the sortie, to enter and reinforce the garrison; but a few shot from the guns on the ramparts, announced that the place had changed the masters. The carnage had been severe, but unavoidable, particularly in the pressure of the fugitives at the Mysore Gate, which at length was completely choked.

Bangalore was the gateway to Mysore, acclaimed as the strongest and most important fortress of the kingdom and called 'Dar-ul-Sultanat' or 'Capital of the Empire'. The fall of Bangalore on 21 March 1791 meant that the very heart of Mysore was threatened. It sounded alarm bells for the Sultan and sent shivers down his spine. Tipu had to make haste if he did not want the situation to change completely to favour the English. Devanahalli, Chikkaballapura and Ambajidurg meekly surrendered to the might of Lord Cornwallis. Realising that the British now looked straight at Srirangapatna from their position of strength in Bangalore, Tipu, along with a strong division of force from Gutti under Qutub-ud-din, stationed himself on the Chennapatna road that led to Srirangapatna. But Lord Cornwallis, with his huge army (one regiment of European cavalry, five regiments of Indian cavalry, three battalions of artillery, seven regiments of European infantry, ten battalions of coast sepoys with seven other such from Bengal and 14,000 irregular horse) gave Tipu the slip and marched towards Srirangapatna via a circuitous route. Facing the greatest hardships on the way—exhausted troops existing on meagre supplies—Cornwallis's grand army reached Arakere, about nine miles east of Srirangapatna, on 13 May 1791.

But lady luck did not seem to favour his Lordship. The monsoons set in earlier than expected that year and with greater severity. This coupled with the acute deficiency of provisions, the tardy attitude of the allies and the death of large numbers of cattle in his army for lack of fodder compelled Cornwallis to beat a retreat. By 26 May 1791, Cornwallis decided to retreat to Bangalore, but with a firm intention to return to Srirangapatna, better prepared. As Lieutenant Colonel L.H. Thornton puts it:

> There were now two courses open to Lord Cornwallis. He might defer his advance on Seringapatam till the cold weather had set in. In the meantime he could place his supply and transport arrangements on a sound basis, and he could render secure his communications with the Carnatic and with the Nizam's and the Mahratta's territory. The second course open to the Commander-in-Chief was to advance without further delay on Seringapatam. This course, as Lord Cornwallis well knew, would be attended with very grave risk. His supply service was in a most precarious state. Since the opening of the campaign, no less than 12,000 bullocks had perished, and this loss had been but very partially made up by the arrival of Colonel Oldham's convoy…nonetheless Lord Cornwallis chose the second course, hazardous though it was.

Thornton also speaks of the 'friction' between Cornwallis and Tejwant Singh, the leader of the Nizam's contingent. There are references to a 'calculated treachery' on Tejwant's part that ensured doom for the British army at Srirangapatna.

Amid all this, Tipu was grappling with personal tragedy. His darling wife Ruqayya Banu had died. He became a near-recluse and all matters of decision-making at the military level passed into the hands of the traitor Mir Sadik.

At around the time Mysore's army had to deal with the forces of Cornwallis and Nizam Ali, it also had a tough time repulsing the attacks of the Marathas. By June 1790, the Maratha army joined the fray under Parashuram Bhau Patwardhan. The first objective of the Marathas was the recovery of the provinces between the five tributaries of Krishna, Gutprabha, Malprabha, Wardha and Tungabhadra, which had been annexed by Haidar during the civil war that had raged in Poona under Raghoba. Dharwad was the deemed capital of these annexed provinces. It was defended by Badr-u-Zaman Khan, who was, H. Rao writes, 'reputed to be a sensible, well-informed old man, whose professional abilities and conduct render him worthy of the trust his master has reposed in him'. A fierce siege of Dharwad began that September and carried on for months on end. Badr-u-Zaman Khan valiantly held the fortress and repulsed the continuous battering of the Maratha forces that were now aided by English detachments. By January 1791, a huge reinforcement of European troops under Colonel Frederick joined Bhau's forces. The shoddy strategies of Parashuram Bhau cost the Maratha army heavily. But it was a battle that had dragged on for so long that retreat at this point seemed the least likely option to boost the already sagging morale of the besieging troops. Already, news of the fall of Bangalore and the threat to the capital city of Srirangapatna was encouraging negative thoughts in the minds of the loyalists of the Sultanat. The old killedar was also running out of provisions and supplies after holding the fort bravely for six months and twelve days. The hopes of reinforcements arriving from Srirangapatna seemed bleak given the precarious position of the kingdom in the wake of Cornwallis's march towards the capital. By April 1791, Badr-u-Zaman Khan capitulated and Dharwad passed into Maratha hands. This was followed by a quick Maratha takeover of everything north of the Tungabhadra.

If the hasty retreat of Cornwallis from the very gates of Srirangapatna shattered the morale of the combined army, the victories of the Marathas brought cheer to them. Cornwallis used the next few months to re-group and strengthen the forces. A few successes, however minor, were the need of the hour. Places like Rayakota, Nandidurg, and Pennagara and so on were annexed between June and November 1791. Tipu also used the breather to realign himself and resolved to reclaim the provinces lost in the course of the previous months. He began a fierce siege of Coimbatore, which was held by Lieutenant Chalmers. But mishaps in the army led to huge and unexpected losses among the Mysoreans. A larger body was despatched under Kumr-ud-din Khan to salvage the position at Coimbatore. A stiff siege ensued. Lieutenants Chalmers and Nash were severely wounded and Coimbatore capitulated to the Mysorean might by November 1791. The Europeans were packed off as prisoners to Srirangapatna.

With every defeat, memories of Yorktown haunted Cornwallis. This also strengthened his resolve to try harder. Since many positions of strength between the British base in Bangalore and Tipu's centre of power of Srirangapatna still remained in Tipu's hands, Cornwallis deemed the reduction of these as his prime task. Savandurg, a place he had long regarded as a giant obstacle in his capture of Srirangapatna, was the first to catch his attention. Colonel Stuart, along with two European and three Indian corps and powerful artillery were sent to reduce this post. After a stiff siege a string of places—Savandurg, Hutridurg and Shivanagiri—capitulated to the British army by the close of the year.

The nizam's armies meanwhile attacked the hill fort of Gurramkonda. Hafiz Farid-ud-din was deployed for the task. There was a long history of clashes between Hafiz and Tipu. Hafiz was in fact the ambassador sent by Nizam Ali in 1789. That Hafiz had refused a marital alliance with Tipu's family was a sore point in the Sultan's mind. Gurramkonda gave Tipu the opportunity to avenge these insults. An unexpected attack led by Tipu's eldest son, Fateh Haidar, assisted by Ghazi Khan and Ali Raza routed the forces of Hyderabad. Hafiz was taken prisoner, stripped and humiliated. It is said that someone took mercy and flung a quilt at him to cover himself. According to H. Rao, a triumphant Ali Raza approached him and said:

'You recollect the disrespectful language you employed towards my sovereign and me at Hyderabad on the occasion of the demanded marriage?'

'Perfectly well,' replied a disgraced Hafiz, 'but we were then serving our respective masters: that day is past. If you are here for the purpose of revenge, murder me at once, but do not dishonour me!'

Wilks states that Ali Raza immediately ordered Hafiz to be led out to a concealed place under the cover of a rock and in his presence to be cut into pieces in cold blood. Hafiz's death was a huge blow to the Nizam. The ego clash between the two Muslim sovereigns of the Deccan seemed to have no end in sight.

Fearing that further procrastination would ruin things, especially in the wake of the upper hand Tipu seemed to be getting, Cornwallis decided to re-attack Srirangapatna. Accordingly, the British made a frontal attack on Srirangapatna in January 1792 and besieged it. The Sultan had made every effort to strengthen the defences of the capital in the preceding six months and was encamped to the north of Srirangapatna awaiting the enemy's arrival. Tipu had however miscalculated the British moves in hoping that they would not attack till General Abercromby's forces joined them from Bombay. He had hoped to intercept the reinforcements that would head towards Cornwallis. But a determined Cornwallis decided to make a surprise attack on the fort of Srirangapatna by night. At about half past eight on 6 February 1792, under a brilliant moonlit sky, three British columns marched in dead silence towards the Sultan's fortified encampments on the northern side of the Cauvery, flanked by the defences of the Karighatta Hills. The British attack was made in three divisions—the right under Major General Meadows, with Lieutenant Colonel Stuart as his second-in-command, the centre under Lord Cornwallis himself and the left under Lieutenant Colonel Maxwell.

Tipu was having dinner in his camp when the first news of the stealthy attack reached him. Taking his position at an outwork of the fort which commanded the scene, he remained there till morning, issuing orders and spending one of the most anxious nights of his life. The fierce fighting continued for two days, during which the losses for the Mysoreans soared upwards of 4,000 compared to about 535 for the invaders. Taking advantage of the confusion, about 10,000 Coorgis who had been forcibly converted and named 'Ahmadi Chelas' changed sides. They tried to cart away a large treasure from the camp that night to pay the troops the following day. But Purnaiya was ever-alert and ensured that their designs were foiled and all the treasure sent back to the fort on camel-back. To add to Tipu's precarious position, the Bombay army under Abercromby repulsed the Mysorean resistance and successfully joined the grand army by 16 February 1792.

Mysore's fall was now inevitable. As Major Dirom records about Tipu's actions during this time:

> He was seen frequently every day on the ramparts particularly at the north face, viewing the English approaches, and giving directions to his own troops. He was constantly bringing guns to the works and cavaliers on that side, and had a multitude of people at work thickening the inner rampart, filling up the embrasures to strengthen the parapet where he could not have guns, and repairing such as had been blown and damaged by the firing of his cannon. He was at work day and night making every preparation possible for a vigorous defence.

Lieutenant Mackenzie describes the other problems a beleaguered Tipu faced:

> But within doors, Tippoo was by no means secure from danger. However faithful their allegiance, it was natural to conceive that

Sultanat-e-khudadad Mysore AD 1782–91

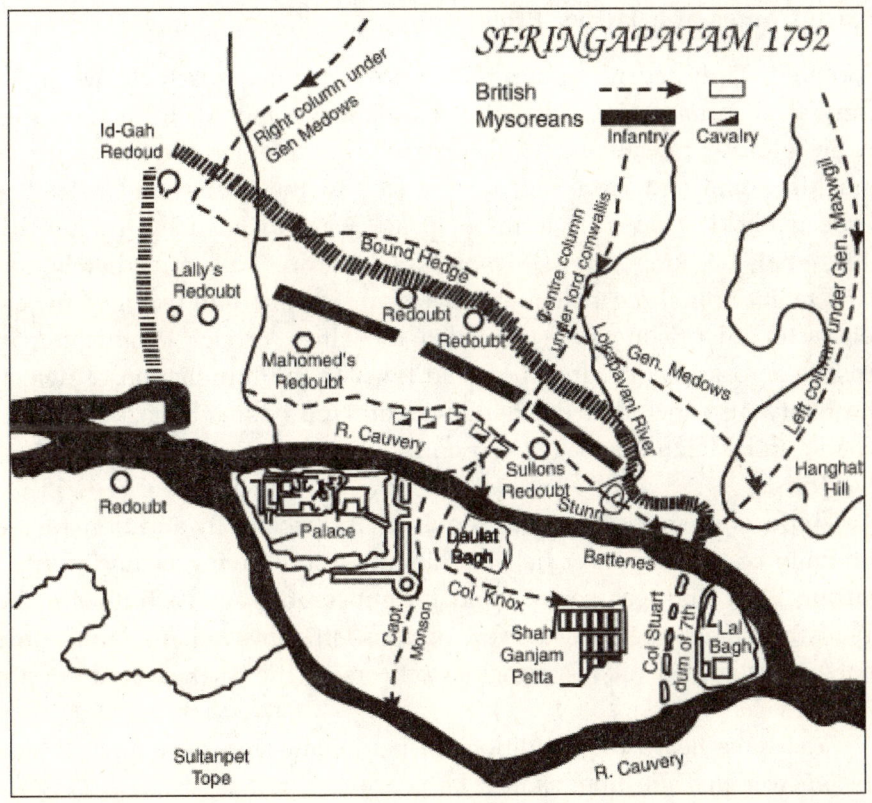

The attack on Srirangapatna in 1792
(Maps are artistic recreations made at Suhaas Graphics, Bangalore)

the multitudes of peaceful people who had flocked to the capital could not relish a struggle of so little expectance, whilst their families and property remained at hazard on the issue.

To add to his woes, Tipu was systematically attacked at the most vulnerable points of his kingdom. Starting December 1791, a corps of 400 Europeans and three sepoy battalions with field artillery under Major Cuppage had reduced Danayakanakote and Satyamangalam. By February 1792 they ascended the top of the Gejjalhatty Pass and facilitated the occupation of the key post of Hardanahalli and the reduction of the new but unfinished fort of Mysore, barely eight miles south of the capital city.

Peace Comes at a Heavy Price

Cornered, Tipu had no option but to open negotiations with the grand army. By February 1792, his vakils Ghulam Ali and Ali Raza were met by Sir John Kennaway and Mr Cherry who represented the British forces and Mir Alam and Hari Pant on the side of the Nizam and Marathas respectively. The possible terms of peace were dictated by the jubilant allies—half the kingdom of Mysore, Rs 3.3 crore, half immediately and the remainder in three instalments over four months, and the unequivocal release of all prisoners of war from the allies' armies languishing in prisons across Mysore. In a personal twist to the humiliation of defeat, the treaty also included the handover of Tipu's sons, Shahzada Abdul Khaliq and Moizuddin, aged ten and eight respectively, as hostages to the British.

Tippu was shocked at the terms of the treaty. In addition to the indignity of handing over half his kingdom and paying heavy tributes, parting with his dear sons would be unbearable agony. But with the enemy at his doorstep, he had few options left. Hayavadana Rao records that he assembled all his principal officers at the mosque and sought their advice:

'You have heard the conditions of peace, and you have now to hear and answer my question: shall it be peace or war?'

The assembled officers unanimously pledged their allegiance to their beloved Sultan and declared that though they were ready to lay their lives for his sake, they had to take into account the fatigue and disillusionment that had set in among the Mysorean troops following the string of reverses. Thus, after a lot of reluctance and trauma, Tipu accepted the terms of the treaty, including the last one. The 'Preliminary Treaty of Seringapatam' was signed on 26 February 1792 and the 'Definitive Treaty of Seringapatam' on 19 March 1792.

Abdul Khaliq and Moizuddin were given a tearful farewell. Major Dirom gives a vivid account of the reception of the hostages:

> Lord Cornwallis...met the Princes at the door of his large tent as they dismounted from the elephants...and led them in, one in each hand, to the tent; the eldest, Abdul Kalick, was about ten; the youngest, Mooza-ud-Deen, about eight years of age. When they were seated on either side of Lord Cornwallis, Gulam Ali, the head Vakeel addressed his Lordship as follows—'These children were

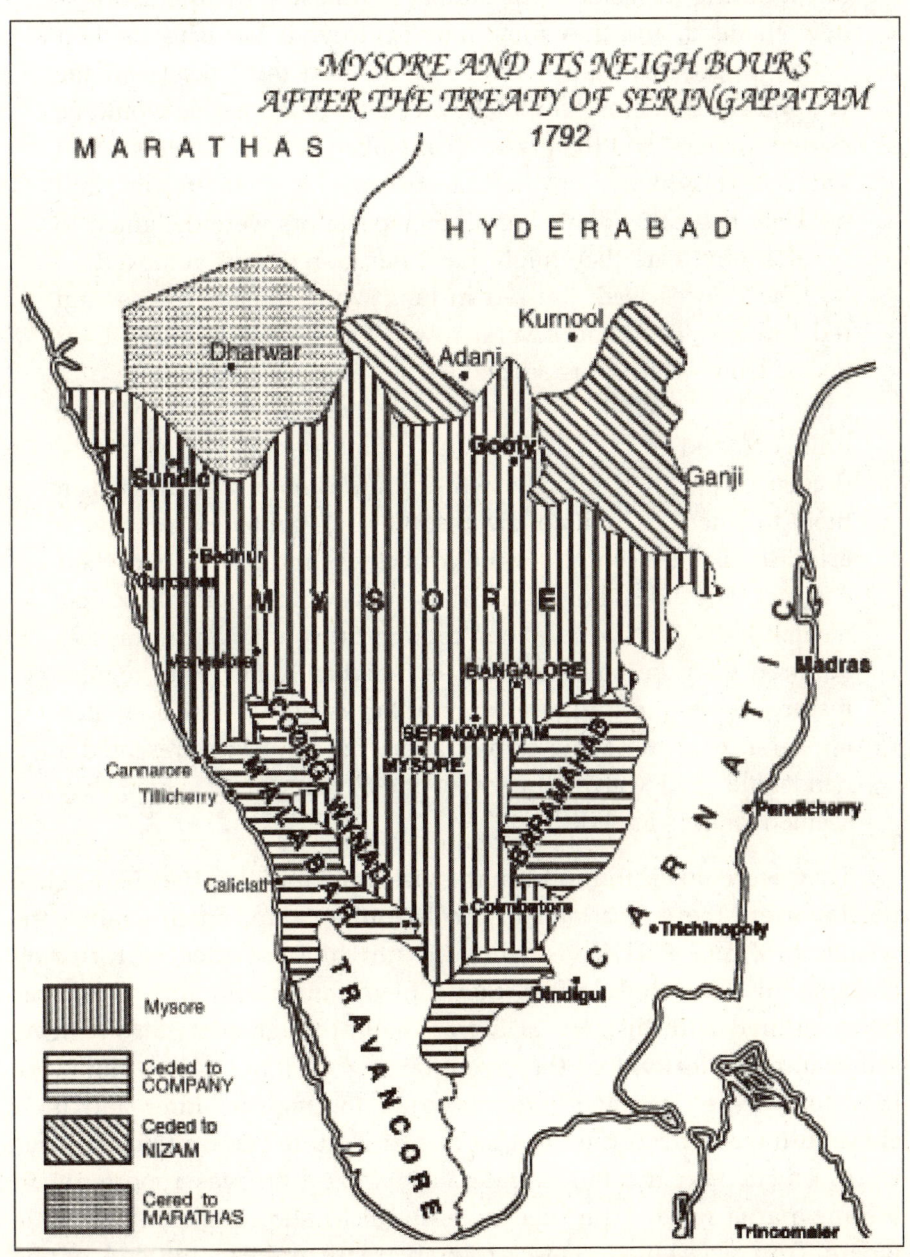

*Mysore and its neighbours after the humiliating Treaty of Srirangapatna, 1792
(Maps are artistic recreations made at Suhaas Graphics, Bangalore)*

this morning the sons of the Sultan, my master; their situation is now changed, and they must look up to your Lordship as their father.' Lord Cornwallis...anxiously assured the Vakeel and the young Princes themselves, that every attention possible would be shown to them, and the greatest care taken of their persons. Their little faces brightened up; the scene became highly interesting; and not only their attendants but all the spectators were delighted to see that any fears they might have harboured were removed...

The Princes were dressed in long white muslin gowns, and red turbans. They had several rows of large pearls round their necks, from which was suspended an ornament consisting of a ruby and an emerald of considerable size, surrounded by large brilliants; and in their turbans, each had a sprig of rich pearls. Bred up from their infancy with infinite care, and instructed in their manners to imitate the reserve and politeness of age, it astonished all present to see the correctness and propriety of their conduct. The eldest boy, rather dark in his colour, with thick lips, a small fattish nose, and a long thoughtful countenance, was less admired than the youngest who is remarkably fair, with regular features, a small round face, large full eyes, and a more animated appearance...After some conversation, his Lordship presented a handsome gold watch to each of the Princes, with which they seemed much pleased.

They were taken to the Carnatic via Bangalore, kept at the English headquarters there and later at the Maratha camp, much against the wishes of Nana Phadnavis who did not like the idea of torturing children in this whole affair. Some historians claim that Tipu was later reunited with his sons at Devanahalli, though some also believe, rather unrealistically, that they were taken to Britain, where they were kept for the rest of their lives, married to English ladies and their children have not returned to this day. It is quite certain that the boys were returned to the family later, as Moizuddin was reportedly in Srirangapatna when Tipu died and Abdul Khaliq fought in the battle where Tipu was killed. This inhuman treaty marked the end of the Third Anglo-Mysore war, which brought much disgrace, humiliation and personal loss upon Tipu. The geography of the kingdom was completely altered after the war.

According to the terms of the Definitive Treaty of Srirangapatna, the English obtained Malabar and Coorg, Dindigul, Shankaridurg, Baramahal and other territories which yielded a total rental of about 13,16,765 Pagodas. The Maratha territory was extended to the Tungabhadra and the cessions to them in the Doab, Dharwad and other places valued at 13,16,666 Pagodas. Areas north of the Tungabhadra and the principality of Cudappah were handed over to the Nizam and valued at a similar sum. The prize money realised from the sale of property captured during the war amounted to £ 93,584. For their phenomenal work in the war, each colonel was paid £ 1,161, £ 29 to a Sergeant, £ 27 to an Indian subedar, £ 11 to a havaldar and £ 5 to other ranks.

Commentators differ in their opinions of the manner in which Cornwallis concluded the decisive war. While some praise him for bringing the Tiger of Mysore to his knees, others criticise him for letting go of Tipu, which resulted in another war seven years later. Below are such contrasting views about the manner in which the Third Mysore War ended. Lieutenant Mackenzie writes:

> This glorious conclusion of the war was celebrated to the utmost extremities of the British Empire, with the most brilliant rejoicings; few indeed affected to disapprove of the treaty, and these were actuated by a desire of seeing the House of Hyder totally extirpated, without attending to the danger of throwing an addition of power into the hands of our northern allies. With men of judgment and experience, the peace was evidently calculated to ensure permanent as well as immediate advantages to the several European settlements in the east, for whilst the loss of half his dominions would be fatal to his plan of conquest, the tranquility of India would, in all human probability, be out of danger from the restless disposition of Tipoo Sultan for many years. His resources crippled, his treasures exhausted, his troops dispersed, his artillery reduced to wreck, the sternest policy could not have demanded further reparation for the insult offered to the British nation in the attack of her ancient and faithful ally, the inoffensive Prince of Travancore.

Lewin B. Bowring adopts a middle-of-the-ground stand on the treaty:

In estimating Lord Cornwallis' policy, it must be remembered that soldiers are ordinarily more generous than other negotiators to a conquered foe and that he deprecated a further conflict which would entail a great sacrifice of life. Moreover, he was probably fettered by restrictions placed upon him by the East India Company, who, while unwittingly founding an Empire, were still walking in commercial leading-strings. Tipu was undoubtedly a usurper, as his father had been before him; the lawful Mysore Raja, though a captive was still alive; and Tipu had not hesitated to avow himself the implacable enemy of the English. The Sultan was hemmed in all sides and Seringapatam must inevitably have fallen had the siege been prosecuted. It must be confessed, moreover, that it was a dubious policy to restore to power a bitter foe, thus enabling him to resume a hostile attitude which eventually compelled Lord Mornington to crush forever the despot's arrogance. Cornwallis was of the opinion that he had effectually curbed Tipu's power of disturbing the peace of India, a mistaken idea of which subsequent events showed the fallacy. The restoration of the lawful Mysore dynasty does not appear to have been contemplated nor would the captive Raja have been able to maintain his rule unsupported by British troops. The territory held by his predecessors at the time of Haidar Ali's usurpation formed but a portion of the Mysore dominions in 1792. These considerations were probably factors in inducing Lord Cornwallis to refrain from the extreme measure of dethroning Tipu Sultan.

As Lieutenant Colonel L.H. Thornton opines:

It would have been noted that Cornwallis had held Tippoo in the hollow of his hand, and there was not wanting critics to say that the Governor General had been too lenient; that he should have crushed the Sultan completely and have erased the State of Mysore from the list of future possible belligerents.

In a similar critical vein, General Meadows writes to Lord Cornwallis:*

---

* Quoted in the *Pall Mall Gazette* of 26 September 1866 in an article entitled 'The Man in Possession—A Story of Mysore'.

I mean that three Governors, the Nizam and the Peishwah should dine at Srirangapatna, with the old Queen of Mysore, sitting at the head of the table. For my own part I freely confess that I should prefer the dignity and justice of dethroning the cruel tyrant and usurper and restoring the Kingdom to the Hindu family—the lawful owner—to the wiser policy perhaps of clipping his wings so effectually that he could soar no more in our time.

In fact, General Meadows was thoroughly disappointed in the way the war had ended and of the supposed lost opportunities for the British. He was angry that, rather than eliminating Tipu once and for all, the Sultan was given a chance to re-align and recover from this shameful defeat. On top of this, when he was asked to receive Tipu's sons, an altercation ensued between him and the governor general. Meadows shot himself in anger and had to be rushed for medical assistance to Madras. Luckily for him, the wound was not too serious.

After the successful campaign in Mysore, Cornwallis left India in 1793, still gloating over his success. Sir John Shore succeeded him as Governor General and stayed on till 1798.

Maharani Lakshmammanni

In 1794, Khasa Chamaraja Wodeyar's wife Kempananjammanni gave birth to a son—Mummadi Krishnaraja or Krishnaraja III—bringing great joy to Mahamathrushree Lakshmammanni. Her anger against the house of Haidar had been accentuated after the ascent of Tipu to the throne. Unlike his father, Tipu had completely discredited the royal family and she hated him for that. Tipu's humiliating defeat encouraged her to make the final blow before uprooting him.

By 1790, she had opened negotiations with Cornwallis and General Meadows; as described earlier, the latter addressed her often as 'Rana' Lakshmi Ammanni.

Maharani Lakshmammanni was also a deeply religious person. The *Annals* state that Lord Venkataramana supposedly appeared in her dream and directed her that His statue, which was in Balamuri, be consecrated at Mysore. The maharani brought the statue to Mysore and installed it at the Kille Venkataramana Swamy temple in Mysore, offering continuous worship and observing strict fasts. Her efforts did not go in vain.

Tirumala Rao and Narayana Rao continued to be her faithful emissaries to the British. This despite the several personal tragedies that struck their families, thanks to the blessings of Haidar and Tipu, for siding with the rani. Both Haidar and Tipu stopped short of taking any severe action against the Maharani, partly out of respect and partly fearing public wrath for misbehaving with a woman, that too one of royal lineage. So the easiest targets were the brothers and their families. The Rani refused to heed the message Haidar and Tipu tried to send her through these actions.

The pradhans tried to utilise Tipu's attack on Travancore to their advantage by mobilising support for the Mysore Maharaja's cause in the courts of Tanjore and Travancore where they had spent sufficient time. They also carried the maharani's messages to General Meadows who had assumed charge as governor and commander-in-Chief on 20 February 1790. Narayana Rao met Meadows at Tanjore and guns were fired from the ramparts of the Tanjore fort to honour the emissary. Meadows stopped short of committing himself to a treaty with the maharani and said he would need to consult his allies, the Marathas and Nizam. He promised to write to the maharani, however, which he did.

His letter, dated May 1790, speaks for itself:[*]

> The repeated greetings of General Meadows, Governor of Channapatna. Your letter was duly delivered by your ambassador Tirumala Rao and I understand the contents thereof. God knows when Tipu may die and leave the country. Victory is God's grace. If He will enable us to restore the Kingdom to the rightful Rulers, we shall indeed be very happy. We cannot now discuss about the distribution of territories. As the Nizam and the Mahrathas are now our allies, we cannot settle the point ourselves. It is right that you should bear the cost of the war, and it is also very good that you promise to pay prize money to the troops. If we can but succeed in restoring the country to you and set things right, we shall feel pleased that we have accomplished a good purpose. We will do our best and the Almighty God should crown our efforts with success. We cannot say more now.

All through the course of the Third Mysore War the pradhans kept the British informed of Tipu's every move. Tirumala Rao supplied spies and

---

[*] This letter appears in a research paper by the descendants of the Mysore Pradhans—M.A. Narayana Iyengar and M.A. Sreenivasachar.

news writers as well to the British. As mentioned in a letter of Captain Macleod to Tirumala Rao (dated 16 September 1790): 'I have received the two Harcars you sent me and I am much obliged to you for them.... if you can get more good harcars and news-writers that will go to stay in Tippo's camp or some of his garrisons I will pay them well and be much obliged to you.'

During Tipu's conquest at Dharapuram, he received intelligence of Tirumala Rao's presence in Coimbatore. He viewed the pradhans as irritants and a life-support system for the imprisoned maharani and wished to eliminate them once and for all. He sent a spy named Singree to ascertain the strength of the fort of Coimbatore and also confirm Rao's presence. Tipu then marched with his forces to attack Tirumala, who was stationed at the fort with 2,200 men and a garrison that consisted of only one officer and 100 troops with little ammunition. The end seemed near for the pradhans. Tipu's huge force was no match for their small and ill-equipped army. But as Providence would have it, a heavy and intermittent rain for three days gave the British time to send in a detachment of 2,000 troops from Nanjnad under Colonel Wahab and Captain Knox. Tipu retreated, dismissing this as a wasteful and costly campaign to nail the two pradhans and marched ahead towards Kaveripuram.

During the Third Mysore War, just around the time Bangalore fell, the discontent among the dispossessed Palegars brimmed over in the form of a fresh attempt to reinstate the old order of the Mysore royal family. Interestingly, the role of Maharani Lakshmammanni in this incident is completely unknown to historians and contemporary commentators. These loyalists were aided and abetted by Lord Cornwallis himself. But the attempt failed.

In the following years, the pradhans again acted as major pawns in the chess game of the times, providing support to British armies all through the Third Mysore War. Of course, Tirumala Rao also faced some unfortunate charges of financial misappropriation of over 10,000 Pagodas from the Treasury at Coimbatore. He denied the charges and blamed his subordinate Amildar Puttaiya, in whose charge he had placed Coimbatore, and left with the British armies on their campaign against Tipu. He was arrested in June 1791. It was left to Narayana Rao to make repeated pleas to the Board of Revenue at Madras to get his brother released. Finally, sensing the potential utility of Tirumala Rao during the war, the British decided to release him.

Throughout the years following Haidar's death, low intensity conspiracies were continuously hatched by Maharani Lakshmammanni and her cohorts. They had even tried measures like setting fire to Tipu's powder magazine in Srirangapatna, overpowering the commander of the fort and his men and taking possession of the city when Tipu was away on the Malabar conquest. But all these efforts failed. The Third Mysore War was seen as the final blow to Tipu and General Meadows had argued with Lord Cornwallis to take Mysore from Tipu following his defeat in the war. But this suggestion was rejected by Cornwallis.

Thus, none of the maharani's efforts or hopes were realised. Lakshmammanni was no ordinary woman, and refused to lose heart. Her one-point agenda was to restore the kingdom to her family.

Even Khasa Chamaraja wrote to the Company's officials wherein he mentioned the 'atrocities' of Tipu and the suffocation and thralldom in which he and his family were held, requesting the British to suppress Tipu and restore power to the family. But in 1796 Khasa Chamaraja passed away. Tipu didn't see the need to install a puppet king on the throne and hence completely ignored Lakshmammanni's pleas to install Mummadi Krishnaraja on the throne. For the first time since 1399, the chain of succession was broken and this strengthened further Lakshmammanni's resolve to vanquish Tipu.

She wrote to Tirumala Rao thus:

> Unless the English defeated the French, victory would remain an impossible dream. If any delay occurred, as on former occasions, the alliance between Tippoo Sultan and the French would be like that of fire and wind. The country would be devastated and the people ruined. There are no able military commanders to oppose the English and everyone wishes Tippu's fall.
>
> If however, it should happen by God's grace that we should be alive and the English conquer Tippu and restore to us our kingdom, we shall pay the expenses of the English army to the extent of one crore pagodas. And for this they must abide by our old treaty with Sullivan and Macartney. You should communicate all this to the English and get the army to march at once. And it cannot be timed to arrive here at a more opportune moment. For Tippu is acting in the most foolish manner. He does not know who are his best friends and who his worst enemies. And hence

he has lost control over his own army. He has no good military officers. And everybody here is wishing for his discomfiture and he is very unpopular. By whatever route the army may come now, it can have ample supplies and good water. If you will therefore exert your best now without delay and with your usual zeal, ability and intelligence, I have no doubt that God will second your efforts and give us victory this time! Let Lord Ranga help us.

On 3 February 1799, she wrote yet another letter to Lord Mornington and Clive, governor of Madras, after narrating in detail the 'sufferings' of her family since the usurpation in 1761.

To their Excellencies Lords Mornington and Clive, ornamented with every noble qualifications—Sallam of Lakshmammanny:

In times of yore, Providence bestowed upon our elders the Raj of Mysore, and got it administered by us with justice and wisdom. Of late our servant Hyder Naik, growing in power, usurped our territories and put to death our Lord Consort, our children, our relations and all our dependents. He plundered our palace several times and with the help of the wealth thereby acquired, conquered several other countries, and committed ravages throughout slaying mercilessly and without cause ryots, poligars and other persons by thousands. Finding it impossible to bear his oppressions any longer and considering the English nation highly virtuous and upright and their friendship very much to be coveted, as certain to yield much good in future, we sent an embassy to the then Governor of Madras, through Mahomed Ali Khan (Nabob of the Karnatic) in the year Pramathi (AD 1760). Certain negotiations followed, as recorded in our letter to the then Governor. Later, in the year Durmukhi (AD 1776) relying on the promises of the illustrious Lord Pigot, we sent our Pradhan Tirumal Row. Unfortunately that Governor could do nothing, as he was himself involved in trouble.

And in the year Subhakritu (AD 1782), Lord Macartney gave us ample assurance of our restoration and hence we got together many of our adherents. Just on the eve of our capturing Tippu and recovering our Kingdom, our object was disclosed to Tippu; and consequently he put to death 700 families from amongst our relations as well as those of Tirumal Row, including men and women and children. You are also aware of the events that transpired in the year Sadharana (1790 AD) in the times of General Meadows and Lord Cornwallis. After the late treaty under the advice of the French, Tippu has caused the death of the Rajah, plundered his Palace and placed us in rigorous custody in a separate house.

While in this state, we learn that you have been sent to this land specially to restore to us our kingdom. Besides, we have also heard of your great nobility of character and purity of heart; and placing implicit faith in you, we seek your protection and aid. And hence with your usual goodness, considering the claims of justice, and with an eye to God and everlasting fame, you should root out the enemy, and restore to us our kingdom, according to the conditions of our last treaty with you. We shall pay you a crore of star pagodas for the expense of the war. We have also written to our Pradhan Tirumal Row in greater detail and he will tell you everything. As he is our best friend, whatever is said or done by him on our behalf shall have our fullest approval, and you may consider them as completely ratified by us. As we are in the hands of the enemy, we cannot count upon our life. Should it happen that we are no more, with the assistance of this our Pradhan Tirumal Row, we request you to establish the Raj with justice and acquire fame for all time to come.

The stage seemed set for the final kill. Tippu was going to face the toughest challenge of his life, encountering innumerable foes, both within and outside his realm.

12

THE SWORD OF TIPU SULTAN AD 1791–99

4 MAY 1799

The inner apartments of the Sultan's Palace at Srirangapatna were deceptively cool. While the mercury soared outside in a typical South Indian summer, at its peak in the month of May, the rooms within seemed to belong to some exotic island. Huge mats sprinkled with water and perfume hung from the walls and balconies and manual fans ran round the clock. In more ways than one, this illusion was symbolic. The man in command was living in a similar world of make-believe, where he was made to believe that things were fine. Just an hour back, Tipu Sultan had personally visited the place where a breach had been reported in the once impregnable fort walls of Srirangapatna. Mir Nadim, an accomplice of his 'trusted' ally Mir Sadik, led him to a place where a few stones lay scattered. 'Sultan! In times of war rumours fly thick; see for yourself, there is no breach here. We are completely in command, Sir, and our troops are stationed at all the main posts. Please rest assured and proceed for your afternoon meal.'

While a relieved Sultan rode away, the breach stood at an opposite end of the fort, welcoming the enemy with open arms. And the troops Mir Nadim was talking about were lured away on the pretext of salary payments and locked up by Mir Sadik. Srirangapatna had seen trouble in the past, but this time treachery permeated virtually every brick and stone of the fort.

Back in the cool environs of his lavish palace, Tipu Sultan sat down to eat. No sooner had he begun than a group of harried soldiers tried to barge in. His trusted aide and physician Raja Khan was enraged.

'You impudent fools! Don't you realise this is the luncheon hour of His Highness? How dare you interrupt at such an hour and with such defiance?' he thundered.

'Sir, I know this is the Sultan's resting hour. But then calamity has struck...we have to meet him...immediately.'

Hearing the din, Tipu left the bread untouched and came out to enquire the cause of the commotion.

'Salutations to Almighty Allah and his favourite Sultan! Sir, the fort is breached, the enemy has entered and is moving menacingly towards the Palace...'

'What? I just came from....' Mir Nadim's nonchalance immediately made sense to Tipu. 'Has he too gone the same way as Purnaiya? Deserted me ultimately? Raja Khan, when is your turn?'

'Sir, hellfire be upon me if such a thought even crosses my mind. The enemy would be here in no time. Your respectful father Haidar Ali Sahab has constructed a number of secret exit routes from the palace after his first loss of trust. Make haste Sir, slip away from Srirangapatna.'

'RAJA KHAN!' roared the Tiger of Mysore, 'I shall sever your head from your body for making such an impudent suggestion. You want me to run away like a mouse from the battlefield? How could you even imagine that I would do that?'

'Huzoor, this is not the time for argument. With each passing second I can sense the enemy's footsteps drawing closer. You can stay in hiding for a few months, realign yourself and storm the city again to regain all that you lost. Isn't that what Nawab Haidar Ali did when faced with Khande Rao's betrayal?'

'I know you wish me well, Raja Khan—you are among the few well-wishers left for me in this hell of doom. But if there is something that I have to defend it is honour—the honour of my clan, the honour of the kingdom of Mysore and that of myself. Running away in the midst of battle is any soldier's worst nightmare. And Allah knows that I have been but a soldier all my life. How can I act against my characteristic nature and flee? I know that I might not survive the treachery that has crippled me. I can see my end is near. But it is far better to live like a lion for a day and die fighting to defend your honour and your Kingdom, than to live like a jackal for a hundred years.'

With these prophetic words, Tipu picked up his legendary sword and hurried towards his horse, with the battle cry 'Sarkar-e-Khudadad'.

The clarion call echoed through the ramparts of the fort on that fateful day of 4 May 1799, for the last time ever.

❖

THE FOURTH ANGLO-MYSORE WAR

Richard Wellesley, the Earl of Mornington, took over as the new governor general in 1798. Before coming to India he had written to Lady Anne Bernard:

> I will heap kingdoms upon kingdoms, victory upon victory, revenue upon revenue; I will accumulate glory and wealth and power until the ambition and avarice even of my masters shall cry mercy.

Wellesley also had a burning desire to spread Christianity in India. Sunday was declared a holiday, the Bible was translated into all the major Indian languages, and Christian missionaries became more active, especially among the illiterate and under-privileged masses. Wellesley appointed a commission of five officers: his brother, Colonel Wellesley, Colonel Close, Colonel Agnew, Colonel Malcolm and Captain Macaulay. He is remembered for introducing the Subsidiary Alliance system with the Indian rulers. These subsidiary agreements between the British and the local rulers ensured that the control of foreign affairs, defence, and communications was transferred from the ruler to the company and the rulers were allowed to rule as they wished (up to a limit) on other matters. This development created what came to be called the native states, or princely states, under a titular maharaja or nawab. Using this agreement he stationed British troops at the Nizam's court in Hyderabad under Captain Kirkpatrick. Slowly, the Nizam lost all power over his own army and dominion and also the option of appointing any Europeans without British consent. Wellesley tried the same trick in Mysore when he tried to get Doveton stationed at Srirangapatna. But Tipu could not be lured into signing such a treaty and with this began the first bickering between the two.

Tipu's soft corner for the French continued. He had heard so much about the heroic Napoleon Bonaparte. There are only a few individuals in history who have captured the imagination of their contemporaries and of historians; perhaps the most compelling of these figures is Napoleon Bonaparte. Actively involved in the French Revolution and a staunch opponent of the British, Napoleon stood for everything Tipu upheld in India. No doubt then, that he sought an alliance with Napoleon. In fact, Tipu had a wide-ranging correspondence with the kings of Afghanistan, Arabia, Constantinople and Mauritius as well in his endeavour to drive the British out of India for good. Napoleon's response to Tipu, addressing him as 'The Sovereign of India', is recorded in Bhagwan Gidwani's novel:

> BONAPARTE, Member of the National Convention General-in-chief to the most magnificent SULTAN, our greatest friend TIPPOO SAIB
>
> You have already been informed of my arrival on the borders of the Red Sea with an innumerable and invincible army full of the desire of delivering you from the iron yoke of England. I eagerly embrace this opportunity of testifying to you the desire I have of being informed by you, by the way of Muscat and Mocha as to your political situation. I would further wish you could send some intelligent person to Suez or Cairo possessing your confidence, with whom I may confer.
>
> May the Almighty increase your power and destroy your enemies!
>
> NAPOLEON BONAPARTE

Tipu's plan was to create an international confederacy that would eliminate the British. He had made friendly overtures to the Nizam earlier and in fact even got a French contingent of 1,400 troops stationed in Hyderabad under Raymond. But that was disbanded by Wellesley following the Subsidiary Alliance system under Kirkpatrick. Tipu had invited Napoleon and Zaman Shah, the King of Afghanistan, to India to aid him in this battle. Things seemed to be moving according to plan, as the letter from Napoleon (intercepted by the British) seemed to suggest. But then suddenly a series of reverses spoilt his plans. Napoleon was defeated at Accre in Syria and forced back to France. Zaman Shah beat a hasty retreat to Kabul because of British machinations that brought about an attack on Afghanistan from the Iranian border. Wellesley was furious at this international plot hatched by Tipu and decided to solve this problem once and for all. He declared war on Mysore and sent the largest army ever assembled in India towards Srirangapatna. This was the Fourth Anglo-Mysore War, and also the last one.

In a political assessment of the situation, Wellesley wrote in 1798:[*]

> In reviewing our political situation in India, particularly with regard to our comparative power of curbing the attempts of Tippu, I ought not to omit the consideration of the relative strength of the prince as it exists at the present moment, and as it stood at the conclusion of the peace at Seringapatam. Since that period of time, he has enjoyed perfect internal tranquility; while our allies all around him have been distracted and exhausted by domestic rebellions, successive revolutions and mutual wars, he has been employed in recruiting the sources of his strength, improving his revenues and invigorating the discipline of his armies... he has been very active for some time past in his applications to the courts of native powers, endeavouring to stir them up against us...But the most remarkable step that Tippoo has lately taken, is his communication with Zemaun Shah...if an invasion of Hindostan should ever seriously be attempted by Zemaun Shah, the diversion of our force, which would be occasioned by such an event, would offer the most favourable opportunity to an attack from Tippoo on our possessions in the peninsula. No mode of carrying on war with us could be more vexatious or more distressing to our resources than a combined attack from the Oude and the Carnatic...if the facts be true which I have stated on both sides of this enumeration of the comparative circumstances of our situation in India, and of those which effect the situation of Tippoo, it must be admitted that he has rather gained than lost weight in the period of time described, and that the consistency, unity and efficiency of our side of the balance has suffered no considerable degree of diminution...the balance of power in India no longer exists upon the same footing on which it was placed by the peace of Seringapatam. The question must therefore arise,

---

[*] This appears in Beatson's account.

how it may best be brought back again to that state, in which you have directed me to maintain it... Of course I fear him greatly. He is not like other rulers of India that we have known. I fear also the example he sets to other rulers. Fortunately all of them are far too pusillanimous to follow his example, but in the long run such an example can have a disruptive influence on the Empire... the movement of our troops and military preparations could not escape the vigilance of Tippoo: his resources are always more prompt than our own; and as a great part of his army is said to be in a state of field equipment, our attempt to strike a blow at him is likely to produce an invasion of the Carnatic before we are in a situation to resist him...a comparison between his own and his father's wars, with the late experience of his own misfortunes has taught him that our strength depends upon our supplies...

The superiority of Tippoo in cavalry and the greater rapidity, with which he moves, would render it impracticable to proceed to the attack of Seringapatam without establishing a systematic chain of posts for depots of stores and provisions. That he had endeavoured to frustrate this is evident from his policy in the destruction of Ossore and Bangalore and in making Seringapatam his only or principal fortification. By the former it is his intention to increase our difficulty of our approach by lengthening the time of our operation, and by the latter to oppose such impediments to make the capture of Seringapatam impracticable in the course of one campaign...nothing therefore short of the capture of Seringapatam can justly be considered as striking an effectual blow against Tippoo...

Thus the vanquishing of Tipu Sultan became the primary objective of the Company in order to maintain its suzerainty over the subcontinent. It is evident that this brave son of Mysore shook the very foundations and the confidence of the mighty British Empire!

THE FOURTH ANGLO-MYSORE WAR

War broke out and three English armies burst into Mysore: the Carnatic army under General Harris from Vellore, the Bombay army under General

Stuart, and the Hyderabad army under Colonel Arthur Wellesley and the Nizam. The allied forces had an army of almost 50,000—26,000 of who came with Wellesley (4,000 European and the rest local Indian sepoys) and the Hyderabad regiment of 10 battalions and over 16,000 cavalry, along with many soldiers supplied by the Marathas. Tipu's defending forces had been seriously depleted by the Third Anglo-Mysore War and the consequent loss of half his kingdom, but he probably still had up to 30,000 soldiers. On 9 March 1799, the English army under General Harris encamped at Kilamangalam and on the next day Lieutenant Colonel Read was sent to protect Baramahal.

A scream of anguish resounded across Mysore as the English army advanced. There was a cry of despair, a broken prayer for mercy. But the invaders had been told that their mission aimed not just to conquer the kingdom, but also to break the spirit of the people and their Sultan. Undefended towns, villages, farms, temples and mosques were burnt down, women were seized and shared among the warring forces, men and children were slaughtered. Tippu rushed from place to place to stall the advancing army. He marched to Siddheshwara to attack General Stuart's army.

The Battle of Siddheshwara

In *Historical Sketches*, Wilks gives an account of the Battle of Siddheshwara, called the Battle of Sedaseer. The final attack on the territory that had proved to be the East India Company's worst southern nightmare was launched under General Stuart, who assembled armies at Cannanore that marched from there on 21 February 1799. Beating the severely harsh Deccan summer, the troops arrived at the top of the Poodicherrum ghats by 2 March, to take up battle positions close to the Mysore frontier.

As Wilks elaborates, the topography of the region—thickly wooded—was so hostile and impregnable that occupying a regular defensive position was almost impossible. With his characteristic military acumen, Stuart was constrained to effect several divisions in his troops so that they could offer mutual help when the need arose. Siddheshwara was a critical military post. By virtue of its altitude, it alone offered an eagle's eye view of signals established between the two armies. Stuart knew only too well that the capture of Siddheshwara would be the key to the capture of Srirangapatna.

The British troops in and around Siddheshwara kept a close watch on the movement of troops in the vicinity. On the morning of 5 March, the very day on which General Harris crossed the frontier into Mysore, the troops reported the pitching of green tents and an extensive encampment in advance of Periapatnam. The news worried Stuart—green tents? They seemed to indicate that the Tiger was not too far away. But Stuart was resolute. His gaze was fixed at the advance towards Srirangapatna and the ultimate goal of seeing the Union Jack flutter on the ramparts of the fort.

The ground at Siddheshwara was occupied by a brigade of three native battalions, under Lieutenant Colonel Montresor. The Company's spies stationed in Srirangapatna had brought in reliable information that the Sultan was somewhere close to the Madoor River and that a detachment under Mohammad Reza, popularly called the Benki Nawab or the Nawab of Fire, constituted the only force west of the Cauvery. Still, Stuart had a great responsibility and an opportunity to prove his mettle. The green tents ruined his sleep and he thought it prudent to send another battalion to a convenient position for reinforcement of the brigade around Siddheshwara.

Accordingly, on the morning of 6 March, the second-in-command, Major General Hartley, was sent to ascertain the exact location and movement of the Mysorean forces. But geography seemed to be on the Sultan's side. The dense forest cover of the region concealed the presence and movement of the green brigade from Hartley's hawk eyes. Between nine and ten in the morning, Tipu's troops made a simultaneous attack on the British troops from both the front and rear ends. Two columns of Mysore forces united at the rear from the right and the left, just at the time when the frontal attack was launched, and prevented any reinforcement from reaching the stranded troops. The Sultan's idea was to strangle the marching armies at the very first frontier post towards Mysore in a typical guerrilla attack. Sadly, the British were not surprised as the traitors had leaked information on the planned attack to the English sixteen hours in advance! This ensured that General Stuart was in a state of perpetual alert and would rush in to help his second-in-command who had ventured into the den of the Tiger.

The minute he received intelligence of Hartley's perilous position, Stuart raced to his assistance. That there was a huge disparity in the sheer numbers of the Mysorean versus British troops, who comprised a pathetic minority, did not seem to worry Hartley and his men. Wilks records that they 'maintained their ground with so much cool resolution, that the utmost efforts of the Sultaun's best officers and troops were unable to make any serious impression on these three sepoy battalions.' They waited for hours, and Stuart, after receiving the urgent message lost no time marching there with the two flank companies of His Majesty's 75th and the whole of the 77th battalion, under Lieutenant Colonel Dunlop. Somewhere around half past two in the midsummer afternoon, this battalion reached Siddheshwara. Small, but efficient, the reinforcement proved fatal for the Mysorean sepoys. Wilks states that 'the energy of the attack' was such that in less than half an hour they had chased the Mysoreans through the woods to join the division attacking from the front. But this was accomplished more by treachery than chivalry on Stuart's part. Qaman-ud-din the traitor ordered the troops to withdraw at a juncture when the victory of Mysore seemed definite. The army was baffled. They were being asked to retreat in the middle of a success? And this disarray ensured the defeat of the Mysorean troops at Siddheshwara.

Stuart then reached Montresor's post to find his men completely overcome by fatigue and exhaustion and their ammunition almost entirely expended. By twenty minutes past three that day, the Mysorean troops had retreated in all directions. Beatson records that General Stuart had a smile of satisfaction on his lips, even as he tried hard to conceal his admiration for the 'immoveable steadiness of the native troops in a protracted encounter of nearly six hours, and the energy of the Europeans whom he had led to their aid'. The bugle of war had been sounded and he was in command of the first step towards victory. This joy was further buoyed for Stuart when the statistics of the dead and injured reached him. While his side had lost 143 men, the loss on the other side was reported to be surprisingly high, amounting to more than two thousand dead. The Maharaja of Coorg, who accompanied Stuart in this encounter, further heaped encomiums on his deft handling of a skirmish of considerable strategic importance. A crucial post had been occupied right in the presence of the Sultan's main army and there could be no better morale booster to start off a war as decisive as this one.

The Battle of Malavelly

Losing on the Siddheshwara front, Tipu rushed towards Malavelly to intercept General Harris. The English advanced to Malavelly where an armed action took place on 27 March 1799. A man Tipu had trusted all along, Mir Sadik wrongly informed him about Harris's intention to conquer Chandagal fort at the right side of the river. Upon arriving there, the Sultan was terrified to see the English forces marching eastward, headed straight towards Srirangapatna.

While the British troops under Harris reached Malavelly, they noticed that the Sultan and his troops were stationed at a considerable distance towards the west. The intentions of the Mysorean troops were misjudged by the fact that they were camped so far from where Harris's men were. But they were caught by surprise when, at about ten in the morning, the guns were opened from the Mysore end on the British cavalry. General Harris quickly ordered the advance of His Majesty's 25th Dragoons and the 2nd Regiment of native cavalry, the three brigades of infantry to form a line towards the left, the whole to make a frontal and left attack on Tipu's forces and Colonel Wellesley to move towards the right flank of the Mysore troops.

The rapid advance of the Mysorean troops baffled the British forces. They made a resolute charge on the British brigade commanded by Major General Baird, but found it difficult to encounter His Majesty's 12th and the Scotch Brigade that ensured a considerable loss for the advancing troops. It was believed that this force was led by the Sultan himself and that it had maintained a heavy musketry attack on His Majesty's 74th Regiment. The Sultan's troops tried to encircle the enemy. While the cavalry charged towards the right of where the British were stationed, a large infantry attacked the side that Colonel Wellesley commanded. But this advance was broken by Major General Floyd and His Majesty's 19th Dragoons, creating complete chaos among the Mysoreans. The division of the army and the attack on its two ends baffled the Mysoreans and this, coupled with the lack of water, left them no choice but to draw off their cannons and retreat.*

Almost 2,000 men of Tipu's army were killed or wounded at the end of this unprecedented attack. A deeply emotional Sultan assembled a council of his principal officers at Bannur and addressed them:

'We have now arrived at our last stage, what is your determination?' He seemed to have some foreboding that this was the end of the road for him.

'To die along with you, Sultan!' was the universal reply, and the meeting ended in tears, as if it were being convened for the last time.

---

* A fuller extract of Harris's report of the encounter can be found in the Appendix to this chapter.

The events of the next few days saw to it that this had indeed been the last meeting.

As decided at the meeting, Tipu hastened to the southern part of the island and positioned himself at the village of Chandgal. But General Harris, by slow yet cautious marches, thwarted his plans—making a circuitous leftward turn and reaching the face of the capital, two miles from the southwest face of the fort.

Thus, spreading loot and disaster along their way, the massive British army reached Srirangapatna for the ultimate siege on 5 April 1799.

The Run-up to the Final Assault

Meanwhile, treachery was at its peak in the troubled fort of Srirangapatna. The commanders of the fort gave the British easy access to Sultanpet Tope—the way to the fort. The English attacked from the western and northwestern sides. Mysore had often known danger in the past, but never such acute danger. Tipu suffered other personal losses as well. His hitherto trusted Prime Minister, Purnaiya left. When it had become obvious to Purnaiya that things were going against Tipu, he decided to leave the fort and bide his time till the British took over and he could go over to their side. Tipu's trusted mentor Ghazi Khan was murdered treacherously by Mir Sadik. The Tiger was virtually the lone defender of the fort of Srirangapatna and the Sultanat-e-Khudadad Mysore.

While Tipu was engaged in defending the frontier posts, Major General Floyd marched to the rear of the camp towards Periapatnam with a strong detachment to meet the army from Bombay. On 14 April, he reached Srirangapatna with this additional army. Richard Wellesley planned the opening of a breach in the walls of Srirangapatna. The location of the breach, as noted by Beatson, the author of an account of the Fourth Mysore War was 'in the west curtain, a little to the right of the flank of the north-west bastion. This being the old rampart appeared weaker than the new'.

Another frontier bastion, Mahtab Bagh was handed over to the British by Zain-ul-Abideen Shustari. The River Cauvery, which flowed around the city of Srirangapatna, was at its lowest level of the year, and could be forded by infantry if an assault commenced before the monsoon. When letters were exchanged with Tipu, it seemed that the Sultan was playing for time. He requested that two persons be sent to him for discussions and also stated that he was preoccupied with hunting expeditions. The

English terms of peace released on 22 April were ridiculous—the cession of half the remaining territories of Mysore, payment of two crores of rupees in two instalments and delivery of four of Tipu's sons and four of his principal officers as hostages! This was completely unacceptable to the Sultan. Sheikh Ali writes that he is believed to have remarked that 'in the short span of human life, it was of little importance whether an inevitable event should arrive a few days or years sooner or later, and it was better to die like a soldier than to live a miserable dependent on the infidels, in the list of their pensioned rajahs and nabobs!'

The Mysorean defence succeeded in preventing the establishment of a battery on the north side of the Cauvery on 22 April 1799. However, by 1 May the British, working at night, had established batteries in the south and brought them up to the wall. At sunrise on 2 May, the batteries of the nizam of Hyderabad succeeded in opening a practical breach in the outer wall. In addition, a magazine of rockets was hit inside the fortress, resulting in a huge explosion.

The British camp was abuzz with hectic planning and strategising as maps were drawn and possible routes for the attack debated. The island of Srirangapatna was about three miles long and one mile broad with a dreary fort of naked rock and mud walls. Tipu had combined the old Indian style of fortification with the French style to try and secure his abode. He had ensured diligently-cut ditches through the granite, but much of it remained unfinished. The fort had long straight walls and square bastions and the glacis was so high and steep in many parts that it could shelter any assailant from fire from the ramparts.

After nearly a month of continued fighting and hardships the brainstorming British army generals saw a glimmer of hope around 3 May. The possibility that a breach could be made in the fort—whose maps they had been scrutinising down to the last brick—sent a wave of cheer through the battle-weary British commanders. They decided to seize the opportunity and immediately ascend the fort through this breach. Accordingly, it was decided that 4 May would be the date for that final and decisive storming of this bastion. The same evening, the troops moved silently down the trenches under the command of Major General David Baird, an old enemy of the Sultan. Held captive by the Sultan for 44 months 20 years ago, he wanted revenge, and to go down in history as a commander who, within an hour, conquered the famed fort of Srirangapatna and inflicted a crushing defeat on the Tiger of Mysore.

While the British soldiers rejoiced at the thought that years and months of fatigue and anguish were finally drawing to a close, they were also aware that Tipu was the most unpredictable of Indian rulers, and that fortunes could change directions any time. They worried that he would give them the slip and emerge victorious despite all their meticulous planning. But the positives far outweighed the negatives this time, and besides Providence, they could definitely count on treachery to finally spell doom for the Sultan of Mysore.

Information regarding the breach in the fort wall was kept secret from Tipu. When he insisted on being led to the place for a first-hand investigation, Mir Nadim led him to a place where just a few stones had fallen and withheld information of the actual breach. Reassured, Tipu rode off. But the actual breach was elsewhere and awaiting the British troops.

The Storming of Srirangapatna

The fateful day of 4 May 1799 dawned like any other day. Perhaps it was the inevitability of what the sunset would bring that caused Tipu to invoke supernatural aid. A large contingent of Brahmin priests were called in to carry on a continuous chanting or *japam* to ensure no harm befell the Sultan. In his youth Tipu had viewed astrology as a false science, but somewhere he had become a great believer in this branch of human knowledge. That morning, he looked at his own horoscope with a grim expression. He was proficient enough to deduce a couple of things. The movement of Mars within a particular circle indicated that the fort could hold on till the completion of this celestial rotation. Sadly, Tipu could see that the journey of the planet had ended the previous night and the new planetary positions were anything but favourable. By about nine in the morning, he proceeded to the palace, bathed and presented the prescribed oblations to avert a calamity—even as his mind seemed reconciled to the inevitable. The Brahmin astrologers assisted him in this ritual. Solemnly trying to ascertain his fortune through the form of his face reflected off the surface of a jar of oil, he presented the final oblations. The incantations were interrupted by the news of the death of Syed Ghaffar, a skilled and able loyalist. Tipu looked at the Brahmin priests questioningly: 'The news of death at the time I seek to conquer it—does it portend a deeper message?' he seemed to ask. The expression on their speechless faces gave him his answer. Tipu decided that this was no time for rituals and invocations. 'Pray for me, holy ones!' he said and stormed out of the inner apartments.

Meanwhile Baird, who was waiting for the afternoon, kept checking his watch and at about one o'clock he exclaimed: 'The time has come... Now, my brave boys! Follow me!'

The storming troops, including men of the 73rd and 74th regiments, clambered up the breach and fought their way along the ramparts. The key position near the breach was held by the traitor Sayyid Saheb. He waved his handkerchief as a signal to the English to come inside—an open invitation to enter the fort and vanquish its Sultan. The troops waited for the signal in the trenches surrounding the fort. From the trench to the river bank was a distance of 100 yards, the river was rocky and varied in depth, ankle-deep to waist-deep. Another 280 yards beyond was the stone wall, a ditch some 60 yards wide and finally, the breach. It was a difficult approach, described by Lieutenant Richard Bayly in his war diary, which is peppered with praise for the heroism of the British army and completely omits mention of the betrayal and intrigue that made the victory possible:

> We experienced little loss, until we were floundering on the rocky bed of the river, when the men began to fall fast. All who were wounded were inevitably drowned in a second afterwards. One step the water scarcely covered the foot; the next we were plunged headlong into an abyss of fathoms deep. Thus scrambling over, the column at length reached the ascent of the breach, where numerous flankers who had preceded us were lying stretched on their backs, killed and wounded, some of the gallant officers waving their swords and cheering our men on. We dashed forward, and the top of the breach was soon crowned by our intrepid lads, and the British flag hoisted. But this was for a moment only. A sudden, sweeping fire from the inner wall came like a lightning blast, and exterminated the living mass. Others crowded from behind, and again the flag was planted. At this time General Baird was discovered on the ramparts. On observing a deep, dry, rocky ditch of sixty feet deep, and an inner wall covered with the troops of the enemy, he exclaimed: 'Good God! I did not expect this!' His presence of mind did not desert him...and we were soon charging to the right and left of the breach along the ramparts of the outer wall.

Without firing a single gunshot, a handful of British soldiers successfully reached the breach and replaced the Sultan's flag (which looked like tiger-

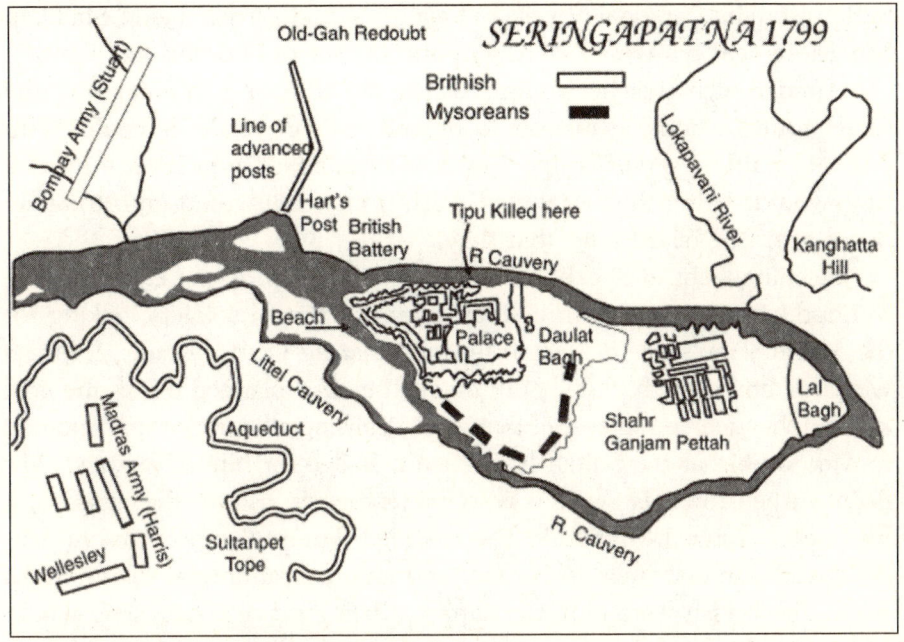

The final attack on the fort of Srirangapatna, 4th May 1799
(Maps are artistic recreations made at Suhaas Graphics, Bangalore)

skin to represent the Tiger of Mysore) with the Union Jack. The traitor, Sayyid Saheb, was betrayed to his death too—the same Major Dallas who had led the forces with General Baird reached the fort's ramparts and pushed Sayyid over the battlements. He fell into the ditch and was drowned in knee-deep water.

The British now divided themselves into two groups to the left and right—one attacking the southern rampart and the other the northern one. They wanted to encircle the Sultan in his own house and give him no opportunity to flee. Both the groups were to meet at the eastern gate. The assault was to begin at 1 pm to coincide with the hottest part of the day when the defenders would take a refreshment break.

The English had entered the once invincible fort of Srirangapatna.

In the middle of such a bloody and decisive war, Mir Sadik called away all the troops defending the fort as if to pay them three months' salary. Mir Nadim imprisoned the faithful soldiers and blocked all the escape routes Tipu could have used. The only faithful allies left to the

Sultan were his personal physician Raja Khan and a trusted aide, Shekhar. Mir Sadik sent his wrestlers Khaliq and Jabbar to find and kill Tipu.

Amidst such treachery Tipu rushed out, refusing to escape by the secret routes, choosing instead to defend his fort while he could, with the very battle cry on his lips 'Sarkar-e-Khudadad', which once upon a time would shatter the morale of British troops; but would unfortunately never again be heard after that day.

Catching sight of Shekhar, Mir Nadim shot him. As he lay wounded, Mir Sadik came along with a small group of British soldiers looking for the Sultan. Tipu's enemies were terrified that he would escape, get fresh weapons, and come back to haunt them. They had planned this as the final kill and they wanted to keep it that way. Realising all this, Shekhar shouted to Mir Sadik that the Sultan had left a message for him. Overjoyed, Mir Sadik rushed towards Shekhar who, pretending to fish for the message in his pocket, stabbed Mir Sadik. The so-called 'Future King of Mysore' was now dead — an evil smile on his face and an unconsummated dream in his heart. The British were only too happy at being rid of a man who would have certainly demanded his pound of flesh. Mir Sadik found his ignoble end. For long, the local populace who revered Tipu's memory were believed to throw stones at the spot where Sadik died, just like the stoning of the devil at Mecca. But since Shekhar died at the same spot, they quickly add 'Not for you Shekhar!' It is said that Shekhar's spirit laughs on hearing this.

THE DEATH OF TIPU SULTAN

The enfilade from the Bombay army, on the northern side of the river, had been so strong that the defendants of the fort had been entirely driven from the ramparts on the right of the breach, and had been prevented from raising any traverses. The British troops who proceeded in that direction faced absolutely no opposition. The flank companies of the 12th regiment, having found a passage across the inner ditch, passed through the town to attack the rear of the Mysorean forces.

The column that rounded the northwest corner of the outer wall near Sallyport faced great opposition. Every twenty-thirty yards, the rampart was crossed by traverses and many of them were immediately involved in a tussle with a group of Mysorean warriors under a short fat officer, who defended every traverse. The officer was observed to be discharging, at Woodhall's British forces, loaded hunting weapons being passed to him by servants at his service. He was seen wearing a richly bejewelled sword belt and was almost fainting from loss of blood. The soldiers pierced his body many times and finally with a shot to his temple, killed him. They snatched away the rich jewels, commenting, 'Who was he? He fought like a tiger.'

The two divisions of the storming army met at an open place surrounding a very fine mosque, into which the remains of the garrison withdrew, and the destruction and fighting seemed to cease even as the day steadily came to an end. The British troops continued to worry about the Sultan's whereabouts. Had he escaped? Was he killed? Commenting on this predicament, Francis Buchanan writes that the last they had heard of the Sultan was that when he was near the narrow Sallyport, he was met with a crowd flying from the flank companies of the 12th Regiment and that a wound, inflicted by a weapon, was discovered in his arm. Though they had blocked all roads to retreat and escape, they were still afraid Tipu would had given them the slip. Buchanan observes:

> The Hindus universally think, that, finding the place taken, he was going to the palace to put all his family to death, and then to seek for his own destruction in the midst of his enemies. But, although such is considered by the Hindus as the proper conduct for a prince in his situation, we have no reason to think that a Mussulman would conduct himself in this manner; nor was Tippoo ever accused of want of affection for his family. I think it more probable, that he was ignorant of the British troops having got into the inner fort, and was retiring thither in hopes of being still able to repel the attack.

By the time the sun had set on the gloomy fort of Srirangapatna on 4 May 1799, the British seemed to be quite in command of all the major frontiers and posts. But fear of the Sultan's return still loomed large. Having fought Tipu for several decades now, the British knew that he could ruin their plans anytime—springing forth from nowhere and launching a fatal attack. They had to see him, dead or alive, to get rid of these apprehensions. Major Alexander Allan and Major Beatson took a round across the southern rampart and saw several persons assembled in the palace, many of whom were of distinguished rank as could be judged by their dress and appearance.

Tipu's whereabouts were as much a mystery to the Mysoreans as to the British. Tipu's few remaining loyalists and his family members were petrified to see the British striding confidently across their once-feared enemy's threshold. At the same time they were puzzled that Tipu was not around to save them and his own fort when the enemy had come so perilously close. The same doubts of his death or escape plagued their minds. Allan and Beatson tried to read the body language of the natives to ascertain Tipu's whereabouts. As Allan states in Beatson's account of those nail-biting hours:

> I particularly remarked, that one person prostrated himself before he sat down; from which circumstance I was led to conclude, that Tippoo, with such of his officers who had escaped from the assault, had taken shelter in the palace.

The troops were left to recover from a long day of battle. In the meanwhile Beatson and Allan apprised General Baird of the circumstances they had been witness to in and around the Sultan's Palace—none of which offered any definitive clue to his whereabouts. Baird ordered Allan to proceed to the palace along with a detachment of the 12th and part of Major Gibbing's sepoy battalion and meet the residents. He was to carry an olive branch of friendship to them with a message that their lives would be saved if they agreed to surrender. Accordingly, Allan proceeded towards the palace with a white cloth fastened to a sergeant's pike and reached the palace where Major Shee and part of the 33rd Regiment were keeping guard. Many of Tipu's family members were on the balcony in a state of deep anxiety. When the message reached the inmates, the killedar along with another officer and a confidante servant came over to the terrace of the front building. They tried to procrastinate so as to buy time—they were all hopeful that their Sultan would not have betrayed them and that he would spring in suddenly and chop off the British heads. They desperately awaited nightfall, which they hoped would facilitate their escape in the event of the Sultan's exit or his death.

After some initial reluctance to allow Allan inside the palace, they finally consented and he made his way to the inner apartments along with Captain Scohey (who was well-versed in the native languages) and Captain Hastings Fraser. It was literally like entering a tiger's den for they had to keep assuring the heavily armed security personnel that their mission was one of peace and negotiation. Allan describes this journey to the inner recesses of Tipu's Palace:

The killedar, and many others affirmed, that the princes and the family of Tippoo were in the palace, but not the Sultaun. They appeared greatly alarmed and averse to coming to any decision. I told them, that delay might be attended with fatal consequences; and that I could not answer for the conduct of our troops, by whom they were surrounded, and whose fury was with difficulty restrained. They then left me, and shortly I observed people moving hastily backwards and forwards in the interior of the place; and, as there were many hundreds of Tippoo's troops within the walls, I began to think our situation rather critical. I was advised to take back my sword; but such an act, on my part, might, by exciting their distrust, have kindled a flame, which, in the present temper of the troops, might have been attended with the most dreadful consequences; probably the massacre of every soul within the palace walls. The people on the terrace begged me to hold the flag in a conspicuous position, in order to give confidence to those in the palace, and prevent our troops from forcing the gates. Growing impatient at these delays, I sent another message to the princes, warning them of their critical situation, and that my time was limited. They answered, they would receive me as soon as a carpet could be spread for the purpose; and soon after the killedar came to conduct me.

Once inside, the visiting British officers met two of the princes, who squatted on a carpet and were surrounded by a large retinue of attendants. They invited the enemy to be seated in front of them. Allan repeated his request to the princes, that if they valued their lives and peace, they must inform him of their father's whereabouts. Gripped with the strongest feelings of fear and dejection, Prince Moizuddin had a quick word with some confidantes and later made a passionate plea that he was unsure where the Sultan was. The British request to have the gates opened in that case alarmed the princes and their attendants, but seeing that as the only option and seemingly convinced by British assurances, they complied.

For Prince Moizuddin it all seemed like *deja vu*. A few years back he had been similarly faced with the British when handed over as hostage to Lord Cornwallis. Allan's suggestion that he quit the palace and proceed to meet General Baird met with violent protests and objections. But being a practical young man, he decided that compliance was the best path. General Baird was consumed with rabid hatred for Tipu and his clan for the murder of many British prisoners of war and the humiliation and suffering he had himself endured in that very place for so long, years ago. But he interviewed the Prince with a sense of equanimity and guaranteed his life, provided he gave them the details of his father. The Prince pleaded helplessness and ignorance of his gallant father's whereabouts.

The British were convinced that the people in the palace were as clueless about the Sultan as they were. So it was decided that a group of English troops under General Harris would form a search party to look for Tipu. The Mysore troops were immediately disarmed as the British search party made its way to the palace yard. A servant told them that in the noon, Tipu had gone to the main gate with Raja Khan while the killedar informed them that the Sultan might have been wounded in the attack and possibly lay somewhere near the northern face of the fort.

The journey of the search party through the ramparts of the fort was like a journey through hell. Heaps of dead bodies lay rotting one on the top of the other and the vultures had already positioned themselves for the feast. The darkness of the night made it worse. Allan says:

> The number of dead, and the darkness of the place, made it difficult to distinguish one person from another, and the scene was altogether shocking; but, aware of the great political importance of ascertaining beyond the possibility of doubt, the death of Tippoo, the bodies were ordered to be dragged out, and the killedar, and the other two persons, were desired to examine them one after another. This, however, appeared endless; and, as it now was becoming dark, a light was procured, and I accompanied the killedar into the gateway. During the search we discovered a wounded person lying under the Sultaun's palankeen: this man was afterwards ascertained to be Rajah Cawn, one of Tippoo's most confidential servants; he had attended his master during the whole of the day.

The only sign of life in this abundance of death was a moan that the British search party heard. It was that of Raja Khan. He was grievously wounded and almost unconscious. Scared out of his wits on seeing the British, he ran to search for his beloved Sultan. Before he had slipped into unconsciousness, he faintly remembered the Sultan having a dizzy fall after considerable loss of blood. He rushed towards a tunnel-like passage that was choked with scores of corpses and there, amidst a heap of dead bodies, lay the brave Sultan of Mysore.

The search might have been over, but the British were shocked to behold Tipu and were in fact scared to even touch him as they weren't completely certain he was dead. They immediately called for the physician. Tipu's body was still warm, his eyes open, his hands clasped the sword in a tight grip and his face bore the same resolute and confident look that the British had shuddered before for decades now. Allan describes it thus:

> When Tippoo was brought from under the gateway, his eyes were open, and the body was so warm, that for a few moments Colonel Wellesley and myself were doubtful whether he was not alive: on feeling his pulse and heart, that doubt was removed. ... His dress consisted of a jacket of fine white linen, loose drawers of flowered chintz, with a crimson cloth of silk and cotton, round his waist: a handsome pouch with a red and green silk belt, hung across his shoulder: his head was uncovered, his turban being lost in the confusion of his fall: he had an amulet on his arm, but no ornament whatever.

He further writes:

> By a faint glimmering light it was difficult for the killedar to recognise the features; but the body being brought out, and satisfactorily proved to be that of the Sultaun, was conveyed in a palankeen to the palace, where it was again recognised by the eunuchs and other servants of the family...Tippoo was of low stature, corpulent, with high shoulders, and a short thick neck, but his feet were remarkably small; his complexion was rather dark; his eyes large and prominent, with small arched eyebrows, and his nose aquiline; he had an appearance of dignity, or perhaps sternness, in his countenance, which distinguished him above the common order people.

It was only after the physician checked for a pulse and proclaimed Tipu dead that the British were relieved. They broke out in jubilation. General Harris shouted in ecstasy, 'India is ours from today!' His laughter echoed through those ramparts that had seen so much death and destruction that very day. It was only then that a few officers who were present during the assault identified the fat, stout Mysorean soldier as the same man whose corpse lay in front of them. Little had they realised when they attacked the officer for the costly jewel he wore that the man they thought was a common soldier of the Mysore army and who fought valiantly till his last breath, was none other than Sher-e-Mysore Tipu Sultan. Kings usually never came out of their palaces to fight and often secretly escaped in the midst of such decisive battles. So they had not imagined that the Sultan might have been among them, fighting with his men to beat the British.

The soul had escaped the body, but the hand still held the sword. Thus Tipu Sultan, along with 12,000 soldiers, attained martyrdom on 4 May 1799—the most grievous fall of any hero in history.

The British took possession of the *toshikhane*, the palace and the remains of the fort. Amidst the wailing and crying of the ladies of Tipu's harem, his body was delivered to his palace. Charles Stuart, who was a witness to Tipu's defeat, reports:

> He had 4 wounds, 3 in the body and one in the temple, the ball having entered a little above the right ear and lodged in the cheek, the countenance was no way distorted but had an expression of stern composure. This fearless soldier fought till the end, nothing could conquer him or make him submissive, except, perhaps death. The deep resentment nursed against the British remained burning in him, till he fell in the battlefield and breathed his last.

Allan records a jubilant letter from General Harris to Richard Wellesley:

> I have the pleasure to inform you that this day at half past two o'clock the palace was completely in our possession. Tippoo fell in the assault.

Thus fell the last bastion of India's defence against the British. Richard Wellesley was apparently entertaining a select group of people at dinner when news of the Sultan's death reached him. He rose, unsteady from the several helpings of whisky he had consumed, raised his glass and said, 'Ladies and gentlemen, I drink to the corpse of India.'

The Rape of Srirangapatna

On 5 May 1799, Tipu's second son Abdul Khaliq, who was commanding the southern face of the fort, surrendered. Once it was confirmed that Tipu was dead, the victorious British army considered it their right to plunder and rape a city that had already been grievously assaulted. What followed was a free-for-all, with each soldier encouraged to fill his coffers as best he could. They looted Srirangapatna down to the last brick. They saw it as a personification of the man who had made them run from one battlefield to the other. The fort, the palace, libraries—everything was destroyed.

As Colonel Bayly recollects:

> The fortress now became one wild scene of plunder and confusion... The rest of the troops had filled their muskets, caps, and pockets with zechins, pagodas, rupees, and ingots of gold. One of our grenadiers, by name Platt, deposited in my hands, to the amount of fifteen hundred pounds' worth of the precious metals, which in six months afterwards he had dissipated in drinking, horse-racing, cock-fighting, and gambling...Tranquility was scarcely restored in the Fort, when the honourable Colonel Wellesley was sent in to take the command, to the great dismay and indignation of General Baird, who had felicitated himself on the certain command of this acquisition of his gallantry; but he was superseded, and at once delivered over to Wellesley the important fortress of Seringapatam to his future guidance, who next day hung up eighteen poor Sepoys, found in the act of plunder, contrary to his orders...

However, Buchanan in his account gives a clean chit to the British troops regarding their behaviour with the people, his claim being that 'our soldiers killed none intentionally but fighting men'. He also makes probably one of the first recorded cases for what in the last century was christened 'collateral damage' when he says that 'terrible things must always happen when an enraged soldiery with firearms are pursuing an enemy through a populous place.' Some justification indeed!

He tries occasionally to flirt with the truth, however, such as here:

> In this, I believe, very little murder was committed; although there can be no doubt that many persons were beaten, and threatened with death, in order to make them discover their property. The women on this occasion went out into the streets, and stood there all night in large groups; I suppose, with the view of preventing any insult... This precaution was probably little necessary. The soldiers had mostly been in the trenches two days; they had been

engaged in a hard day's work; and their hopes and their rage having then ceased, they were left in a state of languor, by which they were more inclined to seek repose, or cordial refreshments, than to indulge in sensual gratification.

The Burial

General Harris made preparations for the last rites as per Islamic rituals. The body was covered with fine muslins and rich clothes, placed in a state palanquin and taken in a long procession till it reached the Lal Baugh Mausoleum where the British gun salute began. Tipu was laid to rest beside his father Haidar Ali and mother Fatima Begum. Several verses were composed in 1799, Hijira 1213 which said: 'Tipu was slain unexpectedly of religion of True God on Saturday 28th Zikad. The day of Judgement manifested itself as the 7th hour from this morning.'

Scarcely had Tipu's remains been committed to the earth than a tremendous storm of thunder, lightning and rain followed for several hours, taking many lives. It seemed that Srirangapatna needed to be washed so as to cleanse the bloodstains of the many patriots who had laid down their lives defending it. It seemed to be nature's last attempt at defending the once impregnable fortress of Srirangapatna and safeguarding the kingdom of Mysore.

Colonel Bayly recounts the terrible thunderstorm that hit Srirangapatna in May 1799 after Tipu's burial:

> I must relate the effects and appearance of a tremendous storm of wind, rain, thunder, and lightning that ensued on the afternoon of the burial of Tippoo Saib. I had returned to camp excessively indisposed. About five o'clock a darkness of unusual obscurity came on, and volumes of huge clouds were hanging within a few yards of the earth, in a motionless state. Suddenly, a rushing wind, with irresistible force, raised pyramids of sand to an amazing height, and swept most of the tents and marquees in frightful eddies far from their site. Ten Lascars, with my own exertions, clinging to the bamboos of the marquee scarcely preserved its fall. The thunder cracked in appalling peals close to our ears, and the vivid lightning tore up the ground in long ridges all around. Such a scene of desolation can hardly be imagined; Lascars struck

dead, as also an officer and his wife in a marquee a few yards from mine. Bullocks, elephants, and camels broke loose, and scampering in every direction over the plain; every hospital tent blown away, leaving the wounded exposed, unsheltered to the elemental strife. In one of these alone eighteen men who had suffered amputation had all the bandages saturated, and were found dead on the spot the ensuing morning.

The funeral party escorting Tippoo's body to the mausoleum of his ancestors situated in the Lal Bagh Garden, where the remains of his warlike father, Hyder Ali, had been deposited, were overtaken at the commencement of this furious whirlwind, and the soldiers ever after were impressed with a firm persuasion that his Satanic majesty attended in person at the funeral procession. The flashes of lightning were not as usual from far distant clouds, but proceeded from heavy vapours within a very few yards of the earth. No park of artillery could have vomited forth such incessant peals as the loud thunder that exploded close to our ears. Astonishment, dismay, and prayers for its cessation were our solitary alternative. A fearful description of the Day of Judgement might have been depicted from the appalling storm of this awful night. I have experienced hurricanes, typhoons, and gales of wind at sea, but never in the whole course of my existence had I seen anything comparable to this desolating visitation. Heaven and earth appeared absolutely to have come in collision, and no bounds set to the destruction. The roaring of the winds strove in competition with the stunning explosions of the thunder, as if the universe was once more returning to chaos. In one of these wild sweeps of the hurricane, the poles of my tent were riven to atoms, and the canvas wafted forever from my sight. I escaped without injury, as also my exhausted Lascars, and casting myself in an agony of despair on the sands, I fully expected instant annihilation. My hour was not, however, come. Towards morning the storm subsided; the clouds became more elevated, the thunder and lightning ceased, and nature once more resumed a serene aspect. But never shall I forget that dreadful night to the latest day of my existence. All language is inadequate to describe its horrors. Rather than be exposed to such another scene, I would prefer the front of a hundred battles....

There was obviously something out of the ordinary about Tipu that extended beyond his life and made itself felt in the immediate aftermath of his death. It touched the rational mind of the white man and sent a shiver down his spine. The events of 4 May 1799 were considered important enough by many eyewitnesses to prompt them to write it all down for posterity, and some of these accounts are provided in the appendix to this chapter.

The celebrated Urdu poet Mohammad Iqbal speaks about the Sultan who literally heralded India's first struggle against colonialism in his book *Javid-Namah* or the Book of Eternity thus:

> I have lighted a different fire in the heart.
> I have brought a tale from the Deccan.
> I have a shining sword on my side;
> I am drawing it out gradually from the scabbard.
> I speak a subtle point about the Martyr Tipu Sultan,
> I fear the festival day may turn bitter,
> I proceed to kiss his dust,
> There I heard from his holy grave;
> If one cannot live a manly life in this world
> Then to sacrifice life, like a man, is life!

In fact, Tippu's persona attracted even the English poets, such as Sir Henry Newbolt in his ode to 'Seringapatam':

> The sleep that Tippoo Sahib sleeps
> Heeds not the cry of man;
> The faith that Tippoo Sahib keeps
> No judge on earth may scan;
> He is the lord of whom ye hold
> Spirit and sense and limb,
> Fetter and chain are all ye gain
> Who dared to plead with him.
>
> Baird was bonny and Baird was young,
> His heart was strong as steel,
> But life and death in the balance hung
> For his wounds were ill to heal.
> Of fifty chains the Sultan gave
> We have filled but forty-nine:

We dare not fail of the perfect tale
    For all Golconda's mine.

That was the hour when Lucas first
    Leapt to his long renown;
Like summer rains his anger burst,
    And swept their scruples down.
Tell ye the lord to whom ye crouch,
    His fetters bite their fill:
To save your oath I'll wear them both,
    And step the lighter still.

The seasons came, the seasons passed,
    They watched their fellows die;
But still their thought was forward cast,
    Their courage still was high.
Through tortured days and fevered nights
    Their limbs alone were weak,
And year by year they kept their cheer,
    And spoke as freemen speak.

But once a year, on the fourth of June,
    Their speech to silence died,
And the silence beat to a soundless tune
    And sang with a wordless pride;
Till when the Indian stars were bright,
    And bells at home would ring,
To the fetters' clank they rose and drank
    'England! God Save the King!'

The years came, and the years went,
    The wheel full-circle rolled;
The tyrant's neck must yet be bent,
    The price of blood be told:
The city yet must hear the roar
    Of Baird's avenging guns,
And see him stand with lifted hand
    By Tippoo Sahib's sons.
The lads were bonny, the lads were young,

But he claimed a pitiless debt;
Life and death in the balance hung,
They watched it swing and set.
They saw him search with sombre eyes,
They knew the place he sought;
They saw him feel for the hilted steel,
They bowed before his thought.

But he – he saw the prison there
In the old quivering heat,
Where merry hearts had met despair
And died without defeat;
Where feeble hands had raised the cup
For feebler lips to drain,
And one had worn with smiling scorn
His double load of pain.

The sleep that Tippoo Sahib sleeps
Hears not the voice of man;
The faith that Tippoo Sahib keeps
No earthly judge may scan;
For all the wrong your father wrought
Your father's sons are free;
Where Lucas lay no tongue shall say
That Mercy bound not me.

Tipu's family consisted of 600 women and his 25 children, of whom the eldest was Fateh Haidar at 25 years of age and the youngest was 8 months old. The other sons were Abdul Khaliq, Moizuddin, Mahizuddin, Yasin Sab, Shuktar Sab, Shaktarullah and Nizam-ud-din. The whole entourage was posted off to Vellore with 2,40,000 Canteroi Pagodas as annual pension. But after they revolted against the British in 1808 in the Vellore Mutiny, they were packed off to Calcutta to fend for their own lives. It is believed that the descendants of Tipu still lead anonymous lives somewhere in the slums of Tollygunge, Calcutta.

APPENDIX TO CHAPTER 12

APPENDIX 12.1

General Harris' account of the Battle of Malvelly

On the 27th March, the army reached Malvelly to the westward of which place, but at a considerable distance, the army of Tippo Sultan appeared, formed on a very commanding ground to oppose our further progress. I had previously arranged the march of the army so as to persevere the right wing and cavalry free from encumbrance of baggage and ready to act as occasion might require, in conjunction with Colonel Wellesley's division, which, lightly equipped, moved at some distance on our left flank, the left wing under Major General Popham being allotted to protect our baggage, provisions and stores, in the event of an action, which although it was not my object to seek, I had determined not to avoid by any movement which might lead the enemy to suppose I could entertain a doubt of the event.

Judging from the distance of the enemy that they did not intend an attack, I directed the ground to be marked out as usual for the encampment of the army, but at 10 o' clock guns were opened from the distant heights on the cavalry and the corps advanced for picquets on our right. The shot falling on the line, I ordered the picquets to be supported by H.M.'s 25th Dragoons and the 2nd Regiment of native cavalry, the three brigades of infantry to form line on the left of the picquets, and the whole to advance on the enemy's left and front, while Colonel Wellesley's division was directed to move towards the right flank of the enemy's line.

The picquets under Colonel Sherbrooke, assisted by H.M's 25th Dragoons, were opposed to a large body of the enemy's cavalry, who hovered on the right flank of our troops during the advance which was too rapid to admit of the fieldpieces attached to corps keeping their position in the line. Encouraged by this circumstance, a small corps of the enemy's cavalry hazarded a resolute charge on the European brigade commanded by Major General Baird, but found it impossible to make any impression on H.M.'s 12th, and the Scotch Brigade, who received them with the greatest steadiness, and by a continued, close and well-directed fire, repulsed them with considerable loss.

This corps was accompanied by its precipitate retreat by a large body of horse, led, as we have since learnt, by the Sultan in person, which had been prepared to sustain the attack if successful; and by a brigade of infantry that for sometime had maintained a heavy fire of musketry principally directed, and not without effect, at H.M.'s 74th Regiment.

Nearly at the same time that their cavalry charged our right, a large division of the enemy's infantry had advanced on our left to attack the force commanded by Colonel Wellesley, and was broken by H.M.'s 33rd regiment, which led his column. At this critical moment, H.M.'s 19th Dragoons and two regiments of native cavalry, commanded by Major General Floyd, charged this retreating corps and nearly destroyed it. The army continued to advance in a well connected line, while that of the enemy retreated before it in the utmost confusion. Their cannon were drawn off, and after a short pursuit, the want of water not permitting to encamp upon the field of battle, the army returned to the vicinity of Mallavelly.

The 19th Dragoons, the 12th, 33rd, 74th and the Scotch Brigade, which alone of H.M.'s corps were engaged, were equally distinguished by their steadiness and gallantry. The 25th dragoons, although prevented by their remote situation from joining in the charge of the cavalry, was most eminently useful with the picquets under Colonel Sherbrooke in checking the advance of the large corps of the enemy's horse which menaced the right flank of the army till the conclusion of the action.

APPENDIX 12.2

Wilks's account of the Battle of Sedaseer

General Stuart, after assembling his army at Cannanore, finally marched from that station on the 21st of April. He arrived at the top of the

Poodicherrum ghaut on the 25th of the same month, and proceeded in obedience to his instructions, to assume a defensive position close to the frontier of Mysore. The nature of the country, every where covered with thick woods, in most places nearly impenetrable, made it impossible to occupy a regular defensive position, and compelled him to place his troops in several divisions, so disposed, as to be capable of affording reciprocal support: the most advanced of these was the height of Sedaseer, indispensable with reference to an early junction, as being the only spot from which the signals, established between the two armies, could be observed.

On the morning of the 5th of March, the very day on which General Harris crossed the frontier, a few tents were descried from the hill of Sedaseer, about nine o'clock, and gradually the pitching of an extensive encampment in advance of Periapatam, and little more than six miles distant, and on further observation, a green tent of large dimensions was perceived, indicating the presence of the Sultaun. the ground at Sedaseer was occupied by a brigade of three native battalions, under Lieutenant-Colonel Montresor, and although the information of trust-worthy spies recently returned from Seringapatam, gave reasonable assurance that the Sultaun, at the time of their departure was still at the Madoor river, and that a detachment under Mahommed Reza, usually called the Binky Nabob constituted the only force west of the river Cavery; General Stuart thought it prudent to send forward another battalion to a convenient position for reinforcing, if it should be necessary, the advanced brigade at Sedaseer.

Early on the morning of the 6th, Major-General Hartley, the second in command, went forward to reconnoitre the enemy's army, which was discovered to be in motion; but their movements were so well concealed by the closeness of the country, that it was impossible to ascertain their precise object, until between the hours of nine and ten, when a simultaneous attack was made on the front and rear of the position; and the battalion destined to reinforce it, was prevented from joining by the intervention of two columns from the right and left, which united in the rear, at the instant of the commencement of the attack in front.

Before the enemy had accomplished this purpose, Major-General Hartley had time to apprise General Stuart of their attack, and remained himself to give any assistance that might be necessary. The best position was immediately assumed, the brigade was completely surrounded on every side, and had to contend with a vast disparity of numbers; the troops were aware that many hours must elapse before they could receive efficient support, but they were also animated by the conviction that aid would ultimately arrive; and maintained their ground with so much cool resolution, that the utmost efforts of the Sultaun's best officers and troops were unable to make any serious impression on these three sepoy battalions.

As soon as General Stuart received intelligence of the perilous situation of his advanced corps, he marched without a moment's hesitation, with the two flank companies of His Majesty's 75th, and the whole of the 77th under Lieutenant-Colonel Dunlop. It was half past two before he arrived with his small but most efficient body in sight of the enemy's divisions, which had penetrated to the rear and possessed themselves of the great road leading to Sedaseer. The energy of the attack rendered it of short duration; less than half an hour was sufficient to accomplish the precipitate flight of the Mysoreans through the woods, to join the division which still continued the attack in front. On arriving at Lieuteant-Colonel Montresor's post, General Stuart found his men exhausted with fatigue, and their ammunition almost expended. At twenty minutes past three, the enemy retreated in all directions, and left General Stuart to admire the immoveable steadiness of the native troops in a protracted encounter of nearly six hours, and the energy of the Europeans whom he had led to their aid. The success was materially enhanced in value, by finding on collecting the reports of corps, that his loss was considerably smaller than might have been expected; amounting only to one hundred and forty-three men, while that of the enemy was unusually severe, amounting according to credible reports to upwards of two thousand; a difference, to be ascribed chiefly to a judicious occupation of ground, and a cool reservation of fire in the defensive position; and in the reinforcement, to the effective consequences of rapid and vigorous encounter.

The raja of Coorg personally accompanied General Stuart, and witnessed for the first time the conduct of European troops in the presence of an enemy. There was a chivalrous air in all that proceeded from this extraordinary man...

... The first impression on the Sultaun's mind, was to renew the attack the following day, with augmented numbers, but in the mean while General Stuart had changed all his dispositions. The chief object for which this advanced post had been occupied, must necessarily cease to exist, during the presence in its front of the Sultaun's main army; and the security of the abundant depot of provisions in the rear, accessible by other routes, rendered necessary a new and more concentrated disposition of the troops: and the evacuation of the post of Sedaseer, afforded to the Sultaun the faint colour of describing as a victory what every officer in his army felt to be an ignominious repulse.

APPENDIX 12.3

Francis Buchanan's account of the events of 4th May 1799

Seringapatam is commonly called Patana, or Patan, that is to say, the city; but the name used in our maps is a corruption from Sri Ranga Patana, the city of Sri Ranga, from its containing a temple dedicated to Vishnu under that name. The temple is of great celebrity, and of much higher antiquity than the city, which did not rise to be of importance until the time of the princes of the Mysore dynasty.

The island is about three miles in length, and one in breadth, and has a most dreary, ugly appearance; for naked rock, and dirty mud walls are its predominant features. The fort or city of Sri Ranga, occupies its upper end, and is an immense, unfinished, unsightly, and injudicious mass of building. Tippoo seems to have had too high an opinion of his own skill to have consulted the French who were about him; and adhered to the old Indian style of fortification, labouring to make the place strong by heaping walls and cavaliers one above the other. He was also very diligent in cutting ditches through the granite; but, as he had always on hand more projects than his finances were adequate to defray, he never finished any work. He retained the long straight walls and square bastions of the Hindus; and his glacis was in many parts so high and steep, as to shelter an assailant from the fire of the ramparts. In the island also, in order to water a garden, he had dug a deep canal parallel to the works of the fort, and not above eight hundred yards distant from them. He was also so unskilled, as to look upon this as an additional security to the place; but had it been deemed necessary to besiege the town regularly from the island, the assailant would have found it of the utmost use. Had Tippoo's troops been capable of defending the place properly, this mode of attack would have been necessary; but the confidence which our officers justly reposed in the superiority of their men, and the extreme difficulty of bringing up the immense stores necessary to batter down many heavy works, made them prefer an attack across the river, where the works were not so strong, and where they ventured on storming a breach, that nothing, but a very great difference between the intrepidity of the assailants and defendants, could have enabled them to carry. The depth of the river was of little importance; but the assailants, in passing over its rocky channel, were exposed to a heavy fire of artillery, and suffered considerable loss.

On ascending the breach, our men found an inner rampart lined with troops, separated from them by a wide and deep ditch, and defended at its angle by a high cavalier. By this they were for a little while discouraged; as, from the information of spies, they had expected to have been able to mount the cavalier from the breach, and to form a lodgement there, till means could be taken to gain the inner works, and expel the garrison, which consisted of about eight thousand men, nearly the same number with that employed on the storming party.

After, however, the first surprise occasioned by this disappointment, the troops soon recovered their spirits, and pushed on, along the outer rampart, towards both the right and left of the breach. Those who went to the left found great opposition. At every twenty or thirty yards distance, the rampart was crossed by traverses, and these were defended by the Sultan in person. The loss of men here was considerqable; but the English troops gradually advanced, and the Sultan retired slowly, defending his ground with obstinacy.

The enfilading fire from the Bombay army, on the north side of the river, had been so strong, that the defendants had been entirely driven from the ramparts on the right of the breach, and had been prevented from raising any traverses. Our people who went in that direction did not meet with the smallest opposition; and the flank companies of the 12th regiment, having found a passage across the inner ditch, passed through the town to attack the rear of the enemy, who were still opposing the Europeans on the left. The Sultan had now been driven back to the eastward of the palace, and is said to have had his horse shot under him. He might certainly have gone out at a gate leading to the north branch of the river, and nothing could have prevented him from crossing that, and joining his cavalry, which, under the command of his son Futter Hyder, and of Purnea, were hovering round the Bombay army. Fortunately, he decided upon going into the inner fort, by a narrow sally-port; and, as he was attempting to do so, he was met by the crowd flying from the flan companies of the 12th regiment; while the troops, coming up behind, cut off all means of retreat. Both parties seem to have fired into the gateway, and some of the Europeans must have passed through with the bayonet; as a wound, evidently inflicted by that weapon, was discovered in the arm of the Sultan. His object in going into this gateway, is disputed. The Hindus universally think, that, finding the place taken, he was going to the palace to put all his family to death, and then to seek for his own destruction in the midst of his enemies. But, although such is considered by the Hindus as the proper conduct for a prince in his situation, we have no reason to think that a Mussulman would conduct himself in this manner; nor was Tippoo ever accused of want of affection for his family. I think it more probable, that he was ignorant of the British troops having got into the inner fort, and was retiring thither in hopes of being still able to repel the attack.

No individual claimed the honour of having slain the Sultan, nor did any of either party know that he had fallen in the gateway. The assailants were, indeed, at that time too much enraged to think of any thing but the destruction of their enemy. Each division pushed on towards the eastern end of the town; and, as they advanced, the carnage increased. The garrison threw themselves from the works, attempting to escape into the island and from thence to their cavalry. The greater part, however, were either killed by the fall, or broke their limbs in a most shocking manner. Meer Saduc, the favourite of the Sultan, fell in attempting to get through the gates. He is supposed to have been killed by the hands of Tippoo's soldiery, and his corpse lay for some time exposed to the insults of the populace, none of whom passed without spitting on it, or loading it with a slipper; for to him they attributed most of their sufferings in the tyrannical reign of the Sultan.

The two divisions of the storming army now met at an open place surrounding a very fine mosque, into which the remains of the garrison withdrew, and their destruction the fighting nearly ceased. The number of burials amounted to somewhat above seven thousand; several of these were towns-people of both sexes, and all ages; but this was accidental, for our soldiers killed none intentionally but fighting men. Those who are disposed to disclaim on the horrors of a town taken by assault, may always find room to dwell on women, infants, and aged persons killed, and on the little protection given to places, however sacred, for such terrible things must always happen when an enraged soldiery with firearms are pursuing an enemy through a populous place.

When our two parties had met, and no longer saw before their eyes the enemy, by whom they, or their countrymen, had been often most barbarously used, they soon cooled, and were disposed, by their officers, in the manner most proper to secure their new conquest; many, however, left their ranks; and the followers of the camp, under pretext of taking refreshment to their masters, poured into the town, and an entire night was employed in plunder. In this, I believe, very little murder was committed; although there can be no doubt that many persons were beaten, and threatened with death, in order to make them discover their property. The women on this occasion went out into the streets, and stood there all night in large groups; I suppose, with the view of preventing any insult, but their exposed situation; few men being capable of committing brutality in public. This precaution was probably little necessary. The soldiers had mostly been in the trenches two days; they had been engaged in a hard day's work; and their hopes and their rage having then ceased, they were left in a state of languor, by which they were more inclined to seek repose, or cordial refreshments, than to indulge in sensual gratification.

APPENDIX 12.4

Lieutenant Richard Bayly's account

After a month's continual fighting and hardships, a breach was reported practicable on the 3rd of May, and the following day was appointed for the storm. Towards evening the troops selected on this interesting occasion moved slowly down to the trenches, under the command of Baird. For nights and days had the troops suffered from excess of fatigue, up to their knees in water, and exposed to the fierce rays of the sun, fired at and rocketted from every direction, and subjected to continual alarms. We were, therefore, all rejoiced at the speedy prospect of a glorious termination to our incessant sufferings, advancing with all that animation and buoyant spirit so characteristic of British soldiers on the eve of a brilliant attack. At one o'clock p.m., on the 4th inst., Baird, taking out his watch, exclaimed: 'The time has expired!' and leaped on the parapet of the trenches, exclaiming in a loud voice: 'Now, my brave boys, follow me!' The enemy were at this moment quietly intent on their culinary preparations for dinner, and we experienced little loss, until we were floundering on the rocky bed of the river, when the men began to fall fast. All who were wounded were inevitably drowned in a second afterwards. One step the water scarcely covered the foot; the next we were plunged headlong into an abyss of fathoms deep. Thus scrambling over, the column at length reached the ascent of the breach, where numerous flankers who had preceded us were lying stretched on their backs, killed and wounded, some of the gallant officers waving their swords and cheering our men on. We dashed forward, and the top of the breach was soon crowned by our intrepid lads, and the British flag hoisted. But this was for a moment only. A sudden, sweeping fire from the inner wall came like a lightning blast, and exterminated the living mass. Others crowded from behind, and again the flag was planted.

At this time General Baird was discovered on the ramparts. On observing a deep, dry, rocky ditch of sixty feet deep, and an inner wall covered with the troops of the enemy, he exclaimed: 'Good God! I did not expect this!' His presence of mind did not desert him; he gave his directions in those cool, decided terms that a great man in the hour of danger and emergency knows so intuitively how to assume, and we were soon charging to the right and left of the breach along the ramparts of the outer wall. In the left attack, Tippoo was himself defending the traverses with the best and bravest of his troops. This impediment caused a sudden halt, but my gallant friend Woodhall impetuously rushed down a rugged confined pathway into the ditch, and ascended the second or inner wall, by an equally difficult road, mounted to the summit, followed by his company, the Light Infantry of the 12th. Here he attained a footing, he had clasped a tuft of grass with his left hand, and was on the point of surmounting the difficulty, when a fierce Mussulman, with a curved, glittering scimitar, made a stroke at his head, which completely cut the bearskin from his helmet, without further injury.

Woodhall retaliated, separating the calf of the fellow's leg from the bone. He fell, and the gallant Light Bob was on the rampart in a moment, surrounded by a host of the enemy, whom, with the assistance of his company, he soon drove before him, thus relieving General Baird and his column on the outer wall from the destructive fire from the interior rampart, thereby saving hundreds of lives. How far this deviation from orders can be justified may be subject for discussion, but a brave man does not often reflect on consequences, when assured that an energetic movement on his part will probably ensure a certain victory and the preservation of a multitude of his fellow-soldiers. Tippoo finding his troops fired on from the inner ramparts, hastened to the Sallyport. Here Woodhall and his men were already in the interior of the town, prepared for the recontre, and a sharp firing ensued. The gateway was filled to the very top of the arch with dead and dying. The column under Baird had pursued the flying enemy to the Sallyport, and whilst Woodhall was bayoneting and firing in the front, they were also attacked in the rear. The body of Tippoo was afterwards amongst this promiscuous heap of slain. Neither Woodhall nor his men obtained a single article of plunder on the occasion, but a private of the 74th Regiment secured a very valuable armlet, which was sold to Doctor Mein of that corps for a few hundred rupees. It was ultimately discovered to be worth seventy or eighty thousand pounds. The doctor purchased the man's discharge, and settled him in Scotland on £100 pension per annum. The fortress now became one wild scene of plunder and confusion, but poor Woodhall and his men were appointed to extinguish the flames of some burning houses in the vicinity of the grand magazine of gunpowder, which, had it ignited, would have blown the whole garrison, friends and foes, into the air. He performed this arduous duty effectually, and although first in the town, his company were the only part of the regiment who did not reap any pecuniary reward for such daring heroism. The rest of the troops had filled their muskets, caps, and pockets with zechins, pagodas, rupees, and ingots of gold. One of our grenadiers, by name Platt, deposited in my hands, to the amount of fifteen hundred pounds' worth of the precious metals, which in six months afterwards he had dissipated in drinking, horse-racing, cock-fighting, and gambling.

Tranquility was scarcely restored in the Fort, when the honourable Colonel Wellesley was sent in to take the command, to the great dismay and indignation of General Baird, who had felicitated himself on the certain command of this acquisition of his gallantry; but he was superseded, and at once delivered over to Wellesley the important fortress of Seringapatam to his future guidance, who next day hung up eighteen poor Sepoys, found in the act of plunder, contrary to his orders...'

APPENDIX 12.5

Major Alexander Allan's account as recorded by Beatson

A short time after the troops were in possession of the works, Major Beatson and I observed, from the south rampart, several persons assembled in the palace; many of whom, from their dress and appearance, we judged to be of distinction. I particularly remarked, that one person prostrated himself before he sat down; from which circumstance I was led to conclude, that Tippoo, with such of his officers who had escaped from the assault, had taken shelter in the palace.

Before any attempt could be made to secure the palace (where it was thought the enemy, in defence of their sovereign and his family, would make a serious resistance) it became necessary to refresh the troops, who were greatly exhausted by the heat of the day, and the fatigue which they had already undergone. In the mean time Major Beatson and I hastened to apprise General Baird of the circumstances we had seen: on our way, we passed Major Craigie and Captain Whitlie, with the grenadiers, and some battalion companies of the 12th regiment. As soon as we reached General Baird, we proposed to him to bring these troops to him, to which he assented. On my return, General Baird directed me to proceed to the palace with the detachment of the 12th, and part of Major Gibbings's battalion of sepoys: he directed me to inform the enemy that their lives should be shared, on condition of their immediate surrender, but that the least resistance would prove fatal to every person within the palace walls. Having fastened a white cloth on a serjeant's pike, I proceeded to the palace, where I found Major Shee, and part of the 33d regiment, drawn up opposite the gate: several of Tippoo's people were in a balcony, apparently in great consternation. I informed them that I was deputed by the General, who commanded the troops in the fort, to offer them their lives, provided they did not make resistance; of which I desired them to give immediate intimation to their Sultaun. In a short time the killedar, another officer of consequence, and a confidential servant, came over the terrace of the front building, and descended by an unfinished part of the wall. They were greatly embarrassed, and appeared inclined to create delays; probably with a view of effecting their escape as soon as the darkness of the night should afford them an opportunity. I pointed out the danger of their situation, and the necessity of coming to an immediate determination, pledging myself for their protection, and proposing that they should allow me to go into the palace, that I might in person give these assurances to Tippoo. They were very averse to this proposal, but I positively insisted on returning with them. I desired Captain Scohey, who speaks the native languages with great fluency, to accompany me and Captain Hastings Fraser.

We ascended by the broken wall, and lowered ourselves down on a terrace, where a large body of armed men were assembled. I explained to them, that the flag which I held in my hand was a pledge of security, provided no resistance was made; and the stronger to impress them with this belief, I took off my sword, which I insisted upon their receiving. The killedar, and many others affirmed, that the princes and the family of Tippoo were in the palace, but not the Sultaun. They appeared greatly alarmed, and averse to coming to any decision. I told them, that delay might be attended with fatal consequences; and that I could not answer for the conduct of our troops, by whom they were surrounded, and whose fury was with difficulty restrained. They then left me, and shortly I observed people moving hastily backwards and forwards in the interior of the place; and, as there were many hundreds of Tippoo's troops within the walls, I began it think our situation rather critical. I was advised to take back my sword; but such an act, on my part, might, by exciting their distrust, have kindled a flame, which, in the present temper of the troops, might have been attended with the most dreadful consequences; probably the massacre of every soul within the palace walls. The people on the terrace begged me to hold the flag in a conspicuous position, in order to give confidence to those in the palace, and prevent our troops from forcing the gates. Growing impatient at these delays, I sent another message to the princes, warning them of their critical situation, and that my time was limited. They answered, they would receive me as soon as a carpet could be spread for the purpose; and soon after the killedar came to conduct me.

I found two of the princes seated on the carpet, surrounded by a great many attendants. They desired me to sit down, which I did in front of them. The recollection of Moiza-deen, who, on a former occasion, I had seen delivered up with his brother, hostages to Marquis Cornwallis, the sad reverse of their fortunes, their fear, which, notwithstanding their struggles to conceal, was but too evident, excited the strongest emotions of compassion in my mind. I took Moiza-deen (to whom the killedar, &c. principally directed their attention) by the hand, and endeavoured, by every mode in my power, to remove his fears, and to persuade him that no violence should be offered to him or his brother, nor to any person in the palace. I then entreated him, as the only means to preserve his father's life, whose escape was impracticable, to inform me of the spot where he was concealed. Moiza-deen, after some conversation apart with his attendants, assured me that the Padshaw was not in the palace. I requested him to allow the gates to be opened. All were alarmed at this proposal; and the princes were reluctant to take such a step but by the authority of their father, to whom they desired to send. At length, however, having promised that that I would post a guard of their own sepoys within, and a party of Europeans on the outside, and having given them the strongest assurances that no person should enter the palace but by my authority, and that I would return, and remain with them until General Baird arrived, I convinced them of the necessity of compliance; and I was happy to observe that the princes, as well as their attendants, appeared to rely with confidence on the assurances I had given them.

On opening the gate, I found General Baird and several officers, with a large body of troops assembled. I returned with Lieutenant-Colonel Close into the palace, for the purpose of bringing the princes to the General. We had some difficulty in conquering the alarm and the objections which they raised to quitting the palace; but they at length permitted us to conduct them to the gate. The indignation of General Baird was justly excited by a report, which had reached him soon after he had sent me to the palace, that Tippoo had inhumanely murdered all the Europeans who had fallen into his hands during the siege; this was heightened probably by a momentary recollection of his own sufferings, during more than three years imprisonment in that very place; he was, nevertheless, sensibly affected by the sight of the princes; and his gallantry, on the assault, was not more conspicuous, than the moderation and humanity which he displayed on this occasion. He received the princes with every mark of regard, repeatedly assured them that no violence or insult should be offered to them, and he gave them in charge to Lieutenant-colonel Agnew and Captain Marriott, by whom they were conducted to headquarters in camp, escorted by the light company of the 33d regiment. As they passed the troops were ordered to pay them the compliment of presented arms.

General Baird now determined to search the most retired parts of the palace, in the hope of finding Tippoo. He ordered the light company of the 74th regiment, followed by others, to enter the palace-yard. Tippoo's troops were immediately disarmed, and we proceeded to make the search through many of the apartments. Having entreated the killedar, if he had any regard for his own life, or that of his Sultaun, to inform us where he was concealed, he put his hands upon the hilt of my sword, and, in the most solemn manner, protested that the Sultaun was not in the palace, but that he had been wounded during the storm and lay in a gateway on the north face of the fort, whither he offered to conduct us; and if it was found that he deceived us, said, the General might inflict on him what punishment he pleased. General Baird, on hearing the report of the killedar, proceeded to the gateway, which was covered with many hundreds of slain. The number of dead, and the darkness of the place, made it difficult to distinguish one person from another, and the scene was altogether shocking; but, aware of the great political importance of ascertaining beyond the possibility of doubt, the death of Tippoo, the bodies were ordered to be dragged out, and the killedar, and the other two persons, were desired to examine them one after another. This, however, appeared endless; and, as it now was becoming dark, a light was procured, and I accompanied the killedar into the gateway. During the search we discovered a wounded person laying under the Sultaun's palankeen: this man was afterwards ascertained to be Rajah Cawn, one of Tippoo's most confidential servants; he had attended his master during the whole of the day, and, on being made acquainted with the object of our search, he pointed out the spot where the Sultaun had fallen. By a faint glimmering light it was difficult for the killedar to recognise the features; but the body being brought out, and satisfactorily proved to be that of the Sultaun, was conveyed in a palankeen to the palace, where it was again recognized by the eunuchs and other servants of the family.

When Tippoo was brought from under the gateway, his eyes were open, and the body was so warm, that for a few moments Colonel Wellesley and myself were doubtful whether he was not alive: on feeling his pulse and heart, that doubt was removed. He had four wounds, three in the body, and one in the temple; the ball having entered a little above the right ear, and lodged in the cheek. His dress consisted of a jacket of fine white linen, loose drawers of flowered chintz, with a crimson cloth of silk and cotton, round his waist: a handsome pouch with a red and green silk belt, hung across his shoulder: his head was uncovered, his turban being lost in the confusion of his fall: he had an amulet on his arm, but no ornament whatever.

Tippoo was of low stature, corpulent, with high shoulders, and a short thick neck, but his feet were remarkably small; his complexion was rather dark; his eyes large and prominent, with small arched eyebrows, and his nose aquiline: he had an appearance of dignity, or perhaps sternness, in his countenance, which distinguished him above the common order people.

13

THE LEGACY OF TIPU SULTAN

Tipu has caught the imagination of people, his critics and supporters alike. The *Annals* and other records are understandably very critical of the Sultan. In almost all references to him, they describe him as 'Loka Kantaka' or an oppressor of the masses. This of course was done more to create a case for the Wodeyar dynasty and to pander to its already crushed ego. But most balanced historians and contemporaries take a more realistic approach and eulogise him no end. As Meadows Taylor says:

> He was a great man, such a one as Hind will never see again. He had great ambition, wonderful ability, perseverance, and the art of leading men's hearts more than they were aware of or cared to acknowledge; he had patient application and nothing was done without his sanction, even to the meanest of affairs, and the business of his dominions was vast. You will allow he was brave and died like a soldier. He was kind and considerate to his servants, and a friend to those he loved. Mashalla! He was a great man.

Tipu often said that 'it was far better to live like a lion for a day than to live like a jackal for a hundred years'. Historians were fascinated by his unique attitude, unknown among contemporary Indian rulers who didn't mind unethical alliances with the British to satisfy their own selfish ambitions.

As James Mill observes:*

> He had the discernment to perceive what is so generally hidden from the eyes of the rulers of a more enlightened state of society, that it is the prosperity of those who labour with their hands which constitutes the principle and cause of the prosperity of states; he, therefore, made it his business to protect them against the intermediate orders of the community by whom it is so difficult to prevent them from being oppressed.... His country was accordingly...the best cultivated and its population the most flourishing in India, while under the English and their dependencies, the population of the Carnatic and Oudh, hastening to the state of deserts, were the most wretched upon the face of the earth.

Despite spending half his life on the battlefield, Tipu did not turn into a crude, bloodthirsty soldier. He managed to maintain the gentlemanliness and decorum that was demanded of him. The ruler of Adoni revolted against Mysore on British instigation a few months after ascending to the throne of Mysore. After sowing the seeds of rebellion, the English conveniently exited when Tipu attacked Adoni. The baffled ruler knew that his army was no match for the grand army of Mysore and its Tiger. He fled, leaving his beautiful wife behind. In those days, it was common for the victor to subjugate his defeated enemy's wives to his desires. Anticipating this, the queen of Adoni sent her veil to Tipu as a symbol of her complete surrender to him. Tipu refused to take advantage of her plight and sent her with due dignity to her parents' house at Bijapur. This contradicts completely Tipu's generally perceived attitude, especially regarding women, but perhaps it reveals his quirky nature.

Wilks states, in a typically cynical English comment on Tipu:

> In person, he was neither so tall nor so robust as his father, and had a short pursy neck; the large limbs, small eyes, aquiline nose, and fair complexion of Hyder, marked the Arabic character derived from his mother. Tippoo's singularly small and delicate hands and feet, his large and full eyes, a nose, less prominent and a much darker complexion, were all national characteristics

---

* Taken from Ali's 1993 book, *Tipu Sultan—A Great Martyr*.

of the Indian form. There was, in the first view of countenance, an appearance of dignity, which wore off on further observation; and his subjects did not feel that it inspired the terror or respect, which, in common with his father, he desired to command. Hyder's lapse from dignity into low and vulgar scolding was among the few points of imitation or resemblance, but in one it inspired fear, in the other ridicule. In most instances exhibiting a contrast to the character and manners of his father, he spoke in a loud and unharmonious tone of voice; he was extremely garrulous and on superficial subjects, delivered his sentiment with plausibility. In exterior appearance, he affected the soldier; in his toilet, the distinctive habits of the Mussalman; he thought hardiness to be indicated by a plain unencumbered attire, which he equally exacted from those around him, and the long robe and trailing drawers were banished from his court...

Of the vernacular languages, he spoke no other than Hindustani and Kanarese; but from a smattering in Persian literature, he considered himself as the first philosopher of the age. He spoke that language with fluency; but although the pen was forever in his hand, he never attained either elegance or accuracy of style. The leading features of his character were vanity and arrogance; no human being was ever so handsome, so wise, so learned, or so brave as himself.

On a slightly different note is the account of Tipu's allies—the French account by Joseph Michaud:

Thus died Tippoo Saib at the age of forty-five. The beginning of his military career had covered him with very great glory throughout Hindustan; fortune had favoured him in allowing him without opposition to sit on the throne of Hyder Aly; and she also did something for him on the occasion in not leaving him to survive the downfall of his Empire. His height was five feet eight inches; he had a thick short neck; his shoulders square and massive; his limbs were small, particularly his feet and hands; his eyes large and his eyebrows arched; he had an aquiline nose, and a brown complexion. Tippoo Saib was a cultured man; he was master of several European languages; he possessed a deep knowledge of the sciences studied in India; but he had not that power of perception, that farseeing and active intuition, which prepares for contingencies, or that wisdom that puts them to profit. Possessed of a boldness, which braves all dangers, he had not the prudence, which avoids them; endowed with an impetuous and irascible spirit, he nearly always preferred violent to slow and prudent measures. In short, it can be said of this Prince, that he occupied himself too much with the means for displaying his power, and not enough with those for preserving and strengthening it.

A completely contrasting picture is presented by the contemporary historian Kirmani, himself a Muslim:

In his courts, the splendour of kingly magnificence and majesty were all well sustained. He was proficient to a considerable extent in all the sciences. He wrote and composed with ease and elegance, and indeed had a genius for literary acquirement, had a great talent for business; and therefore, he was not obliged to rely on the aid or guidance of others in the management of public affairs. He had a pleasing address and manners, was very discriminating in his estimation of the character of men of learning and instruction of the people of Islam. He had, however a great dislike to, or rather an abhorrence of the people of other religions. He held his durbars from the morning until midnight, and after morning prayers, he was used to employ some time in reading the Koran, and he was to be seen at all times with his Tusbih or rosary in his hand, having performed his ablutionary duties. He made only two meals a day, and all his Amirs and the Princes dined with him. But from the day on which the peace was made between him and Lord Cornwallis Buhadur, (to the day of his death) he abandoned his bed and bed-stead and slept or took a few hours rest on certain pieces of a coarse kind of canvas called Khaddi (used for making tents), spread upon the ground. He was accustomed on most occasions to speak Persian, and while he was eating his dinner, two hours were devoted by him to the perusal (from standard historical works), of the actions of the Kings of Persia and Arabia, religious works, traditions and biography. He also heard appropriate stories and anecdotes related by his courtiers. Jests and ribaldry, however, from the repetition of which the religion of Islam might suffer disparagement, or injury, were never allowed in the courts or assemblies of that most religious prince. For the sake of recreation he sometimes witnessed dancing or was present at the performance of Bayaderes.* He was not, however lavish or expensive in any of his habits or amusements, not even in his dress, and contrary to his former custom, he latterly avoided the use of coloured garments. On his journeys and expeditions, however, he wore a coat of gold, or the red tiger stripe embroidered with gold. He was also accustomed to tie a white handkerchief over his turban and under his chin, and no one was allowed to tie on, or wear a white handkerchief in that manner except himself.

Towards the end of his reign he wore a green turban Shumlehdar (twisted appropriately) after the fashion of the Arabs, having one embroidered end pendant on the sides of his head...contrary to the custom of the deceased Nawab, he the Sultan, retained the hair of his eyebrows, eyelashes and moustaches. His beard, however, which was chiefly on his chin, he shaved, thinking it not becoming to him. In delicacy or modesty of feeling, he was the most particular man in the world, so much so that from the days of his childhood to that of his death, no one ever saw any part of his person except his ankle and wrist and even in the bath he always covered himself from head to foot.

One man, three totally contrasting versions! The opinion of the Hindu writers of the time tended to be in favour of the royal family of the Wodeyars and those have been excluded here to save the reader some long reading. But including those would help no better in resolving the paradox. What is a contemporary, unbiased historian to make of such versions? Are we at the end of it, able to make a judgment of the kind of man Tipu was? Certainly not! History seems to have blurred here and each version sticks to its characteristic and expected biases. It is impossible to have clear judgement based on secondary sources more than two centuries after Tipu's time. Yet, even the most eminent historians freely take sides on Tipu Sultan. Isn't that a travesty of the truth, a departure from the scientific and rational representation of history? Dr John R. Henderson offers a more balanced view and in effect mirrors my dilemma on the issue:

---

* Nautch girls.

It is difficult to form an accurate estimate of the character of Tipu Sultan, because the views of contemporary writers, whether English or Muhammadan, are obviously biased. His cruelty and religious bigotry are undoubted and he perpetrated many atrocities in the name of religion; he has been justly censured for his excesses in war, though they never perhaps exceeded a standard set elsewhere in modern times. That he was a brave man cannot be doubted, and while on several occasions he showed considerable military ability, he fell short of his father in this respect. Unlike Haidar, he was a man of education and the changes which he introduced into the calendar, the names of his forts, of Civil and Military officers, and of weights and measures, certainly display a considerable amount of ingenuity, though by more than one writer they have been held to afford evidence of his insanity. Nowhere else is Tipu's love of innovation better seen than in his coinage.

A DAY IN THE LIFE OF TIPU SULTAN

What would a typical day in the life of Tipu Sultan be like when he was not busy heading military expeditions or crushing rebellions? Many contemporary historians—British and Indian—have documented these details. He usually rose with the sun and, after being shampooed and rubbed, he proceeded for a wash followed by a reading of the Quran for nearly an hour. He then held brief meetings with his principal officers and any others seeking his audience. This would be followed by a quick inspection of the Jamdar Khana, where jewellery, plates, fruits and valuables were kept. A breakfast of nuts, almonds, fruits, jelly and milk would thereafter be served, which he would have with a munshi (secretary) and his three youngest children. It was quite a contrast to the spartan food Haidar had enjoyed. His inner circle consisted of Mir Sadik, the Benki Nawab, Purnaiya, Syed Mohammad Asif, Ghulam Ali, Ahmad Khan and his principal secretary Habibullah. The breakfast would always be accompanied by animated discussions that focused more on the Sultan's chivalrous days in the war-front; and even as this discussion carried on scribes would take notes or have letters dictated to them.

The breakfast and gossip would be followed by the royal *durbar* for which he would clothe himself in rich garments. On most other occasions his attire would generally be plain and coarse—a typical, rugged military man. New recruits would be inspected and details of their caste, country, extent of religious knowledge, etc. ascertained. Only then was a decision made regarding hiring them or increasing the pay of deserving candidates. Those found wanting would be packed off to the *qazi* or the Muslim religious scholar for training! These examinations lasted for hours.

After a brief siesta, the evening would see the Sultan inspect on horseback the discipline of the troops and their preparedness. Fortifications and repair work would also be looked into. Beatson had observed that Tipu's mind constantly thought of war and military preparations. Upon his return to the palace, details of arsenals, manufactories, and classified news from the espionage cell which always worked overtime to catch happenings in every nook and corner of the kingdom would be discussed.

Beatson notes:

> He generally passed the evening with his three elder sons, or one or two of his principal officers of each of the departments of state, a Cauzy and Moonshy Hubbeeb Oolah, his Secretary. All these usually sat down to supper with him; and Hubbeeb Oolah asserts that his conversation was remarkably lively, entertaining and instructive. During his meal, he was fond of reciting passages from the most admired historians and poets; and sometimes he amused himself with sarcasms upon the Caufer or infidels and enemies of the Circar and often discoursed upon learned and religious subjects with the Cauzy and Moonshy. Having dismissed his company, which he always did immediately after the repast, he was accustomed to walk about by himself or exercise; and when tired, to lie down on his couch and read a book, either upon the subject of religion or history until he fell asleep.

TIPU THE ADMINISTRATOR

The more significant aspect of Tipu's short and stormy rule was the manner in which he strengthened the administrative and commercial establishments of Mysore. He was a ruler with a vision and believed in translating that vision into concrete action. A perceptible change in the quality of life for the people of the kingdom was also on top of his agenda. His reformist zeal touched almost every department of life, including coinage and calendar, weights and measures, banking and finance, trade and commerce, agriculture and industry and social and cultural life.

Administrative Departments

There were nine major centralised administrative departments in Mysore under Tipu: Revenue and Finance, Military, Ordinance, Garrison, *Zurmana*, Commerce, Marine, Treasury and Mint. The state had twelve mints; gold, silver and copper coins were issued bearing the letter 'H' of Haidar. A gold coin or Mohar was divided into ½, ¼ and so on. A double rupee was called a Hydari, a single rupee (Imani) and a copper coin worth Rs 2 (Osmani) were the popular currency. The kingdom was divided into 37 *asafis* or provinces, and 124 *talukas* or districts. By 1796, kingdom of the Mysore had a total area of 62,000 square miles. Under Haidar, Mysore had included the region south of the Krishna river and, along with a large part of present-day Karnataka, the present Rayalseema tract of Andhra Pradesh, five districts of Tamil Nadu north of Dindigul and northern Malabar of Kerala.

The Organisation of Tipu's Army

The Mysore army became a model army for Indian rulers and even for the British. A well-disciplined army with cavalry, infantry, artillery and 40 ships in the navy were his handiwork. A French engineer was asked to design an engine run by water for boring cannons. Tipu organised a Board of Admiralty, which controlled a navy of twenty-two lines of battle ships and twenty large frigates with seventy-two and sixty-two guns respectively, besides a fleet of merchant ships. In fact, during Tipu's time an elaborate treatise was written on the science of warfare—a seminal work titled *Fathul Mujahidin* or the Triumph of the Warrior. The decades of training and later experience in the rough terrains of Tipu's battlefields have been compiled into eight chapters, which are further divided into many sections. They deal with themes, such as the necessity, importance and value of war against the invaders and oppressors, mechanisms of offence and defence, treatment of the conquered people and territories, loyalty and treachery, treason and conspiracy, prohibition and the evils of intoxicants and tobacco, evils of slavery and submission to foreign rule and signs off by prophetically declaring that attainment of martyrdom is higher than sainthood. It is undoubtedly the first ever military treatise that any Indian ruler might have compiled in a manner as structured and with such a clear goal—eliminating the influence of the colonial powers. The opening paragraph from the translated version of the book reads as follows:

> The Timurid Sultanat had become so weak and disturbed in 1757 AD mainly in account of the treachery of the employees of the house that the English merchants living on the sea coasts of India, under the pretext of trade and commerce were always looking for opportunities. They made use of some unworthy persons who traded their faith for worldly gains for the purpose of colonization and usurpation and took possession of the whole of Bengal, a part of Carnatic in the Deccan and the port of Surat and brought ruin and destruction to the lives, properties and the faith of the people. In these circumstances, Tippu Sultan has appeared on the scene like the sun in darkness who is defending the country and faith. As the fighting of the English people is based on guns and muskets and the Indians are inexperienced in that matter, the Sultan framed new rules and methods for the artillery, arrangement of the army and attacking the enemy, for the individual as well as the whole in detail to face the enemy on equal terms. Hence in the year 1783 AD this courtier received the order to compile them so that this noble science which is not found in India may gain currency and by its help the Sultan's armies may defeat the enemies.

Though Tipu is credited as the author of this book, it is far more likely to have been written by anonymous courtiers and soldiers. Some historians credit Zain-ul-Abidin Shustari, Tipu's commander, as its author. Saki quotes Mir Mahmoode Hussaine about the book:

> It is a masterpiece produced in the court of Tipu Sultan in simple Persian, a creation of his revolutionary mind, based on his own military experience and observation of warfare. It is a brief but comprehensive treatise on military science and the art of warfare... by his royal command many copies of the book were made and distributed among the military officers under his signature...his army was guided by this work all through his reign...

By the time of Haidar's death, the regular Mysorean army had about 1,80,000 men. Two years later by the time of the Treaty of Mangalore the army had 1,44,000 men; Tipu's formula being one soldier in the regular army for every 40 people in the population. He took a keen interest in recruiting the soldiers into the army. Beatson writes:

> It was his custom to review, every morning, the new levies and recruits and to enquire into their caste, country and extent of their religious knowledge. If he was satisfied with their examination, they were in consequence entertained with a higher rate of pay... these examinations often lasted for several hours...From the regular infantry 5000 men being selected, they were named a Kushoon and the officer commanding that body was called a Sipahadar. In each Kushoon there were four Risaldars or colonels of infantry and under the order of each Risaldar or colonel were 10 Jowkidar, and every Jowk or company included two Sur Kheil, 10 Jamadars and 10 Duffadars. In his regiments of troops or regular horse, which was formed and appointed after the manner of Europeans, the Teepdar and Subadar, called Major and Adjutant in the French and English languages, were styled Youzdar and Nakib.

Writing about the general organisation of the Mysorean army, Lally's first-hand account is recorded by De La Tour:

> The Batis (patties) are small writings or warrants. Every person in the military service has one, from the general to the drummer. This writing contains the name of the person, and of his father and grandfather; a description of his person and that of his horse (if he be a horseman), the day he entered the service; his station, and his pay; and as often as he is paid the sum is entered on the same; those of the officers contain simply the name, the station or degree and the sums received. The Batis are triple, and in three different languages—Persian, Maratha and Canarin; and as there are three chancellors, they are preserved in greatest order. Haider signs the state of accounts every month as well as a particular statement for every troop; for no payment is made without the signature of Haider, or in his absence, of the general commandant.

In the early days of Haidar's rule, salaries used to be paid once every forty days. By the end of his reign, however, prompt monthly payments were made with sepoys receiving Rs 8 a month and grenadiers Rs 10.

Not even the British army could boast of such a punctual and timely system of disbursal. Haidar had been through the scourge of frequent uprisings in the army under Immadi Krishnaraja Wodeyar, when, on most occasions, he was the peacemaker and negotiator. No doubt then that Tipu prioritised the streamlining of this process to curb discontent in the army. Lally notes:

> From the time of their first establishment, they were exercised every morning in the handling of their arms, by their own officers; and every afternoon from three till six, five battalions by turns, were exercised in their evolutions by the French commandant; after which they were made to march from six to eight, marching out at the ordinary pace and returning home with a quick step. All the officers, without exception, were obliged to do this exercise as well as the common soldiers…it was thus that this sovereign formed a body of troops, to whose rapid movements the English afterwards attributed all his success.

An intriguing question remains—it is rather strange that the same father and son, who were seized by such rabid hatred for the colonial mindset of the East India Company, did not hesitate to solicit French help! Would the French have been any better in their motives and machinations vis-à-vis the British, had they been the beneficiaries of the great Indian power struggle of the eighteenth century? The answer is uncertain. Why then did these rulers with a vision seek to use one colonial force against another? Would Mysore have turned into a French stooge if not the British one it became in 1799 is a question that remains unanswered.

Lally writes about the military inventory of Tipu in 1786—3,00,000 firelocks, 3,00,000 matchlocks, 2,00,000 swords, 22,000 pieces of cannon, 700 elephants, 6,000 camels and 11,000 horses. Shama Rao writes about the stores in the fort of Maddur in 1799:

> An idea of the military stores generally contained in the forts may be obtained from what was found in this fort. This fort contained 373 guns, 60 mortars and 11 howitzers of brass, 466 guns, 12 mortars and 7 guns unfurnished of iron; in all 929 pieces of ordnance, of which 287 were mounted on the fortification. 4,24,4000 rounds of shot, 5,20,000 pounds of powder, 99,000 muskets, carbines etc of

which 30,000 stand of French and 7000 of the Company's arms. There were also powder magazines, 2 buildings for boring guns and muskets, 5 large arsenals and 17 other buildings filled with swords, accoutrements, rockets and a variety of small stores.

The very name Maddur (*maddu* in Kannada meant gunpowder) signified its strategic importance in the kingdom's defence.

Tipu's army also had a large contingent of 4,00,000 bullocks and cows in 1786. They were sturdy, long-legged and of the Hallikar breed suited mainly for the transportation of materials. It was the quick pace of these bullocks which helped Haidar in many a combat with the British as he raced away at the rate of two feet to one of the British! Lewis Rice writes:

> Principal breeds of horned cattle in Mysore are Amrit Mahal, Madesvaram Betta and Kankanahalli. The Amrit Mahal, literally Milk Department is an establishment for the breeding of a race of cattle peculiar to the country of Mysore and famous for its utility for military purposes. The establishment was founded at some time during the Hindu government with special privileges as regards grazing, but its maintenance for the special purpose of supplying draught cattle for artillery is due to Hydar Ali. He is reported to have introduced a breed of cattle from Trichinapoly country, by a cross between which, and the indigenous breed of Mysore was produced the Hallikar breed, which is considered the best in the establishment.

Rocketry

Another interesting aspect of Haidar and Tipu's lives was their fascination with rockets. In fact, they are considered among the pioneers of rocket technology in India—not surprising then that a lot of research and development of the Indian Space Research Organisation happens at Bangalore, once a key part of Tipu's kingdom!

As Kenneth Macksey writes:

> The first practical rocket missiles were used by Hyder Ally of Mysore against the British in 1780. As a result an Englishman, William Congreve, produced rockets in 1805 which were used in the naval bombardment of Boulogne in 1806.

In fact, a glowing tribute was paid to Tipu by none other than the former president of India Dr A.P.J. Abdul Kalam, who was scientific adviser to the Indian Ministry of Defence during the Hazrath Tippu Sultan Shaheed Memorial Lecture organised by the Al-Ameen Educational Society Bangalore on 30 November 1991:

> Rocket technology engulfed me for two decades since my visit to Srirangapatna in 1960. The question continued to haunt me—'How would Tipu Sultan have led to the world's first war rocket?' 'What environment was responsible for the birth of such a technological innovation in our country?' In August 1974 I received a paper presented by Frank H. Winter of National Air and Space Museum Washington USA, titled 'The Rocket in India from ancient times to the 19th century.' This highly researched paper presented the 'Agni Astra' from Vedic hymns to Tipu's war rocket with eighteen classic references. Winter's conclusion is startling for the Indian Scientific Community. He says, 'Thus, it is fair to suggest that the venerable rocket from the subcontinent of India may well have had its technological impact upon the West. If so, in retrospect, it was an important, if subtle, technological transfer of recent history.' Many such researchers have to spring up in our Universities as well. Soon, I learnt that two of the war rockets captured by the British at Srirangapatana have been displayed in the Museum of Artillery at Woolwich in London. One of my missions during my visit to Europe in 1980 was to study this rocket. Dr V.R. Gowarkar and I visited the museum. It was a great thrill especially for rocket technologists like us, to see an Indian innovation on foreign soil well preserved and with facts not distorted.
>
> Under the heading 'India's War Rocket,' the following details are recorded in the Woolwich Museum London. The motor casing of this rocket is made of steel with multi nozzle holes with the sword blade as the warhead. The propellant used was packed gunpowder. The weight of the rocket is about 2kg. With about 1kg of propellant. 50mm in dia about 250mm length, the range performance is reported 900mts to 1.5 km. Our designers analysed and confirmed their performance. What a simple and elegant design effectively used in war!

The Juzail Burdars were the rocketmen of the Mysorean army and an integral and indispensable part of it as well. The Mysore rockets were massive weapons, with a thick bamboo stalk about eight to ten feet long. A heavy iron tube, weighing between six to twelve pounds, contained the fuse and powder fixed to the end of the tube. In wet weather or on marshy grounds the rockets were pointed horizontally and fired randomly in the enemy's direction, causing huge casualties among the cavalry and troops. As Macksey explains:

> [A] body of cavalry not used to this kind of instrument, would be quickly thrown into disorder by it; for the rockets falling at the feet of the horses, emit a flame resembling that of a forge furnace, which frightens them; and when they burst, they do considerable mischief. It is no small advantage that they describe a curved line, and may therefore be thrown by people that are covered by a line of infantry.

These indigenous missiles traversed a distance of almost 1.4 kilometres. The British, completely unaware of the technology even thirty-seven years after they began their Mysorean campaign, were caught off-guard by this superior and locally designed know-how. No doubt then that after the fall of Srirangapatna, the prime task for the British was to understand and duplicate this technology.

When Tipu was killed, the British captured more than 700 rockets and subsystems of 900 rockets in the battle of Turukhanahally in 1799. His army had 27 brigades, or *kushoons*, and each *kushoon* had a company of rocket men, called Jourks. These rockets were taken to England by William Congreave, a young scientist in charge of this task who made no major innovation in the science, merely replicating what was stolen from the forges, foundries and factories of Mysore. The British then subjected this knowledge from medieval Mysore to what is called 'reverse engineering' today. Of course, the British could do it because there was no GATT, IPR Act, or patent regime at that time, and with the death of Tipu Sultan, Indian rocketry died too. Tipu's rocket science is clearly among India's major military and technological discoveries!

Navy

The occupation of the coastal areas of Mangalore and Malabar led to the establishment of a competent Mysorean navy as well. The aim was to challenge the might of the British navy in the Arabian Sea. Describing the fleet, Peixoto states:

> It consisted of 80 vessels, 13 topsail vessels, several manchoos of war, besides a great many skybars and small craft for the transport of war materials and provisions for the passage of the army across the rivers. The Dutch account differs from the Portuguese. According to the former, the fleet had 2 ships, 7 smaller vessels and 40 gallivats, besides more than 50 other vessels laden with provisions.

Two Mir-e-Yams or chief admirals administered the naval set-up assisted by their admirals or Amirul Bahr. That the initial ideas of Haidar after the conquest of Honnavar, Mangalore and Bhatkal were carried forward by Tippu becomes clear in the consternation expressed by William Kirkpatrick:

> In proportion as the Sultan might have been able to realise his alarming plan of a maritime establishment, we should as a measure of necessary precaution, have been compelled to augment at a heavy expense, our naval force in India, for the purpose of duly watching his armaments, and of keeping them in constant check. This evil at least, was averted by the issue of the war of 1799.

Revenue

Both Haidar and Tipu were greatly suspicious of the Palegars who were notorious for their ambitions and sudden change of loyalties. The Palegar was also a middleman in the process of revenue collection as per the old feudal revenue model of the kingdom. While Chikkadevaraja Wodeyar had begun this campaign against the parasitic Palegar class by eliminating their influence over districts of Mandya, Mysore and part of Bangalore, Haidar and Tipu extended this campaign to cover the districts of Hassan, Shimoga, Dakshina Kannada, Uttara Kannada, Chitradurga, Raichur, Bellary, Dharwad, Tumkur and Kolar in present day Karnataka. Haidar was the one who gave this a serious thought and felt that the state could appropriate more revenue if they removed this middleman. A professional rent-collector would be a more cost-effective and apolitical person—suiting the kingdom's (and Haidar's) interests well. He started replacing a lot of these Palegars under a more systematic tax collection regime—another reason for the innumerable mutinies of the threatened Palegars. Bristow, in his account of a prisoner-of-war, mentions that in 1781 Haidar brought with him about fifty Palegar prisoners to Srirangapatna. During his conquest of Kerala, he vanquished or eliminated all the forty-two Palegars who ruled over Northern Malabar. Buchanan writes about the socio-economic transition from the times of the Rayas of Vijayanagara to the Wodeyars and the times of Haidar and Tipu:

> During the government of the Rayarus, the tributary Polygars of Chatrakal...governed a country valued at 10,000 Pagodas a year...on the decline of the royal family, Vijayanagara, these enterprising hunters, by gradually encroaching on their neighbours, increased their territories until they became worth annually 350,000 Pagodas...Hyder...attacked Chatrakal. The first siege lasted five months, and was unsuccessful. After the second siege had continued six months, there was little prospect of success and Hyder had recourse to corruption...
>
> Gubi...is said to have been founded by about 400 years ago, by a family of Polygars...they were first brought under subjection by the Mysore Rajas, who imposed a tribute of 500 Pagodas. Hyder increased this to 2500, leaving them little better than renters. They were entirely disposed by his son Tippo, and have returned to their original profession of cultivators; but in their own tribe they still retain their hereditary rank...

Haidar's and Tipu's ideas were revolutionary. To tamper with a socio-economic set-up that had been firmly established over centuries of feudal governance would meet with severe opposition and in many cases bloody conflicts. Quoting Buchanan further:

> On the arrival of Lord Cornwallis the Raja of Chica Balapura was reinstated, and, after retreat of the British army, like the other Polygars who had been restored to their countries, he refused submission to Tippoo. Ishmael Khan...was sent with an army to reduce them...the chief officer was hanged, and every soldier had either a hand or leg cut off with a large knife used by...dressers of leather; the only favour shown to the garrison was the choice of the limb that was to be amputated. A similar punishment was at the same time inflicted on 700 of the neighboring farmers, who

had occasionally stolen into the place and assisted in its defence. As they had no means of stopping the haemorrhage, except by applying rags dipped in boiled oil...the messenger of Purnea, who attends me, was present at the execution, as one of Tippo's soldiers...

The Amildars were the professional tax collectors, mostly Brahmins, appointed to replace the Palegars by both Haidar and Tipu. However even the people who established this system were disappointed in it as it was full of corruption. The traditional Palegars had been part of local tradition and custom, whereas the officially appointed Amildars were transplanted from the capital and usually completely clueless about their new environment. Unlike the Palegars, who had integrated themselves into the social milieu they governed, the Amildars were not sensitive enough to the needs of the people. Quoting Buchanan yet again:

> The Amildars, under various pretexts of unavoidable emergency, reported prodigious outstanding balances; while they received, as bribes from the cultivators, a part of the deductions so made... The Brahmin...amildars...who managed the whole of the revenue department were so avaricious, so corrupt...that Tippoo would have entirely displaced them, if he could have done without their services; but that was impossible; for no other persons in the country had any knowledge of business.

Many of the land- and tax-reform measures implemented were thus unrealistic and eventually they impacted the Mysorean economy in the form of a massive peasant revolt several decades later that shook the very foundations of the kingdom! Thus the unification of a large part of present-day Karnataka (barring areas like Belgaum and Bijapur and all of Bidar and Gulbarga) was achieved during the Haidar-Tipu reign. Their reign was also marked by the breaking of the old and defunct social order and the feudal system as mentioned above, setting the 'Bangalore-Srirangapatna axis' as the centre of power. It was a significant axis since it had already witnessed the throttling of Palegar influence for over a century now.

The entire kingdom was divided into 37 provinces under dewans or asophs (fouzdars) and these were subdivided into 1,025 districts under tehsildars or amildars. The *taluk* as stated before had *hoblis* under

Parupatyagaras assisted by two clerks or Shirastedars. In 1792, Tipu prepared and distributed the 'Land Revenue Regulations' which were issued to all the asophs and other officials down the line. It was like an instruction manual on revenue collection practices in the greatest possible detail, as perhaps the regulation clause 29, quoted in Nikhiles Guha's book, elucidates:

> An account shall be taken of all the houses of the ryots and of all the castes throughout your district, specifying the names of villages, the number of ploughs, the quantity of seed sown, and of land tilled; the number of workers, their families and children; with their various castes and occupations. In forming these accounts great precaution is to be observed, to prevent its creating any alarm among the ryots. Every year the increase or dimunition of agriculture and population is to be observed in the manner following: the Shanbhoges of the village are to prepare and transmit the accounts to the Simpt, and the Shanboges of the Simpt are to form the complete account, and transmit it to the Amil of the district, who is to prepare one general statement, giving a full view of the population and cultivation of the country, and deposit it in his Cutchery from whence it will be forwarded to the Huzoor, and as the month if Zeehujee is appointed for the inspection of these accounts in the huzoor, they must be deposited in the Cutchery in the month of Ramzan.

Administrative Set-up

Tipu also sized down the authority of hereditary feudal figureheads in villages, such as the Patels and Shanbhogues. Clauses 5, 11 and 12 make this point clear:

> A Patel has been attached to every village from times of old; wherever it happens that the person holding this office is unfit for it, another who is capable shall be chosen from amongst the Ryots and be appointed to it; and the former Patel shall be reduced to the condition of a Ryot and be made to work at the plough; and the business of the office of the Patel shall be made over to the new ones. *(Clause 11)*
>
> The Shamboges of the Atthavana (royal household) and Ahashaum (low marshy tracts) shall not be employed in the

direction of affairs, nor shall farm of villages be given to them, but they shall be employed in keeping accounts. *(Clause 12)*

The Patels, Taajkaurs (revenue officers) and others have for a long time avoided paying the full revenue of Government lands; this is to be enquired into, and the lands are to be measured and they are to be assessed like other Ryots. The Ryots are not to plough the lands of the Patels; but the Patels shall themselves plough them. If any Patel shall in future employ ryots to till his ground, the whole of the produce shall be taken by Government. His lands which have been cultivated for a length of time by the Shamboges, shall be refused and be delivered over to other ryots to cultivate; and if such Shamboges shall desire to have other land given to them in lieu of their wages, land which is lying waste shall be given to them; if they do not ask for land, they shall receive their wages in money, according to the established rate. *(Clause 5)*

Writing about the administrative set-up, Praxy Fernandes states:

Tippu was of course an absolute monarch...yet his government was not a disorganised chain of personal whims and caprices. The Mysore records found after the fall of Seringapatam indicate the well-organised mechanism of Tippu's central government. Its division into departments under responsible heads and with well-defined jurisdictions will seem familiar to the administrator of today. Each department called a 'Kutcheri' worked under a departmental chief who had the status and rank of a minister and was staffed by competent and specialised civil servants. Tippu introduced the system of Boards in each Kutcheri where officers discussed problems, recorded their views and maintained minutes of the meetings. Decisions were generally taken by a majority of votes. Tippu kept a personal and vigilant eye over these proceedings...on matters of common concern, the departmental chiefs would have conferences before advising the Sultan. The entire atmosphere which emerges from the dusty records of Seringapatam was one which would make a secretariat official in modern India completely at home.

Building on the Attara Kacheri system of Chikkadevaraja Wodeyar, Tipu organised six major Kutcheries or Departments in the administration:

1. **Mir Asaf Kacheri (Revenue and Finance Department):** Maintained accounts of revenue, taxation and expenditure. It was headed by one of the senior-most ministers of the kingdom who was called Diwan or Mir Asaf. Mustaddis and Shirastedars maintained the accounts in Kannada, Persian and Marathi.
2. **Mir Miran Kacheri (Military Accounts and Supply Department)**
3. **Mir Sadar Kacheri (Admiralty):** Looked into the management of ports, merchant-shipping and the navy that had assumed greater importance after the conquests of Kanara and Malabar. The head office was at Mangalore for convenient reasons.
4. **Mir Kazain Kacheri (Treasury and Coinage Department):** Worked under the joint supervision of the *toshikhana*/treasury and the state mint. State jewels, wardrobes, important state documents, bullion and ready money were maintained at the *toshikhana*. The mints were handled by darogas.
5. The postal and intelligence department.
6. **Malik-ut-Tijjar Kacheri (Department of Trade and Commerce)**

Along with these major departments were many smaller ones like Public Works, Temple Department, Amrit Mahal and so on. Tipu was the first Indian king to make civil servants swear an oath of secrecy and loyalty to the kingdom. No doubt then that Dodwell commented that he 'was the first Indian sovereign to apply western methods to his administration.'*

Beatson records that when the Sultan had any important business to transact, or any letters to dispatch that required deliberation, he always devoted one day to his own reflections before he took the opinion of any of his counsellors. After having sufficiently considered the subject in question he assembled the principal officers of the departments of the state, and writing in his own hand the nature of the subject to be referred to their consideration, he required from each person, an answer in writing.

---

* Dodwell's words have been taken from Fernandes' 1969 book, *Storm over Seringapatnam*.

Banking Innovation

Tipu was a creative thinker way ahead of his times. He envisaged a sort of banking organisation in which small investors received higher benefits. It was an experiment in a new type of cooperative banking which encouraged small savings among the masses. Designing such a measure back in the eighteenth century speaks volumes of Tipu's foresight and vision. Farmers were given Takkavi loans at low rates of interest to promote agriculture and help peasants in the lean seasons.* At the beginning of the year, the Amil was to give a *cowl* or security to all the farmers and encourage them to cultivate their lands. To enable the poorer farmers to buy equipment and ploughs, he had to sanction the Takkavi loans at the rate of three to four Pagodas per plough, taking some form of security against repayment. The idea was to recover the loan amount in one to two years. In cases of revenue shortfall, the Amil would bridge the gap by bringing in more ryots, granting them Takkavi loans and new ploughs to enable more cultivation.

Irrigation

Closely linked to the aim of increasing cultivable area was the requirement of water across the kingdom. Irrigation schemes were toned up and nearly forty per cent of the kingdom was irrigated and cultivated. The present Krishnaraja Sagara Dam at Mysore—the lifeline for millions of people in southern Karnataka and Tamil Nadu—was originally Tippu's brainchild, though he did not live to implement it. A detailed look at the irrigation schemes in vogue in Mysore at the time, as described by Buchanan, speaks of the ruler's foresight and attention to agriculture and farmers' welfare:

> The country rises gradually on both sides of the river, is naturally fertile and for some distance from the town is finely watered

---

* Takkavi loans were interest-free and thus non-usurious agricultural loans provided by the government for the peasantry. These loans, provided in the form of material inputs, were repayable in instalments, some within a two-year period and others within a four-year period. They were granted to peasants who desired to bring new lands under cultivation or to those who were ravaged by famines or other calamities and also to those whose lands remained fallow for years on end.

by canals; which, having been taken from the river, follow the windings of the hills, and as they advance horizontally to the eastwards, send off branches to water the intermediate space. The water is forced into the sources of these canals by Anacuts, or dams, which have been thrown across the river, and formed of large blocks of granite of a prodigious strength, and at a great expense...

He describes the Patna Ashtagram irrigation scheme above and speaking about another scheme he saw in Hunsur adjoining Ashtagram across the Cauvery's tributary Lakshmanatirtha, he writes the following:

At a short distance from Sicany Pura is a fine little river called Lakshmanatirtha, which comes from the South West, and rises among the hills of the country which we call Coorg. At all times it contains a stream of water, and in the rainy season is not fordable. It supplies six canals to water the country. The Anas, or dams, that force the water into these canals, are fine works and produce beautiful cascades. One of them is broken down, but the other five are in good repair; and in fact one of them that I saw supplied more water than was wanted; for a quantity sufficient to turn a mill was allowed to run back into the river through a sluice...it is said that the whole land formerly watered by the canals of the Lakshmana, amounted to 7000 candacas sowing; but the candacas are small and contain only from 100 to 140 seers each. If the seed be sown here as thick as in Seringapatam, the 7000 candacas would amount to about 18,000 acres.

He states that the Patna Ashtagram Taluk for example, had 8,487 acres of irrigated land and 22,172 acres of dry lands making the total irrigated area about 38 percent of total cultivated area. Lewis Rice states that there were in all 28 anecuts across the Cauvery and its various tributaries like Hemavathi, Shimsha, Suvarnavathi, Lakshmanatirtha and Nugu. According to Wilks, out of the total cultivated area of 30,12,397 acres in Mysore, 8,13,491 were irrigated by 1803–04. Sadly, in modern day Karnataka, large areas of the northern part of the state remain dry due to a virtually non-existent irrigation system. Our administrators would do well to take a leaf out of Tipu's book.

Trade and Commerce

To strengthen his innovative idea of state capitalism in the form of the banking system, Tipu launched the state control of trade, commerce and industries. Mysore was rich in commercial crops and items such as silk, sandalwood, pepper, cardamom, coconut, betel leaves, horticulture, muslin, ivory and so on, which were greatly in demand in the Western market. Tipu was keen that the trade in these commodities should not fall into foreign hands. Therefore, the state itself became the greatest exporter and importer of goods, which were sent out and brought in by the Sultan's own fleet of merchant ships. Government shops were opened at Jeddah, Muscat, and Karachi to provide a market for Mysorean articles. The hold of private bankers, moneylenders and middlemen was vastly reduced.

Mysore, strategically situated as it was with a good harbour, produced valuable, commercial commodities and also traded in elephants, which were in great demand abroad and also in other parts of India. The Mysore elephant was a brand in itself, just like Mysore silk. Shahar Ganjam, as Tipu renamed Srirangapatna, became a teeming and prosperous commercial hub. Tipu developed commercial relations with a number of foreign kingdoms: the Ottoman Empire, China, Muscat, Pegu, Armenia, Jeddah, Ormuz and Basra but more important than these commercial contacts were Tipu's political objectives.

Today, Karnataka prides itself as a leading producer of silk and in fact the name Mysore silk is synonymous with the state's heritage. This very silk industry of Karnataka owes its origin to Tipu. Efforts were also made to establish pearl fisheries in the Malabar by inviting divers from Muscat. The Chinese were invited to help in the production of fine-quality sugar.

The various initiatives taken by the Sultan led to the specialisation and localisation of agriculture and industry. From Buchanan's accounts, we can deduce that pockets emerged within the kingdom, specialising in particular agricultural or industrial goods and products. For example, in agriculture, Dakshina Kannada and Uttara Kannada were regions that grew pepper, paddy, coconut, cashew, arecanut; paddy and cardamom in Coorg; paddy and arecanut in Chickmagalur and Shimoga; coconut and tobacco in Hassan; tamarind and oil seeds in Kolar; oil seeds, coconut, vegetables, indigo, janupa and fruits in salubrious Bangalore; coconut, arecanut, turmeric and tamarind in Tumkur; sugarcane, paddy, vegetables and fruits in the fertile tracts of Mysore and Mandya; tamarind in Chitradurga; cotton and tamarind in Bellary, Dharwad and Raichur and so on. Similarly, on the industrial front, we observe the formation of areas of excellence within the kingdom. Dakshina Kannada and Uttara Kannada excelled in ship-building and salt; iron and steel in Mysore; armaments, rope-making, sugar and jaggery in Mandya armaments, weaving, dyeing, oil-pressing, indigo, sack-weaving, iron and steel and drugs in Bangalore; iron and steel in Tumkur; blankets, iron and steel and soap in Chitradurga; blankets and cotton-spinning in Bellary, Raichur, Dharwad and Bijapur.

Praxy Fernandes states:

> The bewildering variety of manufacturing enterprises he set up within the space of a few years was truly astonishing - factories for the manufacture of watches, cutlery, hour glasses, scissors, scientific instruments, factories for production of war weapons, guns, musket, carbines and rockets, foundries for casting cannon, a gunpowder factory, a paper mill and glassware units. Hundreds of foreign technicians were brought in; Frenchmen, Germans, Turks, Arabs, Chinese; craftsmen, gunsmiths, watch makers, cutlers bringing with them their technical know-how and the vision of a modern world. No other sovereign in Indian history had given such an impetus to industrial production.

Tipu built a navy both for commerce and war. In 1793, he ordered 100 ships to be built entirely with indigenous material. He paid attention to the manufacture of arms and ammunition. The factory at Srirangapatna converted iron into steel, and manufactured armaments. He named his iron-works Taramandals. These were at Srirangapatna, Bangalore, Chitradurga and Bidnaur.

Arts and Crafts

Not just trade and commerce, but also arts and crafts attracted Tippu's attention for state control as well. He helped the development of sericulture. Weavers also received much patronage. Buchanan describes the life and activities of these weavers or Pattegaras:

> The Puttuegars or silk weavers, make cloth of very rich and strong fabric. The patterns for the first five kinds of dresses are similar to each other; but are very much varied by the different colours

employed and the different figures woven in the cloth; for they rarely consist of plain work. Each pattern has an appropriate name, and for the common sale, is wrought of three different degrees of fineness. If any person chooses to commission them, whatever parts of the pattern he likes may be wrought in gold thread...the fabric of the sixth kind of dress is also strong and rich: but the figures resemble those in the shawls of Cashemire. The turbans are made of a thin fabric of figured patterns, the first three kinds of dresses of silk and cotton. They also made Sada Putaynshina, or thin white muslins with silk borders. These are either plain, or dotted in the loom with silk or cotton thread; and are frequently ornamented with gold and silver. This is an elegant manufacture and is fitted for the first three kinds of dresses. Plain green muslin with silk borders for the first three kinds of dresses is also made by the Puttuegars; but not of so fine a quality as that made by the Devangas...the same may be said of the coloured striped muslin with silk borders called Dutari Huvina, which is used also entirely for female dresses and is wrought of various patterns...

The Puttuegars give their yellow silk to the Niligaru, who dye it with indigo. It is then washed by the Puttuegars in the infusion of tamarinds, and afterwards is of a fine green colour which, if it be dried in the shade, is tolerably well fixed...when the goods are in much demand, it is customary for the merchants to advance one half or even the whole of the price of the goods which he commissions; but when the demand is small the manufacturers borrow money from the bankers at 2 percent a month and make goods, which they sell to merchants of the place...the master weavers keep from two to five servants, who are paid by the piece. Workmen that are employed on cotton cloths with silk borders make daily about a Fanam.* It is not usual for weavers of any kind in this country, except those of the Whalliaru caste to employ part of their time in agriculture. The Cutteries are more affluent than the Puttegars, and these again are more wealthy than any other kind of weavers.

---

* This was the new currency Tipu introduced in place of Canteroi Pagodas and Varahas.

Horticulture

Tipu was so fond of horticulture and gardening that all his correspondence with foreign dignitaries would invariably carry a request for new varieties of seeds and plants. The beautiful Lal Bagh gardens at Bangalore are a result of his tireless efforts. This enthralling 40-acre garden was established by Haidar Ali and it was Tipu Sultan who added the touch of grandeur to the garden, importing shrubs from places, like Turkey, Mauritius, Persia and France. Interestingly, in the midst of one of the battles, Tipu wrote this letter to the killedar of Srirangapatna, Syed Muhammad on 27 September 1786:

> Burhanudeen and Kustury Runga, who were sent to Bengal, for the purpose of securing silk worms are now on their return by way of Sedhout. On their arrival you must ascertain from them the proper situation in which to keep the aforesaid worms, and provide accordingly. You must, moreover supply for their food the wood or wild mulberry trees, which were formerly ordered to be planted for the purpose. The number of silk worms from Bengal must likewise be distinctly reported to us. We desire, also, to know, in what kind of place it is recommended to keep them, and what means are to be pursued for multiplying them. There is a vacant spot of ground behind the old palace, lately used as a Toshehkhaneh…prepare a place somewhere near that situation, for the reception of the worms.

William Kirkpatrick, who hated Tipu from the depths of his heart, could not hide his appreciation for the man as he sat editing some of Tipu's selected letters:

> When the peculiar circumstances under which the foregoing letter was written, are adverted to, it will, no doubt, be allowed to furnish a striking proof, of both the coolness and the activity of the Sultan's mind. He was at the date of it, not only deliberating on the measure to be pursued with respect to Shanoor in planning the future operations of the war on which he was engaged; and in providing for the safety of Burhanudeen's army; but he was in fact, on the eve of a general engagement with the Mahrattas. Yet all these important and urgent considerations united, were not capable of diverting his attention from any of the minor objects of his interest. Thus in the bustle of the camp, and in the face of

an enemy, he could find leisure, and was sufficiently composed, to meditate on the rearing of silk worms!

Tipu gave away wasteland free of rent for cultivation. The existing forced labour was done away with. To discourage needless litigation, he encouraged villagers to settle disputes among themselves. In fact, he hit upon a novel way to dispense justice. For various offences committed by people, he fixed proportionate punishment not in the form of fines or imprisonment, but of making them plant trees, water them, and bring them up to a particular height.

Social Reforms

Tipu realised that liquor ruined millions of families all over the kingdom. He put his foot down on the practice and declared total prohibition in Mysore, even discouraging the use of tobacco. This is amply displayed in his memorandum to Mir Sadik in 1787:

> ...This is a matter in which we must be undeterred and undaunted by financial considerations. Total prohibition is very near to my heart. It is not a question of religion alone. We must think of the economic well-being and the moral height of our people and the need to build the character of our youth. I appreciate your concern for immediate financial loss but should we not look ahead? Is the gain to our treasury to be rated higher than the health and morality of our people?...

He put an end to the purchase and sale of abandoned girls and children. He checked lavish expenditure on the celebrations of weddings. His sense of justice could be guessed by the fact that he punished his eldest son, Fateh Haider, for taking vegetables without the permission of the owner.

Tipu thought of setting up a university at Srirangapatna, naming it Jami-al-Umur. He started Mysore's first newspaper, *Fauji Akhbar*. He was himself an author, and knew, besides Urdu, Persian and Arabic, also Kannada, Marathi, English and French. More than forty-five books were written during his time. His library consisted of over 2,000 manuscripts. Many compilations were created during his reign, and some of them are also credited to him. The *Register of Tipu's Dreams* gives an insight into his mind and the way it worked. It was discovered by Colonel William

Kirkpatrick amongst other secret documents in an escritoire found in the palace of Srirangapatna. Historian Sheikh Ali says that this register was

> written by Tipu's own hand and they are 38 in number. They are valuable for knowing the inner working of Tipu's mind towards the English....dreams...help us to know the psychology of the man...His passion to defeat the English haunted him as much in sleep as when he was awake. Most of his dreams relate his success over the English.

Beatson (as quoted by Hayavadana Rao) has similar thoughts about the dreams of Tipu, when he states

> of some of them it appears, that (war) and conquest and the destruction of the Caufirs were subjects of his sleeping and that of his waking thoughts. ...Habbibulloh, one of the most confidential of the Sultan's servants was present at the time it was discovered. He knew that there was such a Book of the Sultan's composition, but had never seen it, as the Sultan always manifested a peculiar anxiety to conceal it from the view of any who happened to approach while he was reading or writing in it.

Interestingly many of these legendary dreams were also 'divine dictates' to pull down a certain temple here or there, and these Tipu dutifully acted upon. In a letter to his father Munro writes about Tipu's diligence:

> He had an active mind which never suffered him to be idle...he wrote many hours every day, either a journal of orders issued by himself, and of reports received by spies, vakeels or commanders of detatchments; or memorandums respecting intending promotions, embassies, repairs of forts, marriages of his principal officers... Besides this much of his time was consumed in signing papers for he not only signed all public acts, but likewise the innumerable letters and orders which were continually passing from the different officers to all parts of the empire.

A 1786 edict issued by him to his subjects and officials brings out the vision of the legendary Sultan more clearly:

> No man shall be punished save in accordance with the law. The law of immemorial custom and as enshrined in our traditions shall

be honoured by us. So that people know the extent and rigour of the law as also their rights, duties, obligations and responsibilities, we have decided that codification of law shall be undertaken... accordingly we have established a committee of ministers under Prime Minister Purnaiya.

These edicts and messages bear an almost Ashokan or Akbar-like resemblance—the manner of codification of laws and the means adopted to communicate to his masses.

Foreign Policy

Tipu was perhaps the first Indian ruler to apply western techniques in governance. Being well-read and international in his outlook, he was fired by the nascent concepts of democracy and nation-state that had gripped France and America and the successes they charted through their revolutions, freeing their people from the shackles of colonialism and the scourge of medieval feudalism.

He was among the few rulers of his times who actually had foreign affairs on his agenda. Surrounded by a group of kings and contemporaries who couldn't see beyond their own backyards, Tipu looked at building transnational borders. In fact, the cornerstone of his foreign policy was a letter addressed to him by Haidar and it remained his guiding principle on the matter:[*]

> My son, I leave you an Empire which I have not received from my ancestors. A sceptre acquired by violence is always fragile... you have nothing to fear as regards the internal affairs of your State; but it is necessary to carry your vision very far. India, since the death of Aurangzeb, has lost her rank among the Empires of Asia. This fair land is parcelled out into a multitude of sects, who have lost their love of their country. The Hindus softened by their pacific maxims are little able to defend their country, which has become a prey to the strangers. The Mussalmans are more united and more enterprising than the feeble Hindus. It is to them should belong the glory of saving Hindustan. My son, combine all your efforts to make the Koran triumph. The greatest obstacle you have to conquer is the jealousy of the Europeans. The English are today

---

[*] Taken from Diwakar et al.'s 1968 book, *Karnataka through the Ages*.

all-powerful in India. It is necessary to weaken them by war. The resources of Hindustan do not suffice to expel them from the lands they have invaded; put the nations of Europe one against another. It is by the aid of the French that you could conquer the British armies, which are better trained than the Indians'. The Europeans have surer tactics; always use against them their own weapons... remember above all that valour can elevate us to a throne but it sufficeth not to preserve an Empire. While we may seize a crown owing to the timidity of the people, it can escape us if we do not make haste to entrust it to their love. If God allowed me a longer career, you need only have enjoyed the success of my enterprises. But I leave you for achieving them rich provinces, a population of 12 million souls, troops, treasuries and immense resources. I need not awaken your courage. I have seen you often fight my side, and you shall be the inheritor of my glory.

Tipu's external relations were aimed at seeking the support of foreign powers for concerted action against the English. His embassies to distant places like Paris and Constantinople, his numerous letters to France and Turkey, his invitation to Zaman Shah of Afghanistan to rescue the Mughals from the British and his correspondence with Napoleon, were also focused on his confrontation with the English. He sheltered a number of Frenchmen driven out of Pondicherry. Agents of the French revolutionary government were entertained and even allowed to preach their doctrines of Independence and the Revolution openly in Mysore. A Jacobin club was established in Srirangapatna where the French flag was hoisted. Even if such contacts did not bear good political results, he would at least have the satisfaction of promoting the trade and commerce of his country.

THE SWORD OF TIPU SULTAN

General Baird was so consumed with his hatred for Tipu that he wanted to establish his supremacy over everything that belonged to the Sultan. As if mortally hurting him and destroying his township were not enough, Baird's eyes fell on the sword of the Sultan, which had become as famous as its owner and personified valour and bravery.

The sword was found in the bedroom after the storming of Srirangapatna on 4 May 1799 and presented by Major General Harris to General Baird as a token of the army's high opinion of his courage and conduct in the assault which he commanded and in which Tipu Sultan was slain.

The sword is described by the auctioneers as a single-edged weapon with a 91-cm-long blade and an impressive hilt inlaid with Arabic inscriptions. The back edge of the blade bears a Perso-Arabic inscription, 'Sword of the Ruler'. The wooden scabbard, covered in green velvet, has mounts in part decorated with Tipu's favoured tiger-stripe design. James Forbes, quoted in Hayavadana Rao, writes:

> Most of the cannon cast during the reign of Tippu were ornamented with the representation of a tiger devouring a European...he adopted as the emblem of the state...the figure of the royal tiger, whose head and stripes constituted the chief ornaments of his throne and of almost every article which belonged to him.

Tipu's sword was among a number of priceless artefacts looted by British forces at the time and taken back to the United Kingdom. Among the other treasures was a magnificent tiger's head adorned in gold leaf, which was part of Tipu's throne, as well as a jewelled bird of paradise. Both are now part of the Queen's Royal Collection and are stored at Windsor Castle outside London.

In fact, the identification of Tipu with a tiger has much to do with his adoption of the tiger motif as a personal emblem, in several styles and forms. The most obvious examples include the distinctive stylised tiger stripe, commonly referred to as *babri*, from *babr*, (meaning tiger); and the decorative tiger head. Examples of the *babri* motif can still be seen on the inner walls of the Gumbaz mausoleum where there is a complete adornment of yellow walls with red stripes.

The tiger head, on the other hand, is represented in two separate calligraphic representations. The first monogram or cypher is a square design, known as *tughra*, shaped like a tiger's head, and the seal is made up of the name 'Tippu Sultan'. The 'Musical Tiger' was a favourite toy in Tipu's court. It was shipped to London and kept at the India Office Library and now adorns the Albert Memorial Hall. In his memoir *The Library of the India Office*, the assistant librarian A.J. Arberry mentions:

> But we almost forgot our old friend the tiger. Who has not seen, and what is more, heard him at the old India House, and who having suffered under his unearthly sounds, can ever dismiss him

from his memory? It seems that this horrid creature—we mean of course the figure representing it—was found among the treasures of Tipu Sultan, when he fell at the siege of Seringapatam. It was a toy of this great Sultan, representing a tiger preying on the body of an English officer, and so constructed that by turning a handle, the animal's growls mingled with the shrieks of his dying victim. These shrieks and growls were the constant plague of the students busy at work in the Library of the old India House when the Leadenhall Street public unremittingly, it appears, were bent on keeping up the performance of this barbarous machine…luckily he is now removed from the Library; but what is also lucky, a kind of fate has deprived him of his handle, and stopped up, we are happy to think, some of his internal organs; or as an ignorant visitor would say, he is out of repair; and we do sincerely hope that he will remain so, to be seen and to be admired, if necessary, but to be heard no more.

Shama Rao describes this toy as follows:

In a room was found a curious mechanism made of wood representing a royal tiger in life in the act of devouring a prostrate man and within the body of the animal was a row of keys of natural notes acted upon by the rotation of certain barrels in the manner of a hand organ and which produced sounds intended to resemble the cries of a person in distress, intermixed with the roar of a tiger.

The second example is far more ornate and is based upon a style of Arabic calligraphy known as *khatt mukabil* or *khatt ma-kus*. In this case, the monogram of Tipu is the calligraphic merging of the two words Bismillah, and Muhammed. 'Bismillah' is the name of Allah and is derived from the invocatory verse in the Quran: Bismillah-ir-Rahman-nir-Rahim ('In the name of Allah, the Beneficent, the Merciful'); while the name of the Prophet Muhammed is written in the *khatt mukabil* style. To the untrained eye, the words are not readily apparent, overlaid as they are with calligraphic curves, scrolls, decorative lines, ascenders and descenders. The calligraphic tiger motif also includes the epithet *asad allah ul-ghalib* ('the victorious lion of God'); and examples of its use can be found on a banner of Tipu Sultan, as well as on some of his military arms and armaments.

Tipu had adopted the figure of the royal tiger as the emblem of the Sultanate. The symbolism and imagery of the tiger seemed omnipresent. The emblem, the flags, the chief ornaments of his throne and almost every article that belonged to him seemed to bear tiger stripes! His throne was of considerable beauty and magnificence. The support was a wooden tiger as large as life, covered with gold. His head and forelegs appeared in front and under the throne which was placed across his back. It was an octagonal frame, about eight feet by five, surrounded by a low railing which had ten small golden tiger heads. The ascent to the throne was by a small flight of silver steps on either side. From the centre of the throne arose a gilded iron pillar about seven feet high, surmounted by a canopy tastefully decorated with pearl strings. The wooden throne was covered with a thin sheet of pure gold which had on it Arabic verses and tiger stripes inscribed. The statue of a 'huma' bird, considered a good omen, was placed on top of the canopy and seemed to represent unbounded zeal and a flight of courage. It was made of gold and covered with precious diamonds, rubies and emeralds.

Construction and Architecture

Tipu was also a great builder. Beatson quotes an English officer of the besieging army in 1792 who describes the island fortress of Tipu Sultan thus: 'this insulated metropolis must have been the richest, the most convenient and beautiful spot possessed in the present age by any native prince in India'.

About Tipu's fort in Srirangapatna, Major Dirom writes:

> The fort and outworks occupy about a mile of the west end of the island, and the Lal Bagh about the same portion of the east end. The whole space between the fort and the Lal Bagh except a small enclosure, called Daulat Bagh on the north bank near the fort, was filled before the war, with houses had formed an extensive suburb of which the village of Ganjam is the only remaining fort.

Srirangapatna also houses a beautiful mosque with two tall, graceful minarets, which was constructed in 1784 and named as the Masjid-e-Ala. Haidar Ali built the Lal Mahal near the Ranganatha Swamy temple. Monsieur De La Tour, who worked for Haidar, writes that it was a simple yet impressive structure 'with an open balcony or durbar hall overlooking the parade ground, and with another hall opening on to the garden behind.' He goes on to describe the Lal Mahal as follows:

> His apartments are commonly covered with white muslin spread upon the most superb Persian carpets...chandeliers of exquisite workmanship, ornamental with festoons of flowers of the utmost lightness and delicacy.

Tipu had renovated the palace and his garden 'contained many cypresses and fountains and that the trees were grafted and bore many kinds of fruits...'

Lord Valentia wrote about the palace:

> The Loll Mahal or private residence of Tippu Sultan (which was inside the fort, opposite to the Watergate and between two Hindu temples) consists of but one square, three sides of which are divided into two storeys, with a verandah of painted wood in front. Behind were many small rooms used by him as warehouses. The fourth consists of a single room, the same height as the rest of the building. This was the Darbar...where he sat or wrote and received ministers.

The palace was mercilessly pulled down by the British after the fall of Srirangapatna. So was the Lal Bagh palace, which was pulled down and its material used in the construction of St. Stephen's Church and the Holy Trinity Church at Ootacamund.

One of the few remaining structures of Tipu's time in Srirangapatna today is the Daria Daulat Bagh, near the fort. It was his summer palace and is surrounded by a vast, well-maintained garden. The wooden edifice is a fine example of Saracenic architecture and has beautiful paintings and murals depicting the different battles fought by Haidar and Tipu. Haidar started the construction of the Daria Daulat in 1778 and Tipu completed it in 1789.

Tipu's mortal remains are housed in the Gumbaz—an impressive square mausoleum with beautiful ivory-inlaid doors and black marble pillars. His remains were laid to rest beside those of his parents, Haidar and Fatima Begum. On one of the doors is a Persian verse which says: 'Tipu Sultan suddenly attained martyrdom, He sacrificed his life in the way of God.'

SOCIETY IN THE EIGHTEENTH CENTURY

The feudal system that existed in Mysore, as elsewhere in India, had propped up its significant communities and castes, all of which wielded influence and power over the other subservient classes. The biggest landlords happened to be the Gowdas or Patels of the village together with the Shanbhogues, all drawn from the Vokkaliga, Lingayat and Brahmin communities. The agricultural reforms initiated during the time of Haidar and Tipu contributed to the rise of a class of proprietor peasants—small and middle in size—who held lands not by the whims and wishes of the feudal overlords but rightfully sanctioned by the state. Patels and Shanbhogues played a pivotal role in exacting the revenues from the peasants. This was modified through Tipu's land revenue regulations, where the peasant directly negotiated the revenue amount payable as a function of the quantity of seeds sown. Still, it was the Shanbhogue who indulged in activities such as evaluating the quantity and type of seed sown, witnessing the threshing and winnowing operations post harvest and so on. The Patel then transferred the revenues of the village to the Paraputti or Hobli level administrator.

Interestingly, society in Mysore was divided into the guilds of Right Hand and Left Hand (Balagai and Edagai jaatis) on the basis of commodity production and its distribution. Speaking about it at length, Buchanan states:

> In this country the division of people into what are called the left and right hand sides, or Eddagai and Ballagai is productive of more considerable effects than any that I have seen in India, although among the Hindus is generally known...the tribes or castes comprehended in the Eddagai or left hand side are nine:
>
> 1. Panchala comprehending the Cubbinadava or blacksmiths, the Badiga carpenters, Cunsuguru coppersmiths, Cul'badiga masons, Axala gold and silver smiths.
> 2. Bheri Chitty, merchants who pretend to be of Vysya cast.
> 3. Devanga, a class of weavers.
> 4. Heganigaru, oil makers, who use two oxen in their mills.
> 5. Gollur or Golwanlu, who transport money.
> 6. Palwanlu cultivators who are not of Karnata origin
> 7. Palawanlu.

8. Baydaru, hunters.
9. Madigaru, tanners or shoemakers. The Panchala command the whole party.

The castes forming the Ballagai or right hand side are eighteen in number.

1. Banijigaru, who are of many trades, as well as many religions. The two most conspicuous divisions are Panchum Banijigaru, who are traders and wear the Linga and the Teliga Banajigaru, who worship Vishnu.
2. Wocligaru, cultivators of the Sudra cast and of Karnata extraction.
3. Jotiphana, oil makers who use one bullock in the mill.
4. Rungaru, calico painters and tailors.
5. Ladaru, a kind of Musulman traders, who are followed by all the artifices of the same religion.
6. Gujerati, merchants of Guzerat.
7. Jainaru, the worshippers of the Jain.
8. Curubaru, shepherds, blanket weavers and cultivators.
9. Cumbaru, potters.
10. Agasaru, washermen.
11. Besta, palankeen bearers.
12. Padma Shalayvaru, a kind of weavers.
13. Naindaru barbers.
14. Uparu, persons who dig tanks and build rough walls.
15. Chitragaru, painters.
16. Gollaru, keepers of cows and buffaloes.
17. Whalliaru, the people called Parriars at Madras…the Panchum Banajigaru are the leaders of this division.

The different castes of which each division is composed, are not united by any common tie of religion, occupation or kindred; it seems therefore to be merely a struggle for certain honorary distinctions…I must observe, that these lists differ in some respects, from a valuable account of the right and left hand sides, which Colonel Close was so obliging as to communicate. The difference, I suppose, arises partly from his having taken them at Bangalore. Mine I received at Seringapatam by means of an interpreter from the Karnataca language; and have found that in different places though at no great distance, there are considerable variations in the customs of the tribes...

The right hand side pretend that they have exclusive privilege to using 12 pillars in the pandal, or shed, under which their marriage ceremonies are performed; and that their adversaries, in their possessions, have no right to ride on horseback, nor to carry a flag painted with the figure of Hanumantha. The left hand side pretend that all these privileges are confined to them by grant of Kali on the copper plate; and that they are of the highest rank, having been placed by the goddess on her left hand, which in India is the place of honour.

In every part of India with which I am acquainted, wherever there is a considerable number of any one caste or tribe, it is usual to have a headman, whose office is generally hereditary. His powers are various in different sects and places; but he is commonly intrusted with the authority of punishing all transgressions against the rules of the caste...these hereditary chiefs also, assisted by their council, frequently decide civil causes, or disputes among their tribe; or when the business is too intricate or difficult, it is generally referred to the hereditary chief of the ruling tribe or the side of the division to which the parties belong. In this case, he assembles the most respectable men of the division, and settles the dispute; and the advice of these persons is commonly sufficient to make both parties acquiesce in the decision; for everyone would shun a man who could be so unreasonable as to refute compliance. These courts have no legal jurisdiction; but their influence is great, and many of the ablest Amildars support their decisions by the authority of the government.

With such stratification of society, inter-guild and inter-caste conflicts and assertions were common-place. Buchanan describes the manner in which cities, like Bangalore and also other towns of the kingdom, were partitioned into pockets of inhabitants belonging to these guilds and castes. On both sides were the 'lowest of the castes'. The Madigas of the left hand side and the Holeyas/Whalliaru of the right hand side were the most oppressed lot. Unlike other castes, they were denied the possession of arms. Even the so-called soothing balm of Islam under the rule of Haidar and Tipu made little difference to their lives. In the times of the Sultanat-e-Khudadad, Dalits were denied permission to serve as Kandachar militia. The army was largely drawn from the Beda, Kuruba, Idiga, Vokkaliga and Lingayat castes along with the Voddas, Bovis and Lambanies. Writing about Tipu's response to this stratification of society, Wilks states:

> ...on one of these occasions, the Sultan applied his profound research and experience to trace the origin of these sects, and to devise the means of preventing future riots. To the Parias (Holeyas) he had already given the new name Sameree, Samaritans, because as he affirmed, they and their ancient Samaritans were equally distinguished by skill in magic. The Chucklers (Madigas) were Chermdoz, the common Persian designation of their chief occupation. 'In the language of the country', he adds, 'they are called Yere Kai and Bul Kai, that is right and left hand, because these men being the grooms and foragers of the horsemen of Islam, may be considered as their right and left hands, with reference to the important services which they perform'...

LOOKING BACK: SECTION 3

THE CONTROVERSIAL SULTAN

Tipu: Secular or Not?

It is pertinent to mention that unlike most other historical characters, Tipu Sultan and certain aspects of his life continue to ruffle feathers to this day. In September 2006, the Karnataka Minister of Higher Education Mr Shankaramurthy made some vague comments about Tipu Sultan having been 'anti-Kannada', saying that he had ensured the obliteration of Kannada by the imposition and adoption of Persian as the court language. This was enough to send the so-called secularist brigade into a frenzy. Chat shows on television, articles in newspapers and general public debate was diverted from the minister's irrelevant comment to the larger issue of how Tipu was actually one of the most secular and progressive ruler of his times. Both sides hardened their stands and what followed was a free-for-all washing of dirty linen in public by supposed intellectuals and thinkers. Voices of reason and rationalism usually tend to get subsumed by this kind of high-decibel frenzy, which anyway aims to cultivate and nurture strategic vote banks.

Tipu's secularism, or lack thereof, is a subject of great interest, and so merits much focus in this volume. In India, secularism is often little more than the branding of another as communal. We too resort to this game of vivisecting history and categorising the heroes and heroines of the past into air-tight compartments of 'secular' and 'communal', forgetting most often that they were also human beings after all, and, like any of us, were given to their moments of weakness and greatness alike. Two diametrically opposite schools of thought dominate the current scene of Indian historical research and debate. At one extreme we have the so-called 'left-liberal' and 'rational' historians for whom history is but class struggle. Religion and related matters do not hold any significance for them. Their notion of secularism extends to a level where they tend to over-simplify and at times undermine a lot of things that have been revered over the centuries. Completely distinct from this approach is that of the supposed 'right-wing', 'nationalist' historians who would see everything through the lens of religion and judge people thereby. The slanging match between these two groups continues as each tries to portray his version as the 'truth'. Even with respect to Tipu, both sides have arguments and counter-arguments to buttress their claims.

The notion of the rationalists has been that Tipu was a tolerant ruler with deep respect for other religions. There are about thirty letters written in Kannada by Tipu, addressed to the Shankaracharya Swamiji of Sringeri temple, which were found in 1916 by R. Narasimhachar, Director of Archaeology in Mysore. Normally, all Tipu's letters to others would begin with his own name at the top, but these letters mention the name of the Swamiji at the top, with all his titles and Tipu's name is at the bottom without any title. These letters throw a flood of light on his religious policy and seem to clearly establish the secular character of his rule. Tipu wrote to the Swami thus:

> You are the Jagat Guru. You are always performing penance in order that the whole world may prosper and that the people may be happy. Please pray to God for the increase of our prosperity. In whatever country holy personages like yourself may reside, that country will flourish with good showers and crops...

In 1791, during the Third Mysore War, the invading Maratha army under Parsurama Bhau caused a lot of damage to Sringeri—they plundered the temple property and even displaced the image of the Goddess Sharada Devi. The Swamiji left the place and informed Tipu about the Maratha raid, seeking his help to consecrate the image of the Goddess. Tipu responded immediately with funds to reinstall the image. After the idol was installed, Tipu received the *prasada* and shawls, sending in return cloth and ornaments for the Goddess and a pair of shawls for the Swamiji, besides two palanquins—one for the Goddess and the other for Swamiji.

To the Lakshmikantha temple at Kalale in Nanjungud taluk, he gave four silver cups, a silver plate and a silver spittoon. To the Narayanswamy temple at Melkote, he presented gold and silver vessels, besides an elephant and a few jewels. The Srikanteswara temple at Nanjungud was presented with a jewelled cup and some precious stones. To the Nanjundeswara temple in Nanjungud, he gave a greenish *linga*. The Ranganatha temple at Srirangapatana was gifted seven silver cups and a silver camphor burner. This temple was barely a stone's throw from his palace; and the temple of Lord Venkateswara was adjacent to his palace at Bangalore.

Those opposed to the Sultan, however, claim that he made these gestures *after* the Third Anglo Mysore War, when he had been completely routed and even lost his sons to the British. Newly insecure, perhaps he felt the need to mollify the Hindu populace. This was what turned him towards spirituality and the support and blessings of figures like the Shankaracharya. This magnanimity had been conspicuous by its absence in the first half of his tenure, when he was heaping victories over victories, principalities over principalities. The other point of view is that in his zeal to overrun and destroy the Mysore Pradhans who belonged to the Vaishnavite Iyengar sect, Tipu decimated the Ramanujacharya Muth revered by the Iyengars. Were all these gifts to the Shankaracharya therefore a ploy to further divide the already-divided Hindu society by favouring one of the sub-sects and destroying their arch rivals? Shaiva-Vaishnava rivalries have long segmented traditional Hindu society. This book has already discussed similar clashes between the two Hindu sub-sects during the reign of Chikkadevaraja Wodeyar and the king's attempt to force the philosophy of Vaishnavism on all his officers. Keeping these societal divisions in mind, were Tipu's advisers (including Purnaiya) guiding him through a well-planned strategy? There are no definitive answers.

Tipu also gave full freedom for the uninterrupted continuation of the traditional festivals of the kingdom—the Dasara at Mysore and the Karaga at Bangalore. Shama Rao records the writing of an English prisoner–of–war (sadly, without naming him) about the annual Dasara festivities as he saw them under Khasa Chamaraja Wodeyar in 1783.

This Annual Gentoo festival commenced this evening (23rd September 1783) which was continued according to custom for nine days. The King of Mysore made his appearance in a verandah in front of the palace at about 7 o' Clock. It is only on the occasion of this anniversary that he is visible to his nominal subjects. This young prince in whose name Haidar Ali's family assumes the title of Regent, carry on the administration of Government, is allowed for himself and his family an annual pension. He is treated with all those marks of homage that are paid to crowned heads. In his names proclamation is made of war or of peace and the trophies of victory are laid at his feet. Like kings too, he has his guards. But these are appointed and commanded by the usurper of his Throne. Yet people pay good reverence unto the blood of their ancient kings and he is a powerful prince of the peninsula of Hindustan, that it is thought by Haidar Ali not to cut off the hereditary Prince of Mysore but adorn him with the pageantry of a crown.

The spacious Palace in which the young king of Mysore resides stands in a large square in the very centre of Seringapatam in an angle of which our prison was also situated. Hence we had an opportunity of enjoying the sight of Dasara. The curtains with which the gallery was hung being drawn up discovered the king seated on a throne, with numerous attendants on both sides, some of whom fanned him while others scattered perfume on his long, black hair. The verandah was decorated with the finest hangings. The Rajah was adorned with resplendent precious stones among which a diamond of immense size and value shone with distinguished lustre. On an extended square along the front of the Palace, musicians, balladeers and species of gladiators entertained the Rajah with his train in the gallery and the multitude that filled the square with music, dance, tumbling, wrestling, mockery and other diversion. The ladies of His Highness' harem and European prisoners were present and enjoyed it through lattice windows. The king sat motionless for hours, rose up and when he was about to retire advancing to the edge of the gallery showed himself to the people who honoured him with marks of most profound and superstitious veneration. The curtains dropped and His Highness retired to the inner parts of his Palace.

But it must be stated that this very Tipu adopted a slightly different posture in his dealings outside the kingdom of Mysore. Many of his invasions would culminate in forced conversions to Islam—the most pronounced being the ones during his conquest of Malabar. The records speak of similar atrocities in Coorg and Kerala. Let us go over some of these accounts from Coorg and Malabar or present-day Kerala.

It is said that on one occasion, he forcibly converted over 10,000 Hindus in Coorg to Islam. On another occasion, he captured and converted to Islam more than 1,000 Hindu Coorgis before imprisoning them in the Srirangapatna fortress. In the confusion and anarchy prevailing in Srirangapatna during the last war of Tipu Sultan against the British, all the Coorgi prisoners escaped and became Hindus again upon reaching their native kingdom. Dhondoji Wagh, a commander in Haidar's and Tipu's army who was to play a very decisive role later in the history of Mysore, was imprisoned by Tipu, who forcibly changed his name to Sheikh Ahmed and then to Mallik Jehan Khan on Wagh's refusal to accept Islam. On the day of the capture of Srirangapatna, he was found chained to the prison wall and released by a British soldier. He was apparently hysterical with joy on hearing news of the Sultan's death. Stories like these make it even harder to decide which 'compartment' to place our hero in.

Mangalore was a rich and prosperous belt with most of its residents owning vast paddy fields and estates in the mountains, and some of them controlled the diamond and gold mines. Mangalore was also seen by the Portuguese as a vital base from which to safeguard their position in Goa against the Marathas and the Mughals. Haidar's attack on Mangalore following his campaign at Keladi in 1763 left a trail of disaster. Only 204 of the 15,675 Christians of the region captured by Haidar survived; the rest were either killed or converted to Islam.

After the siege of Mangalore, which ended in victory for Tipu's forces in the Second Anglo-Mysore War, the Mangalorean Christian inhabitants were subject to much suffering, with over 5,600 of them killed on a single day. Kirkpatrick's collection of letters has an account of the campaign against the Christians of Mangalore, and details the preparations made by the Mysore army.

> We instantly directed the Divan of the Havur Kutchery to prepare a list of houses occupied by Christians, taking care not to omit a single habitation. After a detailed plan was made, we stationed an officer and soldiers in every place inhabited by Christians, signifying to them that at certain time they would receive orders that they

would carry out in full effect.... On the morning of a specific day, (Ash Wednesday Feb 24, 1784) at the hour of Morning Prayer, let all Christians be made prisoner and dispatched to our presence. Accordingly all orders were everywhere opened at the same moment and at the same hour, namely that of the Morning Prayer.

The churches that existed in Mangalore were destroyed. As Buchanan mentions, '...in Tuluva, the Christians had twenty-seven churches all beautifully carved with statues depicting various saints. Every one was razed to the ground.' The church of Nossa Senhora de Rosario Milagres at Mangalore, Fr Miranda's Seminary at Monte Mariano, church of Jesu Marie Jose at Omzoor, the chapel at Bolar and the church of Merces at Ullal, Imaculata Conceiciao at Mulki, San Jose at Perar, Nossa Senhora dos Remedios at Kirem, Sao Lawrence at Karkal, Rosario at Barkur and many others were destroyed.

Following this round-up, about 60,000 Christians were supposedly taken captive and packed off to Srirangapatna in the most inhuman way. They were asked to traverse the rocky terrain of the Western Ghats by foot to reach the prisons of Srirangapatna—about 210 miles away. Many of them, almost 20,000, died of sheer exhaustion on the way. Those who reached Srirangapatna were tortured in the prisons and freed only if they embraced Islam. The women were all married to Muslim men of the nobility or reached the royal harem as pleasure objects. An English prisoner of war relates the situation in the Srirangapatna prison thus:

> Two risalas were sent daily to Srirangapatna to select girls that they could take as prizes to join their harems. Often, when they seized the girls, their young men would offer resistance .... The officers would capture the men and administer five hundred strokes with whips and canes, from the effects of which many men died.
>
> The Jemadars and Subedars meted out more ignominious punishment by slitting off their ears and noses. One of these, a certain Babli Anton, made the following speech to the Sultan: 'You have disfigured my features by cutting off my ears and nose. May God behold this,' and raising his eyes to Heaven he appealed to God, expressed contrition and expired. Severing the ears and noses of the youth who resisted the Sultan was a common occurrence. Many were made to carry baskets filled

with gobra (cowdung) for three days as a public display of warning to others.

Bowring narrates in his account that:

Tipu demanded the surrender of the daughters of some of these Christians in order to have them placed in his seraglio, and that, on the refusal of their parents, the latter had their noses, ears and upper lips cut off, and were paraded through the streets on asses, with their faces towards the tails of the animals.

The young and able-bodied men who were captured from Mangalore were taken into the Mysore army. One hundred men formed a company, four hundred companies were grouped into a *risala*, four *risalas* into a *sufedar* and four *sufedars* came under a bakshi. It was said that twenty-five young men from each company would be taken and circumcised at the end of each month. These men formed what was known as the Ahmedi Corps for the Sultanat.

By the time of the fall of Srirangapatna, there were just about 10,000–11,000 Christians left of the initial set that was sent to the capital city. Their lands and properties were gone. While many of them lived on in Srirangapatna and Mysore, some moved back to their native places to rebuild their lives after suffering a holocaust of fifteen long years from 1784 to 1799.

A Long History of Strife: Mysore *vs* Malabar

But the region that faced the brunt of Tipu's military-religious onslaught was the Malabar and parts of present-day Kerala. As is clear from the political history of his time, a major part of Tipu's rule was spent conducting military operations to subjugate Malabar.

It was a long and stressful period of strife between Mysore and Malabar, from the times of Haidar. At about the time Haidar grabbed control over Mysore, there were a number of small kingdoms in Malabar. The most important of these were the kingdoms of the rajas of Kottayam, Kolathiri and Kodathanad in North Malabar and the Zamorin in South Malabar. The Kolathiri raja had a Muslim feudatory in the person of one Ali Raja—the senior male member of the Arackal Muslim family. He controlled sea trade through the Cannanore port. The family originated from the Hindu royal Family of Kolathiri, but years after their conversion

Nalwadi Krishnaraja along with the Yuvaraja, Dewan Mirza Ismail and British officers in a hunting camp

Maharani Pratapa Rudra Kumari performing the Gowri Puja in the palace

Yuvarani Kempucheluvajammanni with her children, including Prince Jayachamaraja

The Maharaja and the Yuvaraja with the King of Baroda

Nalwadi Krishnaraja along with the Yuvaraja, Dewan Mirza Ismail and British officers in a hunting camp

Maharani Pratapa Rudra Kumari performing the Gowri Puja in the palace

Yuvarani Kempucheluvajammanni with her children, including Prince Jayachamaraja

The Maharaja and the Yuvaraja with the King of Baroda

The Yuvaraja and his family on a foreign trip

Young Jayachamaraja at the 'Kashi Yatra' ritual during his wedding

In his father's shadow: Jayachamaraja with the Yuvaraja

Pomp and splendour: the marriage of Prince Jayachamaraja

Maharajakumari Gayathri Devi Avaru

Private puja at the palace

The ageing Yuvarani with her daughter and granddaughters

The complete family: Nalwadi (third from left standing) with his mother, brother, sisters and family

Jayachamaraja with British officers at a hunting camp

The royal women of Mysore

Yuvarani Kempucheluvajammanni with grandchild

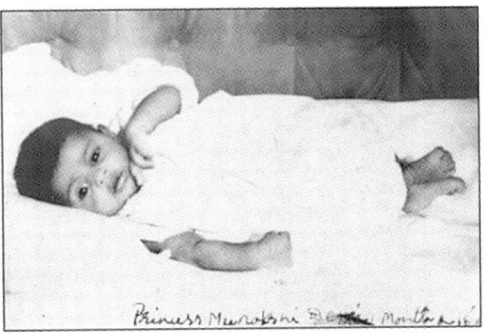

Maharajakumari Meenakshi Devi Avaru

Yuvarani Kempucheluvajammanni with her daughters and grandchildren

Maharani Kempa Nanjammanni with her children

The obedient sons: Maharani Kempa Nanjammanni with her illustrious sons

to Islam, they retained the traditional matriarchal system prevalent among the Hindus of that region. Arackal Bibi was the matriarch and wielded significant authority. Though Ali Raja was a feudatory of the Hindu King of Kolathiri, he nursed ambitions of enhancing his fame and glory. Aligning with the Muslim king of neighbouring Mysore was the best option to realise his dreams.

During Haidar's campaign at Mangalore, when he almost reached the northern borders of Malabar, Ali Raja invited him to invade the region and offered him unconditional support in his campaign. The Malabar campaign began in 1765–66 after Haidar Ali sufficiently armed his forces with the powerful Mysore field-guns. Reaching Cannanore, he appointed Ali Raja the naval chief admiral by virtue of the latter's control and experience over the seaport and his brother Sheik Ali as chief of port authority. Ali Raja had a vast retinue of followers, who were all neo-converts to Islam. They were called the Mappilas—a corruption of the word Mecca-Pillais. They were a violent tribe of fanatically trained Muslims. The Mysore army used their services generously in its Malabar conquest to subjugate the local tribes culturally and politically.

The Malabar invasion was born out of Mysore's desire for territorial expansion. None of the Hindu rajas there had enlisted British support at that time. Even as he overran territory after territory in the Malabar strip Haidar was assisted by Ali Raja and his barbaric Mappila tribe to commit untold atrocities on the Hindu population of the region. Ali Raja also ensured that the palace of his hitherto master, the king of Kolathiri, was set on fire. The king had to flee and seek refuge with the British in Tellicherry. With Kolathiri conquered, Haidar marched towards Kottayam in today's north Kerala, where, after some initial resistance, the betrayal of their king by the Mappilas of Kottayam ensured victory for Haidar.

Kodathanad, his next destination, was where he faced stiff resistance. This was also where the Mysore armies created the maximum havoc. The *Malabar Manual* details the atrocities committed here, recounted by Tipu's son Prince Ghulam Muhammed. These were initially the diary entries of a Muslim officer of the Mysore army:

> Nothing was to be seen on the roads for a distance of four leagues, nothing was found but only scattered limbs and mutilated bodies of Hindus. The country of Nairs was thrown

into a general consternation which was much increased by the cruelty of the Mappilas who followed the invading cavalry of Hyder Ali Khan and massacred all those who escaped without sparing even women and children; so that the army advancing under the conduct of this enraged multitude instead of meeting with continued resistance, found villages, fortresses, temples and every habitable place forsaken and deserted. Wherever he turned, he found no opponent; and every inhabitable place was forsaken and the poor inhabitants who fled to the woods and mountains in the inclement season experienced anguish to behold their houses in flames, fruit-trees cut down, cattles destroyed and temples burnt. By means of Brahmin messengers despatched to woods and mountains, Hyder Ali Khan promised pardon and mercy to the Hindus who had fled. However, as soon as the unfortunate Hindus returned on his promise of mercy and pardon, Hyder Ali Khan, like all the other Muslim tyrants of North India, saw to it that they were all hanged to death, their wives and children reduced to slavery.

It was from here that he proceeded towards Calicut destroying everything that came his way. The Zamorin, after dispatching his family members to safety at Travancore, committed suicide—setting his palace and ammunition depot on fire and then doing the same to himself.

Haidar sent missives to the kingdoms of Cochin and Travancore to submit to the might of Mysore. Cochin capitulated and agreed to pay a subsidy of Rs 2 lakh and eight elephants. Travancore remained defiant. Even while Haidar contemplated action against it, the monsoons set in in Kerala by the end of May, as usual. Haidar therefore retreated to Coimbatore by early June 1766. Taking advantage of his absence, the Keralites besieged the Mysorean strongholds of Calicut and Ponnani to regain their lost territories. Haidar dispatched his General Raza Saib to quell this revolt. But he was caught between the lashing torrential rains and the swell in the Ponnani river. With a huge retinue of 3,000 cavalry and 10,000 infantry, Haidar re-entered the Malabar and ruthlessly crushed the rebellion.

While leaving the Malabar region, Haidar issued edicts that granted special rights and privileges to all the Nairs of the region who agreed to embrace Islam and join the fold. The Hindu Nairs were forbidden from carrying arms. The Syrian Christians of the region also approached Haidar, as reported by Prince Ghulam Muhammad. To safeguard themselves from members of rival sects, they had armed men in their respective folds and these groups beseeched Haidar's mercy on the issue of disarmaments which would make them vulnerable with respect to their opponents. Haidar packed them off with an assurance that he would provide security and that they need not carry arms for this reason. The Syrian Christian community was apparently also instrumental in advancing a loan to General Matthews when he was with Sheikh Ayaz at the conquest of Mangalore. The amount of Rs 3,30,000 was meant to provide a breather to him while the Mysore troops besieged the fortress there.

Before his efforts to conquer the entire Malabar region could succeed, Haidar died in December 1782. Tipu Sultan, who succeeded his father, considered it his primary duty to continue his father's unfinished *jihad*. However, right-wing historians claim that the Islamic fanaticism of Tipu Sultan was much worse than that of his father in the Malabar region. His *jihad* left people with a choice only between conversion and death. The intensity and nature of the suffering of the Hindus during the nightmarish days of Padayottakkalam (military regime) were vividly described in many historical records preserved in the royal houses of Zamorin and Kottayam (Pazhassi), Palghat Fort and the office of the East India Company.

Encouraged by Haidar's death, many of the rajas of the Malabar had declared their independence and also entered into secret alliances with the British. From 1783 to 1791, thousands of Nairs besides about 30,000 Brahmins had fled Malabar, leaving behind their entire wealth, and sought refuge in Travancore State (according to the commission of enquiry appointed by the British soon after Tipu's death). Besides, historians, like Dr M. Gangadharan, claim that there is enough evidence that a few members of the Zamorin family and many Nairs were forcibly circumcised and converted to Islam, and even compelled to eat beef.[*]

As far as the history of the Malabar region is concerned, the most dependable book for basic historical facts is the *Malabar Manual* written by William Logan. Serving in various administrative positions including

---

[*] This is taken from Menon's 1989 book, *History of Cochin State*.

that of a Collector for 20 years up to 1886, he had gone through and extensively researched a variety of documents to prepare his well-acclaimed book. There are plenty of references in the *Malabar Manual* to the cruel military operations and atrocities of Tipu Sultan in Malabar—forcible mass circumcision and conversion, large-scale killings, looting and destruction of hundreds of Hindu temples, and other barbaric acts. Thrichambaram and Thalipparampu temples in Chirakkal Taluqa, Thiruvangatu Temple in Tellicherry, and Ponmeri Temple near Badakara were all supposedly destroyed by Tipu Sultan. The *Malabar Manual* mentions that the Maniyoor mosque was once a Hindu temple. The local belief is that it was converted to a mosque during the days of Tipu Sultan.

Vatakkankoor Raja Raja Varma has written about the loss and destruction faced by Hindu temples in Kerala during the military regime of Tipu Sultan:[*]

> There was no limit as to the loss the Hindu temples suffered due to the military operations of Tipu Sultan. Burning down the temples, destruction of the idols installed therein and also cutting the heads of cattle over the temple deities were the cruel entertainments of Tipu Sultan and his equally cruel army. It was heartrending even to imagine the destruction caused by Tipu Sultan in the famous ancient temples of Thalipparampu and Thrichambaram. The devastation caused by this new Ravana's barbarous activities have not yet been fully rectified.

As per the provisions of the Treaty of Mangalore of 1784, the British had allowed Tipu Sultan suzerainty over the Malabar. 'In consequence, the Hindus of Malabar had to suffer the most severe enormities the world had ever known in history,' observes K.V. Krishna Iyer in *Zamorins of Calicut*, which is based on historical records available from the royal house of Zamorins in Calicut. He goes on to add:

> When the second-in-line of Zamorins, Eralppad, refused to cooperate with Tipu Sultan in his military operations against Travancore because of Tipu's crude methods of forcible circumcision and conversion of Hindus to Islam, the enraged Tipu

---

[*] Varma's writing is taken from the anthology, *Tipu Sultan: Villain or Hero?* compiled by Sita Ram Goel.

Sultan took a solemn oath to circumcise and convert the Zamorin and his chieftains and Hindu soldiers to the Islamic faith.

L.B. Boury writes:*

> To show his ardent devotion and steadfast faith in Muhammaddan religion, Tipu Sultan found Kozhikode to be the most suitable place. It was because the Hindus of Malabar refused to reject the matriarchal system, polyandry and half-nakedness of women that the 'great reformer' Tipu Sultan tried to honour the entire population with Islam.

To the people of the Malabar, the Muslim harem, polygamy and the Islamic ritual of circumcision were equally repulsive, conflicting with ancient culture and tradition in Kerala. Tipu Sultan sought a marriage alliance with the matriarchal Muslim family of Arackal Bibi in Cannanore. Kozhikode in those days had over 7,000 Brahmin families living there. More than 2,000 Brahmin families perished as a result of Tipu Sultan's Islamic cruelties. He did not spare even women and children. Most of the men escaped to forests and foreign lands.

Elamkulam Kunjan Pillai wrote in the *Mathrubhoomi Weekly* of 25 December 1955:

> Muhammadans greatly increased in number. Hindus were forcibly circumcised in thousands. As a result of Tipu's atrocities, strength of Nairs and Chamars (Scheduled Castes) significantly diminished in number. Namboodiris also substantially decreased in number.

The German missionary Gundhert has recorded:**

> Accompanied by an army of 60,000, Tipu Sultan came to Kozhikode in 1788 and razed it to the ground. It is not possible even to describe the brutalities committed by that Islamic barbarian from Mysore.

Thali, Thiruvannur, Varackal, Puthur, Govindapuram, Thalikkunnu and other important temples in the town of Kozhikode as well as those nearby were completely destroyed as a result of Tipu's military operations.

---

* Taken from Goel's *Tipu Sultan: Villain or Hero?*
** Taken from Goel's *Tipu Sultan: Villain or Hero?*

The Zamorin reconstructed some of them after he returned following the defeat of Tipu Sultan in Srirangapatana and the Treaty of 1792.

The records also claim indescribable damage and devastation caused by Tipu Sultan to the ancient and holy temples of Keraladheeswaram, Thrikkandiyoor and Thriprangatu in the Vettum region. The Zamorin renovated these temples to some extent. The Thirunavaya Temple, famous as an ancient teaching centre of the Vedas and revered by the devotees of Vishnu from Tamil Nadu, was also plundered and destroyed by Tipu's army (*Malabar Gazetteer*). As for the Thrikkavu Temple, Logan records that after dismantling and destroying its idol, Tipu converted it into an ammunition depot in Ponnani. It was the Zamorin who renovated the temple later. Kotikkunnu, Thrithala, Panniyoor and other family temples of the Zamorin were plundered and destroyed. The famous Sukapuram Temple was also desecrated. The damage done to the Perumparampu Temple and Maranelira Temple of Azhvancherry Thamprakkal (titular head of all Namboodiri Brahmins) in Edappadu, can be seen even today. The Vengari Temple and Thrikkulam Temple in Eranadu, Azhinjillam Temple in Ramanattukara, Indyannur Temple, Mannur Temple and many other temples were defiled and damaged extensively during the military regime.

Tipu Sultan reached Guruvayoor Temple only after destroying Mammiyoor temple and the Palayur Christian Church. If the destruction caused by Tipu's army is not visible today in the Guruvayoor Temple, it is mainly because of the intervention of Hydrose Kutty who had been converted to Islam by Haidar. He secured the safety of the temple and the continuation of land-tax exemption as earlier allowed by Haidar, besides the renovation and repairs initiated by devotees later. According to available evidence, fearing the wrath of Tipu Sultan, the sacred idol of the Guruvayoor Temple was removed to the Ambalapuzha Sri Krishna Temple in Travancore State. It was only after the end of Tipu's military regime that the idol was ceremoniously reinstated. Till today, daily *pujas* are conducted in Ambalapuzha Sri Krishna Temple where the idol of Guruvayoor Temple had temporarily been installed and worshipped.

The nearby temples at Parampathali, Panmayanadu and Vengidangu carry the scars of Tipu's campaign till date. The damage to the architecture of the sanctum sanctorum of Parampathali Temple is heart-rending. The atrocities committed in Kozhikode during the nightmarish days of the military occupation are vividly described in the works of Fra Bartolomaeo who had travelled through Kerala at that time.

We have already seen how prosperous the Syrian Christian community was, in their generous loan to General Matthews in the conquest of Mangalore. This community suffered a great deal as well. The old Syrian Seminary at Angamaly was destroyed. Some priests there seemed to have had premonition of the impending disaster and fled with the rare manuscripts housed in the seminary. But as luck would have it, the boat they escaped in capsized and the manuscripts were lost forever. Churches in Malabar and Cochin were razed by the invading Mysore armies, as also the Mor Sabor Church at Akaparambu, the Arthat Church, Ollur church, Ambazhakkad seminary and the Martha Mariam Church at Angamaly.

The destruction of coconut, arecanut, pepper and cashew plantations by Tipu's armies, which had been the mainstay of the rich farming classes among the Syrian Christians, totally crippled the community financially. Many of the Syrian Christians fled to save their lives and property and reached Kunnamkulam under the leadership of Father Pulikottil Joseph Kathanar, Vicar of the Arthat Church. Kunnamkulam continues to be a stronghold of the Syrian Christian community even today.

Colonel Wilks' *Historical Sketches*, K.P. Padmanabha Menon's *History of Cochin State* and Sardar K.M. Panicker's, Elamkulam Kunjan Pillai's articles and other writings by several historians do not project Tipu in a better light either. One of the leading Congressmen of pre-Independence days, K. Madhava Nair observes in *Malabar Kalapam* ('Mappila Outrage'):

> The communal Mappila outrage of 1921 in Malabar could be easily traced to the forcible mass conversion and related Islamic atrocities of Tippu Sultan during his cruel military regime from 1783 to 1792. It is doubtful whether the Hindus of Kerala had ever suffered so much devastation and atrocities since the reclamation of Kerala by the mythological Lord Parasurama in a previous Era. Many thousands of Hindus were forcibly converted into Muhammadan faith.

The revolts in south Malabar were led by Ravi Varma of the Zamorin family. To appease him, Tipu had granted him a *jagir*, which he graciously took, but continued to align himself with other powers of the region in defiance of Mysore's authority! Most of the women and men of the royal families of Kolathiri, Parappanad, Calicut and those of the chieftains of Punnathoor, Nilamboor, Kavalapara, Azhvancherry Thamprakkal, etc., fled to the kingdom of Travancore for refuge. Even after Tipu's defeat and the fall of Srirangapatna they remained there in hiding, fearing the atrocities of the Mappilas. In fact, British records as late as the mid-nineteenth century speak of the prevalence of the Mappilas as groups of fanatics who attacked Hindus, burnt their houses and plundered their wealth—thus proving the presence of these tribes and their activities for a long time there.

The continued resistance of the Nairs and the tacit understanding and support they received from the British became a nightmare for Tipu. This was the most decisive event during his reign, other than the attacks of the Nizam and Marathas or subjugating the Wodeyar family in Mysore. He entered into matrimonial alliances with the Arackal family to consolidate his position in the Malabar. His son, Abdul Khaliq, was married to Arackal Bibi's daughter. He even sent formal requests to the British at Tellicherry to refrain from helping the rebels in the Malabar.

To bolster their case against Tipu, rightist historians draw freely from some of Tipu's own correspondences and utterances recorded by his own historians, sons and others. In a letter to Budruz Zuman Khan on 19 January 1790, Tipu himself states:*

> Don't you know I have achieved a great victory recently in Malabar and over four lakh Hindus were converted to Islam? I am determined to march against that cursed 'Raman Nair' (Rama Verma Raja of Travancore) very soon since I am overjoyed at the prospect of converting him and his subjects to Islam, I have happily abandoned the idea of going back to Srirangapatanam now.

Kirkpatrick records another letter from Tipu, dated 13 February 1790 and written to the same gentleman:

> Your two letters, with the enclosed memorandums of the Naimar (or Nair) captives, have been received. You did right in ordering a hundred and thirty-five of them to be circumcised, and in

---

* This quote is taken from an article by K.M. Panicker in the August 1923 issue of the magazine *Bhasha Poshini*. He found Tipu's personal letters and published them in this magazine.

putting eleven of the youngest of these into the Usud Ilhye band (or class) and the remaining ninety-four into the Ahmedy Troop, consigning the whole, at the same time, to the charge of the Kilaaddar of Nugr...

Panicker cites a letter from Tipu, dated 18 January 1790, and written to Syed Abdul Dulai:

> With the grace of Prophet Mohammed and Allah, almost all Hindus in Calicut are converted to Islam. Only on the borders of Cochin State a few are still not converted. I am determined to convert them also very soon. I consider this as Jehad to achieve that object.

Many rightist historians dismiss the grants and gifts sent to various Hindu temples. Tipu was a great believer in astrology and consulted astrologers regularly on his conquest dates and so on. These gifts are claimed to have been made in recompense of those favours. In V.R. Parameswaran Pillai's biography of the Dewan of Travancore, the author states:

> With respect to the much-published land-grants I had explained the reasons about 40 years back. Tipu had immense faith in astrological predictions. It was to become an Emperor (Padushah) after destroying the might of the British that Tipu resorted to land grants and other donations to Hindu temples in Mysore including Sringeri Mutt, as per the advice of the local Brahmin astrologers. Most of these were done after his defeat in 1791 and the humiliating Srirangapatanam Treaty in 1792. These grants were not done out of respect or love for Hindus or Hindu religion but for becoming Padushah as predicted by the astrologers.

These revelations and evidences certainly bewilder the student of history. Was it the same Tipu who, as we saw earlier, made rich tributes to the Sringeri Muth, the Sri Ranganatha Swamy Temple of Srirangapatna, Nanjangud temples and so on? The rightists have an argument for that as well. Writing in *Mathrubhoomi Weekly* (14–20 January 1990), Dr M. Gangadharan says:[*]

---

[*] Taken from an article in *Mathrubhoomi Weekly*, 14-20 January 1990.

In the socio-religious-political conditions prevailing in Mysore of Tipu's days, such things could not be avoided. The financial assistance to Sringeri Mutt meant for conducting religious rites to ward off evil spirits was clearly specified in the letter sent by Tipu Sultan. As such, these cannot be accepted as evidence of Tipu's respect for Hindu religion.

According to Lewis Rice:

In the vast empire of Tipu Sultan on the eve of his death, there were only two Hindu temples having daily pujas within the Sreerangapatanam fortress. It is only for the satisfaction of the Brahmin astrologers who used to study his horoscope that Tipu Sultan had spared those two temples. The entire wealth of every Hindu temple was confiscated before 1790 itself mainly to make up for the revenue loss due to total prohibition in the country.

Even in administrative matters, there was a blatant Muslim bias, especially in the taxation policy. Historian M.H. Gopal observes that Muslims did not have to pay any taxes, and this concession extended to Muslim converts from other religions as well. In the case of employment, Hindus were eliminated to the greatest possible extent. In the 16 years Tipu ruled, the only Hindu to occupy any important official position was Purnaiya. The changing of place-names to Muslim ones—Mangalore to Jalalabad, Cannanore to Kusanabad, Bepur (Vaippura) to Sultanpatanam or Faruqui, Mysore to Nazarabad, Dharwar to Quarshed-Sawad, Gooty to Faiz-Hissar, Ratnagiri to Mustafabad, Dindigul to Khaliqabad, and Calicut (Kozhikode) to Islamabad, etc., are cited as further examples of the intolerance.

With the aid of his innovator friend Zain-ul-abidin, Tipu had envisaged leaving his imprint on every matter of public life. Josyer writes:

Regulations—military, naval, commercial, fiscal; police, judicature and ethics were embraced by the code of this Minos: and his reformation of the Calendar and of the system of weights and measures, was to class him with those philosophical statesmen and sovereigns of whose useful labours his Secretary had obtained some obscure intelligence. It may be briefly stated regarding the whole, that the name of every object was changed: of cycles, years, months; weights, measures, coins, forts, towns, offices—military and civil, the official designations of all persons and things without exception—a singular parody of what was transpiring in France. The administration itself was called Sarkar Khodadad, or God-given Government. Persian was introduced for military commands and official use...he strove, in short, to obliterate every trace of the previous rulers. For this purpose, even the fine irrigation works, centuries old, of the Hindu Rajas were to be destroyed and reconstructed in his own name!

An example that is usually cited to portray Tipu's intolerance was the manner in which he cut the land holding rights of upper-caste Brahmins and their *muths* and temples. Whether this was done for communal reasons or to eradicate the existing feudal structure (only to create a new pecking order in many cases) is uncertain. For instance, Clause 63 of Tipu's Land Revenue Regulations explicitly states this policy:

> The Devasthanam lands are all to be resumed throughout your district; and after ascertaining to what Simpts they formerly appertained you shall re-annex them and include them in the Jumabundy (assessment) of those Simpts.

Francis Buchanan, who made an extensive survey of Mysore during those times, re-emphasises this point with reference to Mandya and Melukote—the stronghold of the Sri Vaishnava Brahmins:

> It (Mandya) was formerly an agaram or village bestowed in charity on the Brahmanas. They were deprived of it by Tippoo; when he annexed to the Circar or public, all the property of that kind... Hyder indeed allowed the Brahmanas the full enjoyment of their revenues but his son reduced their land to 60 thousand Pagodas a year; then to four; then to two; and at length to 1000; finally he entirely took away their land and gave them an annual pension of 1000 Pagodas...The Brahmanas of Nunjinagudu occupied 300 houses and they possessed lands which gave an annual revenue of 14,000 Pagodas...the houses of the Sudras amounted to 700. The town was fortified by Nundiraya who dispersed the Sudras into the neighboring villages, and permitted none to remain in the holy place, but the Brahmanas and the servants who belonged to the temple. Tippoo Sultan gradually deprived the Brahmanas

of the whole of their lands and gave them a monthly pension of 100 Pagodas.

Yet another dead-end for a modern day historian? Even if we commit ourselves to view and assess things with impartiality, how can we gloss over the heaps of evidence, many of which have a lasting impact to this day? At the same time, should a well-meaning and 'rational' historian paint people of the past in colours deemed fit today? Rightist historians rubbish the very claim of Tipu being a nationalist in the first place. Their arguments stem from the question—how can someone who invited foreign powers like Napoleon, Louis XVI, the kings of Afghanistan and Persia to attack India in a confederacy with him against the British be termed as anti-colonial? If the Wodeyar sought the help of the British against Tipu and is thereby dubbed a puppet, then can Tipu soliciting French help against the British be termed as nationalist? Do we have any kind of empirical evidence that had the French managed to win the Fourth Anglo-Mysore War in 1799 against the British, they would have been any less colonial or imperialistic than the British were? The French designs were always those of acquisition of kingdoms and power as was evident from the time of the famed Carnatic Wars. So would a Mysore under French dominion after 1799 have been any different from a Mysore under British suzerainty? Wouldn't the French have claimed their pound of flesh for helping the Sultan in his dark days? These questions haunt every sane mind.

It is noteworthy that Tipu is supposed to have written a letter to American leaders lauding them on their success in the War of Independence against the British:[*]

> Every blow that is struck in the cause of American liberty throughout the world—in France, India and elsewhere—and so long as a single insolent savage tyrant remains, the struggle shall continue.

Does this not demonstrate that Tipu understood the perils of British colonialism (if not of French imperialism or American hegemony) and felt that a united blow was what was needed to throw them out? Even this partial clarity of vision was absent in his contemporaries.

---

[*] Taken from Saki's *Making History—Karnataka's People and Their Past*.

Does one come any closer to solving the mystery that Tipu was? How do we judge his policies towards his subjects, towards vanquished states and his ideas of nationalism? It seems most plausible that Tipu was conscious of the fact that the Wodeyars enjoyed considerable clout in Mysore. Though stripped of his royalty, people swore by his blue blood and always had this at the back of their minds that a Hindu monarch had been displaced by a Muslim upstart who had once been the Wodeyar's protégé. Undoubtedly, he had kept Maharani Lakshmammanni in virtual captivity after her acts of treason against Sultanat-e-Khudadad became known. But he still stopped short of inflicting any harsh punishment on her or other members of the Wodeyar family. Had Tipu treated his own Mysorean subjects with the cruelty he showed outsiders, he would have been completely alienated as a ruler. We therefore see his tyranny in more subtle and indiscernible forms within the Mysore borders. But outside the periphery of the Mysore kingdom, as seen in the Malabar, these compulsions didn't exist. In addition, rather than religion, it was the power of the victor that had to be established, and what better way to do it than by enforcing one's religious identity on the vanquished? His orders in the conquest of Malabar in 1788 seem bewildering:[*]

> Every being in the district without distinction should be honoured with Islam, that the houses of such as fled to that honour should be burnt; that they should be traced to their lurking places; and that all means of truth and falsehood, fraud or force, should be employed to effect their universal conversion.

A state paper in Tipu's own handwriting seems more intriguing:

> There are 500 Coorg prisoners, who must be dealt with in such a manner as shall ensure their death in the course of a month or twenty days; such of their women as are young must be given to Mussalmans, and the rest, together with their children, kept in prison on a small allowance.

At the end of this long narrative of one the greatest sons that the soil of Mysore had seen, questions seem to naturally haunt any rational mind. Does the fact that Tipu showed extreme intolerance to people of

---

[*] This quote and the following one is taken from Goel's book, *Tipu Sultan: Villain or Hero?*

other faiths, especially in his conquests outside Mysore, deny him the greatness he has earned for his name in the hall of fame of history? Are these violent exercises of destruction an assertion of faith or the usual practice of declaring one's supremacy over the vanquished? History does have records of sub-faiths within Hinduism that tried to demonstrate their supremacy over the other through political conquest. Should this be construed as another such exercise or is there a deeper malaise and attitudinal problem in the man who was believed to be so widely read and had the benefits of a liberal and secular education?

In our zeal to construct stereotypes, why must we project 'secular' and 'progressive' as synonyms or 'religious' and 'backward' as synonyms? The ruler could be religious *and* progressive. As in modern India, states ruled by supposedly 'secular' parties do not automatically become progressive or prosperous states. But in Tipu's case, he was not overtly religious—a cause for resentment among many devout Muslims. He could have lined the whole of Mysore with mosques and madrasas. But barring a few, hardly any mosques were built. At the same time, barring two temples in the whole of Mysore there were hardly any temples left untouched by him. So it is a strange contradiction of character that historians find difficult to reconcile.

Some of his own writings, inspired by his dreams, which he had collated in a book recovered after the fall of Srirangapatna, demonstrate his rabid hatred for people of other faiths. Most of Tipu's dreams seem to be exhortations by some unknown force or *fakirs* to demolish one temple or the other. Thus, the definitions that we attribute in today's context to terms like secular and communal definitely do not sit easy on Tipu.

Was he being a true 'nationalist' in the sense that we comprehend the term, at a time when the concept of nation-state or Indianness was unknown? Was he so consumed by hatred for the British that he wouldn't mind enlisting the support of foreign powers and other colonial forces to achieve his goal? How different was he then, from the Wodeyars who enlisted British support against the usurper of their hereditary throne? Though he did have vision and foresight about the serious consequences of British colonialism—something his counterparts singularly lacked—it did not fructify into any major strategy.

Indians in general failed to wake up to the new dangers that had struck their borders in the form of the East India Company. They totally misjudged the Company's intentions, which metamorphosed from trade relations to direct political intervention. They continued to feel that adding one more foe or ally to their long lists of friends and rivals did not make a difference to them. But they did not realise how dangerously different this particular foe would prove.

Also, the profile of the enemy was seldom on religious lines. Tipu and the Nizam were rabid rivals despite being Muslims, and the Marathas committed outrage on the Sringeri Muth and the seat of Jagadguru Shankaracharya himself despite being Hindus. Thus, the notion of religious identity defining friends and foes as it ironically does in modern, 'progressive' India was absent in those days.

Tipu is thus a classic case of a historical character containing too many contradictions. No doubt he has been the object of such varied representations by historians and narrators from across the political spectrum. No narrative on the history of Mysore is complete without assessing this man whose tumultuous reign led Mysore to become the worst nightmare of the East India Company. As Dr N.K. Sinha states, 'Tipu's greatest drawback was his restless spirit of innovations and the increasing bigotry of his later years.'

It seems totally futile to judge people of the past by standards that we have set today in the present ridiculous political syntax of our country. One must realise that these heroes of the past are products of their times and circumstances and one can rarely view their actions or inactions through the prism of contemporary morality and judgment. At the end of the day, Tipu like all other human beings, was a man of grey and there seems absolutely no need to paint him pure black or white. He had his failings and he committed some of the worst excesses among monarchs of his time. To be a modern historian doesn't necessarily mean one needs to brush these cold facts under the carpet and paint a beautiful picture. At the same time, Tippu cannot be denied the greatness he so richly deserves.

Undoubtedly, Tipu was a great ruler and a visionary well ahead of his times. His progressive measures, as discussed, were greatly beneficial to the state of Mysore, which would have collapsed like a pack of cards under the weak Wodeyars of the time. His resistance against the British and his bravery are part of folklore. The reforms in agriculture, the spread of irrigation, the breaking of the old feudal order, the innovations and various other measures discussed earlier bear testimony to this fact. But at the end of the day he was a human being. He had his mindsets and ideas and believed that his faith was the ultimate one. What better way to subjugate the conquered than by destroying them culturally? This was the tactic he lavishly adopted in his conquests.

It would be apt to conclude this rather elaborate treatise on the house of Haidar and Tipu with a quote from Denys Forrest:

> Looking back over his story, I think it can be seen that he had a rare quality of single-mindedness. As in the style of his letters, so in the shape of his life, Tippu Sultan was always recognisably himself. That is why the English feared him, even beyond reason. And he was a brave man. He may have fallen short in wisdom and foresight, but never in courage, never in aspiration, never in his dream of a united, an independent, a prosperous Mysore.

Section 4
Towards Modernism: The Period of Unrest
(AD 1799–1868)

(Mummadi Krishnaraja Wodeyar: AD 1799-1831)

14

THE RESTORATION AND THEREAFTER 1799

NOVEMBER 1799

The inhospitable weather of Tamil Nadu was less oppressive than the volcanoes that seemed to erupt in his heart. Tirumala Rao was a shattered man. As he sat in the open balcony of his little apartment in Madras, he had three letters strewn around him, each conveying a story contrary to the other. He was not sure what his dominant emotion was. Anger? Self-pity? Betrayal? Whatever the feeling, he knew it was certainly not positive. Wiping the tears pooling in the corners of his eyes, he picked up the first letter, written by the woman he had begun to worship and revere in the thirty-odd years of his struggle for her cause—Maharani Lakshmammanni.[*]

Respect to our Tirumalachar

> By the blessing of God and the Brahmins, we have been doing quite well up to date, the 2nd of Jyestha Suddha (3 June 1799). Please keep us informed about your welfare from time to time. We have understood everything from your letter that you sent with Jatavallabha Singri Iyengar. Your efforts so far, living in a foreign land for 24 years and suffering so much on our account, all for the sake of justice and patriotism, have now borne fruit. To such

---

[*] This letter appears in a research paper by the descendants of the Mysore Pradhans—M.A. Narayana Iyengar and M.A. Sreenivasachar.

a wise man and great friend of ours as you are, what more can we say in a letter like this? Even the services of Tirumaliengariah in the days of yore cannot bear comparison to what you have done now. The great good you have done to the state now has brought you everlasting fame, which will last as long as the sun and moon endure. And in future, we shall fully abide by your acts, and shall have nothing to say against them. It is impossible for us to express the fullness of our gratitude for your invaluable services, by means of any letter. It can only be after we meet personally and talk to each other, that we shall be fully pleased and you yourself made to understand everything completely.

(Sd/-) Sriranga

Tirumala's eyes were fixed on 'brought you everlasting fame, which will last as long as the sun and moon endure'. What fame is this, he wondered. It was undoubtedly greed and avarice, the lure of the grand post of Mysore Dewan that had impelled him to help the Maharani in distress. But somewhere down the line, he was so consumed and obsessed by the prospect of the realisation of that dream that it had become a matter of personal success and failure for him. He had welcomed the news of Tipu's death and the fall of Srirangapatna on 4 May by beating drums in Madras and distributing sugar by the cartload to all the citizens. The very next day he had met Lord Clive personally. The latter had assured him of the post of prime minister of the new Mysore. The British were still undecided who to place on the throne. People like Purnaiya—who suggested that one of Tipu's sons be placed on the Masnad*—were already trying to influence the British one way or another, and it seemed like the battle for restoration had only just begun. Clive had asked Tirumala to proceed to Krishnagiri and stay there to wait on Lord Mornington for further discussions.

But while at Krishnagiri he received a letter from the office of the Commissioners of the Company that spelt the death of his dreams. He re-read those terse and judgemental lines—matter-of-fact—with renewed incredulity:

---

* After betraying Tipu, it is rather strange that Purnaiya should have suggested this. But since he didn't have much regard for the Wodeyars either, perhaps his old loyalties came to the fore in the form of this suggestion.

...that having been long absent from the Mysore country, he might not possess that thorough and practical knowledge of the present state of its local resources and other minute particulars, which Purnaiah had been presumed to command in consequence of his long and unremitting residence in the country, and having held offices of importance under Tipu Sultan and his father; that the disorganised and unsettled condition of the country then newly conquered rendered the knowledge, though otherwise of secondary consequence, an indispensable qualification in anyone who should be placed at the head of its affairs at that crisis; that in as much as it was believed that the early tranquilisation of the country chiefly depended upon the said knowledge, they wished he would unite with them in promoting the peace and order of his country from the administration of whose affairs he was not to however consider himself of either totally or long excluded; that in the meantime they would recommend to superior authorities to make a handsome provision for him besides the grant of some present...

When he had first read this letter he had shivered with disbelief and fright. While a man who had recommended the discontinuation of the Hindu dynasty was being promoted to a post of eminence, he—a faithful slave for decades—was being relegated to oblivion. Were his long years of sacrifice in vain? Was the trust he had reposed been misplaced? He wanted answers and for that he had to meet Maharani Lakshmammanni. When he rushed to Srirangapatna to meet his icon, he was denied entry. In a curt manner he was informed that he did not have the requisite permission to meet Her Highness. Tirumala Rao could not believe his ears. He could not meet the rani whose messages he had carried faithfully for twenty-five years, risking his own life more than once? But the message was simple: leave Srirangapatna at once and settle down at Madras. Was it the maharani's message, he asked. No; that of the victorious company bahadars, came the prompt reply.

Totally shattered and disillusioned, Tirumala Rao made his way to Madras, the city he had inhabited for decades as a refugee. He still could not fathom why the maharani had not intervened at least to grant him the courtesy of an audience for all that he had done for her. Almost telepathically, a few days later, a letter—the third one that lay on the floor beside him—arrived from the maharani's new residence at Mysore. The capital city had shifted and she, along with her grandson and future king, Mummadi Krishnaraja, had proceeded to Mysore, leaving behind a wailing Srirangapatna to heal its wounds. In some ways, he thought, Srirangapatna personified him. It was good as long as it was of use; after that it was discarded to fend for itself and the victorious entourage had proceeded to its new destination. Of course, he had heard of the maharani's protests against leaving Srirangapatna before meeting her faithful pradhan and consoling him for the sudden and inexplicable change of fortune. But since she was given an ultimatum by the company authorities, she had no choice but to comply and proceed without further delay to the new capital city of Mysore.

The letter was dated 25 June 1799 and was addressed to Lord Clive and Lord Mornington.*

> You have already been made aware of all our affairs through our Pradhan Tirumal Row. Being unable to put up with the tyranny of the Mahomedan usurpers, and hearing of the nobility and prowess of the English Company, and of the fame due to their extending their protection to many a principality, we sent our Tirumal Row to Channapatna 24 years ago. You know perfectly well of everything that transpired from that time up to date, about our negotiations with you and the promises of restoration made by the Governors and other English Sirdars. You have now overthrown the tyrant Tipu by the strength of your virtue and heroism, conquered the country and spread the glory of your achievement throughout the length and breadth of the land. As you always espouse the cause of justice and truth, you have been pleased to favour us and order Sirdars here to restore to us our Kingdom. To thank you for this act of yours and express our gratitude to you, words will not suffice. Our gratitude to you for what you have done for us now cannot be forgotten even after our death.
>
> Now that your Sirdars here have made up their minds to entrust the conduct of an administration to the officers of the

---

* Since the Rani's letters were always sent to her recipients through Tirumala or Narayana, this one, too, came to him on its way to Clive. This letter appears in M.A. Narayana Iyengar and M.A. Sreenivasachar's research paper.

late government, we press the following on your Excellencies' consideration. We had in the very beginning promised to confer the Ministership upon our Tirumal Row, and on the faith of this, our promise, he put forth his strenuous exertions with the Company for the past 24 years as is very well known to you. We have not at all paid him a single pie for his expenses. And in addition to this, many dependents working on your behalf during the time of the late tyranny, have been completely ruined and reduced to poverty and misery. And you will grant that it is but fair and just that we should provide for them.

And hence as you have been good enough to restore to us our Kingdom, please allow us also to administer it in the manner that suits us best. We have already promised our Tirumal Row to appoint him and his heirs as Ministers in hereditary succession, to grant him 10 per cent of the revenues of the state, and also to pay up all his expenses. It is therefore our request that you will be pleased to permit us to keep up our promise.

Sriranga

8, Bahula Jyeshta, Siddharthi

Even before he could finish reading the letter, a knock on the door informed him that the priest was soliciting his presence. Wiping his tears, Tirumala realised that it was the day of Naraka Chaturdashi—fifteen years ago on this day scores of his family members were brutally killed for no fault of theirs. While the rest of the kingdom celebrated Diwali under the new regime, Tirumala's house bore a pall of gloom. He had to prepare for the annual *shraddha* ceremonies for the peace of his forefathers and murdered kin—now a ritual in his family every Diwali. He flung the three letters away; they meant nothing to him any more.

⁂

THE RESTORATION AND THE TREATY OF SRIRANGAPATNA

With their goal achieved—the defeat of their arch-rival and enemy, Tipu Sultan—the British turned towards the royal family of Mysore, which had been waiting in the wings all this time. Headed by Maharani

Lakshmammanni, the only male support for the Wodeyars had been Nandiraja, the maternal grandfather of Prince Krishnaraja Wodeyar III. Even before the fall of Srirangapatna, back in February 1799, Maharani Lakshmammanni wrote to Lord Mornington recapitulating the negotiations she had been having with the 'Company Bahaddur' for many years now. Josiah Webbe, Secretary to the Madras Government, replied in April 1799:[*]

> With compliments from J. Webbe to Maharani Narapathi Mathoshri Rana Saheb: Three letters you sent, one to me, one to His Lordship of Bengal, and one to His Lordship here, your Pradhan Tirumal Rao delivered, and these gave us much pleasure. Your Pradhan Tirumal Rao has for a long period continued to give us every information respecting you, and their Lordships have solemnly promised to serve you, which your Pradhan must have mentioned to you. You may rest assured that there will be no end to our friendship. We have now declared war against Tipu. But we know not what will be the result. God only knows it. I cannot write much on that head. After it be over they will without doubt attend to your business.

Soon after this letter was written, Tipu was dead and Srirangapatna had been destroyed completely. Maharani Lakshmammanni thanked the British whole-heartedly for saving her and her family from sorrow and humiliation. She sent feelers to the East India Company officials about her eagerness to quickly install Mummadi Krishnaraja on the throne and restore the royal family to its earlier grandeur. The British were in a quandary. Many of them wanted to appropriate this kingdom, won after so many conquests. But a majority of them felt that a situation of power without accountability suited them best and that it was also necessary for them to be seen rewarding someone who had stood by the British through thick and thin. At the same time they wanted their pound of flesh for themselves and their allies—the Marathas and the Nizam.

Finally, it was decided that while the Wodeyar would be restored to his throne, it would be with a diminished dominion, in a position subservient to British authority. Elaborate plans were drawn to partition

---

[*] Taken from M.A. Narayana Iyengar and M.A. Sreenivasachar's 1981 research paper, 'The Mysore Pradhans'.

Mysore among the victorious forces. The Nizam was given the present districts of Bellary, Anantpur, Cudappah and Kurnool. This last, however, was ceded by him in 1800 in lieu of maintaining a British force in his dominion as per the British India policy. The Marathas got the territory north of the Tungabhadra River (Hubli, Belgaum, Dharwad, etc.) except the North Kanara region, which remained with the British. The British also took South Kanara and all the areas west, south and east of the Old Mysore state. At that time Kanara was a single district and it was in 1862 that it was divided into North and South Kanara. The British took special care to keep the entire seacoast under their control; they had bitter memories of Tipu's efforts to enlist the support of the French naval fleets and build his sea-power. The motives behind the partition are detailed in a letter written by the Marquess of Wellesley,* Governor general of India to the Court of Directors in England on 7 June 1799:

> The approved policy, interests and honour of the British Nation therefore required that the settlement of the extensive Kingdom subjected to our disposal, should be formed on principles acceptable to the inhabitants of the conquered territories, just and conciliatory to the contiguous Native States, and indulgent to every party in any degree affected by the consequences of our success.
>
> To have divided the whole territory equally between the Company and the Nizam, to the exclusion of any other State, would have afforded strong grounds of jealousy to the Marathas, and aggrandised the Nizam's power beyond all bounds of discretion and would have left in our hands a territory so extensive, as it might have been difficult to manage, especially in the present state of the Company's service at the Presidency. Under whatever form such a partition could have been made, it must have placed in the hands of the Nizam many of the strong fortresses on the northern frontiers of Mysore, and exposed our frontier in that quarter to every predatory incursion; such a partition would have laid the foundation of perpetual differences, not only between the Marathas and the Nizam, but between the Company and both these powers.

---

* This letter appears in Montgomery's 1885 book, titled *British India*.

To have divided the territory into three equal portions allowing the Marathas who had taken part in the expense or hazard of the war, an equal share with the other two branches of the Triple Alliance in the advantages of the peace, would neither have been just to the Nizam, politic, in the way of example to our other allies, nor prudent in respect of aggrandisement of the Maratha Empire. This mode of partition, also must have placed Chitaldoorg and some of the most important northern fortresses in the hands of the Marathas, while the remainder of the fortresses in the same line would have been occupied by the Nizam, and our unfortified and open frontier in Mysore would have been exposed to the excesses of the undisciplined troops of both powers. To have given the Marathas no larger a territory than is now proposed, while the Company and the Nizam divided the whole of the remainder to the exclusion of any central power, would have been liable nearly to the same objection as that stated against a total exclusion of the Marathas from all participation.

The establishment, therefore, of a central and separate power in the ancient territories of Mysore, appeared to be the best expedient for reconciling the interests of all parties. It would certainly have been desirable that the ancient Mysore territory should have been placed in the hands of one of Tipu's sons, but the hereditary and intimate connection established between Tipu and the French, the probability that the French may be enabled to maintain themselves in Egypt, the perpetual interest that Tipu's family must feel to undermine and subvert a system which had so much reduced their patrimony and power, added to their natural hatred of the English name, and to the aspiring ambition, indignant pride and deadly revenge congenial to the Mohammadan character, precluded the possibility of restoring any branch of the family of the late Sultan to the throne without exposing us to the constant hazard of internal commotion and even of foreign war. Such a settlement would have cherished in its bosom a restless and powerful principle of its own dissolution; we could never have expected harmony or a spirit of friendship or alliance, where no true reconcilement could grow; even submission must have been reluctant and treacherous, where bitter memory of fallen dignity, wealth and power must have united every passion and vice with many of the noblest virtues in a constant desire to recover an empire, originally acquired by an extraordinary combination of falsehood, cruelty and courage, and maintained for a long time with eminent policy and vigour as well as its internal government as in its foreign relations.

You will observe that throughout this view of the subject I have assumed the justice and necessity of the late war against Tipu Sultan and consequently the right of conquest under which I conceive the absolute disposal of the territory to have accrued to the Company and the Nizam. In the exercise of this right if I were to look to moral considerations alone, I should certainly on every principle of justice and humanity, as well as of attention to the welfare of the people have been led to restore the heir of the ancient Rajah of Mysore to that rank and dignity which were wrested from his ancestors by the usurpation of Hyder Ali. The long and cruel imprisonment which several branches of his family have suffered, the persecution and murder of many of their adherents, and the state of degradation and misery in which it has been the policy of both these usurpers to retain the surviving descendants of their lawful sovereign, would have entitled the representative of the ancient family of Mysore to every degree of practicable consideration; but it is also evident that every motive must concur to attach to the heir of the Mysore family, if placed on the throne, to our interests, through which alone he can hope to maintain himself against the family of Tipu.

Thus, it seems clear that it was more of a ploy to consolidate British rule and to maintain the balance of power among the allies, rather than to honour the old friendship with Maharani Lakshmammanni, that the Company decided to reinstate Wodeyar on the throne.

This, however, did not deter Maharani Lakshmammanni. She had achieved her goal and succeeded in bringing her family back to prominence, albeit at the cost of the kingdom's very sovereignty and independence. In a formal letter dated 26 June 1799,* signed by her and her mother-in-law Queen Mother Devajammanni—the adoptive mother of Chamaraja Wodeyar VII and Immadi Krishnaraja—she thanked the British thus:

---

* This letter, and the Commissioner's response, appear in Shama Rao's 1936 book, *Modern Mysore*.

The selection you have made of our boy for the purpose of conferring upon the Government of Mysore, Nagar, Chistel Doorg and their dependencies and the nomination of Purnaiah as the Diwan, has caused us great Joy...as long as the sun and the moon continue to shine on us, we would not render ourselves guilty of any offence against your Government. We will consider ourselves always your protégé and your subordinates.

In the commissioner's words:

The Rana (Rani), in reply expressed through one of her attendants, the lively sense which she entertained of His Lordship's clemency, which had raised her and her family from the lowest pitch of human misery, to that station of which they had been deprived by tyranny and usurpation. She dwelt particularly on the persecution to which she and her family had been exposed from the cruel, savage and relentless disposition of the late Tippoo Sultan; but she added that the generosity of the Company, having restored the ancient rights of her house in the person of her grandson, had opened to her a prospect of passing the remnant of her days in peace.

The Rajah, who is said to be five years old, is of a delicate habit: his complexion is rather fair than otherwise and his countenance is very expressive. He showed some symptoms of alarm on our arrival, but these soon disappeared. He seems to be of a timid disposition, and to have suffered considerably from restraint.

Over one month of looting and arson, Srirangapatna, the ancient capital of the Wodeyars and later of Haidar and Tipu Sultan, had been reduced to rubble. She now stood like an unearthly, wailing damsel and was a mere pathetic reminder of her glorious past. Josyer records a letter written by Lord Mornington to the Board of Directors which reveals the extent of financial benefits that the 'acquisition of Seringapatam' accrued to the Company's coffers:

The establishment of a Hindoo state in Mysore, with the restoration of the Temples and endowments of that religion, must be grateful to the Government of Poona independently of the advantages arising from the substitution of a power of the same religion and of pacific views, in the place of an odious Mohammadan usurpation, scarcely less hostile to the Mahrata than to the British Nation.

By the Partition Treaty of Mysore you have acquired an augmentation of direct territorial revenue to the annual amount of 6,47,641 star pagodas or £ 259056 sterling. By the Subsidiary Treaty of Seringapatam you have secured an annual subsidy of star pagodas 7,00,000 or £ 539056 sterling. But a reasonable expectation is entertained that the territory acquired by the Company under the treaty of Mysore will yield, in the course of a few years, a sum not less than star pagodas 14,78,698 or £ 5,91,479 sterling. If such an advance in the nominal revenue of the acquired districts should actually be realised, the positive augmentation of your available annual resources in consequence of late settlement of Mysore will amount to nearly 20 lakhs of star pagodas, or £ 8,00,000 sterling. Further we retained full sovereignty over Seringapatam as being a tower of strength from which we may at any time shake Hindustan to its center, if any combination should be ever formed against our interests.

Apart from the revenue benefits accrued, as stated viciously above, the British got a huge booty from the plunder of Srirangapatna. The Sultan's golden throne, tiger-shaped with a jewelled canopy and crest was moved to England. As Colonel Wellesley wrote in a letter to his brother:[*]

> By the unrestricted plunder of the town of Seringaptam and its neighbourhood several men of the army became rich beyond the dreams of avarice. Nothing exceeded what was done on 4th May, that scarcely a house in the town was left unplundered, and that in the camp bazaars jewels of the greatest value, bars of gold, and numerous other articles of value were offered for sale by soldiers, at indiscriminate prices, or exchanged for articles of nominal value. Single pearls of great value are said to be exchanged for a bottle of liquor. An army doctor was able to purchase from a soldier two bracelets set with diamonds, and the less costly one is said to have been valued at £300000 sterling or 45 Lakhs of rupees. The other bracelet was declared by the jeweller to be of such superlative value that the jeweller could not fix a price.

---

[*] The letter appears in Josyer's 1929 book, *History of Mysore and the Yadava Dynasty.*

A committee called the Prize Committee was appointed by General Harris to share the booty. General Harris found in the palace

> an enormous and astonishing mass of wealth consisting of ... gold and silver plate, jewels, rich and valuable stuffs, and various other articles of great price and rarity. The jewels were found kept in large dark rooms strongly secured and sealed. In the same manner were stored the gold plate, both solid and in filigree, of which latter there was an endless variety of beautiful articles. The repositories of firearms contained swords most magnificently adorned with gold and jewels. There were also a number of ornamental heavy articles, particularly several doorposts of ivory of exquisite workmanship. A large library in excellent preservation also existed, the volumes being kept in chests and each book having a separate wrapper. Many of them were richly adorned and beautifully illuminated.

The library, except one copy of the Koran, was transferred to the newly formed College of Calcutta. The copy of the Koran, written in beautiful characters with elegant ornamentations, is in the Library of Windsor Castle. The Commander-in-Chief General Harris's share of the prize money amounted to £1,42,202 or an equivalent of nearly Rs 19 lakh.

The rape of Srirangapatna left her totally incapable of recovering her lost glory and grandeur. There was, in fact, no place in Srirangapatna worthy of hosting the coronation of the new king. Also, many of the buildings in old Mysore had been demolished by Tipu as part of the plan of building the new township of Nazarabad. Bangalore was initially chosen for the coronation, but since it was on the border of the raja's domain, the idea was abandoned. The Nazarabad fort would also not do as water supply to the fort had been cut off many years ago. Finally, with not a single palace or house fit for the ceremony, the coronation was held in an open space in a pandal erected outside the Sri Lakshmiramana Swami Temple in Mysore. On the morning of 30 June 1799, the Hindu officers of the kingdom accompanied the British generals and reached the little boy's house. Barely five years old, the loud sound of the *nadaswaram* and other traditional musical instruments that ushered in good luck, and the large crowds that gathered outside, alarmed the boy. He later recovered his royal poise. He was then placed on the Masnad of Mysore as the Khavind Nanjarajabidha Mummadi Krishnarajendra Wodeyar under the tearful gaze of Maharani Lakshmammanni.

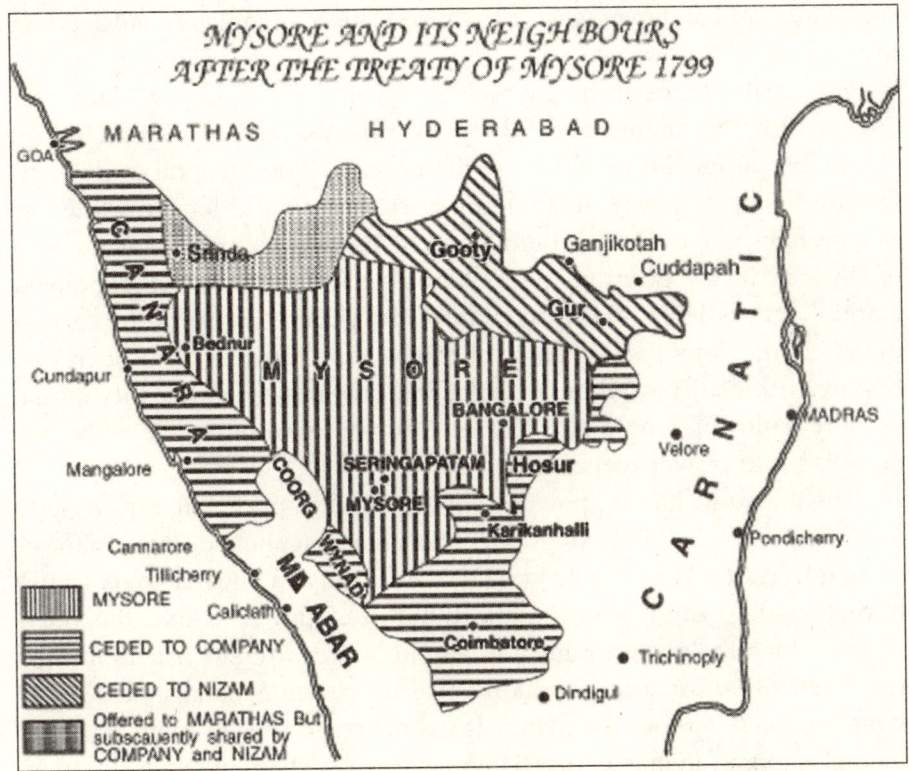

*Mysore and its neighbours after the Partition Treaty of 1799
(Maps are artistic recreations made at Suhaas Graphics, Bangalore)*

Purnaiya accompanied them as the new dewan or prime minister of the state.

To formalise the entire transition process and the appointment of the new king and his dewan, a treaty was signed between Maharani Lakshmammanni and the British on 8 July 1799. The Treaty of Srirangapatna also formalised the partition of the kingdom with Gutti, Gurramkonda, part of Chitradurga and other territories ceded to the Nizam; the Canara coast, Wynad, Coimbatore and Srirangapatna to the British and Soonda and Hardanhalli to the Marathas (which they later rejected). A sum exceeding 25,000 Star Pagodas was assigned to the raja and a group of hill forts in north Mysore and posts away from the Marathas' and the Nizam's territory from Punganoor on the line of Eastern parts to Bidnaur on the Western Ghats. A treaty like this naturally meant the end of suzerainty and independence for Mysore, now completely subservient to the British.*

The treaty imposed the payment of an annual subsidy of 7 lakh Star Pagodas for the maintenance of the Company's body of troops, which would be permanently stationed at the capital for the raja's defence. Extraordinary expenses that might arise due to sudden hostilities or preparations for defence would have to be borne entirely by the raja of Mysore. In the event of the maharaja's pay failure to this stipulated amount, it was left to the discretion of the governor general to assume direct charge over part or parts of the Mysore territory to procure the required funds. The failure to meet his liabilities, such as the annual subsidy payment, would also ensure a loss of territory for the maharaja, be it in times of war or peace.

The maharaja had no power of appeal in case the Company chose to take over territories of the kingdom in the above mentioned circumstances. If the governor general made known such a decision, the maharaja would have to issue orders effecting the transfer of power within ten days, failing which the governor general would be free to issue orders for any regulations or ordinances for taking over the revenue management of the kingdom even without the maharaja's concurrence! As a saving grace for the beleaguered maharaja of Mysore, even in such an adverse situation, the treaty assured him of an annual income that would not fall short of 1 lakh Star Pagodas, along with about one-fifth of the net revenues from the territories ceded to him.

The ability of the maharaja to forge or break alliances with his neighbours was also severely curtailed. He could not do so without the Company's assent. He needed the Company's approval to induct any Europeans in his service and promptly report to the authorities the presence of unknown Europeans within the Mysore territories. The Company was apprehensive of the cordial relations Mysore had shared with the French during Haidar and Tipu's rule and did not want those old ties to be revived at any cost.

The governor general was at complete liberty to garrison or repair any fortress in Mysore with British troops and officers in times of peace or war. The maharaja had to bear half the expenses in case the governor general decided to repair existing forts within the kingdom. The maharaja's

---

* For the full text of this treaty, see the appendix to this chapter.

government was not permitted to employ the troops of the British for day-to-day chores, such as collecting revenue from defaulters, etc., something armies had traditionally always done.

The entry of all provisions and articles required for the British garrison's use at Srirangapatna was to be allowed free of any duty, tax or impediment whatsoever. The maharaja was bound to heed any advice the Company gave him in supposed good faith regarding the state of the kingdom's economy, its finances, the administration of justice, trade and commerce, encouragement of agriculture and industry or any subject they deemed fit. The Partition Treaty was also negotiable in future as and when the allies of the Fourth Anglo-Mysore War wished to change borders by exchanging territories among themselves.

The treaty was signed by General Harris, Colonel Arthur Wellesley, Lieutenant Colonel William Kirkpatrick, Henry Wellesley and Lieutenant Colonel Barry Close—all on behalf of the governor general and by Maharani Lakshmammanni and Dewan Purnaiya on behalf of the infant raja.

The year 1799 thus marked a new milestone in the history of Mysore. A new kingdom was born from blood and strife and the clock seemed to have turned back fully for the Wodeyar family. The worthlessness of the earlier rulers had cost them their kingdom. Lady luck had showered her benevolence on them and destiny did something very rare—she gave them a second chance. Whether they proved their mettle this time, albeit under the iron fetters of the East India Company, was something that only time would tell.

APPENDIX TO CHAPTER 14

I. THE PARTITION TREATY OF MYSORE, 22 JUNE 1799 (TAKEN FROM BEATON'S ACCOUNT)

Article 1

It being reasonable and just that the allies by this Treaty should accomplish the original objects of the war (viz. a due indemnification of the expenses incurred in their own defence, and effectual security for their respective possessions against the future designs of their enemies,) it is stipulated and agreed that the districts specified in Schedule A, hereunto annexed, together with the heads of all the passes leading from the territory of the late Tippoo Sultan to any part of the possessions of the English East India Company Bahadoor, of its allies, or tributaries, situated between the ghats on either coast and all forts situated near to and commanding the said passes, shall be subjected to the authority, and be forever incorporated with the Dominions of the English East India Company Bahadoor, the said Company Bahadoor engaging to provide effectually out of the revenues of the said districts for the suitable maintenance of the whole of the families of the late Hyder Ali Khan and of the late Tippoo Sultan, and to apply to this purpose, with the reservation hereinafter stated, an annual sum of not less than two lakhs of Star Pagodas, making the Company's share as follows:-

Estimated value of districts enumerated in the Schedule A, according to a statement from Tippoo Sultan in 1792...7,77,170 Canteroi Pagodas.

Deduct provision for the families of Hyder Ali Khan and of Tippoo Sultan, two lakhs of Star Pagodas, in Canteroi Pagodas....2,40,000.

Remains to the East India Company.....5,37, 170 Canteroi Pagodas.

Article 2

For the same reasons stated in the preceding article, the districts specified in Schedule B annexed hereunto, shall be subjected to the authority and for ever united to the dominions of the Nawab Nizam-ood-Dowlah Asoph Jah Bahadoor, the said Nawab having engaged to provide liberally from the revenues of the said districts for the support of Meer Kummer-ood-Deen Khan Bahadoor, and of his family and relations, and to grant him for this purpose a personal Jaghire in the district of Gurromcondah, equal to an annual sum of Rs 2,10,000 or of 70,000 Canteroi Pagodas, over and above, and exclusive of a Jaghire which the said Nawab has also agreed to assign to the said Meer-Kummer-ood-Deen Khan for the pay and maintenance of a proportionate number of troops to be employed in the service of His Highness, making the share of His Highness as follows:- Estimated value of the territory specified in Schedule B, according to the statement of Tippoo Sultan in 1792...6,07,332 Canteroi Pagodas.

Deduct personal jaghire to Meer Kummer-ood-Deen Khan, Rs 2,10,000 or...70,000 Canteroi Pagodas.

Remains to the Nawab Nizam-ood-Dowlah Asoph Jah Bahadoor.... 5,37,332 Canteroi Pagodas.

Article 3

It being further expedient, for the preservation of peace and tranquility and for the general security on the foundations now established by the contracting parties, that the fortress of Seringapatam should be subjected to the said Company Bahadoor, it is stipulated and agreed that the said fortress and the Island on which it is situated (including the small tract of land, or island, lying to the westward of the main island, and bounded on the west by a Nullah, called the Mysore Nullah, which falls into the Cauvery near Chenagal Ghaut) shall become part of the Dominions of the said Company, in full right and sovereignty for ever.

Article 4

A separate Government shall be established in Mysore; and for this purpose it is stipulated and agreed that the Maharajah Kishna Raja Oodiaver Bahadoor, a descendant of the ancient Rajahs of Mysore, shall possess the territory hereinafter described, upon the conditions hereinafter mentioned.

Article 5

The contracting powers mutually and severally agree that the districts specified in Schedule C hereunto annexed, shall be ceded to the said Maharajah Mysore Kishna Rajah and shall form the separate Government of Mysore, upon the conditions hereinafter mentioned.

Article 6

The English East India Company Bahadoor shall be at liberty to make such deductions from time to time from the sums allotted by the first Article of the present Treaty for the maintenance of the families of Hyder Ali Khan and Tippoo Sultan, as may be proper, in consequence of the decease of any member of the said families; and in the event of any hostile attempt on the part of the said family or of any member of it, against the authority of the contracting parties, or against the peace of their respective dominions or the territories of the Rajah of Mysore, then the said English East India Company Bahadoor shall be at liberty to limit or suspend entirely the payment of the whole or any part of the stipend hereinbefore stipulated to be applied to the maintenance and support of the said families.

Article 7

His Highness the Peshwa Rao Pundit Pradhan Bahadoor shall be invited to accede to the present Treaty and although the said Peshwa Rao Pundit Pradhan Bahadoor has neither participated in the expense or danger of the late war, and therefore is not entitled to share any part of the acquisitions made by the contracting parties (namely, the English East India Company Bahadoor and His Highness the Nawab Nizam-ood-Dowlah Asoph Jah Bahadoor), yet for the maintenance of the relations of friendship and alliance between the said Peshwa Rao Pundit Pradhan Bahadoor, the English East India Company Bahadoor, His Highness the Nawab Nizam-ood-Dowlah Asoph Jah Bahadoor and Maharajah Mysore Kishna Rajah Bahadoor, it is stipulated and agreed that certain districts, specified in Schedule D hereunto annexed, shall be reserved for the purpose of being eventually ceded to the said Peshwa Rao Pundit Pradhan Bahadoor in full right and sovereignty; in the same manner as if he had been a contracting party to this Treaty; provided however, that the said Peshwa Rao Pundit Pradhan Bahadoor shall accede to the present Treaty in its full extent within one month from the day on which it shall be formally communicated to him by the contracting parties, and provided also that he shall give satisfaction to the English East India Company Bahadoor, and to His Highness the Nawab Nizam-ood-Dowlah Asoph Jah Bahadoor, with regard to certain points now depending between him, the said Peshwa and the said Nawab Nizam-ood-Dowlah Asoph Jah Bahadoor, and also with regard to such points as shall be presented to the said Peshwa, on the part of the English East India Company Bahadoor, by the Governor General or the British Resident at the Court of Poona.

Article 8

If, contrary to the amicable expectation of the contracting parties, the said Peshwa Rao Pundit Pradhan Bahadoor shall refuse to accede to this Treaty or to give satisfaction upon the points to which the Seventh Article refers, then the right to and sovereignty of the several districts hereinbefore reserved for eventual cession to the Peshwa Rao Pundit Pradhan Bahadoor shall rest jointly on the said English East India Company Bahadoor, and the said Nawab Nizam-ood-Dowlah Asoph Jah Bahadoor who will either exchange them with the Rajah of Mysore for other districts of equal value more contiguous to their respective territories, or otherwise arrange and settle respecting them, as they shall judge proper.

Article 9

It being expedient for the effectual establishment of Maharajah Mysore Kishna Rajah Bahadoor in the Government of Mysore, that His Highness should be assisted with a suitable subsidiary force, it is stipulated and agreed that the whole of the said force shall be furnished by the English East India Company Bahadoor, according to the terms of a separate Treaty to be immediately concluded between the said English East India Company Bahadoor and His Highness Maharajah Mysore Kishna Rajah Oodiaver Bahadoor.

Article 10

This Treaty consisting of ten Articles being settled and concluded, this day, the 22nd of June 1799 (recitals follow.)
    Ratified at Hyderabad by His Highness, the Nizam, 13th July 1799.

II. THE SUBSIDIARY TREATY OF MYSORE, 8 JULY 1799 (FROM BEATSON'S ACCOUNT)

Article 1:

The friends and enemies of either of the contracting parties shall be considered as friends and enemies of both.

Article 2:

The Honourable East India Company Bahadoor agrees to maintain, and His Highness Maharajah Mysore Kishna Rajah Oodiaver Bahadoor agrees to receive, a Military Force for the defence and security of His Highness' dominions; in consideration of which protection His Highness engages to pay the annual sum of Seven Lakhs of star pagodas to the said East India Company, the said sum to be paid in twelve equal monthly installments, commencing from the 1st of July Anno Domini 1799. And His Highness further agrees that the disposal of the said sum, together with the arrangement and employment of the Troops to be maintained by it, shall be entirely left to the Company.

Article 3:

If it shall be necessary for the protection and defence of the territories of the contracting parties, or of either of them, that hostilities shall be undertaken, or preparations made for commencing hostilities against any State or power, His said Highness Maharajah Mysore Kishna Rajah Oodiaver Bahadoor agrees to contribute towards the discharge of the increased expense incurred by the augmentation of the military force and the unavoidable charges of war, such a sum as shall appear to the Governor-General-in-Council of Fort William, on an attentive consideration of the means of His said Highness, to bear a just and reasonable proportion to the actual net revenues of His said Highness.

Article 4:

And whereas it is indispensably necessary that effectual and lasing security should be provided against any failure in the funds destined to defray either the expenses of the permanent military force in time of peace, or the extraordinary expenses described in the third Article of the present Treaty, it is hereby stipulated and agreed between the contracting parties, that whenever the Governor-General-in-Council of Fort William in Bengal shall have reason to apprehend such failure in the funds so destined, the said Governor-General-in-Council shall be at liberty, and shall have full power and right either to introduce such regulations and ordinances as he shall deem expedient for the internal management and collection of the revenues, or for the better ordering of any other branch and department of the Government of Mysore, or to assume and bring under the direct management of the servants of the said Company Bahadoor such part or parts of the territorial possessions of His Highness Maharajah Mysore Kishna Rajah Oodiaver Bahadoor as shall appear to him, the said Governor-General-in-Council, necessary to render the said funds efficient and available, either in time of peace or war.

Article 5:

And it is hereby further agreed that whenever the said Governor-General-in-Council shall signify to the said Maharajah Mysore Kishna Rajah Oodiaver Bahadoor that it become necessary to carry into effect he provisions of the fourth article, His said Highness Maharajah Mysore Kishna Rajah Oodiaver Bahadoor shall immediately issue orders to his aumils or other officers either for carrying into effect the said regulations and ordinances according to the tenor of the fourth Article, or for placing the territories required under the exclusive authority and control of the English Company Bahadoor. And in case His Highness shall not issue such orders within ten days from the time when the application shall have formally been made to him, then the said Governor-General-in-Council shall be at liberty to issue orders, by his own authority, either for carrying into effect the said regulations and ordinances, or for assuming the management and collection of the revenues of the said territories, as he shall judge most expedient for the purpose of securing the efficiency of the said military funds and for providing for the effectual protection of the country and the welfare of the people. Provided always, that whenever and so long as any part or parts of His said Highness' territories shall be placed and remain under the exclusive authority and control of the said East India Company, the Governor-General-in-Council shall render to His Highness a true and faithful account of the revenue and produce of the territories so assumed; provided also, that in no case whatever shall His Highness's actual receipt or annual income, arising out of his territorial revenue, be less than the sum of the net revenues of the whole territories ceded to him by the fifth Article of the Treaty of Mysore; which sum of one lakh of Star Pagodas, together with the amount of one-fifth of the said net revenues, the East India Company engages, at all times and in every possible case, to be secure and cause to be paid for His Highness' use.

Article 6:

His Highness Maharajah Mysore Kishna Rajah Oodiaver Bahadoor engages that he will be guided by a sincere and cordial attention to the relations of peace and amity now established between the English Company Bahadoor and their allies and that will carefully abstain from any interference in the affairs of any State in alliance with the said English Company Bahadoor, or any State whatever. And for securing the object of this stipulation it is further stipulated and agreed that no communication or correspondence with any foreign State whatever shall be held by His said Highness without the previous knowledge and sanction of the said English Company Bahadoor.

Article 7:

His Highness stipulates and agrees that he will not admit any European foreigners into his service without the concurrence of the English Company Bahadoor; and that he will apprehend and deliver up to the Company's Government of whatever description who shall be found within the territories of His said Highness without regular passports from the Company's Government, it being His Highness' determined resolution not to suffer, even for a day, any European foreigners to remain within the territories now subjected to his authority, unless by consent of the said Company.

Article 8:

Whereas the complete protection of His Highness' said territories requires that various fortresses and strong places situated within the territories of His Highness should be garrisoned and commanded, as well in time of peace as of war by British troops and officers, His Highness Maharajah Mysore Kishna Rajah Oodiaver Bahadoor engages that the said English Company Bahadoor shall at all times be at liberty to garrison, in whatever manner they may judge proper, all such fortresses and strong places within His said Highness' territories as shall appear to them advisable to take charge of.

Appendix to Chapter 14   393

Article 9:

And whereas, in consequence of the system of defence which it may be expedient to adopt for the security of the territorial possessions of His Highness Maharajah Mysore Kishna Rajah Oodiaver Bahadoor, it may be necessary that certain forts and strong places within His Highness' territories should be dismantled or destroyed, and that other forts, and strong places should be strengthened and repaired, it is stipulated and agreed that the English East India Company Bahadoor shall be the sole judges of the necessity of any such alterations in the said fortresses; and it is further agreed that such expenses as may be incurred on this account shall be borne and defrayed in equal proportions by the contracting parties.

Article 10:

In case it shall become necessary for enforcing and maintaining the authority and government of His Highness in the territories now subjected to his power, that the regular troops of the English East India Company Bahadoor should be employed, it is stipulated and agreed that, upon formal application being made for the service of the said troops, they shall be employed in such manner as to the said Company shall seem fit; but it is expressly understood by the contracting parties that this stipulation shall not subject the troops of the English East India Company Bahadoor to be employed in the ordinary transactions of revenue.

Article 11

It being expedient for the restoration and permanent establishment of tranquility in the territories now subjected to the authority of His Highness Maharajah Mysore Kishna Rajah Oodiaver Bahadoor, that suitable provisions should be made for certain officers of rank in the service of the late Tippoo Sultan, His said Highness agrees to enter into the intermediate discussion of this point, and to fix the amount of the funds (as soon as the necessary information can be obtained) to be granted for this purpose, in a separate Article, to be hereafter added to this Treaty.

Article 12:

Lest the garrison of Seringapatam should be at any time be subject to inconvenience from the high prices of provisions and other necessities, His Highness Maharajah Mysore Kishna Rajah Oodiaver Bahadoor agrees that such quantities of provisions and other necessaries as may be required for the use and consumption of the troops composing the said garrison shall be allowed to enter the place from all and every part of his dominions free of any duty, tax or impediment whatever.

Article 13:

The contracting parties hereby agree to take into their early consideration the best means of establishing such a commercial intercourse between their respective dominions as shall be mutually beneficial to the subjects of both Governments, and to conclude a commercial Treaty for this purpose with as little delay as possible.

Article 14:

His Highness Maharajah Mysore Kishna Rajah Oodiaver Bahadoor hereby promises to pay at all times the utmost attention to such advice as the Company's Government shall occasionally judge it necessary to offer to him, with a view of the economy of his finances, the better collection of his revenues, the administration of justice, the extension of commerce, the encouragement of trade, agriculture and industry, or any other objects connected with the advancement of His Highness' interests, the happiness of the people and the mutual welfare of both States.

Article 15:

Whereas it may hereafter appear that some of the districts declared by the Treaty of Mysore to belong respectively to the English Company Bahadoor and to His Highness are inconveniently situated, with a view to the proper connection of their respective lines of frontier, it is hereby stipulated between the contracting parties that in all such cases they will proceed to such adjustment, by means of exchanges or otherwise, as shall be best suited to the occasion.

Article 16:

This Treaty consisting of 16 Articles, being this day, the 8th of July, Anno Domini 1799, settled and concluded at the fort of Nazzarbah, near Seringapatam by His Excellency Lieutenant-General George Harris, Commander-in-Chief of the Forces of His Brittanic Majesty, and of the Honourable English East India Company Bahadoor in the Carnatic and on the coast of Malabar...the aforesaid gentlemen have delivered to the said Maharajah one copy of the same, in English and Persian, sealed and signed by them, and His Highness the Maharajah has delivered to the gentlemen aforesaid another copy, also in Persian and English, bearing his seal, and signed by Luchummam widow of the late Kishna Rajah, and sealed and signed by Purneah, Dewan to the Maharajah Kishna Rajah Oodiaver. And the aforesaid gentlemen have engaged to procure and to deliver to the said Maharajah without delay a copy of the same, under the seal and signature of the Right Honourable the Governor-General, on receipt of which the said Maharajah and the present Treaty shall be deemed complete and binding on the Honourable English East India Company and on the Maharajah Kishna Rajah Oodiaver, and the copy of it now delivered to the said Maharajah shall be returned.

15

THE SURVIVOR STATESMAN DEWAN PURNAIYA'S LIFE AND TIMES

I

MAY 1811

The clock had struck the end of the day and the British Resident at the Mysore court, A.H. Cole had just finished updating his diary about an issue that had vexed him no end. The year had marked the coming of age of the Maharaja of Mysore, who naturally wanted to now take complete charge of the kingdom from the Regent Dewan, Purnaiya. When the idea was initially floated, Purnaiya readily offered to resign and make way for the young man's direct assumption of power. But Purnaiya had been making numerous representations to the Company through the office of Cole, for many months now, that the post of dewan be made hereditary. Cole was stunned by this preposterous wish of the old man, whom he described as 'very avaricious'. The last paragraph of his memoirs, as quoted by Josyer, read as follows:

> My eyes have been gradually opened to the persuasion that old age, impaired faculties and evil counsel have combined to disappoint my hopes, and have tended to degrade the character of a Minister whose former conduct had deservedly ranked him among the first statesmen who have ever existed in this country. Again to my utmost surprise, he, at one conference used all his abilities to convince me that he should incur the displeasure of

the British Government for having admitted the Rajah into a share of the Government, as he said, to my consternation and astonishment, that he held the Dewanee 'by contract' and that his son or nephew or whoever he should choose to name as his successor would have a lawful claim to the situation of the Dewanee on his death or resignation.

The Honourable Governor-in-Council may believe how much I must have been startled at such a preposterous assertion and the encouragement of such foolish expectations in the breast of a man like Purniah, and I need not state that I used my utmost arguments to convince him that he was grossly mistaken. Butcha Rao, the principal friend and adviser of Purniah, and who had participated in his fortunes through life (he is between 60 and 70, about the Dewan's own age), has been bed-ridden by infirmity for nearly a year, and his intellects have been frequently deranged during this period. The advice and assistance of this man whom we have generally looked upon as the second Dewan, have consequently been denied to Purniah, and as the latter has not had strength and activity for some years to transact matters with the aid of Butcha Rao only (as he used to do formerly), he has had recourse to the members of his own family, and has permitted Coopanna, his brother-in-law, Hirniappah, his nephew, (young men under the age of 25 years) to be his principal agents, he himself generally superintending their conduct. As the old man's faculties have become impaired the influence of these young men has gained ascendancy, and their personal interests have led them to encourage in Purniah, a tenacity of power, that they might benefit under the shade of his authority.

To these young men of whose dispositions I have great doubts, I principally attribute the Dewan's defective conduct, and there is another person of the name of Tippiah, an old follower and an old rogue whose counsels I know to have had great weight. Tippiah was detected in malpractices whilst Killadar of Mysore and Chief Engineer or Superintendent of Public Works, and Major Wilks insisted upon his being expelled from the Capital, but he had influence enough to return to office and the Dewan has employed him in superintending the great nullah.

Just as Cole was about to retire for the day, the Principal Hurcars or messengers from the royal palace sought immediate audience. They sought to convey a message from His Highness. The previous day had been that of salary payments for the government servants and accordingly, the Maharaja had sent the monthly allowance to Purnaiya's son. The Maharaja was baffled when the amount was haughtily returned by his Dewan with no explanation for his conduct. The same morning, when the Maharaja questioned the actions of his Dewan, Purnaiya had risen from his seat with an air of nonchalance and, unmindful of the open durbar he was seated in, addressed the Maharaja with arrogance and disrespect. He told the young king, much to the consternation of other principal officers of the government, that since neither he nor his sons were servants of the Maharaja, he deemed it an insult to accept the money. Saying this, Purnaiya left the durbar in a huff, not even seeking the Maharaja's permission. Surprised and unsure how to respond to such behaviour in a man he regarded highly, the Maharaja sought the Resident's intervention.

Cole knew he had a tough task at hand: pandering to an elderly statesman's ego and humouring his senility. The next morning, he assured the Maharaja in a quick meeting that he would try and reason with Purnaiya. The Maharaja then summoned the Dewan. Both Cole and the Maharaja were shocked by a loud voice at the inner door of the palace.

'I am nobody's servant, I am my own master. Do you people get what I am saying? I am subservient to none!'

Of course, it was Purnaiya, who had reached the Durbar and was arguing with some junior officers. Huffing and puffing, boiling with rage, the old Dewan entered the Durbar Hall. Cole urged him to calm down and hear what he had to say.

'I shall do whatever you ask me to, Sir,' was the cold reply.

'Sir, I am given to understand that your son has been guilty of great misconduct and given the fact that you are an elderly statesman of this Province with years of experience behind you, you would agree with us in condemning this action of his.'

'What misconduct has my son been guilty of?' Purnaiya thundered in a voice bordering on the uncivil.

Cole tried to pacify the old man: 'Sir, I request you to lower your tone as you are speaking in the presence of His Highness,' he said, and narrated the previous day's incidents.

'Oh that!' Purnaiya remarked impertinently. 'My son did no wrong. It was I who returned the wages!'

Cole was startled by this brazen attitude and stole a quick look at the Maharaja's 'I told you so' face.

'Sir, I am stunned. How can someone as wise and senior as you even defend such misconduct? Don't you think it is imperative for your son to fall at the Maharaja's feet and beg his pardon? I am sure you are trying to shield him by taking the blame on yourself, as I refuse to believe that a seasoned diplomat like yourself could even think of acting in a manner as clumsy as this.'

'Of course not Mr Resident Sir,' sneered Purnaiya, 'this was my decision and my son had nothing to do with it. Neither I, nor my sons, acknowledge any master, certainly not the young lad who sits on this Throne,' he said, pointing at the hapless Maharaja. His body trembled violently, and his voice grew louder. 'We have decided that we no longer consider him our Maharaja,' was the final pronouncement.

Irritated, Cole said:

'Your Highness! I am deeply disturbed by your Dewan's manner of speech. His want of self-command and deficiency of respect to his liege Prince is something that I cannot endure any longer. I do not want to subject you to any unbecoming scene of turbulence and madness, as I too am on the verge of losing my temper. I therefore beg you to allow either of us to retire, for so long as I am in your Highness's service, I am bound by duty to protect you from such barbs and insults.'

Mindful of overstretching his case and creating a nuisance in front of the influential and authoritative Englishman, Purnaiya beat a hasty retreat, saying he would prefer to retire, leaving the Resident and the Maharaja to speak with each other. In a final show of defiance, Purnaiya retired, making a salaam only to Resident Cole. The Maharaja showed the greatest respect, rising and making his salaam to the Dewan, which went unacknowledged.

After Purnaiya departed, Cole expressed his astonishment that the Maharaja had allowed things to come to such a pass. The teenaged Maharaja replied:

'I am at a loss to understand the reason for his behaviour. I have been fearful of complaining to you of the Dewan upon this subject, although it is one of serious vexation to me, lest you might suppose that I was impatient of control, or anxious to emancipate myself from the shackles of an old man, whom I should wish to consider as my father, and whom I would ever treat as such, would he but act towards me with common respect, and not always hold me out as a boy and a fool. But you have now been an eyewitness of the fact and have perceived in my demeanour every consideration towards Purnaiya, which he on the contrary forgot himself, in your presence and even made that obeisance to you which he denied to my Throne.'

Assuring the maharaja of a swift solution, Cole departed. Purnaiya's actions and words were still ringing in the young maharaja's ears. He had always known that Purnaiya was opposed to the accession of the Wodeyar dynasty after Tipu's fall. But his conduct in the last ten years had never touched the latest low. It seemed just yesterday that the maharaja had been crowned and Purnaiya had vowed that he would do all he could to protect the maharaja and his dignity. What had changed since then?

II

PURNAIYA'S LIFE AND CAREER

Purnaiya was among the many who had betrayed Tipu. While other traitors like Mir Sadik and Mir Nadim had met their ignoble ends, Purnaiya had stayed on to serve his new masters. Shrewd and greedy, the diplomatic Purnaiya switched sides at convenience and with ease. Master tactician that he was, he transformed even adverse conditions to windows of opportunity and profit.

Born in 1746 at Thirukambur in the Kulitali district of Tiruchirapalli, he lost his father, Madhwa Brahmin Krishnacharya, at the age of ten. His mother, Lakshmiamma, worked hard to bring up her sons Purnaiya and Venkata Rao. A trader, Ranga Setty, noticed Purnaiya's potential and appointed him his gumasta or clerk. The family migrated to Satyamangalam in 1760. Annadana Setty, a friend of Ranga's and the chief supplier to Haidar's palace, took him to Srirangapatna and recruited him as a junior accountant in the daftar. Krishna Rao, the shirastedar of the toshikhane (or treasurer) had an officer called Venkataramanayya, who was in charge of Setty's dealings with Haidar. Purnaiya often settled these accounts and once, when a major discrepancy arose in the tallying, Purnaiya caught Haidar's notice by cleverly resolving the issue.

Now a confidante of Haidar's, he continued to rise up the ranks. It is said that Haidar used to quiz his many officers on various topics and rewarded those who answered intelligently. Once, Purnaiya alone could explain to Haidar why a huge log of timber floated on water, while a small stone sank. Impressed, Haidar decided to make him the head of the toshikhana. By 1770 he was made the head of the daftar where the accounts had to be maintained in Kannada, which had hitherto been maintained in Marathi under Krishna Rao.

A spell of serious trouble with Anche Shamaiya had seemed to augur doom for Purnaiya, but soon his stars were on the rise again. He became the most honoured member of Haidar's durbar and *jagirs* were presented to him. He also had the privilege of the golden umbrella, reserved for the elite few. In 1780, he saved Mysore from Cornwallis's attack and was also badly injured. His sagacity saved the day for Mysore in 1782 in the troubled times that followed Haidar's death at Narasingarayanapet. It was these talents that caught Maharani Lakshmammanni's attention, and she made overtures, inviting him to defect to her side. Purnaiya had also managed to establish friendly ties with the British under Wellesley. In fact, in a letter to Barry Close, quoted by Josyer, Wellesley wrote: 'Purnaiah's abilities have astonished me; he is so different from another man of the same kind, whom I have dealt with...'. The other man was Tirumala Rao, Maharani Lakshmammanni's agent.

Purnaiya led the Mysore side with intelligence and wisdom during the Third Mysore War despite being severely wounded himself. But his sly nature came to the fore in his dealings with his colleague and friend Krishna Rao, who hailed from the same community. As stated before, the dispossessed Palegars staged an insurgency, fanned actively by the British. At Srirangapatna, the suspicion fell on Toshikhane Krishna Rao, one of the ablest and highly trusted officers of the kingdom since the time of Haidar. He had played a pivotal role alongside Purnaiya in the crisis of 1782 following Haidar's death. Purnaiya was naturally jealous of Krishna Rao.

Narrating the unfortunate turn of events for Krishna Rao, Wilks states:

> One of his emissaries was unfortunately detected at this period, with a letter in the Canarese language, concealed in his hollow

bamboo or walking stick. The Sultaun...had reasonable cause for distrusting all Brahmins...A relation of his own who read the Canarese language, was entrusted with the examination of the letter, and the writer was seized; formerly a Brahmin, but forcibly circumcised, and now named Mahommed Abbas. The name of Sheshgere Row, brother of the treasurer Kishen Row, was implicated, and before he could be seized, he had heard of the accusation, and fled to his brother at Seringapatam; the treason seemed alarming and extensive, and Tippoo ordered the writer of the letter to be brought into his presence. Abbas...denied no part of his own imputed guilt, but boldly declared that no torture should compel him to implicate others. 'And how long,' said Tippoo, 'have you been a traitor?' 'From the period,' replied he, 'that you began to circumcise Brahmins and destroy their temples.' He was put to death, by being publicly dragged round the camp, at the foot of an elephant; but the treasurer, Kishen Row, with three brothers, including Sheshgere Row, were privately tortured and dispatched...I could never get Poornea, his colleague, to give an opinion. He kept aloof from enquiry; and of course from interposition, from the natural dread of consequences; and professed to have had no opportunity of forming a judgment.

Krishna Rao's beautiful widow was, according to Kirmani, 'tyrannically forced' into the Sultan's harem. Purnaiya had evidently mastered the skill of survival amidst all adversities. Friendships and people hardly mattered to him; they could all be sacrificed at the altar of his ambitions.

Purnaiya seems to have shared a strange relationship with Tipu. Buchanan details the tragedy of Purnaiya's beautiful daughter, who was heading to the Cauvery in a palanquin one fine morning for a ritualistic cleansing bath after the completion of her periods. It is said that some of Tipu's soldiers, besotted by the beauty of the damsel, misbehaved with her and then raped her. When Purnaiya went to Tipu for justice, the Sultan casually remarked that once a stray dog feeds on the eatable in the earthen pot, the eatable anyway loses its sanctity, becoming public property thereafter. Far from taking any action against these soldiers of his own army, he is said to have 'consoled' Purnaiya by stating that the girl would be honoured with admission into his harem despite her loss of grace. Any father would have surely been furious at such treatment and his helplessness in the face of it, despite being the prime minister of the kingdom.

On another occasion, Buchanan mentions the scene in Tipu's Darbar when Purnaiya demonstrated his characteristic intelligence in solving a problem that seemed insurmountable. So delighted was Tipu by his prime minister's intellect that he seemingly made an open offer to him to give up his false faith and join their ranks as a Muslim. A petrified Purnaiya mumbled something and quickly left. It is said that Tipu's mother who sat in *purdah* beside the throne severely admonished her son for such insolent behaviour towards his father's confidante and warned him of dire consequences if he persisted with his bigotry.

Given these events, could Purnaiya be labelled a traitor? He had been one of the most steadfast and loyal adherents of Haidar after all. What may have changed in those twenty years of Tipu's reign that prompted him to conveniently leave the fort of Srirangapatna three days prior to the storming? The answers are, sadly, unknown.

After Tipu's death, when the British forces reached his house to ask him to surrender, he declared: 'How can I hesitate to surrender to a nation who are the protectors of my tribe from Kasi to Rameswaram?'

He was amply rewarded for his services to the British by being appointed regent for the minor king and the dewan of the state. In fact, the long-standing contender for the post and the maharani's trusted and faithful ally, Tirumala Rao, was completely overlooked by the British. The Maharani was not consulted while appointing the dewan and Tirumala was never again allowed to enter Srirangapatna, even to pay his respects to his queen. Ironically, Purnaiya, who had deserted Tipu in his hour of need, made a strong (though unsuccessful) case with the British after Tipu's death to restore the throne to the Sultan's sons and not to the erstwhile family of Mysore. His rationale was that the Hindu dynasty had lost touch with the administration and the pulse of the people. The real motive was, however, the fact that Tipu's sons held him in great regard and he knew he would be the real master if they took over the reigns of the kingdom. The Wodeyars were unknown to him and he feared the maharani's hostility because Tirumala Rao and not he, was her first choice for the dewan's post. Purnaiya feared that the Hindu royalty would always view him with suspicion as a remnant of the old establishment and so he championed the cause of Tipu's descendants.

In a way, Purnaiya was a complete antithesis to Tirumala Rao. The latter's steadfast loyalty was conspicuous by its absence in Purnaiya. It was indeed a quirk of fate that the man who had single-mindedly worked for the deliverance of the Wodeyar family, albeit with his own personal agendas in mind, was completely relegated to the bin of history; while the man who had betrayed the brave Tipu and opposed the accession of the Wodeyars was recalled to a position of similar eminence even in the new set-up. Tirumala Rao had tried to enlist support for his cause with the British and written to John Sullivan, but received a completely non-committal reply:

> It would have given me the greatest pleasure to have heard that your long and faithful services had been recompensed by your having been placed under your Rana in the situation that would have been most agreeable to you. But as circumstances with which I am not acquainted have opposed such an agreement immediately upon the restoration of the Rajah's Government, you have had an additional opportunity of proving your attachment by retiring from the scene and of showing your judgement by relying on the justice of the English Government.
>
> I most earnestly recommend to you to continue in the same judicious course and to place your whole confidence in Mr Webbe and in Col. Close, whose honour, judgement and abilities are held in the highest consideration...what can I say more than that I am your true friend.

Following this, Lord Mornington recommended his services to the Court of Directors in England and got him an allowance at par with the officers of the erstwhile Tipu regime, distinguished by the title of Meer Meeran, paying him 3,500 Pagodas per annum from the Mysore treasury in addition to his other pension of 120 Pagodas per month. The maharani kept intervening and representing his case to Webbe and others in the Company, but met with little success. In 1811, Narayana Rao breathed his last and Tirumala Rao passed away as well, four years later.

Purnaiya's victory over Tirumala Rao perhaps felt even sweeter to the former as Tirumala had been related to Anche Shamaiya, the man who had implicated him in false cases and almost brought him close to death's door.

Meanwhile, at Mysore, since the king was too young to assume charge, Purnaiya was the de facto ruler. Ambitious and well networked, he shared a very close friendship with the British residents at Mysore—Barry Close, Josiah Webbe, John Malcolm Wilks, A.H. Cole—perhaps closer than he was to the maharaja! As Dr K.N.V. Shastri writes: 'He was submissive to the British Resident, but insubordinate to the Maharaja.' Colonel Wellesley had written to him on 2 March 1805 in a farewell note:*

> Lieutenant Colonel Malcolm will have informed you that affairs having begun to have a more settled appearance in the Deccan, I have obtained permission to go to England, and I shall commence my voyage in a few days. I part with you with the greatest regret; and I shall ever continue to feel the most lively interest for the honour and prosperity of the Government of the Rajah of Mysore over which you preside. For six years I have been concerned in the affairs of the Mysore government, and I have contemplated with the greatest satisfaction its increasing prosperity under your administration. Experience has proved the wisdom of the arrangement which was first made of the Government of Mysore, and I am convinced that under no other management would it have been possible for the British Government to derive such advantages from the country which you have governed, as I have enjoyed in the various difficulties with which we have contended since authority was established.
>
> Every principle of gratitude, therefore, for many acts of personal kindness to myself, and a strong sense of the public benefits which have been derived from your administration, render me anxious for its continuance and for its increasing prosperity, and in every situation in which I may be placed you may depend upon it that I shall not fail to bear testimony of my sense of your merits upon every occasion that may offer, and that I shall suffer no opportunity to pass by, which I may think favourable for rendering your service.
>
> Upon the occasion of my taking leave of you, I must take the liberty to recommend to you to persevere in the laudable path, which you have hitherto followed. Let the prosperity of the

---

* This letter appears in Josyer's 1929 book, *History of Mysore and the Yadava Dynasty*.

country be your great object; protect the ryots and traders and allow no man, whether vested with authority or otherwise, to oppress them with impunity; do justice to every man, and attend to the wholesome advice which will be given to you by the British Resident; and you may depend upon it, that your Government will be as prosperous and as permanent as I wish it to be.

In a letter of 13 February 1802 to the Resident, Barry Close (recorded by Shama Rao), Wellesley had said about Purnaiya that 'he has done everything I could wish him to do.'

III

PURNAIYA AS DEWAN

Administration

Purnaiya took over the reins of the kingdom and sought to make widespread administrative and political reforms. The prime concern was the mobilisation of the state's revenues to meet the huge expenditures entailed in the treaty that had ended the battle. As mentioned earlier, Haidar had appointed Amildars to collect revenue for each *taluk*. Tipu had carried on the same model with slight variations, bifurcating the authority into two offices—that of the Asoph or Head of Revenue and the military commander. Purnaiya abolished the former post. Mysore was divided into three administrative zones—Chitradurga, Patna Ashtagram and Bidnaur or Nagar—modelled on the organisation under Chikkadevaraja Wodeyar. These came under the direct control of the office of the dewan and his three officers or subedars who resided at Bangalore, Chitradurga and Nagar. The divisions had 115–120 *taluks*, each under an Amildar with an area of a little over than 29,000 square miles and estimated population of less than 22 lakh. The civil government had three departments: Finance, Revenue and Miscellaneous. The military was reorganised into cavalry and infantry. A kandachar was appointed for policing work in the countryside and public works as well. The *taluks* had a Golla who guarded the treasury, Shirastedars or accountants and the Amildar or revenue officer. The Shroff examined the treasury in a sort of auditing role and affixed his seal on the bags. There was a general and *huzur* treasury. Land, *sayer* (customs duty), liquor, toddy, tobacco were the main sources of revenue.

Revenue and Taxation

Land revenue formed the bulk of revenues accrued to the treasury. The figures of land revenue over the years Purnaiya served as Dewan appear here. They are proof of Purnaiya's deft 'management' of finances so as to have funds for the state's needs and also to honour the commitment to the British treaty and payable subsidies.

1799–1800	18, 93,793 Canteroi Pagodas
1800–1801	20,33,595 Canteroi Pagodas
1801–1802	23,06,370 Canteroi Pagodas
1802–1803	22,31,618 Canteroi Pagodas
1809–1810	24,10,840 Canteroi Pagodas
1810–1811	22,80,230 Canteroi Pagodas

The land tax had detailed land assessments, house tax and a plough tax (one Canteroi Pagoda from each plough and house). Dry lands paid a third of the total value of crops as tax to the state. In paddy fields, tax was collected in kind at times in lieu of cash.

The second main source of revenue was *sayer*, which denoted the local customs duty on goods passing through the *chowkis*. Some taluks levied *sayer* in contracts while government agencies directly collected it elsewhere. Salt, tobacco, sandal trees, etc., had an annually increasing *sayer* tax imposed on them. The *sayer* tax accounts of the kingdom appear here. These figures again highlight Purnaiya's ingenuous financial management:

1799–1800	2, 26,600 Canteroi Pagodas
1800–1801	2,43,787 Canteroi Pagodas
1801–1802	2,52,690 Canteroi Pagodas
1802–1803	2,57,439 Canteroi Pagodas

Liquor was the next major source of state revenue. Toddy was collected from date and *bagani* trees. The tapping of coconut trees was prohibited.

The receipts and expenditures statement of the kingdom in the year immediately after the disastrous Mysore War appear here and are taken from Shama Rao's book:

Revenues for 1799–1800		Expenses for 1799–1800	
Gross Revenue	15,18,027	Subsidy as per Treat of Srirangapatna, 1799	8,42,592
Net Revenue	15,18,027	Fixed Wages and establishments *	5,16,552
		Extraordinary expenses **	1,50,832

(All figures in Canteroi Pagodas)
*Included wages to Silledar horses, infantry, regular sepoys, physicians, surgeons, harcars, chopdars, pharash, washermen, masalchis, garrison men, artificers for repairing forts and palaces, peons, drummers, 162 gardeners, mustaddis and other junior-level officers, the dalavoy family, company representatives, etc.
** Included gifts to Rajas of other states, bhatta for Kandachar peons, rituals, ceremonies, charities, donations to temples, grains, cattle, poultry, clothes for the Raja's family, utensils, jewels, and personal expenses.

OTHER ADMINISTRATIVE CONCERNS

The miscellaneous department of the administrative machinery had two major heads—regulation of the Maharaja's household, managed by Maharani Lakshmammanni who ensured that there were no lacunae in the pomp and splendour of family rituals, and the other department which looked into judicial records. The judiciary was reorganised. A separate body headed by the Khaji was appointed to look into disputes under the Islamic Shariat law, while the rest of the citizens followed a common civil code. The Amildar of the *taluk* looked into the resolution of petty cases, while the subedar was in charge of the criminal and civil ones. In 1805, Adalat Kutcheries were set up by Purnaiya, consisting of two judges, two Shirastedars, six persons representing the panchayat, one pandit and one Islamic/maulvi scholar.

A glimpse of the changing demographics of the Mysore Kingdom after 1799 is as follows:

	Before 1801	In 1804
Increase in population of villages and Koppals or hamlets	23, 017	25,303
Houses in the villages and Koppals	76, 459	4,87,939
No of families residing in Villages and Koppals	4,25,624	4,82,612
Population of the Kingdom	19,15,326	21,71,754

At the cost of 1,40,000 Canteroi Pagodas, a bridge was built across the northern bank of the Cauvery in 1804. In 1806, seeing the Maharaja's wife suffering from small pox, Maharani Lakshmammanni ordered a massive launch of a small pox eradication campaign across the kingdom, which successfully controlled the dreaded disease.

The maharaja had a narrow escape in 1805–06, when Maharani Lakshmammanni took him to Nanjangud to propitiate Lord Srikanteshwara. They were accompanied by the Resident of Mysore, Major Malcolm and Dewan Purnaiya. As the procession reached Nanjangud the elephant the maharaja was riding suddenly lost its senses and ran helter-skelter causing panic in the crowd. The maharani prayed fervently to Srikanteshwara to save the maharaja's life and after that, the elephant miraculously regained its senses and sat servile in front of the still-terrified crowd.

Purnaiya in the Seat of Power

In 1807, a supplementary treaty was signed by Maharani Lakshmammanni and Dewan Purnaiya with the Company's representative, Wilks. In December of the same year, the Maharaja gifted Yelandur as *jagir* to Purnaiya for his 'extraordinary' services along with *sannads* or certificates in English, Kannada and Persian as well as a rich Khillat. After betraying Tipu during the storming of Srirangapatna, the wily Purnaiya found himself at the helm of affairs as dewan. His annual pay was fixed at a Canteroi Pagoda equivalent of Rs 18,000 and was buttressed with 1 per cent of the net revenue proceeds of the kingdom, amounting to an equivalent of about Rs 62,000. Narasimha Murthy, one of Purnaiya's descendants, writes about the *jagir* of Yelandur:

The taluk of Yelandur selected by Purnaiah for his Jagir is a small but rich tract, one of the most fertile and densely populated in Mysore...The hills have a large forest area abounding in teak, sandal, honne and other valuable trees, which are a source of wealth to the Jagir. The taluk has a large area of compact level ground traversed by the river Suvarnavati, a perennial river which is the sole source of irrigation. The fertility of the soil is conducive to the formation of gardens which yield betel-leaf, areca and coconut. Mulberry is extensively grown and silk is produced in large quantities.

The yearly yield of Yelandur was about the equivalent of Rs 30,000. Purnaiya had embezzled large amounts of money over and above this exorbitant official annual salary. At the time of his retirement, he owed 14,15,729 Canteroi Pagodas to the state. When asked to repay the debts, he paid cash worth 6,69,750 CP and jewellery worth 1,14,000 CP. The deficit of 6,31,978 remained unpaid. The amount he had amassed was nearly what the kingdom of Mysore paid as its annual tribute to the Company. Yet Murthy records this amusing spectacle of the *sannad* being issued by John Malcolm, the Resident, on the Maharaja's behalf and on his recommendation:

> Since the uprightness, rectitude and honesty of the Noble Purniah had been observed, and his ability and sagacity proved and tested, therefore the office of the Minister, which is at all times a trusted and honorable post was conferred to the Nobleman aforesaid...and since it is the intention of our Illustrious Mind that the remembrance of our worthy services and befitting actions performed by the Nobleman should not be totally erased and obliterated from the pages of the record of Time, and more over that the children of this Nobleman shall while contemplating the result of his diligent services, dwell in comfortable and easy circumstances exalted and distinguished for ever and ever; therefore with the advice and the approval of the Government of the Honourable English Company, we have conferred the taluk of Yelandur on the aforesaid Nobleman as an hereditary Freehold (Inam) as long as the course of the Sun and Moon, which are the illumination of the World...

Thus, no effort was spared to pamper and mollify the avaricious dewan. But these only planted more desires in his ambitious heart.

In 1808, an accurate map and survey of Mysore state under Marquess of Wellesley's orders was conducted by Lieutenant Colonel Mackenzie. This was a milestone, as it was the first map of Mysore. In 1809, subsequent to the abolition of an allowance called tentage to the officers in the Madras army, the garrison at Srirangapatna rebelled. After driving the Mysore troops out of the fort, they seized the treasury, blew up the bridges, loaded the guns, formed a committee of safety and sent out a detachment that captured some money on its way to the paymaster. The rebels also got reinforcements of troops from Chitradurga and Bednaur. The resident thereupon called for Purnaiya's assistance to hold them in check till he made haste from Bangalore. The dewan sent 3,000 cavalry for the purpose. The Chitradurga regiment was stopped at Nagamangala by which time the troops arrived from Bangalore and forced the rebels to submit. Srirangapatna was abandoned as a military station and a British cantonment was set up at Bangalore.

Apart from managing the administration of the kingdom, Purnaiya also had the task of tackling armed rebellions that seemed to spring up in different parts of the kingdom and its neighbourhood. The transition of power was something that the different players were yet to get used to and they decided to exploit the flux in the system to assert themselves more effectively. Purnaiya was in charge, and he squashed the rebellions deftly.

The Revolt of Dhondoji Wagh

As early as 1799, Purnaiya was faced with the revolt by Dhondoji Wagh—a Maratha sardar who was born in Chennagiri and joined Haidar's army in 1780. He fled the army during Cornwallis's attack on Mysore and re-entered the army in 1794. It is believed that Tipu tried forcing Islam on him and, when he resisted, imprisoned him and even renamed him Sheikh Ahmed and later Malik Jehan Khan. He left Srirangapatna on 20 August 1799 for Aigur in Hassan's Malnad and thereafter joined the Maratha camp. He opened correspondences with the sardars formerly in Tipu's service and gathered an army of 5,000 cavalry from the remnants of the Mysore army. He occupied Shimoga and proclaimed himself the 'king of the two worlds'. This was followed by the occupation of Nagar and Bednaur as also Gutti in the Nizam's territories. Dhondoji planned to kidnap Colonel Wellesley, who commanded the British troops in Mysore, and to murder Dewan Purnaiya. In the span of a couple of months Dhondoji held possession of a territory spanning Shimoga, Chitradurga, Dharwad and Bellary. From a slender force of 200 cavalrymen he managed to muster a cavalry force of 5,000 men and an army of 80,000 men, enlisting support from the princes of Ramdurg, Sholapur, Kolhapur, Anegundi and Gwalior. Many of the vanquished soldiers of Srirangapatna rallied under Dhondoji.

On Dhondoji's taking of Chitradruga on 14 July 1799, the British forces under Darlimple faced the troops of Wagh, who, according to Shama Rao,

> were immediately attacked, defeated and dispersed...of the 40 prisoners taken 39 were hanged and one man was released after he had witnessed the execution of his comrades to create fear in the country by relating the terrible fate that had overtaken some of Dhondoji's men...

Despite these repeated defeats and the recapture of some of his annexed forts like Honnalli, Shikaripura and Chennagiri, Dhondoji's revolt never seemed to be quashed. He quickly escaped from one place to the other, eluding his enemies and pursuers and avoiding a full-fledged battle. His prime concern seemed to be to conserve the army he had built rather than lose them in reckless pitched wars. Since he was well-acquainted with the terrain, he managed to give his enemies the slip and then prepare for the next 'mobile' attack. But as his army grew steadily in strength it became easier to identify him. Thus, the guerrilla war he had been conducting in typical Maratha style could not be sustained for long. Wellesley's forces pushed him to the banks of the swift-flowing Krishna River. After over a year of armed guerrilla war, Dhondoji finally met his end on 10 September 1800 fighting the combined forces of Colonel Wellesley, Purnaiya and the Dewan at Konagal in Raichur district. Munro now wrote to Wellesley stating that 'Dhondia (Dhondoji) would undoubtedly have become an independent and powerful prince and the founder of a new dynasty of cruel and treacherous sultans,' had he been allowed to roam free.

Between 1799 and 1802 unrest marked the western frontiers of Mysore which were under Company jurisdiction. The feudal lords of the Kanara region—Rajas in their own small way—Vittla, Ravivarma Narasimha Domba Hegde, Nileshwar and Kumbla had been deprived of their lands and fiefs by Haidar and Tipu's anti-feudal drive. Many of these lords escaped to neighbouring Travancore, which was under British suzerainty, and waited for the fall of Tipu. To think that the Company would deliver these scions to their old glory after the fall of Srirangapatna was to expect too much. Many of these disgruntled lords decided that they had nothing left to lose other than their own worthless lives. The British were aware of the discontent fanning the frontiers of Mysore. Speaking about them Burton Stein writes:

> There were ample grounds for Munro's concern about resistance to Company rule over Kanara in 1800. The coastal tract was in a high state of political chaos when he began his work there. A number of armed local chieftains had re-entrenched themselves in territories from which they had been driven by Hyder Ali and Tippu Sultan partly with the aid of firearms obtained from the Company...but above all it was the martial character of the dominant landholding population of Kanara, those private proprietors of small estates, about whom he talked, that had to be appeased, in part by a low level of revenue demand...most of these small estate holders of Kanara were Bunts, a caste of warriors indistinguishable from the Nayars of Malabar, except in language.

Domba Hegde of Vittla openly defied British authority and assumed independent charge on 15 December 1799. He was assisted by Timma Naik, an officer in the Mysore army at Kasargod who formed an alliance for Hegde with Subba Rao—the former shirastedar of Coimbatore. Rao had served in Tipu's army for years and was well-versed in warfare. Subba Rao's contact, Mahtab Khan, the former treasury officer under Haidar and Tipu, could impersonate Fateh Haidar, Tipu's eldest son. The idea was to galvanise the soldiers by showing that the entire movement had royal sanction from Tipu's family. This confederacy was formed at Puttur, from where on 7 May 1800, they marched to occupy Jamalabad, raided Uppinangadi and Buntwal which was a commercial hub of South Kanara. The regions were plundered and the loot transferred to their headquarters at Puttur. The British used devious methods to crush this hill revolt. The chieftain of Bekal, Raman Nair, who knew Timma Naik well, was offered all kinds of incentives to coax the latter into a hunting expedition. In the deep jungles of the region, Timma Naik was hunted down, his head chopped off and personally handed over as a mark of gallantry by Nair to his British masters. Jamalabad, a stronghold of Timma

Naik, fell to the British assault. With one of the most experienced of the rebel, dead, the others fell like a pack of cards. On 15 July 1800, Subba Rao and the impostor were also killed. By 18 July Domba Hegde was captured. Writing to Close, the Resident of Mysore, Munro stated:

> We may now by making an example of him and his associates secure Canara from internal disturbances in the future...it is the mistaken notion of observing on this coast toward every petty chief of a district all the ceremony and attention that is due to a sovereign which keeps alive dead and dangerous pretensions which it ought rather to be our aim to extinguish.

Accordingly, Hegde, his two nephews, brother-in-law, a shanbhogue and jamadar were executed in full public view on 25 August 1800.

This was followed by a string of revolts by the ruler of Balam (present-day Aigur, around Sakleshapura) in 1800–02, the Wynad revolt in 1802, the Munkasira revolt in 1804, the revolt of the Palegar of Chitradurga in 1805 and the European officers' revolt in 1809—all of which were mercilessly quashed by the dewan and the British forces. In the past, Dhondoji Wagh had fled to Aigur before reaching out to the Marathas. The Palegar Venkatadri Naik, who had pledged his support to Wagh's cause, was preparing to attack the British. He had fortified himself at Arakere. After Wagh's death, when the British realised the Palegar had been helping Wagh, the British and Mysorean troops pursued Naik till he was captured on 19 February 1802 by the Mysore forces and executed ten days later. Purnaiya ensured that the fortifications in different parts of Naik's territory were destroyed. Nearly 300 families suspected of being sympathetic to the Palegar's cause were detained and Amildars instructed not to allow trees and hedges to grow in so dense a manner that they might facilitate escape routes for potential rebels.

In 1806, the descendants of Tipu raised their banner of rebellion against the British at Vellore, where they had been posted after Tipu's fall. Writing about the Vellore uprising, Chopra, et al., say:

> In order to make the sepoys appear smart, a new form of turban resembling an European hat was introduced and ear rings and caste marks on the forehead were prohibited...but the sepoys refused to accept the new turban and openly stood against the order even though they were threatened with imprisonment. Consequently

some were arrested. On 7th May 1806 when the sepoys were asked to put on the new turban during their morning parade, they disobeyed the command by putting handkerchiefs on their bare heads and abusively calling the English officers 'dogs'...not long after this incident at Vellore there started at Wallajabad in North Arcot a similar agitation among the sepoys stationed there. In this case the initiative came from the public; they taunted those sepoys who wore the European fashioned 'topis.' Consequently the sepoys threw them away and ridiculed those who continued to wear them...this opportunity was fully exploited by the sons of Tipu Sultan who were living at Vellore in captivity...they tried to attribute a political objective to the revolt...and made clandestine contacts with sepoys and channelled the latter's discontent against the English to violent resistance with the definite object of their expulsion from South India...the sepoys were told that Moinuddin, the fourth son of Tipu would lead the rebellion with support and reinforcement from different parts of South India. It was decided secretly that they should launch their rebellion with violence and 10 July 1806 was fixed for its formal beginning. By night, the sepoys plunged into action; they killed the English sentinels in the main gateway and took possession of the magazine. This was followed by a wanton massacre of the European troops and officers though women and children were spared...There was a scramble for booty and treasure. The unprotected possessions of the English were plundered and there was confusion everywhere.

In all, 14 British officers and soldiers were killed and over 76 wounded. Notably, the rebels received active support from the people of Vellore. As the group chalked out plans to spread the fire to other garrisons and forts in Southern India, the British encircled the fort of Vellore. What followed was a bloody conflict that killed more than 800 people. Philip Haythornwaite describes it as follows:

> ...about 100 sepoys who had sought refuge in the palace were dragged out, placed against a wall and blasted with canister shot until all were dead. John Blakinston, the engineer who had blown in the gates, recalled that although such punishment was revolting to all civilized beliefs, Gillespie writes that 'this appalling sight I could look upon, I may almost say, with composure. It was an

act of summary justice, and in every respect a most proper one.' Such was the nature of combat in India where the 'civilized' conventions of European warfare did not apply.

South India was a prized possession for the British, given that they had spent over three-fourths of a century annexing the region—something they never had to do in their other conquests across India. After the bitter and decisive Fourth Anglo-Mysore War and the death of their enemy Tipu Sultan, the last thing the British wanted was a situation where some captive descendants of Tipu stirred up disturbances in the region they had so carefully secured for themselves through several treaties. Hence, they went into overdrive to ensure that the revolt was fully crushed and also sent out a strong signal to prevent anyone even entertaining such hopes. Tipu's family was packed off to Calcutta, then the seat of British imperialism, to ensure that they stirred up no trouble in the Mysore region.

Writing about the importance and implications of the Vellore uprising to Thomas Munro in August 1806, William Bentinck, then governor of Madras says:[*]

> We have every reason to believe, indeed undoubtedly to know, that the emissaries and adherents of the sons of Tipu Sultan have been most active below the Ghauts, and it is said that the same intrigues have been carried on above the Ghauts. Great reliance is said to have been placed upon the Gurrumcondah poligars, by the princes. I recommend you to use the utmost vigilance and precaution; and you are hereby authorized, upon any symptom or appearance of insurrection, to take such measures, as you deem necessary. Let me advise you not to place too much dependence on any of the native troops. It is impossible at this moment to say how far both native infantry and cavalry may stand by us in case of need. It has been ingeniously worked up into a question of religion. The minds of the soldiery have been inflamed to the highest state of discontent and disaffection and upon this feeling has been built the reestablishment of the Mussalman government, under one of the sons of Tipu Sultan: It is hardly credible that such progress could

---

[*] This letter is quoted in Gleig's 1830 book, *The Life of Major General Sir Thomas Munro*.

Maharaja Mummadi Krishnaraja Wodeyar (1799-1831)

Mummadi Krishnaraja Wodeyar hosting the Europeans and his subjects at a Dasara durbar

An ageing Mummadi Krishnaraja Wodeyar

Portrait of Sir Mark Cubbon

Young princess Kempananjammanni

Young prince Chamarajendra Wodeyar

The bust of Dewan Sheshadri Iyer, Bangalore

The Rangacharlu Memorial Hall, Mysore keeping the Dewan's memories alive

Chamarajendra Wodeyar with his children

A painting of Maharaja Nalwadi Krishnaraja Wodeyar

Empress of India: Queen Victoria

Young prince Chamarajendra Wodeyar

The bust of Dewan Sheshadri Iyer, Bangalore

The Rangacharlu Memorial Hall, Mysore keeping the Dewan's memories alive

Chamarajendra Wodeyar with his children

A painting of Maharaja Nalwadi Krishnaraja Wodeyar

Empress of India: Queen Victoria

*Young prince Krishnaraja
ascends the throne*

*Regent Queen Kempa Nanjammanni
Vanivilasa Sannidhana avaru*

A model of the old palace that succumbed to fire

The magnificent new palace of Mysore

A life-size statue of Nalwadi Krishnaraja in the Mysore palace

Maharani Pratapa Rudra Kumari Lakshmi Vilasa Sannidhana avaru

The Maharaja on one of his foreign trips, with Dewan Mirza Ismail to his immediate left

Brilliance personified: Sir M. Vishweswaraiya

Yuvarani Kempucheluvajammanni

Yuvaraja Kanthirava Narasimharaja Wodeyar

The Yuvaraja on a trip to Rome

An ageing statesman—Nalwadi Krishnaraja Wodeyar (his autograph in the background)

The Yuvaraja with his daughters, Princesses Vijaya, Sujaya and Srijaya

Princess Krishnajammanni

Young prince Jayachamaraja

The lifeline of farmers: the KRS Dam

The imposing building of the Indian Institute of Science, Bangalore

Aesthetic delight: the Brindavan Gardens

His Royal splendour: a painting of Maharaja Jayachamaraja Wodeyar

The princesses at the Royal School

Prince Charming: Jayachamaraja in his youth

Jayachamaraja in Western attire

*Prince Jayachamaraja's marriage with
Princess Satyaprema Kumari Devi*

*Maharani
Tripurasundarammanni Avaru*

Ascending the Golden Throne

In Your Majesty's service: the Royal Durbar in session

The British Resident addresses the Durbar

Maharaja Jayachamaraja addressing a function

The Maharaja with Pandit Nehru

*The Maharaja with the former President of India
Dr Sarvapalli Radhakrishnan*

Rajaji visits the Mysore Palace

*With C. Rajagopalachari at the
Dasara Exhibition*

have been made in so short a time, and without the knowledge of any of us. But, believe me, the conspiracy has extended beyond all belief, and has reached the most remote parts of our Army; and the intrigue has appeared to have been everywhere most successfully carried on. The capture of Vellore, and other decided measures in contemplation, accompanied by extreme vigilance on all parts will, I trust, still prevent a great explosion.

Thus many of the early uprisings Purnaiya faced in Karnataka against British hegemony were one-off incidents of armed struggle by army retinues or by remnants of the former feudal hierarchy. The movement was yet to assume a mass nature, one that captured popular public and peasant imagination. But the countdown to the final showdown had begun.

Meanwhile, far removed from the hurly-burly of politics, wars and intrigues, the family of the maharaja of Mysore revelled in their new status after decades of oblivion. The infant maharaja could not in any case be expected to dabble in affairs of state. The role of Maharani Lakshmammanni, however, was reduced merely to ceremonial niceties. Her advancing age and the long years of struggle and captivity she had endured seemed to have dampened her famed sagacity and she hardly took any interest in affairs of state. Two travellers who visited Mysore during this period, Francis Buchanan and Lord Valentia, have left behind graphic accounts of the state of the kingdom and the maharaja. Buchanan found the reconstruction of the old palace at Mysore, 'so far progressed as to have made it a comfortable residence for the young Maharajah.' He found the Maharaja very much recovered in health, and though he was between six and seven years of age, he spoke and behaved with great propriety and decorum. 'On account of etiquette the Rajah endeavoured in public to preserve a dignified gravity of countenance, but when his countenance relaxed, he was very lively and interesting,' Buchanan wrote.

Lord Valentia, a nephew of Lord Mornington, visited Mysore in 1804. He met the maharaja seated on his heavily-carved, ivory masnad. Dressed in gold tissue with some pearls round his neck, the maharaja returned Lord Valentia's bow. Chairs were placed to the left of the throne for the eminent guest and his friends. Shama Rao quotes Valentia as saying:

I paid the usual compliments through Major Symons and Narasinga Rao assuring the Rajah of the satisfaction I felt at seeing him on the throne of his ancestors, and the confidence the British Nation had in his friendship. The Rajah replied that he owed everything to the British and that his gratitude was unbounded. I turned the conversation to the new town of Mysore, and several indifferent subjects to try if the Rajah's replies would be ready. He never hesitated, spoke sensibly, and I was assured by Major Symons that he was not prompted. He is about 11 years old, of middle size, neither tall nor short for his age, not handsome but of an intelligent countenance. He seemed lively. But on such a public occasion it would have been indecorous even to have smiled. He did so once but was immediately checked by a person who stood by him. I enquired of his pursuits and was informed that he was fond of riding and sports of the field. These were considered as becoming his dignity. But when I observed that he seemed playful, I was instantly assured that he was not so. I therefore ceased my questions as I found that I should not have his doing anything that was not according to rule. I strongly recommended his learning English, and pointed out the advantage it was to the Rajah of Tanjore in his communications with the British Government to be able to write and speak in their language. They assured me that it should certainly be done. I regretted that his youth prevented my having the honour of a visit from him at Seringapatam, and therefore requested that he would oblige me by accepting a sabre as a small memorial. Having procured one for the purpose which had a handle of agate ornamented with rubies after the Asiatic fashion, I delivered it into his own hand and he immediately placed it beside him, assuring me that that it was particularly a valuable present to him as he was a Kshatriya by caste. He in return put round my neck a handsome string of pearls from which was suspended a jewel of flat diamonds and uncut rubies. He also presented me in trays which were as usual laid at my feet, two beautiful chowries, two punkhas and two walking sticks of sandalwood with two bottles of oil which he requested me to accept. Immediately, a salute was fired from the walls of the fort, and the strings of pearls were put round our necks. His mother sent her compliments with inquiries after my health and expressions of satisfaction at my having honoured her son with a visit. Immediately afterwards a paan and atthar were distributed and we took our leave.

In February 1810 the maharani, who had almost single-handedly ensured the restoration of the kingdom to the family, died. That very same year the maharaja turned sixteen and wished to take over the reins of the kingdom from Purnaiya, who readily offered to resign, though he did not follow up his words with actions. A.H. Cole, through whom Purnaiya was pushing his case, mentions in his memoirs:

> It is here requisite for me to mention that great caution was necessary for the security of the public money in the Dewan's house, as two of his family, absolutely took out of the public Toshikhana, whilst His Highness the Rajah was at Nanjangud, jewels etc to the amount of one lakh and fourteen thousand Pagodas (or about Rs 4 ½ Lakhs), which they have acknowledged and offered to restore, and that, after the scene of violence which I had the honour to detail, an attempt was made, and partly succeeded, in the night to remove some of the Sircar property from the house of Purniah which has always been situated in the heart of the Public Treasury forming the Principal part of it.

When a government party of finance officers from the palace reached his house to classify the accounts and arrive at a settlement, Purnaiya became abusive and flung the foulest of invectives against the maharaja. When the final accounting showed a balance of about Rs 43 lakhs due from him, the raja said that despite the insults heaped on him by the dewan, he would forego Rs 19 lakhs and receive Rs 24 lakhs from Purnaiya as full and final settlement. He also agreed to pay him an annual pension of 6,000 Canteroi Pagodas even after his retirement, which would happen in Purnaiya's 65th year.

But on 27 March 1812, Purnaiya died at his house in Srirangapatna. The maharaja sent in his condolences and prepared for the funeral. A monthly pension of 500 Canteroi Pagodas was assigned to his eldest son. Thus ended the story of the ambitious, shrewd and tactful Dewan Purnaiya, who had ably steered the affairs of the kingdom in the troubled times. It also marked the takeover of the maharaja in independent charge, bereft of the two people who had guided him all along—Maharani Lakshmammanni and Dewan Purnaiya.

It was a challenge that he unfortunately could not handle.

16

THE BECKONING OF DOOM AD 1812-30

I

THE REIGN OF MUMMADI KRISHNARAJA WODEYAR

The young maharaja took independent charge of the kingdom in 1811. Rama Rao was the first dewan to work under him between 1812 and 1814. The other dewans who followed during his reign were Siddharaja, Baburao, Lingaraja Urs and Venkataraje Urs (between 1818 and 1831). He took measures to revitalise the administrative set-up.

Eighteen *kacheris* were set up to look into different matters of administration—Dewan, Kille, Katte, Bargir, Sandal, Sawaar, Toshikhane, Piriyad, Modikhane, Kandachar, Barr, Barigath, Duyyambar, Jinasi, Anche, Amrita Mahal, Shagird Pesh and Jillo. Six *tukudis* or *fouzdaries* or administrative units of the kingdom were made—Ashtagram, Bangalore, Chitradurga, Manjarabad, Nagar and Maddagiri with 28, 28, 13, 13, 24 and 19 taluks respectively. A sadar court with two bakshis was set up in Mysore along with three other courts with two presidents called hakims. The fourth court was a magisterial one. Separate courts were set up to try criminal cases. The police system was the same as under Purnaiya with Barr sepoys for assistance. The army had seven major divisions under the joint command of the Silledar at Sindhughat, Katte, Huliyurdurga, Nagamangala, Chennarayapatna, Kunigal and Chennapatna, each under a Tukdidar. A 500-strong infantry, called bargir, was also employed.

The people who managed state affairs after Purnaiya were continuously caught up in internal ego clashes. Rama Rao had been a commander of cavalry under Haidar and Tipu and came from Badami. Bhima Rao of Annigere and Krishna Rao of Hanagal accompanied him. He was made Fouzdar of Nagar in 1799 by Purnaiya. He was the virtual dewan after Purnaiya's exit and filled up most public offices of influence with his friends and family members. Speaking of Rama Rao and his clan, historian Shama Rao states:

> Rama Rao's successors in the office of Foujdar from 1805 to 1825 with only an interruption of a few months were persons nearly allied to him by blood or marriage, namely Survotham Rao, twice Foujdar, whose son was married to Rama Rao's niece Pompiah, Rama Rao's nephew, Balakrishna Rao, his grand nephew and Krishna Rao, another nephew.

Babu Rao, his successor, was also a remnant of the interregnum era. He was shirastedar in the dewan's office and stayed on till his son took over that post in 1818 and he himself rose to the post of dewan. The royal court also had a few persons called moosahebs who were consulted on matters of public interest. Bakshi Rama Rao was a moosaheb for a while. Veene Venkatasubbaiyya—a corrupt official and a great *veena* player—was regarded as a wicked and unprincipled man who had won the favour of the maharaja. He ensured plum posts for his relatives in the Nagar division Amildari and the Customs office at Kavaledurga. He had been removed by Resident Cole once, but using the influence of one Ramaswamy Mudaliar who was close to Cole, Venkatasubbaiyya made a comeback. In fact, all defaulting and corrupt officials knew just where to go to shield their misdeeds—Ramaswamy Mudaliar, who expected huge favours in return for his help. A minor officer under Major Wilks, Cole's predecessor as Resident, Mudaliar had later served Cole as dubash or an interpreter. He soon became anche bakshi or post master general to the maharaja. When Casmaijor became the Resident after Cole, Mudaliar's influence over the palace and the Residency grew phenomenally. The rising clout of this new Brahmin bureaucracy becomes clearer in the case of Mothikhane Narasinga Rao about whom Shama Rao states:

> He had seven brothers in service and he himself was in secret charge of 10 taluks. Veene Venkatasubbiah's relations became Amildars of 7 Taluks in the Nagar Division. Survotham Rao who

was Foujdar of Nagar from 1816–26 employed many of his own relations in government service of that division during the long period of more than 10 years he held office as Foujdar.

Chowdaiyya, Venkatasubbaiyya and Hanagal Krishna Rao became Mudaliar's partners in sin. Other moosahabs who were complicit in the nefarious designs of this famous trio were Gangadhara Rao (son of Purnaiya's deputy Batche Rao), Vyasa Rao and Toshikhane Nanjappa. They pulled the strings from behind the scenes, ensuring that the Resident and maharaja acted according to their convenience. They also poisoned the Resident against the maharaja. Cole was now a different man with his opinion of the maharaja much changed since the time of Purnaiya's exit.

THE FISCAL MESS

Revenue exaction and oppressive taxation became the only solution to the fiscal mess. In 1792, the princely state of Mysore enjoyed a gross revenue of 14,12,553 Canteroi Pagodas. By 1802–03, when the economy was fractured and there was a drastic decline in agriculture and production, this figure had almost doubled to 25,41,571 Canteroi Pagodas. How did Mysore achieve this? Why did the state have to cough up such high revenues? The answer lies in the Subsidiary Treaty of 1799, which dictated that the state had to pay its British masters an equivalent of Rs 24.5 lakh. By 1881, this figure increased by another 10.5 lakhs, and it was only in 1928 that the figure reverted to that specified by the 1799 treaty. It was said that Mysore's tributes formed almost half the total contributions of all the 198 tribute-paying vassal states of princely India.

But did the state have the resources and the revenue to do the same? A look at the revenue figures clarifies the point. In 1809–10, net revenue receipts were an equivalent of Rs 28,24,646, peaking to a gross revenue figure of 60.25 lakhs and net revenues of about Rs 37,18,633 in 1811–12, gradually registering a fall in 1825–26 to about Rs 28,64,950. However, that very year the state incurred the expense of the Maratha wars. To top things, along came a crash in agricultural prices caused by the withdrawal of British garrisons and subsequent fall in demand, and a disastrous drought that hit different parts of the state. By 1818–19, there was a huge fiscal deficit, for the first time, of 7,83,749 Canteroi Pagodas.

Lewis Rice describes the dismal state of affairs:

Purnaiya's system of government was no doubt absolute; and as a financier, the accumulation of surplus revenue presented itself to him, as a prime end to be attained. It may be questioned, therefore, whether he did not to some extent enrich the treasury at the expense of the State, by narrowing the resources of the people; for by 1811 he had amassed in the public coffers upwards of two crores of rupees.

In fact, Josyer writes that the maharaja himself described the avaricious intentions of his dewan after the latter passed away in 1815.

The late Divan Purniya, whose talents lay only in the collection of revenues, directed his attention to the accumulation of money merely for the purpose of displaying his industry and zeal in this branch of the administration and in the course of 12 years he created a separate fund. But he was inattentive to the interests of the people and the inhabitants of the provinces were consequently reduced to great straits and difficulties.

Pinning the blame entirely on Purnaiya ensures that we miss the bigger picture. He was indeed a zealot and despot when it came to revenue exaction. But were there too many options in front of the impoverished state? The annual subsidies had to be paid irrespective of droughts or floods. The state had to play second fiddle to all the British conquests and political ambitions by sending in men, materials and cash during the continuous battles that the Company waged with other Indian states. Agriculture, the mainstay of the people, had been devastated as we saw earlier. The local industries were stripped of the position of eminence that they enjoyed under Tipu. There were natural calamities galore and the economy was under heavy strain. The only option that the administrators found fit to salvage the position of the state was taxation and more taxation. Rice talks about the ridiculous extents to which this theory led, where more than 769 petty items came under the taxman's net.

Among these were such whimsical taxes on marriage, on incontinency, on a child being born, on its being given a name and on its head being shaved. In one village the inhabitants had to pay a tax because their ancestors had failed to find the stray horse of a palegar and anyone passing a particular spot in Nagar without keeping his hands close to his sides had to pay a tax. All these taxes were formally entered in the Government records as part of the resources of the State.

Consequently, from an equivalent of Rs 42 lakh in 1791, the tax revenues of Mysore rose to 93 lakhs by 1809. In 1811 the state revenues stood at 60.25 lakhs and by 1816–17 it stood at 71.25 lakhs.

The continuous dip in revenues set off alarm bells in Madras. On 16 September 1826, Sir Thomas Munro, governor of Madras visited Mysore. He held a high-powered meeting with the maharaja and the state officials on the dwindling revenue scenario. He warned the maharaja that if things were not corrected soon, they would be forced to take recourse to the fourth article of the Treaty of 1799, which authorised the British to take over the state's administration in these circumstances. He suggested that the maharaja must furnish annual accounts to the British government, which would help the latter assess the situation accurately. The maharaja on his part sheepishly agreed with Munro but tried to explain how part of the problem was due to the misconduct of a dewan appointed against his wishes. The Resident jumped in to defend this appointment, claiming that the appointment was made strictly with the maharaja's agreement. Sensing that the situation was getting volatile, Munro reiterated that, notwithstanding political or natural calamities, the continuous dip in revenue was a serious cause of concern. He also turned down the maharaja's suggestion to discontinue the office of the dewan for a while and let him take up the administration independently, on the premise that the administration of a state as large as Mysore was inconceivable without a dewan. Munro thus left Mysore convinced that here was a man who knew nothing about running a state. Thanks to regular exaggerations by the likes of Krishna Rao and Venkatasubbaiyya, the opinion slowly turned to belief even at Madras.

Peasantry in Trouble

The general lot of peasants all over India under Company rule was unenviable and one of abject misery. The country faced a series of famines in the nineteenth century. Unfortunately, nature alone was not to blame for these famines; there were political factors as well. First, India's indigenous textile industries were destroyed by London's high tariffs and the import of cheap British-manufactured products, impoverishing thousands of town-dwellers who were forced into the countryside to compete for dwindling land. Second, India's traditional granary reserve system, designed to offset the impact of bad harvests, was dismantled. Third, India's peasants were pressured into growing crops for exports, making them dependent on fluctuating world-market prices for their means of subsistence. As a result, tens of millions of people died of starvation. These famines were not caused by a shortage of food. They took place at the very same time that annual grain exports from India were on the rise. India actually began importing food under British rule, because Indians were growing cash crops like cotton and tea to be sent to Britain.

Ryots who failed to pay their arrears for four or five years had to auction their properties at the government's behest to repay the dues. If the payable amount was a small figure, the dues would get written off. But these remissions were not allowed for the tenants and therefore added up to the landlord's receipts. The government gave remissions to the landlords though they used to lease their lands for cultivation by their tenants. Thus the benefits of the remission did not reach the man ploughing the fields. The year 1809–10 saw the most impoverished harvests in South Kanara districts. The ryots naturally clamoured for a remission of revenues. This pulled down the net revenues of the state, and they hit rock bottom by 1830–31. Bhat records that the then district collector of South Kanara writes:

> It is now the third year of low price of its staples, and in the last of the three, that price had sunk extremely below the former rates as to have thrown many of the farmers into a state of ruin irretrievable; whilst in many more also amongst those above that class even their kists have not been sent in without a considerable sacrifice of lands or in mortgages.

The happiest in this situation were the moneylenders and *sowcars*. A new class of middlemen who had sprung up under colonial rule, and mainly belonged to the Gowda Saraswat Brahmin and Bunt communities, they ensured that they doled out loans to the helpless farmers at rates that defied repayment. In no time at all, a state that had a rich and teeming agricultural and industrial economy was seen reeling under the severest economic crisis it had ever witnessed. Exploiting the situation were the colonial masters, who cared only about the annual figures. And as a silent witness to all this, sat the maharaja of Mysore. Bound by the terms of the Treaty of Srirangapatna, the maharaja of Mysore sat quiet through all this. Stung by British criticism for lacking financial acumen, he introduced the Sharat System in a desperate attempt to cough up revenues.

According to the Sharat or Contract system, an annual stipulation was made with each amildar that a certain amount of revenue would be realised for the state, and if the collections fell short of that amount, the amildar would be held responsible for the deficit. Safeguards were established to ensure that the peasants were not unduly harassed. The idea seemed to work in its initial years. But for prolonged success of such a mechanism a strong central force—such as the Palegar used to be—was essential. The declining agricultural produce only meant that the amildars would transfer the burden on to the peasant. As arrears began to mount, the system was virtually transformed into an auction of land revenue to the highest bidder for one or two years at a time. The amildars began to subcontract collection of rents and these contractors were ruthless in their task of exaction of revenues. Writing about the Sharat System Rice states:

> All remonstrances failed to check the Raja's downward course. High offices of State were sold to the highest bidder while the people were oppressed by the system of sharti, which had its origin under Purniya's regency. Sharti was a contract made by the Amildar that he would realise for the government a certain amount of revenue; that if his collections should fall short of that amount he would make good the deficiency and that if they exceeded it the surplus should be paid to the government. The amount which the Amildar thus engaged to realise was generally an increase on what had been obtained the year preceding. In the Muchalika or agreement, the Amildar usually bound himself not to oppress the ryots, nor impose any new taxes, or compel the ryots to purchase the government share of garden but this provision was merely formal; for any violation of the contractors in any of these points when represented to the government was taken no notice of. The consequence was that the ryots became impoverished...the distress arising from this state of things...fell heavily on the ryots, who groaned upon the oppression of every tyrannical Sharti Foujdar and Amildar.

In *The Finances of the Mysore State, 1799–1831* historian M.H. Gopal details the manner in which the Sharat system worked:

> In the Nagar Division, the cultivator did not pay the revenue directly to the state. In some taluks (such as Simoga, Tarikere, Holi Honnur, Ajjampura, Honnali, Chandgere, Shikaripur, Basawapatna, Kumsi, Lukkavalli, Muntagatti and Anawatti) the rent was paid through the Patels of the villages who adjusted their accounts with the Amildars, in others (such as Nagar, Anantpur, Kavalidurg, Koppa, Sagara, Chandragutti and Soraba) the rent was paid through a class of people called guttigedars. In other parts of the country the practice of paying through the patels as well as the direct dealing between the ryot and the Amildar prevailed. The latter after arbitrarily fixing the assessment of a village according to his own idea of its ability to pay, compelled the patel or the contractor to collect the amount. In his turn the patel or contractor shifted the burden onto the ryots. Sometimes the patel and the amildar conspired together to squeeze the ryot. Where there was direct contact with the ryot, an arbitrary assessment was fixed directly on the holdings. Further, in waram lands while dividing the crops between the state and the cultivator, an unduly large share of grain appears to have been taken for the State. The amildars also forced the ryots to buy the government share of the grain at prices above the market rates. These grains, of course, did not go into the public treasury but into the amildar's pocket...if the cultivator did not pay, perhaps on account of his inability, his goods and cattle were seized and sold, and his wife and children confined. The result was that the ryot was ruined and cultivation decreased.

Defaulting peasants usually faced severe torture. Historian Shama Rao notes:

> Sometimes heavy stones were placed on the heads of the defaulters and they were forced to stand in the sun with these weights and it was also not unusual to inflict corporal punishments with a cane or a whip.

The amildar emerged as the new power in this sordid and corrupt scheme of things. He exercised authority over both the village as well as town levels and acted as an executive head and as the highest judicial authority at the local level. He was the interface between the state and the peasants. Power corrupts and absolute power corrupts absolutely, and so the office of the amildar degenerated into one infamous for the oppression of ryots and the embezzlements of state resources. They even colluded with thugs and bandits to rob peasants and merchants and fill their coffers. The officials of the kingdom under the cronies mentioned earlier continued to revel in their corrupt and reckless practices. Local officials at the *taluk* or village level related mostly to these influential persons at the court and the residency and, being secure in their protection, indulged in large-scale extortions and misuse of public money. Some officials in Shimoga and Kadur districts were in league with robber bands and committed heinous crimes against the rural population; all going to prove that corruption in the bureaucracy and criminalisation of politics in India is an ancient malaise.

Nature also played its part in this entire mess. Another terrible famine broke out in 1823–24 and a cholera epidemic raged across the kingdom. Natural disaster, such as plague and the pox, raged over the countryside. The ill-prepared, illiterate masses resorted to prayer, propitiating Amma or the Mother Goddess, and her various avatars such as Plague-amma, Pattalamma and the rest of the pantheon.

The peasant was thus severely crippled, physically and financially, which made it all the easier for the amildar to control him entirely. The Sharat System—envisaged to enable the amildars to collect revenues from farmers without exploitation—was a bane for the peasantry. Munro writes about the many reasons for this tragic collapse of the rural peasantry in the years following 1799:

> However unfavourable the season may have been in the Carnatic, the produce will probably be found to be very equal to its consumption; a total failure of the crops is unknown, except in single villages or very small districts. In the very worst years when the crops are everywhere poor, and in particular villages totally destroyed, the produce is always equal to 8 or 9 months consumption, and the deficiency is made up by the grain of former years remaining on hand, and by importation from the neighbouring provinces where the season may have been more favourable. The seed time in India continues so long, it is so easy when one kind of grain

fails, to plough up the land and substitute a second; the produce is in general, so abundant and there is usually so much grain laid up in plentiful years by the farmers and merchants that it may be safely observed that no famine is ever produced in this country by the operation of seasons alone. The scarcity which arises from the seasons is converted into famine in the territories of the native powers by war, by the rapacity of the government in anticipating the revenue by absurd though well meant, regulations for keeping down the price and supplying the great towns, and above all by the endless exactions and robberies by petty zamindars.

Oblivious to these sufferings, the maharaja continued to splurge what little money there was on royal indulgences and pastimes. A light rap on the knuckles or even a stern warning from Company officials—these made no difference. One such letter by the governor of Madras, Lushington, admonishes the maharaja for his reckless spending habits thus:*

> The sources of Your Highness' difficulties are a lavish expenditure of the treasures which you possess ... in the adjustment of Your Highness' debts to sowcars, I learn that your revenues have been in many instances diverted from their proper objects, the payment of your troops and Hoozoor establishments, to your personal expenses, that when your ready-money funds have been insufficient for this purpose you have either substituted donations in lands granted to Sowcars or some particular privileges of collection and that you have alienated a large portion of your revenues, by extensive grants of Enams, in many cases, to persons utterly undeserving of your bounty...Your Highness' extensive grants of Enam lands are another cause of your financial distress, the more alarming because they form a drain upon your resources which is annually increasing. In the Dewan Purneah's time the Enamtee amounted to 1,84,766, 3.14 ¾ Canteroi Pagodas. In 1828 it was 3,53,165, there being an increase of 1,68,998, 3.9 since the time of Purneah. But between 1828 and 1830 a further increase took place, making together the immense sum of 4,34,346, 5.4 Canteroi Pagodas, withdrawn from the resources of the State.

---

* This letter appears in Shama Rao's 1936 book, *Modern Mysore*.

> It is my painful duty to inform Your Highness that an alienation of your revenues by grants of land, in a measure disproportionate to your means, is totally irreconcilable with the mutual engagements existing between your Highness' and the Company's Governments and I recommend your Highness... to refrain from making such grants in future...it is absolutely necessary that you constantly devote a daily portion of your time to the duties of your high station, and then your finances will soon be restored to a proper state...

Constantly funding the British army in its Indian conquests further drained Mysore's dwindling resources. Rupees 20.7 lakh were spent in 1809–10 and 10.5 lakhs in 1824–25 for the Sowar Kacheri and Bargir. The maharaja also organised lavish parties for European guests and spent huge amounts on buying them princely gifts. With so little disposable income left, the arrears for the army's salaries started piling up. Nearly seven lakhs were due to the Kandachar peons during 1824–25. This led to a natural and growing discontent among the civil and military officials owing to non-payment of their salaries because of the constraints on the treasury. Thus, the royal family's careless spending resulted in widespread debt, diminution of revenue from adverse trade and seasonal conditions, growing discontent among the ryots due to the abuse of the Sharat system—all in all the perfect recipe for disaster. Mysore was in for a new round of turmoil.

The kingdom that was born out of blood and war was in the doldrums again. Mummadi Krishnaraja Wodeyar was entirely to blame for throwing away the second chance the Wodeyars had at running the kingdom. He had frittered away his fortune. The tide, as always, turned in favour of the English East India Company.

II

SOCIO-ECONOMIC IMPACT OF PROXY BRITISH RULE

A titular Wodeyar on the throne of a much-diminished Mysore, the British as the all-powerful onlookers—colonialism had arrived in state polity. For the first time, the kingdom's administrative apparatus came under foreign supervision. Colonialism brought with it its cousin, feudalism, something Haidar and Tipu had consciously attempted to wipe out.

Feudalism served as the base over which colonial powers could exert their jurisdiction. And so, among the innumerable changes Mysore underwent after the fall of Tipu was the re-establishment of the feudal set-up. The large number of Palegars who were stripped of their hereditary authority in the Interregnum period saw this as the time when their fortunes, like that of the Wodeyars, might rise. The British were wary of giving these old remnants of feudalism the complete power and autonomy that they enjoyed previously. At the same time, they saw them as an important link to keep the feudal system alive. Palegars who fell in line with this ideology were pensioned off and made Patels of their villages. Those who revolted (and many did) were ruthlessly massacred. In the border regions of Mysore, in present-day Tamil Nadu and Andhra Pradesh, many of these Palegars were made *zamindars*—they not only paid but also collected taxes from the peasantry. Hayavadana Rao quotes historian Kirmani to illustrate this social flux:

> Colonel Read, the Darogah of the Intelligence Department, who was appointed to the command of Amboor Gurh, with great address, and by the liberal distribution of money, sweet words and kind actions, brought over to his side the whole of the Poligars of the Balaghaut, who from the oppression and cruelty of the late Nawab, and the tyrannical character of the Sultan, had abandoned their own country, and had sought refuge in the towns of the Karnatic Payanghaut; such as the Poligar of Gungoondi Pala, the sons of Byreh Kor, the Poligar of Chuk Balapoor; Pud Nair, the Poligar of Vinkut Giri Kote, who was residing at Charkul; Shunk Rayel, or Rawul, the Chief of Punganoor, and besides these, the Poligars of Khut Koomir, Mudunpalli, Anikul, Oonkus Giri, Cheel Naik etc, all being dispossessed of their lands, received written assurances of protection, and were dispatched to their own districts on condition they should collect and forward supplies of forage and provisions to the English army; and they also received authority to retake or recover (by any means) their own districts and talookas...

The sort of ryot Munro's system began to cultivate was a *zamindar* who possessed thousands of acres of land and remained an absentee landlord. This Ryotwari system was introduced in all parts of Mysore. The Karavali region of South Kanara had assessments made on those who held a proprietary right or Mulwarge title over the land irrespective of whether or not they took to actual cultivation. Gleig has reported Munro's description of the way he implemented the task at Kanara:

> After dividing the country into great estates, each of these estates ought to be made over to the potail or principal propreitor of the small estates of which they were respectively composed, in perpetuity. As he has no property in any of the lands composing the great estates, except those which were before his own, he can only be constituted a kind of lord of the manor; but as he must be responsible for all failures, he ought to have the following advantages in order to enable him to perform his engagement: 1st, he ought to have an allowance of 2 ½ per cent on the jama to be included in the reduction which I have already proposed, leaving the remaining per cent, to go as an abatement to the mass of inferior proprietors and farmers. 2nd, he ought to be vested with proprietary of all waste lands to which they are the owners, on condition of his paying the Bidnore assessment the second year after they are brought into cultivation. 3rd, all inferior castes which, on failure of heirs, have heretofore been accustomed to revert to the Sircar, must now revert to him, and become in every respect, as much his respective property as his own original estates...

British motives were as clear as daylight: the reinstatement of the old order in a new form beneficial to their continual survival and hold over the people. The Brahmins were the other pillar in this set-up. In Kanara for example, the Chitrapur Brahmins emerged as the newly appointed shanbhogues of villages. In fact, members of the Saraswat Brahmin and Bunt communities, who were intelligent and qualified, started filling most of the revenue administration posts. In a clear instruction, recorded by Gleig, the governor general tells the Madras government during the takeover of Mysore that 'the existing native institutions should be carefully maintained' and in a memorandum in 1812–13, Munro states: 'The Potails and Curnums of every village, as political instruments holding together the internal frame, are of the highest use to the Government.' The reference here is to Patels and Shanbhogues. Quoting further from Munro's memorandum on the same:

In the infancy of our power, when the great zemindars could afford a formidable resistance, the division of their domains might have been desirable; but in the present state of our power it ought rather to be our object to maintain them as entire as possible. If the whole of the zemindars were swept away...we should have nothing of native rank left in the country. All rank and power would be vested in a few Europeans. Such a state of things could not be but dangerous to the stability of our Government; because the natives could not fail to make the comparison between the high situation of their foreign rulers and their own abject condition; and in the event of any discontent arising, it would be more likely to spread and become general when they were reduced to one level, and consequently more liable to be actuated by feeling. They have no common sympathy with us, and but little attachment to our Government, with the exception of a portion of those who depend upon it for their maintenance; and nothing can tend more effectually to shake what they have, than to behold the destruction of every ancient family and its domains passing into the hands of a set of low retainers of the courts and other dependents of Europeans.

Our power is now too great to have anything to apprehend from our zemindars. They know that they cannot oppose it, they also know that it is not our wish to turn it against them, in order to deprive them of any right which they now enjoy; and that they are as secure in the possession of their zemindaries with a small as with a large armed force. They will all by degrees gather confidence from this safety, abandon their military habits, and attend to the improvements of their possessions; and they will, for their own sakes, be more disposed than any other class of our subjects to support our Government in all times of disturbance...

Not only zemindaries, but the official lands of the village servants have been divided and parceled out among different claimants and, unless measures are adopted to stop this evil, every landowner will in time be reduced to the state of a common cultivator. With this fall of all the upper classes the character of the people sinks; they become less attached to our Government, they lose the principal instruments by which we can act upon and improve them, and the task of conducting the internal

Government becomes everyday more difficult. I am therefore of the opinion that we ought by every expedient in our power to maintain the ancient zemindaries; and official landed estates unbroken. This will keep up a class of native nobility and gentry, and preserve those gradations in society through which alone it can be improved in its condition.

The period also saw the rise of the first set of comprador merchants and bureaucrats. Since the British did not deal with the Kannada, Tuluva and Kodava regions directly, these compradors emerged as agents for their counterparts in Bombay and Madras. The Marwaris settled down in large numbers, coming in mainly from Bombay. They entrenched themselves in remotest villages and ousted the local moneylenders. The British government favoured this class as opposed to the Mysorean local merchant. It was ensured, for example, that the Civil and Military Station in Bangalore was composed of people of non-Mysorean origin. The cantonment area of Bangalore remained an isolated piece of British territory segregated from the rest of Mysore and the Pettah of Bangalore in particular. The objective was to limit the economic interaction between the city and the cantonment. The traders of the Pettah were consciously kept out of the station, prevented from setting up shops in the cantonment and only allowed to sell their goods wholesale to the merchants of the general or regimental *bazaars* within the station. Gowda Saraswat Brahmins and Konkanis also emerged as rich and powerful shopkeepers or powerful bureaucrats in urban areas and as wealthy landlords in villages.

This large-scale churning of the socio-economic order had its own set of implications for the state, some of which had far-reaching consequences. The first impact was certainly on the famed Mysorean army. Tipu's army had had about 1,40,000 men and about 1,80,000 kandachar militia. This army was completely liquidated and the raja's army left with a nominal 12,000 men and 20,000 Kandachars. Hayavadana Rao writes that the man who ensured this was Lieutenant Close, who proudly boasts:

> That Tippu loaded the departments of his Government with dronish Mussalmans cannot be denied, but the characteristic of his domination was to reserve all power to himself and allow no hereditary claims or fixed offices...individuals holding the principal

offices of the state doubtless exercised authority and from such cause possessed some influence, but of these how many remain? Burhanuddin was killed at Seringapatam. The Benki Nawab fell at Siddeswar, and Syed Sahib, Mir Sadak and Syed Gaffar at the storming of Seringapatam. Purnaiya is forthcoming and rests upon our will. Kamruddin rests upon our generosity and is perfectly at our devotion...Where then is the Mahomedan influence to embarrass us or to give a turn to our politics? Tippu's infantry are discharged, his Silledar horse are dissolved, his Killedars pay us obeisance, his Asophs if so disposed have not the means to resist us, the stable horse remain and look to our pleasure for subsistence and at best they are but so many loose individuals connected by no head and kept apart by separate interests. They are ours for actual service at a nod.

The Muslims of Mysore felt acutely the impact of Tipu's death. For over forty years they had revelled in the fact that men from their community had risen from such humble origins and taken over a vast kingdom ruled by an ancient ruling dynasty. Suddenly, the spell was broken and they had to grapple with a vastly different reality. Unable to adapt to the change they sought a false sense of security by retreating among themselves. Buchanan noticed this trend of increased ghettoisation among the Muslims:

> The Mussulmans who were in Tipoo's service are daily coming to this part of the country. Those who have any means carry on a small trade in grain; those who are poor hire themselves to the farmers, either as servants or day labourers. Being unacquainted with agriculture, they are only hired when others cannot be procured. Their wages are, of course low, and their monthly allowance is 30 seers of grain (worth three Fanams) and one Fanam in cash...they however prefer this to enlisting in the service of the Company along with the infidels who killed their royal martyr.

Agriculture and industry were two other pillars that faced most of the brunt of this new reality. The re-establishment of the feudal system, as mentioned before, had its own set of consequences in these two areas. The very system of taxation changed—from taxation based on yield to taxation based on land. This meant that even dry lands of the state paid a fixed rent in cash, amounting to about one-third of the crop. The fixed rent tenure or *kayamgutta* regime severely impacted the agrarian economy. Irrigation, something at which Mysore had excelled, became another casualty of the flux. The total irrigated area fell drastically after 1799. In terms of budgetary allocations and expenditures on the management and repair of tanks and canals, the figures fell from Rs 3,98,754 in 1800 to Rs 1,96,800 in 1804.

Thus, the return of the Wodeyars to power, albeit under British control, saw a feudalisation of the socio-economic set up, the general collapse of urban production and rural migration coupled with no specific incentives for agriculture—all of which contributed to a crisis in the sector. Cultivation of cotton, paddy, sugarcane, oil seeds or arecanut, was hit. The transition from commercial crops to cereals recreated the hand-to-mouth, inward-looking and cloistered feudal village.

On the industrial front, as mentioned before, the new merchant classes displaced the local traders and merchants from their usual thriving businesses. Some of the local factories were shut down, affecting the export of silk cloth, sandalwood, etc., much of which came in from the industrial hub of Bangalore. Buchanan talks about the weavers of Bangalore who had been a thriving and pampered class for long:

> The weavers of Bangalore seem to be a very ingenious class of men, and with encouragement, to be capable of making very rich, fine elegant cloths of any kind that may be in demand but having been chiefly accustomed to work goods for the use of the court at Seringapatam, they must now labour under great disadvantages; for it never can be expected, that the court of Mysore should equal that of Seringapatam nor will the English officers ever demand the native goods as the Mussulman Sardars did. The manufactures of this place can never therefore be expected to equal what they were in Hyder's reign, unless some foreign market can be found for their goods.

Import duties imposed on foreign silks entering Mysore were left unchanged but superior quality silks exported from the state to England were charged duty according to colonial tariffs. This dealt a serious blow to the once-thriving silk industry for which Mysore had been famous. The local cotton industry was also hit by the abolition of *sayer* on imported European cotton thread that entered Bangalore, coupled with the introduction of Bourbon cotton that the weavers were unfamiliar with, and therefore hesitant to experiment with. The destruction of local industry continued unabated ever since the British took over the reins of the state indirectly. The situation deteriorated further with time. To quote Shama Rao:

> In 1843...to the great detriment of the revenues of Mysore the prohibition of Acts XV of 1839 and XI of 1842 of the importation of foreign sugars into the Madras territories was enforced against Mysore on the ground that it was foreign territory, it was in fact ruled that no sugar which was the growth of Mysore could be admitted to the adjacent district of Canara even for local consumption... in like manner, on the same ground, the importation of tobacco from Mysore into Malabar was prohibited altogether and coffee was subjected to a high differential duty and this notwithstanding the fact that Mysore admitted all British produce free and levied on the produce of the Company's districts no higher duty than upon its own.

Krishnaraja Wodeyar III was thus a complete failure in administration and management. But can one entirely blame him? He was bound by a treaty signed when he was still an infant. Each clause spelt destruction for the state. But to remain in power even as the titular head, Krishnaraja had to turn a blind eye to the decadence. It was not long before public ire broke all barriers.

Socially, the re-alignment of feudal powers put many erstwhile powers of the social order back in the driver's seat. The Brahmins, who had long lost their authority in the Muslim regime, began occupying all major posts and public offices. In addition, many groups emerged that challenged Brahmin supremacy. The Devangas belonged to the supposed lower castes but assumed Brahminical Sri Vaishnavite traditions, surnames and practices and declared themselves no less than Brahmins. The State and Dewan Purnaiya were inimical to such groups. Quoting Sebastian Joseph:

> In the circular issued by Diwan Purnaiah in 1807–08 he strongly reprimands the Devangas for violating their respective caste rules and emulating Brahminical practices. It was reported to Purnaiah

that a self proclaimed Guru of the Devangas attempted to introduce sacred thread for the Devangas and to provide religious instruction to them. Purnaiah writes: 'One unknown sudra, claiming to be the so-called Guru of the Devangas has been creating unwanted troubles by insisting that the Devangas should wear sacred thread and receive religious teaching. Where is the sacred thread for the sudras? What do they mean by religious teaching? This is not the work that sudras can do. He should be punished. Those Devangas are supposed to be the disciples of the Sringeri Mutt. Therefore the people from the Mutt should warn the Devangas against such acts and take necessary steps. If the newly arrived Sudra is still adamant to create the troubles, then he should be sent out of the country.'

The *kaditas* or manuscripts of the Sringeri Muth speak of the practice of selling and auctioning of women who had committed adultery. This was testified to by the state and was called *samayachara*. The Dharmasamsthana of the muth seemed to hold the right to openly sell these women like commodities in fairs and markets. In 1818, for instance, the documents speak of the sale of a widow—accused of licentious behaviour—for three Varahas to one Ahobala Somayyaji by the Parupathyagara of the Sringeri Muth, Venkatachala Sastri. Vindicating such a shameful practice was a royal order issued in 1826–27 that instructed all amils and killedars to hand over to the Muth all 'fallen' women they found. The practice thus got institutionalised. The old practice continued even during commissioner's rule in Mysore, with the difference being the soliciting of prior permission before any sale of women by the muth. Rice narrates many such gory practices that existed and were perpetuated by the inefficient regime of the time. He speaks of women among Brahmins and Komtis not only being sold but also expelled from their caste and branded on the arm as prostitutes. Wives and families of thieves were also imprisoned with their husbands for the purpose of satisfying the desires of the corrupt police force. This was done openly, without stealth or fear or justice catching up. In Bangalore, for example, there was supposedly a large building that was meant for this very purpose. Rice further states:

> A peculiar custom is prevalent among one branch of Morasu Vollaigas by which the women suffer amputation of the ring and little fingers of the right hand. Every woman of the sect

previous to piercing the ears of her eldest daughter, preparatory to her bring betrothed in marriage, must necessarily undergo this mutilation, which is performed by the blacksmith of the village for a regulated fee for a surgical process sufficiently rude. The finger to be amputated is placed on a block, the blacksmith places a chisel over the articulation of the joint and chops it off in a single blow. If the girl to be betrothed is motherless, and the boy has not been subjected to this operation, it is incumbent on her to perform the sacrifice.

In this dismal scenario—politically, economically and socially bleak—it was perhaps almost inevitable that public anger should erupt somewhere. That somewhere was a place called Nagar.

17

A COUNTRY ON THE BOIL

I

THE NAGAR REVOLT

23 August 1830
Hosanthe village, Nagar District (now Shimoga)

The sleepy village of Hosanthe near Anandapura of Nagar district seemed abuzz with sudden activity. Sitting under the village peepal tree, octogenarian Thimmappa, a tenth-generation peasant, strained his eyes to see what was raising huge clouds of dust—a noisy advance of a multitude of cattle towards the place where he was sitting. A war was the last thing they needed at this time. Tidings were bad enough for Thimmappa and many of his clan; a bad monsoon, a disastrous epidemic and the continual oppression by the sharat officers had reduced them to a state of abject penury. The very thought that the approaching convoy might spell war caused Thimmappa to tremble in fright. He signalled to his little grandson who was playing marbles with his friends:

'Lo! Putta! Come here! What is this huge noise I hear? Is it the white man's army or the Khavind's forces from Mysore? I can hear a million oxen marching hither. These wretched eyes can't even see what is in front of me. Come, climb this tree and tell me what this commotion is all about.'

The little boys were equally alarmed and stopped their game. Putta climbed the tree and offered a stream of commentary to his near-blind grandfather:

'Ajja! This is no army. They are all like us. I can see some known people too. They are all coming in a huge mass, with sticks in their hands.'

'What? What has come over them? Is it some new trouble we have to face? Oh! Shiva! Don't we have enough on our plate as it is?'

His laments were interrupted by the well-built village headman who asked him to move and make room for the congregation. Thimmappa and his grandson squatted on the ground, anxiety writ large on their faces. Soon, the entire field in front of the peepal tree—the venue for frequent late-night entertainment shows of Yakshagana* for the village folk—was filled with livid peasants from different neighbouring villages. The Patel or head of this *koota* (gathering) stood on the stone slab near the tree and requested the attention of all those assembled.

'Brothers! We have assembled here for a momentous act. The past few years have been the worst in our lives as peasants. We have been oppressed and treated as grime by the white man and his stooge, that spineless Maharaja of Mysore. Fie upon them! How can they hope to revel in luxury when getting a square meal a day has become a distant reality for all of us? The hand that ploughs the field and gives food grains to the rest of the kingdom has not a morsel to feed this stomach with! Is this justice? We are anyway on the path to death, why not put up a fight as we die and shake the foundations of Mysore?'

The crowd burst into thunderous applause.

'As you all know, over the past many months,' the Patel continued, 'headmen, like myself, from several groups of nearby villages have been holding secret council meetings and the deliberations of these have been promptly and transparently passed on to all of you, because this is your fight! We have had many such *kootas* where ideas have been debated and anonymous pamphlets distributed to spread the word amongst our ryot brethren. Just months back our brothers in nearby Kundapura refused to pay the *kists* to the government officers and were bold enough to even

---

* Yakshagana is a folk art-form of Karnataka—a heady combination of music, dance and drama. It would usually be performed in open fields and was an all-night affair.

attack some of the public servants whom we hitherto greatly feared. Not any more!'

There was again deafening applause coupled with jeering and hooting, even as young men raised slogans of 'Long live our rebellion! Death to the Maharaja of Mysore!' With a smug smile, the Patel requested them all to keep silent and listen to him.

'Friends! Today we have gathered here from different parts of the kingdom to pass a unique resolution. We will tell the man sitting on the Throne of Mysore that his kingdom runs because of us, not the Resident and the Madras Company. Our struggle will intensify till all our demands are met. We will prevent all government officials from entering villages. If they refuse to listen, they do so at their own risk. No one can blame us or say we did not warn them. From this day, all revenue payments to the Treasury of Mysore will stop. The government has to recognise that the tiller of the land is its owner and all lands snatched away from the tenant farmers must be returned forthwith. Along with Nagar Khavind and our leader Sriman Budi Basavappa, who would be here shortly, to address all of you, we shall lead a delegation to Mysore and hand over a copy of these demands to the maharaja. Alongside, we also will send copies of our historic resolution to the foujdars of Nagar, Chitradurga and Ashtagram. Come on brothers! This is the time to do or die. Express your solidarity towards this movement which will ensure that the tears are wiped from the eyes of our wives and children and that we do not have to go to bed hungry anymore!'

Chants of 'Long live the Revolution!' filled the skies. Putta was as lost as his grandfather who had heard the proceedings in a state of complete shock.

'Ajja! What is a revolution?' he nudged his grandfather and asked.

'I don't know what it is my son, but I do know these Patels, and they often have something else at the back of their minds. But one thing is for sure. Our kingdom is in for another blood-bath. After Tipu Saib's fall 35 years ago, this is the worst crisis that has hit us all. The coming days portend great disaster, mark my words!' he said wiping his brow.

'Disaster? Does that mean I cannot play marbles with my friends anymore?'

✤

The growing discontent among the ryots found its expression in the form of several mutinies and revolts across the country, of which most were ruthlessly suppressed by those in power. The old, rarely-used weapons of these peasants were no match for the superior arms and ammunition of their masters. In Mysore, the agrarian discontent showed itself in Nagar and Tarikere first and spread across the kingdom like wildfire. In both these places, the farmers, under their erstwhile local leaders—the Palegars, who had been hitherto dispossessed of their privileges—began to revolt against the Sharat system. The Palegars saw this as a brilliant comeback opportunity. Mobilisation of the peasantry was based on force and threat of force, the latter being required due to the use of superstition, curse theories and caste differences. To quote historian Shama Rao:

> As a result of the incitement which emanated from the Palegars and the appeal to caste superstitions by the Nagar ryots by threats of calling down curses of heaven on the members of the caste by the throwing into their houses of bones, horns and margosa leaves combined with the approach of the season for the collection of Government dues, a number of disturbances in several parts of the State broke out…

Though the insurgency had its centre in the Nagar Foujdari comprising the districts of Shimoga and Chikamagalur, it spread to most parts of the state quickly. Uttara Kannada, Chitradurga, Tumkur, Hassan, Mysore, Mandya and Bangalore were rocked by the rebellion, making it one of the most widespread peasant uprisings in British India. The initial spark that ignited the trouble came from the infighting among the different power centres that came into existence under the new colonial order. Shama Rao details the factors that contributed to the revolt:

> Through Bhakshi Rama Rao's influence both when he was Foujdar of Nagar as well as after he became attached to the court of Krishnaraja Wodeyar in various capacities all the important situations in the Foujdari had come to be occupied, as we have seen, by his relations belonging both to his own family as well as the Annigere and Hangal families and a family party was thus formed with powerful interests of their own and this party continued to maintain its position till the beginning of the insurrection in 1830. Many of the members of this party were, it

is believed, given to commit embezzlement and frauds of various kinds and were also suspected of being in league with gangs of robbers who had sought asylum in jungles in that part of the country. In the village of Chetnahalli in the Honnali taluk some families of thugs or Phasegars, as they were locally called, had settled for several years and about the year 1820 a great number more came from the Southern Mahratta country and also settled in the neighbourhood. Another still more numerous gang from North Arcot and the neighbourhood of Bangalore settled at Luckwalli situated at some distance from Tarikere. Among these people were found some of the most notorious robbers who were suspected of receiving encouragement from the members of the above powerful family. As an instance it may be stated that in January 1827 a rich merchant's house in the town of Yedehalli (now called Narasimharajapura) was broken into, several persons were killed, and property was carried off to the amount of about three lakhs and a half of rupees and at the time the belief prevailed throughout the country that the gang of robbers employed on this occasion was directed by Aunnigere Venkata Rao, Amildar of Chennagiri, supported by his relative Hangal Krishna Rao, the Foujdar of Nagar. This belief among the people as well as the frequent gang robberies that occurred in various parts of the country accelerated the occurrence of the agrarian revolt on a wider scale than it could have been otherwise possible.

The initial character of the uprising had little to do with the masses or peasants. It was the typical struggle of the displaced Palegars who tried in vain, time and again, to reassert their supremacy. The notorious Nagar Foujdar Hangal Krishna Rao incited the people in the region to revolt against Viraraja Urs who had been nominated in his place. The protests that followed ensured that Krishna Rao retained his position. But the stooges he had paid to carry out these stage-managed protests continued to wander unleashed and carried on the agitation for personal gain.

Two men are associated with the start of the rebellion: Budi Basavappa and Rangappa Nayak. Both men were frauds, fighting for selfish reasons. 'Budi Basavappa' was actually Hygamalla, a resident of the Chennikatte village, who pretended to be Basavappa, the ruler of Nagar, appropriating the identity of the previous ruler's adopted son. Hyga had always been a trouble-maker and went to prison for his misdeeds. On his release he needed some method to re-enter his old village. He befriended an old Jangama saint who had been the spiritual guide of the last Palegar of Nagar and also possessed his seal rings. Stealing those, Hyga made his way to the zilla court, where he had his name inscribed as 'Budi Basavappa: Nagar Khavind' (the King of Nagar). He was then led to Nagar where opportunity was ripe—the ruler was dead. He took over the seal of the raja, posing as the adopted son of the late raja of Nagar (Dodda Basavappa), and claimed the throne of Nagar. Enlisting the support of the masses, many of whom considered him as a hero, he became all the more popular and was placed on the masnad of Nagar in April 1830 as Srimantha Nagar Khavind. He appointed Manappa as his commander-in-chief. Many of these proceedings had the secret support of people in government at Mysore who were the adherents of former Dewan Rama Rao and opposed Viraraja Urs (who had displaced Krishna Rao, Rama Rao's nephew). Taking advantage of the confusion, Basavappa proudly proclaimed himself a friend of the ryots and promised them full remission of all balances and a reduction in government demand on their lands to only one Rupee for each Pagoda they then paid, if they espoused his cause. The already impoverished and suffering peasants had nothing but their wretched lives to lose by supporting a man who claimed to be their friend and confidante. Many of them readily entered the armed gangs Basavappa had started mobilising.

Rangappa Nayak, the other leader of the rebellion who stayed on in Mysore, was a descendant of the Tarikere Palegar dynasty. He played a pivotal role in mobilising the peasants by declaring that the Wodeyar had sold their state to the avaricious British. He, however, went back to his ancestral territories and proclaimed in the villages that the maharaja of Mysore with the consent of the Company had restored his ancestral throne to him in order to establish law and order in the region and that if the people cooperated with him, he would remit a part of the taxes.

What emerged out of this strange potpourri of deception is interesting. Both the men had nothing but their own petty interests to serve. But in the process of masterminding an insurrection they ended up articulating the burning issues of the people. The masses, especially the peasants, needed a voice to express their oppression and suffering. They rallied behind these two men and later, the movement assumed a mass character, bereft of the leaders who pioneered the whole show.

The struggle took place in three waves: The first wave was that of mass struggles; the second, of mass action, and, the third, when armed struggle predominated. The mass struggle started in early 1830 and assumed many forms. The most important of these was the *koota*, or simply 'gathering'. The *koota* was a broad forum to organise the peasant masses. The *kootas* spread from Nagar to Bellary, and even as far as Mysore. Writing about the *koota* rebellion in South Kanara, Shyam Bhat states:

> The peasant uprising of 1830–31 is also popular as the 'Koot rebellion'. In the context of South Kanara, koots refer to unions or assemblages of peasants expressing their grievances against and seeking redress from the Company Government. The vital factor involved in this peasant uprising was that of land revenue which was a matter of conflict between the peasants and the Company Government. The signs of the peasant unrest could be seen in the closing months of 1830, when the ryots gave general petitions complaining of their losses. But they developed and came to the fore in the early months of 1831. The ryots of Kasargod, Kumbla, Morgal, Manjeshwar, Bungra-Manjeshwar and Talapady sent general arzees (petitions) and complaints of their losses to Dickinson the Collector of South Kanara. In their petitions, the ryots not only complained about the harsh revenue assessment of November 1830, but they also demanded remission to them all at a uniform rate.
>
> In the second stage, around the beginning of January 1831, the ryots started their Koots or assemblages…it was in Bekal that the Koots started in the first week of January 1831 and within a few days it spread to the northern parts of Kanara. Narkur, Brahmavar, Buntwal, Madhur, Manjeshwar, Mulki, Kadri, Kumbla, Malluly, Wamanjoor, Mogral, Udyawar, Uppinangadi and Vittal were some of the important places where the ryots of the respective regions had assembled in Koots…the Manjunatha temple at Kadri was the center of these peasant uprisings, where the Maha Koot or Grand Koot was organised towards the end of January 1831…
>
> In order to organise these Koots the ryots maintained one Patel and two head ryots in each of the villages. There were separate Headmen for the Maganes. When any aspect was

discussed and plan or action was proposed in the Koots, these leaders disseminated them to the ryots in the villages. Further, each of the Koots had its own leaders and all of them met and spoke at the Grand Koot in Kadri. The organisers of these Koots also made use of a Secret Council. It comprised two or three Muktesars (head ryots) of each Magane. The object of this council was to maintain the secrecy of the whole organisational affair of the Koots. However, the result of the deliberations of this Council was communicated to the various assemblies or Koots. Thus the Secret Council played the role of a linking and organizing body in these peasant uprisings. It in fact acted as a think-tank of the rebellion. Further, anonymous pamphlets were made use of by the leaders to spread their ideas and programmes among the ryots. Such papers were circulated in the various Koots.

The participants in these Koots at times made bold to attack the Government servants. Before Dickinson left Kundapura for Mangalore at the end of January 1831 he received reports from the Tahsildar of Barkur that the ryots of that Taluk had assembled in Koot and had assaulted some of the public servants...the ryots were thus determined to refuse the kists to the Government, until a fresh settlement was made, and their mood was so defiant that they unhesitatingly attacked those public servants whom they feared not long back. The growing sense of unity among themselves and faith in their organizational strength had emboldened them to take such postures of defiance. The peasant intransigence, which surfaced in the month of November 1830, continued up to the end of March 1831. It was after Cameron's promise to the ryots that their petitions would be considered and remissions would be made...that they dispersed and stopped organizing the Koots. Thus by April 1831 the rumblings of the Koot rebellions died down.

As the movement built up, on 23 August 1830, at a huge rally organised by Basavappa at Hosanthe village near Ananadapura in Shimoga district, a peasant charter was passed and signed by those assembled. It said:

- The peasant organisation must be built everywhere.
- The struggle must be advanced till the demands are accomplished.

- Government officials must be prevented from entering the village.
- Revenue payment to the government must stop.
- The government must recognise that the 'tiller is the owner' of the land.
- Land must be returned to those tenants who had forfeited it.

The congregation also decided to draft a letter to the maharaja of Mysore articulating these demands and seeking prompt action. Similar copies were made for the fouzdars of all the three divisions—Nagar, Chitradurga and Ashtagram. A ten-member executive council of ryot leaders was formed to tour the state and see the problems of the people with Manappa in command. Manappa, Budi Basavappa's commander, also led a delegation to Mysore that met Krishnaraja Wodeyar. They presented a list of demands to the Sannad which included the restoration of cultivated lands to the ryots, the cessation of the tenancy system, return of auctioned lands to their rightful owners, waiver of revenue arrears, distribution of fallow lands to farmers, issuance of takkavi loans, abolition of Sharat, grants of additional cultivable lands to be made to peasants keeping in view their family size and a termination of revenue collection for a period of ten years by which time the economic conditions would hopefully limp back to normalcy. The maharaja was exasperated by these preposterous demands and, flying into a rage, refused to consider the case. The delegation left Mysore in anger and on its way back, mobilised further support in the villages of Mysore, Mandya, Tumkur, Hassan and Chikamagalur districts.

With assemblies and petitions serving no purpose, the movement graduated to its next logical step. The second stage of the movement was mass action when the rebels built up their armies and attacked officials and bureaucrats of the government. Manappa built up a fighting force of 200 men. These mass actions were directed against the Amildars, corrupt bureaucrats and reactionaries in the villages. Amildars who feared the wrath of the people either fled or surrendered to the groundswell. By the end of 1830, as the phase of mass action began to conclude, the amildar's offices were often seized by the insurgent peasants and collection of revenue was annulled by the new authority in power. Shama Rao writes that on 23 August 1830, Manappa gave a clarion call to his comrades in all districts of the Bangalore and Chitradurga Fouzdaries in particular and across the princely state of Mysore in general:

A Country on the Boil   449

You must positively come to us at the rate of one man per house... set out taking with you the Shanbhogues, the Jamindars and the other inhabitants with due respect without leaving them behind. You must also bring Amildars, Killedars, Shirastedars with as much disrespect as respect is shown to the former class of people. These officials should be kept in custody and made to walk.

Violent incidents followed across the state of Mysore. Shama Rao describes them:

In the month of September 1830 on a demand being made in the village of Basavanahalli in the Chennagiri taluk for the annual land assessment, the ryots insolently inquired for whose benefit the assessments were to be paid whether for the benefit of the Raja of Mysore or of the Nagar Raja. The ryots shut the outer gate of the village against the amildar who was thereupon compelled to break them open to effect an entry...the Foujdar not only sent reports of these excesses to the Maharaja of Mysore but also referred in his reports to the general attitude of the inhabitants... where he said that bodies of people blowing horns and beating drums were moving from village to village inciting residents to join them, or in the alternative, threatening them with curses of bones and horns and that attempts at conciliation had met with failure...

The movement then spread to Chitradurga, Bangalore and Chennagiri. The ryots tried to forcibly take charge of the Chennagiri fort while its Amildar sent messages for help, all in vain, to the Fouzdar of Shimoga to help him. Meanwhile, one Ranga Rao and the farmers at Batterahally were ordered to reach Honnali to reconcile. But they refused and demanded an explanation for the unfair land tenures and the Sharat system. The farmers at Holalakere and Mavinahalli protested and prevented the sale of provisions to the fouzdar. The Chitradurga Fouzdar Sheshagiri Rao and brother of Motikhane Narasinga Rao tried to pacify the mob of 600–700 people at Chitterahalli, but in vain. The group ensured that the bazaars of Chitterahalli shut down. Their power was further augmented by a 500-strong body of ryots joining them from Holalakere. Finally, Sheshagiri Rao surrendered.

The blaze then caught Bangalore as the ryots pursued Venkatakrishnayya, the amildar of Doddaballapur who secretly fled to Bangalore when the ryots came to attack him. The remittances from Bangalore treasury to Mysore, called *irsal*, were cut off. The Bangalore Fouzdar Timmapparaja Urs fled to Hulyar in Tumkur district and invited the ryots for a discussion there. None of the members of the group responded to this invitation but congregated in a show of strength a few miles away from his hide-out in a 6,000–7,000 strong battalion. The terrified fouzdar who had just 8 *sowcars* and 80 Kandachar peons with him was completely at a loss. The group ensured that they secured the release of people arrested by the fouzdar for inciting pandemonium. A letter of the British Resident, Casmaijor dated 5 January 1831 sums up the turmoil:[*]

> Instances of contumacy were daily increasing. The Raja's Tappal was stopped, his Neroops torn and destroyed. Amildars were generally placed in restraint. Their seals of office taken from them, beat and ill-used the Sircar treasuries seized by the Potails. Merchants and travelers arrested by the several gangs of insurgents and money forcibly levied from them...

The mass action succeeded to the extent that it helped vanquish its target—the corrupt and inefficient amildars, who either fled in fright or were captured by the armed mobs.

The ryots in Nagar sent a letter directly to the governor general highlighting the excesses of Krishna Rao:

> The humble petition of the poor kind ryots of the Talooks or Gaudies belonging to the Nuggur country which produces nine lakhs of pagodas...while we were under the dominion of the family of Caladi Sivappa Naik who governed this country for many years, and also in the days of Nawab Bahadoor Tippoo, we were in a state of happiness. When the Company took possession of this country, instead of giving it up to the family of the Rajah of Nuggur who had formerly held dominion over it, joined it to the possessions of the Rajah of Mysore, and without making the least enquiry into the state of our country has appointed a

---

[*] Casmaijor's and the ryots' letters are taken from the New Delhi National Archives: 'Copies of secret correspondence relating to the state of the Mysore government, 1831.'

Foujdar to govern us. This Foujdar, not understanding revenue affairs, has merely looked to supporting himself and has been in the habit of forcibly obeying us to sign an agreement for this Sircar revenue, and then collecting the money. If we delayed to pay for one or two days after the fixed time, he used to torture us to extort bribes…being dreadfully distressed from this tyranny of the Foujdar, we from the end of September to the end of December in this year addressed many petitions to the Rajah, praying that he should enquire into these matters, but he paid us no attention. Afterwards the Foujdar Crishna Roy having sent for some ryots to the village of Hole Honour, under the pretext of giving them satisfaction, having assured them that they might put their confidence in him, took them into the fort, where he killed 500 of them outright, and wounded some others, whom he afterwards ordered to be tied in comlies with large stones attached to them and thrown alive into a deep pool…Crishna Roy and his son-in-law Sreenivasa Roy having assembled some cavalry and sepoys…seized and hung the ryots, ravished the women and cut off their and their childrens' ears and noses, and plundered and burnt down all their houses…Crishna Roy having collected some forces in Anantapur treacherously plundered and burnt down the ryots houses thence. We have no means of preserving our lives against this treachery – from the time that the Company gave our country to the Rajah of Mysore; he has never made any enquiry into our circumstances, but acted as we have written above. The ryots who live in this country…have nothing but death before us, therefore we cannot in any way, remain as subjects of the Rajah of Mysore. Your charitable Government must take into consideration all that we have stated, and quickly give us relief and protection.

Little did they realise they were petitioning the very powers responsible for their condition. Casmaijor advised the Wodeyar to take stern action against the rebellion, which had severely affected the revenues of the state. He advised the maharaja to tour the 'angry state' and to coax the peasants to give up their arms. On 14 December 1830, the maharaja left for Chennarayapatna with Bakshi Rama Rao, Bakshi Dasappa Urs, Baburaya, Bakshi Bhima Rao, Annappa, 1,000 *sowcars*, 200 bodyguards and 4,000 horses. Casmaijor joined him at Kickery. Shama Rao states that at Chennarayapatna

> ...a tom-tom was sent around to proclaim that two men were hanged at Chennarayapatna and two at Kickery and these executions were accordingly carried out on the same day. It had been settled likewise that two persons had to be hanged at Hole Narasipur. But one of them was reprieved at the instance of the Resident and the other was hanged. In all eight or nine persons were hanged at different places as a warning to the inhabitants against joining the cootum or seditious gatherings.

The talks, however, broke down and the apparent show of strength and terror trails didn't yield any constructive results. The peasant movement now took on the form of guerrilla warfare. A guerrilla army was built, with detachments varying in size from twenty to two hundred. The norm was forty. They beat back the maharaja's offensive. They captured the Nagar fort; but retreated into the forests the night before British troops entered. As a major section of enemy forces moved to other areas of combat, they attacked the fort, killed its occupiers and re-took it. In this way the Nagar fort changed hands six times. Each time, they appealed to the town's people who joined them in large numbers. The guerrilla army was given secret training in Brahmagiri, Ulavi, Chennagiri, Chandragutti, Sonale and Sasehwalli. As the battles intensified, enemy troops mutinied and joined the guerrillas. Enemy officers were targeted. The British Government too stepped up its offensive against the rebels and in a series of bloody campaigns—January–June 1831; October 1831 to June 1832 and September 1832 to mid 1833—ensured that the movement was violently and cruelly suppressed. In the first campaign, along with two regiments from Mysore led by Anappa and Lieutenant Colonel Rochfort, a regiment of the Company's army stationed at Harihara led by Lieutenant Colonel Wolfe was deployed. In April another segment from Bangalore under Colonel Evans joined in to make it a 4,000-strong troop. The first campaign was to 'cleanse' Kamanadurga, Masur, Harihara, Nagar, Fathehpet, Anandapura, Sagar, Chandragutti, Mandagadde and so on. By the time of the second campaign, 15,000 soldiers had been mobilised under Anappa.

In many places like Sampige, Kadada, Hebbur, Tumkur, Mallaghatta and Gubbi revolts were suppressed. Rani Bennur became the next spot of riots. Anche Ramayya was sent to Rani Bennur to negotiate with the rebels and was successful. The Regimentdar Srinivasa Rao successfully crushed the revolt at Holehonnur; Venkataraja Urs captured Kaladurga and Kamandurga. Meanwhile Casmaijor sent his troops to Mysore, though with a selfish motive. The principality of Canara was the British dominion of Mysore and when the rumour of a possible outbreak of riots there reached Casmaijor's ears, he chose to react. Till now the British had maintained a comfortable distance from the happenings at Mysore and left the maharaja to his fate. Captain Rochfort and Lieutenant Colonel Wolfe were dispatched to curb the menace at Kamandurga and Kaladurga. The British were, however, unable to stem the growth of the armed struggle. Finally they resorted to infiltration and killing of the leadership.

The ryots meanwhile occupied Honnahalli. The place was looted. A segment of rebels took possession of the fort while the other took shelter in a temple, after a suitable division of their booty was made. Chandra Rao Ranore attacked the fort and Rochfort laid siege to the temple. The rebels managed to escape via the Tungabhadra River. Honnahalli was restored from the rebel's hold. Thousands of ryots were executed, the toll being more than hundred per day on charges of sedition and mutiny. At Honnali, Anappa's forces and those of Rochfort engaged in a pitched battle that saw, by 16 March 1831, the execution of fifty-one ryots around the temple and all the rest hung the next day on the road from Honnahali upto Shikaripura. Shama Rao states that

> ...the callousness with which these executions were carried out may be understood when it stated that on the first day when one of the officers who was passing by at the time wishing to witness how prisoners were hanged and how they died, though the gruesome work had closed for the day, two more men were immediately brought out and hanged in his presence...

The British troops captured Harihar, Shimoga, Anantapur, Sagar and Chandragutti. Colonel Evans took possession of Bangalore. Casmaijor visited the state and toured the troubled areas. Subsidiary troops were stationed at Nagar—the epicentre of the revolt in May 1831. By 1833 the bulk of the leadership were captured and killed and the movement died down.

Interestingly, Budi Basavappa, the kingpin of the whole movement, remained conspicuous by his absence during the entire struggle. By the end of 1830, he moved away to Rani Bennur in Dharwad district and when a search was launched for him, he slipped into the Nizam's territories in Raichur. It is said that he was seen in battle only once. On 27 March 1833 he was captured at Sunda Taluk in Uttara Kannada district. The partners in the whole movement—the Tarikere Palegar family led by one Nanjappa Naik now along with Kengappa Naik and his son Hanumappa Naik—met with Briggs, the Senior Commissioner of Bangalore, in 1832 and surrendered themselves to the Company's mercies. Bragging about his achievements in ensuring the surrender of the Tarikere family, Briggs stated on his return to Bangalore:

> The Commission has received repeated communications from the Palegar of Terrykerrry offering to come in if his life is spared... it appears the desperation arising out of ill-treatment and the execution of several of his clan and kindred by the late government as well as the sympathy for the suffering of his countrymen placed him at the head of a party in opposition to it. Rungappah Naik the chief of the family has paid the debt of nature, his eldest son Annappah was taken prisoner and hanged by the late Dewan and his retainers are now under the command of his nephew who is after all but one of his uncle's followers as a clansman and sues for mercy from the British Government.

The movement, the first of its kind where the oppressed peasants of the state raised the cry of revolt, was ruthlessly squashed no doubt, but it had larger political ramifications for the kingdom. It saw the oppressed souls of the state find a voice. The guerrilla tactics adopted by these mobs terrified the disciplined British troops, who had long forgotten such combats after the times of Haidar and Tipu. Some of the letters that these harassed British Commanders wrote to Casmaijor drive home this point clearly. Rochfort wrote on 4 March 1831:[*]

> I left Avinahally on the morning of 23 and after driving the insurgents from the opposite bank of the Sherwutty encamped at a small village called Husselmacky where there was sufficient plain for the camp to pitch that night. From thence I determined to push on for Nagger about 20 miles, but in consequence of the

---

[*] From the New Delhi National Archives.

insurgents having cut down a number of the largest trees laid them across the road which was this rendered impracticable to even infantry and their having also placed at different distances parties of matchlock men whose fire was very galling, this march was rendered most arduous and trying to the troops and at every 300 or 400 yards it was necessary to detach parties right and left.

It thus took Rochfort three days to traverse just twenty miles.

The Resident Casmaijor and the dewan held a series of interviews with some of the ryot groups in Nagar and came to a settlement that taxes should be collected only on cultivated land while remissions were to be allowed on all waste lands and *bitti* or unpaid work was not to be exacted by the officials for their private purposes.

Thus, the mass movement of the peasants and masses of the state of Mysore was crushed. But it did have its long-term impact on the state and the sacrifices did not go in vain.

THE AFTERMATH OF NAGAR

There were rumblings in the Company's corridors of power about the effectiveness of the maharaja in maintaining order in his kingdom. After much deliberation, a formal letter from the Company authorities, dated 7 September 1831, reached the maharaja while he was in the midst of the annual Dasara festivities. The maharaja's heart sank on reading its contents. The letter berated him for being singularly incapable of managing the affairs of the state and mopping up the budgeted revenues for his kingdom and the upkeep of the British army. It also held him guilty for the complete breakdown of law and order in his kingdom resulting in widespread destruction of peace and tranquility.

However, it was the last paragraph that was a bolt from the blue. Citing the above cases of maladministration and incapability, the Company had decided to depose him and take over direct rule of the state till such time that they felt the situation had returned to normalcy. That being up to the Company's subjective assessment, it was anyone's guess how long this 'transfer of power' would last. The letter concluded with a suggestion for the appointment of commissioners who would take over the complete administration of Mysore.

Given below are the excerpts of that letter addressed to the maharaja, as recorded by Shama Rao:

It is now thirty years since the British Government, having defeated the armies and captured the Forts and overrun the territory of Tippu Sultan, laid siege to Seringapatam, and that city being taken the dynasty and the power of Tippu was brought to an end. Your Highness is well aware of the generosity displayed by the conquerors upon that occasion. Instead of availing themselves of the right of conquest and of annexing the Territory of Mysore to those of the Honourable Company and of the Nizam, the sovereignty was restored to the family of the ancient Raja of the country, who had taken no part in the conquest, and Your Highness was placed on the Musnud. But Your Highness being then a child of three years old, Purniah was appointed Dewan of the State with full powers, and with the aid and countenance of the officers of the British Government he conducted all affairs with exemplary wisdom and success. Up to the period when Your Highness approached the years of maturity, through his good management and as the consequence of his measures, the country prospered, and the State of Mysore attained splendor and exaltation, and the population of all ranks were contented and happy. Further at the time of his resigning the Government to Your Highness, after having conducted its affairs for 10 years, he gave proof of the wisdom and integrity of his management by leaving in the Treasuries of Your Highness' use, no less than 70 Lakhs of Pagodas in cash, which is a sum exceeding two crores of rupees.

From that time which is now more than 20 years, Your Highness has been vested with all the powers and authorities of the Raja of Mysore, and still exercise the rights of sovereignty in the Territory of the State. But I am sorry to be compelled to say that the former state of things no longer exists, and that the duties and obligations of Your Highness' position appear to have been greatly neglected; for it seems that, besides the current revenue of the State, the treasure above stated to have been accumulated by Purniah has been dissipated on personal expenses and disreputable extravagances. An immense debt has been incurred, and the finance of the State has been involved in inextricable embarrassment and although Sir Thomas Munro, the late Governor as well as Hon'ble S.R. Lushington, the present Governor of Madras, frequently remonstrated with Your Highness on the subject, and obtained promises of amendment and of efforts to reduce your expenditure within your income, it does not appear that the least attention has been paid to their remonstrances or advice. The subsidy due to the British Government has not been paid according to the Treaty of 6th July 1799. The troops and soldiers of the state are unpaid and are compelled for their subsistence to live at free quarters upon the ryots. The debt is represented to be greater than ever, and so far from its being possible to entertain, from past experience, the smallest hope that these evils will be corrected under Your Highness' management, more extensive deterioration and confusion alone can be anticipated.

I have in consequence felt it to be indispensable, as well with reference to the stipulations of the Treaty, as from a regard to the obligations of the protective character, which the British Government holds towards the State of Mysore, to interfere for its preservation, and to save the various interests at stake from further ruin. It has occurred to me that in order to do this effectually, it will be necessary to transfer the entire administration of the country into the hands of British officers; and I have accordingly determined to nominate two Commissioners for the purpose who will proceed immediately to Mysore. Your Highness may be assured of the extreme reluctance under which I find myself compelled to have recourse to a measure that must be so painful to Your Highness' feelings, but I act under the conviction that an imperative obligation of a great public duty leaves me no alternative.

This was a ploy the British had repeatedly employed in other princely states of India as well which were under their protection. Using the excuse of maladministration, they had annexed states like Bharatpur, Kachar and Manipur and now it was Mysore's turn to follow suit. The British—who stationed themselves in these princely states to 'guard' the kings of those states against external aggression—conveniently shirked their duties and offered no help to the rulers when their own flawed and exploitative economic policies led to widespread internal rebellion. Then, citing maladministration, they deposed the helpless kings and took over the management of the troubled states.

Thus, on 19 October 1831, Krishnaraja Wodeyar was formally deposed and Colonel Briggs became the first commissioner of Mysore. By this time the British East India Company was at the pinnacle of success in India. The first Burmese War (1824–26) had been a great success. Assam, Kachar, Jaintia, Arakan, Tennasserim, Martaban, Lower Burma and Rangoon were annexed. The Lion of Punjab, Ranjit Singh, was one force who tried to halt British expansion. But he was stopped by the Treaty of Amritsar (1809) and compelled to agree that the Satluj would be the eastern boundary of his empire. After his death in 1839, his three sons were killed in a royal intrigue. His infant Daleep Singh became king with his mother Rani Jhindan as regent. But in the First Sikh War (1846), the Sikhs were defeated at Mudki, Ferozepur, Aizwal and Sobraon. The British annexed Jammu and Kashmir and handed it over to Raja Gulab Singh Dogra. In the Second Sikh War (1848) the Punjab was annexed, Daleep Singh was pensioned off to London and his father's famous diamond, the Kohinoor, was handed over as a gift to Queen Victoria. Thus, in the 100 years since they first began their armed expeditions to India in the Carnatic, the British, who came as traders seeking concessions, had become the permanent rulers of India.

Back in Mysore, from 1831 to 1832, Colonel J. Briggs was the senior commissioner and C.M. Lushington the junior commisioner. Lushington took charge about three months before his senior and in haste tried to bring about radical changes in the system, which further confused the chaotic administration. He attempted to introduce stamp duty and to establish a Huzur Adalat (final court of appeal). These ideas found little favour with the government at Madras. Colonel Briggs reversed these changes after taking charge. He clashed with Lushington—who resigned in a huff—and with Lushington's successors, G.M. Drurry and J.M. Macleod. He also rubbed the wrong way the Dewan of Mysore and the government at Madras. He therefore resigned in November 1832, strongly recommending that a single commissioner rather than two be appointed to Mysore. The suggestion was implemented with the succession of Morrison as the sole commissioner of Mysore. Morrison reduced the number of fouzdaries in the state from the existing six to four in order to prune the administration.

The Company had meanwhile set up a committee to look into the pros and cons of the Nagar Revolt, called the 'Insurrection Enquiry Committee'. The report gave the maharaja a clean chit, exonerating him of all charges. Lord William Bentinck, the governor general, advocated the maharaja's cause even to the court of the Directors in London, asking for the restoration of at least three-quarters of his erstwhile territories. Bentinck visited Mysore in April 1834 and doubted even the legality of the takeover by the Company. Diwakar, et al., write that Bentinck also found that the Company's allegation—that the raja was not paying his subsidies regularly and was thus dishonouring the Treaty of 1799—was completely fabricated and believed that the maharaja would 'make a good ruler in the future'.

But Bentick's proposal to hand over three-quarters of the territory back to the maharaja was turned down by the home government. The maharaja waited patiently, certain that the British would some day judge his claim favourably. He kept a close watch on all the political developments in Mysore, Madras and London in the hope that the tide might miraculously turn in his favour some day.

II

Although the British traders became the political masters of India by the close of the eighteenth century, they could not enjoy their supremacy in complete peace. Even in the immediate aftermath of Tipu's fall, revolts sprang up which they dealt with in their customary ruthless fashion. Purnaiya, whom the British appointed the dewan of Mysore, had to be both administrator as well as British ally in quelling several uprisings: the rebellions of Dhondoji Wagh, the Kanara rajas and the Balam ruler, the Wynad revolt in 1802, the Munkasira revolt in 1804, the revolt of the Palegar of Chitradurga in 1805, the European officers' revolt in 1809, and the Vellore uprising, centred around the sons of Tipu, for which reason they were packed off to Calcutta immediately afterwards.

Interestingly, all these uprisings and disturbances in and around Mysore in the first half of the nineteenth century had political overtones. Usually, such unrest was a struggle for survival led by some disgruntled satrap or displaced ruler. The revolts mentioned above fall into this category. But slowly and steadily, these metamorphosed into a larger expression of the common man's frustration over various socio-economic aspects and religious grounds. The resentment at being commanded by a foreign power simmered constantly and showed itself in numerous small-scale mutinies and uprisings across India. The British were confronted with uprisings by peasants, tribal communities and princely states. Amongst the most significant were the Kol uprising of 1831, the Santhal uprising of 1855, and the Kutch rebellion, which lasted from 1816 until 1832. Some were sustained; others sporadic; a few were isolated acts of revolutionary resistance—but nevertheless they all challenged colonial rule. This period saw a tremendous rise in rural poverty, precipitated by the colonial policy of unchecked extraction of agricultural and forest wealth from various regions, and the masses were reduced to a state of utter deprivation. Added to this was the ever-increasing British sense of cultural superiority, using the 'natives' for their own agendas while despising them, their culture and religion.

Nothing illustrates this as clearly as the life of the Indian sepoy, who worked for the British armies, mostly at the behest of his territory's feudatory king. This led to the growth of unofficial political committees of soldiers who had several grievances against their British overlords. For instance, the 140,000 Indians who were employed as sepoys in the Bengal Army were completely subordinate to the roughly 26,000 British officers. These sepoys bore the brunt of the First British-Afghan War (1838–42), the two closely contested Punjab Wars (1845–46, 1848–49) and the Second Anglo-Burmese War. They were shipped across the seas to fight the Opium Wars against China (1840–42, 1856–60) and the Crimean War against Russia (1854). Although risking death constantly, they had extremely limited opportunities for advancement since the Europeans monopolised all positions of authority. They were paid abysmally low salaries—sometimes as low as Rs 7 per month, expected to work from dawn to dusk, posted at many dangerous locations in India and overseas, often beaten up and manhandled and constantly ridiculed for their religious beliefs.

Despite being smothered by the superior colonial force, Indian political consciousness was by no means totally dead. In fact, even under the white man's heel, it grew and slowly matured, moving towards its first expression as an Indian protest as opposed to disconnected regional flare-ups. The dissatisfaction against the British was not confined to the agricultural communities alone. Every section of society had an axe to grind with the British masters. By rendering the nobility and urban middle class bankrupt, demand for many local goods was almost eliminated. At the same time, local producers faced unfair competition from British imports. Nilakanta Sastri writes that the consequences of this were summarised by the rebel Prince Feroz Shah in his August 1857 proclamation:

The Europeans by the introduction of English articles into India have thrown the weavers, the cotton dressers, the carpenters, the blacksmiths and the shoe-makers and others out of employ and have engrossed their occupations, so that every description of native artisan has been reduced to beggary.

The Indians also resented the Company's attempts to force Christianity down their throats. The hallmark of European colonialism was that wherever the colonial masters and armies went, the missionaries followed. While the former were ruthless, aggressive and cunning while expanding their territories and maximising their incomes, the latter were that and more while spreading the holy word. Driven by this militant zeal to proselytise, Christian missionaries travelled all over the country to harvest souls for Christ. The tenets of Hinduism and Islam were openly ridiculed and Christianity was advocated as the only gospel capable of deliverance of the soul. The *jagirs* of temples and mosques were confiscated while bishops and clergymen were highly paid. According to Malleson, Mr Mangles, the chairman of the Board of Directors of the Company had openly proclaimed that his mission was ordained by providence to make every Indian a Christian. Hindu laws were scrapped in many parts of India. Converts to Christianity were given rich incentives and managed to inherit property and receive preferential treatment in the government services. There was thus an intense feeling of insecurity among the Hindus and Muslims of India.

Amidst all this confusion, Lord Dalhousie became the governor general in 1846. He made numerous annexations on the basis of the Doctrine of Lapse, according to which a subsidiary kingdom automatically passed into the hands of the Company when a ruler died without leaving a direct heir to the throne. Adopted heirs were unacceptable to the doctrine. On this pretext he annexed Satara (1848), Jhansi (1853), Nagpur (1854) and the states of Jaipur, Sambhal, and Baghat Mysore was equally threatened as Krishnaraja Wodeyar was growing older and did not yet have a son. With respect to Mysore, Shama Rao records that Dalhousie had in fact observed:

> I trust therefore that when the decease of the present Rajah shall come to pass without son or grandson, or legitimate male heir of any description, the territory of Mysore which will then have lapsed to the Government will be resumed, and that the good work which has been so well begun will be completed.

The deposed rulers were deprived of all their titles and pensions as well. The Mughal ruler was still acclaimed by one and all. In the beginning the Company chose to be servile to the Mughal, calling itself 'Badshah-La-Fidwi-Khaus' or His Highness's most faithful servant. But once it had established its supremacy across India, the attitude changed. The Mughal ruler was humiliated. In fact, Lord Dalhousie's successor, Lord Canning announced that the successors of Mughal Emperor Bahadur Shah Zafar would lose their title and be known merely as princes. Similarly when Baji Rao II, the symbolic head of the Maratha confederacy, died in 1852, his son Dhondupanth alias Nana Saheb was deprived of his father's position and pension. The annexation of Jhansi by Dalhousie when King Gangadhar died childless is well known.

The situation was ripe for a backlash. Prince to peasant, rich to poor, Pundit to Maulvi—all faced the same common enemy, the British. Only a spark was needed to set the scene ablaze. That spark came in the form of the greased cartridges.

⁕

As Barrackpore burnt and Mangal Pandey made history on 29 March 1857, the countdown began for the final unfurling of the national tricolour ninety years later. A nation which had slept for so long, which had accepted invasions and plunders with fatalism, whose sad story told less of bravery than of the treachery that had brought her under foreign occupation and made her vulnerable to external attacks right from the times of Alexander, had finally woken. This was the glorious year of 1857—the year of the 'Sepoy Mutiny' as the British historians call it and which Indian historians term the 'First War of Indian Independence'. While heroes like Haidar and Tipu had engaged the British in bloody wars in the past, this was the first time the struggle took a broader, pan-Indian approach. This was also perhaps the first time that a spirit of nationhood, of being part of a larger cause called India was at least kindled among the people who never thought beyond the boundaries of their own kingdoms and principalities. It was this valuable sense of 'Indianness' that took birth in 1857, which continues to pervade the minds and souls of all Indians, regardless of millions of divisions of religion, caste, class, creed, language and so on.

⁕

The seeds of the 1857 uprising had been sown across the country by the end of the eighteenth century, and Mysore had not been left out. The Nagar uprising was far more significant than a mere pocket of insurgency, not only because of its scale but because economic issues were articulated by the rebels. That a revolt so widespread and organised could be triggered by an impostor, like Budi Basavappa, proves how volatile the situation was. This was a wake-up call for the British and their feudatory kings, signifying the arousal of the common man's conscience and his readiness to raise his voice against blatant injustice and exploitation.

It was a significant morale-booster and milestone for the people of Mysore that a peasant force could topple the kingdom of the Company's blue-eyed boy. But for the British it was an opportunity to weaken the ruler further. Of course, the British were the cause of the problem but blamed the poor puppet ruler, using this as an excuse to usurp what little power he had left. This is strangely similar to today's Indian politics, where several central governments have tried to dismiss a state government of another political party on unsubstantiated charges of breakdown of law and order, and imposed President's rule.

If Mysore was an early host of a peasant-based revolt, Kittur, its neighbour, did not lag behind where militant political resistance was concerned. As early as 1824, Kittur led an armed struggle against the British when the ruler Shivalingarudra, son of Mallasarja Desai, died. His adopted son was his heir. But Thackeray, the commissioner and political agent of the British at Dharwad misreported to the Madras government that the adoption took place after the demise of the ruler under his forged signature, thus compelling the government to reject the adoption. The British decided to annex Kittur. However, the brave Rani, Chennamma, protested against the move. She wrote a letter to the governor of Bombay to approve the adoption. But when the plea was rejected she resorted to arms. In October 1824 a war broke out. In a spirited address to members of her court on 18 October 1824, she articulated thoughts and feelings that were at the centre of the 1857 uprising:*

> The Britishers have come to our land on the pretext of carrying on trade and now seeing that we are quarrelling amongst ourselves,

---

* Her speech is taken from Saki's 2004 book, *Making History—Karnataka's People and Their Past,* Vol. 2. Saki is the pseudonym for Saket Raman, an author and Naxal leader.

they want to grab our land and rule over us. They want us to pay huge sums of nuzrana. They might have vanquished other rulers in this part of the country by their cunning and wicked manoeuvres. If the Peshwas have done some wrong to us, let us not forget that they are our own kith and kin. Some day they may realise their follies and join hands with us to drive away these foreigners from our sacred land.

Interestingly, Kittur had been a vassal of the British on the lines of Mysore after Shivalingarudra signed the Subsidiary Treaty with the Company. Had the rani's plea not been accepted, Kittur would perhaps have gone the Mysore way in remaining a loyal ally of the British masters.

But things turned out otherwise, and the rani fought fiercely. Thackeray was killed in the battle. The British were routed and two of their leading commanders were taken prisoner. The defeat rattled the British. Elphinstone, Governor of Bombay, ensured that in future plans were more meticulous than ever before. They realigned themselves and re-attacked Kittur in December 1824 with nearly 25,000 troops. Mysore supposedly sent in two guns, 700 infantry and 2,000 cavalry to aid the British.

Unfortunately, the treachery of some of her husband's trusted officers caused Chennamma's defeat. The entire Kittur army retreated to the fort after being pounded to a pulp by the British forces. The town was looted, the palace razed and its wooden decorations auctioned. Rani Chennamma lost the most decisive battle of her life. She was taken prisoner and kept at the Balihongal prison, where she died. Kittur was annexed but continued to haunt British nightmares. Despite her death, Chennamma inspired a series of freedom fighters who led their small armies against the British from Kittur. Sangolli Rayanna, Shankaranna, Narappa Gajapathi, Sheik Sulaiman, Nagappa Beda, Savay Shetty and Rudrappa Kotagi, all led their banners of revolt against colonial hegemony.

In the Kittur battle of 1824, Sangolli Rayanna—one of Chennamma's soldiers—had fought bravely on behalf of the Kittur army. Rayanna now made a small army of his own, looted government treasuries and burnt down post offices. However, he was caught and hanged at Nandagad. Stories of Rayanna's bravery are now part of folklore, local patriotic songs and inspirational stories. Thus, karnataka had been at the forefront of the struggle, pioneering the fight against the British with the likes of Haidar,

Tipu, Chennamma, Rayanna and others leading their armed struggle against the Company forces. Although unsuccessful, these struggles stirred up public conscience and instilled in them the desire to be masters of their own destinies. Though separated by decades in time, it links them in spirit of the heroes and heroines of the 1857 uprising.

In complete contrast to all this was the stance of the royalty of Mysore in 1857. Krishnaraja Wodeyar had the best reason to join the uprising wholeheartedly. He had been, as he always claimed, unlawfully dispossessed of his ancestral possessions and all his efforts in the past twenty-odd years to build a case for himself through pleas, threats and the like had failed. He had nothing to lose. But he actively sided with the British. His opportunism and inability to understand the pulse of the people at large is truly condemnable. He is rumoured to have distributed sweets on the streets of Mysore after news trickled in that the 1857 uprising had failed. He was desperate to demonstrate to the British that despite the unjust treatment meted out to him by the Company, he remained steadfastly loyal. It was as though he was still a terrified five-year-old on the throne of Mysore, propped up and protected by the British. Or perhaps he had a reputation to build and maintain—his failure to control the ryot upsurge at Nagar had gone against his image as a ruler; this was his chance to demonstrate that he could have a grip over things if he so wished.

Whatever the reasons, the British were only too pleased to have his support. Josyer records Commissioner Cubbon's words:

> To no one was the Government more indebted for the preservation of tranquility than to His Highness the Rajah of Mysore, who displayed the most steadfast loyalty, throughout the crisis, discountenancing everything in the shape of disaffection, and took every opportunity to proclaim his perfect confidence in the stability of the English rule. When a small party of Europeans came to Mysore he made manifest his satisfaction by giving them a feast. He offered one of his palaces for their accommodation, and as a stronghold for the security of their treasure; and even gave up his own personal establishments of elephants etc, to assist the 74th Highlanders in their forced march from the Nilgiris to Bellary for the protection of the Ceded districts, a proceeding which, although of no great magnitude in itself, produced great

moral effect throughout the country. In fact there was nothing in his power which he did not do to manifest his fidelity to the British Government, and to discourage the unfriendly.

Viceroy Lord Canning mirrors these thoughts in a letter to the maharaja, reproduced in Josyer's book:

I was well aware that from the very beginning of those troubles the fidelity and attachment to the British Government which have long marked Your Highness' acts had been conspicuous upon every opportunity. Your Highness' wise confidence in the power of England and your open manifestation of it, the consideration and kindness which you showed to British subjects, and to the ready and useful assistance which you rendered to the Queen's troops have been mentioned by the Commissioner in terms of the highest praise. I beg Your Highness to accept the expression of my warm thanks for those fresh proofs of the spirit by which Your Highness is animated in your relations with the Government of India.

True to typical British double-speak, the gesture ended with the 'warm thanks' and no efforts made to even consider the maharaja's old demand of transferring power to him.

18

COMMISSIONERS' RULE AND THE ISSUE OF RENDITION AD 1831-68

ADMINISTRATION UNDER SIR MARK CUBBON

After Briggs resigned in 1832, Morrison took over till, in June 1834, the celebrated Colonel Sir Mark Cubbon became the senior commisioner of Mysore at the age of forty-nine. He had entered the English East India Company's services as a junior officer and risen to positions of eminence through sheer hard work and sincerity. The thirty long years of his administration helped Mysore improve its machinery completely, reforming the flagrant abuse prevalent in several departments. He also put an end to unnecessary expenditures in administration. Fascinated by the city of Bangalore, Cubbon shifted the capital from Mysore to Bangalore with Tipu's palace at Bangalore serving as the new secretariat.

The period from 1831 to 1881, which marked the Commissioners' Rule era in Mysore, saw great progress and prosperity being ushered into the state. There are three distinct phases of the Commissioners' Rule into which historians categorise the fifty-year period. The first phase (1831–55) is called the 'Non-regulation' or 'Patriarchal System' phase, when the main objective was not to make any radical changes in the administration but to consolidate the existing system. The immediate concern was the establishment of law and order following widespread rebellion, redressal of peasants' concerns, prevention of flagrant abuses of power and corruption that had led to the mass uprising and purification of the native system of judicial jurisprudence. The period from 1856 to 1862 is called the 'Transition Phase', and from 1863 to 1881, the 'Regulation System' phase.

To revitalise the administrative set-up, Cubbon reorganised the administrative divisions into four zones: Bangalore, Chitradurga, Ashtagram and Nagar. Each was placed under a European superintendent. There were 120 *taluks* in the state, each under one of these four divisions. Every *taluk* was placed under an amildar and divided into *hoblis* that came under the jurisdiction of a hoblidar or shekdar. The *hobli* comprised many villages that were headed by a Patel or Gowda. The powers of the superintendents in the divisions were enhanced. The amildars could communicate directly with the commissioner and report any problems they faced. The commissioner's secretariat consisted of the first assistant who, as personal secretary to the commissioner, perfomed the duties of the secretary in all branches; the military assistant who also looked after local militia; three junior assistants in charge of different departments and a junior assistant kept as standby.

The amildar collected revenue from villages and *hoblis* and looked after the *taluk* administration. Cubbon also created a secretariat at Bangalore with nine departments: Revenue, Posts, Police, Sawar, Maramat, Medical, Amrita Mahal, Education and Justice, each under a shirastedar. Ten personal assistants were appointed to these shirastedars as personal secretaries. Government proceedings were made known to people at large through circulars, notifications and proclamations. Rules and regulations were publicised in conspicuous places in Kannada, the language of the masses. The Double Daftar system was abolished and the official language was either Kannada or Marathi.

Land revenue was the main source of state income and the land was held by two main systems—the Ryotwari and the Batayi. Under the Ryotwari system the cultivator was recognised as the real owner of the land as long as he paid his revenues (half of the produce, and the poor cultivators were forced to pay even if their crops were destroyed partially or wholly). Under the Batayi system, the government and the ryot shared the produce and the assessment was made in kind. Every effort was made to convert the Batayi to payment of money and to remove irksome procedures where they existed. The establishment of new industries and the improvement effected in the quality of commodities like cotton, wool and silk greatly helped improve the economy.

The judiciary was also improved: eighty-five *taluka* courts were created with eight principal Sadar Munshi courts, four Superintendent Courts, one Huzur Adalat court with three judges and the Commissioner's court. The Huzur Adalat and the Commissioner's courts were courts of appeal. Between 1855 and 1856 Governor General Lord Dalhousie visited Mysore. This was followed by the appointment of a judicial commissioner who would relieve the commissioner of some of his judicial duties. Panchayats at village level for criminal and civil cases continued. While the judicial system was completely overhauled during the commissioners' rule with the areas of jurisdiction of the different courts clearly laid out, there were several cases of delay in dispensing justice that led to uncertainty and discomfort for the parties concerned.

The police force was revitalised. *Taluk* amildars were assisted by killedars, hoblidars, daffedars and kandachar peons. Villagers were authorised to use arms in self-defence. Additional establishments of the police forces were stationed in Mysore, Tumkur, Shimoga and Bangalore. Between 1856 and 1862, steps were taken to form separate departments for important activities, like public works, education, audit, accounts and forests. In order to incorporate engineering skills into the system, the public works or Maramat department was staffed with one chief engineer and eleven upper- and nineteen lower-level engineers. Construction of roads was top priority, with more than 1,600 miles of roads constructed to connect all the district headquarters within the state. Five bridges were built at Maddur, Bhadravati, Hosakote, Shimoga and Hiriyur. About 336 miles of telegraph lines and a railway line[*] from Bangalore to Jolarpet starting early in 1859 can be credited to Cubbon's vision.

A separate Forests Department was set up to promote forests and to safeguard in particular the pride of Mysore—sandalwood. An individual department to preserve forest wealth was set up under a Conservator of Forests. Hospitals were opened in all major towns. Anglo-vernacular schools aided by Christian missionaries sprang up in the state and particularly in cities, like Bangalore and Mysore. Many present-day schools of repute in Bangalore, like the Bishop Cotton Boys' and Girls' schools and the Baldwins schools, were established in the latter half of the nineteenth century under the commissioners' rule.

---

[*] Actual rail traffic began in 1864, connecting the state of Mysore with Madras.

Cubbon also gave an impetus to the coffee industry with 1,60,000 acres of coffee plantations in the state by the end of his rule. His most laudable achievement, however, was a complete reorganisation of the finances of the state. In 1834–35 the state's revenues were at Rs 68 lakh and rose to Rs 84 lakh by 1855–56. Income from other sources like panchabab and sayer (customs duties) also increased markedly. The state had a public debt of Rs 85 lakh when Cubbon assumed office, but all of it was repaid by 1857 and when he left office there were accumulated savings of Rs 40 lakh in the treasury. Cubbon continued to pay the annual subsidy of Rs 24.5 lakh to the Madras government as stipulated in the Treaty of 1799. He abolished unremunerative taxes and octroi, which in the long run helped improve the state's economy.

ADMINISTRATION UNDER LEWIN BOWRING

Mark Cubbon resigned in 1861. He died near Suez, on his way back to England. He was succeeded by Lewin Bentham Bowring as commissioner in 1862. From 1863 onwards Mysore became a 'Regulation Province' and a series of reorganisations were effected in the system.

Bowring was another famed character in Mysore's history, and like his predecessor, continued the reform process to make Mysore a modern and progressive state. He had much administrative experience in the provinces of Bengal and Punjab. He created a wide network of roads all over the kingdom and took steps to connect Bangalore with Jalarpet through railways, in order to reach Madras, the seat of British power in southern India. Bowring divided Mysore into three administrative zones: Nandidurga, Ashtagram and Nagar, each under a commissioner. The state commissioner came to be known as the chief commissioner. Eight districts were created, each headed by a superintendent or deputy commissioner. *Taluks* had amildars and shekdars and *hoblis* the hoblidar as their administrative head.

The Revenue Survey and settlement departments were reorganised. Lands were accurately measured and revenue determined accordingly. In 1863 an officer was appointed as the 'Commissioner for Survey Settlement'. Surveyors were brought in from Bombay Presidency and they completed their assignment by 1888. In 1864, he got the Registration Act passed, by which all property transactions had to be registered. This was intended to curb corruption and *benami* transactions in properties. He set up the

Inam Commission which commenced its work in 1863. A comprehensive Revenue circular was issued in 1864 to systematise revenue cases and records. Committees on the survey system and irrigation matters were formed to deal with important aspects concerning their respective subjects. The Bombay Acts I (1865) and IV (1868) were promulgated, the Survey and Settlement rules framed along those lines, and a uniform set of returns and registers adopted in 1863.

The judicial and police departments received further attention from Bowring. A Judicial Commission was appointed for the whole state. This would be the chief court of all civil and criminal cases. Divisional commissioners, assistant commissioners and amildars came to assume judicial powers. 125 Munsiff courts were set up. Civil and criminal cases were clearly separated. The Indian Penal Code or the Code of Criminal Procedure Act X of 1872 was introduced in Mysore. It defined offences and specified the measures of punishment, abolished the system of fees in lieu of which the stamp rules and stamp papers were issued. In 1873 the separation of civil and criminal functions was attempted, along with the formation of Munsiff courts in the Nandidurga division. Under the revised system, the number of courts went up from 103 to 125.

The police system, on the other hand, was reorganised along the lines of the Madras Presidency. An inspector general and deputy inspector general of police were appointed at district levels and the old Kandachar peons were retrenched. District superintendents of police were appointed to maintain law and order at the district levels.

To Bowring goes the credit of encouraging education on a large scale. Education in Kannada and English ranked high on Bowring's agenda. In 1868 he established the Central Education Agency to set up schools in towns and colleges. Louis Rice, the director of Public Instruction in 1868 started the Hobli School System. The Bangalore Central College building (started in 1860 as Bangalore High School) and the Bangalore Museum building were built during this time. He shifted the Secretariat from Tipu's Bangalore Palace to the Attara Kacheri building. He set up new hospitals and expanded the engineering and horticultural departments. Following the famine of 1866 a reservoir was constructed near the Miller Tank to provide drinking water to Bangalore. Thus, it was the pioneering work done by administrators, like Mark Cubbon and Lewin Bowring, that laid the foundations of a progressive, modern Karnataka.

After rendering such invaluable services to the state, Bowring resigned in 1870. Between 1870 and 1881, Mysore was placed under the command of three chief commissioners—Colonel Richard Meade until 1875, C.B. Saunders for two years and J.D. Gordon from April 1878 to 1881. This fifty-year Commissioners' Rule saw a gradual transformation from the existing Hindu and feudal system of governance to one based on the British model—modern and progressive in its outlook. While all the old institutions of the state, which were worth their name and had stood the test of time, were continued, the defunct and disadvantageous elements were pruned out.

The British rule of this period in Mysore was generally considered benign and helpful, unlike the extremely exploitative role it had played in other parts of the country. Better systems of law-and-order enforcement were put in place under the commissioners, outdated social evils were abolished, as was corporal punishment. Modern amenities like railways, telegraph and roads were introduced, education became more accessible and the revenue system was remodelled in a more reasonable manner. The process of Mysore's modernisation would have lagged by a few decades had it not been for the commissioners and their foresight.

This was perhaps one reason why mass uprisings of the kind that erupted in the North and Bengal never broke out in Mysore after the Nagar revolt. By 1881, Mysore had emerged as an orderly, peaceful, well-administered and progressive state of British India.

But we must remember that behind all these progressive measures lay imperialist designs. It was neither philanthropy nor public welfare that motivated the British. Transport and communication were improved to help carry locally available raw materials to the ports and to England and bring back British goods to local markets across the state. When a proposal was sent to the British government in 1870 to improve the irrigation tank system in the state, the commissioner was promptly instructed that the laying of railway lines and not improvement of tanks needed to take priority. In fact the Mysore Tank Code of 1878 reduced state expenditure on many irrigation tanks. Thus it was incidental, rather than intentional, that the measures adopted seemed to propel Mysore into the realm of modernism and progressiveness.

FRICTION BETWEEN THE COMMISSIONERS AND THE MAHARAJA

The differences between the maharaja and the commissioners were public knowledge. While the maharaja saw the commissioner as a usurper, the latter considered the maharaja an unnecessary obstacle in matters of state that had no *locus standi* under the new dispensation. Ultimately, the maharaja wrote a long letter to the governor general, Lord Ellenborough, in 1846, complaining about the situation where even the payment of one lakh Star Pagodas and one-fifth of the state's net revenue as per Bentinck's formula was denied to him on different grounds. Some excerpts from the letter appear here, taken from Josyer's account:*

> As regards myself I deem it fit to declare that I am perfectly unconscious of ever having in the remotest degree merited anything unfriendly from the Commissioner. But what can be the cause of the Commissioner's past hostilities and continued opposition towards me is an enigma which I am unable to solve. ...
>
> My Lord, I must candidly confess that I have no confidence in him as a friend of my interest or dignity; and I cannot consequently feel assured that in his communications with your Lordship regarding myself or my State he acts an impartial part. I have therefore determined to appeal to your Lordship myself. Your Lordship will deem it no exaggeration when I declare that I feel myself entirely at the mercy of the Commissioner, who as he has by offering me every species of annoyance and hostility in his power, proved himself not to be my friend, neither can I safely calculate upon my security while directly placed under his absolute power as the sole Commissioner of Mysore and also Resident at my Durbar. I feel myself unprotected, and I dread to contemplate the consequence of my defenceless situation. The feeling of opposition and hostility which has so strongly marked the Commissioner's conduct towards me for the last eight years, but especially the undisguised character it has recently assumed is become matter of public observation. I shall therefore, my

---

* All the historical correspondence excerpted in this chapter, unless otherwise indicated, is taken from Josyer's 1929 book, *History of Mysore and the Yadava Dynasty*.

Lord, only add that, after all what I have said, and respectfully urged upon your Lordship's consideration, if your Lordship could possibly consent to leave me even for a moment exposed to the dangers of my present extremely painful situation, I would willingly prefer death to disgrace, and if Your Lordship cannot immediately interpose to rescue me from the latter, implore most earnestly that your Lordship will inflict upon me yourself anything you like, but do not abandon me to the sport of my inferiors.

The war of words continued. When an adversary of the maharaja, Timmarajaiya, was appointed judge of the Adawalat or High Court, a baffled maharaja directly wrote to the commissioner, seeking an explanation:

You are of course aware that this is the first instance in which I have addressed you regarding the distribution of native officers or any other arrangement connected with the public administration of my country since the appointment of the Commission. It may therefore be needless to assure you that I should not have now deviated from the uniform conduct I have hitherto observed, were I not impelled by weighty considerations of what is due to my feelings as sovereign of Mysore, for in the event of the consummation of this appointment in the Government of my own country and before my own eyes, I cannot but regard it as a direct insult offered to my person, and which will doubtless be manifest to yourself on a little consideration, knowing as you do the treacherous misconduct of these men and the fact of my having in consequence ultimately discharged them.

In reply, Cubbon wrote placidly:

It is impossible I can regard Your Highness' communication so much in the light of a remonstrance against an act in contemplation as a deliberate impeachment of the Government of this country for having actually conferred an office of high trust and responsibility upon an unworthy person, whose treacherous and traitorous misconduct, Your Highness declares, I am acquainted with. As your Highness' letter under either interpretation, and more especially when taken in conjunction with the defamatory imputations recently cast by Your Highness upon the highest authorities in this country, imputations calculated, if they could possibly be believed by the people, to destroy their confidence in the administration of justice appears to me to be a clear departure from the course of conduct expected from Your Highness. I consider it my duty to recall to Your Highness' recollection the views and intentions of the Government of India upon this point as first communicated to the Commissioners in 1831 and again in 1836, and to express my most anxious desire that no occasion may arise to impose upon me the painful obligation of representing to the Right Honourable Governor General that Your Highness' interference has a tendency to obstruct and weaken the course of administration, and, in the words of the Government, to frustrate the successful efforts which have been made for the amelioration of the country.

Not one to be cowed down, the maharaja sent another passionate letter to the governor general pleading that he take cognisance of the growing animosity between him and the commissioner:

I had it in contemplation, my Lord, in the absence of a Resident and friend to lay before Your Lordship myself in a formal manner a respectful solicitation for restoration to me of the Government of my country. At this critical juncture the efforts made by the Commissioner to oppose my views have already been submitted to your Lordship, and now, my Lord, after 12 years, he insults me with a threat of expulsion from my own country, by quoting a para of a letter dated 6th September 1831 for the first time for my information. What have I done, my Lord, to merit these insults from the Commissioner? My Lord, in the ordinary obligations of life, according to ancient saying, it becomes part of the maternal duty to cherish her offspring with the sustenance of her own breast, and while I look upon the British Government as my parent for every support, what could have induced the Commissioner to lead me to apprehend that the breast which hitherto nourished me with milk might eventually feed me with poison? I respectfully leave it to Your Lordship's superior judgment to determine. Is it because I venture to say that the rumoured appointment of Thimmapparajiah, one of my 'worst enemies', one of those unprincipled favourites who profited by the past misrule, and one of those treacherous and traitorous men who consummated the ruin of my affairs, if true, could prove a great outrage to my feelings that the Commissioner has thought proper to treat me in this manner? Your Lordship is aware that whatever I may communicate to Your Lordship the Commissioner has the opportunity of knowing, whereas I, my Lord, know not what he writes to your Lordship regarding me. I have no friend to represent any case of mine. I have no support, my Lord, save that of yourself, and in your Lordship's just and generous hands I have unreservedly committed my present welfare and future happiness in full certainty that the exalted nobleman at the head of the British Government in India has not only the power to avenge the grievous indignities unmeritedly inflicted upon me in this my humbled situation, but also the heart to administer to my lacerated feelings the unction of his friendly sympathy.

The war of words continued this way and the maharaja gave spirited replies to the accusations levelled against him. In one of his most vocal pleas he addressed Governor General Lord Henry Hardinge in June 1845:

With reference to my Kareetha of the 7th September 1844, to which I have not as yet had the honour of a reply, I am compelled again to appeal to Your Excellency and to the well known justice of the British Government in reference to my position and my just rights, which the confidence that I feel in British justice persuades me will not be longer refused to me, on a clear and distinct appeal to the Government. It is not unknown to me that my character has been misrepresented and that not only in confidential political communications, but publicly in evidence before the House of Commons in England. I am also aware that it may be the interest and object of others still to keep up this belief in the minds of those who (not knowing me personally themselves) alone have the power to do me justice. But I can with the utmost confidence challenge those who villify me, whether through ignorance or enmity, to the proof, and call on those who best know me and have had the best means of knowing me, the Residents and other European gentlemen who have been at my Court for the last 16 years, to say, whether such terms as my being 'utterly demoralized,' 'fit for nothing,' 'can never show proof of competence to govern,' etc. are not a base and foul slander; these may seem strong terms, but not too strong when the calumny has reference to my character and dearest interests in life, though I donot impute evil motives to the asserter. It may have been said in ignorance or through misinformation. I can call on those who now last know me to say whether at this moment I am not as to mental and physical vigour as capable of governing my country as any man of 50 years of age in India. I am not aware that it has been attempted to show that any reason exists sufficient to render null the Hon'ble Company's treaty with me, or to justify the withholding from me now the Government of my country. That I have been extravagant as to pecuniary matters in my younger days, and have unfortunately in some instances had as confidential advisers, persons who afterwards proved themselves unworthy of such confidence I freely avow, but I will not mock common sense or justice to suppose that any person could assert or believe that because either Prince or private individual had been at one time of his life wasteful in his pecuniary arrangements, or had managed his affairs in some respects but indifferently, he should therefore be disinherited forever. Even now, I confess I have no wish to hoard my income or bury it in the earth, but to spend it in my country and amongst my people from whose industry I derive it.

I believe I could make it plain that the assumption of the Government of my country by Lord William Bentinck was a measure both unnecessary and uncalled for by the exigencies of the time, not to speak of its being unjustified by the Treaty existing between the Hon'ble Company and myself. Disturbances there were in some Districts of my country; but do not disturbances occur in portions of the Company's country without any blame being imputed to the Government's authority? I had contracted debts, it is true; but what were they in proportion to the revenue of my country, and have not the best and most upright Governments in the world debts? But I am willing to let the past rest in oblivion and to draw Your Excellency's attention to the present and ask you and the British Government, with all due deference and respect, what just ground there is now for withholding from me my true, I may say, my unalienable rights? I appeal to the Treaty existing between the Government and myself, that treaty which I have never violated in the slightest particular or degree and which I am sure Your Excellency will consider the Government bound in honour to abide by.

Interestingly all the replies from the side of the Company were highly reassuring; they all began with the addressing mode of 'My Friend' and hoped that very soon the transfer of power could happen and that the Commissioner's Rule was only a temporary and stop-gap arrangement. But nothing ever changed; these were plain and empty words of succour that meant little in reality. The actual verdict had been passed by the Board of Directors in England in a short and crisp judgment:

> We would not willingly, after having assumed the powers of Government, place the inhabitants of any portion of the territory, however small, under the absolute domain of such a Ruler. We are desirous of adhering as far as can be done, to the native usages, and not to introduce a system which cannot be worked hereafter by native agency if and when the country shall be restored to the Rajah or his successors. The real hindrance (of the transfer) is the hazard, which would be incurred to the prosperity and good Government which the country now enjoys, by replacing it under a Ruler known by experience to be thoroughly incompetent.

But the deposed Maharaja Mummadi Krishnararaja Wodeyar was not one to sit quiet. He was the grandson of Maharani Lakshmammanni, who had personified grit and determination. He tried to build a rapport with Governor General Lord William Bentinck, who openly advocated his cause. The maharaja used to hold horse races on his birthdays. A big party of European guests would be invited and there would be three banquets—one on the first day of the race, the second on his birthday and the last at the end of the festivities. He used all these occasions to build a case for himself and the restoration of the throne to the Wodeyars. He kept reminding the British of the long-lasting ties they had enjoyed, right from the times of Maharani Lakshmammanni to the recent times when he had silently supported them in all their tribulations, such as the 1857 upsurge. On their part, the British kept acknowledging his loyalty but postponed the transfer of power on the grounds that the situation was not yet ripe, confirming at the same time that the Commissioners' Rule was only a temporary arrangement and not a permanent feature that he needed to be afraid of. Queen Victoria on her birthday even granted him the title of GCSI or 'The Knight Commander of the Most Exalted Order of the Star of India'. The maharaja waited for eight years for his reinstatement, urging Lord Ellenborough and his successor Sir Henry Hardinge to help him. A committee was formed in November 1845 to investigate the Nagar episode but its report on 14 June 1847 disqualified him.

In 1861, with the concurrence of the viceroy and the secretary of state, the maharaja sent some gem-set necklaces and other jewellery along with some Mysore-bred horses, cows and bulls under the care of the Durbar surgeon Dr Campbell to be presented to Queen Victoria. Commanded by her to acknowledge the same, the secretary of state wrote back:

> The assurances of Your Highness' friendship are very welcome to Her Majesty, who can receive no such precious gifts from the Princes and Chiefs of India as the good words which they send to her from their distant homes. From Your Highness these good wishes are especially gratifying. For more than 60 years you have been the faithful ally of the British Government who felt assured, when trouble recently overtook them, that as Your Highness was the oldest so would you be the staunchest of their friends, if evil and misguided men should seek to sow sedition in Your Highness' country. By the blessing of God the Southern peninsula of India remained undisturbed, but Your Highness nevertheless was enabled to contribute to the success of British arms by the assistance which you rendered to the passage of Her Majesty's troops towards disturbed Districts, whilst by your personal bearing in this critical juncture, you encouraged and sustained the loyalty of your subjects and helped to preserve the tranquility of the country. I am commanded by Her Majesty to send to Your Highness, under charge of Dr Campbell, a few specimens of the manufactures of Great Britain and other articles of which Her Majesty requests your acceptance as token of Her friendship and esteem.

This was followed by a series of high-powered meetings at the Secretary of State's Council to decide on the future course of action with respect to Mysore. The majority held the view that it was not binding on the British government to restore the kingdom to the maharaja, though dissenting voices to the same came through from Sir Henry Montgomery, Sir Frederick Currie and Sir John Willoughby. The final decision was communicated to the Maharaja in the following personal interview:

> On the 3rd February 1864 precisely at 1 P.M. the Commissioner and his Secretary visited the Maharaja, and after mutual enquiries, the Commissioner was silent for a minute or two when it was easy to read in his countenance all that could aggravate the pangs of the blows already sustained once by the heart of His Highness. Conversation was commenced by the Commissioner as follows: 'A Khareetha has been received from the Viceroy to Your Highness' address containing the final decision passed against Your Highness' appeal to the Secretary of State for India.' So saying Mr Bowring handed the Khareetha to His Highness. The Maharaja received it and placing it in his right hand, remained a while silent, grief and horror struck. In the meantime Mr Bowring urged His Highness to unfold the Khareetha. Finding His Highness somewhat slow in untying the strings of the bag, which had contained it, Mr Bowring took it from His Highness' hand, cut the strings with his sword and rehanded it to His Highness. The Maharaja having opened the Khareetha desired Mr Bowring to explain it to him. The purport was made known in a few words. This was enough to disturb the tender emotions of His Highness. Grief and disappointment preyed upon his heart and made him almost distracted. His Highness was a while absorbed on the one hand in endeavouring to compose himself and on the other contemplating what future measures he should adopt. In the meantime Mr Bowring hurried the Maharaja for his reply to the decision. His Highness replied—'I bow to the decision: but I cannot help declaring that in fact justice is denied to me totally by Home Authorities. It is wonderful that the same British government who to secure lasting fame and good faith did justice to my hereditary rights by placing me while a helpless boy of 5 years of age on my ancestral Throne, have now scrupled not to commit breach of faith and subject themselves to infamy by forcing such an unjust decision upon me. If they are to cut down the very tree they themselves nurtured, what can I do? So long as justice sides my cause there is little fear of losing my rights. If one authority refuses me my claims I shall never cease

Composers during Mummadi Krishnaraja's reign: Veene Sambayya

Veene Shamanna and Veene Subrahmanya Iyer

Composers during Mummadi Krishnaraja's reign: Veene Ananthasubbayya

Composers during Mummadi Krishnaraja's reign: Veene Venkatasubbaya

Composers during Mummadi Krishnaraja's reign: Veene Sambayya

Veene Shamanna and Veene Subrahmanya Iyer

Composers during Mummadi Krishnaraja's reign: Veene Ananthasubbayya

Composers during Mummadi Krishnaraja's reign: Veene Venkatasubbaya

The trinity of Carnatic music—Muthuswamy Dikshitar, Thyagaraja and Shyama Shastry

Composers during Mummadi Krishnaraja's reign: Veene Doddasubbaraya

Composers during Mummadi Krishnaraja's reign: Aliya Lingaraja Urs

Pioneer of the Mysore Bani of Veena: Veene Sheshanna

Basappa Shastry

Veene Subbanna

The grand old man of classical music in Mysore: Mysore Vasudevacharya

Bidaram Krishnappa

Vasudevacharya in a musical discourse with his students

Vasudevacharya with Yoganarasimham and Lakshminarasimhacharya

Vasudevacharya in concert

Muthaiah Bhagavathar in the court of Mysore

The innovator and musical genius: Muthaiah Bhagavathar

Muthaiah Bhagavathar, the consummate musician

Veene Venkatagiriappa

Chintalapalli Venkata Rao of the famed Chintalapalli family of musicians who found patronage in Mysore

Mysore T. Chowdaiah

Bangalore Nagaratnamma

Musicians enthrall young Prince Jayachamaraja in a private musical session

to importune another higher authority for a better treatment. Once more I assure you that it is my desire that this State, which from time immemorial has been possessed by my house should be ever continued native and uninterruptedly enjoyed by my posterity.

The maharaja on his part had two allies to stand by him—Dr Campbell, who espoused his cause in the British media and power circles, and Bakshi Narasappa, who stood by the maharaja in his domestic endeavours, though the British tried to use the services of Major Elliot and Major Martin to work on Narasappa to urge the maharaja to give up his claims. In an interview with him, Major Elliot was greatly inflamed:

Both yourself and His Highness are seated on a box of gunpowder and you cannot avoid its taking fire. But you should bear it in mind that sooner or later, it is sure you both will be blown up to the wind. Besides this I quite apprehend that you are giving His Highness every day bad counsels not to accept the present proposition of the Commissioner and to be more firm and steady against the Government who are this moment too powerful and very strong, and that your counsels make deep impression upon His Highness, spoil the business and ruin His Highness and family altogether. Take care you both will ever be in hazard of incurring the displeasure of the Commissioner. His Highness might be put into a cage like a parrot and shown to the world; as to your fate I need hardly say that it will be one similar to the late Venkappaji's, the Vakeel of His Highness.

Despite these threats, Narasappa stood resolute. They sought to create public opinion through mass signature campaigns by the people of Mysore that would be submitted to the viceroy insisting on the reinstatement of their ruler. The maharaja's age, 62, was another minus point for him. Moreover he was childless, the usual occurrence in the Wodeyar family.* Bakshi Narasappa, Kolar Krishnaiyyangar and S. Venkatavarada

---

* Incidentally, Krishnaraja did have a son, Deva Parthiva Bahaddur, in whose name there is even today a street in the city of Mysore. However, since he was not the son of the principal queen, he was denied any right to succession. He filed a case against the British when Chamarajendra was crowned king but this petition was dismissed by the British courts.

Iyengar—the maharaja's confidantes—set up an adoption plan. But this was not accepted by the British till the maharaja turned seventy-one. The wait for the throne continued. The maharaja awaited British permission to ascend the throne. He was like a leafless tree in the autumn with none to succeed him. Finally at the ripe old age of seventy-one, with no hopes of fathering a male heir, he decided to adopt one instead. The lot fell on the son of his daughter Devajammanni and Krishne Urs. On 22 February 1863, a son was born to Devajammanni. He was christened Chamarajendra. He had two brothers and one sister—Gopalaraje Urs, Subrahmanyaraje Urs and Puttalakshmammanni. The boy belonged to the same family of Bettadakote as Katti Gopalaraje Urs and his daughter Maharani Lakshmammanni. On 17 June 1865, the raja formally adopted the two-year-old. The child was brought behind the *purdah*. The traditional function began and at about half past eleven the royal salute was given. Mantras were chanted. The maharaja sat at the centre of the Amba Vilasa Pavilion of the palace with Brahmin priests surrounding him. The family priest of the Wodeyars, the Parakala Muth Swami, was also present. Amid pomp and grandeur the child was adopted and the adoption legally recognised by the British.

Shama Rao writes that after the ceremony, the maharaja sent a telegram to the viceroy and secretary of state:

> The boy I have selected is a child of two and a half years of age, of the purest Raja-Bindy or Royal blood. He is the 3rd son of the late Chikka Krishne Urs and grandson of Gopalaraje Urs, the brother of Lakshmammanni Rani (the Rani who signed the treaty between my family and the East India Company in 1799), who is the daughter of Katti Gopalaraj Urs of Bettada Kotey House, one of the 13 families with which mine is most nearly related. It only remains for me to solicit the protection of the Government of India and England to the heir whom I have adopted, and to request that Your Excellency will do me the favour to issue instructions to the Commissioner for Government of my Territories for the careful observance of all the honors and privileges due to the boy as my heir.

Quite uncharacteristically, a speedy reply arrived from the commissioner:

> In reply to Your Highness' telegram, I have the honour to point out that an adoption by Your Highness will not be recognised

unless it has received the assent, and is in accordance with the orders of the Government of India.

But by now the maharaja knew how to play his cards. Gone were the long letters he wrote earlier beseeching mercy and grace. He decided to take the battle straight into the court at England. He knew the soft corner that some members of the Council of the Secretary of State and also the press in England had for his cause. He decided to utilise the same to his advantage. Sir John Willoughby, Sir Frederick Currie, Sir Henry Montgomery, Sir George Clerk and Dr Eastwick of the Council had strictly opposed any move towards permanent annexation. Sir John Low, member of the Supreme Council, General Fraser, Briggs and Jacob, Secretary Bayley of the Madras government and Colonel Haines, ex-commissioner of Mysore and others sent a joint petition to the House of Commons to preserve the sovereignty of the princely state of Mysore and its ancestral throne. At this time, Lord Cranbourne took over as the new secretary of state from Sir Charles Wood.

On 23 July 1866, the 'Mysore Caucus', along with Sir Henry Rawlinson and Sir Edward Colebrook, a Member of Parliament, impressed upon the new incumbent the need to recognise the adoption made by the maharaja and slowly divest power from the commissioner to the royal family. They were supported by Lord Willian Hay, Member of Parliament who vociferously vouched that any hasty action by the British Government would scar the very reputation of fair play and justice of Her Majesty Queen Victoria. To give credence to their claims, they took along General Briggs, the first commissioner of Mysore, who reported that the cases of maladministration were grossly misrepresented and exaggerated. Overwhelmed by this huge contingent making common cause for a princely state of India, Lord Cranbourne asked them pointedly what they expected him to do. The team requested him to immediately maintain the native state, consent to the adoption and make way for the transition of power. The secretary of state said he would look into the matter deeply and give it active consideration.

The Press of England, known for its free views and thoughts, lashed out at the British government's motives and actions. Josyer tells us that one daily wrote, 'For every shame let us hear no more of Mysore annexation.' Another detailed:

> A fertile and pleasant Province like Mysore, providing a cool summer retreat for Government, and snug berths for sons and

nephews, may seem a rich prize for Indian Officials; but it is marvellous that any English Statesman, taking from a distance a comprehensive survey of the vast Empire of India and mindful of the giant career that, for good or evil, lies before it, should have failed to see that twenty such Provinces as Mysore would be dearly purchased if their possession crippled the influence which it is our high mission to exercise upon the future of India, by shaking the confidence of our native subjects and allies in our moderation and even our good faith.

The candid recollections of John Morley, who became secretary of state forty years later, can be found in Josyer's book:

And there can be no doubt that viewed from the point of higher international morality, measured by the purer standard of the political duty of the superior to the inferior race, which prevails in the present decade of the century—the policy of the Indian government, prompted by men of the old school like Sir Thomas Munro and Sir Mark Cubbon was in the last degree selfish, grasping and hollow—we shall be accused of acting hypocritically from first to last. Lord Wellesley established a Kingdom, which he never meant to be maintained. He made a treaty with the Nizam to last while sun and moon should endure, but he only meant while it should suit English policy. We assumed the administration of Mysore under the pretext of securing a subsidy, but all the time we never intended to give it back again. We declared that we recognized the right of adoption, and on the first opportunity we decline to do any such thing. We declared that we had given up the evil policy of annexation and then we annex the first territory on which we can lay our hands. It is not difficult to see how ugly our conduct can thus, without much forcing be made to look. And all India is said, on creditable authority, to be watching the case. We have abandoned our legitimate influence in the West in order to annex in the East. We preach moral suasion in Europe, so that we may be free to practise material repression in Asia. We make ourselves despised in one continent in order to make ourselves hated in another. It would be paying many of our Cabinet ministers of either party much too high a compliment to say this is their deliberate policy. They have replaced our old, and in many points our bad system of 'Thorough' by the new and in all points, the worse principle of 'Drift'. The story of Mysore illustrates only too perfectly the perils in which the Drift system may involve us in matters not immediately under the public eye. The only consolatory reflection is that in this instance Public opinion may even now come into operation and reverse a policy which is opposed alike to principles of justice, and to the expediency of the hour.

In early 1867, the question was taken for a full-dress debate in the British Parliament and tempers ran high. Dr Campbell, who witnessed the proceedings of the House, sent in a cable to the maharaja on 24 February 1867: 'I heartily congratulate Your Highness. House of Commons decided last night. Mysore Kingdom safe. Prince succeeds Your Highness. Campbell.' The cable was music for the ears of the old and ailing maharaja, who had fought an unrelenting and life-long battle against the powers-that-be for the restoration of his ancestral throne.

The secretary of state, Northcote wrote to the maharaja on 16 April 1867:

> Having regard to the antiquity of the Maharaja's family, its long connection with Mysore, and the personal loyalty and attachment to the British Government which His Highness has so conspicuously manifested, Her Majesty desires to maintain that family on the Throne in the person of His Highness' adopted son upon terms corresponding with those made in 1799, so far as the altered circumstances of the present time will allow.

The adopted son was to be educated under the superintendence of the Indian government. And as though to clear the old maharaja's name of any stigma that might have attached to it by the British government's previous course of action, Her Majesty Queen Victoria in May 1867 conferred on him the title of Knight Grand Commander of the Star of India with these words:

> We are desirous of conferring upon you such mark of our Royal favour as will evince the esteem in which we hold your person and the service you have rendered to our Indian Empire. We have thought fit to nominate and appoint you to be a Knight Grand Commander of the Most Exalted Order of the Star of India.

Thus, towards the end of his life, through his sheer perseverance and grit, Krishnaraja Wodeyar managed to redeem his name and the throne for his family. That he could never again ascend the throne was not such a sore point since he saw it restored to a successor of his clan. Shortly thereafter, Krishnaraja's health deteriorated. By 23 March 1868, his health worsened. Finally on the night of 27 March 1868, Krishnaraja Wodeyar breathed his last. Bakshi Narasappa informed Elliot about his death. The palace and properties, almirahs, treasury and records were sealed. On 28 March 1868 the funeral was held below the Doddakere *bund*. People flocked to catch a last glimpse of their maharaja. Despite having been deposed, he enjoyed a lot of goodwill and affection among his subjects. Prince Chamarajendra was kept away from the sight of mourning and the dead body. The sandalwood-and-camphor cremation went off smoothly. Thus ended the story of Krishnaraja Wodeyar—the man handpicked by the British after Tipu's fall. He lost his kingdom to revolts encouraged by his own lack of foresight and British opportunism.

It must, however, be said that he was a great patron of literature and the arts. A man of great intellect and memory, he was proficient in Kannada, Hindustani, Marathi and Sanskrit. He enriched the Yakshagana folk art of Karnataka. The *Ramayana* and the *Mahabharata* were translated into Kannada. He wrote several literary works, which include *Devatanama Kusumamanjari*, *Sritattva nidhi* (an illustrated encyclopaedia), *Sri Krishna Kathasangraha*, *Ramayana*, *Bharata*, *Dasharathanandana Charitre*, *Grahana Darpana* (on 82 eclipses that would take place from 1841–1902) and *Suryachandra Vamshavali*.

His court was full of authors and artists whom he patronised. Devachandra, the court poet, wrote *Rajavali Kathe*. The *Mudra Manjusha* by Kempu Narayana was a literary masterpiece of the time.

Asthana Vidwan Basavappa Shastri (1843–91) prepared Kannada versions of *Abhigyana Shakuntala*, *Vikramorvashiyam*, *Ratnavali*, *Uttara Rama Charite* and so on. The other books of the period were: *Shurasena Charite*—the Indian version of Shakespeare's *Othello*, *Damayanti* in Champu style and *Savitri Charite* in Shatpadi style.* Ramakrishna Shastri wrote

---

* Champu and Shatpadi are literary styles of varying metres. Champu was a mixture of prose and poetry while Shatpadi was a six-line stanzaic metrical form unique to Kannada literature.

Bhuvana Pradeepika, about the history and geography of South India, while Srinivasa Kavi Sarvabhauma's *Krishnaraja Prabhavodayam* and *Krishnaraja Jayotkarsha Champu* are biographies of the King. Aliya Lingaraja, Srinivasa Kavi and Mahanto Shivayogi were famous poets of the time. Carnatic classical music was given great impetus by the Maharaja. Haridasa Vijayadasa, Gopaladasa and Prasanna Venkatadasa were the acclaimed music composers while Veena Sheshanna, Bakshi Subbanna, Mysore Sadashiva Rao and other great musicians adorned his court.

Singarayya records the viceroy's proclamation, sent with his condolences to the bereaved family on 23 September 1868.

> His Excellency the Right Honourable, the Viceroy and the Governor General in Council announces to the chiefs and people of Mysore the death of His Highness the Maharajah Krishnaraja Wadiyar Bahaddur—Knight Grand Commander of the Most Exalted Order of the Star of India. This event is regarded in sorrow by the Government of India with which the Maharajah had preserved the relations of friendship for more than half a century.
>
> His Highness Chamrajendra Wodeyar, at present a minor, the adopted son of the late Maharajah is acknowledged by the Government of India as the successor and as Maharajah of Mysore territories.
>
> During the minority of His Highness the said territories will be administered in His Highness' name by the British Government on the same principles and under the same regulations as heretofore.
>
> When His Highness shall attain the period of majority, viz. the age of 18, and if he shall be found qualified for the discharge of the duties of his exalted position, the Government of the country will be entrusted to him, subject to such conditions as may be determined at that time.

Meanwhile, rumours were spread that the British had negated the adoption and had planned a permanent annexation of Mysore. This horrified Krishnaraja's widows, who wrote a letter to the commissioner, dated 10 August 1868:[*]

---

[*] This letter appears in Singarayya's book.

To The Commissioner of Mysore, L.B. Bowring Saib, Cheluvajammanni and Devajammani's humble salutes. As per the customs of our Family, after the demise of one ruler and his last rites, his legal heir is invested with all powers. This has been the custom since time immemorial. Therefore, just as your goodselves favoured us and helped us in adopting our son, Sri Chamarajendra Wodeyar, it would be befitting to place him on the Masnad of Mysore after our King's demise. We regret for the actions dissimilar to these customs. Through you we would like to quench our inquisitiveness about the matter and humbly submit to your goodselves to inform the foreign authorities and receive their orders regarding the same. We have been waiting for the Hukm from the British Bahaddars' office. Our annual Dasara festivities are just a stone's throw away from now and if a new king is not nominated by then the festivities would get marred. This would not augur well for our state and it would also be a big blow to our heritage and culture of bygone ages and an affront to out glorious family and kingdom. We hence plead with you to send us the Hukm of coronation by October, before the commencement of the Dasara and thus save our family from disgrace. Kindly send this message through telegram to the State Secretary Saib Bahaddur of England and oblige.

—Queens of Ramavilasa Sannidhana and Seetavilasa Sannidhana

But Dasara arrived and the *hukm* was not yet delivered. The two queens were in a dilemma. On the one hand was grief at their husband's death and on the other the fear of British deceit. They secretly placed Chamarajendra on the Bhadrasana throne and carried on the customs of yesteryears. But on the third day of the festivities, Colonel Elliot came to the palace and delivered the viceroy's Hukumnama on Prince Chamarajendra's coronation. Almanacs were hurriedly looked up to hunt for an auspicious date.

That date was 23 September 1868, when the coronation was held in an exquisitely decorated *pandal*. Preparations were on in full swing. The maharanis bathed the maharaja, dressed him up and the bakshis and Sarvadhikaris led him to the court by 10 am. The throne was worshipped. Bowring held the maharaja's right hand and Elliot his left and led the infant maharaja to the throne. To his right sat the European officers and ladies while the Mysoreans occupied the left. The Arasus and Palegars squatted on the ground on a big, richly embroidered carpet. Near the *thotti* were stationed the state elephant, state horse, state cow, state knife, the chariot, and symbols of Shankha, Chakrankusha, Kuthara were brought in. The sepoys and *bharjis* guarded the venue. The gallery was filled by a large turnout of the citizens of Mysore who had assembled to witness the ceremony—music, the chanting of mantras, a twenty-one-gun salute and a reading from the *History of the Wodeyars since 1399* by Mallarajayya. A poet described the event in Halegannada—the older version of literary Kannada. The royal scribe then read out the list of titles to the king:

> Srimatsamasta Bhoomandala Mandanaaya Mana Nikhila Deshaavatamsa Karnataka Janapada SampadhishTana Vikalakalanidhi Kulakramagatha Rajakshitipala Pramukha Nikhila Rajadhiraja Maharaja ChakravarthigaL Mandalaanubhootam Divyaratna SimhasanaarooDha Srimad Rajadhiraja Raja Parameshwara ProuDha Pratapa Apratimaveera Narapati Birudentembara GanDa, Lokaikaveera Yadukula Payaha Paaravaara Kalanidhi Shankhachakrankusha KuThara Makara Matsya SharabhaSaLva Gandaberunda Dharaneevaraha Hanumagaruda Kantheerava Dayanekabirudaankita Sri Chamarajendrar Wodeyar Bahaddur, Sri Chamundamba Varaprasadodbhava Sri Mummadi Krishnarajendrar Wodeyar Bahhadaravara Sweekruta putrar Srimad Mahamaheshwarar Chamarajendrar Wodeyar BahaddaravargaLige Jayavaagali Jayavaagali Jayavaagali!

This ended the festivities for a family starved of joyous occasions and celebrations. Bowring detailed the events of the day in his diary:[*]

> The young chief was conducted up the steps and when he took his seat was pelted from every corner of the courtyard by a storm of flowers, which lay several inches deep at the foot of the Throne, while a Royal Salute was fired, and the Troops presented arms. The officiating Brahmins then pronounced some

---

[*] While his diary has been excerpted in Josyer's book, Lady Bowring's recollections have been quoted in Singarayya's book, *Sri Chamarajendra Wodeyaravara Charitre*.

benedictory prayers and offered to the young Rajah water of the sacred streams with consecrated coconuts and rice. After this the genealogy of the Mysore Family was read aloud, and at its conclusion where the young Chief's name and titles were recited, the building resounded with the applause of the people. The next step was to present him with a Khillath of 21 trays of shawls, cloths and jewellery on the part of the Viceroy, while all the Rajabundus and high officials of the court came forward in turn, made their obeisance and tendered their offerings, the ceremony being terminated by a distribution of pan, betelnut and garlands of flowers. During the whole time the little Rajah behaved with the utmost decorum, neither allowing himself to be moved by the storm of bouquets, nor by the vociferous adulations of his courtiers. In the afternoon he held a Durbar in the great balcony fronting the courtyard of the Palace, having first walked around the Throne and scattering at its foot flowers in token of taking possession. On his ascending his seat he was again pelted with flowers by the bystanders, while tumultuous shouts of applause rose up from the dense crowds below!

Lady Bowring, who was also present at this occasion, joyfully recounts:

My husband and Major Elliot took the little man by hand and leading him up the silver steps lifted him on his throne. Then you should have heard the row! The lances were clanged, the English hurrahed, the natives shouted and the bands and tom-toms played. I never was in such a din and the crowd surged up and there came a perfect shower of flowers. We were pelted on all sides and Lewin had to protect the little Rajah with his cocked hat, while Major Elliot did his best for me, but it was hopeless and there was nothing for it but to endure. I looked up expecting to see the little Rajah terrified and in tears, but like a high-born oriental, he sat as cool as a cucumber!

The next day Lady Bowring visited the maharanis and recalled the meeting thus:

The Queen is very pretty and her eyes are like her son's. She came with her son to meet me. She placed him on my lap and said 'He is yours from now and not my son!' Then the Guadis offered flowers, sprinkled atthar, granted a rose and gave me betelnuts. The king escorted her downstairs, holding her hand with his tiny ones.

She visited them again on 28 November 1868, when he wished her in perfect English: 'Good Morning!' Thus began a new chapter in the history of Mysore and the Wodeyars.

19

TOWARDS RENDITION

THE EDUCATION OF AN INDIAN PRINCE

Chamarajendra's first tutor was Bhaskar Pant, who taught him the fundamentals of language, arithmetic, *slokas* from the epics and mythological tales. Singarayya records that on 24 April 1867, the late Maharaja Krishnaraja Wodeyar had written a letter to the British government regarding his son, for whom he desired quality education:

> I am very desirous that my son Chamarajendra Wodeyar, who by the blessing of God has now entered his fifth years should receive greater advantage of education and training than I myself enjoyed in my childhood and youth. Although there may be a difference of opinion between Your Excellency and myself as to the actual position and rights of this dear child, I feel that there will be no difference of opinion between us as to the value of education to the princes and nobles of India. I am equally sure that whatever may be the destiny of my son and heir and whatever duties may devolve on him, Your Excellency's successors will never forget that he is by birth a member of this Ancient Royal Family and that he is by Hindu Law the son of the Raja of Mysore, the oldest and staunchest, although the humblest ally of Her Majesty, the Queen Empress of Great Britain and India.

After 1868, the British government deployed Gregorie Hains to tutor the maharaja in politics, English, native languages, swimming, cricket, horse riding, polo, shooting, etc. But he resigned and returned to England halfway through. That very year, the famous historian, Colonel J.B. Malleson, was appointed tutor for the seven-year old maharaja. Malleson decided to put the maharaja in the 'Royal School' or 'Khas Bungalow' where he would study with the royal children of the Arasu and dewan's families. Jayarama Rao, V.P. Madhava Rao, and Ambil Narasimha Iyengar were the English teachers; Basavappa Shastri, Garalapuri Shastri, and Mir Abbas Hussain taught Kannada, Sanskrit and Hindustani respectively. The young maharaja also learnt cricket, swimming, wrestling, horse riding and polo at this school.

Malleson tried to inculcate the habit of punctuality in the young maharaja, something that later became a part of his personality. Once, when the maharaja reached school late, he found the door of the classroom closed on purpose by Malleson. The young student, aware he was guilty of coming late, did not knock but silently stood outside. Suddenly, Malleson came out of the classroom and warned him that this had been his last chance and he should never be late again. Once, during the festivities of his brother Gopalaraje Urs's marriage, the maharaja tried to miss school. An enraged Malleson barged into the Kalyana Mandap (where the wedding was taking place) and dragged the truant back to school!

Malleson knew the value of educational tours in a student's life. He once planned to take the maharaja to the Nilgiris. Singarayya quotes an attendant of the maharaja as saying:

> The Maharaja was 9 years old when he left for Nilgiris. This was the first time he left the capital. Last summer, Malleson wanted to take him to Nandi Hills to meet the Europeans. But since they had not arrived, the idea was dropped. The Queen Mother resented; with tears in her eyes she pleaded the Raja not to leave her and go to an alien land. But the adamant Malleson would have none of such emotional melodramas! So they left the following day. Not many people accompanied. Only the Raja's brother, Bakshi Basappaji Urs and Rangacharlu accompanied him. Since I was the bodyguard, I too followed. On the way we had food in a mantap near Paigere. The roads were very bad and we had to cross forests. After dusk, things became dark and dangerous in the densely forested areas. Wild animals roared. The Raja inquisitively asked, 'Don't these animals sleep at night?' Basappaji

replied 'No Mahaswami, these cruel animals don't sleep but attack nearby villages, kill cattle and sheep.' 'Then we shall hunt them down,' came the pat reply! For night, I had brought dry grasses and prepared a bed for him. We all stayed awake and guarded the young Raja.

In 1872 the maharaja underwent the *Upanayanam* ritual, where the sacred thread was granted to him and he then became eligible to study the Holy Scriptures. Malleson took the maharaja to the Jog Falls in Shimoga district in 1874. The maharaja was reportedly thrilled to see this paradise on earth. They then visited Malnad and Bangalore. After his invaluable help to the royal family and after playing a pivotal role in shaping the maharaja's character, Malleson retired in 1876. By then the maharaja had become proficient in all the areas of study that he had undertaken. Expressing satisfaction on the progress made by the king, Malleson wrote before he left:[*]

From 1868 to 1876 the Rajah has gained a lot of knowledge. He has been taught everything that has to be taught in English schools, other than Latin and Greek. He is capable of horse riding, hunting, playing cricket etc. He is also very punctual, honest and duty loving. He is capable of ruling this land.

The maharaja was, incidentally, a prolific speaker and writer of the English language. Some of the letters he wrote to his friends during this time give us a glimpse of his thought processes and manner of articulation. One such letter, reproduced in Shama Rao's book, appears here:

Wednesday 28th April 1875

Ooty

To

MY DEAR FRIEND MAHMAD IBRAHIM;

We are quite well by the good grace of our creator. I received your kind letter on the 28th of April. I am very glad to see that letter. We are spending time in reading, walking, running and everyday cricket playing. In Physical Geography of India, we finished three chapters. We

---

[*] Malleson's account appears in Shama Rao's 1936 book, *Modern Mysore*.

are also going hunting twice a week and we killed one tiger, twenty porcupines and some jackals...convey my best compliments to Abbas Khan, Bhima Rao and C. Subbaraja Urs. Here all the boys give their compliments to you.

I am yours

Chamarajendra Wadiyar

❖

23rd December 1875

Mysore

MY DEAR SIR RICHARD MEADE

Colonel Malleson delivered to me this morning your letter on the 18th instant, at the same time that he explained to me the reasons of duty which had caused you to accede to the wishes of His Excellency the Viceroy and to leave Mysore for Haidarabad. I can easily understand your preference for a place which you know, when the other is comparatively unknown. I used to experience a similar feeling when it was proposed to take me from Mysore to Bangalore. But I trust the results in both cases may be the same. At all events you have given me the example of sacrificing inclination to duty; though I must admit, since my journey to Bombay, my previous prejudices against change have been removed.

My best wishes will go with you and it will always be a pleasure to me to hear that you and Lady Meade are happy.

I am yours

Chamarajendra Wadiyar

After Malleson, one Wilson and later William Porter served as tutors and Sir James Gordon as Guardian. Porter taught the Raja physics, physical geography, political economy and constitutional history. By January 1880, his education was complete and he was declared a scholar. Shama Rao notes that Gordon wrote to the Indian government as follows:

From the time of Porter, the Rajah's knowledge and etiquette has greatly improved. He can read books, epics, newspapers etc. and write letters with a practised hand. He now discriminates between good and bad and has acquired the judging ability.

When the maharaja turned 16, the Maharani of Seetavilasa Sannidhana decided he should get married. The wedding was fixed for 26 May 1878. The bride was Kempananjammanni, the daughter of Kalale Narase Urs who had served as dewan for some time after Purnaiya retired from public life. She was born in 1866. Her education had begun at the age of five. Everyone praised her beauty, simplicity and honesty. On 23 May 1878, the rituals of *Nischitartha* and *Kankanadharane* were carried out. The next day, *Nandi*, *Kashiyatra*, the installation of the Gods, *Udakashanti*, etc., continued. The city was decorated for the grand event. Dressed in golden robes, riding an elephant, flanked by his brothers, army officers, jesters, dancers, etc., the maharaja led the procession to the bride's house. There he was led to a gorgeously decorated *mantap* with the enchanting music of the *nadaswara* and *thevil* and Vedic hymns resounding everywhere. Bakshi Basappaji did the *kanyadana* as Narase Urs was dead. With the tying of the sacred mangalasutra, Kempananjammanni became the maharani and wife of Chamarajendra Wodeyar X.

THE RENDITION

As per the previous Indian state secretary Northcote's promise to the deceased Krishnaraja Wodeyar, Chamarajendra was invested with ruling powers when he turned eighteen at the 'Rendition of Mysore' on 1 March 1881. 'Rendition' was the term used for the events of 1881 that marked the transition of power from the commissioners back to the Wodeyars. On 25 March 1881, the Palace witnessed a *durbar* whose main objective was to restore power to the maharaja. The Viceroy Lord Ripon was absent due to personal reasons but the Rt. Hon. W.P. Adams, governor of Madras, represented the viceroy. He placed the instrument of transfer in the maharaja's hands and read out the following message:[*]

Your Highness, the Queen and the Viceroy are well aware of the high and responsible trust which the British Government this day

---

[*] The words spoken by Adams and the King are taken from Shama Rao's 1936 book, *Modern Mysore*.

commits to Your Highness' charge. But happily they also know that you have endeavoured to render yourself fit for the great duty that devolves upon you and that under the guidance of Mr Gordon, the Chief Commissioner of Mysore, you have studied the principles of Government and by the interest you have shown therein and also by your own manly life and conduct, you have given every indication of becoming a wise, liberal and enlightened ruler...

The maharaja then spoke:

I beg your Excellency to convey to Her Royal Majesty an expression of my deep, grateful loyalty and attachment to the British crown and my assurance of the welfare of the people to prove myself worthy of the confidence reposed in me...

A group of Indian officers with a dewan as head of executive administration, and a council of three members as presidents under him, was appointed. Sriyutha Settipalyam Veeravalli Rangacharlu became the dewan of the state. A proclamation was read out on behalf of the Viceroy Lord Ripon stating the terms of the Rendition and it had the following clauses:

1. Maharaja Chamarajendra Wodeyar Bahaddur will be given ruling power on the 25th of March 1881.
2. The above Maharaja and his successors can rule independently until and unless they strictly follow the following conditions.
3. For the kingdom of Mysore, Chamarajendra Wodeyar's son or adopted son is the rightful heir of the throne. But if the successors are worthless, the right will be withdrawn. The Governor General in Council's decision is final. If this king has no son or adopted son, the Governor General in Council has the right to nominate the future king.
4. Maharaja Chamarajendra Wodeyar and his successors will be recognised as Maharaja of Mysore if they are loyal and faithful to the Empress of India and Queen of Great Britain and Ireland. They must render help to Her Majesty when the need so arose.
5. The permanent stationing of British troops within the Mysore territory for its protection from all internal and external threats

should be gracefully accepted. For this favour the Maharaja should pay for a year Rs 35 lakh in two instalments to the British Government.
6. From the day the king assumes office, the British control on Seringapatam ceases. The king should act according to those conditions which help him in ruling this land.
7. Without the permission of the Governor General in Council no old fort can be repaired or new forts built anywhere in Mysore territories.
8. No weapons or guns can be bought or stationed without the permission nor should they be illegally manufactured.
9. The king should grant the British government land for cantonments. His authority ceases in these cantonments. He must provide all facilities to the army. No customs or taxes can be put forth by him on the goods bought by the British.
10. The military should have a cap on the number of soldiers. The procedures for the personnel will be put forth by us.
11. The Maharaja should not enter into negotiations with other kingdoms or kings without permission from the British government.
12. He can not employ or retrench civil workers from the service without permission.
13. The same currency should circulate in Mysore as in the rest of British India. The traditional Mysorean currency should be discontinued.
14. For telegraph services the British Government's decision is final when it comes to laying of wires. The Mysore government should readily provide labour for the same.
15. Lands to be provided to build railway lines which come under British jurisdiction.
16. All criminals of British India must be caught and produced to the Government if found in the state.
17. The right of judging criminals of Europe in Mysore must be handed over to the Governor General. The Maharaja must not interfere in British laws.
18. The Maharaja should act according to the British Government's wishes in either reducing or stopping the growth of opium, salt, production of drugs, tobacco, etc. These must not be exported or imported directly by him.

19. No administrative changes can be effected by him.
20. The same revenue settlements of previous years would hold. The revenue should be paid correctly and on time.
21. If the Maharaja does not act as per these conditions the Governor General reserves the right to terminate his rule, seize all powers, property and territories and award him a nominal pension for the upkeep for his family and himself.
22. The previous borders stand cancelled. The right of nominating an heir and capable ruler to the Masnad of Mysore goes to the Governor General.

Ft. William
          RIPON

1st March 1881   The Viceroy and Governor General of India

The details of a proclamation that was issued the same day by the maharaja, as recorded by Shama Rao, are as under:

Whereas the Government of the territories of Mysore heretofore administered on our behalf by the British Government, has this day been transferred to us by the Proclamation of His Excellency the Viceroy and Governor General of India in Council, we do hereby notify and declare that we have this day assumed charge of the said government; and we call upon all our subjects within the said territories to be faithful and to bear true allegiance to us, our heirs and successors. We do hereby further declare that all laws and rules having the force of law now in force in the said territories shall continue to be in force in the said territories. We hereby accept as binding upon us all grants and settlements heretofore made by the British Government within the said territories, in accordance with the respective terms thereof, except in so far as they may be rescinded or modified either by a competent Court of Law, or with the consent of the Governor General in Council.

We hereby confirm all existing courts of judicature within the said territories in the respective jurisdiction now vested in them, and we further confirm in their respective appointments, the judges and all other officers, Civil and Military, now holding office within the said territories. For the conduct of the executive administration of the said territories under our command and control, we have resolved to appoint a Dewan, and we, placing trust and confidence in the loyalty, ability and judgement of C.V. Rangacharlu, C.I.E, appoint him to be our Dewan for the conduct of the executive administration of the said territories. His Excellency the Viceroy and Governor General in Council having complied with our request to lend us the services of the present Judicial Commissioner, J.D. Sandford, M.A, Bar-at-Law to aid us in the administration of justice in our territories, we hereby confirm the said Mr J.D. Sandford in his appointment under the designation of Chief Judge of Mysore.

We have further resolved that a Council shall be formed to be styled 'The Council of His Highness the Maharaja of Mysore' which shall consist of the Dewan for the time being as Ex-Officio President, and two or more members specially appointed by us from time to time. It shall be the duty of the members of the said Council to submit for our consideration their opinions on all questions relating to legislation and taxation, and on all other important measures connected with the good administration of our territories and the well-being of our subjects. We are accordingly pleased to appoint C.V. Rangacharlu C.I.E, Dewan, Ex-Officio President, T.R.A. Thumboo Chetty, Judge, Ex-Officio member, P.A. Krishna Rao, R.A. Sabhapathy Mudaliar, Members, to be Members of the said council and to hold office as such Councillors for the term of 3 years or during our pleasure. Given under our hand and seal this 25th day of March 1881.

With so many strictures and prohibitions the maharaja became a mere titular sovereign, spineless and unable to make independent decisions—a mere tool in the hands of the British.

THE RAJ PERIOD

During the Raj, as it was called after the 1858 proclamation, British rule had incapacitated not just the maharaja of Mysore, but rulers across all the princely states of India. During this period, a tiny number of British officials and troops (about 20,000 in all) ruled over 300 million Indians.

This was often seen as evidence that most Indians accepted and even approved of British rule. There is no doubt that Britain could not have controlled India without the cooperation of Indian princes and local leaders, as well as huge numbers of Indian troops, police officers, civil servants, etc.

Other historians point out that British rule continued because Indian society was so divided, it could not unite against the British. In fact, the British encouraged these divisions. The slightly well-to-do classes were educated in English schools. They served in the British army or in the civil service. They effectively joined the British in ruling their poorer fellow Indians. There are huge arguments about whether the British created or enlarged these divisions in Indian society or whether they simply took advantage of divisions that were already present in Indian society. For much of the 1800s the average Indian peasant had no more say in the way he or she was ruled than did the average worker in the United Kingdom.

The British view tended to portray British rule as a charitable exercise — they suffered India's environment (unfavourable climate, diseases) in order to bring to India good government and economic development (railways, irrigation, medicine, modern education, etc.). Modern-day admirers of British rule also note these benefits.

Other historians point out that ruling India brought huge benefits to Britain. India's huge population made it an attractive market for British industry. In the 1880s, for example, about twenty per cent of Britain's total exports went to India. By 1910 these exports were worth £ 137 million. India also exported huge quantities of goods to Britain, especially tea, which was drunk in Britain or exported to other countries from here. Then there were the human resources. The Indian army was probably Britain's single greatest resource. Around forty per cent of India's wealth was spent on the army. This army was used by Britain all over the world, including the wars in South Africa in 1899–1902 and the First and Second World Wars. It was the backbone of the power of the British Empire. Shama Rao writes that in 1901 the British viceroy of India, Lord Curzon, said, 'As long as we rule India, we are the greatest power in the world. If we lose it we shall straightway drop to a third rate power.'

Britain gained hugely from ruling India, but most of the wealth created was not invested back into the country. For example, from 1860 to about 1920, economic growth in India was very slow — much slower than in Britain or America. The Industrial Revolution in England and the imposition of tariffs on goods imported from India completely ruined flourishing Indian textiles, jute, metal and other industries. Millions of craftsmen starved to death. India, which was the industrial workshop of the world, was reduced to merely an agricultural country and a provider of raw material for British industries.

India's population only grew by about one percent per year, which also suggests there was not much economic growth. India actually started importing food under British rule, because Indians were growing cash crops, such as cotton and tea, for export to Britain.

From 1870 to 1930 Britain took about one percent of India's wealth per year. This was much less than the French, Dutch and Germans took from their lands. The British invested about £ 400 million in the same period. They brought in an irrigation programme, which increased eightfold the amount of land available for farming. They developed a coal industry, which had not existed before. Public health and life expectancy increased under British rule, mainly due to improved water supplies and the introduction of quinine treatment against malaria. Big landowners, Indian princes and the Indian middle classes all gained in terms of job opportunities, business opportunities and careers in areas like the law. Ordinary Indians gained little, but the argument continues as to whether British rule made much difference to their lives.

Section 5
Modern Mysore
(AD 1881–1950)

Four Generations of the Wodeyars: Mummadi Krishnaraja, Chamarajendra, Natwadi Krishnaraja, Kanthirava Narasimharaja and Jayachamaraja

20

THE REFORMER KING CHAMARAJENDRA WODEYAR X

From the achievement of Rendition onwards, the history of Mysore evolves somewhat differently than before. There are three strands along which one can follow its history from this point onwards, but these are not completely separate; they weave in and out of each other, creating patterns as time goes by. However, it is necessary to separate them in this narrative in order to appreciate each of these individually, and to see how their interplay ultimately created the modern identity of Karnataka, a state hailed today as the hub of the IT revolution in India and a leading industrial destination of the country.

Our three strands are as follows: firstly, the rule of the Wodeyars, especially Nalwadi Krishnaraja Wodeyar, (also known as the Rajarishi); secondly, the administration of the dewans of Mysore, especially the outstanding quartet of Rangacharlu, Sheshadri Iyer, Sir M. Vishweshwarayya and Sir Mirza Ismail, and the impact this administration had on the political institutions, economic development and society of Mysore, and finally, India's freedom movement under Mahatma Gandhi and the role Karnataka played in it. The context in which all this took place, namely, nineteenth-century India, also needs to be briefly reviewed.

NINETEENTH CENTURY INDIA

The later half of the nineteenth century saw the country ravaged by innumerable famines. Large parts of the country, especially Bengal, reeled under the effects of the devastating Zamindari system and the Permanent Settlement that Lord Cornwallis had introduced. The Collector was converted into a *zamindar* or landlord and the peasants were mere tenants. The Company received a fixed revenue on a regular basis at the due time, thus was saved the bother of making frequent changes in the revenue system.

In 1875–76 famine struck Mysore as well and millions lost their lives and properties. Epidemics spread like wildfire. Bangalore alone had railway service in the entire state and so transportation of relief material to far flung areas was difficult. More than 500 tons of food grain were imported into Mysore from Rangoon and Madras. Almost one-fifth of the population of Mysore succumbed to the famine and related diseases. The Viceroy Lord Lytton made a survey of the state and appointed Sir Charles Elliot as famine commissioner and Sir Collin Scott Moncrieff as Chief Engineer. The maharaja personally spent over a crore of rupees for the relief operations. A special commissioner, Sir Richard Temple, was deputed by the Indian government to superintend the campaign against famine and Lord Lytton visited the affected areas.

By September 1878 it rained and the famine seemed to abate. But mortality was high, with epidemics and sickness ruling the roost. A Mansion House Fund was raised in London to help reinstate agriculturists who had been left destitute. The famine severely hit state revenues. The surplus of Rs 63 lakh dwindled and a debt of Rs 80 lakh mounted. The revenue collections, which had been Rs 109 lakh in 1875, fell to Rs 82 lakh in 1876 and to Rs 69 lakh the next year. A retrenchment committee was appointed to meet the fiscal deficit and on its advice the government was 'right-sized' through the abolition of unnecessary posts.

The second half of the nineteenth century was also marked by a widespread churning in Indian society in the social and religious spheres. An exposure to modern education led Indians to question age-old superstitions and practices, such as Sati, human sacrifice, caste system and so on. Maharashtra and Bengal were the main breeding grounds for such revolutionary ideas, perhaps because they had borne the brunt of the ill-effects of the Raj and also of social ills. Social reformers, such as Raja Ram Mohan Roy, Dayananda Saraswati, Jyotiba Phule and others, took it upon themselves to transform society. There were several thinkers and spiritual leaders on the philosophical front as well—Ramakrishna Paramahamsa, Swami Vivekananda, Aurobindo Ghose, Ramana Maharshi, to name a few.

Amidst all this flux were the pompous princes of regal India—nonchalant and indifferent—throwing lavish parties and pandering to their white masters. They had little to lose as long as the British looked favourably on them. Administration or reforms were not a priority for them since it was not so for their British masters. The treaties they had signed with the Raj forbade them any firm decision-making whatsoever. So they lived luxurious lives, oblivious to the suffering around them.

But what set Mysore apart from the stereotypical princely state under the Raj was that alongside the pomp, splendour and wasteful expenditure, serious and sincere efforts were made to bring about reforms in areas over which the maharaja had jurisdiction. It was a state with a heart, and it felt the pulse of its people. The situation was helped more by a succession of extraordinary dewans—from Rangacharlu to Sheshadri Iyer to the celebrated Sir M. Vishweshwarayya and Sir Mirza Ismail, all these dewans strove hard to put Mysore on the rails of uninterrupted progress, a determination hitherto absent in other Indian princely states.

CHAMARAJENDRA WODEYAR (1868–94)

Lady Bowring's 'little man' grew into a capable ruler, and one of the best things he did for Mysore was to appoint Rangacharlu as its dewan.

The two councillors—Rangacharlu and Thumboo Chetty—were exceptional statesmen. Thumboo Chetty came to Mysore as judicial shirastedar in 1867, just before Mummadi Krishnaraja Wodeyar's death. He in fact recalled his interview with the late maharaja:[*]

> As I stood up and made my obeisance and craved leave to depart, His Highness gave a gentle tap on my shoulder and with a majestic look and powerful voice said: 'Young as you are, you have a long career of usefulness before you. You are new to Mysore, but I am sure you will be kind and sympathetic to the Mysoreans, always treating them as your own countrymen.'

Rangacharlu also joined the year after the late king's demise. Born in Madras, Dewan C. Rangacharlu had served as deputy collector in the

---

[*] His words are recorded in Josyer's 1929 book, *History of Mysore and the Yadava Dynasty*.

English East India Company for eighteen years. He was sent to Mysore as revenue secretary. As palace comptroller, he ended many malpractices prevalent in the palace. Earlier, as Head Shirastedar in Nellore, he had published several articles on that and used this new post as a means to implement those ideas. In 1874, he published in England an article on 'The British Administration of Mysore', which brought him into the limelight and also earned him the title of C.I.E. (Companion of the Indian Empire) in 1877 and the post of revenue secretary in 1878.

Coming into office at this difficult time, after the famine and when the state's finances needed expert management, Rangacharlu came up with a formula that worked—downsizing the administration and opening up the state's economic potential by connecting its area through the railways. The posts of native secretary and revenue commissioner substituted for the three commissioners. The salary of the deputy commissioners was reduced from Rs 1000–1500 to Rs 700–1000. Eight of the twenty-seven assistant commissionerships were abolished. Within a year, his financial management yielded to the treasury a surplus of Rs 2.5 lakh. Hassan and Chitradurga were discontinued as separate districts for civil and criminal administration, nine *taluks* were reduced to deputy amildars' stations, four munisff courts and three sub-courts were abolished as also travellers' bungalows meant for European officials.

Rangacharlu was a strict disciplinarian and encouraged honesty and efficiency. An interesting anecdote involving him is as follows: Music had been introduced into the curriculum in government-run institutions. Some wild gossip about the music teacher and the wastefulness of the subject as a part of the curriculum reached the ears of Mrs Rangacharlu, who took her husband to task. An angry dewan rushed to the school and fell like a ton of bricks on the hapless music teacher. As the latter was turned out of the room, Rai Bahadur Narasimha Iyengar entered. He writes:[*]

> I then asked him to go in notwithstanding and found Mr Rangacharlu quite furious against me. I begged him to have patience for an hour, and see what kind of music was being taught and then judge for himself. He very kindly agreed to it,

---

[*] His recollections are recorded in Josyer's 1929 book, *History of Mysore and the Yadava Dynasty*.

and the cause of music won the day! He was very sorry he had been misled, said that he was convinced that not only was there no harm in music, but that it was essential to the education of girls. He further advised me to invite his wife to see the school. I waited upon her that very afternoon, and her visit to the school the next morning completely changed her opinion! She was thoroughly pleased with all that she saw of the school and herself being a lady of some education and accomplishments gave several valuable suggestions, and from that day sent two of her daughters to the school!

Rangacharlu weeded out all corrupt officials from the government. Unfortunately, his excellent administration ground to halt when he died in Madras on 21 December 1883, within two years of his tenure.

The maharaja then appointed as Dewan Sheshadri Iyer—who had entered the state services in 1868 along with Thumboo Chetty and Rangacharlu—and the good work continued in this and other areas of economic and social importance. Sir William Hunter described Iyer as 'a statesman who had given his head to Herbert Spencer and his heart to Parabrahma'.

One of the pioneering projects to which the king lent his wholehearted support was women's education. He encouraged the dewan, who in turn—with the aid of academics like Durbar Bakshi and Rai Bahadur Ambil Narasimha Iyengar—established a Kannada-medium girls' school with twenty-eight students in Mysore in 1881. In 1889, a new building was commissioned for this school. Josyer records the King's words on the occasion of its inauguration:

> You are all aware that this school, which was started only a few years ago, is now one of the most popular institutions in Mysore. I have watched its progress with great attention, and have hitherto accommodated it in a part of the Jaganmohan Palace premises. I believe that it has now acquired those dimensions, which make it desirable that it should have a proper, separate school house. The importance of female education to the well-being and progress of Hindu society has long been recognized. But the difficulty has hitherto been, how to interest the conservative classes in the movement and secure their active sympathy. The revival of female education in this country, after a long period of neglect,

had come to be looked upon with the suspicion which innovation always rouses in the Hindu mind. Taking therefore a just estimate of the forces they had to deal with, the leaders of the movement in Mysore established this school, upon principles, which while aiming at imparting useful knowledge, avoided all unnecessary shock to longstanding prejudices, and by that means enlisted the active cooperation of even the most conservative classes. The result they have achieved has been pronounced by native gentlemen from all parts of India as a grand solution of one of our great social problems. It is this concurrence of opinion from persons of different nationalities and religions that has encouraged me and my officers to persevere with the institution and to endeavour to place it on a stable footing.

He also supported the opening of a college for the study of the ancient classical language of Sanskrit in 1882 at Mysore as well as the Oriental Library, which housed a prized collection of books and manuscripts.

It was not long before the British government began contemplating conferring on the Maharaja the title of G.C.S.I. (or Knight Grand Commander Star of India), about which Sheshadri Iyer wrote to M. Thumboo Chetty in 1884.[*]

FERNHILL PALACE

OOTACAMUND

April 16th 1884

My Dear Sir

We are all enjoying Ootacamund very well this year. It is much drier than usual and there are no unpleasant chills to fear. It is very probable that His Highness' stay here will be a very short one this year. Mr Layall will be here on the 23rd and may return to Bangalore after a fortnight's stay. As His Highness likes to receive the Insignia of G.C.S.I. from his hands, and as Mr Layall is on furlough about the end of May, His Highness will probably

---

[*] This letter appears in Singarayya's book, *Sri Chamarajendra Wodeyaravara Charitre.*

return to Mysore about the 10th of May after which arrangements will be made for a little ceremony, for the investiture which may perhaps better take place at Mysore, the historical capital of 50 years standing. This seems to be His Highness' present idea, and if it is finally decided that the ceremonial is to take place at Mysore we must arrange for the principal officers of the State coming there for the occasion. If you think of coming to Ooty, this is the best time for it. A Tonga from Mettapolyam will bring you in 6 hours. I have a small separate house here and you are quite welcome to occupy a part of it. Probably Dr Dhanakoti Raju will be here for a short time, also Ramachandra Iyer and a few other friends.

Yours sincerely,
K. Sheshadri Iyer

Accordingly, on 10 May 1884, the Resident, Layall, came over to Mysore and conferred the title of G.C.S.I. on the king.

On 27 November 1885, the raja embarked on an extensive tour of the entire state. He visited a number of places, Chunchunahalli, Malnad, Sringeri, Agumbe, Kolar, Sagar, Ikkeri, Sorab, Belgaum, Shimoga, Benkipura, Kallatagiri, Galikere, Chickmagalur, Belur, Halebid, Hassan, Chennarayapatna, Shravanbelagola, Kunigal and Bangalore, finally reaching Mysore on 19 January 1886.

Back home, the raja's family had been growing since 1881, when his wife, Maharani Kempananjammanni Vanivilasa Sannidhana gave birth to a daughter, who was named Jayalakshmammanni. On 8 June 1883, another girl was born to the couple and named Krishnajammanni. They were blessed with the much-awaited male child and heir on 4 June 1884. He was named Krishnaraja Wodeyar. Between 1888 and 1892, the royal couple were blessed with three sons—Kanthirava Maharaja Wodeyar was born on 5 June 1888, Raja Wodeyar III on 7 July 1890 and Devaraja Wodeyar in July 1892.

On 20 June 1887, Queen Victoria completed fifty years of her rule as queen of England. The message sent out by Chamarajendra Wodeyar, recorded by Singarayya in his book, was read out at the jubilee function by Colonel E. Bowen, the chief engineer of Mysore:

> Ladies and Gentlemen—It gives me sincere pleasure to be able today to take the first step towards the fulfilment of a promise I made in February last to establish in my capital a Victoria Jubilee

Institute—an institute designed to commemorate a special occasion and to promote a special object.

The occasion is the celebration of the fiftieth anniversary of the accession to the throne of Her Most Gracious Majesty Queen Empress of India, and I need scarcely add that on this day, all English speaking races and their fellow subjects of other races scattered over every part of the earth's surface unite with one voice to give expression to those sentiments of loyalty and devotion which half a century of affectionate and beneficent rule has fostered and strengthened to a degree without parallel in the history of the world. To India, it was given to anticipate by a few months the rejoicings peculiar to this most auspicious day for, on the 16th of February last, the princes and people of this country joined together to celebrate the 50th anniversary of Her Majesty's regime and to submit to the foot of her throne the homage of their heartfelt gratitude for the complete fulfilment of that gracious message she sent when assuming the direct administration of India, so full of goodwill and generous assurance that 'in your prosperity is our strength, in your contentment our security and in your gratitude our best reward.'

On that day, we in Mysore, I may be permitted to say were not behind the other nations of India in doing honour to the occasion but for this day which terminates the half century of the most beneficent reign in the history of modern times, I reserved the foundation of a special and permanent memorial which will do fitting honour to whom it is dedicated. This memorial will be devoted to the study and promotion of the Arts, Industries and the Literature of Mysore. It will from its character be indicative of peace and prosperity and I am sure there could be erected no more fitting edifice to Her Most Gracious Majesty, the first aim and object of whose reign has been the promotion of peace and goodwill amongst all states and peoples. I may add that as the Victoria Jubilee Institute will be a temple of peace and prosperity, so the occasion for its dedication is an appropriate one also for laying, in close proximity, the foundation stone of another building, which will in the future be intimately connected with the prosperity of this province.

I allude to the new Public Offices of Mysore. As the end of all good government is the preservation and promotion of peace and prosperity of its subjects the time and labour of those for whose official accommodation these offices are about to be erected, will, I feel certain, be always directed to that subject. So I may say in conclusion that these two buildings, although diverse in immediate design, are destined for the same ultimate purpose and that therefore the ceremonial attendant of their foundations are most appropriately linked together on this most auspicious day which in the Annals of Mysore, as in those of other parts of Her Majesty's Empire serves to mark the period of special material progress and social advancement.

Chamarajendra's appreciation was not directed wholly towards his British sovereign. He is credited with having lent support to one of India's most illustrious sons, Swami Vivekananda, who faced financial constraints while planning to attend the Parliament of Religions at Chicago where he was invited to represent India and the Hindu religion. Despite the vast geographical distance that separated them (the Swami hailed from Dakshineshwar in Calcutta), the maharaja decided to help him reach America. On reaching American shores, Swami Vivekananda wrote a long letter to the king which reads as below:[*]

June 23rd 1894

Sri Narayana bless you and yours! Through your Highness' kind help it has been possible for me to come to this country. Since then I have become well known here and the hospitable people of this country have supplied all my wants. It's a wonderful country and this is a wonderful nation in many respects. No other nation applies so much machinery in their every day work as do the people of this country. Everything is machine. Then again, they are only one-twentieth of the whole population of the world. Yet they have fully one-sixth of all the wealth of the world. There is no limit to their wealth and luxuries. The wages of labour are

---

[*] This letter appears in Josyer's 1929 book, *History of Mysore and the Yadava Dynasty*.

the highest in the world; yet the fight between labour and capital is constant.

Nowhere on earth have women so many privileges as in America. They are slowly taking everything into their hands, and strange to say, the number of cultured women is much greater than that of cultured men. Of course the higher order of geniuses are mostly from the rank of males. With all the criticism of the Westerners against our caste, they have a worse one, that of money! The almighty dollar, as the Americans say, can do anything here!

The theories of creation out of nothing, of a created soul, and of a big tyrant God sitting on a throne in a place called Heaven, and of the eternal hell fires have disgusted all the educated, and the noble thoughts of the Vedas about Eternity, of creation and the Soul, about the God in one's own soul, they are imbibing fast in one shape or other. Within fifty years the educated of the world will come to believe in the eternity of both soul and creation, and in God as our highest and perfect nature as taught in our holy Vedas. Even now the learned priests are interpreting the Bible in that way. My conclusion is, that they require more spiritual civilisation, and we, more material!

One thing that is at the root of all evils in India is the condition of the poor. The poor in the west are devils; compared to them ours are angels, and it is therefore so much the easier to raise our poor. The only service to be done for our lower classes is to give them education, to develop their lost individuality. That is the great task between our people and the princes. Up to now nothing has been done in that direction. Priest power and foreign conquest have trodden them down for centuries and at last the poor of India have forgotten that they are human beings. They are to be given ideas, their eyes are to be opened to what is going on in the world around them, and they will work out their own salvation. Every nation, every man and every woman must work out their own salvation. Give them ideas, that is the only help they require, and then the rest must follow as the effect. Ours is to put the chemicals together, the crystallization comes on the Law of nature.

This is what has to be done in India. It is this idea that has been in my mind for a long time, I could not accomplish it in

India and that was the reason of my coming to this country. The great difficulty in the way of educating the poor, is this. Supposing even Your Highness opens a free school in every village, still it would do no good, for the poverty of India is such that the poor boys would rather go to help their fathers in the fields, or otherwise try to make a living than come to school. Now if the mountain does not come to Mohammed, Mohammed must go to the mountain. If the poor boy does not come to education, education must go to him. There are thousands of single minded self-sacrificing sanyasins in our own country going from village to village teaching religion. If some of them can be organised as teachers of secular things also, they will go from place to place, from door to door, not only preaching, but teaching also. Suppose two of these men go to a village in the evening with a camera, a globe, some maps, etc., they can teach a great deal of Astronomy and Geography to the ignorant. By telling stories about different nations, they can give the poor a hundred times more information through the ear than they can get in a life-time through books. This requires an organisation, which again means money. Men enough there are in India to work out this plan, but alas! They have no money. It is very difficult to set a wheel in motion but when once set, it goes on with increasing velocity. After seeking help in my own rich country, and failing to get any sympathy from the rich Bengalis, I came to this country through Your Highness' aid. The Americans do not care whether the poor in India die or live. And why should they, our own people never think of anything but their own selfish ends!

My noble Prince, this life is short, the vanities of the world are transient, but they alone live who live for others, the rest are more dead than alive. One such high, noble-minded and Royal son of India as Your Highness, can do much towards raising India on her feet again, and thus leave a name to posterity, which shall be worshipped. That the Lord may make your noble heart feel intensity for the suffering millions of India sunk in ignorance, is the prayer of Vivekananda!

Such a noble and inspiring letter from a man, veritably acclaimed as a hero of his times. But sadly, while the letter made a profound impact on the maharaja, he didn't have an opportunity to put these ideas into practice. The last paragraph of the Swami's letter of life being short was prophetic.

The maharaja embarked on an extensive tour of northern India, returning only in 1893. On 9 December 1894, he left Mysore for Calcutta, where he stayed at the Sealdah House. By 23 December, the king was down with high fever. Chamarajendra was a tall, well-built and extremely handsome man, but his smile and bright eyes were dimmed by the fever that oppressed him for about fourteen days. By 26 December, his condition worsened, affecting his hearing as well. Doctor McConnel examined him the next day and concluded that he was suffering from diphtheria.

The King insisted on his daily bath even in his sickness. He would stagger to the Puja room and offer his prayers to Goddess Chamundeshwari. But soon that became almost impossible for him. Unable to leave the bed, he prayed lying down and sought forgiveness for a less elaborate prayer. By nightfall on 27 December, he could barely speak. He was placed on an easy chair by attendants but soon a grave discomfiture pulled him back to bed. Stimulants were fed to him, which, after much resistance, he was forced to consume. Around dawn, he softly stammered 'Mother Chamundeshwari', closed and opened his eyes thrice in reverence and breathed his last.

Darbar Bakshi Narasimha Iyengar informed Kempananjammanni of her husband's death. Grief-stricken and hysterical, she rushed to the room where the cold, lifeless body lay. The baffled dewan rushed to the spot and tried consoling her. She cried and lamented loudly, cursing her fate and the will of Destiny, finally falling unconscious. The dewan informed Foreign Secretary Cunningham, who in turn informed the viceroy about the tragedy. Mysoreans could hardly believe the news when it began trickling in. The young and dashing ruler was no more! It was decided to carry out the cremation at Calcutta itself. The bed on which the body lay was used as the palanquin for the final procession. The body was dressed in royal garments for the last time. The Bengal army arrived to attend the procession. It started around 2 pm, passing through Lower Circular road and Rusa road and reached its destination in Kalighat by 6 pm. Prince Krishnaraja was just ten years old and so Bakshi Basappaji Urs performed the final rites.

The next day the Government of India sent a telegram informing the bereaved family that the government of Britain had granted permission for the accession of Prince Krishnaraja as the future King of Mysore with the maharani and the dewan as regents.*

> Pending the issue of orders on the form of administration to be finally approved as that best suited for the period of minority, the administration of the state will continue for the immediate future in the manner in which it is now conducted under the Dewan, Sir. K.Seshadri Iyer, K.C.S.I. The Dewan will ask for, and follow the advice of the Resident on all matters of importance, and as it is practicable and desirable, he will consult the wishes of Her Highness the Maharani Vani Vilas Sannidhana, C.I.

On 30 December the family left Calcutta for Mysore in a pall of gloom. In moving a resolution, the president of the Congress, Alfred Webb, MP, spoke thus:**

> Friends and fellow subjects, you all feel the heavy and dark clouds under which we meet today. The bright sunshine and the blue sky outside are in accord with the feeling of depression and sadness which reign in our hearts. There is no need for me to mention the reason for the fact that we all know and feel since last night when we heard of the death of the Maharajah of Mysore, that this Congress could not end in the joyful manner in which it commenced. There is no need that I should say anything relating to the character, the services, the patriotism and the life of the deceased Maharajah. That of course will be properly spoken on other occasions by men who have known him and who are fully aware of his services to his country and his race. It remains for me to propose the resolutions which of course will be received by you standing in solemn silence.

Thus ended the life and rule of the twenty-third ruler of the Mysore royal family, a man remembered for his strength of character and all he did for his kingdom.

---

* The text of the telegram is taken from Singarayya's book, *Sri Chamarajendra Wodeyaravara Charitre.*

** This speech is taken from Singarayya's book, *Sri Chamarajendra Wodeyaravara Charitre.*

The Times of London published a long article in its obituary column, praising the maharaja. Written by Sir William Lee-Warner, KCSI, it appeared on 29 December 1894. The text of the article is as follows:

A Reuters telegram from Calcutta states that the Maharajah of Mysore died there on Friday morning of diphtheria. The sudden death of the Maharajah of Mysore cuts short the career of one of the most promising and prominent princes of India. In his brief life, little more than 30 summers, he had done much in the cause of good government, but it was only regarded as the earnest of the greater achievements that would follow during what seemed likely to be a lengthy reign. These hopes are nipped in the bud by his having fallen victim to the fell disease diphtheria during the annual visit he regularly paid to the Viceroy's court at Calcutta; but still be accomplished enough to mark out his tenure of authority as a distinct epoch in the modern history of his state.

The relations of the British Government with Mysore have been of a peculiar kind, and might fill a volume, but it must suffice here to say that the Mohammedan conquerors, Hyder Ali and his son Tippo Sahib, dispossessed the old Rajput family which had established itself as Wodeyars or Lords, of Mysore at the end of the 14th century. On the final overthrow and death of Tippoo at Srirangapatam in 1799, we restored the old ruling Hindu family in the person of Krishnaraj; who retained the style and state of Maharajah until his death in 1868. During the early years of this prince's rule the administration was well conducted by the Dewan Purniah but during the 15 years that followed his retirement in 1811, matters were so mismanaged that the British Government assumed charge of affairs in 1831, and retained it during the last 37 years of the life of Krishnaraj. On the death of that prince, the lately deceased Maharajah, a scion of the house who had been adopted as his heir by Krishnaraj some years before was proclaimed ruler, but the responsible authority remained in our hands. But it was not until 1881 that the famous Rendition of Mysore to its natural prince was carried out. By that time the young Maharaja Sri Chamarajendra Wodeyar who was born on February 22, 1863, had given promise of such ability and good sense that it was deemed possible to entrust to his hands the control of

The Reformer King Chamarajendra Wodeyar X

a Government that had been British for fifty years. It is only just to the late prince to say that the confidence was not misplaced and that he discharged his task to the complete satisfaction of the Viceroy and the benefit of his own people. The statement has been made that in all ordinary duties of an India Government such as the dispensation of justice, the collection and expenditure of revenue, the protection of life and property, the promotion of public works, sanitation etc, Mysore was well abreast of British India, and that in some matters, especially female education and schemes for developing latent resources it was ahead of it.

Mysore is one of the parts of India that have been most visited by the ravages of famine and the Maharaja's Government earned special distinction in coping with the terrible visitation and in devising a permanent remedy for it. In the year 1892 precautions on a most elaborate scale were taken. The private forests and plantations of the prince were thrown open for free grazing and half a million of the ryots' cattle found sustenance which was unobtainable elsewhere. Large sums were expended on public works, principally tanks and ten lakhs of revenue were either remitted or held in suspense. The result of these efforts and precautions was that no lives were lost and that the famine was averted. The Maharajah's wishes in this and other directions have been ably carried out by his Chief Minister Sri K. Seshadri Iyer, who has earned a reputation in Southern India equal to that of the late Sir Madhava Rao. Among other points it should be mentioned that the Maharajah was a strong supporter of female education and that he was the first Hindu prince to found a school for girls. This step was rendered more remarkable by the school being intended for only the children of high caste families and it numbered as many as 500 scholars. The mining laws and regulations passed in consequence of the extensive discovery of gold during the last 15 years in Mysore have been frequently praised for their simplicity and have given the state a large and increasing revenue. The Maharajah who was a Knight Grand Commander of the Star of India leaves several sons and daughters. It is unnecessary to assure the officials and people of Mysore that nothing will be done to disturb the order of succession and that every assistance will be given by the Supreme government to those who may have to administer the affairs until the new Maharajah can govern for himself.

Not a few Englishmen who have lived in India must feel that by the death of this young prince they have lost a true friend of singularly sympathetic and amiable character. From his natural shyness of disposition which was increased by a slight impediment in his speech and which he never entirely overcame he did not always make a favourable impression on strangers; but any impression of this kind soon disappeared on better acquaintance, and it may be said to his credit that those who knew him best were those who were most warmly attached to him. Certainly he was fortunate in finding such an able, upright and conscientious Dewan as Sir K. Seshadri Iyer; but on the other hand it is equally true that this remarkable native administrator was fortunate in finding such an enlightened, high principled, benevolent master as the late Maharajah.

21

THE RAJARISHI

Maharaja Krishnaraja Wodeyar IV also known popularly as Nalwadi Krishnaraja Wodeyar was one of the most celebrated rulers among those of the Indian States. He was a philosopher-king and had been compared to the Emperor Ashoka by the English statesman Lord Samuel. Mahatma Gandhi called him 'Rajarishi'—a saint among kings—a tag that remained with him all his life.

Paul Brunton, a Western philosopher who came to India seeking oriental wisdom, saw the raja as living the ideal expressed in Plato's *Republic*. His impression of Krishnaraja Wodeyar is analysed by Annie Cahn Fung as follows:

> In the philosopher-king Brunton not only met a benefactor who so generously gave him residence, servants, various material resources, and even the company of his Rajaguru; he also met the supreme embodiment of his ideal of the sage as philosophic man of action. Later Brunton would contrast this ideal to what he considered a lesser type: the reclusive, solitary mystic. The Maharaja, open to science and modern technology, had founded the great iron and steel industry of Bhadravati, one of the most important in the British Empire. His strong example was both a source of inspiration for the English author and a reassuring confirmation of the latter's belief that philosophy and the active life are not incompatible. The Maharaja's life, which unfolded before Brunton's eyes during those years, was proof of the point:

You have rescued philosophy from those who would make it a mere refuge from disappointment, and converted it into a dynamic inspiration to higher action for service,

wrote Brunton in his dedication to *The Quest of the Overself*.

The circumstances under which young Krishnaraja ascended the throne of Mysore as its twenty-fourth ruler were anything but pleasant. The untimely death of a young, charismatic, popular and reformist maharaja had jolted the public of Mysore. It was all the more shocking for the young maharani and her little children. She had to cope with her loss and assume a new responsibility—regent to her infant son, who would be placed on the musnud of Mysore.

The British were forthright in anointing young Krishnaraja as the successor. In a *kharita* (official letter) addressed to the young king-designate, the Viceroy Lord Elgin said:*

My Honoured and Valued friend, at the time when the melancholy death of His Highness Sri Chamaraja Wodayar Bahadur, G.C.S.I., Your Highness' father, occurred in Calcutta, I conveyed at once to Her Highness, your mother, as well as to yourself, the sincere sympathy which was felt both her and in England with Her Highness' family in consequence of so untoward a catastrophe. I have already made known the approval given by the Government of India to your succession to the Chiefship of Mysore State. I now formally confirm that approval and assure you that if you are fitted by character and ability when you are qualified by age to assume so high and honorable a position, you will be entrusted with the ruling powers so well discharged by your father. A grave responsibility devolves meanwhile upon the British Government in supervising your own education and the Provincial Government of the Mysore State, and this is a matter to which I have devoted anxious thought. Happily the present circumstances are auspicious. A fitting central authority must be provided during Your Highness' minority. The Government of

---

* This letter appears in Swami Rao's *Sri Nalwadi Krishnarajendra Wodeyaravara Charitre*.

India by conferring upon Her Highness Maharani Vani Vilas, C.I., the dignity and position of the Regent of the Mysore State, mark in a special manner their confidence that they will find in Her Highness, in the Minister who has ably filled the difficult post of Dewan, and in the experienced officials who may be associated with him, the means of continuing under their own special care a system of administration which has stood with success the test of time. I will, in conclusion, assure Your Highness and, through you, Her Highness, the Maharani, that the Government of India will continue to watch over your interests and those of the Mysore state with jealous regard for the welfare of both. My endeavor will be to secure the continued prosperity of the State. I sincerely trust that Your Highness may prove worthy to fill the place of your lamented father, whose untimely removal I cannot cease to deplore. I desire to express the high consideration, which I entertain for Your Highness and to subscribe myself Your Highness' sincere friend.

Elgin

Viceroy and Governor General of India.

Fort William, the 25th January 1895.

After the tragic circumstances following the sudden and untimely death of his father, young Krishnaraja, barely ten years old then, was crowned King on 1 February 1895 with his mother Maharani Kempananjammanni Vanivilasa Sannidhana and Dewan K. Sheshadri Iyer as regents.

With a statesman as senior as Sir K.C. Sheshadri Iyer by her side, the young maharani was quick to rise to the occasion and soon learnt the art of administration and realpolitik. She had a dual role to play—caring and concerned mother to her children and a loving and efficient administrator for the state and its people. She rose to the occasion and fulfilled both these tasks to the fullest of her abilities.

In February 1897, during the festivities for the marriage of Princess Jayalakshmammanni with her maternal uncle Kantharaje Urs, the existing wooden palace at Mysore succumbed to an accidental fire. Maharani Kempananjammanni decided to get the new palace built on the model and foundations of the older one. She met Mr Henry Irwin, architect of the Viceregal Lodge of Shimla and inaugurated the construction of the new palace in October 1897. The palace was completed in 1912 at an expense of Rs 41,47,913. It has a 145-foot high tower with a golden flag on its summit. The façade has seven big arches flanking the central arch supported by all the pillars. Above this is a statue of Gajalakshmi. The star attractions of the palace are the Kalyana Mandapa, Diwan-i-Aam or Darbar Hall, which is forty-two feet wide, Amba Vilasa or Diwan-i-Khas and so on. It continues to remain a major tourist attraction in Mysore today.

Displaying courage, wisdom and dedication, the maharani steered the affairs of the state with the able help of Sheshadri Iyer from 1894 to 1902. In the words of a contemporary historian quoted by Josyer:

> She rose to the occasion with great courage and aided by her able Dewan and Councillors, she succeeded in her task magnificently, commending herself to Her Imperial Majesty the Queen Empress and the British Government, while the people all over the State were loud in her praise. If she found the State prosperous and its people contented when her consort died, she left the State still more contented when she laid down the reins of her Regency on the accession of her son to the throne.

During the regency of the maharani, the young maharaja was being groomed into the skills of kingship. In his sixth year he began his education. Sri Purnaraghavendra Rao was his tutor between 1890 and 1892 and Sri Sosale Ayya Shastry was his Kannada tutor. In June 1892, he was sent to the Royal School and in the course of his study here he befriended a boy called Mirza Ismail. The two became the best of friends and Ismail was to become the dewan of the state later. For 18 months, M.J.J. Whitely taught the King English, mathematics, history, geography and science and the Indian teachers taught him Sanskrit, Kannada and Urdu. He was also trained in sports, such as swimming, horse riding, cricket, polo and so on. In his twelfth year, 1896, the British government appointed Sir M. Stuart Fraser as his tutor, and what Malleson was to the late Chamarajendra Wodeyar, Fraser was to Krishnaraja Wodeyar. At the age of sixteen, in June 1900, the king was married to the daughter of the Rana of Kathiawad Vanavar Sri Pratapa Kumari Bai. She was named the maharani of the Lakshmi Vilasa Sannidhana.

Meanwhile, several members of the Representative Assembly under Mr Venkatakrishnayya, popularly called 'Tataiah' or Grand Old Man of Mysore, put forth virulent pleas against the dewan and his schemes. Tataiah was an enlightened school master, who later became the king's adviser. He held that Sheshadri Iyer being an 'outsider' who came into the Mysore service from Madras Presidency, displayed regional bias by employing many people from there. They complained that he did not allow sufficient representation and scope to the local Mysoreans and their talent. This group always maintained their opposition to the views of the Dewan. Iyer was very upset with these allegations levelled against him. He retired from the post of dewan in 1901, and passed away a year later.

Acknowledging his services upon his death, the maharani said: 'The many reforms, which have brought the Mysore administration to a high level of efficiency, are attributable in great part to his talents, forethought and resourcefulness.'*

Even Dinsha Wacha, president of the Indian National Congress, expressed his condolences, which were recorded by Josyer:

> In him the administration loses an administrator of the highest capacity and most matured experience. He was the latest instance of the Indian statesman who had shown himself capable of governing fully an indigenous State with as much skill and capacity, judgement and discrimination, tact and sympathy, as some of the greatest English administrators, who have left their mark on British Indian History. Sir K.C. Sheshadri Iyer has now gone to swell the roll of honour of Modern Indian Statesmen!

The dewan's progressive initiatives won him the title of 'Rajadurandhara' (adept administrator) from the regent queen. Lord Curzon spoke of him as one who, for eighteen years, wielded an authority that left its mark on every branch of the administration, and indicated that the deeds and services of such great men need to be honoured by public commemoration, not merely as a posthumous compliment to them, but to inspire others and set an example. In Bangalore, the Sheshadri Iyer Memorial Hall with the statue of the dewan, unveiled by Viceroy Lord Hardinge himself, reminds us of this able leader even today.

---

* These words are taken from Josyer's 1929 book, *The History of Mysore and the Yadava Dynasty*.

The year the king attained majority, Maharani Kempananjammanni laid down the regency of the state she had so ably handled over the past eight years. Describing her sagacity, Rajadharmapraveena T.R.A. Thumboo Chetty, who was a judge and senior councillor from 1881 to 1901 and a close friend of Dewan Sheshadri Iyer says:*

> In my repeated official visits I was really struck with Her Highness, the Maharani's capacity for business, fair knowledge of things and amiable character. She listened to everything with exemplary patience. Her mind was bold and acute, and whatever be the subject of discussion, she came directly to the point and brought it to a happy completion. Sometimes her enlightened suggestions and direction most agreeably surprised me and afforded ready solution of many difficulties. Her anxiety to promote the highest and best interests of the country was always perceptible. I invariably retired from the interviews I had with a strong sentiment of devotion, as well as admiration and respect, for Her Highness' high character and intellectual qualities.

On 8 August 1902, the young maharaja was installed on the throne with ruling powers. The function was held in the Darbar Hall Mandapa of the palace. A twenty-one-gun salute followed the entry of Lord Curzon, the Viceroy who had come to preside over and conduct the proceedings on behalf of the British government. The stage was well decorated with two silver chairs beneath it, occupied by Lord Curzon and to his left, the Resident. The viceroy led the maharaja to the platform and made him sit on the masnad and reaffirmed his commitment to the throne of Mysore.

Speaking on the occasion Lord Curzon said:**

> The young Maharaja whom I am about to install has recently attained his 18th birthday. He has passed through a minority of nearly 8 years. They have not been idle or vapid years spent in enjoyment or dissipated in idleness. They have been years of careful preparation for the duties that lay before him, and of laborious

---

* These words are taken from Josyer's 1929 book, *The History of Mysore and the Yadava Dynasty*.
** Curzon's words and the Maharaja's response are taken from Swami Rao's book, *Sri Nalwadi Krishnarajendra Wodeyaravara Charitre*.

training for his exalted state. It is no light thing to assume charge of 5 millions of people, and it is no perfunctory training that is required for such a task. He has studied their wants and needs at first hand. He has thereby acquired the knowledge, which will enable him to understand the problems with which he will be confronted. Fortified by this knowledge, his naturally business-like habits and instinctive self-reliance should enable him to steer a straight course. Youth is his, and health and strength. He enters upon a splendid heritage at an early age. May God guide him in his undertaking and speed him on the straight path!

In reply to the viceroy's address King Krishnaraja said:

How important are the responsibilities, which now devolve upon me I fully realise, and it is my intention to prove by performance rather than by words. The inheritance to which I succeed is no ordinary one, and I appreciate what Mysore owes to the administration of wise statesmen, and the care of the British government under the Regency of my revered mother. But at the same time, I know fully well that I cannot rest on the laurels won by others, and that my utmost efforts are needed, not only to maintain for my subjects the benefits they already enjoy, but to press onwards to a yet higher standard of efficiency. How far I may be granted the ability to cope with the problems before me, the future can only show, but it is a comfort to me to feel that I shall for sometime at any rate, enjoy the assistance of my well proved friend, the Hon'ble Col. Donald Robertson, as the Resident of the State. And speaking with all deference, I am able to say that I begin my task with some knowledge of its difficulties, thanks to the education I have received from Mr Fraser, to whom I have to prove that his labours for the past six years have not been without fruit. This much at any rate can confidently be affirmed that the desire and the effort to succeed shall not be lacking. I have now seen a great deal of my State, with its beautiful scenery and its loyal people, and it would be a poor heart indeed that was not filled with pride and love for such an inheritance. May Heaven grant me the ability as well the ambition to make a full and wise use of the great opportunities of my position, and to govern, without fear or favour for the lasting happiness of my people.

Sir P.N. Krishnamurthy, great grandson of the late Dewan Purnaiya, was appointed the new dewan of the state. He was assisted by a Council consisting of two able and trustworthy statesmen, V.P. Madhava Rao and T. Ananda Rao. Inaugurating this council a week after the installation ceremony, the maharaja said:[*]

> We are once again at the beginning of a new experiment in Mysore. Whether that experiment is a success or the reverse, will depend greatly on you. Of your devotion to myself personally I am well aware. In your devotion to the interests of the State, I have full confidence. No human institution can be perfect and the new scheme of administration will no doubt disclose defects of one kind or another. As the fruit of the labours of my Dewan, aided by the advice of my good friend, the Resident, I myself hope and expect much. This object can only be attained by single hearted and unselfish cooperation between Members of Council of the State. It cannot be expected that you will always agree with one another or that I shall always agree with you. It may be that, at times, you may feel soreness individually or even collectively at being overruled. At such times I ask you to give credit to those who disagree with you for being actuated by the same sense of public duty as yourselves, and reflect that, in giving your honest opinion and urging it to the utmost of your power, you have done your duty and retained your self respect. I ask you to banish all sense of resentment and to address yourselves to the next question before you with undiminished courage and goodwill. If this is the spirit that animates our labors, I can, relying on your mature experience and proven abilities, look forward with confidence to the future.

The Prince of Wales, Queen Victoria's heir, visited Mysore in 1906. Expressing delight at the rapid strides made by the state he said:[**]

---

[*] The Maharaja's words are taken from Josyer's 1929 book, *The History of Mysore and the Yadava Dynasty.*

[**] His words are taken from Swami Rao's book, *Sri Nalwadi Krishnarajendra Wodeyaravara Charitre.*

If any proof were required of the wisdom of the policy of 1881, which restored to your father the Province of Mysore after 50 years of British Administration, it is surely to be found in the contentment and prosperity which the people of Mysore enjoy under the Government of Your Highness. It is interesting to hear of the many enterprises, notably that of the Cauvery Electric Works, and the general policy of irrigation and public works. Under the lead which we may expect from such a capable and enlightened Ruler as our kind host, with the assistance of statesmen of the type of the late Sir. K.C. Sheshadri Iyer, your Province may look forward with confidence to making still greater strides.

The same year the maharaja was given the title of G.C.S.I. from the British government. The Mysoreans organised a congratulatory gathering to felicitate the maharaja. Speaking on the occasion the maharaja said:

You allude in your address to this honour as being a fitting recognition of my four years' personal rule. Though I appreciate the depth of feeling, which has prompted you to express this opinion, yet, I must candidly confess that I cannot altogether endorse it. I feel that there is a very great deal to be done, and that very little has yet been achieved. My responsibility is a heavy one, but I fully realise it, and as it has pleased providence to call upon me to discharge it, I can only submit to the Divine will. It shall ever be my aim and ambition in life to do all that lies in me to promote the progress and prosperity of my beautiful State and the happiness of my beloved people. I can assure you that I shall not spare myself in the endeavour to accomplish this. Neither perseverance nor effort will, I trust, be found wanting in me in fulfilling this aim.

On 30 March 1906, Sir P.N. Krishnamurthy resigned from the post of dewan and was succeeded by V.P. Madhava Rao as dewan. He was earlier dewan of Travancore and entered the service of Mysore. He was known for the wide range of administrative reforms he brought about in the system. But Rao became unpopular because he forbade the elections of M. Venkatakrishnaiya and D. Venkataramanaiya to the Legislative Council.

By doing this he created a second legislative chamber. He got the Mysore Newspapers Regulations Act passed in 1908, imposing regulations and restrictions on the Press. This was perhaps the most repressive action by any statesman of Mysore. This also earned him public wrath and unpopularity. Many newspapers in the state stopped publication as a mark of protest against this Act. The seeds of democracy might have been sown in Mysore through the establishment of the Representative Assembly and the extension of franchise, but the fact remained that it was still a centrally controlled monarchy, a nascent and immature democracy that was on the path of evolution. The newspapers of Mysore were known for their free and frank espousal of causes of national and public interest, many of which were tangential to the Dewan's purposes. This forced him to undertake this draconian measure. Due to rising public opinion against him, Madhava Rao was forced to retire in early 1909.

He was succeeded by T. Ananda Rao, the son of the great statesman Raja Sir T. Madhava Rao. He had entered the Mysore Civil Service in 1873 and had been revenue commissioner and council member. On the advice of his Chief Engineer, M. Vishweswaraiya, the dewan gave shape to the Kannambadi irrigation project. He also organised an Economic Conference for the purpose of achieving the economic development of the state. Addressing the conference, the maharaja declared:

> Here is an opportunity for public work, as to the necessity of which all parties and interests in the State are agreed. The political element, which has caused so much bitterness elsewhere, has been entirely eliminated from the peaceful work of this organisation. We want earnest workers. It is our object to reach all people who desire to cooperate. Those who have brains must organise, those who have money might contribute to the expenses of the movement the aim we have in view, namely, the economic security and vital efficiency of the people, must appeal to every right thinking person. We want no ornamental members. I hope everyone associated with you will work earnestly and persistently, and that your combined efforts will achieve some measure of progress calculated to be of lasting good to the State. This movement will be what your activities and wisdom make of it. I appeal to you, and through you, to every citizen of the State, to become skilled and capable, and to train your children and children's children in some skilled

calling. There is no royal road to success. I hope I shall not appeal in vain if I ask everyone, official or private citizen, to actively promote the objects of this movement.

By 1910, the Mysore Palace had been completed and lavishly decorated with the paintings of celebrated artist Raja Ravi Verma and others. A railway line was laid from Bangalore to Chikkaballapur via Kolar. Pradhanashiromani Ananda Rao was a man of rigid sense of duty and discipline of conduct. He was the son of a dewan, had married the daughter of a dewan and was himself a dewan, which prompted his wife (herself the daughter of Dewan Rama Rao of Baroda) to exclaim that she was perhaps the only Indian woman to be daughter, daughter-in-law and wife to dewans! Ananda Rao retired in 1912.

Ananda Rao was succeeded by one of the most illustrious men of modern Mysore—Sir M. Vishweswaraiya. He was the first 'local' Mysorean to become dewan. Even decades after his death, he was voted the most popular Kannadiga in a recently conducted television poll.

Sir M.V. as he was fondly called, was born to Srinivasa Sastry and Venkachamma at Muddenahalli village in the Kolar district. His father was a Sanskrit scholar and an authority on the Hindu scriptures, besides being an Ayurvedic practitioner. The family was a pious Telugu-speaking Smartha Brahmin family belonging to the Vaidiki Mulukanadu sub-caste. Sir M.V.'s ancestors actually hailed from the village of Mokshagundam near Giddalur in the Prakasam district of present-day Andhra Pradesh; they had migrated to Mysore perhaps three centuries earlier. The family name, 'Mokshagundam', preserves the memory of this distant association.

The young Vishweswaraiya lost his father at the age of fifteen, when the family lived at Kurnool; they moved back to Muddenahalli immediately. Sir M.V. attended primary school at Chikballapur and high school at Bangalore. He earned his B.A. from Madras University in 1881 and later studied civil engineering at the College of Science, Pune, now known as the College of Engineering, Pune (COEP).

Upon graduating as an engineer, Vishweswaraiya took up a job with the Public Works Department (PWD) of Bombay, and was later invited to join the Indian Irrigation Commission. He implemented an extremely intricate system of irrigation in the Deccan area. He also designed and patented a system of automatic weir water floodgates, which were first installed in 1903, at the Khadakvasla reservoir near Pune. These gates were employed to raise the flood-supply level of storage in the reservoir to the highest level likely to be attained in a flood, without causing any damage to the dam. Based on the success of these gates, the same system was installed at the Tigra dam in Gwalior and later at the celebrated Krishna Raja Sagara (KRS) dam in Mysore. Vishweswaraiya achieved celebrity status when he designed a flood protection system to protect the city of Hyderabad from floods. He was also instrumental in developing a system to protect Visakhapatnam port from sea erosion. In 1909, as chief engineer of the state, he made significant contributions to the construction of the Kannambadi Dam across the Cauvery, irrigating 1.5 lakh acres of dry land in the regions of Mandya and Malavally. This dam created the biggest reservoir in Asia at the time it was built.

During his period of service with the government of Mysore state as its dewan (1912–18), Vishweswaraiya was responsible for founding, under the aegis of that government, the Mysore Soap factory, the Parasitoide Laboratory, the Bhadravati Iron Works, Sandal Oil Factory, spun silk works, the SJP polytechnic, a school at Hebbal, which grew into the University of Agricultural Sciences in Bangalore decades later, the State Bank of Mysore, the Mysore Sugar Mills and numerous other industrial ventures. He also encouraged private investment in industry during his tenure as dewan. He was known for his sincerity, time management and dedication—a true Kannadiga.

When public gatherings were organised to felicitate him on assumption of office, he modestly remarked:[*]

> It will, I hope, not be regarded an affectation of modesty on my part if I say that all I have wanted is opportunity for work, and that thoughts of personal advancement have not influenced my action in recent years. With the important duties now graciously entrusted to me by His Highness the Maharaja, I have all the scope for work that I may have ever longed for. I seek no further reward. The pleasure of working for a few more years, of serving my Sovereign and my country, is enough for me. Their interests will be my constant thought and their appreciation, if I am able to secure it, will be my best reward.

---

[*] These words are recorded in Josyer's 1929 book, *The History of Mysore and the Yadava Dynasty*.

Fiercely conscientious and dutiful, Vishweswaraiya was constantly seeking to improve himself and all he encountered, to serve better and to learn more. All these ennobling qualities, honed through contact with the stalwarts of the Indian Nationalist movement like Ranade, Gokhale and Wacha—with whom he was associated during his engineering days at Bombay—made him a perfectionist and workaholic. His panacea for the ills facing the state and the country was simple—cut slackness, and work. As early as 1907 he wrote *A Vision of Prosperous Mysore*, in which he outlined his plans for economic development of the state. The book stressed the need for the spread of education, technical knowledge and proposals for irrigation, industrialisation and commercial progress. He firmly believed that the investment of the state's finances in income-yielding projects would completely preclude the need for maintaining reserves out of its income.

Josyer records his words:

> Slackness is the worst curse of the country. At first sight, everybody seems to be taking part in some common toil; as a matter of fact several persons are looking at the labour of one. The Public works department is not altogether free from this taint of slackness. We are too much accustomed to soft conditions. The number of working hours is fewer here than in Europe. There are more government holidays in the State than even in British India. Official employment is sought for because once a man gets into service whether efficient or weak, wise or imprudent, he is practically sure of a competence for the rest of his life. Closely associated with slackness is lack of initiative. 'The more energy we put forth,' said an eminent German to me, 'and the more we use our intelligence, the greater the pleasure provided we do not overdo it to the point of fatigue.' With industry, and by studying technical books and papers, even men of mediocre talent can excel. But unless people consider slackness a disgrace, there is no hope of improvement.
>
> Our efficiency as a country depends not on our better position compared with our past but on our progress in relation to the

---

* This speech appears in Josyer's 1929 book, *The History of Mysore and the Yadava Dynasty*.

other civilized countries of the world, to the other members of the family of nations. For instance the percentage of the entire population actually attending school is as high as 21 in some of the advanced countries. In Mysore it is less than 2 ½. The expenditure on education in advanced countries like the United States is as high as Rs 12 per head. Our expenditure is less than Rs 6 per head. We should dismiss from our mind the idea that any great work can be accomplished, that any reputation in the profession can be made, without drill, discipline and iron labour!

The far-sighted Sir M.V. seems to hold up quite a mirror to the slack bureaucratic machinery of governments in modern India.

Economic progress became the *mantra* of the dewan. He made his vision amply clear in the address to the Mysore Economic Conference in 1913, which was expanded with three committees, one each for industry and commerce, education and agriculture:[*]

> The great bulk of our people are uneducated, and agriculture is their chief occupation. They have no industries or trade on modern lines worth mentioning. No country so largely dependent as ours on agriculture can be said to be prosperous. The margin between the ordinary standard of living and distribution among our people is very narrow. Out of 57 lakhs of people in Mysore, only 3 ½ Lakhs can read and write, that is, only 6 persons out of every 100. In advanced countries it is 85 to 95 persons per 100. In the USA, the expenditure on education is Rs 14 per head of population. In Mysore it is 6 annas per head! In progressive countries 1/5th of the population are at school. In Mysore 1/50th! Although we have a population of nearly 6 millions, we have no Universities in Mysore. In Canada, with a population scarcely 25% more than in Mysore there are 20 Universities!
>
> The value of manufactured produce in the United Kingdom is Rs 326 per head or about 30 times that produced in Mysore. The earning power of an average Mysorean is about Rs 30 per head per annum, an average European earns about Rs 400 per head per annum and an average Englishman Rs 600 to Rs 700. Hitherto

---

[*] This speech appears in Josyer's 1929 book, *The History of Mysore and the Yadava Dynasty*.

thinking work was left chiefly to Government officials. In future it will be shared by both officials and non-officials. Eventually the work should be transferred largely to non-officials.

No country can prosper unless the agricultural and manufacturing industries were equally fostered. When all the world around is making marvellous progress, the 200 million people in this country cannot much longer continue in their long sleep, simply following the traditions of their ancestors of 2000 years ago and earning a miserable subsistence, ready to be crushed on the first occurrence of a famine or other calamity. When nations so incomparably richer than ourselves who already possess a connected scheme of national life, are thinking of reconstruction, are we, who have no prosperity at all worth mentioning, to sit still? Shall we remain content with our low standard of life and work, or adopt a policy of development and progress? If the latter, are the standards I have indicated too ambitious in the present circumstances of the country, or are they reasonable and practicable? If the answer to the question be also in the affirmative, you will agree that the present drift and traditional inaction should give place to a reasoned policy and a courageous initiative. We must begin work at once with a changed outlook and new ideals. In these days of open door, free communication and world competition, it would be unpardonable neglect on our part to omit to organise the resources and working power of our people in every walk of life.

The greatness of a man, they say, lies in the timelessness of his thoughts. If one were to sit back and just go through the thoughts expressed in this stirring speech, how many of us would deny that the thoughts remain as germane and as relevant to the India of today as it was about a hundred years ago when Sir M.V. first articulated his thoughts. He was thus a man far ahead of his times in terms of his vision, his dedication and single-minded devotion to work for the all-round development of the state. The reign of Maharaja Krishnaraja Wodeyar under whom dewans as illustrious as these served, has rightly been called the Golden Era of Mysore's history and if Karnataka today boasts of industrial, technological and social progress vis-à-vis its other counterparts, the credit lies largely with the robust foundation laid by these illustrious statesmen and thinkers—for whom public service was not a chance to fatten one's purse, but to serve the people in the truest sense of the word.

The good work that was going on in Mysore compelled the British government to rethink the status they had so far accorded the vassal kingdom and its chief. During a visit to the state in 1913, Lord Hardinge observed:[*]

> I have now the pleasant duty of making an announcement, which it is as gratifying to me to deliver, as I trust it will be to Your Highness to receive. Some four months ago Your Highness wrote me a letter in which you took exception to certain features in the Instrument of Transfer of 1881 under which the Government of Mysore was restored to Your Highness' father, and you urged that the document should be revised both in substance and in form, in such a manner as to indicate more appropriately the relation subsisting between the British Government and the State of Mysore. After a very careful consideration of the question, I have decided with the concurrence of His Majesty's Secretary of State for India, to substitute for the Instrument of Transfer a new Treaty which will place the relations between us on a footing more in consonance with Your Highness' actual position among the Feudatory Chiefs of India. His Majesty's Government in accepting my proposal has observed that Your Highness' views on this question were stated with much force and moderation, and that they derive additional weight from the high character and reputation which Your Highness has always borne.

In 1914, war broke out in Europe and soon engulfed the entire world. The damage caused by the war was unprecedented in history. In earlier wars, civilian populations were generally not involved and casualties were confined to the warring armies. But this war affected the economy of the entire world—the casualties suffered by the civilian population from the bombing of residential areas and the famines and epidemics in its aftermath far exceeded losses suffered by the armies. No wonder, then, that it is called the First World War. It was a turning point in the history of the entire world.

---

[*] Taken from Swami Rao's book, *Sri Nalwadi Krishnarajendra Wodeyaravara Charitre.*

Besides conflicts resulting from rivalries over colonies and trade, the major European powers clashed over certain developments within Europe. There were six powers in Europe at this time—Britain, Germany, Austria-Hungary, Russia, France and Italy. The two major camps were the Triple Alliance of Germany, Austria-Hungary and Italy and the Triple Entente comprising France, Russia and Britain. The USA also joined the war in 1917 along with Russia, though Russia withdrew after the Bolshevik Revolution in 1917.

The First World War ended on 28 June 1919 with the signing of the Treaty of Versailles. Mysore placed its imperial service troops under British command, granted Rs 50 lakh to the war fund and Rs 2 lakh to the Imperial India Relief fund. Mysoreans donated Rs 30 lakh and the maharaja an additional sum of Rs 20 lakh between 1918 and 1919. The Mysore army fought in Palestine, Egypt and Mesopotamia. The dewan appointed a food controller, prevented the export of food grains and established fair price shops to counter the outbreak of epidemics, influenza, food scarcity and also financial malpractices like hoarding.

The dewan made it clear to the people that the government intended to foster economic development despite these global hiccups and fallouts. As recorded by Josyer, the dewan declared:

> Government is prepared to render State aid to the extent such aid is given in other countries. It may be rendered in various ways, by experimenting and starting industries, and when successful handing them over to private bodies, by guaranteeing interest for a term of years on private capital invested in new or infant industries, by offering Takavi loans, by granting subsidies to enable companies to declare a dividend in the first few years, by giving bounties to stimulate production, starting workshops for experimental work and training artisans, by providing experts at Government cost, by employing foreign skilled workmen to instruct the people in minor industries, by providing expert advice in forming joint stock companies, by purchasing articles required for the Government's use from local manufacturers as far as possible, by collecting and publishing correct statistics and circulating foreign publications containing useful information, by means of Exhibitions, Conferences etc., by carrying on as State concerns some of the larger industries such as the manufacture

of iron and steel, and sandalwood oil, and by exempting new industries from octroi duties and other taxes for a term of years. Had it not been for this terrible war, we might have made much more rapid progress. The times are out of joint, machinery is hard to produce and the money market is tight. But we hope that with the close of the war better times will come for the Empire and for ourselves.

You will be glad to hear that His Highness' Government has made all reasonable financial provision for State aid required. His Highness the Maharaja has been pleased to authorise us to announce that a sum of Rs 5 Lakhs per annum will be available for the next five years for loans and encouragement of industries generally. His Highness has also been very particular that funds should be provided for education to the fullest extent permitted by resources. As I was leaving for Ootacamund to attend a Council meeting at Bangalore, for the preparation of our budget for the coming year His Highness said to me 'be sure that you do not stint money for education.' His Highness watches over your interests with an unceasing vigilance and solicitude, and I know His Highness' dearest wish is that the Government and the people should cooperate on a basis of common ideals and aspirations, and work with mutual goodwill, confidence, and hope for the future.

Meanwhile, the social churning in Mysore resulted in demands for greater representation for the traditionally backward and oppressed sections of society. The Praja Mitra Mandali that was founded in 1917 for the espousal of this cause put forth vociferous demands for reservations in government jobs for backward classes. The Justice Miller Committee was appointed to look into this demand. Sir M.V., however, firmly believed that merit alone ought to be the criteria for government jobs. When his voice was lost in the clamour of populist demands, he resigned from the post of dewan in 1918—an act that brought him much criticism from the social-justice lobbies of society.

While his resignation severed his ties with the state's political class, it didn't prevent him from continuing to participate in economic and developmental activities. He became the chairman of the Board of Management Bhadravati Iron Works in 1923. He established a model institute for Polytechnics—Jayachamarajendra Occupational Institute. He served as chairman of the Cauvery Canal Committee, guided the Thippagondanahally water supply system that supplies water to Bangalore city. The establishment of the Hindustan Aircraft Factory (later HAL) in 1941 goes to his credit. In 1949, at the ripe old age of 88, he forwarded a scheme for rural industrialisation and financial corporation. For all his pioneering services, the master brain was awarded the highest civilian honour of Independent India—the Bharat Ratna in 1955. This great son of Mysore died on 14 April 1962 at the ripe age of 101. The then Maharaja Jayachamaraja Wodeyar said in a condolence message:

> I am deeply grieved to hear the sad news of the demise of Dr Mokshagundam Vishweswaraiya...indeed he was the first to think of a master plan for the industrialisation of India, which we are happily realising through our five year plans. In his demise, we have lost a great statesman, economist and engineer...

Sardar M. Kantharaje Urs, brother of Maharani Kempananjammanni and brother-in-law of the maharaja succeeded Sir M. Vishweswaraiya as dewan. The Miller Committee gave its recommendations during this time, favouring reservation for backward castes in government jobs.

Kantharaje Urs retired in 1922 due to ill-health. He was succeeded by Sir Albion Rajkumar Banerji, a retired officer of the Indian Civil Service and formerly the dewan of Cochin who was taken into the State Executive Council under Sir M. Vishweswaraiya.

Banerji faced two major challenges on assuming the post: managing the finances of the state, which suddenly seemed to spin out of control with mounting debts, and tackling the increasing demand for popular reforms triggered by the Montford Reforms of British India. An able administrator, Sir Albion Banerji decided to meet these challenges head-on. The abolition of extravagant state expenditure and tapping neglected sources of revenue tilted the balance in favour of a surplus budget. In 1923, the income was Rs 331 lakh and expenditure was Rs 313 lakh; in 1924 it was Rs 333 and Rs 319 lakh respectively and by 1925 the same figures stood at Rs 345 and Rs 321 lakh respectively; while 1926 saw a further improvement of Rs 346 and Rs 323 lakh respectively.

Sir Albion Banerji was succeeded by another illustrious dewan, Sir Mirza Ismail, in 1926. His grandfather Ali Askar had migrated to Bangalore from Persia and gained the favours of Mummadi Krishnaraja Wodeyar.

His father Aga Jaan was the personal bodyguard of Chamarajendra Wodeyar. To this Aga Jaan was born, in 1883, the illustrious Mirza Ismail. He studied at Bangalore's St. Patrick School, Weslin Mission and Central College. When Krishnaraja Wodeyar IV was a student at the Royal High School, Mirza was his classmate. The friendship strengthened over the years and in 1926, Mirza Ismail was invited to occupy the post of the dewan of Mysore. He can rightly be called one of the makers of modern Mysore and his 15-year tenure marked tremendous progress in the history of the state.

The year 1927 was one of joyous celebration all over Mysore—it had been 25 years since the king's ascent to the throne. Governor General Lord Irwin, visiting Mysore around this time, observed:[*]

> On the eve of a most auspicious occasion, the celebration of the 25th anniversary of Your Highness' accession to power, I take the liberty of offering Your Highness on behalf of Lady Irwin and myself, the most sincere congratulations on Your Highness' Silver Jubilee. I was naturally attracted by the prospect of visiting a State, which had played so large a part in the history of Southern India from remote times. For many years we have watched and admired the maintenance and development of those high standards of administration, which you have inherited from the great British administration who nursed your State. We have not forgotten the noble services you have rendered to the British Government when the need for service was the greatest, and we are not blind to what Your Highness personally has done to set an example of the fashion in which the Government of a great State should be conducted. Mysore has perhaps a longer tradition of progressive Government than any other State in India, and the Government of India can feel assured that any relief, which they may feel it in their power to give, will endure to the benefit of the people of your state. The Government of India have accordingly decided to remit in perpetuity with effect from next Financial year, Rs 10 ½ Lakhs out of the annual subsidy you now pay, thus reducing the amount to the sum originally fixed by the Treaty of 1799.

---

[*] Irwin's remarks, and Malaviya's which follow, are taken from Swami Rao's book, *Sri Nalwadi Krishnarajendra Wodeyaravara Charitre*.

Many illustrious Indians sent their congratulatory messages as well. Pandit Madan Mohan Malaviya, founder of the Benaras Hindu University of which the maharaja was the first chancellor, said:

The purity of life of His Highness, his solicitude for the welfare of his people, his desire to see that there was no oppression and injustice, but on the other hand development and progress, his impartiality for all his subjects, his appreciation of whatever was good and noble, rightly entitle him to the loyalty and love of his subjects.

C.R. Reddy, vice-chancellor of the Andhra University notes:[*]

What a transformation Mysore has undergone under him! Life everywhere, activity, hope, and aspiration in the entire rural masses, who have till now been sleeping partners in the State's concern merely paying their taxes and helplessly dependent on the powers that be, slaves of the bureaucracy, the women awake to their rights and interests; modern industries installed and encouraged; local banks to finance and sustain those industries; railways, irrigation projects, electrical power plants; the most forward and systematic educational policy; the mere narration of all of which sounds like the poetry of administration, a lyric in statesmanship!

Swami Rao records in his book a message from the maharaja to all his subjects on 8 August 1927:

On this day when I complete the twenty-fifth year of my reign, I send my loving greetings to each one of my dear people, with a full heart of solicitude for their happiness. With unceasing effort I shall, while life lasts, endeavor to promote their welfare and prosperity, and I pray that God may give us light and strength to achieve this—the supreme object of my life and rule.

❖

Travelling was Krishnaraja's passion. He especially had a penchant for pilgrimages. He had visited Amarnath in 1918 and Badrinath in 1925, where he walked 150 miles of hilly tract from Nainital in thirteen days!

---

[*] Taken from Josyer's 1929 book, *The History of Mysore and the Yadava Dynasty.*

On 18 June 1931, the king left for a tour of Northern India. He visited Manasarovar and after bathing in the holy Ganga, the entourage reached the camp 15,000 feet above sea level. After some days, they went on to Mount Kailash, the mythological abode of Lord Shiva. After visiting a number of towns and cities of the north, they returned to Bombay and then Bangalore to meet Maharani Kempananjammanni. On 16 September 1931, the king returned to Mysore.

The dewan however went through a rough patch around this time. Mirza Ismail had to face a lot of criticism and unpopularity on the charge that recruitment to public services and justice to backward classes was biased. This led to widespread agitations. The year 1928 was marred by ugly communal riots due to the government's removal of a Ganesha idol from the open quadrangle of a middle school in the heart of Bangalore. The atmosphere was deeply communalised, and people began to suspect the Muslim dewan's hands in the whole affair. The Hindu leaders staged an unprecedented walkout of the Mysore Council and Assembly protesting the insult to the idol of Lord Ganesha. Widespread disturbances and Hindu-Muslim clashes broke out in Sultanpet in 1928, which had to be forcefully suppressed by the government. Arrests on charges of sedition followed. The government refused to allow the Congress to hold its flag-hoisting ceremony in 1929 and this led to further clashes between the state and the public.

Several new establishments were inaugurated in this time. These include the Sir K.P. Puttanna Chetty Hall in Bangalore, the Town Hall or Pura Sabhe of Bangalore, the Bangalore City Corporation building and the Professional Training College at Bangalore set up by Sir M. Vishweswaraiya, which taught mechanical engineering, electrical engineering, agricultural technology, chemistry, mathematics, physics and so on. The Thippagondanahally Dam, again a brainchild of Sir M.V., was inaugurated on 15 March 1933.

The Maharaja was aware of the enormous progress the state witnessed in the past few decades and made it a point to impress the same upon visiting dignitaries, though a lot of it was there for all to see. When Viceroy Lord Willingdon visited Mysore in 1933, the maharaja hosted a banquet. Before the toast, he addressed the gathering and spoke about the material progress that Mysore had achieved in the decade:*

---

* Taken from Swami Rao's book, *Sri Nalwadi Krishnarajendra Wodeyaravara Charitre.*

We have much to show Your Excellency since you last visited us in 1922. We have carried through the project that you had then so much at heart, of a division of the waters of the Cauvery with Madras, and while the Mettur Project is almost complete, the Irwin Canal with a 9,000 feet tunnel is in active working. We have added nearly 50 miles to our railways, though we still cry in vain for the 14-mile link from Chamarajanagara to Satyamangalam. The whole generating station at Sivasamudram has been remodeled to a capacity of 36,000 kilowatts; the addition of another 6,000 kilowatts is in progress; and lights and power have been supplied to nearly 250 villages and towns. We have built immense new water-works at a cost of nearly 60 Lakhs for the City and Cantonment of Bangalore. Our Silk and Soap and porcelain industries have all made good progress, and our Bhadravathi Works continue to make splendid iron, though alas! We find it hard to transmute it into gold. We have great hopes of doing that, however, with the production of the sugar factory, which is rapidly approaching completion.

The sharing of waters between Mysore and Madras, which the maharaja refers to in his speech, would soon become a bone of contention between the two states—the Cauvery water dispute which haunts the governments of Karnataka and Tamil Nadu, as well as the central government to this day. The history of this dispute dates back to 1892, when the agreement was first signed. An award was given by Sir H.D. Griffin in 1914 but rejected by the then Madras Presidency. Josyer records Griffin's words:

> The resolution we have arrived at recognises the paramount importance of the existing Madras interests, has for its primary object the safeguarding of those interests and does, we believe, safeguard them effectually.

This was, more or less, the basis of the agreement arrived at in 1924 between the then Madras Presidency under British rule and the princely state of Mysore.

On 7 July 1934, Queen Mother Kempananjammanni Vanivilasa Sannidhana, who had so ably headed the state during her regency years, passed away at the age of sixty-nine. The maharaja—deeply attached to his mother—was terribly upset. In her memory, he inaugurated in Bangalore the Vanivilas Hospital and the Parvati Chandrashekara Clinic on 8 June 1935. This maternity hospital serves women and children to this day.

The loss of his mother and the political unrest in the state in the wake of the freedom movement seemed to take a toll on the king's health as well. On medical advice, he took a trip to Europe in 1936. Leaving Mysore in the last week of June, he sailed from Bombay in a steamer in which separate accommodation was provided for the royal party to allow for their orthodox lifestyle. He visited Paris, London, Scotland, Turkey, Berlin, Budapest, Australia, and Zurich and returned to Bombay on 29 September. Unfortunately, as he was still coming to terms with his mother's loss, his younger brother Yuvaraja Kanthirava Narasimharaja Wodeyar died. This grief turned the king into a complete recluse. He only attended two public events after that—the lavish anointment and ablution of the Gomateshwara Statue at Sravanabelagola—an event that happens once every twelve years called the Mahamastakabhisheka—and the silver jubilee of the Kannada Sahitya Parishat in June 1940. But the loss of his dearly loved ones ate away at him from within.

Maharaja Nalwadi Krishnaraja Wodeyar breathed his last in the Bangalore Palace on 3 August 1940. With that came to an end the 'Golden Era' and 'Ramarajya' of Mysore.

YUVARAJA KANTHIRAVA NARASIMHARAJA

It would be worthwhile to turn our attention to the life and times of Yuvaraja Kanthirava Narasimharaja Wodeyar who, like a devoted Lakshmana, stayed in the shadow and guidance of his illustrious brother. Born in 1888, his early education commenced at the Royal School, after which he was sent to the Rajkumar College at Ajmer. Within a few months of getting there, he fell very sick and was brought back to Mysore and educated at the Royal School. In 1910, he married the daughter of Dalavoy Devaraja Urs—Kempucheluvajammanni. In fact, his was the first marriage ceremony to be celebrated at the Kalyana Mandapa of the Mysore Palace.

He was sent on a trip to Europe in 1913, speaking of which Sir M.V., the then dewan says:

The Yuvaraja who has been traveling abroad for the past 6 months, with a staff of three officers and a young gentleman of the Ursu

An ageing danseuse: Padmabhushan Dr K.Venkatalaskhamma

The Dashavatara Ganjifa card of Mysore

Mysore Ganjifa

The Dasara procession at the old palace in Mysore

The European durbar hosted by the Maharaja during Dasara

Galaxy of Mysore dancers at the Mysore Sangeet Natak Academy conference of 1964 (from left)- Jejamma, Vankatalakshamma, Balasaraswati, Sundaramma Nanjangud and Nagaratnamma.

Jetti Thayamma

Venkatalakshamma in performance

Nalwadi Krishnaraja Wodeyar and Jayachamaraja at the Dasara Durbar

Prince Jayachamaraja offering his respects to his uncle, Maharaja Nalwadi Krishnaraja during Dasara

Galaxy of Mysore dancers at the Mysore Sangeet Natak Academy conference of 1964 (from left)- Jejamma, Vankatalakshamma, Balasaraswati, Sundaramma Nanjangud and Nagaratnamma.

Jetti Thayamma

Venkatalakshamma in performance

Nalwadi Krishnaraja Wodeyar and Jayachamaraja at the Dasara Durbar

Prince Jayachamaraja offering his respects to his uncle, Maharaja Nalwadi Krishnaraja during Dasara

Nalwadi Krishnaraja Wodeyar and Jayachamaraja atop horses during the Dasara procession

Nalwadi Krishnaraja Wodeyar takes a salute from a horse cart

The Jambu Sawari—the Maharaja, Yuvaraja and the Prince atop the elephant in procession to the Banni Mantap on Vijayadashami day

The Dasara procession through the streets of Mysore

Dasara parade near the Chamaraja Circle

Galaxy of durbarees at Jayachamaraja Wodeyar's Dasara

Jayachamaraja Wodeyar worships the state palanquin during Ayudha Puja

Jayachamaraja Wodeyar atop the Chamundi Hills during Dasara

A riot of colour, theatre, music and dance: the Yakshagana folk art

Mural painting of the Dasara procession, on the walls of the Mysore palace, by artist Y. Subramanya Raju

The Jambu Sawari immortalised in paint, by Keshavayya (1941)

*The private Dasara Durbar of present scion of the Wodeyar dynasty
Sri Srikantadatta Narasimharaja Wodeyar*

A mix of tradition of modernity: the state festival in current times with the goddess in the Ambari

An illuminated Mysore palace — a sight for sore eyes!

'The Glow of Hope':
the masterpiece of Haldenkar

Artist beyond comparison:
Raja Ravi Verma

The Mysore School of painting

The gold Kanthirava fanams of Ranadhira with an image of Lord Narasimha in a yogic posture

Half pagoda gold coins of Chikkadevaraja with the image of child Krishna atop the serpent Kaliya

Bahaduri pagodas of Haidar Ali retaining the Hindu figurines of Shiva and Parvati and 'He' inscribed in Persian on the reverse side

Ahmadi pagodas issued by Tipu Sultan, with verses in Persian

Shiva and Parvati on the gold coins issued by Mummadi Krishnaraja Wodeyar

The Golden Howdah or Ambari in the Gombe Thotti

The Kalyana Mantapa

The intricate paintings on the roof of the Kalyana Mantapa

Painting of baby Nalwadi Krishnaraja, by Raja Ravi Verma

Painting of Nalwadi Krishnaraja with his sisters, by Raja Ravi Verma

The armoury

The magnificent Durbar Hall

The expansive courtyard of the Durbar Hall

The Amba Vilasa

Silver doors in the Amba Vilasa

The fort walls of the Mysore palace

Silver Jubilee Tower erected in Mysore to commemorate the silver jubilee of Nalwadi Krishnaraja Wodeyar

community, has just been welcomed home with great warmth and enthusiasm. In his travels in Europe, the Yuvaraja spent a life of ceaseless toil, visiting numerous institutions and studying the varied activities of the countries he passed through. From all sources we learn that he met with a cordial reception wherever he went and he has come back to us, leaving pleasant memories of his visit behind him, rich with experience and an ardent desire to help in the uplift of the people.

He was soon appointed extraordinary member of the Executive Council. He had worked as military secretary to the maharaja earlier and was also the Chief Scout. In 1915, the British government conferred the title of G.C.S.I. on him. On 18 July 1919, Princess Kempucheluvajammanni gave birth to a baby boy who was christened Jayachamaraja Wodeyar, the prefix *'Jaya'* being added to indicate the victory of the allied forces in the First World War. He was also blessed with two daughters, Princess Sujayakanthammanni and Princess Vijayalakshmammanni. The Yuvaraja established a number of organisations across the state relating to cooperation, scouting, the Red Cross, child welfare, and the welfare of the depressed classes. He also served as the president of the Karnataka Sahitya Parishad and was pro-chancellor of Mysore University.

The London press referring to him as a conversationalist said that 'He often contributed words, which if spoken in the House of Lords, would have been front page news!' An African prince was struck by his intolerance of snobbery and said, 'His Highness seemed to symbolise the union of what was best in East and West.'

One can glimpse the depth of knowledge and power his speech possessed in his address to the Eighth All India Oriental Conference, where he traced the past of Mysore in a beautiful manner:

> A fair country, like a fair lady, generally has a more eventful history than her less favoured sisters. And Mysore is no exception to the rule. We have cromlechs, dolmens and rude stone implements belonging to the Paleolithic age. There are many beautiful spots associated with great Sanskrit epics. It was Rama's arrow that made a great fissure in the Yadugiri hill. The waterfall at Chunchanakatte enshrines the bath of Sita. Tradition tells us that the Bababudan Hills were formed from a portion of the Sanjiva Mountain, which fell from the hands of Hanuman as he was flying

to restore Lakshmana to consciousness. Bhima, the terrible tore Bakasura in twain on the French-Rocks hills and slew Hidimba on the Chitradurga. The sage Gowthama performed penance on a rock in the sacred Cauvery near Seringapatam, while Agastya had a hermitage at Kalasa, Parashurama at Nanjangud, Jamadagni at Chandragutti and Rishyashringa at Shringeri.

In the historical period, we have records of the Mauryan and Satavahana Empires, of the wars between the Pallavas and the Chalukyas, between the Hoysalas and the Yadavas. It was a minister of the Ganga Empire that gave us the largest monolithic statue in the world, the Gomata image. We have relics too, of the Vijayanagara Empire, of the rule of Bijapur and Golconda, of the Mughal Governorship at Sira, and of the Mahratta Jagirs at Bangalore and Kolar. The city of Seringapatam has a history stretching back through the ages, and under the Mysore Kingdom it became a centre of learning.

We can show you also the premier monastery of the great Shankaracharya at Sringeri; the place where the large-hearted Ramanuja found asylum from the persecution of his king, the many Muths founded in pursuance of the tenets of the devout Madhwa, and many relics of the reformer Basaveswara. Our Oriental Library can show you over 11,000 valuable manuscripts and our Archaeological Department has published more than 10,000 inscriptions and is conserving some 200 ancient monuments.

Nor are we altogether neglectful of the modern arts. Here you will find master musicians like Vidwan Subbanna, Vasudevacharya and Venkatagiriappa, who have won the admiration of Southern India, while the Indian styles of painting and sculpture have also their honoured representatives in artists of fame, like M. Venkatappa and Mr Siddalinga Swami, and technical institutions are doing what they can to revive the ancient craftsmanship and to develop in modern work an ancient simplicity of form and design.

In our Mysore we have mosques, temples, churches and viharas erected for devotion and consecration of man to the service of God. Sacred spots like Dattatreya Peetha in Bababudan mountain ranges show that Hindu and Mussalman can worship with equal fervour and devotion at one and the same shrine. Let us therefore work for mutual understanding between the two great sister communities, the Hindus and Mussalmans, which is so essential for India's political and economic regeneration. Let us try to remember that these and other religions are alike in all fundamentals, and that the differences, if any, pertain only to matters of external form, such as rituals and ceremonies, which are comparatively of little consequence in enabling an individual to lead a pure, devotional and spiritual life.

Thus ended the lives and times of the two illustrious and worthy sons of Chamarajendra Wodeyar, each brilliant in his own way. The Maharaja's forty-year reign marked an era of all-round progress never before seen in Mysore.

Education had received the highest priority. In 1915, when the Kashi University was set up, the maharaja became its first Chancellor. In 1916 the Mysore University was set up and all colleges in Mysore and Bangalore were affiliated to it. In a far-sighted speech recorded by Josyer, the maharaja, addressing the University's senate, said:

> I feel that I ought to say a few words as to what I think should be the aim of our University. In the first place we should spare no efforts to gain for the Mysore University the respect of the educational world. This end can only be achieved by maintaining a really high standard of teaching and examination, and also by never allowing that standard to be lowered, however strongly you may be tempted by the lure of numerical results.

The king evinced keen interest in the spread of Sanskrit and Kannada. In fact, the expenses of the Sanskrit college at Mysore were met out of his own purse. He also contributed Rs 60 lakh annually for spastic children. On 28 December 1937, the Benaras University conferred him with an honorary doctorate. Mysore became a seat of learning, music and fine arts. Many kings passed out of Mysore University, such as the Maharajas of Akkalkot, Bannira, Nagod, Janjira, Gwalior, Narasinghpur, Travancore, etc.

Gandhiji's epithet of Rajarishi for this King was extremely apt—simplicity and dedication were his forte. He was a reservoir of goodwill and affection for all fellow beings. He was also a great connoisseur and composer of music and wrote his own compositions or *kritis* in the Carnatic classical music style. He was also an expert of the Western classical music styles and the piano and patronised Hindustani classical music in the kingdom. As Lord Sankey said: 'His State is not only a pattern to India, but a pattern to the world!' The concept of the mythical Ramarajya or ideal government was translated into reality by the series of progressive steps initiated under his benevolent rule—guided by the best dewans any maharaja could ever ask for. The golden period in the history of Mysore came to an end with the passing away of Nalwadi Krishnaraja Wodeyar.

The trademarks of the way he lived his life can be summed up through his own address to the graduates of the Benaras University in the Annual Convocation in 1919:[*]

> I would impress on you that you should endeavour to combine in your lives a real sense of religion with true culture; to believe that you owe a duty to God and to your fellow countrymen, and to aim at faith without fanaticism, deference without weakness, politeness without insincerity and above all integrity of character in thought, word and deed.

---

[*] This address is taken from Swami Rao's book, *Sri Nalwadi Krishnarajendra Wodeyaravara Charitre.*

22

POLITICAL, SOCIAL AND ECONOMIC DEVELOPMENT OF MYSORE

The dewans of Mysore were a stark contrast to the avaricious dalavoys who had held similar positions of eminence in politics in earlier periods. Unlike the semi-literate, militarily trained, ambitious dalavoys, this new genre of officers were suave, English-educated, well-read, exposed to modern Western philosophies of freedom, liberty and justice and were appointees of the Raj, rather than self-appointed dictators of the kingdom. They knew that their professional performance would be the only way to earn fame, rather than the tactics followed by the dalavoys, infamous for storming palace doors with elephants and deposing the king unceremoniously. Education and exposure ensured that the dewans had a broader vision of development—one that included the welfare of the common people and projects of public utility. These measures, carried out successfully over decades of nurturing by the dewans, catapulted Mysore into the forefront of successful states of imperial India.

In describing the successes and achievements of the dewans, we must not forget to praise the foresight of the maharajas who made all this possible. Rather than the autocratic maharajas of earlier centuries, who appointed and dismissed dalavoys at whim, the later Wodeyars, especially Krishnaraja Wodeyar IV, gave their dewans the freedom and power to make Mysore a better, a more modern kingdom. In an environment free of interference, with a supportive and broad-minded maharaja, the dewans could make full use of their powers to make a difference during their tenure. So, while the planning and implementation of various developmental projects is to the dewans' credit, we must not neglect the significant role played by their maharajas in this scenario.

AT THE THRESHOLD OF GLORY

By the turn of the nineteenth century, Mysore was poised to take off into the skies of progress and development. Her fundamentals were all right—politically stable, socially progressive and administered by a set of remarkable men who called themselves her maharajas and dewans.

The Rendition of Mysore on 25 March 1881 followed fifty years of progressive and efficient administration by the British commissioners. The commissioners' stint had, to a large extent, laid the foundations for a modern Mysore. If one were to take stock of the financial health of the state in 1910–12 vis-à-vis the Rendition, most of the fiscal parameters point to a surge, thereby bolstering the statement we set out to make about Mysore being poised for a confident take-off.[*]

On the downside, the period was marred by famines, with the one in 1875–78 the severest of its kind in the region in half a century. It cost the state exchequer Rs 160 lakh and embroiled the government in debts of over Rs 80 lakh. The province also lost one million people to the famine and subsequent epidemics. From 50,55,402 in 1871, Mysore's population fell to 41,86,188 by 1881—a fall of 17 per cent. The number stabilised, however, to 58,06,193 by 1911.

The demographics of the state also saw interesting change during this time. The population in the towns, which was about thirteen percent of the state's total population, fell to eleven percent in 1911. This could be attributed to the lack of employment opportunities in towns and migration to cities—a trend that caught up during this time. The agriculture-dependent population in Mysore rose from thirty-three lakhs to forty-two lakhs between 1881 and 1911. The same period also saw a healthy increase of 79 per cent in the area occupied for agriculture—mainly extensive and not intensive agriculture—to about 74,38,463 acres in 1911–12.

These changing socio-economic dimensions had a natural impact on the state's revenues as well. From about 50 lakhs at the time of transfer

---

[*] The information presented as part of this stock-taking exercise is taken from Sir M. Vishweswaraiya's speech, recorded in Josyer's 1929 book, *The History of Mysore and the Yadava Dynasty*.

of power to the royal family after the fall of Tipu, the revenue rose to 101 lakhs by the time of Rendition. Including the accidental income that was accrued due to the gold mines at Kolar, the revenue figures jumped to a healthy 247 lakhs by 1910–11. Between Rendition and the early decades of the twentieth century, the land revenue also increased from 60 lakhs to 106.5 lakhs; excise saw a hike from 10 to 67 lakhs and income from forests shot up to 21 lakhs from 7 lakhs. But along with the rise in revenues, the expenditure also doubled from 101 lakhs to 223 lakhs in the said period. Law and justice, jails, education, medical expenses and public works were the main expense items that saw an increase. This was comforting, however, as the expense was intended to create a sound socio-economic infrastructure for the state and its people. Education in particular saw a healthy increase in fund allocations from Rs 3,91,028 in 1881 to Rs 18,79,135 in 1911—a whopping 80 per cent increase, clearly demonstrating where the administration's priorities lay. Consequently, the school-going population within the kingdom of Mysore also increased from 53,872 in 1881 to 1,38,153 in 1911.

The railways was an area that was given primary importance by both, the commissioners and the rulers of Mysore. It might have begun as a means of transport for the British (especially between Mysore and their headquarters at Madras) and as a facilitator of trade activities, but in the long run it played a vital role in building a robust economy for the state. The railways, which covered only 50 miles in 1880–81, rose to 411 miles in 1910–11 and the capital outlay on them in the same period from 25 to 250 lakhs—a sharp rise indeed! The mileage of the province's road networks were also doubled since the time of Rendition. Channel irrigation was extended during this period in the Cauvery and Kapani valleys, numerous tanks were restored and repaired, the two major works of public interest—the Cauvery Power Scheme which was a pioneering electrical undertaking in the whole of India and the Marikanave Reservoir, also one of its kind in contemporary times—were completed. Urban development and planning, especially in the cities of Bangalore and Mysore, received royal attention. Industries like the gold mines of Kolar, the manganese mines of Shimoga and a few cotton and other mills sprang up across the state.

The officials of the Madras Presidency would often remark that Mysoreans resided in one of the most beautiful and picturesque provinces of the country.

While the above description of the state's financial health in the early decades of the twentieth century sets a context for discussing the enormous strides Mysore made on all fronts, it is important to delve deeper into the various aspects of this growth saga.

THE CRADLE OF INDIAN DEMOCRACY

George Bernard Shaw had once famously commented, 'Democracy is a device that insures we shall be governed no better than we deserve.' That Mysore and her people deserved the best in the country in those times becomes amply clear when we see some of the pioneering experiments in democracy in India being successfully tried in this small southern kingdom. India was a blend of several contrasts back then. The presidencies that came under direct British rule depicted a deceptive picture of modernism, while feudal barons and kings continued to hold sway and preside over medieval practices in many provinces.

Against such a backdrop, the first Representative Assembly or Praja Pratinidhi Sabha, was set up in Mysore in 1881 under the stewardship of the first dewan, Rangacharlu. It was truly the first of its kind in India and it was indeed laudable that while parts of India, like Bengal, still reeled under the old and antiquated feudal forms of government and *zamindari*, Mysore had become a pioneer in sowing the seeds of people's representation in government affairs. A representative arrangement of this kind did not exist even in the British Presidencies.

The Assembly had 144 members appointed by the deputy commissioners of the districts and were chosen from among the leading merchants, planters and agriculturists. A proclamation of Maharaja Chamaraja Wodeyar X dated 25 August 1881 brought this assembly into existence. It was during the time of the Dasara festivities that the assembly was born. The dewan served as its ex-officio president. The policies of the government, measures it undertook, and its balance sheet were placed before the assembly, which would then plan and budget for the coming year. It was not a statutory body nor was it elected directly by the people—a concept that gained momentum much later. Nonetheless, it was a bold and innovative step in the direction of representative government and is said to have paved the way for measures undertaken to extend the concept of local self-government in British India during the viceroyalty of Lord Ripon.

In his inaugural speech, recorded by Josyer, Rangacharlu described the main aim of the Sabha:

> His Highness hopes that by this arrangement the actions of the government will be brought into greater harmony with the wishes and interests of the people. Such an arrangement by bringing the people in immediate communication with the Government would serve to remove from their minds any misapprehension in regard to the views and actions of the Government and would convince them that the interests of Government are identical with those of the people.

The first assembly consisted of two cultivating landowners from each *taluk* and three to four leading merchants from each district invited officially. In all, 144 members attended, with the dewan presiding over the sessions. The second session met the next year and Dewan Rangacharlu in his address dwelt on the importance of local self-government and urged the people to take active interest in administrative matters. He observed:

> If the spread of any high degree of education among the great mass of the people were to be insisted as a *sine quo non*, we may have to wait forever. Meanwhile every year under an autocratic system of Government we find the people less fit for Representative Institutions. The real education for self-government can only be acquired by the practical exercise of administrative functions and responsibilities under the guidance of officers of administrative tact and experience.

He also warned people against letting such representative institutions 'fall into apathy or breed a factious spirit among the members'.

Dewan Sheshadri Iyer furthered the reforms process by effecting changes to the Representative Assembly and thus making it truly representative of the people—elections were held to elect the members in 1891. This happened in phases. In 1887, representation to agricultural classes with property qualification was added to the Assembly Charter for membership. It also included the nomination of eminent citizens and nominations by the elite and enlightened sections of society. The objective of the assembly was widely publicised to the masses as a forum to voice their grievances. From 1887 onwards the names of the members of the assembly were gazetted. Finally, by 1891 came the phase of complete election of all members to the Assembly. The assembly had a term of three years. Praising the work done by the assembly, the dewan said:*

> The moderation, the intelligence and the practical good sense, which have characterised your discussion in the past years, the material help that you have given the government in discussion of important questions and the sustained interest you have evinced in public affairs have convinced the Maharaja that the time has come when the wealthier and more enlightened classes may, with safety, be left to themselves to choose the members of the state.

A property qualification was imposed for the effective representation of the varied interests in the state. In 1891, the people were given the right of universal franchise. A land tax of Rs 100–300 a year or a municipal rate of Rs 13–17 was fixed as the qualification to vote. This raised the number of elected members to the Representative Assembly to 357. In 1894, the property qualification was reduced and 78 minor municipalities were disenfranchised, bringing down the number of members to 275. As before, they were elected for a three-year term.

A system of Mysore Civil Services for which men of proficiency were picked up was started. In November 1891, a competitive examination was held to appoint young men to fill high posts in the executive and judicial services of the state. The examination also helped in the recruitment of probationary assistant commissioners.

The maharaja, and also his able dewans, understood the importance of local self-government as the building blocks of a democracy; how the sum of the parts makes the whole. The system of local self-government prevailed in Mysore from the Commissioners' Rule onwards. On 20 March 1862, a municipal institution was formed in Bangalore with the amildar as executive officer. It looked into the local issues, public works and infrastructural problems of the city. The Bangalore Town Municipal Regulation was passed in 1871 and in 1881 it was extended to all governing bodies prevailing in municipalities. Sanitation and town planning received great attention, with over Rs 28 lakh spent on sanitation and improved water supply for Mysore, Bangalore and other *mofussil* towns.

---

* Taken from Josyer's 1929 book, *The History of Mysore and the Yadava Dynasty.*

The system of local self-government got a further boost under Dewan P.N. Krishnamurthy who extended eight District Boards, seventy-seven Taluk Boards and thirty-eight Unions constituted according to the rules promulgated in September 1903. The British system of maintaining records and files was introduced and a secretariat manual was prepared by the dewan to guide the officers and bureaucrats.

The most remarkable work of Dewan V.P. Madhava Rao was the founding of the Mysore Legislative Council in 1907, which commemorated its centenary in the year 2007. It had ten to fifteen additional members besides the existing three councillors. Previously, legislative measures formed part of the duties of the Executive Council consisting of the dewan and his two councillors. It was felt that the character and composition of the council, the limited membership and want of communication of its proceedings to the public at large, made its functioning rather unworthy of attention. So the dewan envisaged the enlargement of the council in this manner. These additional appointees to the council would bring their political acumen, knowledge and experience to the table and facilitate the smooth functioning of the council. Two-fifths of them were non-officials nominated by the government. Two members were elected from the Representative Assembly to the Council on Resolutions, while it was customary in the assembly to take a consensus of opinion. The elective principle was promised to be introduced soon. The council came into being on 22 June 1907.

Under Sir M.V. the membership of the Mysore Legislative Council was increased from eighteen to twenty-four in 1914. Three members were to be elected from the Representative Assembly and four others from the eight districts. The council was also given the powers to discuss the budget. The assembly was to have a second session in April (from 1917 onwards) called the budget session.

The Mysore Local Boards' and Village Panchayats Regulation was passed in 1918 and provided for an elected majority in District and Taluk Boards, otherwise dominated only by officials. Municipalities came to be provided with elected vice-presidents and panchayats with elected chairmen.

But the story of democracy in Mysore was not a perfect one throughout. The same Madhava Rao — visionary enough to form the council — lost support because of various unpopular measures he implemented, as described in the previous chapter. The press, too, revolted against him.

Every democracy undergoes a process of churning and this was certainly the emergency period in the history of Mysore's democratic sojourn. But the inherent strength of the idea ensures that such obstacles only help the system emerge stronger, more robust and more vigilant against the perils of autocracy, which rear their head from time to time.

Opportunities for this revitalisation came in the form of the Morley-Minto reforms and then the Montford reforms propounded by Secretary of State Edwin S. Montague and the Governor General Lord Chelmsford, offering a mixed sort of responsible government to the elected public representatives in British Indian provinces. The people of Mysore demanded similar reforms. Dewan Sir Albion Banerji appointed a committee with the vice-chancellor of Mysore University, Dr Sir Brajendranath Seal, as chairman to look into the details and suggest changes. The Seal Committee's report submitted in March 1923 met with a mixed response. Krishnaraja Wodeyar issued a proclamation on 27 October 1923 outlining the changes to the assembly.

The assembly became a statutory body and had to be consulted on all matters regarding taxes, general principles of all bills, etc. It could pass resolutions regarding the budget and public administration. The assembly strength was of 250–75 members. There was a widening of franchise with voting powers allotted to people paying Rs 25 land revenue or Rs 5 municipal taxes. Women also got the power to vote.[*]

Standing committees consisting of members of the Representative Assembly and Legislative Council were to be constituted to advise the government. Labour was represented, together with education, trade, commerce, mining and planning in the two houses of legislature; 35 seats were to be reserved for minorities in the assembly, while 150 members were to be elected from rural areas. The strength of the Legislative Council increased to 50 (excluding ex-officio members), of which 60 per cent were non-officials and not more than one-third were to be nominated members; eight were to be returned from the assembly, eight from districts, one each from Bangalore and Mysore, four from the municipalities, two Muslims, one Christian, and one backward caste member.

The assembly included veterans, like Tathaiya, G. Srinivasa Rao, Karnit Krishnamurthy, B. Narsinga Rao, and younger ones, like Hosatoppa

---

[*] It is noteworthy that women in Mysore got the power to vote around the same time as women in the USA and UK.

Krishna Rao, G. Paramashivaiya, D.S. Mallappa, publicists like K.P. Puttanna Chetty, B.K. Garudachar, D. Venkataramaiya, Rao Bahaddur N.S. Nanjundaiya, S. Venkataiya and so on. On 17 March 1924, the maharaja formally inaugurated the new Legislative Council and Representative Assembly at a joint session.

Speaking on the occasion, he said:*

> You, Gentlemen, represent an enlarged electorate, you have been returned under a wider franchise and you start with increased powers and responsibilities. The changes, which I am inaugurating today, are fundamental, providing as they do for a far closer association of the people with the administration. I am aware that a section of my people were in favour of further radical changes, including a wider franchise and increased powers. While fully sympathising with the ideals, I may state that our decision was made after prolonged consultations. Each State must evolve its own constitution, suited to its own needs and conditions and the genius of its people. Without departing from the fundamental principles of development common to all forms of polity, it has been deemed necessary to maintain the character of the Representative Assembly as essentially a body for consultation and reference, as well as representation, directly voicing the needs of the people, and with a constitution sufficiently flexible to expand with the expanding political consciousness of the people, leaving the Legislative Council the more formal work of legislation and other functions usually associated with such bodies.
>
> It is the ambition of my life to see the people of my state develop self-sustaining qualities, exhibit initiative and enterprise, and take a front rank in all progressive movements and activities in the country. In making our plans for the future, we have got to take note of the tremendous changes of the recent past. India, under the beneficent guidance of the British nation, is shaping into a federation of Provinces and States. We in Mysore, form, as it were a nation within a nation. While cooperating with both, the Government of India and the rest of the Indian public in

---

* Taken from Josyer's 1929 book, *The History of Mysore and the Yadava Dynasty*.

measures, which lead to the prosperity of the country as a whole, we, in our local sphere should promote education and economic growth to the fullest extent permitted by our resources, so that our people may not fall behind other Provinces and States in the race of progress.

I would have you apprehend with mind and heart this vital fact that the interests of Government and people are identical. The happiness of the people is both the happiness and the vindication of Government. Any differences of opinion between the Executive and yourselves, and such differences naturally occur in all lands and all along the road of progress can refer only to the means, never to the end. You can count upon responsiveness and goodwill in government, as they certainly count upon them in you. This day, therefore, marks the dawning of a new era in the history of Mysore. My faith in the power and willingness of my people to render patriotic service is finally rooted in experience and you may rely on my abiding sympathy in your aspirations. You will help to build up the prosperity and reputation of our State and will become custodians with me of its permanent interests.

How timeless and thought-provoking are these words of advice from a man who undoubtedly deserved to be called Rajarishi.

Implementing the recommendations of the Local Self-Government Conference of 1923, the maharaja's government abolished Taluk Boards and established Village Panchayats on a statutory basis. This had well-defined powers for collection of taxes, functions relating to transition, communication, extension of franchise to women, etc. A department of industries and commerce came into being as also the Apex Bank. The year 1924 saw floods ravage Mysore and cause a lot of damage. Dewan Banerji initiated a series of relief measures.

In January 1938, the Conference of the Legislative Council was held. Mr D.V. Gundappa demanded the setting up of a committee in connection with the problems and challenges facing the council and the Mysore Federation. The government accordingly set up a standing committee called Rajyaanga Vyavastha Samiti consisting of fifteen members. It had to also examine the Government of India Act of 1935. The Act provided for a Federation at the centre consisting of Indian states and provinces. In the states, the system of dyarchy was abolished and provincial autonomy introduced. The Provincial Executive consisted of the governor and his council of ministers—appointed by him from among the members of the Provincial Legislature. The leader of the majority party was called the chief minister. Only fourteen percent of the population could vote. The committee had its first sitting on 27 April 1938, its first chief minister and president was Rajamantrapraveena S.P. Rajagopalachari. A political reforms committee called Rajakeeya Sudharana Samiti was set up and it began work on 28 April 1938, with Dewan Bahaddur Rajasabha Bhushana K.R. Srinivasa Iyengar as president. It had 120 members, and 3 more members were later admitted. It scrutinised the work of district boards, municipalities and gram panchayats.

Thus, by the time of India's independence, the foundations of democracy were well-entrenched in the soil of Mysore. Of course it was not the perfect recipe and naturally had its own problems and prejudices. But seen from a pan-Indian perspective it was undoubtedly a great inspiration for the rest of the country.

FUELLING INDUSTRIAL GROWTH AND ECONOMIC REVITALISATION

Every Dewan—right from the first, Rangacharlu—had his finger on the pulse of the kingdom's fiscal situation and strategised to vitalise a sagging economy battered by repeated famines and droughts. When Rangacharlu took charge of the dewani, the kingdom had undergone its worst natural calamities. Land revenue could not be collected regularly and a debt of Rs 80 lakh was due to the British government. In charge of finance for the state, Rangacharlu resorted to downsizing government machinery and the money saved went to pay a major part of the debt, while the remaining was paid up in instalments. Negotiating tactfully with the British government he got the interest rate on the loan taken by Mysore during the famine years reduced from five percent to four percent and extended the payment period to forty-one annual instalments of Rs 4 lakh each. This, along with floating public loans and undertaking public works to provide jobs to unemployed peasants, gave the state financial scope to focus on socio-economic improvement.

Realising the importance of the Kolar gold fields in the state's economy, Rangacharlu signed a pact with the British firm, John Taylor and Company, to start mining operations. Five percent of the Company's profits in the scheme were given to the Mysore treasury as royalty. These measures helped raise funds through routes other than public taxation. The Anglo-Indian community that had established itself in large numbers in Bangalore was given 400 acres of land to utilise for farming. This area came to be known as Whitefield.

The net liabilities of the State in 1881 exceeded the assets by over Rs 30 lakh and an annual fiscal deficit of 1.25 lakh. But after an initial stationary period and the great slump following the drought, over ten years the revenues increased steadily to Rs 180 lakh from 103 lakh in 1895. The net assets rose to over 176 lakhs. The increase was not due to the introduction of new taxes, but the impetus to overall economic development through the building of new roads, laying of railway lines, irrigation works, industrial growth, mining of gold, etc. There was also a stipulated increase in the taxes from excise, mining and forests. In 1892, the financial year was changed so as to end on 30 June instead of 31 March. The Land Revenue Code was passed.

In 1907, during the annual Dussehra celebrations, an Industrial and Agricultural Exhibition was held in Mysore to boost the climate of industrial activity. This was the first such exhibition in Mysore's history. Industrial and agricultural products from Mysore and other parts of India were on display. Inaugurating the exhibition, Maharaja Krishnaraja Wodeyar said:[*]

> It is not to be expected that exhibitions of this kind should have an immediate and revolutionary influence on the Agriculture and Industries of the country. But they offer to all classes an opportunity of seeing what their neighbors are producing; to craftsmen they are of special use in indicating the directions in which their skill must be most usefully directly, whilst distributors may learn from them of new markets on the one hand and on the other of new sources of supply. Whatever disappointments may be in store for us, I have no doubt whatever of their educational value and of their far-reaching influence in the cause of progress. I attach great importance to the policy that we propose to follow of holding these

---

[*] Taken from Josyer's 1929 book, *The History of Mysore and the Yadava Dynasty.*

exhibitions annually. Experience shows that when they are held at long intervals, the lessons learnt from the successes or failures of one year are forgotten when the opportunity of profiting by then next occurs. Exhibitors are apt to remember their disappointments and the trouble and expense incurred, rather than benefits gained, and the result is, inexperience on the part of the executive and misdirected energy or apathy on that of the exhibitors. It is our hope that an annual exhibition will produce continuity of effort and steady progress on both sides.

Sir K.C. Sheshadri Iyer followed the footsteps of his predecessor. The enhancement of subsidy by Rs 10.5 lakh had been waived till 1886. The dewan's vigorous pleas to waive the amount till 1896 were conceded by the Indian government. With some relief on the liabilities front of the kingdom's balance sheet, he decided to boost the revenues by charging a royalty of five per cent on gold mining, which resulted in revenue of Rs 47,000 in 1886–87. Extensive plantations were undertaken to increase the forest cover of the state. Revenues rose from 180 lakhs to 191 lakhs by 1902; railway receipts rose from Rs 5.74 lakh to Rs 6.35 lakh; land revenue from Rs 96 lakh to Rs 98.25 lakh in the period. The total expenditure on public works from 1801 to 1901 exceeded Rs 5.5 crore, irrigation and major water supply works alone consuming about Rs 2 crore.

Raichur Doab Gold mines, the Mysore Spinning and Manufacturing Co. (set up in 1883 by a Bombay firm), the Bangalore Woollen-Cotton and Silk mills Ltd., the Davanagere Cotton Ginning factory in 1884, the coffee works (Bangalore, by M/s Binny and Company), M.S.K. Mills (in 1884 in Gulbarga), Cauvery Hydroelectric Scheme (1900), Shimoga Manganese Company and by 1914 oil mills, rice mills, saw mills, tile factories, printing presses, cigarette factories, distilleries, iron and brass foundries were all set up.

During the dewanship of Sir Krishnamurthy, the good work of the past continued with added vigour. Steps were taken to train artisans in iron work, carpentry, rattan work, lacquer work, weaving, etc., in Chennapatna and other places by opening training colleges for the same. Scholarships were awarded to meritorious students to pursue the arts in Madras and Bombay. The Mysore City Improvement Trust for the beautification and development of the city was established in 1903. An Ethnological Survey, consequent to the 1901 census, was inaugurated and H.V. Nanjundayya, the then secretary of government, was entrusted with this work.

In 1904, a cooperative movement began in India, and was adopted in Mysore in 1905. This led to the spread of banks and cooperative societies all over the state of Mysore. The Central Cooperative Bank was established at Bangalore to finance the cooperative societies. Even the maharaja placed large fixed deposits in the bank to patronise it.

The greatest impetus to industrial growth came about during the dewani of Sir M.V. Between 1914 and 1924, the sandal oil factory at Mysore, the soap factory (Bangalore, 1918), the chrome tanning factory, Central Industrial Workshop (Bangalore), Mysore Iron Works, the Minerva, the Krishnarajendra and Mahalakshmi Woollen and Silk Textile Mills, the Mysore Premier Metal Factory, the Standard Tile and Clay Works Ltd., the Bangalore Printing and Publishing Co., Kaolin Syndicate, Mysore asbestos, Sindhuvalli Chromite, and wood distillation plants (Bhadravathi) were established. The Government Central Industrial Workshop and a weaving factory were set up with the objective of giving a special thrust to the hallmark of Mysore: silk production. Sericulture and production of silk was taken up under the auspices of the government and greatly encouraged.

The Mysore Economic Conference was expanded; it came to have three committees for industry and commerce, education and agriculture. It started publishing two journals, one in English and the other in Kannada. The conference met periodically and generated popular interest in the economic progress of the state.

In 1913–14 there were 72 factories in Mysore exclusive of mines employing 4,451 people and earning profits of Rs 1.6 crore. The 15 gold mining industries employed 24,300 men and 5 lakh ounces of gold worth Rs 19 lakh were annually extracted.

The year 1913 saw the emergence of the Mysore Bank, today's State Bank of Mysore and also the Mysore Chamber of Commerce and Industry at Bangalore. An organisation was set up to collect statistics regarding trade; commercial correspondents were appointed in Bombay and Madras and the inputs helped the government to calibrate the industrial progress and policies of Mysore with the rest of the country.

During this period, the number of factories for the manufacture of paper, cement, agricultural implements, porcelain ware, electric goods, glass and enamelware, bakelite products, matches, machine tools, lac, paints, pipes, pottery, sugar, power alcohol, chemicals, fertilisers, chrome and leather were established. Interestingly, many of these achievements occurred at the time of the First World War when the state had to contribute substantial amounts of money to the British war efforts.

These progressive measures of Sir M. Vishweswaraiya were enhanced by the other star of the famous Mysore Dewan quartet—Sir Mirza Ismail. His stint in office saw a rapid increase in the number of industries across Mysore in both the public and private sectors. The steel plant, the paper mills and cement works all at Bhadravathi, the Hindustan Aeronautics Limited, the porcelain and glass factories at Bangalore, the chemicals and fertilisers factory at Belagola (India's first fertiliser factory), the sugar factory at Mandya, the Shimoga Match factory, a khadi production centre at Badanval—these were all due to his personal initiative. Efforts were made to export Mysore Sandal Soap, *agarbattis*, sandal oil and Mysore silk—all signature items of the state—abroad. A trade commission was set up in London, to find lucrative incentives and markets for Mysorean products.

RAILWAYS—THE LIFELINE OF INDUSTRIAL GROWTH

To achieve this kind of industrial growth, the kingdom's infrastructure needed to be strengthened. One of the biggest contributors to this growth story was the railways. Lower costs of transportation, creation of a beneficial circle of expansion and connecting people from villages and the countryside to towns and cities—it was truly the lifeline for economic resurgence and one of the greatest boons of the British Raj.

The dewans understood the importance of this mode of transport and hence devoted considerable attention to its development in the budgetary allocations of every fiscal year. Exhibiting tremendous far-sightedness, Rangacharlu said:[*]

> The urgent want of the Province is not irrigation, but life and enterprise in the cultivator and what can evoke them as successfully as that great civiliser of modern days, the Railways? With the increase of activity and intelligence which are sure to come in the train of these quicker means of transport and

---

[*] Taken from Josyer's 1929 book, *The History of Mysore and the Yadava Dynasty*.

communications, we may hope for a considerable increase of private irrigation and garden cultivation for which the Province is peculiarly adapted.

For the railways project he borrowed a capital of Rs 20 lakh and planned to set aside for the proposed lines Rs 5 lakh each year out of the revenues. Railway lines were established throughout the state after 1881. The Mysore-Bangalore section was opened in 1882 at an expenditure of Rs 4,56,690. The Bangalore-Tumkur line was opened on 11 August 1884 and the Tumkur-Gubbi section on 26 December 1889 at a combined cost of Rs 19,37,480. The Gubbi-Harihar section was constructed out of foreign capital. From 58 miles of railway line in 1881, 315 miles of lines had been laid by 1894.

Subsequently, railway lines were extended up to Harihar, Shimoga and Nanjangud. By 1893, the railways were extended up to the Kolar gold fields. The state transferred the Mysore railways to the Mysore Southern Maratha Company for Rs 68 lakh.

In 1906, the Mysore-Chikkaballapur railway line was laid. Dewan Madhava Rao entered into an agreement with the Madras and Southern Maratha (M.S.M.) railways for the working of railways by Mysore.

Under Sir M.V. the Mysore-Arsikere railway line via Hassan was opened. Bangarapet or Bowringpet was connected with Chikkaballapur via Kolar by narrow gauge loop railway line. For the transportation of timber from the Malnad forests, a narrow gauge railway line was started from Tarikere to Narasimharajapura. The management of 327 miles of M.S.M. railway line in the state was taken over by the dewan. Due to the treaty of Srirangapatna in 1799, Mysore had no access to the sea. He negotiated with the British Government to develop Bhatkal (in Bombay province) as a seaport for the state, but met with little success. The interior of the state was opened up through new road connections and also through several railway lines to the extent of 231 miles at an outlay of Rs 85 lakh.

IRRIGATION AND POWER

Mysore, like any other state of India, was a largely agrarian economy. The frequent famines and droughts necessitated an effective system of irrigation and water conservation. Blessed with great natural resources, the challenge before the state was a proper utilisation and harnessing of these bounties of nature.

Among the earliest irrigation projects to begin in Mysore was the Marihalla Project across the Vedavathi River, started by Sheshadri Iyer. It created the Vanivilasa Sagar (or Marikanave Dam), which gave a big boost to irrigation schemes in the riparian states. The dam project aimed at bringing 25,000 acres in the dry areas of Chitradurga district under wet cultivation. Water supply schemes were augmented for the cities of Mysore and Bangalore. It was the biggest reservoir in India at the time of its completion.

The Hessarghatta project, which provides water to Bangaloreans even today, goes to the credit of Sheshadri Iyer. A sum of Rs 1 crore was spent on original irrigation works during this time, adding 355 square miles to the area under wet irrigation and mopping up additional revenue of Rs 8.25 lakh; 1078 irrigation wells were completed to protect against famines; Rs 67 lakh were spent on building road infrastructure and Rs 18 lakh for roads in the Malnad district. Sheshadri Iyer initiated a series of other progressive projects as well, such as the Cauvery Electricity Systems.

But one name that comes to mind in the context of irrigation measures is undoubtedly Sir M. Vishweswaraiya. His vast experience as an integral part of the Indian Irrigation Commission, his implementation of an intricate system of irrigation in the Deccan area, design of automatic weir water floodgates which were first installed in 1903 at the Khadakvasla reservoir near Pune and later replicated at Gwalior's Tigra Dam made him an unequalled expert in the design of irrigation schemes. In 1909 as chief engineer of the state, his expertise was utilised in the construction of the Kannambadi Dam across the Cauvery, irrigating 1.5 lakh acres of dry land in the regions of Mandya and Malvelly. This reservoir was Sir M. Vishweswaraiya's brainchild, and was a boon to the farmers of the riparian state as it brought huge expanses of dry land under irrigation.

But the Kannambadi Dam had a long history of its own and many eminent personalities contributed to its completion. It had been Tipu's dream to construct a dam at the site to harness the water and utilise it for irrigation purposes. Interestingly, when the actual construction work of the dam began in 1911 and the excavations were carried out by the engineers, they recovered an inscription written in Persian, which dated back to Tipu's times.

AD 1794

YAFATTAH! IN THE NAME OF GOD, THE COMPASSIONATE, THE MERCIFUL

On the 29th of month Taqi of the solar year Shadab 1221.

One thousand two hundred and twenty one. Dating from Mowlood of Muhammed (may his soul rest in peace) on Monday at dawn before sunrise under the auspices of the planet Venus, in the constellation Tanrus, Hazrath Tippoo Sultan the shadow of God, the Lord, the bestower of gifts laid the foundation of the Mohyi Dam across the river Cauvery to the west of the capital. By the grace of God and the assistance of the Holy Prophet the Caliph of the worlds, and the Emperor of the Universe. The start is from me but its completion rests with God.

On the day of commencement the planets, Moon, Sun, Venus, Neptune, were in the sign Aries in a lucky conjunction. By the help of God, the most high, may the above mentioned Dam remain till the day of resurrection like the fixed Stars. The money amounting to several lakhs which the God-given government have spent is solely in the service of God. Apart from the old cultivations, any one desirous of newly cultivating the arable land, should in the name of God be exempted from various kinds of production whether of corn or fruits, of the one fourth part levied generally from other subjects. He will only have to pay 3/4 of it to the benign government. He who newly cultivates the arable land, himself, his posterity and other relatives will be the masters of the above as long as earth & heaven endure. If any persons were to cause any obstruction or be a preventer of this perpetual benevolence, such an inhuman being is to be regarded as the enemy of man-kind, as the accursed Satan of those cultivators, nay of the entire creation.

Tipu's plans were certainly grand, but he did not live to see them being fulfilled.

The impetus for the KRS or Kannambadi Dam was driven by British selfishness. It was not due to the altruistic motive of providing water to the ryots of the region. The gold mines at Kolar were a pot of gold for the British government. Frenzied mining was carried out there to excavate as much gold as they could, using high-power dynamos and generators. The electric power to run these came chiefly from the Sivanasamudram hydroelectric project. This project was the first of its kind in India and was implemented in 1899–1900. The burgeoning needs of the gold fields at Kolar necessitated at least 32,000 HP of electric power—something that Sivanasamudram could barely provide, especially in the dry months. If this power was not made available by July 1914, John Taylor and Company threatened to end the initial agreement. By 15 July 1908 the third phase of the Sivanasamudram project was built—small check dams 8 feet high and 2,300 feet long—and this ensured a timely supply of the required power.

But the British government knew only too well that this was a temporary measure. And so they began seeking permanent solutions to the power issue. The chief engineer of Mysore, Captain W. McHutchin and his assistant engineer, Captain Bernard drew up a plan to raise the height of the dam at Sivanasamudram from its current 70 feet to about 115 feet. The excess water so harnessed could generate up to 23,000 HP of electric power. Such a scheme would however have turned the entire riparian area into a virtual desert and deprived the region's farmers of water for irrigation. Also, the British planned to divert most of the power to the gold fields and the remainder to Madras and Coimbatore. The kingdom of Mysore stood to lose here as well. The maharaja, then barely in his teens, firmly rejected this proposal.

In 1908, McHutchin retired and Bernard took over as the chief engineer. Since the original proposal on the Sivanasamudram project was shot down by the maharaja, alternative sources of power were being explored. It was Bernard who envisaged and laid out the project plan for the Kannambadi Dam. It was to be a 97-foot high dam that could store water up to 80 feet and gradually increased to 124 feet (with water stored up to 118 feet). It could store up to 37,100 million cubic feet of water. To please the maharaja, the plan provided for irrigating the farmlands of the region through canals at the northern end which would be about 100 miles long and carry water to the regions of Mandya, Nagamangala, Malavally and Chennapatna *taluks*. After the initial survey works were completed in 1909, it was estimated that the yield from the dam would be about 46,000 HP power. The approximate cost of the project was Rs 2.5 crore. The Government of Mysore was shocked to see this hefty expenditure as it overshot the State Budget by a great deal!

But the project would prove to be a boon for the state. Not only would it help irrigation to a large extent, the government stood to gain revenue to the tune of 10 dollars per horsepower of electricity. It was then that Maharani Vanivilasa Sannidhana and the young maharaja came up with the most ingenious and unparalleled solution to the problem. The jewels, costly diamonds, ornaments and gold and silver plates of the royal family were dispatched to Bombay and sold at competitive prices there. The money so obtained was used as seed-capital for the project. How often in the history of princely India do we have such instances of selflessness in the royal family? The interests of the people were uppermost on the maharaja's mind—when the earlier project was considered detrimental to the state's interests, he opposed it tooth and nail, but when the new plan suggested bounties for the people and farmers of the agricultural state, he was willing to even pawn his personal wealth to see the project through! This kicked off the dam project.

A tragic story accompanies the construction of the dam. On 30 July 1909, Chief Engineer Bernard was engrossed in work in the Kannambadi village. The Cauvery was overflowing its banks that day after a night-time surge in water levels. Despite the turbulence of the river, the British engineer and his seven local aides, who perhaps belonged to the fishermen community, sat in a theppa or coracle and tried crossing the river. The upsurge ensured that the fragile coracle capsized. Six of the seven aides managed to swim to safety. But seeing the last man desperately calling for help, Bernard risked his life and—though he himself could not swim—managed to push the labourer towards the banks. But sadly, the turbulence claimed Bernard's life, sucking him into the gushing waters of the Cauvery. His body was recovered some four days later a considerable distance away. So moved were the villagers by the heroism of this white man that they contributed and collected about Rs 600, which was deposited with the government at an interest rate of about 6.5 per cent. An award was instituted with this money in the name of the deceased chief engineer and presented to any student of the Mysore University who demonstrated acts of courage and bravery in rescuing others. What a humane and unexpected gesture from a British officer towards an Indian labourer, and what a touching reciprocation from the locals!

It was after this tragic incident that Sir M.V. took over as chief engineer. His skill, experience and knowledge added great value to the Kannambadi Project. The work continued even after his retirement from the post of Dewan. The project's iron and steel requirements were met by the Bhadravathi Steel Plant. Successive dewans, like Kantharaje Urs, Sir Albion Banerji and Sir Mirza Ismail, oversaw the progress of the project, which finally saw its completion in 1931. Under Mirza Ismail, a 9183-foot- long canal, called the Irwin Canal, was constructed to irrigate 1,20,000 acres and the dry tracts of Mandya, Malavally and T. Naraseepura *taluks*.

This dam created the biggest reservoir in Asia at the time it was built. It was second only to the Aswan Dam across the Nile in Egypt. It remains the biggest reservoir of its kind in India and stands as true testimony to the foresight and progressiveness of the rulers of Mysore and their dewans.

Agricultural implements factories were started at Bangalore, Mysore and Hassan. The Krishnarajendra Mills and Electrical Goods Factory were also set up. The Vishweswaraiya canal for the Cauvery was created, as also additional irrigation facilities for Mandya.

On 8 November 1935 the Minister for Industrial Development Sir Frank Nauis inaugurated the completed Vanivilasa Bridge across the Kapila River near Tirumakudlu and Naraseepura. The bridge was built under the guidance of the Chief Engineer of Mysore Sir Dewan Bahaddur N.N. Iyengar, at the confluence of the Cauvery and Kapila Rivers. Work began in 1928 and ended in 1932 at a cost of Rs 6,02,000

Closely linked to the issue of irrigation was the generation of hydroelectric power to satisfy the burgeoning needs of a vibrant industrial economy and social sector. The Sivanasamudram hydroelectric project, the first of its kind in India, was implemented in 1899–1900. Electricity was provided to the Kolar gold fields in 1902 and the city of Bangalore was provided with power in 1905. In fact, Bangalore became the first city of India to be electrified! This was also the first and remained the longest transmission line in the world then.

Sir Mirza Ismail embarked upon an ambitious project of rural electrification—the first of its kind in India. By 1940, about 180 villages all over Mysore were electrified. Speaking of the advantages electrification had brought to Mysore, the maharaja said:[*]

---

[*] Taken from Josyer's 1929 book, *The History of Mysore and the Yadava Dynasty.*

It was only in 1882 that electric light was first used on a commercial scale in London, and it was another ten years before the possibility of utilising electric power at a distance from the generating station was accepted as a safe and paying undertaking. In Mysore we are exceptionally favoured in respect of sources of power to be put into harness, and in the genius of our administrators, who have seized upon the opportunity to make this power of the utmost value to the State. Compare with the dates that I have just given you the date of 1894, on which Sir K.C. Sheshadri Iyer first took up the question of the harnessing of the Cauvery Falls at Sivasamudram, and you will see that Mysore was not behind the times. In fact when in 1902 the transmission line from the Cauvery Falls to the Kolar Gold Fields, 93 miles long, and operating at 35,000 Volts, was put into service, it was the longest high voltage transmission line in the whole of Asia and the second or third longest in the world! The success of that undertaking is an eloquent testimony to the boldness of spirit, the farsightedness and the statesmanship of those who were responsible for it. The work thus auspiciously begun has never halted. Installation has followed installation, and the output of power has increased from 6000 H.P. in 1902 to 67,000 H.P. in 1937! In the meanwhile the uses of the power have been extended far beyond the original purpose of supply to the gold mines, Electric power was supplied to the two cities of Bangalore and Mysore in 1905 and 1908 respectively, and now it is issued to nearly 150 towns and villages. Meanwhile the demand for industry has also increased, and at the present time we have nearly 32,000 lighting installations and nearly 4000 power installations in operation!

URBAN AND SOCIAL INFRASTRUCTURE

Building an urban infrastructure to support this economic spurt was an equally important task, as also creating social amenities that would benefit the people of the state.

From 19 hospitals in 1881, the state had 114 in 1894; five being maternity and childcare hospitals at district headquarters. The Victoria Hospital was established in Bangalore in 1897 to commemorate the diamond jubilee of the queen of England. Towards the end of the maharani's Regency period, the number of hospitals in the state increased to 134 from 116; 124 municipalities in place of 107; educational institutions increased to 4,009 from 3,897 with the outlay on education expenditure also seeing an upward trend from Rs 8 lakh to Rs 10 lakh.

The state and Bangalore in particular suffered the scourge of plague in 1897–98 and this led to the laying out of new extensions and settlements in Bangalore like Malleswaram and Basavanagudi, which heralded the rapid expansion of the city. Dewan Iyer pressed for the surplus revenue from the Bangalore cantonment area to be transferred to the Mysore kitty to augment the state's treasury.

The maharaja was extremely fond of his elder sister, Princess Krishnajammanni. On 22 November 1904, at the young age of twenty-one, she succumbed to the dreaded disease of tuberculosis that was spreading its tentacles across the state. Sadly three of her daughters, aged between fourteen and sixteen, also died of the same disease. This tragedy completely shook the maharaja and the regent queen mother. They were determined to ensure speedy and timely treatment for this disease for the people of the state at large. To this end, the Princess Krishnajammanni Tuberculosis Hospital was started in April 1918. A sum of Rs 75,000 from the personal wealth of the deceased princess was donated for the treatment and cure of needy patients. On the inauguration of the hospital on 18 November 1921 the maharaja made an emotional and touching speech recalling fond memories of his sister and her daughters and hoping that no one had to endure such tragedies. He would also arrange to send the palace music band on certain Sundays to entertain the patients in the hospital! Such was the empathy of the benign ruler of Mysore.

A medical college in Mysore and the mental hospital and craft institute at Bangalore were founded in the time of Dewan Mirza Ismail. To him goes the credit for the establishment of the Cheluvamba Maternity Hospital, railway offices, radio station—all at Mysore and MacGann hospital at Shimoga and Narasimharaja hospital at Kolar. During Sir M. Vishweswaraiya's stint in office, the Minto Ophthalmic Hospital was set up as a specialty hospital for eye ailments.

In 1889, the model Mysore Postal System was merged with the Indian Postal System for Rs 50,000. The Bangalore Century Club and Mysore Cosmopolitan Club were set up in the early decades of the twentieth century.

The Bangalore cantonment area, which was under British control, was purchased by Mirza. He had a great sense of aesthetics and beauty. The general thrust was on the cleanliness, tidiness and elegance of towns and cities. To this end many measures, like the terrace gardens at Krishnarajasagara dam called the Brindavan Gardens (inspired by the king's fascination for the Shalimar Gardens on a visit to Kashmir and his desire to replicate it in Mysore), its illumination, as also that of the Mysore Palace on festive occasions, lighting of the contours of the Chamundi Hills, well-laid parks, boulevards, well-lit squares, the greening of Bangalore, which earned it sobriquets of the 'Garden City' were undertaken. He toured the state extensively and established an excellent rapport with eminent citizens and philanthropists, using their help to build hospitals, maternity wards, schools and the like. He had great affection for Gandhiji, though he was critical of many policies of the Congress. Gandhiji visited Mysore on his invitation and stayed at the Nandi Hills near Bangalore in 1927.

EDUCATION AND SOCIAL REFORM

One of the greatest indices of human resource development in any economy is undoubtedly education. It is universally acknowledged that the maharajas of Mysore and their dewans contributed significantly to the cause of education, particularly for women. While practices like Sati were rampant in other parts of India, here was a state where women's education and social reform received such a boost, thus creating a sound social infrastructure.

During the dewani of Rangacharlu and Sir K.C. Sheshadri Iyer, elementary and secondary education to all classes of society was given through the state and by private efforts, to promote the vernacular and ancient classical languages. Efforts were made to encourage female education, higher education among the masses, training young people in professional and technical courses like engineering sciences and medical sciences. By 1888 the number of pupils had increased by 20 per cent and by 1890 the total number of schools increased to 2,902, with 83,278 pupils enrolled. In 1892, an industrial training school was set up.

Women's education remained the primary area of attention. In 1889, the Prince of Wales visited Mysore and was taken to the Girls' School started during Rangacharlu's dewanship in 1881. He was awestruck by what he saw there and promised to report the school's progress to the queen. Many other royal visitors—Their Highnesses Maharaja and Maharani Gaekwad of Baroda, and Sir Robert Lethbridge (quoted by Josyer) who remarked that the school stood 'absolutely in the van of female education in India and owing so much to the Maharaja's enlightened care and interest, may be regarded by His Highness as one of the brightest jewels in his crown!'

In 1894 a Department of Geology and in 1898 a Department of Agriculture were started at the Mysore University. To the girls' school started in 1881 were added higher education courses as well. This led to the founding of the Maharani's college for women's education in 1895, which became the first of its kind upon its inauguration in Mysore. The course curriculum, examination scheme and certification were done by Madras University. The year 1906 was a golden one in the history of women's education: for the first time, three women students from Mysore—Smt K.D. Rukminiamma, Srirangamma and Subbamma—obtained their B.A. degree with meritorious results, awarded by the Madras University. By 1916, the College was affiliated to the newly founded Mysore University.

An Archaeological Department was created with B.L. Rice as its head. A library housing ancient texts, manuscripts, documents and historical archives of immense value was thrown open to the public in 1891, during the rule of Chamarajendra Wodeyar. This was named the Oriental Library.

Schools sprang up by the hundreds and special scholarships were given to the needy and backward-caste students. An adult education scheme was begun in the year 1912. That very year, the S.S.L.C., or Secondary School Leaving Certificate examination system was adopted uniformly across the state. Foreign travel for post-graduate male students was fostered and a scholarship scheme instituted for promising students seeking to study abroad. Many hostels were built for the benefit of students who were staying away from home in order to study at a good school or college.

In 1894, the Mysore Infant Marriages Regulation was passed. The social evil of child marriage was eating into the very vitals of society. This social termite had to be eradicated. Young girls would be married off, pre-pubescent and sometimes even in their cradles. If, to their misfortune, they were widowed, they would be condemned to lead a life bereft of all pleasures and abused and ridiculed by society as an evil omen. They would be compelled to shave their heads, wear saffron and forget all worldly pleasures, though they often fell prey to the intentions of lecherous men of their own family. The Act aimed to stem this evil by forbidding the marriage of girls below the age of eight—a major step in the right direction back then. In 1909, the Devadasi system, which had slowly degenerated into institutionalised prostitution over the years, was abolished by the government. Smoking by minor boys was banned by an act passed in 1911.

At around the same time, there was a competitive bid by Roorkee for their town as a possible location. But what clinched the deal in favour of Bangalore was the vision of a lady who herself was not too highly educated. The city would have lost the prestigious Indian Institute of Science but for the timely initiative of the Recent Queen of Mysore—Vani Vilasa Sannidhana. She immediately seized opportunity and quickly signed a contract offering 371 acres or prime land in the city and a generous grant of Rs 50,000 a year. The overjoyed Committee that was looking for an ideal venue looked no further and Bangalore became the chosen city. The spin offs that came with the establishment of the IISc in Bangalore were amazing. It catapulted the city into a knowledge capital of India—and an ideal destination for the Space Research, Aeronautics and Information Technology industry to find its roots here, many decades later. The institute's first director was Morris Travers FRS, Ramsay's co-worker in the discovery of the noble gases.

This institute is today well known as the Indian Institute of Science or IISc, and acclaimed worldwide as a worthy institution in fields of scientific research and post-graduate study. The institute has been able to make many significant contributions, primarily because of its unique character. It is neither a national laboratory which concentrates solely on research and applied work, nor a conventional university which concerns itself mainly with teaching. However, the institute is concerned with research in frontier areas and education in current technologically important areas.

Under Dewan Madhava Rao, primary education was made free and compulsory for all. A grant of Rs 5 lakh was made for the Indian Institute of Science. A Veterinary Department was also set up in Mysore. Two students were sent to Oxford and Dehradun for the study of forestry.

Being an academic and thinker himself, Sir M.V.'s natural thrust was on education and on the increase in the number of primary and middle schools. His pet project was female literacy and education for the backward classes of society. The Mechanical Engineering College, Commercial and Agricultural Schools, Chamarajendra Technical Institute (Bangalore), Industrial Schools at the District headquarters, Bangalore Engineering colleges (1917), Karnataka Sahitya Parishad at Bangalore (1916), libraries in Bangalore and Mysore, the famed Mysore University (in 1916) were all established by his zealous personal efforts. The maharaja was the chancellor of the Benaras Hindu University of Pt. Madan Mohan Malaviya. The dewan contributed Rs 2 lakh and made an annual grant of Rs 12,000 to this University. At the time of Nalwadi's coronation in 1984, there were about 3884 schools in Mysore state and the same number stood quadrupled at a staggering 12,869 by the time of his Silver Jubilee in 1927. Education also formed almost a quarter of the State's expenditure when one sees the annual reports of administration. The presence of the benign Regent Queen also ensured the spread of female literacy.

One of the hallmarks of the education revolution in Mysore was its all-inclusive nature. It was never restricted to a particular class, group, gender or community. In fact in the Maharaja's own words, he had said that education is not the reserve of a few privileged souls and that like hospitals, courts and public utility services were open to all, so also were schools, irrespective of any discrimination. Numerous schools came up for the backward classes, tribals, communities like the Lambanis, Kurubas, Kumbis, Vaddas, women of the backward castes and so on. Special schools were set up to promote Urdu as well. In 1890 Urdu primary schools came up in all the taluks of the State. Unlike now, the emphasis however was that while the medium of instruction might be Urdu, the content needs to be modern and secular. So fresh textbooks were created for this purpose on par with the other schools of the State. Mysore was also perhaps the only province in India to have a school for the physically challenged in 1906. About 150 blind and deaf children were admitted into this residential school that gave them vocational training. It attracted students slowly from neighbouring Bombay and Madras Presidencies and the Nizam's kindgdom. Bu 1912, 7000 Saksharata Centres or night schools were set up all over Mysore State for adult education, as also a chain of libraries. The Government actively took part in the campaign of 'Vayaskara Akshara Prasara' to spread adult education along with the Congress and many NGOs like the Ramakrishna Mission. Technical and

Occupational Institutes in different parts of the State provided skills to the young workforce.

Josyer writes that a visiting minister from Orissa was very impressed with what he saw. Referring to the progress of the state by 1947, the minister stated:

> The standard of education in Mysore is high. There are enough institutions and workshops to give instruction to its young men in various arts and crafts and in machinery. The Occupational and Technical Institutes, one at Bangalore and other at Mysore, are institutions unique in kind. The prospect of an army of qualified young men in not less than about 20 or 25 arts and crafts, spreading out into the world, thrills me. There are two Polytechnical institutions to the credit of the Mysore State. How I wish that a few such institutions in our Provinces had been established!
>
> The progress of Mysore is due as much to its administrators as to its officers, who are patriotic and whose aim and object is to improve the Mysore State and the people. I find them to be sincere to the core. The several contacts with many of their officers gave me this impression. By the time I reached Mysore, another minister from the Central Provinces, was already in Mysore. It is no wonder that such a progressive state like Mysore has been drawing to it visitors of eminence from all parts of India. Mysore is a beautiful city. It is a Garden city. I was struck by the methodical fashion that pervades every branch of the administration of Mysore and the public life in Mysore state. It is an achievement of no mean order.
>
> Mysore is a premier State with a long-standing reputation for progressive and modern outlook. It has also the reputation for embarking on big development schemes and projects. The purpose of my visit to this premier State is to imbibe and emulate as much as I can. I have fulfilled this object to the maximum limit!

Thus we see at the end of this long and chequered saga that, despite being surrounded by mediocrity and suppressed by colonialism, Mysore achieved pioneering and stunning results and was deservingly acclaimed a 'Model State' by the time of India's independence. These sound economic and social fundamentals, so painstakingly laid over years of labour by the benevolent maharajas and their able dewans, placed the state of Karnataka on a unique growth trajectory.

23

THE STRUGGLE FOR SWARAJ

THE INDIAN POLITICAL CONSCIOUSNESS

The 1857 uprising had kindled a sense of nationalism among the Indian masses, who, till then hardly envisaged themselves as fellow citizens of the same country. India's aspirations to remain as an independent entity had always remained scattered till the second half of the nineteenth century. Due to the lack of an organised effort against the well-organised British, these murmurs of protest and assertions of independence were easily subdued.

The coming of the British brought Western influence, which inspired Western education. The liberal and radical ideas of Europe influenced the Indians and created a new educated class. The use of Western education and English as a language for communication brought closer the populations of various regions. Thus, it helped in an exchange of ideas and developing aspirations for liberation from foreign rule. The socio-religious movements initiated by various social reformers across India inspired national consciousness to improve social conditions and invoked the spirit of patriotism in the Indian masses. The promotion of vernacular languages and their use in the Indian and vernacular papers infused a feeling of nationalism in the people. Throughout British rule in India there was a section of Indians who were discontented and exploited politically, socially, economically and spiritually. They took up the mission of subduing the British and reviving self-rule. The development of means of communication and transport eased the exchange of ideas that inspired freedom.

Events like the passage of the Vernacular Press Act in 1878 and the Ilbert Bill of 1882, as well as the reduction of the age limit for the Civil Services Exams in 1876, resulted in a wave of opposition from middle-class Indians. Consequently, some of them came together and formed a number of small political parties that took to the streets for protests and rallies. The British foresaw it quickly becoming another rebellion on the pattern of the War of Independence of 1857.

To avoid such a situation, the British decided to offer an outlet to the local people where they could discuss their political problems. In order to achieve this goal, Allan Octavian Hume, a retired British civil servant, had a series of meetings with Lord Dufferin, the viceroy. He also visited England and met people like John Bright, Sir James Caird, Lord Ripon and other members of the British Parliament. Hume also had the support of a large number of Englishmen in India, including Sir William Wedderbun, George Yule and Charles Bradlaugh. On his return from Britain, Hume consulted the local Indian leaders and started working towards the establishment of an Indian political organisation. He invited the convention of the Indian National Union, an organisation he had already formed in 1884, to Bombay in December 1885. Seventy delegates, most of whom were lawyers, educationalists and journalists, attended the convention in which the Indian National Congress was established. This first session of the Congress was presided over by Womesh Chandra Bonnerjee and he was also elected the first president of the organisation.

To begin with, Congress acted as a 'King's Party'. Its early aims and objectives were:

- To seek the cooperation of all Indians in its efforts.
- To eradicate the concepts of race, creed and provincial prejudices and try to form national unity.
- To discuss and solve the social problems of the country.
- To request the government for a greater share in administrative affairs to the locals.

As time went by, the Congress changed its stance and became the biggest opposition to the British government.

The turning point for the Congress was the partition of Bengal in 1905, enforced on 16 October during the viceroyalty of Lord Curzon (1899–1905.) It proved to be a momentous event in the history of modern India. Bengal, which included modern day Bihar and Orissa since 1765, was admittedly much too large to be a single province of British India. This premier province grew too vast for efficient administration and required reorganisation and intelligent division.

The lieutenant governor of Bengal had to administer an area of 189,000 square miles and by 1903 the population of the province had risen to 78.5 million. Consequently, many districts in eastern Bengal that were isolated lay neglected, making good governance almost impossible. Calcutta and its nearby districts attracted all the energy and attention of the government. The condition of peasants was miserable under the exaction of absentee landlords; and trade, commerce and education were heavily impaired. The administrative machinery of the province was under-staffed. Especially in the eastern Bengal countryside—cut off by rivers and creeks—no special attention had been paid to the peculiar difficulties of police work till the last decade of the nineteenth century. Organised piracy in the waterways had existed for at least a century. Along with administrative difficulties, the problems of famine, of defence, or of language had at one time or other prompted the government to consider the redrawing of administrative boundaries.

The publication of the original proposal of partition, towards the end of 1903, had aroused unprecedented opposition, especially among the influential educated middle-class Hindus. The educated Bengali Hindus felt that it was a deliberate blow inflicted by Curzon at the national consciousness and growing solidarity of the Bengali-speaking population. The partition evoked fierce protest in west Bengal, especially in Calcutta, and gave a new fillip to Indian nationalism. Henceforth, the Indian National Congress was destined to become the main platform of the Indian nationalist movement. It exhibited unusual strength and vigour and shifted from a middle-class pressure group to a nation-wide mass organisation.

The leadership of the Indian National Congress viewed the partition as an attempt to 'divide and rule' and as proof of the government's vindictive antipathy towards the outspoken *bhadralok* intellectuals. Defeating the partition became the nationalists' immediate target. Agitation against the partition manifested itself in the form of mass meetings; rural unrest and a swadeshi movement to boycott the import of British manufactured goods. Swadeshi and Boycott were the twin weapons of this nationalism and Swaraj (self-government) its main objective. Swaraj was first mentioned as the Congress goal in 1906, in the presidential address of Dadabhai Naoroji at the Calcutta session of the Congress.

The new tide of national sentiment against the partition of Bengal spilled over into different regions in India—Punjab, the Central Provinces, Poona, Madras, Bombay and other cities. Instead of wearing foreign-made outfits, the Indians vowed to use only swadeshi (indigenous) cottons and other clothing materials made in India. Foreign garments were viewed as hateful imports. The Swadeshi Movement soon stimulated local enterprise in many areas; from Indian cotton mills to match factories, glassblowing shops, iron and steel foundries. The agitation also generated increased demands for national education. Bengali teachers and students extended their boycott of British goods to English schools and college classrooms. The movement for national education spread throughout Bengal and beyond, reaching as far as Benaras, where Pandit Madan Mohan Malaviya founded his private Benaras Hindu University in 1910.

In 1907, the Indian National Congress at its annual session in Surat split into two groups—one moderate, liberal, and evolutionary; and the other extremist, militant and revolutionary. The young militants of Bal Gangadhar Tilak's extremist party supported the cult of the bomb and the gun while moderate leaders like Gopal Krishna Gokhale and Surendranath Banerjea cautioned against such extremist actions, fearing it might lead to anarchy and uncontrollable violence. Surendranath Banerjea, though one of the front-rank leaders of the anti-partition agitation, was not in favour of terrorist activities.

The consequence of the agitation was the growth of communalism and a deepened Hindu-Muslim divide. The economic aspect of the movement was partly responsible for encouraging separatist forces within the Muslim society. The superiority of the Hindus in the sphere of trade and industry alarmed the Muslims. Fear of socio-economic domination by the Hindus made them alert to their own interests, which they then needed to safeguard. Muslim groups openly advocated partition and to give their voice a forum, the All-India Muslim League came into being at Dacca on 30 December 1906.

Thus the partition of Bengal and the agitation against it had far-reaching effects on Indian history and national life. Swadeshi and Boycott became a creed with the Indian National Congress and were used more effectively in future conflicts.

AND THEN CAME GANDHI...

The Indian political spectrum changed radically with the arrival of a short, skinny man in the second decade of the twentieth century. He was Mohandas Karamchand Gandhi, a British-trained lawyer of Indian origin from South Africa. He had won his political spurs organising the Indian community there against the vicious system of apartheid. During this struggle, he had developed the novel technique of non-violent agitation, which he called satyagraha, loosely translated as moral domination. Gandhi, himself a devout Hindu, also espoused a total moral philosophy of tolerance, brotherhood of all religions, ahimsa and of simple living. He adopted an austere traditional Indian lifestyle which won him wide popularity and transformed him into the undisputed leader of the Congress. As Jawaharlal Nehru, the Congress leader said, 'He was a powerful current of fresh air that made us stretch ourselves and take a deep breath,' and revitalised the freedom movement.

Gandhi returned to India in early 1915, and would never leave the country again except for a short trip to Europe in 1931. Though he was not completely unknown in India, Gandhi followed the advice of his political mentor, Gokhale, and took it upon himself to acquire a familiarity with Indian conditions. He travelled widely for one year. Over the next few years, he was to become involved in numerous local struggles, such as those at Champaran in Bihar, where workers on indigo plantations complained of oppressive working conditions, and at Ahmedabad, where a dispute had broken out between the management and workers at textile mills. His interventions earned Gandhi a considerable reputation, and ensured his rapid ascendance to the helm of nationalist politics. His saintliness—though not uncommon in other walks of life—was unique in the world of politics. He had earned from Rabindranath Tagore, India's most well-known writer, the title of 'Mahatma', or 'Great Soul'.

The Jallianwala Bagh massacre of 13 April 1919 was one of the cruellest examples of British suppression in India. People had gathered on the auspicious day of Baisakhi at Jallianwala Bagh, adjacent to the Golden Temple (Amritsar), to lodge a peaceful protest against persecution by the British Indian Government. General Dyer appeared suddenly with his armed police force and fired indiscriminately at innocent, unarmed people, leaving hundreds of people, including women and children, dead. The massacre stirred the collective conscience of all Indians as thousands of unarmed women, children, senior citizens and men were fired at amidst a peaceful protest meet.

Over the next two years, Gandhi initiated the Non-Cooperation movement, which called upon Indians to withdraw from British institutions, to return honours conferred by the British, and to learn the art of self-reliance. Though the British administration was at places paralysed, the movement was suspended in February 1922 when a score of Indian policemen were brutally killed by a large crowd at Chauri Chaura, a small market town in the United Provinces. Gandhi himself was arrested shortly thereafter, tried on charges of sedition, and sentenced to imprisonment for six years. At The Great Trial, as it is known to his biographers, Gandhi delivered a masterful indictment of British rule.

Meanwhile, the Civil Disobedience Movement launched in 1930 under Gandhi's leadership was one of the most important phases of India's freedom struggle. The Simon Commission, constituted in November 1927 by the British Government to prepare and finalise a constitution for India and consisting of members of the British Parliament only, was boycotted by all sections of the Indian social and political platforms as an 'All-White Commission'.

Following the Indian rejection of commission's recommendations, an All-Party Conference was held at Bombay in May 1928 under the presidentship of Dr M.A. Ansari. The conference appointed a drafting committee under Motilal Nehru to draw up a constitution for India. The Calcutta Session of the Indian Congress (December 1928) virtually gave an ultimatum to the British government, that if dominion status were not conceded by December 1929, a countrywide Civil Disobedience Movement would be launched. The British government, however, declared in May 1929 that India would get dominion status within the empire very soon.

Gandhi began a new campaign in 1930, the Salt Satyagraha. He and his followers set off on a 200-mile journey from the ashram at Ahmedabad to the Arabian Sea, where Gandhi wanted to pick up a few grains of salt. This action formed the symbolic focal point of a campaign of civil disobedience in which the state monopoly on salt was the first target. Prior to the beginning of the action, Gandhi sent a letter to the Lord Lieutenant:

> Dear Friend. Whilst, therefore, I hold the British rule to be a curse, I do not intend harm to a single Englishman or to any

legitimate interest he may have in India. My ambition is nothing less than to bring round the English people through non-violence to recognise the injustice they have done to India. I do not intend to be offensive to your people. Indeed, I would like to serve your people as I would my own.

After a 24-hour march to the Indian Ocean, Gandhi picked up a few pieces of salt—a signal to the rest of the subcontinent to do the same. This raw material was carried inland before being processed on the roofs of houses in pans and then sold. Over 50,000 Indians were imprisoned for breaking the salt laws. The entire protest was carried out almost without violence. It was this that annoyed the police.

Margaret Bourke White records a report by the English journalist Webb Miller, who witnessed one of the clashes, has become a classic description of the way in which satyagraha was carried out at the forefront of the battle lines; 2,500 volunteers advanced on the salt works of Dharasana:

> Gandhi's men advanced in complete silence before stopping about one-hundred meters before the cordon. A selected team broke away from the main group, waded through the ditch and neared the barbed-wire fence. Receiving the signal, a large group of local police officers suddenly moved towards the advancing protestors and subjected them to a hail of blows to the head delivered from steel-covered Lathis (truncheons). None of the protesters raised so much as an arm to protect themselves against the barrage of blows. They fell to the ground like pins in a bowling alley. From where I was standing I could hear the nauseating sound of truncheons impacting against unprotected skulls. The waiting main group moaned and drew breath sharply at each blow. Those being subjected to the onslaught fell to the ground quickly writhing unconsciously or with broken shoulders. The main group, which had been spared until now, began to march in a quiet and determined way forwards and were met with the same fate. They advanced in a uniform manner with heads raised—without encouragement through music or battle cries and without being given the opportunity to avoid serious injury or even death. The police attacked repeatedly and the second group was also beaten to the ground. There was no fight, no

violence; the marchers simply advanced until they themselves were knocked down.

Following their action, the men in uniform, who obviously felt unprotected with all their superior equipment of violence, could think of nothing better to do than that which seems to overcome uniformed men in similar situations as a sort of 'natural' impulse: unable to break the skulls of all the protesters, they now set about kicking and aiming their blows at the genitals of the helpless on the ground. 'For hour upon hour endless numbers of motionless, bloody bodies were carried away on stretchers,' according to Webb Miller.

THE FREEDOM STRUGGLE TAKES ROOT IN MYSORE

The winds of nationalism, inspired by the Mahatma's clarion call, blew over Mysore as well, though the magnitude of the movement was much more evident in the parts of today's Karnataka, popularly known back then as Bombay Karnataka and Hyderabad Karnataka. The people in these regions were under the repressive rule of the Bombay presidency and the Nizam respectively. Their counterparts in the kingdom of Mysore enjoyed a greater degree of prosperity and did not feel the pinch of foreign rule.

Renaissance in Mysore

The freedom struggle in Mysore was preceded by a period of renaissance that facilitated the spread of new ideas and technology. The spread of education, the introduction of printing, the activities of the Christian missionaries and their impact on Hindu society, and the spread of liberal and democratic ideas widened people's outlook towards their own lives and their political consciousness. These invariably affected the fine arts, like music, dance, drama, literature and painting. The birth of prose as a literary form and the increasing popularity of secular literature occurred around this time.

The emphasis on education by the Mysore Maharajas has been discussed in depth. Supplementing the efforts of the kings and dewans were the Christian missionaries who, despite their hidden agendas, contributed to the spread of modern, English education. The missionaries who came to Mangalore from Basel in 1834 had started two English schools in South Kanara district and Dharwad. The London Mission was active in Bangalore, Bellary and Belgaum and the Wesleyans in Mysore and Bangalore. All the district headquarters across Mysore state came to have English schools between 1840 and 1854. In 1858, the department of education was founded in Mysore and the Bangalore High School (later christened Central College) was established. By 1881 about 2,087 schools existed across the state. These were important agents in awakening the consciousness of the masses.

Coupled with the spread of English education came the boon of printing. Initially conceptualised by the missionaries to spread the gospel, the technology made available to the masses books and journals from varied thinkers and revolutionaries on Western political and philosophical ideas from across the world. The first printed book in Kannada was released in 1817, followed by a Kannada Bible in 1820. To accelerate the proselytisation drive, missionaries were zealous in learning Indian languages so as to connect better with the masses. So we see a spurt of dictionaries and grammar books in Indian languages. In 1824, the English-Kannada dictionary was compiled by Rev Reeve. To belittle Indian mythology and religion, the missionaries needed to understand them first. So a number of Indian religious texts were also translated to English and Kannada. Indirectly this helped in the classical revival of Kannada and interest in ancient Kannada literature. The Mysore government initiated the 'Bibliothica Carnatica' series from 1891 through the efforts of Louis Rice, wherein works of celebrated Kannada poets of yore like Pampa were printed.

Almost at the same time, the Backward Classes Movement began in Mysore. The quest of backward castes of traditional Hindu society to seek political and social participation could be termed a by-product of the spread of modern ideas. The Lingayats, followed by the Vokkaligas, Kurubas and other communities, spearheaded the movement in Mysore. The destruction of local industries in the nineteenth century caused large-scale unemployment among traditional craftsmen. This, coupled with the horrific famines of that century, led to widespread starvation deaths. Bangalore had been a hub of textile activity in the early nineteenth century, but the primacy was lost to competition from the Manchester and Liverpool mills. The Goniga castes were primarily involved in the flourishing gunny-bag weaving trade. But this too faced severe competition from Dundy mills of Scotland. Iron and steel units that the kingdom was famous for were also shut down in the nineteenth century in the face of British competition. The Uppars of the State were traditional producers of saltpetre or potassium nitrate, which is used to manufacture gunpowder. The British introduction of a chemical substitute for saltpetre caused thousands of Uppars to lose their livelihoods. The two-rupee excise duty on salt made matters worse for salt miners inland and salt-pan workers in the coastal areas. Similar misfortunes befell the Ganigas who produced kerosene, local potters and braziers. Thus, a vast section of society was keen to mobilise itself to educate its youth and help them secure government jobs as the last resort for livelihood. The other offshoot was their internal grouping to seek rights and privileges for their communities.

The Miller Committee appointed to look into the demands of the backward classes recommended reservations. The government took the recommendations seriously and decided to include backward classes in government jobs. The Praja Mitra Mandali however lost its focus. Many of its members were elected to the Representative Assembly but their tone was always one of support for the government and the Dewan.

Also the derisive attitude of the missionaries led Hindu society to look inwards and introspect on existing social evils. The Karnataka chapter of the Brahmo Samaj was formed in Bangalore in 1866, the Theosophical Society in Bangalore in 1886 and the Arya Samaj in 1894 in the same city. By 1904 the Ramakrishna Mission too had established its base in Bangalore. Influenced by all these groups, the Indian Progressive Union of Bangalore was founded in 1903 as a local body to propagate social reforms. The Mysore Social Progress Association was formed in 1915 and held its conference at Bangalore in 1917 where the Ashakta Poshaka Sabha was formed to empower weaker sections of society.

The maharaja's government, as we have seen, was no less committed to social reform. The 1894 law banning child marriage (girls below the age of 8), the first Indian state to enfranchise women (1923), pioneering strides in female education—these were all significant milestones in Mysore's social history. R. Gopalaswamy Iyer in Mysore and Govindacharya Swamy in Bangalore made significant efforts in the eradication of untouchability much before even the Congress could take up the issue. In fact, Dewan K.C. Sheshadri Iyer had founded separate schools for 'untouchables' and Sir M.V. had instituted scholarships for them.

The time thus seemed ripe for a social movement that sought representative and responsible governance for the state.

The Freedom Movement in Mysore

The freedom movement in Mysore needs to be viewed in two dimensions—the general patriotic demand that the British quit the country and the demand to provide to the people a responsible government. It was when issues connected with native interests clashed with those of the Imperial British government and when the unscrupulous way in which the latter was run became evident, that the clamour began for a government that sought to protect the interests of the people of the state. One such instance was the agreement on the sharing of Cauvery waters between princely Mysore and Madras Presidency. The British bulldozed the interests of their dominion, Madras, over those of subservient Mysore. The rumblings of the British government against the industrialisation drive of Sir M. Vishweswaraiya, such as the opposition to a proposed automobile factory in Bangalore, made the stepmotherly treatment all too obvious. The British, while heaping encomiums on Mysore, were also wary of the pace at which it was progressing. While the maharaja put his foot down frequently in protest against British decisions, he could not always prevail over the British, given his position. All he could do in such difficult situations was to hold his ground and watch mutely. The people did not see his protests, only his meek submission to British will. Gradually, they began to resent being slaves to a slave maharaja.

If the discriminatory actions of the British government hurt Mysorean pride, the advent of the modern age and easy access to newspapers and information from across the country, alerted them to developments elsewhere. Tilak's *Maratha*, *New India*, *Hindu* and local newspapers, like *Karnataka Prakashika* (1874), *Suryodaya Prakashika* (1888), and those of the legendary Venkatakrishnaiya, like the *Vrittantha Chinthamani*, stirred people's political consciousness. Many of these local newspapers also carried bold statements on national issues that helped the local Mysorean connect to events occurring across India.

Coupled with the political angle was the religious one. The efforts of Christian missionaries at evangelisation and the foul means employed for the same stirred people, like Tagadur Ramachandra Rao, to begin a campaign against the missionaries' vilification of Hindu religion. The Swarajya Mandira, an organisation he established at Tagadur in 1919, was set up for this very cause. It also initiated a clean-up within Hindu society by campaigning against casteism and untouchability.

Tilak's death in 1920 saw huge mourning processions on the streets of Mysore, even as shops remained shut as a mark of respect to the departed leader. The students of the Maharaja College and boys of the Marimallappa High School and other schools of Mysore ensured the closure of even the District Court on this occasion. Venkatakrishnaiya, who was also the principal of the Marimallappa High School, initiated leaders, like Tagadur Ramachandra Rao, M.N. Jois, Palahalli Sitaramayya and Agaram Rangayya, to the national cause. Swami Rao, G. Virupaksha, Rangaswamy Iyengar and Narayana formed a Tilak National Union in Mysore to propagate the late leader's views and ideas on freedom.

The Karnataka Pradesh Congress Committee (KPCC) was established in 1920 by the 'Lion of Karnataka', Gangadhara Rao Deshpande, at the Nagpur Congress Session. Deshpande became the committee's first president in 1920. It opened branches and District Congress Committees by 1921 at Mysore, Bangalore, Tumkur and Kadur and had Venkatakrishnaiya as the first president of the Mysore city local committee. Vishweshwara Gowda, T.S. Subbanna, T. Rama Rao, Siddhoji Rao, T.P. Boraiah, Advocate M.A. Srinivasa Iyengar, G. Krishnamurthy, Ganapathi Sastry and others were the early leaders of the KPCC. The Congress in Mysore demanded a responsible government for the state—run by elected representatives under the aegis of the maharaja. The government, they demanded, must be responsible to the elected assembly.

But unlike the rest of India, the Congress in Mysore had a tough task endearing itself to the masses. It was branded a band of Mysorean Brahmins and this image changed only with a great deal of effort. The social atmosphere was already charged by the categorisation of the dominant Lingayat sect as Shudras in the 1891 Census Report—something that the community saw as a Brahmin conspiracy to marginalise them. Lingayat leaders protested widely against this move. Yajaman G. Veerasangappa of the community even wrote fiery articles in the newly started journal, *Mysore Star*, which initiated a long public debate on what status needed to be accorded to the Lingayats. To counter Brahmin dominance in administration and public life, the Praja Mitra Mandali was formed by non-Brahmin groups. It opposed the demand for responsible government in Mysore, pointing out that the non-Brahmins had a very small share in the government service and demanded special privileges to amend this. Their activities were encouraged by Yuvaraja Kanthirava Narasimharaja Wodeyar, who believed in the concept of social justice.

Thus, the social friction translated itself into an opposition to the Congress. In fact, the *Mysore Star* editor, G. Virupakshayya, opposed the Congress, its Swadeshi movement and Savarkar and his ideology.

A lot of the disconnect between the masses and the Congress also had to do with the way the Congress conceptualised its role. Gandhi wanted all law-breaking activities to be strictly confined to the British Presidencies like Bombay, Madras, Calcutta and so on. Princely states like Mysore were to enrol members in the Congress but engage themselves in constructive activities, like production of khadi, cow-protection, propagation of Swadeshi, Hindi, etc.

It was the untiring efforts of people, like Tagadur Ramachandra Rao that helped the Congress bridge this gap. As mentioned earlier, his efforts to eradicate untouchability won him, and through him the Congress, public acceptance. He struggled to ensure entry of untouchables to the Gunja Narasimhaswamy Temple at T. Naraseepura, as also allowing them to use public wells and tanks. His Khaddar Sahakara Sangha started in 1925 in Tagadur helped the villagers earn a living. Rao's efforts to uplift one of the most backward communities, the Kanniyars, won him great praise from national leaders, including Gandhi.

To further accentuate this growing acceptance for the Congress, Gandhi toured Mysore in 1920–21 and visited Bangalore in 1927. At Gandhi's calling, many lawyers, like Mahali, Karaguppi, Joshi, Ajrekar, Kaujalagi, Janvekar, Jayarao Deshpande and others from the Bombay Karnataka region, gave up practising law. Gandhi visited Mysore and Krishnarajanagar again in 1927 to propagate the use of *khadi*. The Government also opened a *khadi* production centre at Badanwal.

The Mysore visit of the Prince of Wales in 1921 was opposed by Congress leaders. The protest against the Simon Commission of 1927 had its echoes in Mysore as well. Ramachandra Rao published a work titled, *Simon Commissionge Dhikkara*, against the Simon Commission. His subsequent address in Mysore led to his imprisonment for fifteen days—making him the first political prisoner in Mysore.

The Second and Third Political Conferences of the Congress were held at Mangalore and Gokarna in 1922 and 1924. Santakavi's *Mathrubhoomi Janani Ninna Charanaseve Maduva* and *Udayavagali Namma Cheluva Kannada Nadu* by Huligol Narayana Rao stirred patriotic fervour among the masses. The Hindi Premi Mandali started by Jamuna Prasad and Siddhanath Pant at Dharwad to propagate Hindi among the masses as a unifying language brought many women into the freedom movement. The organisation called Tuntara Thanda (literally meaning 'band of mischief-makers') established by G.R. Swamy and others in Chamundipuram was also a nucleus of nationalistic activity.

The first demand for responsible government in Mysore was made in the journal *Satyavadi* in 1918. To project the demand further, the Mysore State Congress was formed and in May 1928, its first session was held in Mysore through the efforts of Venkatakrishnaiya and Hosakoppa Krishna Rao of Chikkamagalur. The Congress held its next session in Bangalore the following year.

The Ganesha idol events in Bangalore's Sultanpet in 1928 vitiated the communal atmosphere and generated anti-dewan feelings among the people. These protests, along with the anti-Simon Commission disturbances, created strong nationalist feelings in the minds of teenagers and youngsters of Mysore.

Meanwhile, the completion of the Irwin Nala/Canal turned out to be another focal point of mobilisation. The heavy betterment levies imposed on the peasants of Mandya on completion of this canal propelled Congress leader H.K. Veerana Gowda to espouse the cause of the peasants. Even here the Praja Mitra Mandali, originally conceived to protect the rights of the backward, was caught napping. Gowda led a huge agitation in 1930–31 and brought a large group of about 4,000 peasants from the Maddur-Mandya region, which bore the brunt of the canal's levies, to Bangalore for protests. He published *Chitragupta*, a popular daily that helped carry his message to his readers.

Thus, in keeping with the national mood, the patriotic spirit was fast catching up in Mysore as well.

Towards Conciliation

The Labour government returned to power in Britain in 1931, and a glimmer of hope ran through Indian hearts. Labour leaders had always been sympathetic to the Indian cause. The British government decided to hold a Round Table Conference in London to consider new constitutional reforms. All Indian politicians, Hindus, Muslims, Sikhs and Christians were summoned to London for the conference.

Almost 89 members attended the conference, out of which 58 were chosen from various communities and interests in British India, and the rest from princely states and other political parties. Prominent among the

Muslim delegates invited by the British government were Sir Aga Khan, Quaid-i-Azam, Maulana Muhammad Ali Jouhar, Sir Muhammad Shafi and Maulvi Fazl-i-Haq. Sir Tej Bahadur Sapru, Mr Jaikar and Dr Moonje were among the Hindu leaders. Sir Mirza Ismail attended this conference as the Representative of South Indian states and favoured a federation of Indian states and British Indian provinces.

The Muslim-Hindu differences cast their shadow over the conference as the Hindus pushed for a powerful central government while the Muslims stood for a loose federation of completely autonomous provinces. The Muslims demanded maintenance of weightage and separate electorates, the Hindus their abolition. The Muslims claimed statutory majority in Punjab and Bengal while Hindus resisted their imposition. In Punjab, the situation was complicated by inflated Sikh claims.

The conference broke up on 19 January 1931, and what emerged from it was a general agreement to write safeguards for minorities into the constitution and a vague desire to devise a federal system for the country.

The Gandhi-Irwin Pact that was signed following the First Conference made the parties agree that the Congress would give up its Civil Disobedience Movement and return to the negotiating table and the government would withdraw all ordinances issued to curb the Congress and release all persons undergoing sentences of imprisonment for their activities in the movement.

The second session of the conference opened in London on 7 September 1931. The main task of the conference was done through the two committees on federal structure and minorities. The communal problem represented the most difficult issue for the delegates. Gandhi again tabled the Congress scheme for a settlement, a mere reproduction of the Nehru Report, but all the minorities rejected it. As a counter to the Congress scheme, the Muslims, the depressed classes, the Indian Christians, the Anglo-Indians, and the Europeans presented a joint statement of claims which they said must stand as an interdependent whole. As their main demands were not acceptable to Gandhi, the communal issue was postponed for future discussion. Three important committees drafted their reports; the Franchise Committee, the Federal Finance Committee and the States Inquiry Committee.

On the concluding day, the British prime minister, Ramsay MacDonald, appealed to the Indian leaders to reach a communal settlement. Failing to do so, he said, would force the British government to take a unilateral decision. Mohammad Ali Jinnah of the Muslim League did not participate in this session of the Second Round Table Conference.

Attending the Round Table Conference Sessions gave Sir Mirza Ismail an opportunity to acquaint himself with the current political scenario of the country and also to voice Mysore's viewpoint, rather the viewpoint of all South India, which he represented there.

The Agitation Intensifies

Over 300 volunteers from Mysore participated in the Civil Disobedience Movement at Karwar and Dharwad districts as also in the Madras Presidency. Many spent time in jail. In a way, these events propelled the Responsible Government Movement in 1938, starting with the Shivapura Congress.

In 1938, the leaders of Mysore set up a Mysore State Congress after merging the existing Congress party in the state with the Praja Samyukta Paksha and agitated against the maharaja's government. It held its first session at Shivapura near Maddur presided over by T. Siddhalingaiya and attended by Congressmen of Mysore—S. Nijalingappa, Talakere Subrahmanya, K.C. Reddy, H.C. Dasappa, M.N. Jois, K.T. Bhashyam, K. Hanumanthaiya, Bellary Siddamma, Sahukar Chennaiya and so on.

The government had promulgated prohibitory orders against the hoisting of the tricolour at Shivapura. It deployed hundreds of armed policemen to enforce the order. But thousands of Congress workers and volunteers gathered at Shivapura and, in violation of the prohibitory orders, the flag was hoisted by T. Siddhalingaiya. Many Congress leaders were immediately arrested. But flag-hoisting continued every day for a month at Shivapura and the maharaja's government could do precious little about it.

Buoyed by the success of the agitation, the Congress decided to conduct a Flag Satyagraha in the whole state. Hundreds of Congress workers were arrested for hoisting flags at important centres. On 25 April 1938, at Vidurashwatha in Kolar District at a similar flag-hoisting ceremony, the police deployed by the government seemed to go berserk. It resorted to indiscriminate firing on a group of peaceful protesters who had gathered to merely hoist the flag at the centre. Ten innocent people, including pregnant women, were killed in the process. The event sent shock-waves across the state and people were alarmed by the barbaric behaviour of a hitherto benevolent government. This event was widely condemned by eminent national leaders such as Sardar Vallabhbhai Patel and J.B. Kriplani and came to be known as the Vidurashwatha tragedy. It only helped intensify the Congress agitation and its mass appeal. In the elections, the Mysore Congress won 101 and 16 seats in the Assembly and Council respectively, along with a thumping victory in local body elections.

In 1939 a satyagraha was organised, demanding responsible government in the state. Labourers of Bangalore, Bhadravathi and other industrial centres decided to organise themselves into unions affiliated to this new Congress entity. Their strength was tested for the first time in the Binny Mills strike in 1941, which carried on with great success for twenty-five days. The Mysore Government was forced to accept the workers' right to organise unions as a result. The Congress had also organised the peasant force and held peasants' conferences at *taluk* levels in 1939 and 1940 across the state of Mysore. Thousands of peasants participated in the 1939 Satyagraha of the Congress and over 1,700 of them courted arrest.

In 1940, the Government of Mysore introduced reforms based on the recommendations of the K.R. Srinivasa Iyengar Committee. But the Congress was not satisfied.

The intensity of these agitations at both the state and national levels indicated that soon the desires of the people would be consummated. The winds of change had begun to blow over the kingdom of a dynasty that had seen so many transformations in its 600-year history.

24

THE BEGINNING OF THE END

It was a time of chaos and pandemonium—a fire spread across the whole world; a moving cry of the injured and the wails of widows and orphans of the dead. It was the time of the First World War. But a great beam of joy and hope illuminated the inner recesses of the palace of Mysore from which was heard a cry—the shrill cry of a newborn boy. A ray of hope and satisfaction was to be seen, especially on the face of the child's heirless uncle, who could now rest assured of a successor to the throne of his ancestors. That ray of hope was Jayachamaraja, born on 18 July 1919 to the couple Yuvaraja Kanthirava Narasimharaja Wodeyar and Kempucheluvajammanni.

THE EARLY YEARS OF PRINCE JAYACHAMARAJA

Like all other members of his family, he too attended the Khas Bungalow or royal school for his studies. As a contemporary historian notes, he was not an aloof and stuck-up prince, but a Prince Charming, who treated his schoolmates as equals, and conducted himself like a commoner in the midst of commoners. He was at ease with himself, he set the professors at ease, and he rendered the students delighted. He was as modest, shy and quiet as the rest of them and as studious as the best of them.

My study of Mysore's history introduced me to a plethora of people and one such close family friend of ours, Mrs Lakshmi (who is fondly called 'Paapu') surprisingly had many secrets to reveal. The octogenarian was a classmate of the royal princes and princesses between 1932 and 1935. It was joy and a sense of a lost past that gripped her as she narrated to me numerous anecdotes of those three wonderful years she spent as a child, barely six, at the royal school. Her father, the late Sri Yoganarasimham, was a musician and composer par excellence. She was chosen to be the companion to the sisters of Prince Jayachamaraja Wodeyar, mainly the last one Jayachamundammanni. She recalled the first meetings with the royals when she was given a big banana and orange on the inaugural day and introduced to them.

The venue was the royal school—the Chamundi Vihara, where the prince and princesses studied with the children of the nobility. The schedule there, as recounted, was never a rigorously academic one. It was more to do with frolic and experiential learning, as also picking up skills, like embroidery, painting, etc. Both boys and girls had to wear a compulsory uniform of a coat and trousers. The older girls were allowed to wear saris. Sports and games predominated in the evenings. Paapu proudly narrated how she would manage to 'defeat' Prince Jayachamaraja Wodeyar in the 'running and catching' games—his weight a major disadvantage in such games!

Paapu narrated how the princesses admitted to feeling stifled by the aura of royalty around them and wished they could be more like ordinary children, doing things that befitted their age, which they were often forbidden due to the superficial garb of royalty and sophistication though their inner selves continued to be wild. They would ask Paapu to get salt, chilli powder and such ingredients stealthily from the kitchen, coax her to climb mango trees, pluck the sour ones before the gardener could chase them and add copious amounts of the stolen treasures for freshly-made pickles—a real treat!

But children at an impressionable age, when treated like royalty usually, develop certain airs. Paapu bitterly recalled being bullied, pinched and bruised by the princesses, who thought it was their royal right to do so. She complained to her father and refused to attend school any longer. When her father complained, Prince Jayachamaraja, a teenager of about fifteen-sixteen and a typical big brother, in a laudable step decided to discipline his erring siblings. He tried all means—persuasion, then coercion, to make the guilty apologise and seek forgiveness in public. It was an earnest effort to divest them of the false airs of superiority. The very motive behind the royal school would otherwise be defeated, since its purpose had been to allow the royal children to mingle with the 'commoners' children' and shed their superiority complex. Finally his efforts bore fruit in the form of a not-so-wholehearted apology in front of all the other students. It is this that helps ease Paapu's bitterness in these memories!

The prince's sister, Vijaya Devi writes about his early education thus:

> The humble prince was a studious student in school, bagging five gold medals for the command over economics and political science. My brother was always a good student. He went deeply into whatever he took up.

Prince Jayachamaraja was trained in this school for ten to twelve years; he passed the S.S.L.C. examination with distinction and joined college like any ordinary young man in 1938. He passed out of the Mysore University with a B.A. degree—the first in his family to get a degree! He excelled, winning five gold medals on graduation. Mr Elwin supervised his education in political science and public administration. Academic stalwarts like Prof Wadia, Prof Ralo, Dr Krishna, Dr Gopal, Prof Satyagirinathan, Prof Nagesh Rao and others took him under their tutelage. He distinguished himself by his robustness and modesty of deportment. He was the leader of the Cubs and fulfilled all the sanguine executions of the role of the Chief of Boy Scouts in his early teens.

Mr J. Turner superintended his education. Turner had predicted a bright future for the young prince as he witnessed his remarkable understanding of international affairs and knew that only knowledge could wipe out the evils of factious strife, communal jealousies and all the other evils plaguing society. He was very particular that he receive no preferential treatment vis-à-vis the other students. The prince was soon proficient in swimming, horse-riding, hunting, squash and tennis. On joining the Maharaja's College at Mysore, he developed an aptitude for history, economics and politics. Contemporary problems fascinated him and his attention rose from the mere study of parochial and national events to the evaluation of international current affairs and events.

On 15 May 1938, the prince was married to Smt Satyaprema Kumari Devi, the sister of Charakari Raj's kingdom's Maharajadhiraj Shifadar-ul-mulk Arimardan Singh Judheo Bahaddur. His second wife was Smt Tripurasundarammanni, whom he married on 30 April 1944. He had five daughters—Maharajakumaris Smt Gayatri Devi, Smt Meenakshi Devi, Smt Kamakshi Devi, Smt Indirakshi Devi and Smt Vishalakshi Devi and one son, Sri Srikantadatta Narasimharaja Wodeyar—the present scion of the Wodeyar dynasty. After the demise of Nalwadi Krishnaraja Wodeyar in 1940, Sri Jayachamarajendra Wodeyar was crowned the twenty-fifth and last ruler of Mysore on 8 September 1940.

In a proclamation issued to the people on the occasion of the coronation, he said:*

> My Beloved people, in succeeding to the throne of Mysore, I follow a great ruler who loved you all, and who won your love by his love of God, by his wisdom, his graciousness, his humility, his faithfulness to duty and his Kingly greatness. It is now for us to dedicate ourselves to the fulfilment of his great task. And we shall succeed in fulfilling it if we so consecrate ourselves in the spirit of unity and self-sacrifice that we can win through. In this spirit, I look upon this ceremony of ascending the throne of my ancestors as a dedication of myself, my life and all I have to the service of the people of Mysore. But I am fully conscious that no effort of mine can succeed alone. I need your help and your cooperation, your confidence and your love. May God grant me the light and strength in the discharge of the sacred duty entrusted to me and His blessings in abundance rest on every hearth and brighten every home in Mysore!

Sir Mirza Ismail did not wish to continue in the post he held after the death of his beloved friend and king. He retired in 1941 and Nyapati Madhava Rao became the dewan. He had been a member of the Council. He implemented the Srinivasa Iyengar Committee recommendations based on which the strength of the Representative Assembly was raised to 315 out of which 26 seats were reserved for Muslims, 26 for depressed classes, five for Indian Christians, one for Europeans, 28 for the special interest category, 11 for women and 10 for government nominees. The Legislative Council's strength was increased to 68, with four seats for Muslims, four for depressed classes, one for Indian Christians, one for Europeans, 10 under the special interests category and 24 nominees including 16 officers. The maharaja would nominate the president of the council for the first term and thereafter he would be nominated by the council's

---

* This and the next speech of the Maharaja's are reproduced in Josyer's 1929 book, *The History of Mysore and the Yadava Dynasty.*

non-official members. Three non-official members were to be chosen as ministers from among both the Houses. A vote of no-confidence against non-official councillors or ministers was not guaranteed. This, however, was no fulfilment of the strong demand for responsible government as the Council was not responsible to the elected Assembly.

Addressing a joint session of the two Houses, the maharaja announced:

> The reforms that are now to come into operation are thus a natural corollary to the honourable record established by these bodies and a recognition of the experience they have gained in Parliamentary methods of business. At the same time, I am sure that these reforms will be recognised as a generous response to the desire of important sections of the people for increased participation in the administration of the State. It will be useful to recount a few of the special features of the reforms, which are being inaugurated today: wider franchise in the case of both Houses; substantial increase in their strength; larger representation for special interests and minorities and for women; representation of minority communities by direct election; extension of the life of each House from three to four years; provision of a statutory elected majority of nearly 2/3rds; in the Legislative Council power to elect a non-official President and Deputy President for the body; increased power for the Representative Assembly in the matter of Legislation and control of state expenditure; and freedom of speech and immunity from arrest, under certain conditions, for members of both Houses. Above all I am sure you will appreciate the decision to give a place to the elected representatives of the people in my Executive Council with regular portfolios of administration. For my part I am convinced that a variety of experience on the part of my Ministers can only add weight and value to the advice that I receive from my Council. It is now for us all, working together with the welfare of our state as our united objective, to take steps to ensure that our future is worthy of our past.

The new maharaja spent the first two years of his reign touring the districts of his state, acquainting himself with the needs and problems of the people there. He announced a special grant of Rs 2 lakh for the development of the Malnad area, construction of a new general hospital and a regulated market at Davanagere and a water supply scheme for Chitradurga. The establishment of an Occupational Institute or Polytechnic and an Institute of Indian Medicine was taken up in Bangalore.

Government grants to education rose from Rs 54 lakh in 1940 to Rs 2 crore 75 lakh in 1948. The number of primary schools had risen from 6,400 to 9,800 and the number of pupils from 2,31,000 to 4,80,000. The number of middle schools by 1948 was 319 with 59,000 students while there were 46 high schools with 31,700 pupils. In addition, 4,500 adult literacy classes were started at a cost of Rs 5 lakh.

In 1942, the Benaras Hindu University conferred the honorary degree of Doctor of Laws on the maharaja. In 1945 the British Government conferred on him the title of G.C.S.I and in 1946, the G.C.B. or Grand Commander of the Order of Bath. Several conferences and meetings were organised across the state of Mysore during the king's short rule: the All India Economic and Political Science Conference in 1940, the Indian Historical Records' Commission and Indian Academy of Sciences in 1942, the 91st District Rotary International in 1942, the All India Olympic Games and the Indian Central Advisory Board of Education in 1946 and the All India Educational Conference in 1948. Big schemes could not be launched due to the volatile political conditions prevailing in the country in the 1940s, except for the launch of the Sharavathi Project to produce power and the Bhadra Project Plans.

A TUMULTOUS WORLD—THE SECOND WORLD WAR

The world had never known such intensity, turmoil and turbulence as in the 1940s. Both nationally and internationally, the situation was precarious. The world was bracing itself for yet another bloody conflict that was to take a huge toll of men and material. The humiliation mounted on Germany after the Treaty of Versailles in 1919 led to a simmering discontent in that nation, finding expression in the form of fascist leader Adolf Hitler, who made his way to the corridors of power in Germany with his Nazi party. He led Germany through a chain of events: rearmament, reoccupation of the Rhineland, incorporation of Austria, dismemberment and occupation of Czechoslovakia and finally the invasion of Poland. Hitler's counterpart in Italy, Benito Mussolini, helped brew the conflict. In Asia, Japan's efforts to become a world power and the rise of militarist leadership led to conflict first with China and later the United States. Japan also sought to secure additional natural resources, such as oil and iron ore, due in part to the lack of natural resources on Japan's own home islands.

The League of Nations that was formed after the First World War was powerless and mostly silent in the face of many major events leading to the Second World War, such as Hitler's re-militarisation of the Rhineland, annexation of Austria, and occupation of Czechoslovakia. The League commissioner in Danzig was unable to deal with German claims on the city. This was a significant contributing factor to the outbreak of the Second World War — a large-scale military conflict that took place between 1939 and 1945. It engulfed much of the globe and is accepted as the largest and deadliest war in human history.

The war was initially fought between Germany and the Allies — at first consisting of the United Kingdom, France and Poland. Germany was later joined by Italy, jointly known as the 'Axis Powers', and Japan. Some of the nations Germany conquered also sent military forces, particularly to the Eastern front, while others joined the Allies. The Soviet Union had signed a non-aggression treaty with Germany, but on 22 June 1941 Germany invaded the Soviet Union, pulling that country into the war as well.

On 7 December 1941 the USA entered the war on the Allies' side after first Japan and then Germany attacked and declared war on the US and Japan attacked the US naval base at Pearl Harbor. China, which had been engaged in war with Japan since the mid-1930s, also entered the Allies' camp. Thus it ended up as a war that entangled almost all the nations of the world in its web.

Initially, while the Axis powers seemed to be gaining the upper hand, a series of reverses they suffered, especially Germany, weakened their position. The Red Army (including 78,556 soldiers of the Polish Army) began its final assault on Berlin on 16 April 1945. By now, the German Army was in full retreat and Berlin had already been battered due to preliminary air bombings. Most of the Nazi leaders had either been killed or captured. Hitler, however, was still alive, and was said to be slowly getting desperate. As a final resistance effort, he called for civilians, including children, to fight the oncoming Red Army as part of the newly created *Volkssturm* militia. When this failed, Hitler became increasingly paranoid and delusional, believing that everyone was against him and that he still had battalions of troops to send into battle. Hitler and his staff moved into the Führerbunker, a concrete bunker beneath the Chancellery, where, on 30 April 1945, he committed suicide. Admiral Karl Dönitz became leader of the German government, but the German war effort quickly disintegrated. German forces in Italy surrendered on 2 May 1945; those in northern Germany, Denmark, and the Netherlands on 4 May; and the German High Command under Generaloberst Alfred Jodl surrendered unconditionally all remaining German forces on 7 May in Reims, France. The Western Allies celebrated V-E Day on 8 May and the Soviet Union celebrated Victory Day on 9 May.

EFFECTS OF THE WAR

But it was truly a Pyrrhic victory—humanity suffered and even the victors were actually losers in some way or the other. Germany and Hitler might have lost the war physically, but the world at large was torn apart by these bloody years of organised carnage. The fascists had converted Europe into a vast graveyard and a slave camp. Hitler, known for his unstinting hatred of the Jews, had had them mercilessly butchered in gas chambers that were opened all over Germany. They were fed to toxic gases or injected with poison to meet traumatic deaths. New destructive weapons like the atom bomb were used in this war. To avenge the attack on Peal Harbor, the US committed the greatest sin in human history—bombing the two Japanese cities of Hiroshima and Nagasaki with the deadly atom bomb, killing over 3,20,000 people. The effects of these bombs on the health of those who survived and the genetic effects on subsequent generations are still visible. The war ended in 1945 with the unconditional surrender of both Germany and Japan.

Approximately sixty-two million people died due to the war. This figure includes acts of genocide such as the Holocaust and General Ishii Shiro's Unit 731 experiments (conducting lethal tests on prisoners using bacillus bombs) in Pingfan, incredibly bloody battles in Europe, North Africa and the Pacific Ocean, and massive bombings of cities, including the atomic bombings of Hiroshima and Nagasaki in Japan, the firebombing of Dresden and Pforzheim in Germany as well as Tokyo and other Japanese cities, and the blitz on British cities such as Coventry and London. Few areas of the world were unaffected; the war involved the 'home front' and bombing of civilians to a greater degree than any previous conflict. Atomic weapons, jet aircraft, rockets and radar, the *blitzkrieg* (or 'lightning war'), the massive use of tanks, submarines, torpedo bombers and destroyer/tanker formations, are only a few of many wartime inventions and new tactics that changed the face of conflict. It was the first time that a number of newly developed technologies, including nuclear weapons, were used against either military or civilian targets. It is estimated to have cost about 1 trillion US dollars in 1945, not including subsequent reconstruction. The vast outcomes of the war, including new technology and changes to the world's geopolitical, cultural and economic arrangement, were unprecedented in human history.

While it might have won the War, Britain's position as a colonial power was severely weakened and her financial position severely impoverished. The myth of the sun never setting for the mighty British Empire seemed to have shattered. The peoples' movements in different parts of her colonies started gaining momentum. India could not be far behind.

INDIA AFTER THE SECOND WORLD WAR

Gandhiji's call to 'Quit India', and 'Do or Die' in 1942 pushed the last phase of the Indian freedom struggle following the failure of the talks between him and Sir Stafford Cripps, the Cabinet minister deputed by the British Parliament. The Cripps Mission, with its vague proposals of post-war Dominion Status for India, a constitution-making body elected by provincial legislatures and the native states, a provincial opt-out clause, the immediate participation of Indian leaders in the war effort but the retention of control over Indian defence by the British, satisfied none and threatened to fragment the Indian subcontinent.

The second phase of the movement started around the middle of August. Militant students fanned out from various centres, destroying communications and leading peasant rebellion in northern and western Bihar, eastern UP, Midnapore in Bengal, and pockets of Maharashtra, Mysore and Orissa. A number of short-lived local national governments were also set up.

The third phase of the movements began around the end of September and was characterised by terrorist activities, sabotage and guerrilla warfare by educated youths and peasant squads. Parallel national governments functioned at Tamluk in Midnapore, Satara in Maharashtra, and Talcher in Orissa. All the three phases of the movement were crushed by brutal atrocities including the use of machine-guns from the air.

QUIT INDIA AND ITS IMPACT ON MYSORE

'Quit India' sparked off a series of mass protests in Mysore, as it did all over the country. The workers in Bangalore, Bhadravathi and Kolar gold fields called for a strike in protest against the imprisonment of national leaders. Students did not attend school and college; railway stations were burnt, post offices sacked, the Bangalore-Guntakal railway line was damaged, disrupting traffic for over two weeks. Leaders, like Sardar K.A. Venkataramaiya, A.G. Ramachandra Rao, N.D. Shankar, M.V. Krishnappa, Maganlal Shah, Kotre Nanjappa, H.S. Doreswamy and others, directed underground activities in Mysore as all the senior leaders had been arrested in the initial stages of the movement itself. The agitation continued with enhanced intensity for a whole year. Twenty-five railway stations were burnt or damaged across the state. Post offices in Bangalore and Nippani were among the many to be destroyed. At Nippani, a punitive fine of over Rs 2 lakh was levied for having burnt many government offices, including the sub-registrar's office.

Bangalore became the epicentre of the political agitations. The police began lathicharging and firing on the mobs that had gathered there in 1942 even as news trickled in of the death of Gandhiji's trusted confidante, Mahadevbhai Desai, in jail. In Bangalore the police fired on an unruly mob in the Mysore Bank Circle killing 11 and injuring over 450. Law and order seemed to be spinning out of control. Five persons were killed at Davangere and seven at Bailahongal as a result of police firing. Seven persons from Nippani *taluk* died at Gargoti, Kolhapur State, while trying to loot the state treasury. A school boy was killed at Nippani when police opened fire on processions. In Hassan district, picketing of shandys or weekly fairs was organised and people implored not to pay the shandy toll to the government. There was police firing at Sravanabelagola on a shiny day, 6 October 1942. The police, unable to control the large peasant gathering, resorted to firing and killed seven people.

In a village called Isur in Shikaripura *taluk* of Shimoga district, villagers hoisted the tricolour on the Veerbhadraswamy temple, burnt village records and humiliated the Shanbhogue and Patel of the village. When the *tehsildar* (police inspector) and his men visited the village, he was killed by the village freedom fighters for walking over Gandhiji's photograph and for firing a shot at young boys who had requested him to wear a *khadi* cap to express solidarity with the freedom struggle. Five people were later hanged in March 1943 in this context. The police began firing; a number of arrests followed and the fighters were lodged at the Bangalore Central Jail. Many were executed or tortured in captivity. At least 15,000 people were jailed all over Karnataka in 1942–43 at the height of the Quit India agitation and of these more than 10,000 came from princely Mysore. Jails were full and barracks were erected to house political prisoners. Many died in jails due to lack of hygiene and the spread of dangerous epidemics.

Perceiving this as an isolated law-and-order problem, and also on British urging, the dewan followed a ruthless repression policy. Firings took place all over the state, leaving hundreds of thousands of people dead or wounded, and 2,500 arrests in the state. The infantry and cavalry were perpetually on the scene in Bangalore. Four villages in the state paid heavy collective fines and a total amount of Rs 2,000 was levied on them. Railway stations at Davanagere, Tiptur, Mayakonda, Banavar, Banasandra, Kodaganur, Holalakere, Chikkajajur and Hosadurga were attacked. Thirteen railway lines were derailed and eight removed. In about twenty-five major incidents, culverts and bridges were either destroyed or partially damaged. About thirty-five incidents of cutting of telegraph wires were reported. The Bangalore Head Post Office and three other branch post offices of the city were badly damaged. Letters were burnt in the Head Post Offices of Siddhapura, Sirsi and other *taluks*. Eleven toddy and *ganja* shops were damaged. There was toddy-shop picketing at four places in Mysore state. About fifty toddy trees were cut down near Hassan. At Hebbal, Rs 3,000 worth of government revenue was looted. The agitation came to an end when leaders, like Dr Diwakar, who were spearheading the underground activities, were instructed by Gandhiji to call off the agitation.

In the 1945 elections, the Congress members won with a thumping majority in both houses. In the Representative Assembly, K. Hanumanthaiya became the party leader while K.C. Reddy was the one in the council. Meanwhile in 1946, Nyapati Madhava Rao resigned and became a member of the Constituent Assembly and Drafting Committee. Sir Arcot Ramaswamy Mudaliar succeeded him as the last dewan of Mysore.

The national situation had gone completely out of control for the already tottering British government, fresh from a war that had drained its resources completely. It finally decided to form a Cabinet Mission that would discuss the transfer of power.

THE FINAL MARCH TO FREEDOM AND THE BIRTH OF TWO NATIONS

When the Cabinet Mission arrived in Delhi in March, it had three members—Stafford Cripps, A.V. Alexander and Lord Pethick-Lawrence. They would work in close conjunction with the viceroy to try to get the leaders of the principal Indian political parties to agree on two matters: the method of framing a constitution for a self-governing, independent India and the setting up of a new Executive Council or interim government that would hold office while the constitution was being hammered out.

After marathon meetings and teething problems with Jinnah's Muslim League, which wanted a separate Muslim state, the mission went about the formation of a new executive council or interim government. The viceroy announced that discussion with the parties would not be prolonged any further and that he was issuing invitations to fourteen pre-determined names to serve as members of an interim government—six were Hindu members of Congress including one member of the Scheduled Castes, five were members of the Muslim League, and the remaining three a Sikh, a Parsee and an Indian Christian. But Gandhiji's objection to the non-inclusion of a Congress Muslim member to the government saying it was detrimental to the secular interests of that party delayed the process.

Wavell wrote identical letters to Nehru and Jinnah on 22 July 1946 asking them whether the Congress and the Muslim League would be prepared to enter an interim government on the basis that six members (including one Scheduled Caste representative) would be nominated by the Congress and five by the Muslim League. The viceroy would nominate three representatives of the minorities. Jinnah replied that the proposal was not acceptable to the Muslim League because it destroyed the principal of parity.

The negotiations with the League reached a deadlock and the viceroy decided to form an interim government with the Congress alone, leaving the door open for the League to come in later. A communiqué was issued on 24 August, which announced that the existing members of the Governor General's Executive Council had resigned and that new persons had been appointed in their place. It was stated that the interim government would be installed on 2 September.

Jinnah declared two days later that the viceroy had struck a severe blow to Indian Muslims and had added insult to injury by nominating three Muslims who did not command the confidence of Indian Muslims. He reiterated that the only solution to the Indian problem was the division of India into Pakistan and Hindustan. The formation of an interim government consisting only of the Congress nominees added further fuel to the communal fire. The Muslims regarded the formation of the interim government as an unconditional surrender of power to the Hindus, and feared that the viceroy would be unable to prevent the Hindus from using their newly acquired power to suppress Muslims all over India.

After the Congress had taken the reins at the Centre on 2 September, Jinnah faced a desperate situation. The armed forces were predominantly Hindu and Sikh and the Indian members of the other services were also predominantly Hindu. The British were preparing to concede independence to India. If they withdrew, the Congress was to be in undisputed control, and was also to be free to deal with the Muslims as it wished.

Jinnah realised that the Congress would not give up the right to nominate a nationalist Muslim and that he would have to accept the position if he did not wish to leave the interim government solely in the hands of the Congress. On 13 October, he wrote to Wavell that though the Muslim League did not agree with much that had happened, 'in the interests of the Muslims and other communities it will be fatal to leave the entire field of administration of the Central Government in the hands of the Congress.'* The League had therefore decided to nominate five members for the interim government. On 15 October, he gave the viceroy the following five names: Liaquat Ali Khan, I.I. Chundrigar, Abdur Rab Nishtar, Ghazanfar Ali Khan and Jogindar Nath Mandal. The last name was a Scheduled Caste Hindu and was obviously a tit-for-tat for the Congress insistence on including a nationalist Muslim in its own quota.

The British government sent the Cabinet Mission to India in March 1946 to negotiate with Indian leaders and agree to the terms of the transfer of power. After difficult negotiations, a federal solution was proposed. Despite initial agreement, both the British and the Congress eventually rejected the plan.

However, as leader of the Muslim League, Jinnah accepted the Cabinet Mission's proposal. However, when Nehru announced at his first press

---

* Taken from Margaret Bourke White's 1949 book, *Halfway to Freedom*.

conference as the re-elected president of Congress that 'no constituent assembly could be bound by any prearranged constitutional formula', Jinnah took this to be a repudiation of the plan, which was necessarily a case of all or nothing. The Muslim League Working Committee withdrew its consent and called upon the Muslim nation to launch direct action in mid-August 1946. A frenzy of rioting between Hindus and Muslims ensued. As Jinnah thundered to his supporters about his attitude towards India and the Congress: 'If you want peace, we do not want war. If you want war we accept your offer unhesitatingly. We will either have a divided India or a destroyed India.'*

By the end of 1946 communal violence had escalated and the British began to fear that India would descend into civil war. The British government's representative, Lord Wavell, put forward a breakdown plan as a safeguard in the event of a political deadlock.

Lord Mountbatten replaced Lord Wavell as viceroy of India in 1947. Mountbatten's first proposed solution for the Indian subcontinent, known as the May Plan, was rejected by Congress leader Jawaharlal Nehru on the grounds that it would cause the balkanisation of India. The following month the May Plan was substituted for the June Plan, in which provinces would have to choose between India and Pakistan. Bengal and Punjab both voted for partition. By accepting the Mountbatten Plan/Partition, the Congress was only accepting what had become inevitable because of the long-term failure of the Congress to draw the Muslim masses into the national movement and stem the surge of Muslim communalism which, especially since 1937, had been gathering momentum and fury.

The Congress leaders felt by June 1947 that only an immediate transfer of power could forestall the spread of Direct Action Day and other communal disturbances. Sardar Patel rightly said: 'A united India even if it was smaller in size was better than a disorganised and troubled and weak bigger India.'

Difficulties created by the obstructionist policies and tactics of the League proved to the Congress that the League's leaders were only concerned about their own interests and that the future of India would not be safe with them in the government—they would act as a stumbling

---

* Jinnah's quote taken from Ayesha Jalal's 1994 book, *The Sole Spokesman*.

block in the path of India's progress. The Congress leaders also felt that continued British rule never was and never could be in the best interest of Indians. The sooner they left India, the better it would be.

In July 1947, Britain's Parliament passed the Indian Independence Act, which set a deadline of midnight of 14–15 August 1947 for 'demarcation of the dominions of India'. As a result, at least 10 million Hindus, Muslims and Sikhs fled their homes to seek sanctuary on whichever side of the line was favourable to them. The ensuing communal massacres left at least one million dead, with Sikhs—caught in the middle—facing the brunt of the suffering.

Margaret Bourke White in her eyewitness account of the gory events of 1946–47 vividly portrayed in her book *Halfway to Freedom* says:

> With the coming of Independence to India, the world had the chance to watch the most rare event in the history of nations; the birth of twins. It was a birth accompanied by strife and suffering... the roads connecting the Union of India with Pakistan looked as our Pulaski Skyway or Sunset Boulevard looks during the rush hour. But instead of the two-way stream of motorcars there were endless convoys of bullock carts, women on donkey back, and men on foot carrying on their shoulders the very young or the very old. Babies were born along the way. People died along the way. Some died of cholera, some from the attacks of hostile religious communities. But many of them simply dropped out of line from sheer weariness and sat by the roadside to wait patiently for death. The name 'Pakistan' means Land of the Pure: many of the pure never got there. The way to the Promised Land was lined with graves ... the division of India into two separate nations based on religious differences blew fanaticism to such an extent that great caravans of desperate, terror stricken refugees began to crawl along the inadequate roads, millions of them, Hindus and Sikhs to India, Muslims to Pakistan.

Finally, amidst strife and blood, the severe backlash of communal riots that raged all over the country, India and Pakistan emerged as two independent nations on 15 and 14 August 1947 respectively. It was a momentous occasion for India. Centuries of subjugation had come to an end and she was now free to manage her affairs in the way she wanted. Summing up the mood of the nation aptly on this occasion,

Pandit Jawaharlal Nehru, the new prime minister of independent India made the famous 'tryst with destiny' speech:

> Long years ago we made a tryst with destiny, and now the time comes when we shall redeem our pledge, not wholly or in full measure, but very substantially. At the stroke of the midnight hour, when the world sleeps, India will awake to life and freedom. A moment comes, which comes but rarely in history, when we step out from the old to the new, when an age ends, and when the soul of a nation, long suppressed, finds utterance. It is fitting that at this solemn moment we take the pledge of dedication to the service of India and her people and to the still larger cause of humanity.

CREATION OF A NEW INDIA—MERGER OF THE PRINCELY STATES

Attaining freedom was no doubt an achievement in itself. But what haunted the new rulers was a more daunting challenge—integration of pre-Independence British India with its numerous kingdoms that were hitherto British puppets. Deputy Prime Minister and Home Minister Sardar Patel took it upon himself to integrate the warring kingdoms into a composite nation. During the transition period before Independence, assisted by civil servant V.P. Menon, Patel worked towards the integration of the numerous Indian states into the Indian Union. Patel and Menon persuaded the princes of 565 states of the impossibility of independence from the Indian republic, especially in the presence of growing opposition from their subjects. He also proposed favourable terms for the merger, including creation of privy purses for the descendants of the rulers. While encouraging the rulers to act with patriotism, Patel did not rule out force, setting a deadline of 15 August 1947 for them to sign the instrument of accession. All but three of the states willingly merged into the Indian union leading to the popular perception that Patel liquidated the princely states without liquidating the princes. Only Jammu and Kashmir, Junagadh, and Hyderabad did not fall into his basket.

Junagadh was especially important to Patel, since it was in his home state of Gujarat. The Nawab had, under pressure from Sir Shah Nawaz Bhutto, acceded to Pakistan. It was, however, quite far from Pakistan and eighty percent of its population was Hindu. Patel combined diplomacy with force, demanding that Pakistan annul the accession, and that the Nawab accede to India. To show his resolve, he sent the army to occupy three principalities of Junagadh. Following wide-spread protests and the formation of a civil government, or Arzi Hukumat, both Bhutto and the Nawab fled to Karachi, and under Patel's orders, the Indian Army and police units marched into the state. A plebiscite later organised produced a 99.5 percent vote for merger with India.

Hyderabad was the largest of the princely states, and included parts of present-day Andhra Pradesh, Karnataka and Maharashtra. Its Muslim ruler, the Nizam, presided over a kingdom with over 80 percent Hindu subjects. The Nizam sought independence or accession to Pakistan. Militant Muslims called the Razakars, under Qasim Razvi, pressed the Nizam to hold out against India, while organising attacks with militant Communists on the Indians. Even though a Standstill Agreement was signed due to the desperate efforts of Lord Mountbatten to avoid a war, the Nizam constantly rejected deals and changed positions. Finally, in September 1948, Patel reconciled Nehru and the Governor General, Chakravarti Rajagopalachari, and sent in the Indian Army to integrate Hyderabad. After Operation Polo commenced, thousands of Razakar militants were killed and Hyderabad was comfortably secured into the Indian Union.

MYSORE AT THE TIME OF INDEPENDENCE

On his part, the dewan of Mysore, Arcot Ramaswamy Mudaliar, announced that seven Mysorean representatives would participate in the Constituent Assembly of India as Mysore, unlike Hyderabad, had readily decided to merge with the Indian Union. Of the seven, the Assembly and Council would elect two each, and three would be nominated by the government. On 5 July the Assembly members staged a walkout in protest. As a preliminary to the end of the British rule the Civil and Military Station area was retroceded to the maharaja and on 26 July 1947 the Residency was wound up.

The maharaja signed the Instrument of Accession to the Indian Union on 9 August 1947, but never in reality considered establishing a responsible government. All along, he was completely misguided by his council, headed by the Dewan Arcot Mudaliar, who assured him that this was a mere storm in a tea cup and would pass. They tried to make light of the brewing clamour for self-governance that was manifesting itself in widespread public outbursts.

The Mysore Congress continued to demand a responsible government in the state. It launched a campaign called 'Mysore Chalo' from 1 September 1947. A Satyagraha called 'Aramane Satyagraha' or Palace Satyagraha was launched on 14 September. Congress volunteers toured the entire state to enlist people's support in the agitation. Rallies were taken out in Mysore. But the government remained indifferent, giving strict orders to the Press not to publish news about the agitation or incite people. Yet the rebels, armed with slogans like 'Arcot Boycott', 'Thambu Chetty Chatta Katti' (Death to Thambu Chetty) and 'Mysore Chalo', trooped into the palace. En route, at Bangalore's Banappa Park, K.C. Reddy declared the Congress manifesto, which aimed at setting up a responsible government in the state, forming an interim government till assembly elections took place, and releasing all political prisoners.

There was unprecedented popular support for this movement. The volunteers were openly welcomed and fed by common people en route to Mysore. The government followed a policy of suppression of the planned 4 September march to Mysore. Many leaders were even arrested the previous day. But what the government did not anticipate was the large-scale participation of students, workers, officials and women all over the state. They organised mass demonstrations and protest rallies. Labourers went on strike in all industrial centres, like Bangalore, Mysore, Davanagere, Bhadravathi and Kolar gold fields. The Press lent its full support to them. As jails could not accommodate all these protesters, they were severely beaten and taken away to remote places. To paralyse the administration, government offices were picketed by thousands of agitators—men and women alike. At places like Hosadurga, Tumkur, Tirthahalli, Challakere and Sidlaghatta, the mob surrounding the taluk office had to face police bullets in which many lost their lives—the toll being six at Hosadurga itself and seven on Bangalore's Sepping Road. Over twenty people, including a school boy, were killed in police firing in the city of Mysore.

Camps were organised across the border in neighbouring Bombay and Madras states in many centres and volunteers from the camps raided the state of Mysore and organised sabotages to cripple the administration. A journal called *Pauravani* was being printed from Hindupur in Anantapur district of Andhra Pradesh and circulated in Mysore. The government had absolutely no control over the hundreds of villages along the borders that had got liberated. These acted as buffers to assist the main stock of agitators of the state. The fear of police wielding *lathis* and firing guns at them seemed to have disappeared.

The government could not prevent the mobs from marching to the city of Mysore. As an immediate measure the maharaja declared curfew in the city. However, post offices, railway stations and public buildings were burnt, telephone and telegraph lines were cut off. Finally, the maharaja consented. An understanding was reached between the dewan and the president of the Mysore Congress as per which:[*]

> The present Ministry shall be dissolved and a fresh ministry constituted. The Mysore Congress will make recommendations for the Ministry after consultation with such other parties as may be deemed appropriate regarding non-Congress ministers. The Ministry shall consist of not less than nine members, and not less than three members chosen from parties outside the Congress. The Ministry shall remain in office so long as it enjoys the confidence of the Legislature. The Ministry shall function as a Cabinet with the Dewan, who will continue in office, and act on the basis of joint responsibility in all matters. The decisions of the Cabinet will be arrived at by a majority vote. One of the Ministers chosen from the Congress will be appointed the Chief Minister. The new Ministers shall immediately set up a Constituent Assembly composed of elected representatives of the people, for framing a Constitution Bill for the State based on full responsible Government under the aegis of His Highness. The new Constitution shall come into force on or before 1st July 1948.

In a proclamation dated 24 September 1947, the maharaja announced:

> It is my earnest desire that my people, conscious of the great opportunity that has been afforded to them, will work harmoniously, and I am confident that my Council of Ministers will discharge their duties fairly and justly for the peace, progress and prosperity of the State and its people.

---

[*] The text of this understanding, the Maharaja's proclamation and Patel's response are taken from Josyer's 1929 book, *The History of Mysore and the Yadava Dynasty*.

In a telegram to the maharaja, Sardar Patel conveyed his thanks as follows:

> Please accept warm congratulations on the display of wisdom and statesmanship befitting the dignity and responsibility of a Ruler in gracefully recognizing the strength of popular will. I have no doubt this generous action will meet with full and appropriate loyalty and cooperation and will raise the prestige and prosperity of the Mysore State.

By 7 October 1947, all arrested leaders were released. On 11 October the KPCC President K.C. Reddy met Dewan Mudaliar, resulting in the formal acceptance of the Maharaja's government to grant a responsible government to Mysoreans.

K.C. Reddy became the first chief minister of the independent state of Mysore on 27 October 1947 with a team of nine—six Congressmen and three others. Josyer records Reddy's inaugural words at the new Assembly:

> Mysore's progress has been steady and has been a model to others. It is unnecessary for me to narrate the course of Mysore's political history. The first Representative Assembly was constituted so far back as 1881, and the Legislative Council in 1907. There were instalments of reforms in 1924 and then again in 1941. in the last one decade, however, the people of Mysore urged for quick progress and I may say, paid the price for the same. It may not be appropriate to lift the veil over the past, and apportion either blame or praise. It is enough to record that there has been a happy ending for which every one deserves congratulations and over which there is general joy. The decision to evolve a new Constitution for Mysore on the basis of Responsible Government was magnanimously taken by His Highness the Maharaja last year and it is in pursuance of that we are meeting here today.

The constitution-making process of the Mysore government was however halted by the Central Government, which decided to implement a federal system of bicameral legislature on India and its Union of States. The central Constituent Assembly was framing the world's longest Constitution for this purpose. These deliberations ended on 26 November 1949 and were enforceable all over India. With it ended the jurisdiction of the State

Constituent Assembly and also the lives of the existing Representative Assembly and Legislative Council. A single body, the Mysore Legislative Assembly, was to be brought into being with newly elected members, a new Cabinet and a single party leader as Chief Minister.

Accordingly, the old Assembly and Council were dissolved on 15 December 1949. On 26 January 1950, the new Indian Constitution came into force. It guaranteed to all Indian citizens Justice, Liberty, Equality, and Fraternity. India became a Sovereign Socialist Republic and a federal power shared between the Central and State Governments.

The maharaja was appointed as the 'Rajapramukh' of the state of Mysore. On 5 February 1950, the chief minister tendered the resignation of the entire ministry announced earlier and on the same day, as leader of the Congress Assembly Party, K.C. Reddy submitted the names of the new ministry, consisting of himself and five of his old colleagues, dropping the three non-Congressmen and taking in T. Siddhalingaiya, the president of the State Congress. The new ministers were R. Chennigaramaiya, H. Siddaiya, H.C. Dasappa, K.T. Bhashyam Iyengar and T. Mariappa. Preceding this were agitations on the presence of the dewan and the very existence of that post, which Congressmen saw as symbol of the ruthless suppression they suffered during the satyagraha years. In August 1949, the post of dewan was finally abolished. Jayachamaraja Wodeyar later became the governor of Mysore state.

MYSORE IN 1947: AN ECONOMIC SNAPSHOT

The earlier chapters have extensively documented Mysore's material progress in the twentieth century. Taking stock of the geographic and economic conditions of the state at the time of transition of power, a contemporary historian quoted by Josyer notes:

> It has an area of 29,458 square miles, equal in size to Scotland, and two and half times Belgium. It has a population of over 75 Lakhs. It has 2,665 major and 20,368 minor tanks, and 2,135 miles of channels, 11,30,000 acres of land under irrigation and 61,34,000 acres under cultivation. It has 49 Lakhs of cattle, 269 centers of cottage industries, 433 large industrial establishments and 10 cotton mills. It has 81,200 acres under mulberry and produces 3 lakh pounds of filature silk worth Rs 1 ¼ crores. Its gold mines produce

about 1,68,000 ounces of silver. It produces 17,500 tons of sugar, 2,500 tons of pig iron, 23,300 tons of steel, 1,23,700 tons of cement, 2,600 tons of paper, 5,000 tons of soaps, 2,900 tons of fertilizers, 3,700 tons of sulphuric acid, 500 units of electric transformers and 3,200 gallons of varnishes. It generates 3,036 lakhs of units of electric power supplying electricity to 225 cities and towns and to 822 irrigation pumps. It has 2,026 Cooperative Societies and 248 Joint Stock Companies. It has 409 Medical institutions and 9,372 educational institutions with 21 Colleges, 90 High schools, 524 Middle schools and 8,572 Primary Schools. It has 757 miles of Railways and 5,748 miles of Roads. It has a Broadcasting Station of its own and 4,700 receiving sets.

Mysore has the highest waterfall and the tallest statue in the world, taller than those of Rameses in Egypt. The Mysore Representative Assembly was the most ancient democratic House in all India. Mysore was the first Indian State to establish a University. It was the first to establish a hydro-electric station in India. Its gold mines produce the entire output of gold in India. The sandalwood of Mysore is the best anywhere and supplies the world market. Its Iron and Steel Works are the second largest in the Commonwealth and contain the only charcoal blast furnace in the East. The first spun-silk mill in India was established in Mysore and its output of raw silk is the highest in India. Its sugar factory is the biggest single-unit sugar manufactory in India. The electric tunnel kiln in its porcelain factory is the biggest in the East. Its aircraft factory is also the first of its kind in India. The flood-lit garden at Brindavan has no rival in the East and is compared to the Versailles of the French Emperors. And as the new Chief Minister recently testified—it is a matter of great joy, it is a matter of gratification that today, whether it be in Jodhpur, whether it be in Jaipur, whether it be in Kashmir, whether it be in any other major State, the agencies that they are bringing into existence, the set up that they are deciding upon, are on the lines indicated by Mysore.

Cottage industry thrived in Mysore at the time of Independence. Iron smelting, steel and metal work, gold lace bangles, brass casting, copper work, musical steel work, bidriware, nakki weaving, lac turnery, sandalwood carving, musical instruments, scents, *agarbattis*, carpentry, mat weaving were the major occupations. Sericulture was given great impetus in Nanjangud, Chamarajanagar, Chennapatna, Devanahalli, Kankanahalli, Kunigal, Magadi and Kolar. Modern industries were set up following the effects of the Industrial Revolution in England.

In 1913–14 there were 72 factories in Mysore exclusive of mines employing 4,451 people and earning profits of Rs 1.6 crore. The 15 gold mining industries employed 24,300 men and 5 lakh ounces of gold worth Rs 19 lakh were annually extracted.

Between 1939 and 1945, the Hindustan Aircraft Limited and Indian Telephone Industries (ITI), radio and electrical goods manufacturing companies, Kirloskar Ltd, chemicals and fertilisers companies sprang up. The joint stock companies increased from 117 with a capital of Rs 8 crore in 1921 to 315 with Rs 20 crore by 1947.

By 1939, railway lines extended 1,400 miles, nearly double what they had been before. In the 1930s, a large network of roads was laid all over the state. There was an average of 36 miles of road-length for every 100 square miles in Mysore state. The number of motor cars, lorries and buses rose from 2,972, 384 and 572 respectively in 1936 to 4,478, 1,175 and 794 respectively in 1947.

Pepper, betel nut, coconut and rice were exported through Honnavar, Ankola and Kundapara. Salt, sulphur, tin, lead, zinc, copper, European steel, paints, glue, nutmeg, cloves, camphor, raw silk, dates and almonds were imported, while betelnut, sandalwood, pepper, cardamom, tamarind grain, hides and horns were exported. The value of imports increased from about Rs 175 lakh in 1880–81 to Rs 281 lakh in 1890–91 and Rs 673 lakh in 1913–14, while exports went from 92 lakhs to 253 lakhs and then to 547 lakhs in the same period. By 1947, the major exports were the products of the iron and steel works, sugar factory, the textile mills and cigarette factory while the imports were coal and coke, brass, copper, tin, mineral oils, petrol, chemicals, manure, paper, matches, drugs, cycles, motorcars and leather goods. *Santhes* and *Jathres* or trade fairs formed a part of the internal trade.

Between 1871–91 the rise in population was about 14.72 per cent and the proportion of urban to total population was only 9.7 per cent. There were 27 towns with a population of over 5,000. Bangalore and Mysore grew into large cities with populations of 88,651 and 71,306 respectively. The Mysore government also favoured the Khadi cottage industry. The first khadi centre was set up in Badanaval with the help of the All India Spinners' Association and it rose to 23 centres in 1947, with the number of spinners increasing from 1,052 in 1927 to 9,560 in 1947.

That Mysore was hailed at the time of Independence as India's model state—self-sufficient and progressive in all respects—has been stated before. Diplomats, visiting dignitaries, rulers of other kingdoms, statesmen and national leaders lavished praise on this well-administered and progressive State. The most glorious encomiums came from none other than Chakravarthy Rajagopalachari, the first Indian governor general, in his visit to the state in 1948.

No wonder then that with such sound macroeconomic foundations and a large pool of educated, English-speaking masses, Karnataka, (particularly Bangalore) became the first choice of the information technology and business process outsourcing industry, leading to the emergence of Bangalore as the veritable knowledge hub and IT capital of India.

IN PASSING: AN UNFINISHED AGENDA—THE FORMATION OF KARNATAKA[*]

The attainment of freedom however did not consummate the aspirations of the people in toto. It was a long-cherished dream that all the Kannada-speaking areas be unified under one big state to be named 'Akhanda Karnataka'.

Historically, the concept of Kannada nationalism and statehood was unknown. This could largely be attributed to political and geographical reasons, arising out of a fragmented territory. In different time-spans of its political history, the region was ruled by various dynasties of southern India—the Satavahanas, Kadambas, Gangas, Chalukyas of Badami, Rashtrakutas, Hoysalas, Yadavas, Vijayanagara and Bahamani Empires, Wodeyars of Mysore and so on. Except during the reign of the Satavahanas, Rashtrakutas, Rayas of Vijayanagara and Haidar Ali and Tipu Sultan of Mysore, most parts of present day Karnataka never came under a single direct rule. The fall of Tipu Sultan in 1799 led to the restoration of the

---

[*] The history of the Wodeyars ends with 1950. This section goes on to prepare the context for present-day Karnataka.

Wodeyar dynasty. But it came at a heavy price. Erstwhile Mysore was partitioned among the victorious parties—the Nizam of Hyderabad, the Peshwas and the British. What remained was handed over as the princely state of Mysore to the Wodeyars. The terms 'Hyderabad Karnataka' and 'Bombay Karnataka' that are used so frequently even today, testifies to this historical tragedy of partition.

But partition on political grounds was not the only dividing factor. The feeling of separatism and unique identity looms large among the Tulu, Kodava and Konkani groups of the state. They have their own indigenous culture, a language distinct from Kannada, customs and traditions that set them apart. Coorg for example, had a long-standing agitation against the hegemony of Haidar and Tipu's Mysore. The stories of Coorgi valour and their resistance against being politically and culturally subsumed are part of folklore.

Despite all these political and cultural differences, the undercurrents of 'One language–one province' continued to subtly spur people into action. The early years of the twentieth century saw a number of books and publications that sought to inspire Kannadigas across the provinces about the glory and heritage of their culture.

As early as 1903, people had begun envisaging this new state. Benegal Rama Rao delivered a speech in Dharwad in 1903 urging the unification of the people into a new state and so did Justice Setlur of Bangalore in 1906. Driven by the patriotic fervour that the partition of Bengal had created, Alur Venkata Rao wrote in his *Vagbhushana* magazine in 1907 propounding the creation of a Karnataka state on the model of Bengal. He also organised an All Karnataka Writers Conference at Dharwad and made a concrete demand for a unified province for all Kannada-speaking people.

The Karnataka Sahitya Parishad established by the maharaja in 1915 at Bangalore and the Karnataka Sabha at Dharwad in 1916 furthered this cause. It also led to mass movements to encourage Kannada language and literature. In 1920, the Karnataka Sabha organised the Akhila Karnataka State Political Conference at Dharwad, presided over by Dewan V.P. Madhava Rao. The conference unanimously passed a resolution demanding the unification of all Kannada-speaking territories. The demand was put forth at the Nagpur Congress Session that conceded to grant Karnataka a separate Provincial Congress Committee that covered Kannada-speaking areas including the Mysore state, Bombay, Madras and Hyderabad Karnataka regions.

In 1924, the Belgaum Session of the Congress was presided over by Gandhiji at a venue named Vijayanagara—a subtle reminder of the glorious unified past. Veene Sheshanna gave a scintillating veena recital at the Congress and Huligol Narayana Rao sang his famous *Udayavagali Namma Cheluva Kannada Nadu* poem for the first time here. The first Karnataka Unification Conference was held after this session at Belgaum presided over by Sir Siddappa Kambali. But the inaction on the part of the new Indian government in 1947 disappointed the group. It strongly resented the postponement of the creation of linguistic provinces by the Central Government. The Conference at Kasargod decided to send a delegation headed by S. Nijalingappa to impress upon the central leadership the urgent need to satisfy the peoples' long-standing demands. The government appointed the Dhar Commission to study the formation of states on linguistic lines; but the commission gave its verdict against such a move.

In 1948, the Jaipur session of the Congress was forced to reconsider the demand and a committee was formed under Jawaharlal Nehru, Vallabhbhai Patel and Pattabhi Sitaramaiya (and therefore popularly called JVP) to consider the case for Karnataka, Andhra Pradesh and Kerala. The committee propounded the cause of Andhra but, strangely enough, rejected the demand of Karnataka and Kerala! All members of the KPCC resigned in protest. Interestingly, though the JVP Report sanctioned the formation of Andhra Pradesh, the Central Government chose to remain inert even on that issue.

The Congress made this an issue in the first General Elections in 1951, but conveniently went back on its promise after returning to power. The Akhanda Karnataka Nirmana Parishad was formed and this led to a period of mass agitations and violent protests all over the state. Potti Sriramulu died in Andhra after a hunger strike undertaken for the cause of Andhra. The whole of Andhra raged under fire.

Immediately taking cognisance of the situation going steadily out of hand, the prime minister announced the immediate formation of the Andhra state in 1953. The Wanchoo Committee recommended that the Bellary District without the taluks of Alur, Adoni and Rayadurg be merged into the old state of Mysore. The formation of Andhra Pradesh and the rejection of their demand angered the KPCC, which issued a direct-action call that year. It called on the Kannada members of the legislatures in the provinces and the Centre to resign. Many leaders including Andanappa Doddameti embarked on a fast-unto-death.

On 22 December 1953, the prime minister announced the appointment of a high-power Fazal Ali Committee to examine the question of formation of Karnataka. The Committee was headed by Fazal Ali, H.N. Kunzru and K.M. Pannikkar. They issued a press note in 1954 and visited various parts of the state after which, in 1955, they submitted their recommendations in favour of the formation of a new state of Karnataka.

On 1 November 1956, the long cherished dream of millions of Kannadigas was fulfilled through the integration and formation of the new state of Karnataka—an event celebrated as Karnataka Rajyotsava. However, the name 'Mysore' was retained for this state. It contained the whole of Mysore state including Bellary district, Belgaum district except the Chandgad *taluk*, entire Dharwad, Bijapur and North Kanara districts of the Bombay state, South Kanara district except Kasargod *taluk*, Kollegal *taluk* in Coimbatore district, whole of Coorg or Kodagu, the whole of Gulbarga district without Kodagana and Tandur taluks from Hyderabad state, Raichur district without Alampur and Gadwal taluks and from Bidar district the entire *taluks* of Bidar, Bhalki, Ourad and Humnabad. Bangalore was made the new capital of the State and S. Nijalingappa became the first chief minister of the unified state.

On 1 November 1973, the then Chief Minister Devaraja Urs renamed the state Karnataka. It is worth mentioning that a number of border agitations with neighbouring states can still be seen, with Maharashtra clamouring for Belgaum and Kasargod urging a reunion with Karnataka, even in this 'Suvarna Rajyotsva' or fiftieth year of the state's formation.

Sri Jayachamarajendra Wodeyar, whose rule saw so many revolutionary changes, died on 23 September 1974 of cardiac failure. Devaraja Urs expressed shock and grief over his demise and referred to him as a 'man of the masses'. Crowds raised cries of 'Jayachamaraja Wadiyar ki Jai' as the body draped in spotless white was brought out in a stretcher and placed in an open car for the last procession.

Thus ended the life and times of the last ruler of the Wodeyar dynasty, bringing to an end a 600-year regime—one of the longest reigning Indian ruling houses. Like every end that heralds a new beginning, the demise of Royal Mysore led to the formation of an independent and vibrant State of Karnataka—one that could build on the sound foundations of its predecessors.

Section 6
The Cultural Legacy

'Galaxy of musicians': Painting by Raja Ravi Verma, Mysore

25

DEFINING CULTURE

No history of a region is complete without an account of the people inhabiting it—the people who ultimately shape the way of life and the term we so loosely define as the culture of a place. Mysore, like any other region, has, over the centuries evolved its own distinctive socio-cultural identity and when I speak of Mysore here I refer to the Mysore state, a large part of present day Karnataka. Its people mostly display a genial, cordial and hospitable disposition and have, over the years, established a unique cultural individuality for themselves. Known for the many characteristic and traditional symbols of its identity—the sandalwood, the sandal oil and perfumes, ivory, the world-famous Mysore silk, *agarbattis*, the Mysore jasmine (*Mysuru Mallige*), the Mysore brinjal (*Mysuru Badanekayi*), the bounties of nature in the form of waterfalls, greenlands and plateaus in the rocky Deccan, foliage, varied horticulture, the avian and animal diversity in its numerous sanctuaries, the rich cultural heritage bequeathed over the generations—all collectively add a unique dimension to the state's identity. This is what I hope to document in brief in the coming pages.

DEFINING CULTURE

Before getting into the details of the various components of Mysore's cultural persona, it would be worthwhile to attempt a definition of the term 'Culture' itself, in a more pan-Indian context. The spirit of India has always fascinated the world with its very mystique. A subcontinent with a 5,000-year old history; a civilisation united by its diversity, the richness of its culture, the glory of the past, the turbulences and triumphs, the landmarks of each era, the achievements of each age, the legacy of its many rulers—as you walk through history, through India's geography, and her linguistic and artistic contributions, your individual interpretation will be your very own discovery. In a sense, each one of us who has made an attempt to 'feel' India could well become a Jawaharlal Nehru and author our very own *Discovery of India*! Such is her enigma. India—she can move you to question what you have taken for granted and touch you so deeply as to remain a memory forever. Seers and savants for centuries have been trying to discover this very soul of India—the soul that shows up in our traditional musical forms, dance styles, in the rusticity of the myriad folk arts, in the linguistic brilliance of the literary works, in theatre, in our philosophy and religions, in paintings—yet this image is so transient; like lightning, that it disappears even before we've caught full sight of it! It is like a nymphet trying to play a game of hide and seek with you, for centuries now!

Going by the above, how are we then to define something as lofty as the 'culture' of a place—be it a Mysore or an India? Culture has always been defined in numerous ways and the definition given by the British anthropologist Sir Edward Burnett Taylor seems to be one of the most satisfactory. He defines it as 'That complex whole which includes knowledge, belief, art, morals, law, custom and any other capabilities and habits acquired by man as a member of society.'

A set of cultural traits adopted by a group to, as Taylor said, 'meet its needs and ensure its survival' constitutes its culture. In this sense, culture could be associated with a nation, town, village or a tribe. In terms of Tylor's definition, man acquires culture or becomes cultured by being a member of a society or a group and there are various elements in that complex whole called culture. Has India a culture of her own? It seems difficult to arrive at a lowest common denominator by this definition for a country like India with its diversities of race, religion, language, customs and traditions. However Sardar K.M. Panicker states, 'That India has a life view of her own, a special outlook on essential problems, which has persisted throughout her history, would hardly be denied by anyone.'

T.S. Eliot in *Notes towards a Definition of Culture* argues that the basis of culture is religious belief. It is undeniably true that it is Christianity that forms the basis of European culture. In the same way, the pre-eminence of the Hindu shade in the many colours of India gives to its culture its special characteristics. And this is not to be berated as any fundamentalist or exigent political philosophy—it is a fact that needs to be gracefully accepted! There is absolutely no need to be defensive or apologetic about the Hindu-ness of India and its supreme contribution to the psyche of Indians. Non-dogmatic and encouraging its followers to question and commit 'heresy' in the quest for the truth, Hinduism does impart an all-embracing and tolerant shade to the Indian way of life—one that has helped her to assimilate the goodness of all points of view and religions and enrich itself in the process by bringing out a unique and composite Indian culture, so to say. Concepts of 'heretics' and 'non-believers' being condemned to hellfire for challenging the might of the 'gospel truth' and 'divinely ordained laws' which are the 'only True revelation' are Semitic ideas alien to Indian way of life. Of course, the beauty of the Indian context, which cannot be conceived by other mono-cultural civilisations, is the synthesis and amalgamation of numerous other faiths and beliefs, which, even while maintaining their identity in the midst of the larger framework, are intertwined like the warp and weft of the same fabric.

ART AS A VISIBLE MANIFESTATION OF CULTURE

Having attempted to define something as elusive as 'culture', I may now descend to the individual components which I think define this complex whole. Art, in its various forms, is the first thing that comes to our minds when we talk of 'culture'. But then art itself is such a complex organism! To define it and its further sub-components is also an onerous task.

Art is one of those ideas that evade clear definition. Abstract in its nature, it does not lend itself to being expressed and defined in concrete terms that our logical mind can easily comprehend. Several definitions, have no doubt, been attempted. Goethe called it 'the magic of the soul', Wagner defines it as 'the pleasure one takes in being what he is... the accomplishment of our desire to find ourselves again among the phenomena of the external world' and defining an artist not as 'one who makes, but one who finds,' while Brock says 'when all the knowledge, skill and passion of mankind are poured into an acknowledgement of something greater than themselves, then that acknowledgement is Art.' Of course, art is all this; but much more. It is the essence of existence, a way of revelation of life and its true meaning, an expression of the 'soul of fact'.

In India, art has always been considered as a path of realisation of the Ultimate Reality. It has always been spiritual in its outlook, idealistic in expression and sublime in interpretation. It is not merely a matter of sensuous enjoyment or amusement or a fiefdom of the rich and wealthy. It might have been that too, in one of its numerous manifestations, but it certainly had a deeper basis and a more exalted aim. It was considered as vital for human progress as devotion, knowledge or love. God was considered the fountain of all beauty and what an artist—a musician, a dancer, a painter or a sculptor—attempted was to bring that Godhead and its beauty nearer to us. So art is verily a path to the Supreme, it is a yoga, soundarya yoga so to say and artists ought to be *yogis* in their own way.

In ancient India, art went hand in hand with religion; so much so that it would not perhaps be wrong to say that art turned inward is religion and religion turned outward is art. Our temples have long been repositories of all types of art. Indian art has thus been idealistic and symbolic rather than realistic. For an artist, a work of art is an expression of one's experience, a universal language of deep human emotions. Art is a great unifier and a real artist is above all false division among humans, because a good work of art is appreciated everywhere, as human experiences are fundamentally the same—people weep everywhere, smile everywhere, love everywhere! These unsophisticated expressions of one's inner being have a universality about them.

While culture itself is an abstract and complex idea to grasp and assimilate, it manifests itself in different forms at different times. These could be the complex and structured forms of classical music and dance or the rustic and energetic folk art forms. Literature, architecture, painting and theatre are other visible forms of this enigma that we loosely call culture. In the coming chapters, let us explore the growth of culture in Mysore by tracing the evolution of these visible facets of culture.

26

THE LIVES AND TIMES OF MYSOREANS: CLASSICAL MUSIC

It was a lazy winter afternoon in Mysore. The nip in the air added a dash of charm to the beauty of the place. The horse-driven vehicle of the eminent court musician, Mysore Sadashiva Rao[*] halted in front of his palatial house. From within the cart emerged the man himself. Of medium height, with a broad forehead and sparkling eyes, his persona and the quiet humming of a melody that had occurred to him on the way back from the palace clearly indicated that he was a man of music. He bade the obedient driver a farewell and made way to his house.

Sundara Bai, his wife, waited for him at the doorstep. She hurried to inform him of the sudden arrival of a musician from a neighbouring state. She had received him with all due respect and told him about her husband's daily duties at the palace and that he would be back soon.

'Has he had his lunch?' quizzed Sadashiva.

'Yes, he had a small nap too…he is currently in the study room waiting for you.'

Sadashiva Rao hastened to welcome this unsolicited guest. On meeting him he realised that the man was considered an expert when it came to the rendition of the Raga Todi. The visitor stood up and folded his hands with reverence, as the great musician, teacher and composer approached him.

---

[*] It is common practice among South Indian musicians even today to be addressed by the name of the place they represent. Thus we have Mysore Sadashiva Rao, Bangalore Nagaratnamma, and so on.

'Sorry to have kept you waiting Sir! I was not aware of your coming. What, if I may ask, brings you to my humble abode?' asked Sadashiva Rao with characteristic humility.

Pat came the reply, 'It is an honour to stand before you Sir. I have wanted to meet you for long for music-related discussions. As you know, I am a very reputed singer. I could only gain from the enormous knowledge that you have and so willingly share!'

'A very reputed singer!' the words rang in Sadashiva's ears. Music, he thought, could teach one nothing but humility. The deeper one explored the ocean of music, the more one realised how little one knew and how many more lifetimes it would take to explore a fraction of this vast ocean. Rao firmly believed that only by subsuming the ego of the 'I' did the birth of a true musician become possible. But here was a man who unabashedly proclaimed that he was a reputed singer. Of course he had heard stories of the latter's proficiency when it came to the Raga Todi, 'But that gives him no right to assume he is great!' thought Sadashiva Rao.

Choosing to ignore the pompous statement, he sat down with the visitor and the two spoke at length on a number of technical aspects related to music. The visitor was indeed talented and had a sharp brain that absorbed all that Sadashiva Rao spoke.

At the end of the discussion, Sadashiva Rao asked him

'I have heard so much about your Todi. Can you sing something for me? May be a little *alapana* that exposes this beautiful raga? I am desirous of knowing what makes you renowned as a specialist of this raga.'

'Oh! No! Sir! Anything but that! I am sorry I cannot sing for you,' came the unexpected refusal.

'Why? You deem it below your dignity to sing in front of me?' quizzed Rao, amused.

'Hell fire on me, Sir if I thought that way. But the matter is I have pledged the raga to one of my patron zamindars. I cannot sing for anyone but him. I would be guilty of misconduct and he would strip me of the monthly allowances that he gives me if he learns that I have sung Todi for you. Any other raga that you desire Sir, I shall oblige. Spare me the Todi.'

It was common practice those days for the rich and famous to gag the voices of eminent musicians and make them pledge that the ragas they were supremely good at would be sung in their presence alone and at no public performances. It was a haughty practice of buying music by the sheer power of money and popularity and many musicians capitulated to this practice for the huge monetary benefits.

Sadashiva Rao was thoroughly vexed. The opening sentence of the impudent visitor had already irked him. This angered him further. He was the host and so chose not to pick a fight with this shallow musician—one for whom music meant entertainment and money. Determined to teach the man a lesson, Sadashiva Rao bade him farewell, requesting him to attend a concert of his that night.

The news of this incident reached the ears of Maharaja Mummadi Krishnaraja Wodeyar. He knew that Sadashiva Rao would come up with an ingenious way of teaching the man a lesson. He wanted to witness this in person and decided to attend the concert disguised as a commoner.

That night at the concert, after a couple of opening pieces, Sadashiva Rao geared up to propitiate Todi. With a meditative smile he seemed to be invoking the *raga devatha*, or the god of the raga.

As the first strains of the magnificent Todi emanated from Sadashiva's throat, the audience sat spellbound. The *ghana* raga that Todi is, it assumed an other-worldly shape through the instrument of Sadashiva Rao's mellifluous voice. The majestic vibrations, the meandering of the *gamakas* laden with *bhava* brought the characteristic of the melodic identity of Todi to its fullest. With *Ga* and *Dha* acting as the nuclei of the melodic entity, the *Ma* gliding as a swing in between, connecting the lower and higher ends of the *raga* created a magical effect. Even as Sadashiva Rao meandered from one note to the other with ample elaboration around the resting or *nyasa swaras* of *Ga, Ma, Pa, Dha* and *Ni*, the audience was transported to an ethereal world.

The exercise might have begun as one to teach an impudent young musician a lesson. But once the exploration began, Sadashiva Rao lost himself and forgot the agenda behind singing Todi. With closed eyes and a voice steeped in emotion, he was exposing every contour of the glorious raga. Someone in the audience recognised the maharaja sitting amidst them, equally lost in the music. A small flurry and murmur ensued in the crowd. The maharaja made a quick exit and returned, dressed in his royal robes. But none of all this activity distracted the musician on stage. He was on a journey, and the arrival and departure of listeners had absolutely no relevance.

It was the chirping of birds that made the audience aware that a full night had passed and they had heard nothing but Todi through those long hours! Finally, as if reluctantly abandoning a deep, spiritual slumber, Sadashiva Rao wound up the *alapana*. As he opened his eyes, he was surprised to see the maharaja seated right in front of him.

But even before he could address the maharaja, the visiting musician rushed to the stage and fell at his feet with tears rolling down his eyes.

'Sir! Sir! Forgive me for my sins. How presumptuous of me to have thought I was a great musician or that I was an expert at Todi. I have not only sold my music to that zamindar, but my soul as well. In the last few hours, I realised I knew nothing of this Raga. It seemed to take on a different dimension through you. I don't know what catastrophe beckons me in the other world for making a commodity of this divine art. But if I can atone for my sins, it can only be by serving you for the rest of my life as a faithful and obedient student and hoping that at least by the time of my death, I get a fraction of your expertise in Todi.'

✧

INDIAN CLASSICAL MUSIC AND ITS CONTEXT: A BIRD'S-EYE VIEW

The origin of Indian music is said to lie in the Vedas. It is said that God himself is 'musical sound'—the sound that pervades the whole universe—Nadabrahma. It is said that the musician has to abandon himself in order to fuse with the Supreme Reality, the Parabrahman.

Music has a pervasive influence on an Indian's life—right from birth to death, in religious rites and seasonal festivals. The rules of music as they developed were originally passed on by word of mouth, in the guru-shishya *parampara*—a system of a *gurukula* where knowledge was imparted to deserving students. It took a long time for music to evolve to its present state.

The most important advance in music was made between the fourteenth and eighteenth centuries, during which period the music of the North came in contact with Persian music—through the Pathans and Mughals—and assimilated with it. It is then that the two schools of Indian music—Hindustani and Carnatic—came into existence. It would be an oversimplification to classify them as merely the music of the North and South of India, as they share several common features. The difference, if any, lies in the style of presentation and raga exposition. Both have a distinct personality and yet are so similar—something so reflective of the 'unity in diversity' concept of Indian culture.

In the Carnatic tradition, the singing saints and famed Trinity* had made the art much safer to learn. God legitimately existed and no one disapproved of His presence. But with the arrival of Sufi influence on Hindustani musical tradition, religion went out and was substituted with the life of the spirit. This made the raga an interior ocean for discovery and exploration and made music more personal. Music took on the mantle of time and seasons and of festivals and celebrations in all of which God remained unnamed, yet always present. This was among the reasons why the best of Hindustani musicians had to run away from home on a regular basis! This journey needed privacy and inner silence and family was the worst place to seek that! This was another reason why music was banished from middle-class homes in the north. It is a happy irony that it was essentially middle-class homes where Carnatic music flourished and continues to do so to this day. Western classical musician Leopold Stokowski had this to say about Indian music:

> One of the great characteristics of the music of India is its flexibility and freedom. While giving due consideration to traditions stemming from the past, Indian music is free and improvised so that all powers of imagination in the musician is brought into play. This way the music of India is always creative and never a reproduction of what is written or played.

In India there has always been a subtle difference between a 'musician' and an 'artist'—the former is one who knows music while the latter improvises with the music he knows.

The period from the end of the eighteenth century to the beginning of the nineteenth century was unique in the history of Indian music. In one sense we may say that today's Carnatic music is mainly the outcome of the musical upheaval that resulted from the contributions of the great composers of that period—Thyagaraja, Shyama Shastry and Muthuswamy Dikshitar.

---

* The Trinity consisted of Thyagaraja (1767–1847), Shyama Shastry (1763–1827) and Muthuswamy Dikshitar (1775–1835), three great composers of that period.

Although Thyagaraja shunned publicity all his life and even rejected the king's offer to join his court, he is hailed as the King of Carnatic music. He renounced all worldly pleasures and devoted himself to God and this submission finds expression in his compositions. He is credited with the invention of *sangatis* and numerous other creative ideas in rhythm. A study of his compositions clearly indicates that he was a mystic to the core and his entire life was dedicated to the service of Lord Rama, who was a living reality to him, a constant companion and a loving guru. The perpetual source of pathos for him was that the people around him were not able to enjoy the bliss of Ramabhakti and were making their own and others' lives miserable.

Shyama Shastry's contribution to Carnatic music is unique. He had great mastery over the technique of the art and commanded a polished diction. His compositions are replete with *ragabhava*. He gave a special charm and beauty to his favourite raga, Ananda Bhairavi and enriched it to a remarkable degree. His compositions are dedicated to Goddess Kamakshi of Kanchi.

Art is essentially considered a matter of personality; the artist can never be divorced from his work and his personality gets stamped on or revealed in every work of art he creates. But a striking feature of Muthuswamy Dikshitar's compositions is the remarkable absence of the personal element. He sublimated his human personality and raised it to the level of the impersonal. This is the only possible explanation for the magnificent richness, all-embracing completeness, lyrical dazzle and vibrant perfection of his *kritis*. He was also a *veena* player and expert astrologer. The texts of his *kritis* were rich in symbolism, using a wide variety of terminologies drawn from Indian mythology, philosophy and astrology. His *kritis* are difficult to master due to the excellent lyrics, the strict adherence to the rules of musical prosody, the appropriateness of the raga, *tala* and tempo used to express an idea. He was more of an academic and spent considerable time in the North studying Hindustani music, which influenced him deeply and he adopted the Dhrupad system of Hindustani to double the pace of compositions.

The Bhakti movement that ushered in a cultural and spiritual renaissance in medieval India had a deep impact on Carnatic music too. The period saw a spurt in the growth of the Vachana Sahitya of Basaveshwara, Akka Mahadevi, Guheshwara and others, which later led to the growth of a new sect in Hinduism—the Lingayat sect, and the Dasa

Sahitya. The Haridasas or nomadic bards brought the rich philosophy of the Indian scriptures to the common man's doorstep even as they sang in the local language. Purandara Dasa, Kanaka Dasa, Vijaya Vitthala Dasa, Vadiraja, Kamalesha Dasa, Bhadrachala Ramadasa, Annamacharya and others are but a few luminaries of the Dasa family.

Of these there is perhaps no figure in the history of Indian music more unique and revered than Saint Purandara Dasa, hailed as the 'Pitamaha' or Grandfather of Carnatic music. The present-day practice of Carnatic music is entirely due to him. It is he who fixed the Mayamalavagowla *raga* scheme of preliminary teaching and prescribed the elementary lessons in music like Saralivarase, Jantivarase, Geeta, Alankara, etc. He was a prolific composer and is believed to have composed more than 4,75,000 songs in Kannada. His compositions cover a wide range from the simplest bhajans to highly technical pieces. He used his songs as a medium for his work as God's messenger. His compositions abound in allegories, proverbs and epigrams. He is viewed to this day as a divine mediator interpreting God and His joy to humanity through the medium of music. It would not be an exaggeration to say that the works of Purandara Dasa gave a stimulus to the Trinity and also to Kshetrajna, an eighteenth-century musician.

Meanwhile, to systematise and coordinate the systems that existed in North Indian music, Burhan Khan of Khandesh invited Pundarika Vitthala (1562–99) to settle in the North. Vitthala was a native of Satanor, near Sivaganga in Bangalore district and was proficient in both styles of music. Many of the ragas of modern Hindustani music have retained the scale of Pundarika Vitthala. Under the patronage of the king of Jaipur, he later authored a revolutionary book in the history of Indian music called *Ragamala*, or garland of ragas. This book classifies the ragas under six male ragas of the Hindustani style—Bhairav, Malkauns, Deepak, Hindol, Shree and Megh and five raginis to each. Vitthala also specified the time for singing the ragas and authored books, like *Ragamanjari* and *Nartana Nirnaya*, the former dealing with twenty melas or parent scales and comparing 16 Persian ragas with the Northern melas being analogous.

It is interesting to note that music is so intrinsic to the Indian imagination that miniature paintings are found in the North, inspired by the *Ragamala* series, and are an ideal synthesis of music, poetry and painting. The series of paintings visualises music as having a visible or bodily form besides an auditory form. Depending on the moods they evoked, *ragas* were classified as male or female.

What exactly is the raga, which forms the bedrock of Indian classical music? In its primary sense, a raga is a musically sound and sensible combination of the seven basic notes. But in its aesthetic definition, a raga assumes a more sublime meaning. With deep spiritual undercurrents, a raga and its study or exploration is akin to self-discovery and self-realisation. Of course, on the surface it also entertains and soothes the mind. 'Ranjayati ithi raga' or 'that which pleases' is the usual definition attempted for this abstract concept.

Poetical forms have been woven around these *ragas*, *raginis* (female ragas) and *ragaputras* in this work of Pundarika Vitthal, as mentioned above. Different seasons, sounds and times of singing came to be associated with the Hindustani style of music. The earliest reference to this is in the *Natyashastra* of Bharata. Hanumana, a musicologist, had visualised ragas in the personalised forms. Each *raga* or *ragini* denoted various aspects of life; they varied technically, spiritually and emotionally. Hindustani music, with its major thrust on improvisation—unlike Carnatic music that depicts a delightful blend of both improvisatory and composed music—aims to bring this very aspect of *raga swaroopa* or an introduction to the nature of the raga just as one introduces one's friends to a newcomer.

CLASSICAL MUSIC AND ITS GROWTH IN MYSORE

Music, like all the arts, depends on royal patronage or the support of the powers that be. The royal family of Mysore extended unbridled support to music, so much so that Mysore and Tanjore emerged as musical centres of southern India. Chamaraja Wodeyar V was a great patron of the arts. Vocal and *veena* concerts were a daily affair. Ranadhira Kanthirava Narasaraja Wodeyar was also a great patron of the arts. In his court were such great musicians, as Bharati Naiya, Veena Narasayya and Veena Krishnayya. Govinda Vaidya's *Kanthirava Narasaraja Vijayam* has graphic accounts of the ubiquitous role played by music in the king's daily life. The fact that Mysore had separate streets for *vainikas*, singers, percussionists, and so on, speaks for itself. The role of music would be further highlighted during the annual Dussehra festivities. The poetry of the times has verses which state that the ladies sang melodiously to the tunes of *ragas* like Dhanyasi, Bhupali, Gundakriya and Desakshi. Veena Krishnaiya's recitals have also been mentioned.

Chikkadevaraja Wodeyar had authored a musical treatise called *Geeta Gopala* containing compositions that dealt with the theme of Krishna Leela akin to those of the famous composer Jaideva. Each piece has seven *padas* or Saptapadi instead of the Ashtapadi or eight-stanza style of Jaideva's *Geeta Govinda*. It has its own specific melodic notes or raga and rhythm or *tala*. The ragas employed range from Bhairavi, Kambodhi, Kedaragowla, Asavari, and Mukhari to Nata, Pantuvarali, Ghantarava, Kannadagowla, Narayani, Huseni, Kapi, and Kuranji and so on. Various musical instruments were played in the recitals that took place in his court. These have been named as *thambura, veena, maddala, mukha veena, sankha, bheri, thaala, jambaka, dindima, muraju, dakka, thambata* and *venu* (flute). In his court, dance performances were accompanied by many musical instruments.

When Haidar Ali took over the Mysore throne, one of the *asthana vidwans* (court musicians) was Pachimiriam Adiappayya, whose *Ata tala varnam* in Bhairavi has remained an unsurpassed musical composition popular on the Carnatic music concert stage till date. It is an authentic example of the shape of the *raga* from the days of Purandara Dasa down to the earlier years of the twentieth century. The sudden increase in the use of *Chatusruti dhaivata* since then has changed the complexion of the raga itself. Adiappayya migrated to Thanjavur and became a court musician under King Sarabhoji. Adiappayya's son Kuppiah had four children—three sons: Kuppayya, Appayya and Sheshappa, and a daughter Narasamma, whose son was Veena Chikkaramappa. His son was Veena Sheshanna. It was this family that laid the foundations of the famous Mysore Bani or Mysore style of music, especially with regard to the playing of the *veena*. The very name of Mysore evokes memories of great *vainikas*. 'Veeneya bedagidhu Mysooru'—this line from a popular Kannada poem describes Mysore as the splendour of *veena*.

Music under Mummadi Krishnaraja Wodeyar

Mummadi Krishnaraja Wodeyar was himself a great music composer and his court glittered constantly with the presence of musicians. The courts of Tanjore and the Peshwas having ceased to exist in the early half of the nineteenth century, there was a mass exodus of scholars and musicians to Mysore who received a warm welcome from the benevolent king. It is said that the maharaja once ordered Dewan Purnaiya to invite one of the greatest musicians of the time and a composer from Tanjore—Veene

Venkatasubbaiya, Adiappayya's grandson. The maharaja presented him with a golden *veena* studded with diamonds! He was appointed as the maharaja's guru. He is credited with composing a Saptataleshwari Githe in Raga Rithigowla. The specialty of this composition is that seven singers are supposed to start the composition simultaneously, each in one of the seven *suladi sapta talas* of the Carnatic style. At the end of the composition, all the singers would finish their respective *talas* simultaneously. It is believed that only those extremely proficient in the art of *laya* or rhythm as well as *sahitya*[*] or poetry can attempt such a challenging task. Veene Venkatasubbaiya was certainly one such gifted and learned musician.

The maharaja's musical knowledge translated itself into other forms of art, like painting. Krishnaraja Wodeyar is believed to have got two sets of paintings done—one for the *Sritatvanidhi* and the other for *Swara Chudamani*. In fact the main theme of *Swara Chudamani* is the portrayal of the seven notes or *sapta swaras* as demi-gods. Each note has a *dhyana shloka* or meditative verse considered essential to propitiate it. The seven notes, believed to have arisen from the divine sound of Omkara, have always caught the imagination and reverence of musicians. Thyagaraja in his *kriti Mokshmau Galada* similarly eulogises the seven notes as having emerged from the cosmic union of life and fire leading to the hallowed Omkara. It is this very reverence to the divine sound that comes across in *Swara Chudamani*. To make the notes less abstract and perceivable to the human mind they were personified as demi-gods and contain detailed descriptions of their being with the help of 32 characters or Dwaatrimsha Lakshanaatmakaha.

From notes the progression naturally moves to combinations of these notes, which are nothing but the *ragas*. The maharaja selected 36 ragas of his choice, not following the traditional Batteesa Ragas then prevalent in South India. These ragas were portrayed as human beings and depicted different *rasas* or emotions among the nine classified ones or *navarasas*. Saindhavi, Dhanyasi and Velavali depict Veera Rasa or valour; Malavashri and Megha portray Shringaara or romance; Asavari for Karuna or kindness; Bhupali for Shantha or peace and so on. The *ragas* have also been given genders. For example, Bhairavi, Malava Koushika,

---

[*] In the case of music, the word 'sahitya' always means a poem, unlike its usual meaning encompassing all literature. The poem becomes the literary device or structure for the music.

Hindola, Deepaka, Sri and Megha have been classified as *purusha ragas* or male ragas; the first four of which have five raginis or female ragas; Sri has six and Megha has four raginis.

The *raga lakshanas* or features of each raga that he brings out are equally marvellous. Raga Deepaka for example has been beautifully described in the following picturisation:

> A shy heroine waits for her hero in a reclining cot. When the hero enters, the maid moves out with the lamps, thus making the room dark. But the shine of the jewel from the hero's crown is so bright that the entire room is illuminated, and the heroine posing shyness turns to the other side, hiding her face from the hero.

Thus Deepaka, a classified male raga, brings with it the masculinity associated with light and heat. It uses its inherent power to create a romantic atmosphere. Similarly, *talas* too have pictures and stories associated with them. Dhruva Tala for example has been described as

> born on a Sunday; and of a goat; his birth sign is Karkataka; birth star Pushya; belongs to the race of Devas; with large eyes; dressed in clean clothes. He wears a necklace of precious stones and is under the power of Hrinkara, the Brahmi Shakti...he belongs to the Brahmin caste and is seated on the Laksha Dwipa riding a single-wheeled chariot and exuding Shringara Rasa. He has three angas like divya laghu and dual laghu.

This personification of ragas and talas made them identifiable beings who could be invoked through *sadhana* or dedicated practice.

It was during the reign of Krishnaraja Wodeyar III that such famous musicians, as Veene Sambaiya, Veene Anantha Subbayya, Veene Chikkaramappa, Veene Chikka Lakshmiramanappa, Veene Krishnappa, Mugur Subbanna, Veene Dodda Subbaraya, the great vocalist 'Janjaa maaruta' (cyclone) Subbayya, Shyama Shastry's disciple Appukuttan Nattuvanar, Thyagaraja's disciple Lalgudi Rama Iyer, his sons Guruswami Iyer and Radhakrishna Iyer, Mysore Sadashiva Rao, and Thatchur Singarachar, were all *asthana vidwans*.

Shunti Venkataramanaiya, a friend of Veene Venkatasubbaiya, was another eminent musician in the court. The prefix 'shunti', which means ginger, has an interesting anecdote to it. It is said that while singing, he would go into a trance. To revive him, someone would chew ginger and with its juice in their mouth blow air into the ears of the rapt singer! And hence the name. Aliya Lingaraje Urs (1823–74) is another eminent composer of the times, whose composition *Shringaara Lahiri* in Raga Nilambari is famous on concert stages to this day. Twenty-five *kritis* dedicated to the Goddess and compositions for Yakshagana dance form are his other achievements. Chinnaih, the eldest among the famous Tanjore Quartet of dancers and musicians, was also a court musician at Mysore. He is said to have composed many *varnas*, *kritis*, *javalis* and *tillanas* and created a repertoire for dance lyrics also.

Music recitals were a regular feature of the Mysore court, especially during festivals like Dussehra and Sivaratri. The court also invited famous musicians from the neighbouring state of Tanjore, like Patnam Subramanya Iyer, Tirukodikaval, Krishna Iyer and Mahavaidhyanatha Iyer for musical recitals and discourses.

Mysore Sadashiva Rao (1790–1880)

Among the early musical luminaries of the Mysore court was the gifted musician-composer Mysore Sadashiva Rao. Born in Chittoor District of Andhra Pradesh, Sadashiva Rao was a child prodigy. An interesting anecdote tells of him as a young child stretching his hand out for an extra helping of *ghee* from his mother. She taunted him with sharp words, suggesting that he had better earn for himself instead of reaching out for *ghee*. So insulted did young Sadashiva feel, that he decided to leave home and prove his mettle to his mother.

This self-imposed exile led to the discovery of music by the young man. He decided to move to Walajapet and train under one of the three direct disciples of Saint Thyagaraja—Venkataramana Bhagavathar and the Umayalapuram Brothers—Krishna Bhagwathar and Tillaisthanam Rama Iyengar. They had kept the saint's tradition and compositions alive. The years under Venkataramana Bhagavathar groomed Sadashiva's technical and aesthetic skills in the art. The exposure to *katha kalakshepas* or long discourses intertwined with philosophy, music and poetry, so characteristic of the Bhagavathar clan, honed his compositional skills as well. It is said that he had the fortune of receiving the blessings of the holy Saint Thyagaraja himself when the latter came to Walajapet to his student's house. Sadashiva's extempore composition and rendition of *Thyagaraja Swamy Vedalina* in Raga Todi won him the appreciation and blessings of the Saint.

During his trips to neighbouring states, it is said that he was so overcome with emotion at the Prasanna Krishna Swamy temple at Mysore and sang his own composition *Dorakenu Nedu Sri Krishna* in Raga Devagandhari with such devotion that he mesmerised the other devotees. Two traders, Pedda Muniswamy Shetty and his brother Chinna Muniswamy Shetty, who were present there, informed the maharaja about this young and talented musician. A special concert was arranged at the maharaja's durbar. The beauty of Sadashiva Rao's music floored the maharaja and the thirty year old was appointed court musician at a monthly salary of Rs 30.

Many interesting anecdotes revolve around the life of this musician, who was a mystic in his own right. A staunch devotee of Lord Narasimha, he had composed several *kritis* in praise of his favourite deity. The worshippers of this god needed to follow strict practices when it came to the rituals of worship. Sadashiva is said to have followed these rules even with regard to the *kritis* and their rendition. But on one occasion, intense public demand made him forego these practices and render his *Narasimhudu Dayinchenu* in Raga Kamalamanohari. It is said that as he progressed towards the Anupallavi line *Sarasijasanandamu Pagula*, a portrait of Lord Narasimha that hung on the wall beside the stage cracked and the glass smashed into smithereens! It is believed that he immediately realised his folly, stopped the concert and offered his sincerest apologies to the deity.

Sadashiva Rao is said to have named eminent musician-composer Patnam Subrahmanya Iyer as Begade Subrahmanya Iyer for the latter's extraordinary rendition of the Raga Begade. He is also credited with having given a new dimension to the Rama Navami celebrations in Mysore, making it an occasion for religion and music to blend beautifully. He would personally invite many musicians from all over the country to perform at this occasion—a tradition that most parts of South Karnataka follow to this day during Rama Navami.

Rao was a prolific composer and composed many forms prevalent in the Carnatic style like *swarajatis, tana, varnas, pada varnas, kritis* and *tillanas* in Sanskrit and Telugu. Currently we have about 90–100 compositions of his available for use. They bear his *nom de plume* of 'Sadashiva'. From standard compositions centring on *bhakti*, like the famous *Ramabhi Rama* in Raga Hamsadhwani, *Devadideva* in Raga Mayamalawagowla, *Gangadhara Tripuraharana* in Raga Purvikalyani, *Paramabhuta Maina* in Raga Khamas,

Sita Lakshmana Sametha in Raga Kambodhi, *Sri Kamakotipeetha* in Raga Saveri *Saketa Nagara Natha* in Raga Harikambodhi, Sadashiva Rao has been an iconoclast and penned erotic *kritis*, obviously in anonymity, like *Ye Maguva Bodhinichine* in Raga Dhanyasi. Apart from using his *nom de plume* in the compositions, he has also used the Dikshitar style of *raga mudra*, or incorporating the name of the *raga* in the *kriti*, as also the *Raja mudra* or the name of the maharaja, 'Krishnaraja' in many of his compositions. Some of his compositions cannot be handled unless one has a good grip over *kala pramana* or time measures of *tala* and *laya* and also a rich and flexible voice.

Prominent among his disciples were the eminent Veene Sheshanna, Veene Subbanna, Hanagal Chidambaraiah, Ganjam Surya Narayanappa, Chikkanayakanahalli Venkateshaiya, Bettadapura Shamanna and others.

Music under Chamarajendra Wodeyar

Chamarajendra Wodeyar X followed his father's footsteps when it came to patronising the arts. Many noted musicians adorned his court. The greatest musical change to occur during his reign and patronage was the clear evolution of the distinctive style of playing the *veena*, known as the Mysore Bani/Mysore Shaili. It gave Mysore a place of eminence in the Carnatic music firmament along with other centres of excellence like Tanjore or Travancore. Tanjore continued to maintain its supremacy in vocal music.

Veene Sheshanna (1852–1926)

Veene Sheshanna is perhaps the most renowned musician of the Mysore royal court and proponent of the famous Mysore Bani.[*] Hailed as the king among *veena* players by Margaret Cousins in her book, *Music of Orient and Occident*, Sheshanna brought grace, elegance, style, innovation and melody of execution to the Mysore Bani.

Born into a family of musicians, he learnt music from his father Bakshi Chikka Ramappa—the court musician for Maharaja Mummadi Krishnaraja Wodeyar. He was a child prodigy and gained acceptance at the court at the young age of ten. Later he learnt vocal music under the

---

[*] Details on the technical aspects of the Mysore Bani are given in the appendix to this chapter.

famous vocalist Mysore Sadashiva Rao. Apart from *veena*, he was adept at playing various other instruments, like piano, *sitar* and violin. He also learnt Hindustani and western classical music and was a prolific composer.

His foray into the Mysore Court was an interesting incident in itself. Mummadi Krishnaraja would invite several musicians during the Sivaratri celebrations for night-long concerts. To add spice to the whole performance, these concerts would be formatted as teaser contests between musicians. The visiting musicians would throw up a musical challenge in the form of a *pallavi* and the local musicians would have to elaborate on, improvise and continue the same. On one such occasion, the musical challenge of the visiting stalwart stumped all the court musicians. A six-year old Sheshanna, who had accompanied his father, pestered him to be allowed to sing and completed the *pallavi* in an aesthetic and perfect manner. The delighted king presented him with a pair of shawls and his own pearl chain. He also ensured that the young boy received the right training thereafter to develop his innate talents.

Now there could be no looking back for Sheshanna's musical journey. Under able gurus, like Sadashiva Rao for vocal music and Dodda Sheshanna for *veena*, his fertile *manodharma* or musical imagination blossomed fully. Ragam Tanam Pallavi, the epitome of a musician's mastery of the art, was his forte. His sense of *tala* and *laya* was so immaculate that people swore by it. Elaboration of ragas for hours on end without sounding repetitive came naturally to him. His method of playing gave the Mysore *veena* a special flavour. Speaking to veteran musician Mysore Vasudevacharya, which he narrates in his book *Naa Kanda Kalavidaru*, he described the technique one must employ while playing the *veena*:

> The nada should be so melodious like a cuckoo's voice. The pluck should be so soft, that neither the sound of wood nor the string should be heard. All that one should hear is the shuddha nada or pure melodic sound from the strings of the instrument.

Sheshanna was appointed court musician by Maharaja Chamarajendra Wodeyar X in 1882. Rulers from other kingdoms, such as Ramnad, Travancore, Baroda, Tanjore, etc., invited him for performances and musical discourses. The maharaja of Baroda is said to have arranged for him to be carried around in a golden palanquin when he invited him to the court for the music festival. On his return, when the maharaja of Mysore wanted to carry him around the city in a similar fashion, he decided that the honour should go to his instrument rather than him. So he placed his *veena* on the palanquin and walked beside it! The maharaja conferred the title of 'Vainika Shikhamani' or the crown jewel among *vainikas* on him.

The Raja of Ramnad organised a week-long concert by the maestro at his durbar. At the National Congress convention at Belgaum in 1924, he had the rare honour of playing before leading Congress leaders of the day. His recital won him a standing ovation and the title of 'Vainika Chakravarthi', and held leaders, like Gandhi and Rabindranath Tagore, spellbound at the beauty of his music. It is said that even the British Emperor George V was so impressed by his music that he requested a photograph with him, which he later displayed in the art gallery of Buckingham Palace.

As a composer, he has to his credit 12 *jati swaras*, nine *varnas* in Telugu and Kannada, one *saptaragamalika githa*, 17 *tillanas* and *javali*. He used the names Shesha and Srinivasa. His *varnas* are in major and minor ragas and are set to a variety of *talas*. Among his *kritis* too he has employed rarely-used Melakartha ragas like Ganamurti, Dhenuka, Natakapriya, Gamanashrama, Hemavathi, Dharmavathi, Rishabhapriya and Vachaspati. Most of them are medium tempo or *madhyamakala kritis*. Many of his *tillanas* were composed as reminders to the maharaja of his promised loan of Rs 8,000 for him, which the maharaja seemed to have forgotten!

Despite the innumerable awards and titles bestowed on him, Sheshanna's heart lay inside the hidden beauty of ragas, to which he had surrendered his soul. He had the humility to say that his fingers had still not captured the inordinate grandeur of a Todi or Kambodhi in full. His greatest delight lay in taking the *veena* lovingly in his hands and playing for hours.

Sheshanna's eminent disciples include Veene Venkatagiriappa, the brothers Srirangam Ramaswamy and Govinda Iyengar, Bhairavi, Lakshminaranappa, Shermadevi Subrahmanya Shastry, Tirumale Rajamma, M.S. Bheema Rao, painter K. Venkatappa, Narayana Iyer, Veene Shivaramaiya, his adopted son Veene Ramanna, and grandsons A.S. Chandrashekaraiya and Swaramurthy V.N. Rao.

Sheshanna passed away on 25 July 1926 at the age of seventy-four.

Other *vainikas* who shone with their musical brilliance were Veene Shamanna (1832–1908), Veene Padmanabhaiya (1842–1900) and Veene Subbanna (1861–1939). Shamanna, popularly called Tala Brahma, was as proficient with the violin, *ghatam* and *swarabath* as he was with the *veena*. It is interesting to note that great rivalry existed among some of these musicians and their schools and styles of playing. The Mysore Bani is supposed to have had two sub-styles—the Agrahara group of Shamanna and the Kote group of Sheshanna. The two groups always indulged in one-upmanship about whose style was the better one! Vasudevacharya recollects that the Agrahara group, which excelled in *tala* and *laya* would openly ridicule the ignorance of the same among the Kote group. Similarly, the Kote group, which laid great emphasis on the melodic and *bhava* aspects of music, derided their counterparts as the 'Ta dhi gin a tom gang', which meant that their music was soulless and exhibited only skilful mathematics and rhythmic jugglery.

Veene Subbanna, the other stalwart of the times, is credited with a number of compositions. He is said to have been generosity personified. During the visit of musician Poochi Srinivasa Iyengar to his house, Subbanna, on coming to know that the latter was depressed at the loss of a diamond ring presented to him by the maharaja of Ramnad, apparently opened his complete treasure of rings and precious stones and asked him to pick all he wanted!

Devottama Jois made valuable contributions through compositions in Kannada. Sangeetavidya Kantheerava Karigiri Rao (1853–1927), who composed under the pen name of 'Narasimha', was another celebrated musician patronised by the maharaja and had illustrious disciples like Bidaram Krishnappa and Chikka Rama Rao.

Court poet Basappa Shastri (1843–91) is credited with composing the first Mysore anthem. When the British Resident fixed the coronation of young Prince Chamarajendra, they were surprised to know that the kingdom had no state anthem. Accordingly, Basappa was asked to pen the anthem: *Kayau Sri Gowri Karuna Lahari Toyajaakshi*. It was rendered by both the Carnatic and the Western bands in their respective styles.

Mysore Vasudevacharya (1865–1961)

Mysore Vasudevacharya was a musical genius beyond description and his compositions adorn Carnatic music concerts to this day. They are noted for their spontaneity of expression, easy flow and rich *ragabhava*.

His compositions were mainly in Sanskrit and Telugu and most, such as *Brochevarevarura, Bhajare Manasa,* and *Devadideva Sri Vasudeva,* are very popular with performing musicians. But very few know that he was a writer too. In fact, he wrote two books in Kannada, *Naa Kanda Kalavidaru* (The artistes I knew) and *Nenapugalu* (Memories). The first is a collection of essays on fellow artistes, while the second describes his experiences as a musician in the Mysore court. Vasudevacharya's prose is laced with gentle humour. He assesses the music of some of our greatest artistes without being overwhelmed by their greatness. At the same time, he is generous in praising their genius. His simple and lively style makes his essays interesting reading even today.

Vasudevacharya was born in Mysore on 28 May 1865. Young Vasudeva learnt music initially from Veene Padmanabhayya of Mysore. Having come to know of his prodigious talent for music, the maharaja of Mysore arranged for the teenaged Vasudeva to be sent to Tiruvaiyaru to learn music under Patnam Subramania Iyer. There, Vasudeva started his *gurukula* training at his mentor's. After finishing this stint in Tiruvaiyaru, Vasudeva came back to Mysore and was appointed an *asthana vidwan* of the royal court of Mysore palace. Much later in his life, he came to Madras on the invitation of Rukmini Arundale to join the faculty at the famed Kalakshetra School of Music and Fine Arts. He eventually became the principal of the school. His contemporaries at the Kalakshetra were stalwarts, like Tiger Varadachariar, Veene Krishnamachariar and Mazhavaraya-nendal Subbarama Bhagavathar.

He was extremely close to Maharaja Chamarajendra and would accompany him on many of his tours. In fact he even performed the maharaja's last rites in Kashi upon his untimely death in 1894. This perhaps made him something of a father-figure for the young Prince Krishnaraja and gave him referral power over the boy. He was also given the responsibility of teaching Sanskrit to the young prince. It appears that Vasudevacharya took his job a little too seriously and did not think twice before smacking the knuckles of his own maharaja! So much so that the prince had to plead: 'please be soft Gurugale, it pains!' He was a prolific composer, creating more than 200 compositions, which include *pada varnas, thana varnas, kritis, javalis, tillanas* and *ragamalikas.*

Strangely enough, he began his career as a composer in 1905, when the plague struck Mysore. In those days around 3,000 families still lived inside the Mysore Fort. Even some of the senior musicians like Veene

Sheshanna, Subbanna and Subba Rao had their houses inside the fort. Outside, on the eastern side was a vast sheet of water known as Dodda kere. During the Great Plague of 1905 most of the people were shifted to temporary tents in what is known as Alanahalli. Vasudeva also found refuge there due to his proximity to an old Urs gentleman called Gopala Raja—his father's contemporary—who liked young Vasu immensely and used to play dice with him to kill time.

Sitting in front of the temporary tents outside the fort, with death staring them all in the face, Gopala Raja coaxed Vasudevacharya to compose music for posterity and beseech the Lord's mercy. Thus was born the first *kriti*, *Chinthayeham Janaki Kantam* in Raga Mayamalawagowla. After that, there was no looking back.

He has used Telugu and Sanskrit as the media for his *kritis*. The lyrical Telugu in his *kritis* is chaster than that of his contemporaries. He was not too comfortable with the usage of Kannada in classical music compositions and seems to have had many an argument with the maharaja in this regard. For his compositions, he has used common ragas alongside several unusual ragas, like Megharanjani, Sunadavinodini, Pushpalatika, Shudda Salavi, etc. He has also employed several types of *talas* such as *chaturasra rupaka, tishra rupaka, adi, ata, tishra triputa, khanda triputa, mishra triputa, mishra jhampa*, etc., in his compositions.

Vasudevacharya has composed captivating *chittaswaras* for some of his *kritis*. Two examples will suffice here: *Ra-ra-rajeeva lochana* in Raga Mohana and *Sri Chamundeshwari* in Raga Bilahari. It is noteworthy that Vasudevacharya has elevated the stature of minor ragas like Abheri (*Bhajare re manasa*), Behag (*Bhavayeham Raghuveeram*) and Khamas (*Brochevarevarura*) by composing major *kritis* in them. Note that these *kritis* were composed at the turn of the century even before these *ragas* were popularly rendered. He introduced *kakali nishada* for his Khamas instead of the conventional *kaishiki nishada* as in Saint Thyagaraja's Khamas. Vasudevacharya's Khamas is an equally appealing raga.

Around the 1930s, Maharajapuram Vishwanatha Iyer rendered Vasudevacharya's *kriti*, *Brochevarevarura* in Khamas with much polish in his concert. Vasudevacharya, who happened to be at the concert remarked to Vishwanatha Iyer: 'My composition like a simple girl was metamorphosed into a beautiful damsel. That is how well you beautified the composition with your embellishments.'

His forte lay in the singing of Ragam Tanam Pallavi and Neraval passages. Another distinct feature of his style was the singing of Sanskrit *shlokas* in *ragamalika* or a garland of ragas with the appropriate *bhava* or emotion. He was at ease with many Hindustani ragas as well. He always stressed practice and mastery over the lower octaves to gain control over the voice at higher reaches, explaining that only when one strikes a ball forcefully on the ground does it bounce up with the same force! He performed at Bhopal, Baroda, Bombay and other bastions of Hindustani music and won the praise of the stalwarts, there like Abdul Karim Khan, Faiz Khan and Pandit Vishnu Digambar Paluskar. Karim Khan supposedly learnt a few *kritis* from him as well.

The Hindu of March 1912, gave a delightful 'review' of Vasudevacharya:

> A correspondent writes from Bombay under third instant; Vidwan Vasudevachar, the well-known vocal musician of the Mysore Durbar is now here on his return journey from Jallandhar where he had gone to attend the great Congress of Indian musicians which held its sittings from the 26th to 29th of December last. He scored a brilliant success at Jallandhar (being one of the fortunate four who carried away the highest awards), for his originality in composing Sanskrit songs and setting to happy music even ordinary every day Mantras such as Kayena Vacha. He was also awarded a gold medal at Bhopal. The public of Bombay had the pleasure of hearing him yesterday when a concert and entertainment was organised in his honour at Hira Bagh Hall by the South Indian residents of Bombay. He kept the whole audience spellbound throughout those three hours of the entertainment and especially the 'coronation song' which the vidwan has composed in Sanskrit and set to three different kinds of music (Karnatic, Hindustani and English) won repeated applause....

Vasudevacharya was honoured with numerous awards and titles: Sangeetha Shastra Ratna and Sangeetha Shastra Visharada by the maharaja of Mysore; Sangeetha Kalanidhi by the Madras Music Academy in 1935, Sangeetha Kala Kovida by Gurudev Rabindranath Tagore and so on. After Independence he was also the recipient of the Central Sangeet Natak Academi Award and the Padmabhushan from the Government of India.

Vasudevacharya trained a number of disciples while he was in Mysore and later in Madras, like N. Chennakeshavaiya, H. Yoganarasimham, B.K. Padmanabha Rao, Veene Shivaramaiya, D. Pashupati, his grandchildren S. Krishnamurthy and S. Rajaram and so on. He published 150 of his compositions himself.

On 17 May 1961, this celebrated musician died at the age of 96 in his house at Kalakshetra, Madras.

Bidaram Krishnappa

Bidaram Krishnappa (1866–1931) was another famous and gifted musician at the court of Mysore. His father, Vishwanathaiya Kini was a talented Yakshagana artist who hailed from Nandalike village of South Kanara. He excelled at enacting female roles. On attending a Yakshagana performance specially arranged for him when he visited Dharmasthala, Mummadi Krishnaraja Wodeyar was highly impressed by Viswanathaiya's role and invited him to join the royal theatre at Mysore.

Unfortunately, Vishwanathaiya's early death orphaned his two gifted sons Subba and Krishna at a young age. They began singing in Mysore's Anjaneya Temple for a living. Sahukar Timmayya, a great philanthropist who happened to listen to young Krishna's devotional songs, was so impressed with his singing that he arranged music lessons for him under the well-known music teacher Karur Ramaswamy. Later, Krishnappa trained under court musicians Karigiri Rao and Veene Sheshanna.

At the age of 19, Krishnappa was recognised as the palace musician. He started performing in public at well-known centres of music, such as Bangalore, Madras, Tanjore, Tiruchinapalli, Madurai, etc. In an age before microphones, he had a rumbling, resonant voice that could reach more than a thousand people. This he would always attribute to the long hours of practice he had put in during his early years, standing in waist-deep water. His knowledge of *tala*, which is of prime importance in Carnatic music, was extraordinary. That won him the title of 'Tala Brahma', or master of rhythm, and 'Shuddha Swaracharya' for his tonal perfection and the adherence to *shruthi*.

Later he became court musician and the title of 'Ganavisharada' (one who excels in music) was bestowed upon him by the maharaja of Mysore. He won several other titles, like 'Gayaka Shikhamani' and 'Gana Kesari'. A disciplinarian, he led a pious and virtuous life and expected similar dedication from his disciples as well. T. Chowdaiah, the legendary violinist who studied under Krishnappa for more than twenty years, worshipped him. A whole band of good musicians, like B. Devendrappa, R.R. Keshavamurthy, B. Naranappa, and musicologist, Sanskrit scholar and Telugu and Kannada writer Rallapalli Anant Krishna Sharma as well as Bangalore Nagaratnamma, trained under him.

His punctuality at concerts was legendary. Even if the accompanying artists were late, as often happened, Krishnappa would be unfazed, beginning his recital on the dot, with just two drone *tamburas* behind him! The accompanists would be embarrassed when they arrived much later, and sheepishly join in.

Bidaram Krishnappa left a permanent mark as a devotee of Anjaneya. He built the famous Prasanna Seetharam Mandir at Mysore, spending his entire savings and gold medals, and the mementos he had acquired. A temple with an auditorium, it became a historical place where several eminent musicians came and performed. The building is known today as Krishnappa's Temple. Krishnappa was the first musician who began singing Purandara Dasa's compositions in classical music concerts. He has composed some *kritis* under the name Srikrishna.

On his death on 29 July 1931, the Madras Music Academy brought out an obituary in its journal:

> As a vocalist his rank is high. His stately appearance, his winning manners, his mellifluous voice, his mastery over the intricacies of the science and art and his exuberant fancy contributed not a little to the success and popularity of his performances. Of him it must be said of few others, that he did full justice to the Sahitya of the pieces he sang and fully conscious of their import. He was an authority on the proper rendering of Devaranamas and the Kirtanas of Sadashiva Rao...his loss will be particularly felt by the Music Academy, Madras with which he was ever ready to cooperate on all occasions. He was an ardent member of its Advisory board of experts. He was present at its conferences, gave performances and what is more, took part in the discussions...the world of music has lost a notable savant and the Academy a staunch supporter.

Music under Nalwadi Krishnaraja Wodeyar

Along with material progress for Mysore, the reign of Nalwadi Krishnaraja Wodeyar ushered in a grand era of cultural renaissance. Innumerable *vidwans* from all over India were invited and honoured by the maharaja who was himself a musician of repute. A good singer, he could play the *veena*, flute, violin, *mridangam*, *nagaswaram*, *sitar*, saxophone, *harmonium* and the piano! It is said that he would wake up at 5 am for his daily music practice. He began the system of orchestras, which included instrumental and vocal components. For the first time, microphones and speakers were introduced in Mysore by him to allow a larger audience to enjoy the music, especially on festive occasions.

Sheshanna composed innumerable *swarajatis*, *varnas* and *tillanas* in this period. Sambaiya was another famous composer of *swarajatis*. Other outstanding musicians of the time were Veene Subrahmanya Iyer, Harikesanallur Muthaiah Bhagavathar, Veene Shivaramaiya, Veene Venkatagiriappa, Belakawadi Srinivasa Iyengar, Chikka Rama Rao, Mysore T. Chowdaiah, Gotuvadyam Narayana Iyengar, Tiruvayyar Subrahmanya Iyer, Anavati Rama Rao and others.

Dr Harikesanallur Muthaiah Bhagavathar (1877–1945)

'Where do you have your bath?'

'There is the river, by God's grace. Three dips in it and my bath is over. I need neither a boiler nor any fuel!'

'What about your food?'

'It is enough if I get a few morsels of rice from a couple of houses. I am a Brahmachari, my Upanayana having been already performed. If I ask for alms, some kind-hearted woman gives me food. Each day I have a different sort of food and a different relish!'

'You bathe in the river, you get your alms, it need hardly be said that you must be living in some choultry.'

'Your guess is right. Right from my twelfth year, this dharma chatra has been my home. What else do I need?'

Recollecting this first encounter with the genius, his contemporary and another genius in his own right, Vasudevacharya writes:

> This in brief was my very first conversation with Muthaiah Bhagavathar when we were students at Thiruvayyar. Even when he was speaking of the misfortunes he had faced, he maintained a cheerful countenance. One evening, when we were sitting in the front verandah of his choultry, we talked about our younger days and thought the Creator had made both of us sail in the same boat. Thereafter, we became fast friends.

Born on 15 November 1877, Dr Harikesanallur Muthaiah Bhagavathar is one of the most important post-Trinity composers and an important vocalist as well. Muthaiah Bhagavathar was born to Lingam Iyer and Anandambal in 1877. After the early death of his father, he was brought up by his maternal uncle Lakshmana Suri of Harikesanallur, who taught him Sanskrit and the Vedas. The uncle was an orthodox Vedic scholar who believed that music and dance were not respectable pursuits and tried very hard to turn his nephew towards the study of Sanskrit. Muthaiah Bhagavathar studied Sanskrit for about two years but his heart was not in it. Finally, he left Tirunelveli for Tiruvayyar without telling anyone. He had resolved to learn music even if it meant begging for a living.

Bhagavathar wandered about in search of an able guru. At last, a reputed *vidwan* named Sambashiva Iyer, who belonged to the Thyagaraja *shishya parampara*, agreed to teach him. Muthaiah Bhagavathar studied under him for seven years and acquired proficiency in music. He got further musical training from Sambasiva Iyer's son T.S. Sabesa Iyer.

Muthaiah Bhagavathar was twenty when he returned to Harikesanallur. He stayed in his hometown for about five years, and gave a few concerts. In those days music concerts did not receive as much encouragement as musical discourses did, and Muthaiah Bhagavathar decided to switch over to that form for a career. He had good scholarship in Sanskrit; he had fluency of speech, an excellent knowledge of music and a rich voice. No wonder his discourses became popular within a short while. He was able to make ends meet at last.

As a vocalist, his big break came when in 1887 he sang before Maharaja Mulam Tirunal of Travancore who honoured him as a court musician. This established him as one of the front-ranking musicians of the time. Later he started giving Harikatha performances, for which he earned the name Bhagavathar. This was when he began creating compositions for his Harikathas.

At the age of 25, Muthaiah Bhagavathar settled in Madurai. He started a small music school where he himself taught. Shortly after this, he went to Karur, where he befriended a wealthy landlord of Andipalli named Petta Chettiyar. Fortune smiled on Muthaiah Bhagavathar now. The Chettiyar, who admired his learning, honoured him. As suggested by Muthaiah Bhagavathar, he celebrated the Skanda Sashti festival every year at Karur. He invited well-known vidwans from all over South India to give concerts, and rewarded them liberally. This gave Bhagavathar an opportunity to come into contact with the famous artistes of the time and to further his scholarship. But the happy days came to an end when Petta Chettiyar passed away. Dejected, Bhagavathar left Karur and after touring places, like Calcutta and Rangoon, he settled in Madras.

The next phase of his life, at the age of 50, was from 1927 as a court musician in Mysore. Most of his compositions were created in this period. Bhagavathar composed over 108 *kritis* in an equal number of ragas in praise of Goddess Chamundeshwari. Many derived *ragas* or *janya ragas*, which were hitherto unused, were used in his compositions. Initially, he composed mostly in *madhya kala* or medium tempo, like Shri Thyagaraja. After 1931, he was influenced by Muthuswamy Dikshitar's compositions and started composing in *vilambita kala* or the slow tempo. His compositions of the *dhatu* or notation for the *Ashtottara shata nama kritis* in Kannada dedicated to Goddess Chamundeshwari, the *mathu* or lyrics being composed by Devottama Jois, are ample testimony of his devotion and knowledge.

The scholar in him was always ready to absorb other forms of music, assimilate those aspects into the Carnatic style and innovate on his own. It is said that on a visit to Benaras, he heard Rag Sohini of the Hindustani style and was so captivated by its haunting beauty that he wished to adapt it to the Carnatic System. On omitting the occasional *panchama* usage, he found its *lakshana* agreed with that given in the South Indian music books. Thus was born Raga Hamsanandi, in a beautiful song *Needu Mahima Pogada Naa Tarama Rama*, an instant hit, which took South India by storm and was rendered by all musicians of the south in their concerts. Similarly he created popular ragas like Mohanakalyani, Valaji, Budha Manohari and Gauda Malhar, to name a few. His musical brilliance comes to the fore in his compositions in several similar sounding ragas, like Saranga Malhar, Nagabhushani, Gowda Malhar and Pashupatipriya.

It is said that on one occasion Bhagavathar was so moved by the Maharaja's agony due to severe mouth ulcers that he went home and composed the *kriti Rajarajaraadhite* in Raga Niroshtha (the name of the raga literally meant 'no contact with the lips'!) and prayed for the speedy recovery of his benefactor.

In 1936, he was again invited by Maharani Sethu Parvathi Bai of Travancore and spent several years there. During that time, one of his major contributions was in popularising Travancore Maharaja Swati Tirunal's compositions and systematising the notations of over 300 *kritis* of Swati Tirunal. He was also the first principal of Travancore's Swathi Tirunal Academy of Music. He wrote and published a book in Tamil on the theory of music, entitled *Sangeeta Kalpadruma*. In 1940, Bhagavathar composed *Srimat Thyagaraja Vijaya* in Sanskrit, which sketches the life, achievements and compositional characteristics of the saint. Consisting of 487 *shlokas*, the work is divided into seven *sargas* or cantos—the number seven reflecting the seven notes of music, even as the *shloka* of each *sarga* starts with the letters *sa ri ga ma* and so on.

Apart from being a vocalist and composer, Muthaiah Bhagavathar was also a learned musicologist. He was actively involved in the Annual Conference of Experts conducted by the Music Academy of Madras. In 1930 he was awarded the Sangeetha Kalanidhi by the academy. He also wrote a book on the science of music, *Sangeetha Kalpadhruma*, for which he was awarded an honorary doctorate in 1943 by the Travancore state.

Vasudevacharya fondly recollects:

Muthaiah Bhagavathar, who had endured several hardships in life, had great compassion for the poor. No musician who visited him returned empty-handed. His was a small family: he, his wife and his daughter. Even the daughter passed away shortly after his coming down to Mysore. Though they were only two at home, husband and wife, they had to ensure food for at least 15 people—morning, and evening. Friends and relatives always flocked around him but Bhagavathar never encouraged idle talk; his life was dedicated to music and he spoke only about music. Those who went to him rarely returned without learning something valuable. Occasionally, if bored, he played cards. On many occasions, he invited me to join him in the game.

Before he composed his kirtanas in Shankarabharana and Kharaharapriya, he sent for me and made me sing half-a-dozen times the kirtanas I had composed in those ragas, namely, Harini Bhajinche and Rara Yenipilichithe. He then remarked: 'Acharya, I now have a complete picture of the emotional shades of ragas and I shall begin my composition.'

Apart from his varnas and kirtanas which are rich specimens of melody and emotion, I had a great admiration and liking for his tillanas and darus. Many a time, when I sang at the palace, he accompanied me on the mridanga. No one could question his skill. After all, he had learnt under no less a vidwan than Narayanasamappa of Tanjore. He possessed an accurate knowledge of rhythm which explains the excellence of his tillanas and darus. He first sang his compositions before vidwans and welcomed their suggestions and comments. He accepted all the criticism he found valid, and incorporated the necessary changes. Though he could render all ragas equally well, fully elucidating their emotional content, Mukhari was his favourite and his rendering of that raga was unique.

Veene Venkatagiriappa (1887–1952)

Along with the family of Adiappayya and his successors, including Sheshanna, the other family that greatly contributed to the Mysore Bani was that of Veene Ramakrishnaiya, the court musician in Haidar Ali's time. In his family were born many musicians, including his grandson Dodda Subba Rao and his son Chikka Subba Rao. Venkatagiriappa was the maternal grandson of this Dodda Subba Rao. He unfortunately lost his parents at a young age and that brought him under the loving tutelage of his maternal family. He also had the opportunity to learn under Veene Sheshanna.

His maiden concert was held at the Khas Bungalow in the presence of Nalwadi Krishnaraja Wodeyar. An interesting event occurred then. The maharaja sat through the performance motionless, a stoic expression on his face. The budding artist was nervous but continued playing with grit. At the end of the concert the maharaja did not say a word. He merely gave him Rs 2 as a gift and left. Chikka Subba Rao was deeply disappointed at what he thought was his nephew's maiden failure. To make matters worse for him, attendants from the court taunted him about the wholesome reward that he had received. Subba Rao maintained his composure and told them that the very fact that the maharaja heard his nephew play would remain a cherished honour. But in reality all this was a ploy by the maharaja to test the true mettle of the musician. He was actually greatly impressed with the young man and this began Venkatagiriappa's entry into the Mysore court.

He soon won the maharaja's heart and was appointed to several positions of eminence. He was the director of the Palace Band, headed the supervisory committee that assessed upcoming musicians for palace performances, taught the *veena* to Yuvaraja Kanthirava Narasimharaja's daughters and the students of the Government Training College and Maharani's High School. He learnt Western music and made some valuable contributions to it at the behest of the maharaja. He gave performances at many places in and outside the state and was honoured by the raja with the title of 'Vainika Pravina'.

Maharani Sethu Parvati Bai of Travancore was so overwhelmed by his performance that she is said to have literally worshipped him by showering him with a variety of flowers. He is also credited with composing the music for the Travancore Anthem and for composing twenty-six *kritis*, five *varnas*, three *ragamalikas*, four *tillanas* and three *naghmas*. This last was a new genre in the Carnatic style that he created, resembling the *gats* prevalent in the Hindustani style.

Among his celebrated disciples were the world-famous *veena* player Mysore Dr V. Doreswamy Iyengar, Prof R.N. Doreswamy, M.J. Srinivasa Iyengar, M. Cheluvaraya Swamy, N. Chennakeshaviah, Rajamma, Rajalakshmi, V. Desikachar, Ranganayaki, C. Krishnamurthy and others. His celebrated disciple Veene Doreswamy Iyengar recounts:

> I did not undergo gurukulavasam. Our house was very near to Venkatagiriappa's. I would go to my guru's house in the morning. He would teach and watch me as I played. If I committed any mistake, I had to repeat the portion at least 15 to 20 times till I could play perfectly. Unless he was satisfied he would not proceed further. He always said, 'You must get siddhi in playing.' In this way he taught me Chitta Tânam that Veena Sheshanna had specially composed for Vainikas to understand the method of playing Tânam. They are studded with gamakas and that gave me excellent training in gamakaful Tânam and also improvised Tânams. Muthaiah Bhagavathar was then the Asthana Vidwan. Chamundeswari is the deity of the Royal house. Muthaiah Bhagavathar has composed many kirtanas on Chamundeswari. Venkatagiriappa taught me several of those songs.
>
> The Mysore Maharaja was very particular that the second line of Vainikas, Vocalists and others were prepared. So one day he asked my guru whether he had given training to young persons to take on his mantle. Then, along with me, Ranganayaki Parthasarathy and Nallar Rajalakshmi were also learning Veena. The Maharaja asked my guru to bring his disciples one day to

the Palace so that he could hear them. I remember I played for half an hour. The Maharaja heard me and asked my guru, 'Who is that boy?' pointing to me. 'He is our orchestra Veena Vidwan, Venkatesa Iyengar's son.' The Maharaja told my guru, 'Train this boy well. He is full of promise.' I was pleasantly surprised when the Maharaja gave me Rs 50. In those days you can imagine the value of Rs 50.

Mysore T. Chowdaiah (1894–1967)

Here was another towering musical personality who dazzled under the royal patronage of the Wodeyars. It is said of him that

> in the field of Karnatak music, Violin Chowdiah is a towering personality like that of a delicately carved, rich and imposing Gopuram. His perfect knowledge of Shabda jala, his innate ability to traverse the entire spectrum of raga with supreme ease and his capacity to give perfect solace to his listeners are beyond the frail capacity of words.*

Born in T. Naraseepura district, Chowdaiah showed a natural inclination for music right from childhood. Eighteen years of strenuous tutelage under the strict disciplinarian, Bidaram Krishnappa, transformed him into an ace violinist. His break came when he was barely seventeen. It came by chance when he was honoured with a request to accompany his guru when the violinist failed to turn up. After that there was no looking back for him. He accompanied all the stalwarts of the then pantheon of Carnatic music—Mysore Vasudevacharya, Chembai Vaidyanatha Bhagavathar, Ariyakudi Ramanuja Iyengar, Tiger Varadachariar, Musiri Subrahmanya Iyer, G.N. Balasubramaniam, the Alattur brothers, T.R. Mahalingam, Semmangudi Srinivasa Iyer—to name a few. His mastery of both the left- and right-hand techniques and his unique bowing style earned him great accolades from connoisseurs and artists alike. He is credited with over twenty-five *kritis* and eight *tillanas*, one of which is a *nadai tillana* where the tempo or *nadai* changes successively.

Few women entered the musical profession in those days. Among the few women musicians of the times, mention must be made of Bangalore Nagaratnamma, who was popular all over South India for her musical

---

* Taken from the 1962 souvenir of the Rasika Ranjani Sabha, Calcutta.

brilliance. She was earlier an exponent of the Bharatanatyam form of classical dance. In honour of the memory of Saint Thyagaraja she undertook to renovate his *samadhi* or resting-place at Tiruvaiyur in Tanjore, where to this day, Carnatic musicians assemble to pay tribute to the saint at the famous Thyagaraja Aradhana conclave. Her recitals were marked by purity of diction and style.

It was the tradition of the Mysore Court to honour prominent artists by inviting them to perform in the royal presence and to accept the title of *asthana vidwan*. It is said that in 1937 Maharaja Krishnaraja Wodeyar extended an invitation to Chembai Vaidyanatha Bhagavathar to perform. Chembai accepted the invitation and gave a performance which was hailed as excellent by the maharaja as well as by his courtiers. Next day Wodeyar presented the *vidwan* with a shawl and other tokens of appreciation. Muthaiah Bhagavathar also honoured Chembai and a photograph showing the two Bhagavathars together is on display at the Mysore palace till this day.

The maharaja then expressed his wish to have Chembai recognised as an *asthana vidwan*. Though pleased to hear this, Chembai declined, saying that he would be unable to discharge the obligations of a court musician, which required his attendance at the court frequently and especially during Dasara. The *vidwan* was already committed, for many years now, to perform Navaratri puja privately at home and therefore he was not available for any public engagements during that holiday period. His sense of priorities was such that he did not wish to break this commitment. Far from being upset, the maharaja appreciated Chembai's sense of priorities. The courtiers too were struck by his dedication. In subsequent years, Chembai is said to have performed at the court several times at the Maharaja's invitation.

Not only did the maharaja invite to Mysore famous Carnatic musicians of his times, such as Tiger Varadachariar, Veene Dhanammal and Ariyakudi Ramanuja Iyengar, he also patronised the Hindustani style. Maharaja Krishnaraja Wodeyar IV invited the legendary Hindustani musician Ustad Faiz Khan of the Agra *gharana* or style and also Ustad Abdul Karim Khan of the Kirana *gharana* to Mysore. The legendary singer of her times, Gauhar Jaan of Calcutta (1875-1930), who was among the first musicians of India to be recorded on the gramophone, was patronized by the Maharaja in the last days of her life when she was in great misery in her home town of Calcutta. She was appointed a court musicians with a monthly allowance of Rs 500 and a bungalow in Mysore. Gauhar also breathed her last in Mysore in 1930. Many Hindustani musicians were specially invited to perform during the Dasara celebrations, and some of them settled in Mysore to teach music. Abdul Karim Khan stayed in the city and was a guest of the maharaja for six months while Aftab Barkatullah Khan of Calcutta a well-known sitar artiste of his times was another visitor who stayed on in Mysore at the behest of the maharaja.

The Cultural symbiosis that this interaction among musicians created was immense and added to the cosmopolitan character of Mysore. It facilitated an erudite Muthhaiah Bhagavathar to incorporate many Hindustani ragas into Carnatic music; Ustad Abdul Karim Khan learnt many Carnatic kritis from Vasudevacharya and in fact incorporated the kalpana swara technique into the Hindustani sargams which are an integral part of his Kirana Gharana. The short stay of about 2 years of Sarala Debi Choudhrani, Rabindranath Tagore's niece, in Mysore at the Maharani Girl's School, exposed her to Carnatic music and the Veena of Mysore. On her return she sung these to her uncle Tagore, who was so impressed by the Carnatic tunes and composed songs based on these. This in turn gave birth to a new genre of Rabindra Sangeeth called the 'Bhanga Gaan.' So many of the Carnatic kritis like *Lavanya Rama, Meenakshi Me Mudam dehi* etc have their Bengali counterparts as well! Thus the idea of cultural exchange among different genres was actively encouraged in Mysore.

Nalwadi's reign also saw Mysore playing a very modernizing role in musical development. The palace records have interesting details about individual musicians who came forward to collaborate in musical reform and education. The court took an active interest in developing a royal school of music for teaching music and setting it to notation. The main features of this project were scientific theory and systematization.

Instrumental orchestras in Carnatic, Hindustani and Western styles and many times an amalgam of all the three was another prominent feature of the music of Mysore. Otto Schmidt conducted the Western Orchestra. Carnatic vidwans were commissioned the job of harmonizing. Carnatic tunes and transcribing them in staff notation. In today's democratic world while many purists frown upon creative collaborations between genres, in the early decades of the 20th century, Mysore encouraged a grand instrumental ensemble of three varied musicians of varied nationalities-

Otto Schmidt on the violin, Dr Margaret Cousins on the Piano and Sheshanna on the Veena!"

Krishnaraja Wodeyar also patronised Western music and founded a European band with a German conductor to popularise Western classical music. Artists selected for the European band of the Mysore Palace had to train and clear the music examination of Trinity College of Music, London, for which the examiners had to come from England to Mysore. They were provided accommodation by the maharaja. Instrumental orchestras of Carnatic and Hindustani music also received much attention during his reign. He introduced the public address system (microphones) on the palace premises, facilitating the enjoyment of music by the common people as well.

MUSIC UNDER JAYACHAMARAJA WODEYAR

The music of Mysore reached its zenith during the rule of Jayachamaraja Wodeyar.

He was a prolific composer and a greatly talented musician himself. The atmosphere of music and culture that existed in the Mysore Palace inspired the young prince to take up music. His sister, Smt Vijaya Rani recounts:[*]

> I think the cultural atmosphere prevailing in the Mysore Palace at the time of our childhood did undoubtedly have a profound influence on us...though we grew up steeped in Carnatic music and dance, etc., we strangely enough were not taught Carnatic music until a later stage. Our musical lessons commenced with piano for my brother and myself and violin for my sister. Sister Ignatius was from the Good Shepherd Convent in Mysore. After basics we went through the Annual Examinations held by the Trinity College of Music in London starting with the grade examinations and on the diploma...Western music was a passion with him. He devoted whatever little time he could get in to its study. He played and read extensively, thereby enlarging his repertoire of piano music. This habit continued till the end of his life.

---

[*] Taken from the Mysore Association Silver Jubilee Souvenir, 'A Tribute from a Sister—His Highness Jayachamaraja Wodeyar'.

In fact, an essay that he penned in his early years, titled 'Aesthetic Philosophy of India', provides an insight into his views on music:[*]

> Music has been called the finest of fine arts. In a sense it is also the most elusive and apparently unsubstantial of the fine arts. A musician builds a palace of sound which vanishes into nothingness, even as it is being raised. But induces no feeling of frustration since the musician builds his structure right in the heart of his listeners. We may well say Wordsworth 'The music in my heart I bore long after it was heard no more.'…in Indian music, there is a clear emphasis on the resemblance between the joy of music and the joy of spiritual experience. The final purpose of music is to create a deep joy, similar to the joy that artists get out of the realisation of God…the release or the realisation of the latent Ananda through the medium of musical sound is to help the ordinary man to attain moksha, An aesthetic experience lasts only a short time, no doubt it is temporal. But it is nonetheless worth having since it helps us, even though temporarily, to attain the highest plane.

His 94 compositions are an invaluable contribution to the treasure of Carnatic music and have made their way into the repertoire of South India's reputed musicians. He used rare *ragas* such as Durvanki (*Gam Ganapathe*), Prathapavarali (*Bhooribhagyalahari*) and Bhogavasantha (*Amba Sri*). Composers have traditionally played a very important role in the development of Carnatic music. It is they who through their compositions established the grammar and *bhava* of the many hundreds of *ragas* that are vogue in Carnatic music today.

As mentioned earlier, Jayachamaraja Wodeyar had a brilliant academic track-record and was first taught Western music on the piano, along with his sister Vijaya Devi, by Sister Ignatius. He received high honours in the annual examinations conducted by Trinity College of Music, London. Western classical music became a passion with him. He not only became a good musician but also a composer. He was responsible for forming the Medtner Society in honour of the Russian composer Nikolai Karlovich

---

[*] This essay can be found in Sukanya Prabhakar's 2005 book, *Karnataka Sangeetakke Sri Jayachamarajendra Wodeyaravara Koduge.*

Medtner. On hearing one of his compositions on the B.B.C, the Maharaja made enquiries with his friends in London about the composer. When he was told that Medtner was too poor to have his works recorded and published, he graciously took it upon himself to sponsor the genius and twelve of the composers' best pieces were recorded and published under the aegis of the 'Maharaja of Mysore's Medtner Society' established in London in 1949! Despite his failing health, Medtner recorded his three piano concertos, as well as his sonatas, chamber music, numerous songs and shorter works. Though he never got an opportunity to meet him in person, Medtner conveyed his gratitude to the Maharaja by dedicating his third Piano concerto to him!

The Medtner project brought the Maharaja in touch with Walter Legge, an influential British classical record producer, who was invited to Mysore. Legge recollects this as a fantastic experience, being totally astonished by the royal library with over 20,000 rare records and a large range of loud speakers and several grand pianos. Legge had nurtured dreams of founding a new orchestra, the Philharmonia. His joy knew no bounds when the Maharaja readily agreed to give him an annual subvention of £ 10,000 for three years to enable him to establish the Philharmonia Orchestra and the Philharmonia Concert Society in London on a firm basis. The Maharaja also became the first President of the Philharmonia Concert Society in 1948.

One of the last wishes of German opera composer, Richard Strauss, was that Kirsten Flagstad should be the soprano to introduce the four songs which he finished in 1948. The Maharaja sponsored this even with a $ 4,800 guarantee for the performance. Strauss was overwhelmed by emotion to see a packed royal albert Hall, with German conductor Wilhelm Furtwangler in the lead and Soparno Flagstad singing his 'Four Last songs' (Going to sleep, September, Spring and At Sunset) in 1950!

The Maharaja also sponsored Louis Kentner's recording of Balakirev's Piano Sonata and Etudes d'execution transcendante Op 11 — the series 12 compositions written for the piano by Sergei Lyapunov.

After 1940, when he came in contact with many eminent Carnatic musicians, like Vasudevacharya, Ariyakudi, Tiger Varadachariar and others, his interests gravitated more towards the Carnatic style. His knowledge of music, Sanskrit and philosophy was the basis of his 94 *kritis* in Sanskrit. He has followed the Muttuswamy Dikshitar style in composing *pallavi* and *anupallavi* portions. The lyrical beauty and complexity of words are the hallmarks of his *kritis*, many being set to the *mishra jhampa tala*. He was a Srividya Upasaka or a devotee of the Goddess. His compositions therefore use phrases like *Sri Vidya Shodashakshari, Akaradi Khshakaranta* in the *kriti Amba Sri Rajarajeswari* (Raga Bhogavasanta), *Shodashakshari kundalamale* and *Navantaragata vasarathe* in *Bale brihat shrishti mule* (Raga Simhendra Madyama) which are rich in symbolism of the divine feminine and tantric lore.

Apart from the usual ragas, he also composed in rare and new ragas, like Bala Chandrika, Bhanu Chandrika, Hamsanatini, Hamsavinodini, Bhupala Panchama, Suranandini, Jayasamvardhini, Neelaveni, and so on. Of the 94 kritis, 11 are in praise of Lord Ganesha, 13 for Lord Shiva, 4 for Lord Vishnu, 2 for Goddess of whom the Maharaja was a great worshipper.

The royal insignia was the mythical bird Gandabherunda and the bracelets given away as gifts to renowned musicians were embossed with this symbol. Other eminent musicians at the royal court of Mysore during this time were Tiger Varadachariar, Chennakeshavaiah, Titte Krishna Iyengar, S.N. Mariappa, Chintalapalli Ramachandra Rao, R.N. Doreswamy, H.M. Vaidyanatha Bhagavathar and others.

By this time new and strange developments had caught up with the world of Carnatic music. It had come a long way now from the temples and *puja* rooms of the Trinity and singing bards to the houses of the *devadasis* followed thereafter by lavish royal patronage in the courts of Mysore, Tanjore, and Travancore, etc., as seen earlier. The freedom movement was gathering momentum and it had an indelible impact on all walks of life. Music—a part of society—could not remain untouched. Madras emerged as the new centre for music around this time for strong political and social reasons. As eminent author T.J.S. George puts it:

> 'Madras', the first city of Tamil, was also the political headquarters of the British administration in the south. In fact the Madras Presidency covered virtually the entire south, subsuming large chunks of present day Andhra, Karnataka and Malabar regions. Madras was the pan-south seat of power from where all decisions flowed. That eminence also elevated Madras to the status of the premier centre of cultural and intellectual activities in the south. The Madras benchmarks set the pace in education, dance and painting. In Carnatic music too, Madras developed into the hub

of authority. By the end of the nineteenth century, it was not enough for a musician to be established in Thanjavur or Madurai or Mysore or Tirupati. For true recognition, he or she had to go to Madras and be acknowledged there. After the Madras Music Academy was established in 1928 by leading residents of Mylapore, the Brahmin citadel of Madras. Carnatic music acquired an instant 'Vatican Council' of its own, the ultimate symbol of establishmentarian power. The academy's approval could build careers and disapproval could destroy them.

Thus the seat of authority seemed to gravitate away from the places where this musical form had actually taken birth and grown. With this came numerous allegations of step-motherly treatment of musicians from other states, be it Mysore or Travancore or Andhra. Ace violinist Dwaram Venkataswamy Naidu or a Chowdaiah always felt the discrimination, not feeling wholeheartedly 'accepted'. It was a sad truth that strangely seems to dog the Carnatic music world even in present times.

But it would be worthwhile to conclude this elaborate chapter, which sketches the growth of classical music in Mysore, with the assertion that Karnataka presents a rich synthesis that perhaps few other states would, when it comes to musical tolerance. Sadly, musical forms in India have got ghettoised in the citadels of their promotion. While Chennai and the Cauvery belt remains the most distinctive proponent of Carnatic classical music, places, like Pune, Kolkata, and Gwalior, etc., remain the citadels of the Hindustani style. But there is very little tolerance for the other style or even an acknowledgement of them in these places. However, in Karnataka, while the old Mysore state was a rich citadel of Carnatic music and to an extent Hindustani music, the northern parts of the State—known as Bombay Karnataka—were centres of Hindustani music. No wonder then that the veritable greats of contemporary Hindustani music, like Pandit Bhimsen Joshi, Smt Gangubai Hangal, the late Mallikarjun Mansoor, the legendary Kumar Gandharva and others, hail from Northern Karnataka; while the Carnatic greats like Veena Doreswamy Iyengar, Violin Maestro Chowdaiya, Vidwan R.K. Srikantan, Mysore Manjunath and Nagaraj, Flautist Shashank and others hail from Mysore! A unique synthesis of styles here! And it speaks of the Mysorean ethos of tolerance, acceptance, assimilation and enrichment that I have tried to capture in this section.

APPENDIX TO CHAPTER 26

THE MYSORE BANI OF VEENA—FOR THE TECHNICALLY ORIENTED

*B**ani* is nothing but a style that is cultivated carefully over a period of time by a set of people or one person. This style or *bani* is then passed over to the next generation of *shishyas* or disciples who want to follow that particular style of rendition. Its usage is similar to the word *gharana* in Hindustani music. To the lay listener, all *veena* recitals my sound alike, but the discerning ear can distinguish different styles of playing. The four southern states evolved their own *veena* traditions and vied with each other for excellence. Karaikudi Sambasiva Iyer, Subbarama Iyer and Dhanammal of Tamil Nadu, Venkataramana Das and Sangameswara Sastri of Andhra Pradesh, Sheshanna and Subbanna of Mysore and Venkatadri Bhagavathar (who belonged to Palghat Anantarama Bhagavathar's family), of Kerala were legends in their own lifetime. Each of these *vainikas* had their field of specialty. If one excelled at speed, another mastered subtle nuances and dynamics.

THE STRUCTURE OF THE MYSORE VEENAS[*]

Not only the style, but also the structure of the *veenas* varied from one state to the other. In the Mysore *veenas*, the main resonator (*kudam*) and the *dandi* are manufactured with the best kind of jackwood, which has

---

[*] This section of the appendix has been taken from the Ph.D. thesis of eminent *veena* artist and teacher, Vidushi Dr Jayanthi Kumaresh.

good grains. These *veenas* are polished with colourless polish. In the old Mysore *veenas* the *birudais* are made of ebony wood with ivory *shikamani*. The wood used for the neck is a kind different from the one used for the main body. The *yali* (head) is carved directly from the neckpiece of the *veena*. The thickness of the wood used for the round *kudam* in the Mysore *veena* is very little as compared to the Tanjore *veena*. It is only about 2.5 to 3 mm. This increases the resonance of the instrument. The main resonator is absolutely plain with no decorations whatsoever.

The top board or the soundboard of the main resonator plays a very important part on the final quality of the timbre of the *veena*. In the Mysore *veena*, this soundboard is made from good quality rosewood with parallel grains. Following the craft tradition of the city, the soundboard is relatively thin (around 4 mm) and its profile is completely flat. These characteristics, which render it very flexible, bring about a low resistance to the vertical pressure exerted on to its centre by the bridge. In fact, because of the absence of any bar, there is a slight sinking at this spot. The flexibility of the sound boards of the Mysore *veenas* favors the emission of the low register, but forbids all excessive use of string deflection which, due to considerable increase of pressure on the bridge, deforms the sound board and alters the accuracy of the instrument, in particular the stability of the *tâla* strings. No sound hole is visible on the surface of the soundboard and the instrument is therefore a completely closed unit.

The absence of decorations could be because of the thinness of the wood used on the main resonators. But it is said that the *veenas* of court musicians were decorated in some places with silver and ivory.

The neck of the *veena*, also known as the *dandi*, is attached to the main resonator with the help of pegs that go through these two parts. Five pegs go through the *dandi* and the main resonator to attach it and three pegs go through the *dandi* and the peg box to attach it. Fine strips of deer antler conceal these two joints exteriorly with indented edges. This constitutes the sole ornamentation of this part.

The *dandi* is made out of a different kind of jackwood. The *dandi* is rather slender and thins greatly from one end to the other. It is hollow inside. The hollow curvature of the elongated neck is covered on the top by a *dandi palakka*, on which is fixed the fingerboard. The *dandi palakka* in the Mysore *veena* is made of rosewood. This fingerboard is fixed on the *dandi* by skin glue, and joined to the soundboard by a brass screw. Three small knobs made out of antler, which are fixed to its side, serve as nuts for the drone strings. The wax made out of beeswax, rosin and lamp black is applied on the two ledges of the *dandi palakka* and the frets are placed on this. The frets in the Mysore *veena* are of increasing length.

The peg box is made out of rosewood and is attached to the *dandi* by a pegged tenon and as stated before, its *yâli* is carved at its extremity, from the same block. Access to the pegs is largely open, without a cover, and no storage space (for plectrums) has been arranged at the top. The tuning pegs are arranged on both sides of the peg box in two groups: firstly those of the two highest strings, *sârini* and *panchama* and secondly those of the two lowest strings, *mandhara* and *anumandhara*. A fine decoration made from strips of engraved antler, the only one on the entire instrument marks the two exterior edges.

In Mysore, where there is a strong tradition of woodcarving, the making of the *yâli* is realised with particular care. Each instrument maker has for this piece his own canons which he reproduces with slight variations depending on the instrument, and which forms a sort of signature. The *yâli* in the Mysore *veena* is more of a lion than a dragon. The piece is both voluminous yet slender and is made with extreme care. It forms just one piece with the peg box and a petal-like finish, imitating fur extends itself widely underneath it.

Regarding the strings, the first two strings are made of steel and the lower octave strings are made of bronze. The bridge's characteristics are substantially responsible for the particular timbre of the *veena*. The bridge is formed from a wooden base onto which is glued using lacquer, a plate of brass or bronze with a slightly rounded profile that serves to support the four melodic strings. The profile and the incline of this surface are of capital importance in the quality of the timbre of the instrument and are subject to very minute adjustments. The three *tâla* strings rest on another plate of brass, curved, immobilised between a foot of the bridge and the soundboard simply by the pressure of the strings. Two small bamboo or steel nails, embedded into the soundboard hold in place the two feet-like extensions of the bridge onto which a lateral push is exerted due to the *tâla* strings. The bridges from Mysore have the characteristic of using a small independent plate of steel to support the *sârini* string with the other strings normally resting on brass. According to the musicians, the use of steel gives the tone a slight 'sharp' colour, which no doubt favours its perception.

The *meru* is constructed from a small parallel fret-like structure made from deer antlers, rounded on the upper side and equipped with four notches. The four knobs on which the *tâla* strings pass though are made out of antler and are fixed on the side of the *dandi*.

The tailpiece or the *nagapasha* is a rectangular outgrowth from the main resonator and the soundboard, which is reinforced by a plate of the antler, and pierced with nine holes. Each string is attached to the tailpiece by a metal buckle (*langar*). This device called *langar* allows the string to be easily tuned with precision. The Mysore *veena* uses a simple twist of brass wire for a runner.

The tuning pegs are made out of rosewood and are made from one piece and are decorated with small buttons of antler, which are fixed in the middle of the handle. The secondary resonators, which now serve the purpose of only providing the required height to play the instrument, were initially made of scooped out gourd (*sorakkais*). It was said that this too complemented in enhancing the quality of sound.

But now in the Mysore *veena*, since the beginning of the twentieth century, metal resonators made from plates of welded steel, coloured either green or black, are used.

The Style

Among all the styles, Mysore *veena* Bani with its *meetu* (style of plucking at the strings) and presentation has a charm of its own. The style can be described as basically instrumental, and seeks to retain the melodic purity of the notes. Therefore, deep *gamakas* are generally not used. The Mysore style exhibits the significance of *veena*-playing with *gamakas* and the correct *kalapramana* with which they should be rendered. Shallow *gamakas*, playing the notes on the frets, a pleasing *meetu*, use of *tribhinna* (plucking the three strings simultaneously or successively) for a pianoforte effect, use of *janta swaras* in phrases like *sa-ni-ni-dha-dha-pa-pa-ma* and *dhatu swaras* such as *ri-pa-ga-dha-ma-ni-pa-sa* are typical of this style. The fingers of the left hand are separated to facilitate fast passages. The secret of producing a mature sound lies in the plucking of strings. A special fingering technique was introduced whereby a fast musical passage could smoothly be negotiated with a single stroke. Inflecting the string produced certain nuances. The effect of 'Pause' while rendering *alapana* and *swara prayogas* is another important characteristic that highlights this Bani.

The *raga* Alapana is presented on these lines, and the *tanam* typical of Mysore is full of melodic effects achieved by the use of appropriate plucking modes. According to *veena* exponent Doreswamy Iyengar, an interesting feature used to be the *chitta tana* (preset *tanam*). These were extensively used for practice to help the student gain speed and clarity. *Tanas* are played in three degrees of speed that add colour and liveliness. The employment of *dhatu swara prayogas* while rendering *kalpana swaras* is another noteworthy feature of the Mysore school. Compositions like *darus* and *tillannas* are well-known for representing the *dhatu swara prayogas*.

The interpretation of a particular note in Mysore style can be well portrayed by introducing special effects. There are various possible modes with which a particular musical note can be presented in Mysore style.

Many ragas such as Behag, Jhenjooti or Khamas played by *vainikas* of the Mysore school have a distinct North Indian touch, due to the proximity of Karnataka's northern districts to Maharashtra and the resulting influence. It is very pleasing and reposeful. Playing *veena* in Mysore style is unique. It is played with the nails of the right hand, without using the metal plectrums usually required. This helps the strings to resonate more naturally. The mellifluous touch comes the closest to soft vocal tones. 'Veena as such is a soft and melodious instrument and needs delicate handling,' says Doreswamy Iyengar, in whose hands the *veena* was never a loud instrument.

The structure of an instrument tends to affect the way it is played. The top board of the Mysore *veena* is so thin that exerting pressure through inflexion of strings or deep *gamakas* would dent it. So, unconsciously perhaps, the Mysore *vainikas* play in a more fret-based style. The resulting tone, sweetness and lilt are characteristic of the Mysore style. Finally, mastering the technique is only a means to an end and the sensitivity of the Mysore Bani can be appreciated more in a close and intimate gathering. These are some of the characteristics of the Mysore Bani:

- Preference for straight notes
- Liberal usage of *meetus*
- Tonal sweetness
- Using natural finger nails instead of plectrums
- Preference for sharp Veena tone
- Less deflection of strings
- Increased instrumental effects to bring out the beauty of *veena* as an instrument
- Split fingering techniques

27

THE LIVES AND TIMES OF MYSOREANS: CLASSICAL DANCE

The first rays of the sun had just touched the dew-soaked blades of grass. The rest of the city was still curled up in bed. But at 5 am on that auspicious day began a new chapter in the saga of dance. The house of Jetti Thayamma was abuzz with activity. The ritual was the Sadhaka Puje—the initiation of a new student to the fold. Today, little Venkatalakshmi, aged 9, was entering the tutelage of the celebrated dancer of Mysore, Jetti Thayamma.

The Ganapati and Saraswati pujas began the initiation process. Paddy was spread on the ground and on that were placed a pair of spotless white cloths. A *swastika* on the paddy heap signified all auspicious things. The guru led her little student by her hand.

'Venkatalakshmi! Place your right foot on the cloth there and take five steps on it!' she commanded.

The little girl complied, and there was much jubilation in the gathering. A new student, after careful screening, had been chosen to follow the art of classical dance and the few girls there now had a new companion.

Each day now began at 5 AM for Venkatalakshmi. After an initial warm-up exercise, the regimen began. From the *poorvaranga* to the *jatiswaras* and the *varnas*, she was privileged to have the most intense coaching anyone could aspire for.

'Lakshmi! It isn't enough for you to just learn dance. Go and tune the *tambura* there! What is dance if you have no musical sense? Alignment with the *shruti* is the most fundamental aspect of any fine art. It gives you a sense of balance and grounds you to the earth,' would be her guru's constant advice.

Three years later...

The girl was twelve and ready to perform publicly. The date of performance was nearing and once again there was a flurry of activity like the day of her initiation. The Vaddige Puje ritual involved her worship of all the instruments and seeking the blessings of the musical accompaniments. This was followed by the Gejje Puje (worshipping the anklets).

Young Venkatalakshmi bathed in fragrant and scented waters and put on her nine-yard sari in a delightful twist. Her friends beautified her with some fine jewels. With anxiety and nervousness written large on her face, the young girl entered the courtyard of her guru's house where her Rangapravesha or debut in the world of dance was to happen.

The *pushpanjali shloka* and *choornika* were sung delightfully by the musician ensemble. Thayamma then placed a pair of anklets, newly woven in thread, in a brass plate and took it around the courtyard to seek the blessings of all the assembled elders. She then went to Venkatalakshmi and lovingly placed her arms around the girl.

'Today is when your journey truly begins. What you do from now on will show the world whether I was competent or not. Don't bring me a bad name, my dear!' she whispered and herself tied the anklets around the young girl's ankles.

The dance that began on that auspicious day in Mysore carried on ceaselessly for decades after that. It won the hearts of millions and established the beauty of the special Mysore Shaili of Bharatanatyam. It brought fame not only to the revered guru Thayamma, but also the deserving student, Padmabhushana Dr K. Venkatalakshamma.

❖

CLASSICAL DANCE IN INDIA

The *Natyashastra* of Bharata—an authoritative treatise on the music and dance of India—attributes the origin of Indian classical dance to the creation of a fifth Veda by the Creator, Lord Brahma, called Natyaveda on the insistence of Sage Narada. It drew from the other four Vedas—the Word came from the Rigveda, Music from the Samaveda, Histrionics from the Yajurveda and *Rasa* or emotions from the Atharvaveda. The emotional involvement in any dance performance transports the dancer and the audience to a realm of beauty, binding them together in the thread of *rasa*. Dance is an outward manifestation of expression and is deeply spiritual in its outlook. Even the seemingly sensuous pieces have a deeper philosophical import of the soul craving for the super soul—an imagery common in music as well. All dance forms have the mechanical body and foot movements or the *nritta* aspect as well as the *abhinaya* or histrionic representation. This in itself is four-fold: *angika* (body language), *vachika* (speech), *aharya* (ornamentation) and *sattvika* (aesthetic abstract). The seven classical dance forms of India are Bharatanatyam, Kuchipudi, Mohiniattam, Kathakali (all from South India), Kathak from the Indo-Gangetic belt of northern India, Odissi from the south-western region of Orissa and Manipuri from the north-east.

The Bharatanatyam dance form is among the oldest of them all and finds mention in the classic Tamil literary work, *Silappadikaram*. With a spurt in temple-building activities after the sixth century AD, the dancers were employed in temples to propitiate the gods. Thus began the practice of the *devadasis*, literally meaning the servants of God. The literary content came from medieval composers and later from the Carnatic music of the South, with *varnas*, *tillanas*, *padams* and *javalis* being the main items of performance.

Classical dance, particularly Bharatanatyam, has been practised professionally as well as academically from ancient times in Karnataka, as is evident in Kannada literature, inscriptions, and paintings. All the evidence points to a rich tradition of dance in Karnataka through the centuries to the present day. The Chalukyan sculptures at Badami and Aihole proclaim that the sculptors of Karnataka had a good knowledge of the *Natyashastra* in the fifth century itself. In fact, the very first dancing figurine of Shiva as Nataraja, sculpted in the *chaturbhangi mudra*, was found in Karnataka's Badami—the erstwhile capital of the Chalukyas. Classical dance was studied as a regular course in the great universities of Talakadu, Talagunda, and Bulligavi between the fourth to the thirteenth centuries. Karnataka's royalty not only patronised the art form, but also learnt it, like the great danseuse, Queen Shantala, of the Hoysala Empire.

The *madanika* (*shilabalike*/sculptures) figures representing dancing figurines are found in the temples of Halebid and Belur. The Vijayanagara empire patronised the various classical art forms. After the fall of the empire, the art of dance was nurtured by the *devadasis*—temple dancers. It was Mysore that took on the mantle of patronising the arts.

Classical dance in Mysore

Kanthirava Wodeyar set up a Bharatanatyam school in Srirangapatna while Chikkadevaraja Wodeyar wrote two dance dramas, *Geeta Gopala* and *Saptopadaki*. The kings honoured local artists as well as those from other kingdoms.

Mummadi Krishnaraja Wodeyar was a contemporary of the 'Tanjore Quartet', consisting of the four brothers, Chinayya, Ponnayya, Shivanandan, and Vadivelu, who gave a *marga* (format) to the Bharatanatyam solo recital. He also patronised many dancers, among whom Jetti Thayamma was the most famous. Daughter of the wrestler Dasappa, she trained under several *gurus*, like Kavisvar Giriappa, Chandrashekara Shastry and Karibasappa Shastry. Jetti Thayamma was not a *devadasi*, and due to some misunderstanding, she did not dance at the royal court of Mysore for a long time. She was very popular for her *abhinaya* both in the Bharatanatyam style and Hindustani nautch—where she rendered *thumris*, *ghazals*, etc. Chamarajendra Wodeyar felicitated her when she was eighty years old, and she received the title of 'Natya Saraswathi' from Dr S. Radhakrishnan.

Other famous dancers of the Mysore school were Chandravadanamma, Puttadevamma, her daughter Chikkadevamma, Kolar Kittappa of Bangalore whose famous students were Nagaratna, Varaalu and Kolar Puttappa, Konamara Deviamma, Ramamani, Mugaloor Tripurasundaramma and others. These dancers and musicians had to pass a vigorous and painstaking test held by the palace officers to choose artists whose art was worthy of exhibiting before the king. One such fastidious officer who sent cold shivers down the spine of many a budding artist was Ambil Narasimha Iyengar.

Chamarajendra Wodeyar continued the patronage and brought Chinnayya to his court, where the latter not only composed several *varnas* and *tillanas* suited to dance, but also influenced to a great extent the dance teachers and musicians of the court. Hence, the indigenous tradition of dance absorbed the other traditions and arrived at a continuous stream of dance art in Mysore.

In the past two centuries, Mysore has produced many illustrious dance teachers, such as Muguru Subanna, Amritappa, Dasappa,

Bangalore Kittappa, Kolar Puttappa, and great dancers like Amritamma, Coimbatore Tayi, Nagaratnamma, the incomparable Jetti Thayamma, and her disciple—the celebrated Venkatalakshamma. Alongside the palace dancers (the *asthana vidushis*) existed the *devadasis* like Rangamma, and Jeejamma—a veritable galaxy of dancers with high standards of excellence and profound scholarship.

However, Maharaja Krishnaraja Wodeyar IV's apathy towards what he considered cheap performances during marriages and functions, called *taphe*, discouraged the tradition to some extent. The banning of dance in temples in 1909 also dealt a blow to the *devadasi* system, which had nurtured the dance form for centuries.

The Mysore Style of Bharatanatyam

Though the Tanjore tradition and Kanchi tradition of Bharatanatyam had mingled with the local modes of dance, the Mysore school encompassing all the artistes of the state had a distinct flavour of its own. The Jetti Thayamma School excelled in *abhinaya*, with an exceptional observance of the *poorvaranga vidhi*. The performance used to be packed with *shlokas, asthapadis, padas* and *javalis* from *Geeta Govinda, Amarushataka, Niti Shataka, Mukunda Mala* and also many Kannada compositions of rare beauty.

Other *banis* that existed within the Mysore school were those of Kittana, Nanjangud Rajamma and the Mugoor School. Kittanna's school was known to observe palace traditions, temple traditions and social performances, which included *choornika, prabandha, ashtadhik paalaka aradhana, swarajati, swara prabandha, saptataleshwari varnas, nava sandhi nritya, ugabhoga, suladis,* etc. This was a rich, relatively lesser-known repertoire.

The Nanjangud style of Rajamma carried on by the late Guru Kaushik was replete with *bhava* or emotion and fascinating *nritya*. The Mugoor School was famous for its strict adherence to *nritta* and various *adavus, jathis* and also a regular string of *jatiswara, varnas, tillanas, padas* and *javalis*.

The Jetti Thayamma school comprised a vast repertoire of *abhinaya* as its forte. The *poorvaranga vidhi* was an elaborate ritual preceding the dance performance—following the rules laid down in the *Natyashastra*—and had a spiritual purport. The dancers at the court stood behind the musicians before commencing the dance. They paid obeisance to their guru and musicians and then came around to start their performance. Besides being good singers, the dancers were also proficient in Sanskrit and *sahitya* (literature). She would sing a *choornika* (a prelude) in Raga

Arabhi in praise of a Rangadhi *devata* (stage goddess) or *natya* (dance) itself in other *sabhas* (gatherings). After the *choornika*, a *sabhavandana shloka* (salutation to the audience), and a *natyaprashamsa shloka* from Kalidasa's play *Malavikagnimitra* were regularly sung and a *pushpanjali shloka* came at the end of it all. Then they danced a *Ganapathi shabda* or other *shabdas* instead of an *allarippu* as is common in the Tanjore style.

As the Mysore dancers were influenced by the presence of Chinnayya, one of the brothers of the famed Tanjore Quartet, they used to perform *jatiswaras*, *shabdas*, *varnas*, and *tillanas*, which were similar to any Tanjore-style dancer. The whole performance would be danced without any break. When it came to the *abhinaya* numbers—*Geeta Govinda*, Kshetragna Padas, *javalis* in Kannada and Telugu, *shlokas* of Amara, *Krishnakarnamrita*, *Mukundamala*, and Bharatahari's *Niti Shataka*—were the chosen ones. The artists danced to many poems by the Dasarakoota composers* and *vachanas* of various poetic works, like *Rajeswara Vilasa*, etc. *Devaranamas*, *kritis* of several well-known composers like Mutthaiah Bhagavathar, Mysore Sadashiva Rao, and Mysore Vasudevacharya were also added to their repertoire.

It is here in the *abhinaya* that the flavour of Mysore was evident. The dancers nearly always rendered a *shloka* before a *pada*, which came as a prelude in the same mood or a *kandha padhya* before a *javali*, which suggested the mood of the particular *nayika* (the heroine) of the *javali*. The *jaru adavus* (slide or rest steps), which embellished the *javalis*, were unique and made the *javali* lively and crisp. *Abhinaya* while seated was also common (unlike today, where the dancers stand throughout), with the dancers themselves singing the lyrics.

THE LEGEND OF THE MYSORE SHAILI: DR K. VENKATALAKSHAMMA

K. Venkatalakshamma was not a *devadasi*. She belonged to the Lambani/Banjara/gypsy community. Born on 29 May 1906 at Tangali Tandya in Kadur, the young girl migrated to Mysore along with her family members.

---

* The Dasarakoota composers were wandering saints who composed devotional music. They were called the Haridasas and created a rich repertoire of devotional music called *Dasa Sahitya*.

A kind *tongawala* suggested a shelter for the nomads. The girl showed great promise in music and dance from a young age. She was taken under the tutelage of the famous royal dancer, Jetti Thayamma. Besides dance, equal importance was given to music and literature. Bidaram Krishnappa and his disciples trained her in music; while Devottama Jois, Shanta Shastry and Giri Bhatta guided her in Sanskrit and literature. She made her mark in the field of dance from the time of her entry at the age of twelve.

Thayamma, as a good teacher, accompanied her students wherever they performed and in fact even provided vocal support on many occasions. The troop would mingle with the public and dance at marriage parties as well. They would reach the marriage venue a few days in advance and befriend the family. So emotionally attached would they get that departing after the function would be a tough proposition for both parties.

Her audition for the palace performance happened at the house of Mysore Vasudevacharya. Many scholars and musicians had assembled. Thayamma was on the *natuvanga* or vocal accompaniment. Young Venkatalakshamma was made to sing a *varna* and a few *kritis* at the outset and later asked to perform while sitting. This way the dancer's expressions acquire greater prominence as the body is still. Naturally, this makes things harder for the dancer. Venkatalakshamma performed a *shloka*, *Yuktakim Thava* followed by a *pada* in Bhairavi, a few *javalis*, Ganapati *shabda*, Bhairavi *jatiswara* and a Kapi *tillana*. An elaborate viva-voce of sorts followed where all the gathered scholars quizzed her on aspects of music, dance and literature. Her brilliance convinced them of her capability to perform in the maharaja's presence and she was appointed a court dancer in 1939.

Dance formed an integral part of all festivities in the Mysore palace. Apart from Dasara, Ganesha Chaturthi was another occasion where dancers rendered their services. Ganesha idols would be placed at different locations in the palace and the dancers would go in troops to each one of these and display their talents. The special *durbars* of the maharaja also called for dance. After the maharaja's entry into the *durbar* hall and the requisite formalities, the dancers would be summoned. If the maharaja was in a mellow mood, the dance would carry on for a while. Otherwise an eye-signal from the Darbar Bakshi would bring the performance to a quick halt. Regular entertainment for Maharani Pratapa Kumari Bai was also a part of the court dancers' responsibilities.

Venkatalakshamma was at the royal court for thirty long years, dancing in front of Nalwadi Krishna Raja Wodeyar and the last king Jayachamarajendra Wodeyar. Later, she became a reader of dance at the fine arts college founded by the University of Mysore. Many central and state academy awards were conferred on her—Natya Shantala (the highest award for a dancer in Karnataka), Padma Bhushan by the Government of India and others. Among the other honours she received are Karnataka Sangitha Nritya Academy Award, an honorary doctorate from the Mysore University in 1977, Mumbai Mysore Association Award in 1986, Karnataka Rajyotsava Award in 1988, Bangalore Gayana Samaja Award in 1989 and so on. She had the rare privilege of performing at the Rashtrapati Bhawan in the presence of the then President of India, Dr Sarvepalli Radhakrishnan.

THE FUTURE OF CLASSICAL DANCE AND THE MYSORE STYLE

The art of dance declined steadily in the early twentieth century due to the social boycott of dancers. The stigma attached to it and the abolition of the *devadasi* system by law due to its gradual degeneration into prostitution, ensured that women from 'good' families were prevented from learning the art. However, important changes have taken place, bound to impact the art form's development. The most important is the shifting of the art from the temple to the western type of theatre with a high stage bound by a proscenium, and with the audience seated in the front. This has, naturally, led to several changes in the choreography, lighting, make-up, costume, and also to an all-round improvement of the supporting musical ensemble.

Patronage of the art and its exponents is no longer exercised by the maharajas, who were great *rasikas*. This has now been taken over by the representatives of the people in a democratic government. Thus, dance has ceased to be elitist and under the monopoly of a particular community, becoming instead the art of the people. The dancer has become an important member of society and is educated, articulate and self-sufficient.

The Mysore School of Bharatanatyam survived in the temples in places, like Moogur, Nelamangala and Kolar, Mulbagal and Kollegal. Sadly, none of these places have dance in the temples anymore. The Mysore

School, too, has not survived in its original form, though there still are a few practitioners. Only shades of the glorious style remain today and the rest of it is merely reminiscent of those *durbars* of grandeur in royal Mysore where the practitioners of this unique style, which was steeped in *abhinaya*, demonstrated their art to a connoisseur maharaja.

28

THE LIVES AND TIMES OF MYSOREANS: FOLK ARTS AND POPULAR TRADITIONS

Folklore and folk arts, they say, mirror our society and its history in a way that few other art forms do. Mark Twain had commented:

India is the cradle of the human race, the birthplace of human speech, the mother of history, the grandmother of legend, and the great grandmother of tradition. Our most valuable and most instructive materials in the history of man are treasured only in India.

Our folk arts are living repositories of the tradition to which Twain was referring. They comprise a bookless world carrying messages to the present, which likes to read about itself.

In an earlier chapter, we had assessed the importance of folklore in the reconstruction of history. Here we seek to examine its relevance in the comprehension of a region's culture. The advent of folklore could be attributed to the fact that man, faced with the wrath and vagaries of nature, dedicated various rituals to Mother Nature in the hope of gaining her benevolence. In folklore, music and dance blend beautifully with literature and poetry—more in tune with the 'spoken' language of the masses—to present a wonderful catharsis of emotions. The tale varies from teller to teller, the performances change based on the audience and the song changes from singer to singer.

What constitutes folklore and tradition? These are all-encompassing words that represent the practices of a society and include myths, legends, folktales, proverbs, folk beliefs, superstitions, customs, folk songs, folk dances, ballads, folk cults with their own set of gods and goddesses, rituals, festivals, magic, witchcraft, art and craft; in short, everything that binds the society together in one cohesive unit.

As with other parts of India, the Mysore state has had a rich cultural tradition in the folk arts. These unsophisticated expressions of the common people mirror the nature of society, the turbulence of the times, the political overtones and the psyche of its people at large.

Traditional clothing in Mysore was also unique. The men, especially the learned ones or the ones in the nobility, loved to sport the elaborate turban famous as the 'Mysore peta' in white silk with golden borders. They also wore a long, black coat and a nine-yard dhoti neatly tucked up at the waist. The coat usually sported a looking glass or a watch suspended by a golden chain from within the pocket. Women of the upper classes and nobility usually wore a nine-yard saree—though some preferred the six-yard saree—tucked from underneath the legs to the back. The famous Mysore jasmine had to adorn their hair. The beautiful paintings of Ravi Verma capture many of these traditional forms of dress of the Mysoreans.

Mysore has contributed a great deal to India's folk arts scenario: plays performed on stage; epic episodes enacted through the Yakshagana form and puppet shows.

Yakshagana

'Yakshagana'—roughly translated as 'Celebration of the Celestials'—is a complete theatre form that includes song, dance and drama and is extremely popular in Malnad, Uttara Kannada and Dakshina Kannada districts of the state. The three different styles of Yakshagana include Karavali Yakshagana of coastal Karnataka, Doddata Yakshagana in northern Karnataka and the Mysore Yakshagana of the old Mysore state. It is essentially a stage form that entertains and educates rural folk. A team of fifteen to twenty actors, mostly nomadic, performs its shows in an open place or field; hence the name 'Bayalaata' or 'open-place play'. In content and format it draws from many regional performance traditions and art forms. Having a history of more than 400 years, Yakshagana evolved into a complete theatrical form during the reign of Mummadi Krishnaraja Wodeyar. He revived and changed many forms in this art and extended patronage to a great exponent, Parti Subba.

Aliya Lingaraja Urs, who was a poet and composer at the court of Mummadi Krishnaraja Wodeyar, has composed a number of Yakshaganas with plenty of songs and *dwipadas*. His famous composition *Girija Kalyana*, on the celestial marriage of Lord Shiva and Parvati, has been composed in both *sangatya* metre as well as in the form of a Yakshagana. The songs blend with the story of the birth of Girija, her youth, her penance, her pining for Lord Shiva as a husband and the final wedding. Various poetic forms, like *padyas*, *kandas* and *shatpadis*, which are broadly classified as *prabandhas* have been utilised here. Classical ragas like Nata, Shankarabharana, Kambodhi, Navroj, Jhunjooti, Surati, Desh, Kalyani, and Punnaga Todi and so on have been used.

With its all-pervasive element of grandeur, the stage of Yakshagana is a parade of colourfully attired heroic characters, with magnificent headgear, costumes and elaborate make-up. The singing by the Bhagavathar and the roaring of percussion instruments like *chande*, *maddale* and cymbals heightens the overall impact. This art form embodies the richness and plurality of music, dialogue, dance, action and colour. Performed in an open-air theatre, a Yakshagana performance takes place at night. Generally, stories from *Ramayana*, *Mahabharata* and the *Puranas* are taken up for performance. The show begins with *Ganesh Stuti*—an invocation to Lord Ganesh or the *Vighna Vinashak* (remover of obstacles. The Bhagavathar offers prayers before taking up the dual role of a singer and of the *sutradhar* or the master of ceremonies. He is a key figure on stage throughout the performance. The invocation is followed by the appearance of the *vidushaka* or jester. Also known as *kodangi*, he brings in the element of buffoonery to the show. *Kodangis* enjoy great liberty and can get away with witty and daring remarks.

The makeshift stage of Yakshagana, set in the open, is deceptively simple. It contrasts with the magnitude of the heroic acts staged on it. As the show progresses into the late hours of night, the story unfolds. There is a lot of scope for heroism as the *rasas* of Roudra (anger) and Veera (heroism) predominate in the performance. Though not devoid of other *rasas*, it mainly portrays heroism.

During a Yakshagana performance, the Bhagavathar sings a verse and the characters interpret it through expressional dance, following it up with dialogues. The actors move majestically, portraying gods, goddesses, *kiratas* or mischief-mongers, demons and other mythological figures. Heavy make-up is used to depict the celestial characters. Heroes and kings are attired in gilded crowns and colourful costumes. Noble kings have a sacred red mark on their forehead and sport a large black moustache. Red and yellow checked sarees tied as *dhotis* are the typical lower garment for the main characters. The key characters display an air of refinement, elegance and authority in their dialogue delivery, facial expressions and gait. The heroic exploits of these characters reach epic proportions as the show progresses into the night. Traditionally, women do not perform in Yakshagana and so the male actors play the female roles as well. However, recent years have seen women entering the field.

Puppetry

Puppetry—string and leather/shadow puppets have been another popular folk form of the state. Many traditional Brahmin puppeteers are found even today in and around Nelamangala near Bangalore. Some of the string puppets in Hallare in Nanjangud *taluk* are more than 300 years old. They are manipulated from above by strings invisible to the audience. The puppeteers are called Gomberamas or Kille Kyatas.

The puppets of south Karnataka, i.e. Mysore are about three feet high at an average and have no legs. Most of the puppets have two eyes in profile—a rare combination of realism and the abstract. The technique of these artistic creations reveals wonderful imagination and skill that breathes life into an inanimate puppet.

In the past, village artists were supposedly given privileges to cut whatever part of the animal hide they needed to make these puppets. Generally, the skins of goats, cattle and hunted deer were used. The raw leather is carefully cleaned and after being soaked in water and tanned well to suit the purpose, the resultant hard and rough leather becomes almost transparent. With their nails, the artists then carve out figures of men, women, gods, goddesses, demons, and so on. Traditionally, indigenous herbs and minerals were used to provide the much-needed dash of colour to these lifeless leather figurines. They retained their innate lustre and brightness for a long time. Red occupied a prime place in the hierarchy of colours, followed by indigo or jungle green and black. Black was made from the soot of a burning lamp. Lighter shades and combinations of these colours offered a wider array of hues to choose from.

Leather puppetry is extensively found in Chitradurga, Bellary and Kolar districts even today. Shadow puppetry—where the actual puppet is concealed behind a screen and only the shadow is visible to the audience—creates a magical world of fantasy and colour.

The themes were drawn from the epics. The motions of the puppets were caused by dexterous manipulation from behind the curtain using bamboo splints. The puppeteer performed the dual role of narrator of the episode and manipulator of the puppets and his work demanded great dexterity to combine these two actions effectively into one. Shrill music was provided by a woman outside who rubbed a reed on the back of a flat dish of bell-metal to accompany the recital. Frequently, musical instruments like *mridangam, maddale, mukhaveena*, cymbals and harmonium were also used, particularly by the richer and more affluent puppet troupes. These shows, like those of Yakshagana, commenced late at night and continued till daybreak. The oil lamp behind the curtain radiated its light, casting coloured shadows of the puppets and making a delightful spectacle.

The puppets were held in profile to enable the audience to recognise them. The size and colour combinations indicated the importance and nature of the character. Contemporary themes were also chosen and the stage would recreate the beauty of a queen's inner apartments or a garden with birds and animals. Besides being thoroughly entertained, the villagers also believed that the staging of such a show would bring rain, good luck and drive away epidemics and diseases.

The puppeteers would set up a simple stage for their performance. It usually consisted of a thick black backdrop, two or three wooden poles, and a curtain to conceal the puppeteers from the audience. A white screen slanted across the stage slightly above the audience. Below the screen was a thick carpet and the three sides and top of the stage were covered with rugs. The puppeteers sat on the platform invisible to the audience.

Sitting in those open fields on a moonlit night and witnessing dancing figures narrating tales from mythology and folklore would have been an experience in itself, far more enriching than the multitude of TV channels we surf today in the name of entertainment!

Harikatha

Harikatha is another folk art form popular all over Mysore state. It combines literature and lilting lyrics to reflect a rich musical and literary content, drawing heavily on Hindu mythology. Over 150–200 years old, this art form has a principal protagonist called Dasa or Bhagavathar or Kirtankar. His accompanists play the *mridangam, tabla,* violin and *harmonium*. He himself holds a pair of castanets or chinking instruments made of wood. In a high-pitched voice the Dasa conveys to an attentive audience messages related to religion and social causes. The Bhagavathar tradition also finds a place in the Carnatic music firmament with the likes of Muthaiah Bhagavathar. He trained under Karandattangudi Govinda Bhagavathar at Tanjore and Krishna Bhat of Maharashtra in this art and learnt the techniques of Harikatha, like Nirupanas, rare and attractive *varna mettus* and so on. A mellifluous voice that can reach and captivate a large gathering with an excellent narrative style are the essential qualities of a Bhagavathar. The Kathakalakshepas were regular all-night features at religious festivals and town fairs.

Nagamandala

Rural masses living mostly in villages, unprotected from serpents and snakes, manifest their fear and reverence for this reptile by worshipping it (the serpent or *Nagaraja* is worshipped as the son of Lord Shiva—Subrahmanya) and portraying it in various art forms. Nagamandala is one such form. It is a drawing created through *rangoli* where serpentine coils numbering four, eight, twelve and sixteen represent the full mandala. Two sets of priests are required for this art form—one set acting as the physicians or *vaidyas* and the other as *patris* or participants. The *vaidyas* hold instruments called *dhakke* and are accompanied by a musical chorus and instrumentalists. While the *vaidyas* beat and sing, the *patris* face them, dancing to their tunes just like a snake-charmer makes a cobra dance to his tunes. Such a folk practice is quite like a physician healing a mental ailment, as the performance is believed to exorcise ghosts possessing the victim. It is a common practice in large parts of the state, especially the coastal areas, to this day.

The Ganjifa Cards

Mysore is famous for yet another interesting artefact—the characteristic Ganjifa cards. The Ganjifa cards have a history of more than 300 years. 'Ganj' is a Persian word meaning treasure, treasury or hoard. Mughal Emperor Babur wrote in his memoirs: 'The night we left Agra, Mir Ali the armourer was sent to Shah Hasan in Tatta to take him playing cards (ganjifa) he much liked and had asked for.'

Babur's son Humayun also enjoyed playing these cards, which remained popular even in Akbar's time. A pack of ganjifa cards consists of ninety-six cards with eight suits of twelve cards each (comprising the numerals one to ten and two 'court' or trump cards). They are generally circular and made of ivory, tortoise shell, thin wood or hard board material. Dancing, hunting, worshipping, playing *chaupar* (gambling boardgame) and processions are some of the subjects painted on the cards.

It was a game that people in Mysore took to, thanks to the revival of the art by Mummadi Krishnaraja Wodeyar, who was an ace at the game. A specific branch of Mysore Ganjifa, distinct from the Mughal style, emerged under his royal patronage. Ganjifa was a popular game among all sections and age-groups of Mysore society. The cards used by the royals were of course beautifully designed whereas the commoners used similar cards, though they were neither as grandly designed nor based on specific themes.

The Mysore cards are distinct, their complicated structure using numerous suits, up to six court cards and a number of loose cards comparable to tarot cards and jokers in European games. Figures and suit signs completely fill the card face. There is also an elaborate chapter in Krishnaraja Wodeyar's *Sritatvanidhi* titled 'Kautuka Nidhi' meaning 'treasure book of sports and pastimes' that lays down elaborate rules and tricks of the game.

In the great audience hall of the Jagan Mohan Palace of Mysore, the walls are covered with paintings of astrological charts and tables and an endless series of board, dice and card games. The court artists produced beautifully designed playing cards for him including the numerous Chad[*] cards for the games he must have invented. Some of his card games required packs of 320 or 360 cards populated by the Hindu pantheon. The Chad games were probably played mainly inside the palace. The structure of Chad cards is derived from the normal Ganjifa, with the suits consisting of court cards and numeral cards. These games are mainly built on religious or astrological themes.

A list of the thirteen popular categories of Chads of Mysore appears here. These Chads were part of the king's collection and so were particularly artistic and ornamented.

---

[*] The Mysore Ganjifa cards were given this unique name, Chad. These cards wee distinct from the Mughal and Persian cards by virtue of their complicated structures. Their themes were also different, drawing on Hindu mythology.

1) Chamundeshwari Chad: A set of 320 cards. It consists of an assembly of the south Indian pantheon. The cards are made of layers of paper, lacquered and painted by hand.
2) Jagad Mohan Chad: Means 'conqueror of the world', this is a name given to Vishnu the Preserver. This Chad set is the largest listed. An almost complete set of round, beautifully painted cards as well as Chamundeshwari Chad in their wooden boxes are in the Leinfelden Museum, Germany.
3) Navin Dashavatara: Navin Dashavatara or the 10 new incarnations of Lord Vishnu is a set of 240 cards in 12 suits of 18 cards each plus extra cards. The description of this Chad in 'Kautuka Nidhi' differs somewhat from the actual composition of the above set. This Chad is an interesting one as two of its suits of 12 cards feature only female divinities. The first shows *apsaras* (divine mistresses in charming poses with birds and trees) and the second shows various poses of Devi or Durga.
4) Nava Graha: or the nine planets. A complete set is in the Leinfelden Museum, Germany. The Chad has 216 cards in a pack. The 12 suits are three supreme divine powers: Durga, Shiva and Vishnu, plus the nine planets.
5) Pancha Pandava Chad: The name signifies the five Pandavas, heroes of the epic *Mahabharata*. An incomplete set of this Chad is in the Leinfelden Museum, Germany and in the Jagan Mohan Palace in the city of Mysore.
6) Devi Dasavatari Chad: The 10 incarnations of Devi with 10 suits of 18 cards each. Sadly, there are no known specimens of these cards in existence.
7) Dikpala Chad: The name designates the guardians of the eight regions of the world or compass. This Chad is supposed to have 10 suits of 16 cards each or 160 in all. There are two Dikpala sets from the Deccan but they may not necessarily be from Mysore.
8) Manohar Chad: Captivator of the mind (Krishna).
9) Sarva Mangala Chad: Bringer of universal bliss (Durga).
10) Navaratna Chad: The nine jewels. Again, there is no longer any specimen available and perhaps these cards have been lost forever.

11) Sadye Jyatadi Chad: No traces of these cards have survived and so there is no description available either.
12) Krishnaraja Chad: Named after the royal inventor. This handy game of 72 cards in four suits must have enjoyed great popularity in and outside the palace. It was a game of the quartet type. This Chad is considered the most beautiful of all the Mysore Chads. One complete set is known to exist, and we know of three incomplete sets and stray cards of five further packs.
13) Navin Chad: This is an Indian adaptation of the four-suited piquet pack with numerals from 6 to 10 and a king, queen, knave and ace. This must have been popular among certain classes of South Indians who were at the time strongly influenced by the French.

Thus, we see in these unsophisticated and rustic forms of art—so close to the common man—a revelation of the socio-cultural history of the region and how it evolved. It also brings to the fore the concerns, aspirations and apprehensions of the common man, remote from the power games and conspiracies of palaces and emperors. All over India, millions of such forms are dying out for lack of encouragement and awareness. But as long as there are people, and as long as they feel joy, sorrow and fear, folk forms will continue to flourish in one way or another. The list above of the various folk arts that came to prominence in the Mysore state is in no way exhaustive and is only the tip of the iceberg. There are as many manifestations of folk art forms as there are human emotions.

APPENDIX TO CHAPTER 28

THE MYSORE DASARA

The culture of a place is intrinsically linked to the festivities that the people there indulge in and the message it conveys to society at large. This festival marks the triumph of good over evil. It also seeks to imply the invincibility and power of the Divine feminine energy—one that sustains and protects the Universe. The Dasara happens to be celebrated as 'Nada Habba' or State Festival in Karnataka to this day— a reminiscent of the past when it was the State festival of the erstwhile Wodeyar Royal Family. It was started by Raja Wodeyar to seek continuity with the Vijayanagara traditions and was fostered further by Ranadhira Kanthirava Narasaraja Wodeyar and successive kings. Even during the interregnum period, the lingering Royal Family carried on the private celebration of the Dasara festival—one that marks the victory of good over evil. Come September—October, Mysore would be engulfed in a plethora of activities and merry—making.

Contemporary observers recount the details of the manner in which the festival was celebrated during Nalwadi Krishnaraja Wodeyar's times. On the morning of the 1st day, the brighter half of the Hindu month of Ashvayuja, the King worshipped Goddess Chamundeshwari, the family deity and presiding Goddess of the State, after a ceremonial bath, prayed to Lord Ganesha and tied the *Kankana* or the sacred thread around the wrist signifying the inauguration of the 10-day festival. Reaching the Durbar Hall, he would worship the *Navagrahas* or nine planets, the throne, circumambulate it thrice and then ascend it. He would then worship the State sword and receive the offerings and honours sent by pontiffs of principal muths and temples of the State. A few Brahmin priests would offer consecrated coconuts and coloured rice; *muzre* (homage) and *nazar* (tribute) by officers, the dewan, citizens and merchants would follow. Then the state horse and elephant would be worshipped.

Then the royal ladies would enter, bless the king and retire to their harems. This mode of worship would follow for the Nine days or *Navaratras*. On the eve of the 1st day by 7 pm a Durbar would be held. After floral offerings, *nazar* and *muzre*, the king would enjoy the wrestling matches at the courtyard below the Durbar Hall. These matches would turn out to be bloody in the true sense of the word as the victor was the one who could ensure that his opponent fell to the ground bleeding.

On the 7th day, Goddess Saraswati, the Hindu Goddess of knowledge, learning and the arts was propitiated. All the books in the palace and the king's musical instruments would be worshipped. On the 8th day, the ceremony to mark the destruction of Demon king Mahishasura by the Goddess Mahishasuramardini or Durga was conducted at night in the palace. On the 9th day of 'Ayudha Puja,' arms, ammunitions, the State horse, elephant, etc., would be worshipped; a *Chandi Homa* sacrifice performed and the *Kankana* tied on the first day untied. That evening a European Durbar would be held. The courtyard would be lit up. Wrestling matches, musical and dance performances and other amusements would be a part of this Durbar.

On the 10th day of 'Vijayadasami,' the king would take bath, worship the State arms, place it in the State Palanquin, which would carry them to *Banni Mantap*, the sacred place where the *Sami* tree (*prosopis spicigera lin*) stood. It was believed that during the times of incognito, the Pandavas hid their arms on the Sami tree and when they retrieved them after the one-year incognito imposed on them by their cruel cousins, the Kauravas, they achieved success in the ensuing Mahabharata War. So the tree was considered a good omen and a harbinger of success. The procession to *Banni Mantap* was the most spectacular part of the 10-day fest. The function would begin by 4 pm in the noon after a 21-gun salute, a fanfare of trumpets and the Mysore Anthem. The royal elephant would be bejewelled with gold-embroidered robes, massive chains, anklets, bells, and ropes of pearls, pendants, tassels, bosses of pure gold with paintings on its face, trunk, legs and ears. It would carry the resplendent Golden Howdah or *Amburi* in which would sit the maharaja, the yuvaraja and Prince Jayachamaraja Wodeyar. The palace has illustrated mural painting gallery of the order of this procession held in 1929, which gives us a flavour of the kind of procession that would enthrall the citizens of Mysore city each year.

The gala procession would traverse a mile's length making its way through the fort's north gate, through Doddapete to reach *Banni Mantap*, where troops worshipped the sacred *Sami* tree. The procession would be lit by electric bulbs and naphtha oil torches and firecrackers burnt along the way. The troops would return by 9.30 pm to a small concluding durbar. The palace and principal roads and squares would be fully illuminated with electric bulbs after dusk—a real sight for sore eyes! This would conclude the 10 day-long grand Dasara festivities of Mysore.

So synonymous this festival and the procession has become with the cultural identity of the state, that the democratic government of Mysore State and later unified Karnataka decided to continue this festival and the procession with as much pomp and gaiety and celebrate it as a 'People's festival'. The deity of Goddess Chamundeshwari replaces the king atop the *ambari* or golden howdah, though the royal family continues its rituals and celebrations, including the worship of Rani Alamelamma, in the private recesses of the palace.

But the real heroes of the Dasara are truly the elephants who participate in the procession, year-after-year, with utmost meticulousness. The stories of the Dasara elephants itself is a matter of great fascination for the local population. The participant elephants over the years, and especially the lead elephants (the recent ones named Biligiriranga, Rajendra, Drona and Balarama) have become part of history and folk legends.

Most of these Dasara-elephants were caught by the elephant trainers via the *Khedda* operations. During the Wodeyar rule, the elephants thus caught were inspected in an open field for strength, personality, and character. The walking styles, weaknesses to seduction, and the facial charisma were some of the factors considered for selection! Then the chosen elephants were trained for the festival. It is said that the king himself would overlook the training.

Biligiriranga was a majestic beast, about ten feet in height. The king Jayachamaraja Wodeyar was known to be very fond of him. After the festivities, Biligiriranga would return to the forest and live there till the next Dasara. According to the forest officials, he was a virile bull and was responsible for the increase in the elephant population in the area!

There would be no exaggeration to state that Biligiriranga enhanced the glory of the festival in Mysore.

Rajendra was caught in the year 1971, and was the last to serve the Wodeyar dynasty. Soon after Indira Gandhi annulled all royalty in India. The idol of Goddess Chamundeshwari replaced the king during the procession. Rajendra was the chosen one to have the privilege of carrying the Goddess for the first time. He was a soft bull and was easily influenced by presence of female elephants. His trainers felt that Rajendra never found true love in his life and kept pining for a soul mate till his demise. The Goddess somehow did not seem to be kind on this poor soul who carried Her dutifully every year!

The elephant Drona was named so because of his amazing ability to learn and correct himself. When the *ambari* shifted left or right during the procession, Drona could move his muscles selectively and stabilise the weight! Such was his dexterity. His trainers were very surprised because they had not trained Drona in this skill. Drona was shrewd enough to fathom for himself that walking slowly, early in the procession, was the best way he could conserve his energy during the long ride. He was also supposedly very particular about his diet and always ate in solitude. Drona led a durable family life with his two wives Kokila and Shanti. Unfortunately, on one fateful day in the jungle, Drona went grazing and pulled down a trunk of a tree to eat the leaves. The falling trunk also brought down a high-tension power cable and instantly electrocuted the celebrated bull. Drona was mourned in the state just like any other celebrity.

Altogether 13 elephants participate in the festival. Each one of them has to go through a rigid conditioning. At least two of them have to be female as per the tradition. The chief elephant is followed by a row of five elephants. There is one elephant dedicated to pull the chariot containing the Karnataka police band. Thus, these mute but adorable creatures have become as much a part of the state's culture and legacy as the many celebrated and talented personalities from various walks of life!

29

THE LIVES AND TIMES OF MYSOREANS: PAINTING, COINAGE AND ARCHITECTURE

TRADITIONAL MYSORE SCHOOL OF PAINTING

Painting as an art has been nurtured in Karnataka from ancient times. The inscriptions and manuscripts of the Rashtrakutas bear testimony to the existence of painting as an art form. The earliest murals, dating back to the sixth century AD, were found in the Badami caves. The Vijayanagara school of painting (1336–1665) was quite distinct from the earlier styles and has made a great contribution to Indian art. The pupils of this school specialised in drawing war and hunting scenes, folk dances, commercial transactions and the everyday life of the common people. The Mysore and Tanjore traditional paintings are offshoots of the Vijayanagara school.

After the disintegration of the Vijayanagara empire, there emerged a distinct style of painting popularly known as Mysore painting. Raja Wodeyar was known for his patronage and encouragement of artists. Painters were engaged in creating eye-catching illustrations on the walls of temples and palaces. He is also credited with the construction of two shrines, one at Srirangapatna and the other at Ganjam, for Goddess Nimishamba Devi, who is revered by artists. Mysore painting got its impetus during the reign of Mummadi Krishnaraja Wodeyar. He was a great connoisseur of the traditional paintings and commissioned more than a thousand portraits of the royal family and important public men. The portraits of historic figures can be seen even today on the walls of Jagan Mohan Palace in Mysore. The murals can also be seen in the temples of Prasanna Krishnaswamy, Shwetha Varaha Swamy and Prasanna Venkataramana Swamy in the palace compound. They are refined and the colour scheme, with bright reds and greens, enhances their spectacular quality.

Mummadi Krishnaraja Wodeyar also coaxed the painters to prepare their own portraits and that is why painters like Narayanappa and Chinnakrishnappa can be seen immortalised in gesso art even today. The *Sritatvanidhi* of the maharaja is a pictorial digest divided into nine sections and contains 1,000 paintings. It is a compendium of illustrations of gods, goddesses and mythological figures with general instructions to painters regarding composition, placement and choice of colour, mood, etc. The *ragas*, seasons, animals, and plant world are effectively depicted in these paintings as co-themes or contexts. As stated earlier, it is also perhaps the only pictorial representation of music in South India—a tradition that existed widely in the North. Another work of the maharaja's titled *Sara Sangraha Bharata*, is dedicated to dance, illustrated with colourful paintings depicting the various elements of the art form.

The artists used locally available material for their paintings. Goat, camel or squirrel hair was used for brushes, tying the hair with a silken thread and inserting it into the narrower end of a quill. The painting board was made by pasting cloth or paper on wooden planks. They prepared a paste of zinc oxide and Arabic gum, called the 'gesso paste', which was applied to this base. In order to make the picture larger than life, a small raised effect was made, on which the images of thrones and arches were painted with a thin brush. The primary sketch was made on the canvas. Burnt tamarind sticks were used as sketching charcoal. The motifs were drawn with a crayon. The sky and river were painted, followed by animal and human figures. The gold foil was pasted last and the paintings polished only when perfectly dry. The foil used here was much thinner than that used in the Tanjore style. Grass blades were used to give a sharp-edged effect to the painting. These paintings were illustrated with water colours, using only subtle colours. The artists of yore were skilled not only in the art of painting but also in the process of preparing the required resources, like brushes, colour paints, canvas and the gold foil. Paints were made from plant extracts and minerals.

The stories from the *Ramayana, Mahabharata, Bhagavata Purana* and the Jain epics are the primary basis of traditional Mysore paintings. Individual deities, epic heroes, court scenes, and battlegrounds are also depicted. The most popular themes are Goddess Rajarajeshwari, Shri Rama Pattabhisheka, Kodanda Rama, Dashavatara, Tandaveshvara, Ambegalu Krishna, Lakshmi, Saraswati, Chamundeswari, Visvarupadarsha and Samudramanthana. Some of the well-preserved gesso paintings can be seen in Mysore, Nanjangud and Bangalore. Sringeri, Melkote and other pilgrimage centres also have many gesso paintings.

It is natural to wonder about the differences between the Mysore and Tanjore styles of painting. At first glance, they appear similar in their layout, design and decorations. But on closer scrutiny the differences in the materials and technique used become clearer. The faces of the gods in the Mysore school are rounder and the gesso work is also in low-relief compared to the high-relief of the Tanjore style. The former uses pure gold leaf, while the latter uses a silver leaf coated with gold. The usage of the pure gold leaf gives the Mysore paintings lustre and permanence. Tanjore School employs glass pieces or pearls in its ornamentation—a trait absent in the Mysore style. Most Mysore paintings that feature a sitting deity portray them as seated on the throne of Mysore with backgrounds and surroundings similar to the palace. This made the figures seem more familiar. Some paintings also use the *makki safeda* or gesso work without gold leaf, creating an illusion of gold lustre with delicate lace-like ornamentation. Lustre and line work seem to be the forte of Mysore painting.

MODERN MYSORE ART AND RAVI VERMA

Modern European art, Roman model art and the art of Raja Ravi Verma led to a decline in the demand for traditional Mysore painting during the nineteenth and twentieth centuries. The celebrated artist Raja Ravi Verma was patronised by the maharajas of Mysore.

Raja Ravi Verma was born on 29 April 1848 at Kilimanoor, a small town in Kerala. As a boy of five, he filled the walls of his house with pictures of animals and illustrations from everyday life. His uncle, the artist Raja Raja Verma, recognised his talents and gave him elementary art lessons. He was taken to Thiruvananthapuram at the age of 14 to stay in the royal palace and learn oil painting. During these formative years the young Ravi Verma had many opportunities to discover and learn new techniques and media in the field of painting. His later years spent in Mysore, Baroda and other parts of the country enabled him to sharpen and expand his skills and blossom into a mature and complete painter.

The glittering career of Raja Ravi Verma is a striking case study of academic art in India. A year after his death on 2 October 1906, the *Modern Review* described him as the greatest artist of modern India, a nation-builder who showed moral courage by being a gifted 'high-born' who took up the so-called 'degrading' profession of painting. He was courted assiduously by the British empire as well as by the Indian maharajas. The less expensive prints of his Hindu deities hung in every home.

Raja Ravi Verma owed his success to a systematic training, first in the traditional art of Tanjore, and then in European art. His paintings can be broadly classified into portraits, portrait-based compositions, and theatrical compositions based on myths and legends. Though the artist's immense popularity stemmed from his work in the third category, the first two types of work prove his merit as an exceedingly sensitive and competent artist. No other painter has been able to supersede Ravi Verma in portraiture in the oil medium.

Ravi Verma is considered modern among traditionalists and a rationalist among moderns. He provided a vital link between traditional and contemporary Indian art, between the Tanjore school and Western academic realism. He brought Indian painting to the attention of the larger world. His paintings, including large life-size portraits of the kings, queens and members of the royal family and nobility, adorn the Mysore palace to this day.

Many celebrated painters like, K. Keshavaiya, S.N. Swamy, Y. Nagaraju, S. Shankararaju, S.R. Iyengar, Y. Subrahmanyaraju, Venkatappa and others adorned Mysore and made valuable contributions in the beautification of the palace. A brilliant painting titled *Glow of Hope* by S.N. Haldenkar can be found at the Jagan Mohan Palace. The colour combinations and contrasts used give the perfect ambience of radiating light in the midst of an envelope of darkness—a testimony of the brilliance of the artist.

COINAGE IN MYSORE

Ranadhira Kanthirava Narasaraja Wodeyar was the first to issue coins with inscriptions. These coins or *fanams* became famous as Kanthirava Fanams. They carried images of Lord Narasimha. The other series of *fanams* that gained popularity were the Shiva–Parvathi (originally minted by Sadashiva Naik of Ikkeri) and the Hoysalas' stylised Lion/ Boar *fanam* which was called Viraraya Fanam.

There are two noted Kanthirava types of *fanams*. They both have the Narasimha on the obverse. Narasimha is the fourth incarnation of Lord Vishnu with a human body and a lion's head. The 'Yogabhanda' pose is well depicted in the earlier Kanthirava coinage. The meditation pose shows the legs folded inward and the holy thread going around both his knees, which virtually supports the posture. He holds in his upper hands the stylised attributes of a flaming *chakra* and a conch, his lower arms resting on his knees. The earlier dies seem to have been engraved with the superior workmanship of the engraver, and the one or two legible characters lead us to conclude that they are the prototypes.

The popularity of the Kanthirava Fanams influenced the coinage of many other southern dynasties like the Nayakas of Sira, the British at Madras and even the Dutch at Pulicat, Nagapattinam and Tuticorin. These *fanams* eventually carried the name Kantheerva or were corrupted to Canteroi. During his rule, Haidar Ali used the same obverse device on his coinage but inscribed the letter 'He' in Persian to indicate his name. His coins were renamed Bahaduri Pagodas.

Tipu changed the names of these coins to Sultani and Faruqi pagodas and they were inscribed in Persian. Though partially Mughal in lineage, Tipu's coins are a unique series in themselves, showing evidence of French influence especially in the copper variety where ancient Hindu devices are found fairly intact. His was perhaps one of the most remarkable individual coinages in the history of India, comparable in ways to that of Muhammad-bin-Tughlaq, and these coins exist in greater variety and number than those of his father. His mint towns were Puttun (Srirangapatna), Nagar (Bednaur), Bengalur (Bangalore), Faiz Hissar (Gutti), Farrukhyah Hisar (Chitradurga), Kalikut (Calicut), Farukhi (Feroke), Salamabad (Satyamangalam), Khilayabad (Dindigul), Zafarabad (Gurramkonda), Khwurshed Sawad (Dharwar) and Nazarabad (Mysore). These places were chosen as mint towns for their military, strategic and political importance, though not all of them were equally active during Tipu's reign. With few exceptions most of them are gold and silver issues and bear the name of the mint as well. Hence, we also learn that while Srirangapatna and Nagar were the only mints in the first few years of his reign, their spread and importance varied with every passing year, more so after the Third Anglo-Mysore War when Tipu lost a major part of his dominions to the British.

The coins issued in the first four years of his reign bear the Hijri date, the numerals reading from left to right. From the fifth year onwards till the end of his reign, they are dated in the special Mauludi era and the figures read from right to left. Tipu followed the *abjad* and later the *abtah* system of naming cyclical years—both of which are Islamic nomenclatures of years where a certain numerical value is assigned to the letters of the Arabic alphabet.

After the Mauludi system was adopted, he also invented names for his coins, which appear on the reverse. The gold and silver coins are named after Muslim saints, Khalifas in the earlier version and after Imams in the latter version. Copper coins generally bore Persian or Arabic names of stars. About fifteen types of these coins with their names are in existence. The Ahmadi coins were struck in the Srirangapatna and Nagar mints and the Pagodas in Dharwar as well. In addition to these three mints, *fanams* were struck at Calicut, Feroke and Dindigul. His coins though largely unmilled betray a distinct French influence as well, perhaps owing to some French workmen who were hired to design and cast them.

With the restoration of the kingdom to the Wodeyars, Dewan Purnaiya implemented the old coinage system with 'Sri Krishna Raja' inscribed on the obverse.

ARCHITECTURE IN MODERN MYSORE

The architectural splendour and beauty of Mysorean monuments, especially those of the modern era, speaks volumes about the aesthetic tastes of the rulers who got them built. Foremost on this list of spectacular buildings is the Mysore Palace in all its majestic beauty and characteristic elegance.

The early Wodeyars lived in a palace at Mysore. Ranadhira Kanthirava Narasaraja Wodeyar had rebuilt the palace in 1630 after it was struck by lightning. During Immadi Krishnaraja Wodeyar's rule Haidar Ali invited him to visit the new palace that was constructed for the royal family.

Tipu Sultan demolished all the old buildings at Mysore to rebuild the city as Nazarabad and even the palace came under the bulldozer. As stated earlier, there was no place worthy of the coronation of Mummadi Krishnaraja Wodeyar in 1799. Maharani Lakshmammanni then hurriedly got a palace constructed within two to three years and many parts of it were, by 1897, crumbling and easily caught fire. Rice describes the old palace thus:

> The Palace of the Maharaja, which is situated inside the fort facing nearly due East is built in the Hindu style and with the exception of a few paintings executed by European painters at various times in the Palace employment, contains little trace of the influence of European art. The front, which is gaily painted and supported by 4 elaborately carved wooden pillars comprises the Sejje or the Dasara Hall, an open gallery where the Maharaja is in the habit of showing himself to the people on great occasions seated on his throne...its principal gate opens on a passage under the Sejje, leading to an open yard. At the further or west side of this courtyard is the door leading to the women's apartments, which occupy most of the western portion of the Palace. The northern side comprises various offices such as the armoury, library etc and on the south are the rooms occupied by the Maharaja. Of these the most interesting is the Ambavilasa, an upstairs room, 65 ft square and 10 ft high with a raised ceiling in the center. It was here that the former Raja was receiving his European guests and transacted ordinary business of the day. A wooden railing separated that portion of the room in which the Raja's seat was placed from the rest and the adjacent wall was hung with pictures, principally of officers connected at different periods with Mysore, which His Highness was accustomed to uncover and point out to his European visitors. The floor was of chunam and with the exception of the doors, which were overlaid with richly carved ivory or silver there was no attempt at magnificence or display. This hall has been recently renewed in more modern style and the ceiling raised on handsome iron pillars.
>
> The sleeping and eating apartments of the Raja, which are for the most part small and confined all opened upon the Amba Vilasa and just outside it was the stall in which was kept the cow worshipped by His Highness. The chapel is adjacent. Although the

Palace had been almost entirely built, since the year 1800, it was in very bad repair and many of the tenements attached to it were crumbling to ruin. The only remaining portion of the Palace of the old Hindu dynasty, which Tippoo Sultan had not demolished is a room in the interior with mud walls of great thickness and stability. This is known as the Painted Hall, owing to the decoration of its ceiling and is said to have been the state room of the old palace, which was a much less pretentious building. As with most oriental courts, there was no attempt at isolation and except in front, where is an open space, the Palace was pressed closed on all sides by the dwellings of the poorest inhabitants.

The Palace that we see today in Mysore was the result of the efforts of the then Regent Maharani Kempananjammanni to erect a residence that suited the status of their dynasty. With the aid of Mr Henry Irwin, architect of the Viceregal Lodge of Shimla, the new palace was completed in 1912.

The Mysore Palace has a vast, sprawling fort with five entrances built in the Indo-Saracenic style. The Jayamarthanda gate is the main gate and the central archway is sixty feet tall and forty-five feet wide. The other gates are the Balarama-Jayarama gates to the north, the Varaha on the south, the Brahmapuri and Karikal Thotti on the west. The inside area of the fort is 55 acres. Lewis Rice reports:

> The fort is quadrangular ground plain, three of the sides being about 450 yards in length and the remaining on the North, South and the West; those on the North and South are protected by outworks. Flanking towers command the curtain at frequent intervals. There is a casemate to the South-Eastern and a parapeted cavalier at the North-Western gate...

To the east of the ground floor are the Gombe Thotti (dolls' pavillion,) Kalyana Mandap (marriage pavillion,) to the north are the Ayudhashala (armoury) and Trophy room. On the first floor are the Diwan-e-Aam (public durbar hall) and a Diwan-e-Khas (private durbar hall). The Gombe Thotti has seven firing and four ammunition cannons, the firing ones used on festive occasions. Four of the cannons are made of firths steel bearing the Old French inscription *Honi soit qui mal y pense*[*] while the other

---

[*] Shame upon him who thinks evil of it.

three are made of bronze by A. Brome. The dolls were worshipped by the maharaja during Dasara. The common people in southern India and Mysore usually celebrate Dasara in their homes by making elaborate doll arrangements and floral decorations, inviting neighbours for a friendly competition as to who had the best dolls' exhibition!

The Gombe Thotti contains figurines and Rajasthani marble sculptures of Lord Rama, Hanuman, Lakshmana and Goddess Sita, wooden *mandaps* with pillars and *yalis* with *vimanas* and housing a Ganesha idol, Krishna, Lakshmi, Saraswati and Chamundeshwari. It also contains the royal emblem of Mysore—the Gandabherunda with the slogan *Satyamevoddharamyaham* or 'I shall always uphold the Truth'. The Gandabherunda is a mythical double-headed eagle and, according to ancient Indian literature, it symbolises power and authority. One can find several examples of this bird in the architecture, art and textiles of the city of Mysore. Similar mythical two-headed birds can also be found in other ancient cultures, like those of Egypt and Mesopotamia. The golden *howdah* or *ambari* made of approximately 80 kilograms of gold is also found here.

The Kalyana Mandapa walls have been decorated with the paintings of celebrated artists like K. Keshavaiya, S.N. Swamy, Y. Nagaraju, S. Shankararaju, S.R. Iyengar, Y. Subrahmanyaraju and others who have immortalised the world-famous Dasara procession of Mysore on canvas. The Mandapa is octagonal and has a stained-glass ceiling with a peacock motif, designed by Walter Macfarlane. English mosaic tiles adorn the floor in a peacock design, giving the Mandapa its name: Peacock Hall. A balcony for royal guests and ladies and murals depicting epics are also found here.

The Portrait Gallery houses the portraits of Krishnaraja Wodeyar IV with his brothers and sisters, Maharani Kempananjammanni (in 1897) (both taken by Del Tufo and Co.), portraits of Krishnaraja III, Chamaraja X and so on, the celebrated painter Raja Ravi Verma's paintings of the child Krishnaraja with his sisters and Harold Speed's portraits of King Edward VII and Queen Alexandra of Britain. The furniture room has two silver chairs, one made by Bartonson and Company, Bangalore and the other by T.R. Tawker and Sons, Madras. Two cutglass or crystal chairs of Belgium, two marble flower vases and two dressing-tables and mirrors adorn the room.

The *ayudhashala* houses many old weapons of the royal family. In 1575, Bola Chamaraja Wodeyar founded the armoury at Mysore but it was

Krishnaraja Wodeyar III who got his name and serial number inscribed on weapons. The *Mysore Gazetteer* says:

> Several of them are of interest both from a historical and artistic point of view. An elastic sword bearing the number 186 and named Nimchaa, which can be worn as a belt is said to have belonged to the Mysore King Ranadhira Kanthirava.

This is one of the oldest weapons of the armoury. A knife bearing the inscription 'Chura De' is said to have belonged to Chikkadevaraja Wodeyar. A sword named Nimchaa bearing the number thirty-six and another heavy one named Sanva are said to have been used by Haidar Ali and Tipu Sultan respectively.

From the inscription of a knife named Pesh Kabza we infer that the weapon was used by Krishnaraja Wodeyar III. Another knife named Herige Katthi or delivery knife bears the inscription 'Khasa' or the king's very own. This however was not actually used during delivery by midwives, but merely worshipped to bring about speedy and safe delivery. Among the names of the other weapons found here are Mudgara, Surayi, Buriya, Jambaya, Baku, Pancha, Kathari, Sabdar, Birudangichura, Tabbar, Bagunakha, Gaddara, Khandva, Abbari, Saipu, Madu, Sosan, Aleman, Parang, Singoti and Bharji. Many of the weapons bear Persian inscriptions.

There are also several state gun models in the armoury. Three of them bear the inscription that Mummadi Krishnaraja Wodeyar was placed on the musnud of Mysore on 30 June 1799. The inscription on another names the above king along with Haidar Ali Khan, Tippu Saib, Nandaraja, Devaraja, Lally and Mir Muhammad Sadak. Another inscription tells us that the gun on which it is engraved represents the 'Moolke Maidan of Beejopore'—captured by Arthur Wellesley in 1803. There are also two *chauris*, one of which bears an inscription stating that they were sent as presents to Krishnaraja Wodeyar III by Lord Dalhousie. Another object worthy of notice is a tiny four-pillared *mandapa* of black stone surmounted by a turret with a seated figure of Ganapati inside.

The Durbar Hall was the place where ceremonial Durbars were held during Dasara. It has marble floors and rows of brick and mortar pillars covered with plaster of Paris. Arches connecting pillars are in Mughal style, with floral designs in bright hues. To the east of the hall is a large open courtyard for the assembly of people during festive occasions. The beautiful paintings of Ravi Verma adorn the walls.

There is a small shrine inside the Palace called the Atmavilasa Ganesha which is inaccessible to the public. It was the private daily-worship hall of the maharajas. The idol is over 250 years old and is made of 450 *saligramas*—holy stones revered by Vaishnavas as remnants of Vishnu—brought from over 300 pilgrim spots. This deity did not succumb to the 1897 fire that destroyed most of the other items of the palace and so it holds a special significance for the royal family.

The last part of the palace is the Amba Vilasa or Diwan-e-Khas having a rosewood door inlaid with ivory motifs depicting baby Krishna on a peepal leaf—the Vatapatrashayi Krishna. There are many doors, all depicting the Dashavatara of Lord Vishnu and the Ashtadikpalas. The stained-glass ceiling, chandeliers, the steel grillwork and carved wooden ceilings provide a pleasing atmosphere.

The royal throne that was handed over to Raja Wodeyar is described thus in the *Devatanama Kusumamanjari* composed in 1859 by Mummadi Krishnaraja Wodeyar:

> The throne is decorated with a golden pillar and mango leaves. The balustrades of the steps leading to the seat are embellished with female figures. The golden umbrella has festoons. The seat has the Kurmasana tortoise seat. The 4 sides of the throne are decorated with Vyalas and creepers. Elephants on the east, horse on the south, soldiers to the west and chariots at the north decorate the royal seat. Brahma to the South, Maheshwara on the North and Vishnu in the center form the Trinity. In the corners are found Vijaya and 4 lions, two of the mythical Shardulas, 2 horses and swans in the 4 corners. It is further adorned with Naga nymphs and Ashtadikpalas.

The throne would earlier be placed in this hall for public viewing but has now been removed, making its way back there only during Dussehra. The credit for decorating the hall goes to the celebrated artist K. Venkatappa who devoted his life to the work, about whom Nalwadi Krishnaraja Wodeyar once said:

> You have devoted your whole life for the study of fine arts, you have made name in your life, you have brought credit to my state, I consider it a pride having you here. My only ambition is to show you, through your art, to the distinguished visitors that come here, and say to them proudly that it is my countryman's work!

One cannot leave the Mysore palace without a sense of awe and admiration for its magnificence coupled with innate simplicity and aesthetics.

Some of the other architectural works of the later Wodeyars are described here. Mummadi Krishnaraja Wodeyar, who was known for his zeal in renovating dilapidated temples, got the Shweta Varahaswamy temple at Srirangapatna and Thrineshwara Swamy temple in Mysore renovated. The Shweta Varaha Swamy temple was constructed by Chikkadevaraja Wodeyar and the idol was brought from Srimushnam in Tamil Nadu. It is said that the temple was destroyed by Tipu Sultan. Purnaiya got the idol from Srirangapatna to Mysore and the maharaja donated a large sum of money to consecrate the idol in the palace complex in a newly constructed temple. The Chamundeshwari Temple atop the hills in Mysore was extended and the spire that Raja Wodeyar had conceived was taken up and completed. He got the numerous crevasses and potholes on the hilltop filled up and levelled, making it safe and accessible. The Lakshmiramanaswamy Temple in the palace complex was also renovated. The Krishnaswamy Temple in the complex was constructed during his reign. The Srikantheswhara Temple at Nanjangud was improved and provided with a new spire. The Gayatri Devi and Bhuvaneshwari Temples in the complex were constructed during Jayachamaraja Wodeyar's reign.

During the mid-nineteenth century when the Mysore PWD building was being constructed, European engineers were employed and they introduced the Ionic, Doric, Corinthian and composite styles. Therefore, many of the buildings built after this period exhibit a synthesis of all these styles. Some of the noted buildings from this era onwards are the Attara Kacheri (1869), the Museum (1879), the Daly Memorial Hall (all in Bangalore in European style), while the Maharaja's College (1894), the Jubilee Institute (1894), Public offices (1895) and the Law court buildings (1889) in Mysore are simpler structures. The Central College, Bangalore (1901) is in the Gothic style.

The Victoria Hospital (1896), the Indian Institute of Science, the Government High School, Minto Ophthalmic Hospital, the Sheshadri Iyer Memorial Hall (all in Bangalore) and the Chamarajendra Technical Institute in Mysore are other elegant and well-laid buildings of the era. The Krishnarajendra Hospital of Mysore (1918) is built in the American Rennaissance style. The Lalitha Mahal (now an ITDC Hotel) and

Rajendra Vilas Palace atop the Chamundi Hills in Mysore are magnificent architectural pieces. The Sri Krishnarajendra S.J. Technological Institute and the K.P. Puttanna Chetty Town Hall in Bangalore are other buildings worth the mention.

Another integral aspect of the lives of times of common Mysoreans is the Devaraja Market, with a century-old history behind it. It was one of the oldest commercial establishments of Mysore and was built in memory of Chikkadevaraja Wodeyar. It was built near the Sayyaji Rao Road, which in turn was named to commemorate the visit of Sayyaji Rao Gaekwad to Mysore in the 1900s. The Devaraja Market was very well planned, with separate sections allocated for fruits, plantains and plantain leaves, betel leaves, flowers, jaggery blocks or *bella*, condiments, coconuts, groceries, onions, potatoes, and other vegetables. The cellar underneath the granite stone of each shop was a small store-house for the shopkeeper to stock items of sale. The stone slab was the place for him to sit and sell his item, while the covered portion was the walk-through for the customers to walk in the shade, protecting themselves from sun and rain. The hollowed cast iron pillars and the metal domes facilitated the easy flow of rain water from the roofs into the covered drains, leaving no trace of water even after a heavy downpour. The office-rooms in surrounding areas provided accommodation for advocates and other professionals. Interestingly, the century-old market still serves a majority of Mysore's population. What was built when the population was less than a lakh continues to serve a population of over 10 lakhs, much like the Krishnaraja and Cheluvamba hospitals. This shows the far-sightedness of the Mysore rulers in matters of town planning.

30

THE LIVES AND TIMES OF MYSOREANS: LITERATURE, THEATRE AND JOURNALISM

One of the greatest aspects of culture is the spurt in the growth of language and literature, coupled with opportunities of freedom of speech and expression manifesting itself in the journalistic endeavours of the press. Let us briefly look into this aspect of Mysore's glorious culture.

THE BACKGROUND OF KANNADA LITERATURE

The Kannada language belongs to the Dravidian family of languages and is the oldest language (after Tamil) currently spoken in India. Kannada literature is also one of the oldest literary traditions in India. It includes early writing dating from 2,000 years ago to modern-day literature.

The first example of Kannada writing can be found in the Halmidi inscription dated 150 CE. The famous Badami inscriptions from the seventh century provide more examples of early Kannada writing. However, the first available book in Kannada is the *Kavirajamarga*, written in the ninth century by Amoghavarsha Nrupatunga. The book is a treatise of sorts on Kannada poetry and language and Kannada-speaking people in general. Based on its references to earlier Kannada works, historians estimate that literature in Kannada must have begun a couple of centuries before, in the sixth or seventh centuries CE. However, none of these earlier works have been found.

The history of Kannada literature is usually studied under four phases: Purva Hale Gannada (pre-old Kannada); Hale Gannada (old

Kannada); Nadu Gannada (middle Kannada); and Hosa Kannada (new Kannada).

The Old Kannada phase marks the period between tenth-twelfth centuries. This period consists mainly of Jain religious literature. The famous poet from this period is Pampa (902–75 CE), one of the most celebrated writers in the Kannada language. His *Vikramarjuna Vijaya* (also called *Pampa Bharatha*) is hailed as a classic even today. With this and his other important work, *Adipurana*, he set a trend of poetic excellence for future Kannada poets. The former work is an adaptation of the celebrated *Mahabharata*, and is the first such adaptation in Kannada. Noted for the strong human angle and the dignified style of his writing, Pampa has been one of the most influential writers in Kannada. He is identified as the *adi kavi* or first poet of Kannada literature.

Ponna (939–66 CE) is also an important writer from the same period, with *Shanti-Purana* as his magnum opus. Another major writer of the period is Ranna (949–? CE). His most famous works are the Jain religious work *Ajita-Tirthankara Purana* and the *Gada-Yuddham* (The Mace Fight), a birds'-eye view of the Mahabharata set in the last day of the Battle of Kurukshetra and relating the story of the Mahabharata through a series of flashbacks. Structurally, the poetry in this period is in the Champu style—essentially poetry interspersed with lyrical prose.

The Middle Kannada period gave birth to several genres in Kannada literature, with new forms of composition coming into use, including Ragale (a form of blank verse) and metres like Sangatya and Desi. The works of this period are based on Jain, Hindu and secular principles.

Two of the early writers (thirteenth century) of this period are Harihara and Raghavanka, trailblazers in their own right. Harihara established the Ragale form of composition, and most of his works are based on the Shaiva and Veerashaiva traditions. Raghavanka popularised the Shatpadi (six-lined stanza) metre through his six works, the most famous being *Harishchandra Charitre*, based on the life of the Hindu mythological character Harishchandra. The work is noted for its intense attention to human ideals. Raghavanka also wrote *Siddharama Charitha* and *Somanatha Charitha*. Thr former describes the story of Siddharama and his accomplishments in building a sacred pond and a Shiva temple at Sonnalige.

A famous Jain writer of the same period is Janna, who expressed Jain religious teachings through his works, *Yashodhara Charite* and *Ananthanatha*

Purana. A seminal work on Kannada grammar from the same period is *Shabda Mani Darpana* by Keshi Raja.

Kannada had poetry similar to the Japanese haiku as far back as the twelfth century! This form of poetry, called Vachanas, were three-lined pithy comments on contemporary social, religious and economic conditions. More importantly, they hold a mirror to the seed of a social revolution, which caused a radical re-examination of the ideas of caste, creed and religion. Some of the important writers of Vachana literature include Basaveshvara (1131–67 CE), Allama Prabhu and Akka Mahadevi, the first woman writer in Kannada.

Arguably, Kumara Vyasa has been the most famous and most influential Kannada writer of all time. His grand work, *Karnata Bharata KathaManjari*, is a sublime adaptation of the first ten *parvas* (chapters) of the Mahabharata. A devotee of Krishna, Kumara Vyasa ends his epic with the passing of Krishna in the 10th chapter of the Mahabharata. The work is easily the most celebrated in Kannada literature. Its fame arises from the fact that it has appealed to people of all strata of education and intellect over the centuries, till today. The work is entirely composed in the Bhamini Shatpadi metre, a form of six-lined stanza. The range of human emotions Kumara Vyasa explores and the versatility of his vocabulary are extensive. The work is particularly known for its use of sophisticated metaphors, earning Kumara Vyasa the title 'Rupaka Samrajya Chakravarti' (Emperor of the Land of Metaphors).

Literature under the Wodeyars

Kannada literature assumed a new dimension with the coming of the Wodeyar dynasty and the generous patronage they extended to its growth. The literary works under early Wodeyars, like Raja Wodeyar, also indicate the growing influence of Vaishnava philosophy on the polity. *Sriranga Mahatmya* (1600) and *Karnavrittantha Kathe* (1615) are two major works during Raja Wodeyar's rule.

Chamaraja Wodeyar VI was a great patron of literary activities. He is credited with writing the *Brahmottara Khanda* and *Maniprakasha Vachana* (1630) in colloquial Kannada prose format dealing with the philosophy and rituals of Shaivism. The *Chamrajokti Vilasa* is another prose work in Hosa Gannada on the seven cantos of the Ramayana. Though the king is said to have composed this work, differences exist on whether he actually got it written by the scholar Virupaksha.

Lakshmisha, believed to be a native of Devanur in Kadur Taluk was a shining poet of the times and is known for his masterpiece *Jaimini Bharata*. He is adorned with such titles as 'Upamalola' and 'Nadalola'—reveller in similies and melody. His is a superb art of story telling in verse. His contemporary was Virupaksha Pandita whose brilliant work *Channabasava Purana* is another milestone in Kannada literature. In the *History of Kanarese Literature*, E.P. Rice comments

> Channabasava is regarded as an incarnation of Siva. The work relates his birth and his greatness at Kalyana; but is mostly taken up with the instruction he gave to Siddharama of Sonnalige on the entire body of Virasaiva lore, the creation, the wonderful deeds (lila) of Siva, the marvelous efficacy of Saiva rites and stories of Saiva saints. It has, consequently been very popular among Lingayat readers. It is also very useful to the historian of Kanarese literature, because it gives much help in determining the approximate dates of the early Virasaiva saints and poets.

It might be worth mentioning here that the Veerashaiva faith or the Lingayat sect that developed from the teachings of the medieval saint and reformer Basaveshwara, in opposition to the dogmatic practices of traditional Brahminical Hindusim, became the state religion and had a huge following. E.P. Rice writes that Lingayetism was the state religion of the early Wodeyars of Mysore and Ummattur from 1399–1640 and of the Nayakas of Keladi from AD 1550–1763. Their principal *muth* in the Mysore country is at Chitaldoorg. The drift towards Sri Vaishnavism began with Chikkadevaraja Wodeyar and its impact on the literature of the times is also obvious.

The reign of Chikkadevaraja Wodeyar was truly the golden period in the history of Kannada literature. Experts categorise the growth of the language into the pre-Chikkadevaraja era and post-Chikkadevaraja era. In the former era, writings were in the Shatpadi style.

Chikkadevaraja Wodeyar was himself a poet of great repute and wrote works, like *Geeta Gopala* and *Chikkadevaraja Binnapam*. The latter is written in prose form. It contains 30 *binnapas* or prayers addressed to Lord Cheluvanarayana of Yadugiri. They contain the essence of the Dwaita and Vishishtadwaita philosophies of Hinduism propounded by Saint Madhawacharya and Saint Ramanujacharya respectively. Other works credited to him are *Bharata Vachana*, *Chikkadevaraja Sukti Vilasa* and

Sacchoodraachara Nirnaya. The last among these is an important document on the social conditions of the times. It details the maharaja's prescriptions and codifications on the dos and don'ts of a good Shudra. His court was adorned with numerous poets and scholars.

Tirumalaraya (1646–1706) was a court poet and later minister. He authored two historical works in Kannada, *Chikkadevaraja Vijaya* and *Chikkadevaraja Vamshavali*. The former is considered the best in the Champu style in Kannada literature. His *Apratimavira Charita* is a treatise on rhetoric, drawing freely on ancient Sanskrit works on the subject. They are all important sources of contemporary history, though one needs to take the information provided therein with caution, as it abounds with sycophantic superlatives. His undated works also include a series of hymns or *stavahas*.

Chikkupadhyaya was another prolific author and has over 30 works in the Champu, Sangatya and prose styles of Kannada literature to his credit. Most of his works tend to propagate the faith of Sri Vaishnavism and also narrate the heroic deeds of Chikkadevaraja Wodeyar. *Vishnu Purana* in two volumes in the Champu and prose style, *Divyasuri Charitre*, considered as the best among his Champu works and dealing with the 12 Alwar or Vaishnavite saints, *Arthapanchaka* and *Tiruvoymoli* translated from Tamil as also the many Mahatmyas describing the greatness of pilgrim centres like Srirangam, Srirangapatna, Kanchi, Melukote, Tirupati, etc., are to his credit.

Singaraya, brother of Tirumalaraya, wrote the first drama extant in Kannada literature entitled *Mitravinda Govinda*, adapted from the Sanskrit drama *Ratnavali* by Sri Harsha. Giving a Vaishnavite touch to the play, he has substituted the original lovers of the drama, Udayana and Ratnavali with Krishna and Mitravinda.

Sanchiya Honnamma was among the few women writers of repute in Kannada. The prefix to her name came on account of her occupation of carrying the bag of betel leaves and nuts for the maharaja. An unlettered Vokkaliga woman with inborn literary talent, she seems to have caught the maharaja's notice by her brilliance and was sent for literary education under Singaraya by the king himself. She wrote the *Hadibadeya Dharma* in Sangatya metre, which describes the duties of a faithful wife. It is a masterpiece in the Sangatya style. She also wrote the *Padmini Kalyana* in the same metre, describing the divine wedding of Lord Venkataramana and Padmavathi.

The following timelines are drawn when analysing the growth of Kannada literature under Chikkadevaraja Wodeyar's reign:

1) 1673–76: Earliest Sangatya metre compositions in honour of Lord Ranganatha, the presiding deity of Srirangapatna, were composed. Some of the works of this era include *Aksharamalika Sangatya, Paschima Ranga Sangatya, Rangadhama Stuti Sangatya, Shringara Shataka Sangatya*, etc., most of which have been composed by Chikkupadhyaya.

2) 1676–77: *Kamandaka Niti* and *Shuka Satpati* were prose renderings at Chikkadevaraja's behest. While the former deals with the ancient science of politics, the latter is a compilation of maxims in the form of 70 didactic stories narrated by Sage Shuka to King Vahniraja.

3) 1678: Completion of the *Divyasuri Charitre* of Chikkupadhyaya.

4) 1678–80: Creation of historic accounts/merits of holy places (Mahatmyas), mostly done by Chikkupadhyaya. *Kamalachala Mahatmya, Hastagiri Mahatmya, Sriranga Mahatmya, Venkatagiri Mahatmya, Paschimaranga Mahatmya* and *Yadavagiri Mahatmya*—in both prose and poetry styles—are some of the works of this genre.

5) 1680-91: Vaishnavite works composed by Chikkupadhyaya. *Sheshadharma, Satvika Brahmavidya Vilasa* and *Vishnu Purana*.

The Hosa Gannada prose style evolved in Mysore towards the end of Chikkadevaraja's reign.

Around 1750 is when Helavanakatte Giriamma shot to brilliance. She was a Brahmin writer who wrote *Chandrahasana Kathe* and *Uddalika Kathe* in Sangatya and *Seeta Kalyana* in the form of songs. Ranganatha or Mahalinga Ranga of 1675 was another brilliant author/poet. He wrote the *Anubhavamrita* where he speaks extensively of the Advaita philosophy of Adi Shankaracharya. Simple, lucid and direct exposition of a philosophy as abstract as Advaita in language so sweetly rendered is the hallmark of this work. His follower Chidanandavadhoota wrote more extensively on his teacher's pet topic in *Jnanasindhu*.

The 1700s saw the pinnacle of Kannada literature with the advent of the ace poet Sarvajna. Unconventional in every sense, he was a wandering minstrel and his mission was to spread the spiritual message to the people. His 2,000 verses in the Tripadi metre with his name Sarvajna, narrate no stories or epics but deal with the philosophy of life and spirituality. He pokes fun at the superstitions and dogmas of society in the most cynical way and is most reflective in other verses. The stamp of Kavi Sarvajna on Kannada literature and his impact on its growth is remarkable.

A few other Kannada writers and poets of the time were Chidananda Kavi, Pandit Mallikarjuna, Venkataraya Shishya, Timmarasa, and Sarpa Bhushana and so on. The growth of Kannada seemed to get stunted in the Interregnum period between 1760 and 1799; it was revived by Mummadi Krishnaraja Wodeyar. The maharaja was himself a man of letters and translated the *Ramayana* and *Mahabharata* into Kannada. He wrote famous books, like *Devatanama Kusumamanjari, Sritatvanidhi, Srikrishna Katha Sangraha, Ramayana, Bharata, Dasharathanandana Charitre, Grahana Darpana* (predicting 82 eclipses from 1841–1902), *Suryachandra Vamshavali*, etc. The masterpieces of his reign include *Ganita Sangraha, Swarachudamani, Sowgandhikaparinaya, Sankhyaratnakosha, Chamundambalaghunighantu, Mahakoshasudhakara, Chaturangasarasarwasva, Sankhyaa-malay, Dashavibhaga Padaka* and so on.

Asthana Vidwan Basavappa (1843–91) prepared Kannada versions of Kalidasa's *Abhigyana Shakuntala, Vikramorvashiyam, Ratnavali*, and *Uttara Ramacharitre*, etc. The other books of this period were *Shurasena Charita* (the Indian version of Shakespeare's *Othello*) and *Savitri Charitre* in Shatpadi Style. Ramakrishnashastry wrote *Bhuvana Pradeepika* on the history and geography of South India, while Srinivasa Kavisarvabhauma's *Krishnaraja Prabhavodayam* and *Krishnaraja Jayotkarsha Champu* are biographies of Krishnaraja Wodeyar. Aliya Lingaraja, Srinivasakavi, Mahanto Shivayogi were other famous poets of his time.

Parti Subba, a Yakshagana exponent from South Kanara, received royal patronage and this enriched the Yakshagana Kannada literature. In fact it was under Mummadi Krishnaraja that the foundation of modern Kannada prose literature was truly laid. The *Mudra Manjusha* of Kempu Narayana (1823) was a landmark in Kannada prose literature. It was based on the Sanskrit drama *Mudra Rakshasa*. He retold the story in a more elaborate way and in his peculiarly individualistic prose style. It marks the beginning of prose fiction in Kannada. Aliya Lingaraja has over 47 works to his credit in different literary styles like Champu, Shatpadi, Saangatya, Yakshagana, Shataka, song, ballad, etc. Muddanna, whose real name was Nandalike

Lakshminaranappa is the author of *Adbhuta Ramayana, Rama Pattabhisheka* and *Ramaswhwamedha* and is considered the morning star on the horizon of modern Kannada literature. Blending the old and new in his delightful inimitable style, Muddanna used chaste old Kannada language, but his prose was modern in idiom and style. His death at the young age of 31 was a great loss to the world of Kannada literature.

The northern parts of Karnataka, coming as they did under the severe influence of the Maratha regime, could not produce much fine literature in Kannada due to the predominance of Marathi. However, painstaking efforts by numerous luminaries dispelled this notion. William Russell and Deputy Channabasappa started Kannada schools and introduced Kannada textbooks in those regions. Christian missionaries like Rev. Kittel, Mr Ziegler, B. Lewis Rice, Dr Caldwell, E.P. Rice and others were fascinated by the simplistic beauty of the Kannada language and did a lot to propagate it and to prepare standard works in Kannada. Kittel is credited with creating the first Kannada–English dictionary. Eminent people, like R. Narasimhachar, recorded the historical growth of Kannada in a three-volume book spanning 10 centuries from 900–1900 AD. These Western influences greatly revolutionised the Kannada literary forms both in style and content. Older forms like Champu were discarded; prose was established as the principal mode of literary expression, giving rise to diverse literary forms, like drama, novels, short stories, biographies, essays, etc., and the writings became more secular in nature.

The Navodaya (literally meaning new birth) phase of Kannada literature was indeed the period of renaissance in the late nineteenth and early twentieth centuries. This period saw greats, like Srikanthaiah, Kuvempu, Bendre, Shivaram Karanth, and Betgeri Krishnasharma.

Many educated Kannadigas, especially those in the teaching profession, realised that they needed to express themselves in their mother tongue and started writing in Kannada. Modern Kannada literature is the outcome of creative work, which was looked down upon by the traditionalists and was more experimental in nature. Eminent figures like B.M. Srikantaiya (1894–1946), Masti Venkatesha Iyengar, D.V.G., Govinda Pai, Panje Mangesha Rao, Santa Kavi and others heralded this modern era, being influenced by the English poets of the romantic era, like Wordsworth, Coleridge, Byron, Shelly and Keats. Srikantaiya's *English Geetegalu* set the tone for the romantic school in Kannada literature. The era was made further memorable by some of the greatest figures of

Kannada literature, such as Rashtrakavi 'Kuvempu' (Dr K.V. Puttappa) and 'Ambikatanayadatta' (D.R. Bendre) who still hold sway over popular literary imagination. Numerous other writers sprang up in this era—Sali Ramachandra Rao, V. Sitaramaiya, P.T. Narasimhachar, Kadangolu Shankar Bhatta, Betageri Krishna Sharma, V.K. Gokak, Madhura Chenna, R.S. Mugali and younger turks like G.P. Rajaratnam, S.V. Parameshwara Bhatta, K.S. Narasimhaswami, B.H. Sridhara, Pandeshwar Ganapati Rao, Gopalakrishna Adiga and others. G.P. Rajaratnam's *Ratnana Padagalu* and Narasimhaswami's *Mysuru Mallige* became very popular. And Gokak and Adiga, under the influence of the English poet T.S. Eliot, tried to break fresh ground and have been responsible for the emergence of yet another new, or *navya*, school of poetry.

Early Kannada novels were merely translations of Bengali or Marathi novels. But things changed with B. Venkatachar and Galaganatha who pioneered independent novel writing. The first original novel in Kannada was written in 1899 by Gulwadi Venkata Rao called *Indira Bai*, followed by *Vagdevi* (1905) by Bolar Babu Rao and Kerur Vasudevachar's *Indira* in 1908. *Madiddunno Maharaya* by M.S. Puttanna was the first and an outstanding novel depicting socio-economic conditions during Mummadi Krishnaraja Wodeyar's reign. The themes of society and socialism crept in with the works of A.N. Krishna Rao as also Kuvempu and Karanth. *Marali Mannige* by Karanth and *Kanuru Subbamma* by Kuvempu are brilliant pieces in the history of the Kannada novel. Many new popular novelists sprang up, like Niranjana, Basavaraja, Kattimani, T.R. Subba Rao, Krishnamurthi Puranik and women novelists, like 'Triveni', whose novels, which deal with very contemporary and modern issues, have been made into many old Kannada movie classics.

LITERATURE AND KANNADA THEATRE

The changes in the literary world greatly influenced the Kannada stage as well. Traditionally a people who love telling stories, as amply displayed in the Yakshagana Bayalaata art forms, theatre came naturally to the people of the Mysore state. The earliest available Kannada play is the *Mitravinda Govinda* written in the last quarter of the seventeenth century by Singaraya who was at the court of Chikkadevaraja Wodeyar. Scholars agree that traditional Kannada theatre flourished in the region in two distinctive styles, one nourished by the royal courts and providing entertainment to the educated and elite sections of society, and the other that sprang from the soil and literally mirrored the culture and aspirations of the commoners. The latter is believed to have been more ancient than the court theatre. Court theatre was more like a theme-dance with too many dialogues than a drama. The Kannada stage claims to be older than any other regional theatre in the country. The Yakshagana, Bhagavatara Aata, Doddaata, Sannaata and other forms of dance-drama have always been a delightful blend of music, dance, drama and poetry.

The commercial Kannada stage is about a hundred years old but in this short period it has brought many eminent figures, like Basavappa Shastri (*Abhinava Kalidasa*), Kerur Vasudevachar, Narayana Rao, Garud, B. Puttaswamaiya, A.V. Varadachar, Mohammad Peer, K.V. Subbanna, Handiganur and Master Hiranaiya. Many well-equipped troupes with bands of talented artists frequently went around the state and created a taste for dramas not only in Karnataka but the whole of South India.

When it comes to dramatic writing or scripts for plays it was perhaps the translation of *Shakuntala* by Churamuri Sheshagiri Rao in 1870 that set the ball rolling. Dhondo Narasimha Mulabagil, Subba Shastry, Anantanarayana Shastry, Mysore Seetarama Shastry and others joined the bandwagon of play-writing in Kannada. Many well-known plays by Shakespeare, Moliere, Ibsen, Goldsmith, etc., have either been translated or adapted into Kannada by scholars like D.V. Gundappa, Masti Venkatesha Iyengar, A.N. Murti Rao, Kuvempu, Parvatavani, S.G. Shastri, Devudu and others. The plays of T.P. Kailasam, Sriranga and K.S. Karanth introduced new and experimental methods in Kannada literature. Being social satirists they tried to lampoon social evils. While Kailasam did so by making a joke of them, Sriranga took it to the extremes of anger and retaliation. T.P. Kailasam's legendary tongue-in-cheek remarks were always a delight.

One-act plays by K.S. Karanth, D.R. Bendre, 'Parvatavani' Kaiwar Raja Rao, N.K. Kulkarni, 'Ksheerasagara' and others have been another challenging and interesting aspect of the growth of this area of literature. Essay writing under writers, like A.N. Murthi Rao, Goruru Ramaswamy Iyengar, N. Kasturi, Sriranga, Karanth, 'Nagemari' and others has developed into another form of literary expression.

From religious and epic descriptions, like in literature, theatre also transformed itself into a vehicle of social statement. The trend began with T.P. Kailasam whose satires were very popular among the masses and struck at the root of many social evils. His famous remark in view of the mammoth size of Maharaja Jayachamaraja Wodeyar: 'Three chairs for the ruler of Mysore!' would send the audience into splits! A galaxy of old and young writers, like K.T. Puranik, M.N. Babu, Kumara Venkanna, K. Gundanna, Sadasivaiya and Dasharathi Dixit contributed to the new dramatic literature. Kannada theatre also drew inspiration from similar forms in neighbouring states, like Maharashtra, Andhra Pradesh and Tamil Nadu and in turn influenced the forms there. It was said that a Yakshagana troupe that went from North Kanara to Sangli in 1842 at the invitation of the Raja of Sangli, Srimanth Appa Sahib Patwardhan, bowled the raja over so that he decided to write Marathi plays on the lines of Yakshagana.

In the context of Yakshagana literature, mention must be made of the immense contribution of Dr Kota Shivarama Karanth—a great litterateur, novelist, researcher and linguist who continued writing throughout his lifetime and contributed more than 100 books belonging to various categories in Kannada literature. Loved by children as Karanthajja, Dr Karanth was famous for his straight-forward nature and active involvement in his fields of interest. There is no category in literature that Dr Karanth did not touch. He has written novels, short stories, plays, music dramas, literary criticism, and books for children, travelogues, books on nature, science, and on folk culture. In addition, Dr Karanth was the exponent of Yakshagana, the folk art of coastal Karnataka and had experimented a great deal with the art form. Some of his famous novels include *Bettada Jeeva*, *Mookajjiya Kanasugalu*, *Chomana Dudi*, *Marali Mannige*, *Battada Tore*, *Alida Mele*, and many others. He wrote many plays including *Kisa Gouthami*, *Savitri-Sathyavan*, *Somiya Soubhagya*, *Katte Purana*, *Garbha Gudi*, *Geddavara Samkhye*. *Tereya Mareyalli* and *Hasivu Maththu Havu* are short shories. *Huchchu Manasina Haththu Mukhagalu* (The Ramblings of a Lunatic) is his autobiography.

Patronage to Sanskrit

It was not just Kannada that the maharajas of Mysore patronised. Sanskrit—the classical and ancient language of the Aryan civilisation—was a close contender for their attention. After the disintegration of the Vijayanagara empire, Keladi and Mysore inherited the Hindu traditions and Sanskrit was prime among them. Apart from royal patronage, religious institutions like the three Vaishnava *muths*, the eight *muths* at

Udupi, the Advaita Peethas at Sringeri, Koodli, Sankeshwar and Kanchi were centres of learning for Sanskrit and the Vedanta. It is difficult to categorise Sanskrit and its scholars on a regional basis as they usually moved from one place to another under the patronage of different kings. The language had no regionalistic connotations attached to it and was viewed as the language of the intellectuals. Some of the early Sanskrit scholars of Mysore include Devaraja, Yaska, Narahari, Mysore Anantacharya, Shadaksharadeva, Surpur Venkatacharya, Mysore Pradhana Venkata Bhoopati and others. The infamous Dalavoy Nanjarajayya, known for his many political misadventures and machinations in the time of Immadi Krishnaraja Wodeyar, was a great Sanskrit scholar and translated many works from Sanskrit to Kannada, even composing *Sangeetha Gangadhara* in Sanskrit. It is in four cantos in the *Gita Govinda* style.

Mummadi Krishnaraja Wodeyar was a scholar of Sanskrit as well and most of his earlier mentioned works were either in Kannada or Sanskrit. Many poets and scholars of Sanskrit adorned his court— Ramakrishna Shastry of Hassan, Srinivasa Kavisravabhauma, Tirumala Bukkapatnam Venkatachar, Udeyendrapuram Anantacharya (who wrote the famous poem *Yadava-Raghava-Pandaviya*), Chincholi Venkannachar (*Ashtadhyayadarpana*) and others. This trend continued in the latter half of the nineteenth and early half of the twentieth centuries with the maharajas extending their benevolence and patronage to scores of Sanskrit *vidwans* and scholars. Many books were written in Telugu, such as *Vachana Bharatamu*, *Halasya Mahatmyamu*, Kundalakurki Chandrakavi's *Krishnabhupaliyamu* and Amble P. Laksminarasimha Shastri's *Bhanu Shatakamu* and *Neethi Shatakamu*.

Growth of Urdu

During the Interregnum period, Urdu was patronised in Mysore. Persian and Kannada became the state languages. Zainul Abidin Shustary wrote the *Fathull Mujahideen*. Kirmani, the historian, wrote a biography of Haidar Ali called *Haidar Nama* and *Bahadur Nama*; Tarab's *Fatheh Nama* on Tipu Sultan and his achievements was another great piece of Urdu literature.

The Wodeyars too were great patrons of Urdu and Hindustani. Latiff Arcoti, Shah Muhammad Arif, Mir Hayyat, Banke Nawab Nassim, Ghamshad, Jadu, Salim Dil, Athar, Ah, Alwi, Barq, Tahshil, Muqbil and others were the great Urdu poets patronised by the later Wodeyars. Nalwadi Krishnaraja Wodeyar was himself proficient in Urdu and in fact he even *spoke* in Urdu during the inauguration of the Jama Masjid in Mysore in 1929. In 1927, during the silver jubilee celebrations of his coronation, he made his public announcements in Urdu for the Muslim brethren of Mysore and also instituted a chair for Urdu and Persian at the Mysore University. Thus we see a delightful blend of languages flourishing in Mysore, which contributed a great deal to its largely cosmopolitan and tolerant social ethos.

THE FOURTH ESTATE

Besides propagating the language, the press acts a watchdog over democracy and has the power to make or break rulers and kingdoms. We have all seen the important role played by the newspapers in India's freedom movement.

Mysore has the distinction of having an old and illustrious journalistic history. In 1850, the first printing press came up in Mysore and the first newspaper was the *Bangalore Herald* in 1859, edited by James. Other papers that followed were *Mysore Vritthanhta Bodhini* edited by Bhashyachari, *Arunodaya* (1862) edited by R. Rice, *Qasim-ul-Akbar* (1863) edited by Janab Mohammad Qasim 'Gham' and the first monthly Kannada journal *Hitabodhini* by Ramanuja Iyengar.

The first Kannada weekly newspaper *Karnataka Prakashika* was published in 1865 and revived in 1874 as a Kannada-English bilingual weekly by T.C. Srinivasachar, an eminent Sanskrit scholar. It championed the cause of a pro-Mysorean political party that also had radical views about non-Mysoreans infiltrating into the Mysore services and enjoying posts of great privilege and authority, while not doing much to promote employment for the locals. The *Mysore Gazette*, a government publication, began in 1866 in Kannada and English and continues to this day.

After the Rendition of Mysore in 1881, the press received a fresh impetus. Kannada weekly *Deshabhimani*, started in 1894 by B. Srinivasa Iyengar, ran into serious problems due to misunderstandings between Mr Iyengar and Dewan Sheshadri Iyer. The *Vrittanta Patrike* was founded by the Wesleyan mission, had a sober news service and furnished constructive suggestions. It ceased to exist in 1942.

No treatise on journalism in Mysore would be complete without a reference to M. Venkatakrishnaiya, fondly addressed as Tathaiya (1844–1933). Called by many names, like Dayasagara and Bhishmacharya, he was a veritable pillar for budding journalists. In his long career spanning over sixty years he started many newspapers: *Vrittantha Chintamani* (1885), *Sampadabhyudaya, Vidyaadaayini* and *Saadhvi*, so much so that he was rightly considered the 'Pitamaha' of Kannada journalism in the then Mysore state. A horde of newspapers entered with *Hitabodhini, Udanta Chintamani* and *Poorna Samajika Patrike*, all in Kannada and *Mysore Patriot, Wealth of Mysore, Mysore Herald* and *Nature Cure* in English, all owing to the patronage and support of M. Venkatakrishnaiya.

Though he had great respect for the maharajas of his time, he acted as a true watchdog and made it a point to protest any administrative lapse. This cost him his headmastership of the Marimallappa High School in 1918, but that was no deterrent to the outspoken man. The maharaja held him in high regard, sanctioning a pension of Rs 50 for Tathaiya from the palace funds after his forced retirement from the school. However, a supposedly seditious article in the *Sampadabhyudaya* led to the closure of the newspaper by the maharaja's government in 1922 along with a quasi-judicial enquiry. Resident Barton insisted that the paper be discontinued forever and his will prevailed. He also ensured that the maharaja terminated the pension sanctioned to the old man. Tathaiya did write many letters to the maharaja, the dewan and Charles Toddhunter, the personal secretary of the maharaja, seeking that the order for cancellation of pension be revoked, but in vain. Tathaiya died a pauper in 1933.

Tathaiya firmly believed that newspapers would go a long way in establishing democracy and that some of the repressive measures of the dewans were stifling democracy by trying to gag the press. Though a course in journalism had not yet begun in Mysore University, Tathaiya made an endowment for a prize for the best journalism student that actually took shape in 1951, thirty years after he had sponsored it. Tathaiya played a pivotal role in Mysore's history as a representative of the fourth estate with his liberal and progressive outlook.

The students of Tathaiya, M. Gopala Iyengar and M. Srinivasa Iyengar, started the *Kannada Nadegannadi* and *Mysore Standard*, a move that severely displeased the dewans—P.N.Krishnamurthy and V.P. Madhava Rao. In 1908, the council passed the infamous Newspaper Regulations Act, earning the wrath of many journalists including Tathaiya. The editor of *Nadegannadi* was ordered to be deported from the state.

Dr D.V. Gundappa started the English bi-weekly *Karnataka*, edited *Arthasadhaka Patrike* and the English journal *Indian Review of Reviews*. Other

The Lives and Times of Mysoreans: Literature, Theatre and Journalism 717

newspapers of the time were *Vishwakarnataka* (1921), a weekly edition by Tirumala Tatacharya Sharman, *Tainaadu* (1926) by P.R. Ramaiya, *Janavani* (1934) by B.N. Gupta, *Chitragupta* by H.K. Veeranna Gowda, *Veerakesari* by Sitarama Shastry and *Navajeevana*, edited by Ashwath Narayana Rao. Of these, the *Vishwakarnataka* served as the best mouthpiece of the freedom struggle and Quit India Movement under its new editor Siddhavanahalli Krishnasarma. The government banned its publication in 1944 on charges of sedition when it carried an open letter to the Viceroy Lord Linlithgow. It was revived in 1945, but could not last too long due to financial problems and wound up in 1956. *Prajamatha,* started in 1931, was very popular among the masses. These newspapers strengthened democratic institutions in Mysore and also contributed a lot to the freedom struggle by inspiring people to work towards an independent India.

At the end of this elaborate treatise on the cultural story of Mysore, we are struck by the all-round evolution and elevation of Mysore and its people. Material progress was of course easy to define. But more important was the evolution of the distinct way of life and social ethos of the 'Mysorean', that revealed itself more often than not in the various forms of human expression—music, dance, theatre, literature, folk forms, architecture, painting and the press. This is just a humble sketch and a bird's-eye view of the path of socio-cultural development that Mysore followed under the long and benevolent rule of its culturally conscious maharajas.

CONCLUSION

The beginning of one era stems from the end of another. Thus ended the grandeur and splendour of the Yadu royal family of Mysore. As I walk away from the Kodi Bhairava Temple, from where this whole story began, the sun has set, birds are returning to their nests and quite symbolically, a chapter in the history of the land is over.

But it goes to the spirit of Mysore that it has always had the fortune of being ruled by some of the best minds of the country. Each time the person at the helm dithered, a new force would emerge that took the land to greater glory. The fall of Vijayanagara catapulted Raja Wodeyar to the fore. When his successors rendered themselves unworthy of the throne, stalwarts, like Ranadhira Kanthirava Narasaraja Wodeyar and Chikka Devaraja Wodeyar, led the kingdom to its zenith. With the state being milked by the machinations of the dalavoys and the members of the royal family remaining mute and powerless spectators, it was left to the valour of Haidar Ali and his heroic son Tipu Sultan to steer the state in troubled times. The British shivered at the very mention of Mysore, which was rightly the first Indian state to take up arms against the foreign power. When Mummadi Krishnaraja Wodeyar's administration bungled in its duties, the state passed on to the able hands of Commissioners, like Mark Cubbon and Lewin Bowring, who only helped accelerate the pace of growth.

It must be admitted that the Mysore state after its Restoration in 1799 was geographically a weak reflection of its earlier might and that the later maharajas were vassals of the British Crown. But it is to their credit that unlike other contemporary Indian princes, they utilised the British technical know-how and combined it with their own ingenuity and the statesmanship of illustrious dewans, like Rangacharlu, Sheshadri Iyer, Vishweswaraiya and Mirza Ismail, to help the state achieve unparalleled progress on all fronts. The number of firsts that Mysore has had in the Indian context are truly laudable.

Women played a prominent role in this extensive and chequered history of the state, where female power has long been worshipped in the form of the Goddess Chamundeshwari—the slayer of the mythical demon Mahishasura. From an irate Rani Alamelamma who supposedly cursed the Wodeyars to the unsophisticated and raw energy of an Onake Obavva of Chitradurga; from the diplomatic and courageous Rani Lakshmammanni who strove to salvage the fortunes of her family to the suave Rani Kempa Nanjammanni Vanivilasa Sannidhana who steered the state ably during her regency—women have always proved their mettle and played a pivotal role in state polity.

At the end of this long saga of Mysore over six centuries, I return to the theme with which I began—the objectives of history that one needs to keep in mind while documenting it. If this work of mine has instilled a sense of pride and achievement among even one reader, about the greatness of the cultural heritage bequeathed to him/her and at the same time instilled a feeling of responsibility and ownership towards the present and future of the state, I would consider my work truly successful and worth the effort.

REFERENCES AND BIBLIOGRAPHY

Ahmed, Tahsin. 'The Mysore Palace'. Tourist booklet. Mysore: Royal Palace authorities.

Ali, B. Sheikh (Ed.). 1993. Tipu Sultan: A Great Martyr. Bangalore: University of Bangalore.

Allan, Captain. 1799. An Account of the Campaigns in Mysore. Calcutta.

Aparanji, N.R. 1982. History of Karnataka.

Arberry, A.J. 1938. The Library of the India Office. London: India Office.

Azer, Rehman. 1982. Tiger Sultan. Bangalore: Nayab Publications.

Bartolomaeo, Fra. Voyage to East Indies.

Bayly, Lt. Richard. 1896. Diary of Colonel Bayly, 12th Regiment 1796–1803. London: Army and Navy Cooperative Society.

Beatson, A. 1800. A view of the origin and conduct of the war with Tippoo Sultan; comprising a narrative of the operations of the army under the command of Lieutenant General George Harris and the siege of Seringapatam. London: G. & W. Nichol.

Bhat, N. Shyam. 1987. 'A Study in Colonial Administration and Regional Response'. Mangalore: Mangalore University.

Bowring, L.B. 1893. Hyder Ali and Tipu Sultan (Rulers of India series). Republished. New Delhi: Asian Educational Services.

Bristow, J. 1794. Narrative of Suffering during Ten Years of Captivity with Hyder Ali and Tipu Sultan. Calcutta.

Buchanan, Francis. 1807. A Journey from Madras through the Countries of Mysore, Canara and Malabar. London: East India Company.

Carey, Henry. 1853. The Slave Trade, Domestic and Foreign. Groningen: Department of Alfa-Informatica, University of Groningen, the Netherlands. Republished (2004). IndyPublish.com.

Chalmers, George. Collection of Treaties between Great Britain and Other Powers, Vol. 1. Piccadilly: John Stockdale.

Chopra, P.N., Ravindran T.K. and Subramanian. 1979. *History of South India, Vol.3: Modern Period*. New Delhi: S. Chand and Co.

Cousins, Margaret. 1935. *Music of the Orient and the Occident*. Madras: B.C. Paul and Co.

De Pradt, Abbe. 1902. *Les Trois Ages des Colonies*. Paris.

Dirom, Major Alexander. 1793. *A Narrative of the Campaign in India which Terminated the War with Tippoo Sultan in 1792*. London. Reprinted (1985). New Delhi: Asian Educational Services.

Diwakar, R.R. et al. 1968. *Karnataka through the Ages, Vol I & II*. Mysore: Literary and Cultural Development Department, Government of Mysore.

Edwards, Michael. 1961. *A History of India*. Bombay.

Eliot, T.S. 1949. *Notes towards a Definition of Culture*. New York: Harcourt, Brace and Company.

Fernandes, Praxy. 1969. *Storm Over Seringapatam, the Incredible Story of Hyder Ali and Tippu Sultan*. Bombay: Thackers.

Forbes, James. 1813. *Oriental Memoirs*. London.

Forrest, Denys. 1970. *Tiger of Mysore: The Life and Death of Tipu Sultan*. London: Chatto and Windus.

Fryer, John and Thomas Roe. 1873. *Travels in India in the 17th Century.*

Fryer, John and William Crooke. *A New Account of East India and Persia, Being Nine Years' Travels, 1672–81*. Oxford University Press.

Fung, Annie Cahn. 1992. 'Paul Brunton: A Bridge between India and the West'. Paris: University of Paris.

George, T.J.S. 2005. *M.S.—A Life in Music: A Biography of Bharat Ratna M.S. Subbulakshmi*. New Delhi: Harper Collins and India Today.

Gidwani, Bhagwan. S. *The Sword of Tipu Sultan*. New Delhi: Allied Publishers.

Gleig, Rev. G.R. 1830. *The Life of Major General Sir Thomas Munro*. London: Henry Colburn and Richard Bentley.

Goel, Sita Ram. *Tipu Sultan: Villain or Hero? An Anthology*. New Delhi: Voice of India.

Gopal, M.H. 1960. *The Finances of the Mysore State. 1799–1831*. Bombay: Orient Longman.

———. 1971. *Tipu Sultan's Mysore, An Economic Study*. Bombay: Popular Prakashan.

Guha, Nikhiles. 1985. *Pre-British State System in South India, Mysore 1761–1799*. Calcutta: Ratna Prakashan.

Hall, Richard. 1996. *Empires of the Monsoon*. London: Harper Collins.

Haythornwaite, Philip. 1806. *The Colonial Wars Source Book, Mutiny at Vellore: 1806.*

Henderson, John R. 1921. *Coins of Haidar Ali and Tipu Sultan.* Madras: Government Press.

Huberman, Leo. 1976. *Man's Worldly Goods.* People's Publishing House: New Delhi.

Iqbal, Mirza. *Ahwali Hyder Naik.* (A supplement to Kirmani's *Nishani Hydari*).

Iyengar, M.A. Narayana and M.A. Sreenivasachar. 1981. 'The Mysore Pradhans'. Reprinted by Asuri Sreenivasa Iyengar and R.N. Tirumala Iyengar. Bangalore: Mandayam Sree Vaishnava Sabha.

Iyer, K.V. Krishna. 1938. *Zamorins of Calicut: From Earliest Times to AD 1806.* Calicut: Norman Printing Bureau.

Jalal, Ayesha. *The Sole Spokesman: Jinnah, the Muslim League and the Demand for Pakistan.* Cambridge University Press.

Joseph, Sebastian. *State and the Ritual Realm in Nineteenth-century Mysore.* Monograph.

Joyser, G.R. 1929. *History of Mysore and the Yadava Dynasty.*

Kamath, Suryanath. 1988. *Gazetteer of India—Karnataka State—Mysore District.* Bangalore: Government Press.

———. 2002. *A Concise History of Karnataka.* Bangalore: Jupiter Books, MCC Publications.

Keswani, K.B. 1996. *International Relations in Modern World 1900–1995*, 3rd ed. Himalaya Publishing House.

Kirkpatrick, William. 1811. *Select Letters of Tippoo Sultan to Various Public Functionaries.* Arranged and translated by William Kirkpatrick. London: Cox, Son and Baylis.

Kirmani, Mir Hussain Ali Khan. 1890. *Nishani Hydari.* Translated from Persian by Col. W. Miles.

———. 1997. *History of Tipu Sultan—Being a Continuation of the Nishani Hydari.* Translated from Persian by Col. W. Miles. New Delhi: Asian Education Services.

Krishna, B. 1995. *Sardar Vallabhbhai Patel—India's Iron Man.* New Delhi: Harper Collins.

Kumaresh, Jayanthi. 2007. 'Analytical study of different Banis and playing techniques of the Saraswati Veena'. Mysore: University of Mysore. Ph.D. thesis.

Lockman, John. 1995. *Travels of the Jesuits.* Originally published in 1743. London: John Noon.

Logan, William. *Malabar Manual.* Trivandrum: Charitram Publications.
Mackenzie, Lt. Rodrick. 1794. *Sketch of the War with Tipu Sultan (1789–92)*, 2 Vols. Calcutta.
Macksey, Kenneth. 1973. *The Guinness History of Land Warfare.* London: Guinness Superlatives Ltd.
Malcolm, Major General Sir John. 1836. *The Life of Robert, Lord Clive: Collected from the Family Papers*, Vol. 1. London: J. Murray.
Malleson, George Bruce. 1858. *The Mutiny of the Bengal Army: A Historical Narrative.* Bosworth and Harrison.
Manucci, Niccolao. 1906. *Storia do Mogor, 4 Vols.* Translated into English by W. Irvine. London: John Murray. Reprinted (1981). New Delhi: Oriental Books.
Martin, Robert Montgomery. 1885. *British India: Its History, Topography, Government, Military Defence, Finance, Commerce and Staple Products.* London: London Printing and Publishing Co. Reprinted (1983). New Delhi: Mayur Publications.
Menon, K.P. Padmanabha. 1989. *History of Cochin State.* Mathrubhoomi Publication.
Michaud, Joseph Francaise. 1801. *Histoire des Progres et la chute de l'Empire de Mysore Sons les Regnes d'Hyder Ally et Tippoo Sahib*, 2 Vols. Paris.
———. 1809. *Historie des progress de la chute de l'empire de Mysore, sons les regnes d'Hyder –Aly et de Tippoo Saib.* Paris.
Mukerji, R. 1794. *Rise and Fall of the East India Company.*
Munro, Innes. 1789. *A narrative of the military operations on the Coromandel coast, from the year 1780 to the peace in 1784.* London.
Murphy, Veronica. 1990. 'Europeans and the Textile Trade', in John Guy and Deborah Swallow (eds) *Arts of India, 1550–1900.* London: Victoria and Albert Museum.
Murthy, N.K. Narasimha. 1976. *Purniah.* Bangalore.
Murthy, Srinivasa. '*Karnatakada Itihasa*'
Nair, K. Madhava. 1921. *Malabar Kalapam.*
Newbolt, Henry. 1898. 'Seringapatnam', first published in *The Island Race.* London: Elkin Matthews. Republished (1912) in *Poems: New and Old.* London: John Murray.
Orme, Robert. 1782. *Historical Fragments of the Mogul Empire, of the Morattoes and of English Concerns in Indostan from the Year 1659 to 1689.*
Panicker, K.M. *Freedom Struggle in Kerala.*
Peixoto, Eloy Jose Correa. *Memoirs of My Service under Hyder Ali, from 1758 to 1770.*

Pillai, Ananda Ranga. 2004. *The Private Diary of Ananda Ranga Pillai, 1736–1761.* New Delhi: Sudeep Prakashan.

Pillai, V.R. Parameswaran. 1973. *Life History of Raja Kesavadas.* Kottayam: N.B.S. Publications.

Pirenne, J. 1950. 'From Trade to Colonization: Historic Dynamics of the East India Companies', in *History of the Universe.* Paris.

Prabhakar, Sukanya. 2005. *Karnataka Sangeetakke Sri Jayachamarajendra Wodeyaravara Koduge.* Mysore: D.V.K. Murthy.

Pranesh, Meera Rajaram. 2003. *Musical Composers during the Wodeyar Dynasty.* Bangalore: Vee Emm Publications.

Puttaiya, B. 1921. 'Maharaja Chikka Devaraja Wadiyar of Mysore'. *Quarterly Journal of the Mythic Society*, Vol. XI, No. 2 (January).

Rao, B.R. (Ed.). 1916, 1922. *Annals of the Mysore Royal Family — Srimanmaharajaravara Vamshavali.* Parts I and II. Mysore.

Rao, Gopal H.S. 1996. *Karnataka Ekikarana Ithihasa.* Bangalore: Navakarnataka Printers.

Rao, Hayavadana C. 1930. *Mysore Gazetteer*, Vols. I–V. Bangalore: Government Press.

———. 1945. *History of Mysore, 1399–1799 AD*, Vols. I–III. Bangalore: Government Press.

Rao, Nagaraja. '*The Mysore Palace*'. Tourist booklet. Mysore: Royal Palace authorities.

Rao, Shama. 1936. *Modern Mysore*, 2 Vols. Bangalore.

Rao, Swami. *Sri Nalwadi Krishnarajendra Wodeyaravara Charitre.*

Rebellow, I. *History of Karnataka.*

Records of Fort St. George: Diary and Consultations Book, 1694. 1910. Madras: Government Press.

Rice, E.P. 1982. *History of Kanarese Literature.* New Delhi: Asian Education Services.

Rice, Lewis. 1877. *Mysore and Coorg: A Gazetteer Compiled for the Government of India*, 2 Vols. Bangalore: Mysore Government Press.

———. *History of Mysore.*

Robbins, Nick. 2006. *The Corporation that Changed the World.* Hyderabad: Orient Longman.

Saki. 2004. *Making History—Karnataka's People and Their Past*, Vol. 1 (1998) and Vol. 2 (2004). Bangalore: Vimukthi Prakashana.

Sastri, Nilakanta and G. Srinivasachari. *Advanced History of India.* Allied Publishers.

Sewell, Robert. 1990. *A Forgotten Empire (Vijayanagara).* London.

Shastri, K.N.V. 1934. 'Cash contributions of Mysore to the British Government, 1799–1881'. Mysore.

Shourie, Arun. 1998. *Eminent Historians: Their Technology, Their Line, Their Fraud.* New Delhi: ASA Publications.

Singarayya. *Sri Chamarajendra Wodeyaravara Charitre.*

Sinha, N.K. 1941. *Haidar Ali.* Calcutta: A. Mukherjee and Co. Pvt. Ltd.

Sivaramakrishna, Sashi. 2005. *The Curse of Talakad: (Re)situating and (Re)contextualizing a Legend in History.* New Delhi: Rupa & Co.

Smith, Vincent. A., C.I.E. 1981. In Percival Spear (ed.) *The Oxford History of India,* 4th ed. New Delhi: Oxford University Press

Spear, Percival. 1981. *The Oxford History of Modern India 1740–1975.* New Delhi: Oxford University Press.

Srinivasan, R. 1990. *Facets of Indian Culture.* Bombay: Bharatiya Vidya Bhawan.

Stein, Burton. 1989. *Thomas Munro, the Origins of the Colonial State and His Vision of Empire.* New Delhi: Oxford University Press.

Taylor, Meadows. 1986. *Tippoo Sultan: A Tale of the Mysore War.* New Delhi: Asian Educational Services.

The Dasara Souvenir. 1994. Government of Karnataka Publication.

Thornton, Lt Col. L.H. 1927. *Light and Shade in By-gone India.* London: John Murray.

Tour, De La. *Histoire d'Ayder-Ali-Khan, Nahab-Bahader.* Translated (1976). *The History of Hyder Shah, alias Hyder Ali Khan Bahadur, and of His Son Tippoo Sultan.* New Delhi: Cosmo Publications.

Toynbee, Arnold J. 1934. *A Study of History,* Vol. I. London: Oxford University Press.

Urs, Nanjaraja. 2007. *Mysuru: Noorinnooru Varshagala Hindhe.* Mysore: Abhiruchi Prakashana.

Valentia, Lord. 1809. Voyages and Travels to India, Ceylon, etc. *London.*

Varma, Vatakkankoor Raja Raja. *History of Sanskrit Literature in Kerala.*

Varma, Vatakkankoor Raja Raja. *Tipu Sultan: Villain or Hero? An Anthology.* New Delhi: Voice of India.

Vasudevacharya, Mysore. 1985. *Naa Kanda Kalavidaru.* Kavyalaya, 2nd ed.

White, Margaret Bourke. 1949. *Halfway to Freedom.* New York: Simon and Schuster.

Wilks, M. 1810. *Historical sketches of the South of India in an Attempt to Trace the History of Mysoor,* Vols. I and II.

———. *History of Mysore,* Vols. I & II

INDEX

Alexander the Great, 153
Ali, Haidar, *vii, xi, xx*, 59, 137, 141, 143, 145, 146, 147, 148, 149, 151, 153, 154, 155, 157, 159, 160, 161, 163, 165, 167, 169, 171, 172, 173, 175, 177, 178, 179, 181, 183, 184, 185, 187, 189, 191, 193, 195, 197, 199, 201, 203, 205, 207, 209, 211, 212, 213, 215, 216, 217, 219, 221, 258, 266, 288, 333, 340, 349, 353, 617, 653, 693, 694, 698, 713
Ali, Sheikh, 276, 335
Anglo-Mysorean Wars, 179
Ashoka, Emperor, 521
Atharvaveda, 669

Baird, General, 274, 278, 279, 282, 283, 284, 287, 294, 301, 302, 303, 305, 306, 337, 338
Balamuri, 145, 259
Banerji, Sir Albion, 539, 556, 569
Barrackpore, 462
Battle of Plassey, 154, 206
Battle of Porto Novo, 207
Beg, Latif Ali, 160, 224
Begum, Majida, 146, 147
Bentinck, William, 416, 459, 477, 478
Bhagavata Purana, 691

Bhagavathar, Dr Harikesanallur Muthaiah, 649, 650, 652, 654, 681
Bhakti movement, 632
Bharata, *x*, 125, 486, 634, 656, 668, 669, 670, 671, 672, 674, 690, 704, 705, 706, 708, 713
Bharatanatyam, *x*, 125, 656, 668, 669, 670, 671, 674
Bhat, Shyam, 446
Bonaparte, Napoleon, 268
Bourchier, Charles, 181, 182
Brahmo Samaj, 586
Brunton, Paul, 521

Caliph, Ottoman, 211
Canning, Lord, 462, 466
Chamaraja, Khasa, 196, 234, 259, 262, 348
Chelmsford, Lord, 556
Chowdaiah, Mysore T., 649, 655
Clive, Robert, 154
Cornwallis, Lord, 241, 246, 248, 249, 252, 254, 256, 258, 261, 262, 264, 283, 311, 323, 506
Crimean War, 460
Cripps, Sir Stafford, 602, 605

de Pradt, Abbe, 176

728 Index

Devarajayya, Dalavoy, 133, 134, 146
Dikshitar, Muthuswamy, 631, 632, 651
Doctrine of Lapse, 40, 461
Dow, Alexander, 234
Dupleix, 136, 149, 150, 151, 152

East India Company, *xi, xxi*, 93, 94, 95, 96, 97, 98, 99, 100, 154, 176, 181, 190, 202, 229, 234, 258, 271, 318, 355, 366, 367, 376, 385, 386, 388, 389, 390, 391, 392, 393, 394, 395, 430, 458, 467, 482, 508
Elphinstone, 464

First British-Afghan War, 460
First Sikh War, 458
First War of Indian Independence, 462

Gandhi, Mahatma, 505, 521
Ganjifa cards, 681, 682
Ghouse, Muhammad, 189
Golconda, 546
Gopal, M.H., 362, 427

Haidar, Fateh, 215, 251, 292, 413
Hardinge, Lord Henry, 476, 479
Harikatha, 650, 680, 681
Harris, General, 270, 271, 272, 273, 274, 275, 284, 285, 286, 288, 293, 295, 337, 382, 385
Hastings, Warren, 195, 206, 228, 229
Hobli School System, 471

Ilbert Bill, 578
Iqbal, Mohammad, 290
Ismail, Sir Mirza, *xi, xvi, xxiii*, 505, 507, 524, 539, 540, 542, 563, 569, 571, 591, 592, 597

Iyengar, Tirumala, 85, 86, 87, 116, 125, 143
Iyer, Sheshadri, 505, 507, 509, 510, 511, 523, 524, 525, 526, 529, 553, 561, 565, 570, 572, 574, 586, 700, 714

Jung, Basalat, 168, 172, 178, 194, 237
Jung, Muzaffar, 149, 151
Jung, Nasir, 149, 150, 151, 154

Kalam, A.P.J. Abdul, 320
Karim, 163, 175, 178, 220, 225, 646, 656, 659
Khan, Abdul Rasool, 147
Khan, Dost Ali, 149
Khan, Ghazi, 155, 176, 180, 184, 190, 210, 237, 251, 275
Khan, Malik Jehan, 350, 411
Khan, Qasim, 149
Kirkpatrick, William, 322, 333, 334, 385
Krishnappa, Bidaram, 643, 647, 648, 655, 673
Kunzru, H.N., 620

Lakshmammanni (Maharani of Mysore), *xx*, 75, 136, 143, 146, 159, 166, 177, 188, 195, 197, 199, 201, 215, 219, 227, 259, 261, 262, 365, 371, 373, 376, 379, 382, 383, 385, 408, 409, 417, 419, 478, 482, 695
Lawrence, Major, 150
Louis XVI, 245, 364

Mahabharata, 4, 486, 678, 683, 686, 691, 703, 704, 708
Malabar Manual, 353, 355, 356
Malcolm, John, 150, 405, 410

Marathas, *xvi*, 88, 90, 98, 99, 102, 104, 106, 107, 108, 109, 130, 131, 132, 133, 137, 149, 153, 158, 160, 163, 164, 168, 170, 171, 173, 176, 177, 179, 183, 184, 185, 189, 190, 191, 192, 195, 197, 201, 205, 208, 226, 234, 235, 236, 237, 238, 242, 243, 245, 249, 250, 254, 260, 271, 350, 360, 367, 376, 377, 378, 383, 414
Marihalla Project, 565
Meadows, Major General William, 243
Michaud, Joseph, 310
Mill, James, 309
Mitravinda Govinda, 706, 710
Mohammad, Fateh, 146, 147, 149
Mohammad, Prince Ghulam, 210
Morley-Minto reforms, 556
Mornington, Lord, 258, 263, 372, 374, 376, 380, 404, 417
Mughals, *xvi*, 16, 64, 88, 97, 98, 99, 107, 108, 109, 110, 130, 132, 133, 137, 148, 172, 213, 337, 350, 630
Muhammad, Prince Ghulam, 355
Munro, Thomas, 416, 424, 456, 484
Muthaiah Bhagavathar, 650
Mysore Palace, 531, 544, 572, 657, 694, 696

Nadim, Mir, 265, 266, 277, 279, 280, 400
Nagamandala, 681
Naik, Rangappa, 191
Natakashala, 79, 143, 196, 219
Natyashastra, 634, 668, 669, 671
Nayak, Rangappa, 444, 445

Opium Wars, 100, 460

Pandey, Mangal, 462

Pandit, Kala, 236
Pannikkar, K.M., 620
Patel, Vallabhbhai, 593, 619
Pethick-Lawrence, Lord, 605
Phadnavis, Nana, 191, 192, 235, 236, 242, 256
Pigot, Lord, 197, 263
Plato, 521
Portuguese, 91, 92, 95, 96, 98, 185, 322, 350
Prince of Wales, 528, 572, 589
Purnaiya, *viii*, 189, 210, 211, 215, 252, 266, 275, 313, 336, 348, 362, 372, 383, 385, 396, 397, 398, 399, 400, 401, 402, 403, 404, 405, 406, 407, 408, 409, 410, 411, 412, 413, 414, 415, 417, 419, 420, 421, 422, 423, 435, 437, 459, 496, 528, 635, 694, 700

Raja of Malabar, 170
Ramakrishna Mission, 586
Ramayana, 4, 50, 81, 486, 678, 691, 704, 708, 709
Rangacharlu, 493, 497, 500, 505, 507, 508, 509, 552, 553, 559, 563, 572
Rao, Appaji, 178, 185, 188
Rao, Berki Srinivasa, 179, 183, 189, 191, 203
Rao, Hayavadana, 71, 118, 127, 170, 173, 175, 187, 194, 198, 216, 220, 225, 228, 239, 243, 254, 335, 338, 431, 434
Rao, Khande, 155, 157, 159, 160, 161, 162, 163, 164, 165, 166, 173, 187, 214, 266
Rao, Mysore Sadashiva, 487, 627, 637, 638, 641
Rao, Peshwa Madhava, 170, 173, 177, 183, 190, 205

730 Index

Rao, Raghunath, 170, 190, 191, 203
Rao, Shama, 318, 339, 348, 379, 406, 408, 412, 417, 421, 427, 429, 437, 443, 448, 449, 452, 453, 455, 461, 482, 494, 495, 496, 499, 501
Rao, Tirumala, 197, 198, 226, 227, 232, 259, 260, 261, 262, 371, 373, 401, 403, 404
Register of Tipu's Dreams, 334
Republic, 521
Rice, Lewis, 319, 329, 362, 423, 696, 709
Rigveda, 669

Sadik, Mir, 237, 242, 245, 249, 265, 273, 275, 279, 280, 313, 334, 400
Sahib, Chanda, 149, 151, 152, 178
Samaveda, 669
Sastri, Venkatachala, 438
Seal, Dr Sir Brajendranath, 556
Second Anglo-Burmese War, 460
Second Sikh War, 458
Shamaiya, Anche, 188, 197, 226, 401, 404
Sharat System, 426, 428
Shastri, Asthana Vidwan Basavappa, 486
Shastri, Basappa, 643
Shastry, Shyama, 631, 632, 637
Shaw, George Bernard, 552
Sheshanna, Veene, 619, 640, 644, 647, 653
Simon Commission, 582, 589, 590
Singh, Daleep, 458
Singh, Hari, 158, 159
Singh, Ranjit, 458
Siraj-ud-daulah, Nawab, 154
Sitaramaiya, Pattabhi, 619
Smith, Colonel Joseph, 178

Srirangapatna, 24, 25, 26, 27, 29, 30, 31, 32, 33, 37, 38, 39, 45, 46, 49, 52, 55, 65, 66, 67, 68, 69, 70, 71, 76, 77, 78, 80, 82, 84, 85, 86, 87, 96, 103, 104, 105, 106, 113, 119, 120, 123, 127, 130, 133, 137, 144, 147, 149, 151, 155, 157, 158, 159, 160, 161, 162, 164, 165, 169, 170, 173, 174, 177, 178, 183, 184, 190, 191, 194, 195, 200, 202, 203, 211, 213, 214, 219, 223, 225, 226, 227, 236, 239, 248, 249, 250, 251, 252, 253, 257, 259, 262, 265, 266, 267, 269, 271, 272, 274, 275, 276, 277, 279, 281, 286, 287, 288, 320, 321, 323, 324, 330, 331, 333, 334, 335, 337, 340, 341, 350, 351, 352, 360, 361, 366, 372, 373, 374, 375, 376, 380, 381, 382, 383, 385, 400, 401, 403, 408, 409, 411, 412, 413, 419, 426, 564, 670, 689, 693, 694, 700, 706, 707
Subsidiary Treaty, 381, 390, 422, 464
Sufism, 155, 175
Sultan, Tipu, *viii, xi, xvi, xix, xx, xxi*, 120, 155, 157, 163, 174, 175, 176, 177, 178, 179, 180, 184, 201, 203, 205, 206, 208, 209, 210, 211, 223, 224, 225, 226, 227, 228, 229, 230, 232, 234, 235, 236, 237, 238, 239, 240, 241, 242, 243, 244, 245, 246, 247, 248, 249, 250, 251, 252, 253, 254, 256, 257, 258, 259, 260, 261, 262, 265, 266, 267, 268, 269, 270, 271, 272, 273, 274, 275, 276, 277, 279, 280, 281, 282, 283, 284, 285, 286, 287, 288, 289, 290, 291, 292, 308, 309, 310, 311, 312, 313, 314, 315, 316, 317, 318, 319, 320, 321, 322, 323, 324, 325, 326, 327, 328, 329, 330, 331, 332, 333, 334, 335,

Index   731

336, 337, 338, 339, 340, 341, 342,
343, 345, 346, 347, 348, 349, 350,
352, 353, 355, 356, 357, 358, 359,
360, 361, 362, 363, 364, 365, 366,
367, 368, 372, 373, 374, 375, 376,
377, 378, 379, 380, 382, 384, 400,
402, 403, 404, 406, 409, 411, 412,
413, 414, 415, 416, 421, 423, 430,
431, 434, 435, 442, 454, 459, 462,
465, 467, 471, 486, 551, 565, 566,
617, 618, 693, 694, 698, 700, 713
Swamy, Kille Venkataramana, 259

Takkavi loans, 328
Tanjore School, 691
Tata, Jamsetji Nusserwanji, 574
Thayamma, Jetti, 667, 670, 671, 673
Theosophical Society, 586
Third Mysore War, 257, 260, 261, 262, 347, 401
Thyagaraja, 631, 632, 636, 637, 638, 645, 650, 651, 652, 656
Tiger of Mysore, 234, 257, 266, 276, 279
Treaty of Alliance, 235
Treaty of Amritsar, 458
Treaty of Mangalore of 1784, 356
Treaty of Salbai, 192, 208

Urs, Katti Gopalaraje, 136, 137, 148, 152, 196, 482

Vasudevacharya, 546, 641, 643, 644, 645, 646, 647, 649, 652, 655, 659, 672, 673
Vasudevacharya, Mysore, 641, 643, 655, 672, 673
Venkatagiriappa, Veene, 642, 649, 653
Venkatalakshamma, K., 668, 672
Verma, Raja Ravi, 621, 677, 691, 697, 698
Victoria, Queen, 458, 479, 483, 485, 511, 528
Vijayanagara, *xi*, 13, 14, 16, 17, 18, 23, 24, 26, 29, 30, 31, 33, 40, 42, 45, 49, 58, 63, 64, 68, 70, 71, 75, 76, 78, 79, 84, 88, 112, 113, 122, 124, 168, 172, 193, 196, 323, 546, 617, 619, 669, 685, 689, 712
Vishweshwarayya, Sir M., 505, 507
Vivekananda, Swami, 506, 513, 574

Wagh, Dhondoji, 411, 414, 459
Wellesley, Richard, 267, 275, 286
White, Margaret Bourke, 583, 606, 608

Yajurveda, 669
Yakshagana, 441, 486, 638, 647, 677, 678, 679, 680, 708, 710, 711, 712

Zamorins of Calicut, 356